D0943763

Self Psychology
Comparisons and Contrasts

Self Psychology
Comparisons and Contrasts

edited by

Douglas W. Detrick
Susan P. Detrick

THE ANALYTIC PRESS
1989 Hillsdale, NJ Hove and London

The Analytic Press

Distributed solely by

Lawrence Erlbaum Associates, Inc., Publishers
365 Broadway
Hillsdale, New Jersey 07642

Library of Congress Cataloging-in-Publication Data

Self psychology: comparisons and contrasts / edited by Douglas Detrick, Susan Detrick.

p. cm.

Includes bibliographies and index.

ISBN 0-88163-077-2

1. Self psychology. 2. Psychoanalysis. 3. Psychology-philosophy. I. Detrick, Douglas. II. Detrick, Susan.

(DNLM: 1. Ego. 2. Psychoanalysis. WM 460.5.E3 S4655)
BF697.S444 1989
155.2—dc19
DNLM/DLC
for Library of Congress 88-14541
CIP

Printed in the United States of America
10 9 8 7 6 5 4 3 2

To the Memory

of

John Bradley Schaupp

Contents

CONTRIBUTORS xi

ACKNOWLEDGMENTS xv

FOREWORD – Arnold Goldberg xvii

PART I
Freud and the Historical "Dissidents"

CHAPTER 1
A comparison of Freud and Kohut: Apostasy or Synergy? 3
Michael Franz Basch

CHAPTER 2
Kohut and Jung: A Comparison of Theory and Therapy 23
Lionel Corbett

CHAPTER 3
Adler, Kohut, and the Idea of a Psychoanalytic Research Tradition 49
Paul E. Stepansky

CHAPTER 4
Otto Rank and Self Psychology 75
Esther Menaker

CHAPTER 5
Ferenczi's Contributions to the Evolution of a Self Psychology Framework in Psychoanalysis 89
Arnold Wm. Rachman

CHAPTER 6
Karen Horney's Theory of the Self 111
Henry A. Paul

PART II
Existential-Humanistic Thinkers

CHAPTER 7
Narcissism and Nihilism: Kohut and Kierkegaard on the Modern Self 131
Jane Rubin

CHAPTER 8
Kohut and Husserl: The Empathic Bond 151
Marilyn Nissim-Sabat

CHAPTER 9
On Maurice Merleau-Ponty and the Psychology of the Self 175
Robert J. Masek

CHAPTER 10
Psychoanalytic Phenomenology and the Thinking of Martin Heidegger and Jean-Paul Sartre 193
George E. Atwood

CHAPTER 11
Carl Rogers and Heinz Kohut: On the Importance of Valuing the Self 213
Edwin Kahn

Part III
English Object Relations Theorists

CHAPTER 12
Klein, Balint, and Fairbairn:
A Self-Psychological Perspective 231
Bernard Brandchaft

CHAPTER 13
Winnicott and Self Psychology: Remarkable Reflections 259
Howard A. Bacal

Part IV
Contemporary Contributions

CHAPTER 14
Interpersonal Psychoanalysis and Self Psychology:
A Clinical Comparison 275
Philip M. Bromberg

CHAPTER 15
Conflict and Deficit Models of Psychopathology:
A Unificatory Point of View 293
Helen K. Gediman

CHAPTER 16
Masterson and Kohut: Comparison and Contrast 311
Ralph Klein

CHAPTER 17
Kernberg and Kohut: A Critical Comparison 329
Salman Akhtar

CHAPTER 18
Lacan and Kohut: From Imaginary to Symbolic
Identification in the Case of Mr. Z 363
John P. Muller

CHAPTER 19
Mahler, Kohut, and Infant Research: Some Comparisons 395
Estelle Shane and Morton Shane

CHAPTER 20
Self Psychology: A Post-Kohutian View 415
John E. Gedo

PART V
Summarizing Reflections

CHAPTER 21
Self Psychology, Psychoanalysis, and the Analytic Enterprise 429
Douglas W. Detrick

AUTHOR INDEX 465

SUBJECT INDEX 471

Contributors

Salman Akhtar, M.D., Professor of Psychiatry and Director, Adult Outpatient Service, Jefferson Medical College; Faculty Member, Philadelphia Psychoanalytic Institute.

George E. Atwood, Ph.D., Professor of Psychology, Rutgers University, New Brunswick, NJ; Co-author, *Structures of Subjectivity* (The Analytic Press, 1987).

Howard A. Bacal, Ph.D., Training Analyst and Former Director, Toronto Institute of Psychoanalysis; Associate Professor, Department of Psychiatry, University of Toronto.

Michael Franz Basch, M.D., Professor of Psychiatry, Rush Medical College; Training and Supervising Analyst, Institute for Psychoanalysis, Chicago.

Bernard Brandchaft, M.D., Training and Supervising Analyst, Los Angeles Psychoanalytic Institute; Assistant Clinical Professor of Psychiatry, UCLA School of Medicine.

Philip M. Bromberg, Ph.D., Faculty Member, Training and Supervising Analyst, William Alanson White Psychoanalytic Institute, New York City; Clinical Professor of Psychology, New York University Postdoctoral Program in Psychoanalysis and Psychotherapy.

Lionel Corbett, M.D., Assistant Professor of Psychiatry, Rush

University Medical School; Clinical Director, Department of Psychiatry, Rush-Presbyterian-St. Luke's Medical Center, Chicago.

Douglas W. Detrick, Ph.D. (editor), Director of Psychology Training, Outpatient Clinic, Department of Psychiatry, Stanford University Medical Center; private practice, San Francisco and Palo Alto.

Susan P. Detrick, Ph.D. (editor), Member, Clinical Faculty, Department of Psychiatry, Stanford University Medical Center; private practice, San Francisco and Portola Valley, CA.

Helen K. Gediman, Ph.D., Clinical Professor of Psychiatry,New York University Postdoctoral Program in Psychoanalysis and Psychotherapy; Faculty Member, The Training Institute of the New York Freudian Society.

John E. Gedo, M.D., Training and Supervising Analyst, Institute for Psychoanalysis, Chicago; author of eight books, most recently *The Mind in Disorder* (The Analytic Press, 1987).

Arnold Goldberg, M.D., Professor of Psychiatry, Rush Medical College; Training and Supervising Analyst, Institute for Psychoanalysis, Chicago.

Edwin Kahn, Ph.D., Professor of Psychology, Queensborough Community College, The City University of New York; private practice, New York City.

Ralph Klein, M.D., Clinical Director, The Masterson Group for the Treatment of the Personality Disorders and The Masterson Institute for Teaching and Research; Co-editor with James F. Masterson, *Psychotherapy of the Disorders of the Self.*

Robert J. Masek, Ph.D., Graduate Clinical Faculty Member, West Georgia College, Carrollton; private practice.

Esther Menaker, Ph.D., Clinical Professor, New York University Postdoctoral Program in Psychoanalysis and Psychotherapy; Member, Senior Faculty, National Psychological Association for Psychoanalysis.

John P. Muller, Ph.D., Chief of Psychology and Director of Psychotherapy, Four Winds Hospital-Chicago; Candidate, Institute for Psychoanalysis, Chicago.

Marilyn Nissim-Sabat, Ph.D., Chairperson, Department of Philosophy, Lewis University, Romeoville, IL; Member, Husserl Circle.

Henry A. Paul, M.D., President, American Institute for Psychoanalysis of the Karen Horney Psychoanalytic Institute and Center; Faculties, Department of Psychiatry, Columbia University, and Department of Psychiatry, Mt. Sinai Medical Center, New York City.

Arnold Wm. Rachman, Ph.D., Chairman, Board of Directors, New York Institute for Psychoanalytic Self Psychology; Training Analyst, Senior Supervisor, and Faculty Member, Postgraduate Center for Mental Health, New York City.

Jane Rubin, Ph.D., Visiting Assistant Professor, Program in Religious Studies, University of California, Berkeley; Lecturer, School of Nursing, University of California, San Francisco.

Estelle Shane, Ph.D., Founding President, Center for Early Education and College of Developmental Studies, Los Angeles; Visiting Lecturer, Department of Psychiatry, UCLA.

Morton Shane, M.D., Director of Education, Training and Supervising Analyst in Adult and Child, Los Angeles Psychoanalytic Society and Institute; Associate Clinical Professor, Department of Psychiatry, UCLA.

Paul E. Stepansky, Ph.D., Editor-in-Chief, The Analytic Press; Research Associate, Department of Psychiatry, Cornell University Medical College, New York City.

Acknowledgments

This book is the direct result of the support and encouragement given to us by Arnold Goldberg. His conviction that the time was now right for a book comparing Kohut's work with the ideas of others provided the necessary impetus for us to undertake this project. He not only provided help and encouragement along the way, but in the early stages suggested some possible contributors from that small group of people who are experts both in psychoanalytic self psychology and other theoretical perspectives.

James Fosshage and Robert Stolorow aided us in our task of finding appropriate authors for a number of the chapters.

Eleanor Starke Kobrin of The Analytic Press has been unfailingly helpful as the various chapters went through successive versions.

Foreword

Arnold Goldberg

Heinz Kohut has made us take notice. Not all of us, to be sure. I well remember a luncheon address that I gave some years ago in which I spoke of the history of the so-called self psychology movement in psychoanalysis. While some of the audience sipped their coffee or finished their desserts, and others seemed to be attending to my talk, at least one member in that group was writing furiously without looking up at all. I soon learned that he certainly was not taking notes, for the movements of his hand had no possible connection to my words. And no effort of mine to be witty or profound or engaging seemed to modify his determination in any way. When my talk was over, he was one of those who came up afterwards to say a few polite words. Only later did I learn that his own talk, to be given later that afternoon, had been composed primarily during my lunchtime exercise. I subsequently listened to what he had written and had to say. It was good; but I could never still my regret that he had not been able to put down his pen and listen to me. Not that what I had to say was so significant, but rather that he, like many others, had to my mind robbed himself of something enriching that self psychology might have offered to him. It is not difficult to shut our ears to disturbing voices, but we always run the risk of missing out on things of importance. In our field of psychoanalysis there often seems to be a sea of competing voices and not enough time to hear them all. But on occasion one must pause and take notice. All of the contributors to this book have done that; they have all looked up from their own work to hear and read about self psychology. And no matter if they have returned to their main concerns with renewed or diminished interest, they have all been affected. That is one of the peculiar strengths of Heinz Kohut and self psychology: if one will only listen, what Kohut and self psychology have to say is very hard to ignore.

As I read through the many contributions to this volume I rediscovered a feeling that has not commonly accompanied my usual reading: it is simply that I wanted to talk directly to the author. The quality of the imagined conversations was quite varied. Sometimes, I just wanted to ask a question or gain a clarification. Quite often in this book, I wanted to set the author straight, to explain things and (I must confess) have the author admit his or her misunderstandings. But I also experienced a variant of the feeling that has been much neglected: I wanted to know a lot more about some of the persons and topics discussed, to learn in a leisurely way about some areas of interest that once seemed peripheral but now appear to be moving to the center of our concern. Being both teacher and student as a reader may be my own particular manner of getting "turned on" by a book. And so, rather than discuss or comment on each paper in the book in the manner of a tour guide, I prefer to move between these two other roles and extend my own imaginary conversations with the authors, thereby alerting the prospective reader to what lies ahead. These reflections are intended to encourage the reader to formulate his or her own dialogue with certain of the authors and perhaps with me as well. They range from the usual and now familiar arguments about Kohut's omissions and commissions, his failings and his follys, and even, albeit at times reluctantly, his successes.

We must recognize at the start that Kohut's work, as well as the field of self psychology, is unfinished business. Kohut really did not write a great many pages; he was a very careful and deliberate writer, and his main creative efforts were begun rather late in life. He spent a great deal of time in administrative work, was an active teacher and supervisor, and maintained a full clinical practice. The overall incompleteness of psychoanalytic self psychology is also a developmental testimony to its relative infancy. But to focus for just a moment on its founder, there is no doubt that Kohut failed to acknowledge the work of many other scholars, that he neglected to discuss many important psychological problems, and that he seemed to dismiss many issues that remain current and cogent even today.

Once all the deficiencies of Heinz Kohut and self psychology are admitted, I confess that my own prejudice is that the carping should stop. The need now is to look to the future. For instance, one example of such a need lies in the relative lack of study of separate objects, that is, those objects that are not selfobjects. I think Kohut felt both that this broad topic had been well examined by others and that it had little immediate relevance to his work. But it was never a settled issue. In his later work he indicated that the usual trials and tribulations of such object relations were secondary issues in psychopathology. However, such a position need not be read as purposeful neglect; it can be seen as a call for much more clinical study and research. This lack of detailed study of issues that beg for more consideration runs through the literature on self psychology. It is cause for much encouragement about the potential scope of research in the field. I remember some of the discussions with Kohut about this very issue of separate objects. Kohut's position, with his concept of two lines of development, was the most classical, while certain colleagues felt that the whole idea of separate objects was untenable. If the gods had been kinder, Heinz Kohut might be writing on the subject right now. It should be remembered, however, that most sciences live in various degrees of incompleteness, and this lack of completeness is more often due to intellectual limitations than to simple neglect.

The failure to acknowledge the work of others is a very common criticism leveled at Heinz Kohut and, even today, at all of self psychology. A book such as this highlights the issue by its detailed comparison of Kohut with the work of significant scholars. I am sure that the personal reasons for this neglect are undeniable, but I would like to suggest another reason that has to do with the aforementioned issue of time and thoroughness. As any of the notable contributors to this volume will testify, it takes an enormous amount of study to become well enough acquainted with a creative mind to represent it accurately. It is doubly difficult to undertake that task with two sets of ideas contributed by separate thinkers. Imagine the effort required of Kohut had he been required to detail the similarities and differences between his work and that of the many others who made overlapping or even tangentially related contributions. With his need for careful and deliberate study, I suspect he would never have gotten beyond his first book. I say this because an idle reference to a person who worked in the field may lend some narcissistic satisfaction to the cited author but is often little more than a tip of one's hat. At times it is even unfair. Take, for example, the common currency in the concept of self among scholars from Mead to Jung. Who and what can be omitted? Then focus on a significant concept such as Winnicott's notions of true and false selves. Just where and how should one include consideration of these concepts in Kohut's work? I know of no careful self-psychological exploration of these particular terms and ideas, but I do know that Kohut would have been satisfied with nothing but the most thorough examination. That may well be why he chose not to even begin this type of task. As a continuation of this defense, I can claim some expertise in self psychology, and I am continually amazed at the many references to Kohut's work that are simply wrong. Frequently, such references are no more than the perfunctory "tip of the hat" to which I have referred: an author's proclamation that he has done his homework, even though it is often the case that he has not. Bibliographic references are one thing; an elaboration of how an earlier contributor has foreshadowed some of one's own ideas is another. Indeed, this present volume is the first comprehensive answer to this question of attribution and provides proof that such recognition of continuity of ideas is no easy matter.

One other major contribution of this present volume has to do with the philosophic underpinnings of self psychology. Many of us who became involved with this new body of ideas were alerted to questions about the scientific basis of self psychology, as opposed to classical analysis, as well as questions that had to do with a search for just why self psychology seemed so different from what we had learned. Some earlier efforts to tackle these questions touched on the postmodernist approach of self psychology, and those in this volume stress the phenomenological roots of Kohut's work. A word of caution is in order. Although the case is made that phenomenology need not be devoted solely to conscious experiences, there still is more work to be done to encompass a psychoanalytic conception of the unconscious within the phenomenological viewpoint. For psychoanalytic self psychology there can be no compromise on the issue of the unconscious. Though we aim to grasp the experience of another person, we can never consider our empathy to be only a conscious phenomenon. Kohut utilized the phrase "frameworks of introspection" to explain unconscious and preconscious issues. In so doing, he was referring to the fact that the psychoanalyst gathers data with the notion of the unconscious as a preconception or a guiding theory. His empathy must therefore include unconscious considerations. And this last point allows me once again to urge the reader to ignore all clinical writers now and forever who claim to listen without any preconceptions at all, or with more humane considerations than those accruing from classical psychoanalysis, or without any wish to foist their own ideas on patients. Such listening hears nothing. Such claims are special pleading that speaks to a false sense of innocence. Our theories are our eyes, and we cannot see without them.

There are many other areas of concern and interest in the book that beg for more extended and lengthy deliberation. I do not believe I am negligent in passing the job on to the reader for, after all, the task at hand asks the reader to engage in his own imagined conversations, with his own questions, comments, and arguments.

In sum, this is a book that cannot be ignored. It is written by a group who are uniformly attentive to issues that matter. It is an impressive record of those who have studied self psychology and reached the point of being able to criticize with authority. My own dialogue with the authors lasted long after the book had been read, and there is nothing so satisfactory as this lasting impact of a good book.

Part I

Freud and the Historical "Dissidents"

1

A Comparison of Freud and Kohut

Apostasy or Synergy?

MICHAEL FRANZ BASCH

What was for many psychoanalysts Kohut's divergence from Freudian psychoanalysis did not begin with the introduction of what has come to be known as self psychology (Kohut, 1971), but much earlier, with what he often told us was, as far as he was concerned, his most important contribution, namely, "Introspection, Empathy, and Psychoanalysis" (1959). In that essay, Kohut outlined the historical and epistemological evidence showing that the essence of psychoanalysis lay in Freud's discovery of the psychoanalytic method, the investigation of human thought and motivation through the cooperative venture in which the deeper meaning of a patient's verbalized introspections came to be understood through the analyst's immersion in the patient's psychological life, which led to empathic understanding.

Although that paper was presented in 1957 as the plenary lecture celebrating the 25th anniversary of the founding of the Chicago Institute for Psychoanalysis, it, as Kohut told me, was accepted for publication only through the intercession of Maxwell Gitelson and over the objections of several other influential leaders in the field. The latter recognized that in the paper, by making the case that its method and not its theory was the foundation of any science, Kohut indirectly challenged the supremacy of Freud's instinct theory for psychoanalysis. Kohut was quite innocent of any such intention; it was years before he (1977) reluctantly concluded that the manifestations of unintegrated infantile sexuality and aggression in the analysis of psychoneurotic patients did not represent biological bedrock, as Freud had thought it did, but, instead, was a byproduct of deeper, further analyzable self pathology. However, the self-appointed guardians of Freud's legacy were quite right to object to Kohut's empathy and introspection paper. Resting as it does on simplistic and long-since falsified biological speculation and on an epistemological fallacy (Basch, 1975a), the instinct theory was (and to some extent still is) supported only by belief grounded in convention—any threat to that belief could bring the whole house of cards tumbling down. So, in making a comparison between the contributions of Sigmund Freud and Heinz Kohut, one has to ask, which Freud are you comparing Kohut with? The Freud in search of a scientific psychology on a footing with other natural (physical) sciences, or the Freud who almost incidentally discovered the psychoanalytic method for the investigation of the unconscious motives behind human behavior? A historical appraisal shows that the method of psychoanalysis, along with the clinical findings to which it gave rise, and the theory of the mental apparatus that Freud developed to explain those clinical findings are not of a piece. Only by clarifying the difference can one judge whether Kohut's work enhances or undermines Freud's contributions.

HISTORICAL BACKGROUND

Freud came to study the neuroses quite by accident (Jones, 1953). In 1885, at that time a 29-year-old Viennese neurologic researcher, he had gone to Paris to further his interest in pediatric neurology by studying children's brain specimens at the Salpêtrière Hospital. Though he was disappointed in the pathological laboratory there, he soon became very interested in the weekly lectures given by the chairman of that department, Jean Martin Charcot.

Most doctors of that day, frustrated by their inability to cure neuroses by talking common sense to patients and exhorting them to use willpower to overcome imaginary problems for which no anatomical basis could be found, blamed neurotics for their own suffering and wrote them off as malingerers or frauds who deserved no further attention. It was unusual, but in retrospect certainly fortuitous, that Charcot, the preeminent neurologist of his day, thought he could discover order where others saw only chaos and became convinced that neuroses were after all a form of illness attributable, he suggested, to the effect of emotional trauma on a hereditarily weakened brain and, therefore, worth studying, classifying, and treating. Charcot would demonstrate to his audience how a hypnotic trance could be used to regress a patient in time until he relived the forgotten trauma, often a life-threatening shock like a railroad accident, for example, that had precipitated his illness and to which his symptoms, unbeknownst to the patient, referred. Freud started to investigate such patients himself, corroborating Charcot's findings, but soon disagreed with his teacher's explanation for the origin of these problems. Charcot, taking for granted the Cartesian doctrine that reason and consciousness were identical, postulated that, since the origin of the neurotic symptom was not known to the patient, the symptom had to be the result of other than rational thoughts produced by the cerebral cortex. He suggested that, as there was no anatomic evidence of cortical damage in the autopsied brains of deceased neurotic patients, the cortical damage must be an as yet unknown physiological impairment that at certain times precluded the cortex from discharging strong emotions through reason, leaving the resultant emotional charge or energy free to agitate the lower centers of the brain. It was this agitation of the subcortical, nonreasoning part of the brain that created the symptoms of hysteria, obsessions, compulsions, or anxiety states. These symptoms made no sense in themselves and were to rational thought what the sounds produced by a child's banging on piano keys was to real music.

Freud, however, was apparently not subject to these preconceptions and soon saw that far from being brain damaged, his neurotic patients were, if anything, of above average intelligence. Their symptoms, once understood, proved to be extremely cleverly reasoned and designed to deal, in disguised fashion, with a conflict between need and morality; the symptoms, like a game of charades, portrayed both the nature of the forbidden desire and its gratification, as well as the punishment the patient expected to be visited upon him for his transgression. Furthermore, as a neurologist, Freud (1888) could see no reason why consciousness had to accompany the cortical problem-solving activity that we call thought. Eventually, as is now well known, Freud came to realize that evidence for reasoned thought unaccompanied by consciousness was to be found in everyone once the motives behind dreams and such errors of everyday life as slips of the tongue, forgetting, and mistaken actions were studied and deciphered.

After his exposure to Charcot's work, Freud combined Charcot's hypnotic investigative method with the cathartic abreaction of traumatic emotional experiences that he had heard about from another of his teachers, Josef Breuer. This technique became the basis for both treating and studying neurotic pathology and provided the precursors for what was to become the psychoanalytic method of therapy (Breuer and Freud, 1893–1895; Basch, 1983b).

THE ORIGINS OF THE PSYCHOANALYTIC THEORY OF THOUGHT FORMATION

The goal of establishing a general scientific psychology led Freud first to create what Andersson (1962) has called the "brain mythology" of the "Project for a Scientific Psychology" (Freud, 1895a) and later to attempt its transmutation into the various versions of the nonanatomical mental apparatus (Basch, 1975b, 1976a, 1983a). These included the so-called picket fence model (Freud, 1900); the topographic model (Freud, 1915a), with its division into unconscious, preconscious, and conscious mental states; and the final version of ego and id (Freud, 1923).

To understand what makes all these models of brain functioning and thought processing operational, we have to go back to a work that was never included in the various collections of Freud's psychological writings, *On Aphasia* (Freud, 1891). In this book Freud first adopted the model for thought formation that remained throughout his lifetime the basis for his theory of cognition and that he repudiated only in one of his last publications (Freud, 1940). His hypothesis was that thought was made possible by a union of sensory images with the words that appropriately describe them and, *per contra,* that without words sensory images were blocked from both consciousness and participation in cognitive maturation. He attributed motivation for action to the amount of instinctual force attached to a sensory image. Conflicts would spring up between the need to discharge instinctual tension and the restrictions placed on uninhibited behavior by conscience and convention. Unable to control the strength of the instincts, which were somatic givens, the brain or mind would withdraw the speech associations from forbidden sensory images. These images were then isolated both from thought, which precluded their maturation, and from consciousness, which blocked their direct fulfillment in action. This theoretical construct corresponded to the conflict Freud saw in his neurotic patients, whom he cured by helping them to find the words to express their hidden desires and fears so that they could then either dismiss or sublimate them. For Freud, neurotics were essentially functional aphasics, and he made the error of thinking that the success of his therapy established the validity of his hypothesis regarding the development of thought. Unfortunately, Freud was studying the one psychological illness that seemed to corroborate his theory. In the long run, this success prevented the full implications of psychoanalysis from being appreciated by either Freud or the analysts that followed him.

It should be emphasized that none of the foregoing hypotheses is part of psychoanalytic theory, although they have come to be known as such. They were all formulated before Freud discovered the significance of dreams, psychic reality, and the transference and before he deciphered the code of the preoperative (Piaget and Inhelder, 1969) or presentational (Langer, 1982) symbolism that he termed the primary process (Basch, 1977). Because Freud never published the "Project" and because the significance of "On Aphasia" went unrecognized until recently, analysts did not know the origin of these concepts. They assumed, as Freud's later writings had led them to believe, that these conclusions had somehow been reached through psychoanalytic investigation (Basch, 1983a).

THE ORIGIN OF THE PSYCHOANALYTIC THEORY OF MOTIVATION

To understand Freud's theory explaining human motivation, one must realize that it too was a hypothesis and did not come out of his clinical observations, but, rather, was derived from other fields in an attempt to explain those observations. Between 1885 and 1900, when most of Freud's basic theorizing about mental processes took place, was the time in biology when hormones were discovered. The discovery that there were in the blood powerful chemical forces with which one part of the body influenced the activity of another part—for example, that the brain secreted a chemical (hormone) that influenced the thyroid gland to produce its secretions, which stimulated growth—was a revolutionary explanation, and it is not surprising that Freud drew on it to try to explain what he observed in his work with neurotic patients.

What intrigued Freud was the power of neurotic ideas—they could overcome common sense and literally paralyze an otherwise perfectly healthy person. Where did they get this power from?

Clinically, Freud discovered by hypnotizing and age-regressing his patients that sexual experiences and/or fantasies of childhood were responsible for laying down the basis for what later became neurotic phenomena. He put this clinical finding together with a biological speculation: Testicular secretions either chemically or mechanically, by stretching the connective tissue around the testicles, send messages to the brain, which then energize sexual ideas present there. Freud could not explain the mechanics of this transformation—he called it the "mysterious leap" between the somatic and the psychic. In any event, it was this somatic sexual secretion converted into sexual energy that provided the motivating power for behavior. Neurotic ideas were so strong because they attracted more of this power to themselves than did other ideas and motives and therefore dominated mental life (Freud, 1895b, p. 108).

This very primitive, purely speculative, and long-since disproven notion is the basis for Freud's instinct theory and the idea that sexuality is the basis for all motivation.

At first Freud postulated that there were two basic instincts or drives:[1] the self-preservative and the species-preservative, or sexual. Later (Freud, 1933) he changed this to sexual and aggressive drives, with the sexual drive being responsible for both self-and species preservation, the aggressive drive being attached to a "death" instinct that worked in opposition to the sexual drive. Freud never made it clear what the somatic source of the self-preservative, or ego, instinct and, later, the aggressive drive might be. (It is hard to believe, but this is really the foundation on which rests this theory that has dominated the field for 100 years.)

Once Freud had established in his mind the correctness of this hypothesis of the sexual basis for motivation of behavior, he modified it in various ways, giving rise to the tension-reduction theory of motivation, also known as the pleasure-unpleasure principle. Again, this is a very simplistic idea: the body keeps producing sexual stimulation, which in its raw form seeks blind expression in sexual behavior. The culture, first in the form of parents, later as society at large, cannot permit such purely selfish expression and imposes barriers to discharge. This constraint creates tension as the

[1]A drive, or, in German, *trieb,* is a modified form of instinct. In primitive animals instinct determines behavior in a very narrow, rigid fashion; higher animals have some choice about how their instinctual needs (hunger, thirst, respiration, and sex) will be met. When there is some choice of behavior we speak of drives rather than of blind instinct.

sexual excitation builds up in the brain or mental apparatus. This tension is experienced as unpleasure. The part of the brain or mental apparatus that is attuned to the needs of society—what Freud first called the reality principle, later the *ego*—tries to find compromises that will let the sexual excitation be discharged without incurring punishment. The best way is through sublimation, that is, finding substitute outlets for sexual energy in work and play that will be rewarded rather than punished by society. If this does not work, the defenses try to repress the instinct, pushing it into the unconscious and not letting it get entrance to the preconscious, reasonable, reality-oriented part of the mental apparatus. Once repressed, these forbidden ideas, because they still have an instinctual force attached to them, continue to exert pressure and seek forbidden fulfillment. If they should escape from repression, a second line of defense is the formation of a neurotic symptom—a form of discharge that both gratifies the wish and punishes the patient for having it. So, for example, a hysterical woman can release her tension in quasi-sexual "fits," but at the same time is punished for her underlying ideas by being invalided by her sickness and prevented from finding a man whom she might marry—and so on.

So the mental machine that Freud devised is one in which there is a basic source of power (sexuality) that accumulates in a tank (the brain) and requires venting when the pressure gets too high. Actually, there were not one but two tanks. One was the system unconscious, later called the id portion of the unconscious, in which the raw instinct poured and got connected with nonverbal perceptions. The second was the system preconscious—conscious, later called ego, in which the modified, neutralized instinctual energy could be used for work and love in an acceptable way.

Freud himself made it explicitly clear that his theories about drives and instincts were *biological* speculations that he adduced to explain his clinical findings. As he said, these ideas were imposed upon rather than derived from psychoanalytic observations (Freud, 1915b). He acknowledged that these hypotheses were vague and unsatisfactory at best, and he referred to the instinct theory as the "mythology" of psychoanalysis (Freud, 1933, p. 95). Freud anticipated that eventually his theory of the libido and the nature of instincts would have a proper organic foundation, but in the absence of a definitive theory of instincts he felt justified in speculating about their biological substrate on the basis of psychological findings (Freud, 1914). Now, it is true that when Freud found them useful, the initially tentative nature of extra-analytic speculations tended to be forgotten, as if repeated usage had made these hypotheses more factual (Basch, 1976a). So it was with the theories of instinct and drive.

THE ORIGIN OF THE PSYCHOANALYTIC METHOD

Psychoanalysis as an investigative method began when Freud realized that (1) much of what adult neurotic patients advanced as memory was actually childhood fantasy; (2) when it came to influencing later behavior, psychic reality was as significant as external reality; and (3) the attempt to transform childhood fantasy into adult reality by projecting into the present situation what the patient had wished or feared was an ongoing process that manifested itself in the relationship between doctor and patient. In his practice, it was brought home to Freud that it was the interpretation of this transference that led to the resolution of the neurosis. It is the reliving of the old trauma in a new edition with the analyst that engages the emotional as well as the intellectual life of the patient and ultimately proves to be curative. The management, examination, and resolution of the transference became the basis for psychoanalysis and remains so to this day. It is what identifies the psychoanalytic method and is probably the one principle whose cardinal importance all analysts would accept.

The problem for psychoanalytic theory was that the psychoanalytic method worked too well, at least at first. It worked so well, in fact, that the theory whose formulation should have been stimulated by the application of the psychoanalytic method and that would truly have deserved the label "psychoanalytic" never came into existence. Instead, Freud felt that the success of the psychoanalytic method was the experimental proof of his general theory of the development of thought and his concept of how the mind or brain worked. He seems to have reasoned along the following lines: The vicissitudes of infantile sexuality are fundamental for the eventual onset of a neurosis. Dreams, slips of the tongue, and other errors of everyday life in healthy people show that infantile sexuality is a part of normal development. Therefore, development as reconstructed in the analysis of neurotic patients mirrors the development of all people: the neuroses show in bold relief what is ordinarily hidden from view by the resolution of the oedipal conflict in others. Similarly, Freud saw neurotic development as the result of a form of thought process that did not follow the rules of everyday adult logic. Everyone shows the universality of this type of thought process in dreams and errors of everyday life. On this basis Freud concluded that he had discovered the primary process, the earliest form in which the brain or mind attempted to adapt itself to the problems of life (Basch, 1983a).

In retrospect, of course, such conclusions are non sequiturs. The insight into development offered by an analytic study of a neurosis does not in itself offer a guarantee that all infantile development or all that is significant about early development is now understood. Nor is it to be taken for granted that the ability to decode a manner of processing thought that precedes logic has put us in touch with the earliest or "primary" process (Basch, 1977).

The psychoanalytic view of development, which formed the basis for the explanatory theory that is called psychoanalytic metapsychology (Basch, 1973), rests on five postulates about general psychology. These postulates, which were developed by Freud before the discovery of the psychoanalytic method, are the following:

1. The goal of the brain or mental apparatus is to avoid stimuli, or at least minimize them to the greatest extent compatible with the preservation of life.
2. Thought development is linear; the infant's appreciation of self and the world, although less complex, is essentially based on the same principles of perception and cognition found in adults.
3. The intensity of thought—its affective component—is determined by the quantity of a postulated "psychic energy," which attaches itself to a wish and determines its influence on behavior.
4. Development of speech precedes and is essential for thought.
5. True thought is equated with verbal logic and is made possible by a union of sensory, pictorial images with the more sophisticated and later-acquired word images (Basch, 1983a).

We know today that every one of these postulates is false. True, the evidence that makes possible an alternative and more acceptable theory of development was, for the most part, not yet available to Freud or the co-workers who eventually gathered around him. The experimental disproof of Freud's developmental hypothesis was to come shortly, however, although it was not recognized then and even now is not acknowledged as such by many analysts. In short, the symptoms of patients coming for treatment should, in principle, have been relieved by the investigation and interpretation of the vicissitudes of infantile sexual development but were not helped by that approach.

WIDENING THE APPLICATION OF THE PSYCHOANALYTIC METHOD

Psychoanalyts have always had patients who were suffering not from neuroses but from what we now call narcissistic personality and behavior disorders. We find the following comment by Freud (1919).

> We cannot avoid taking some patients for treatment who are so helpless and incapable of ordinary life that for them one has to combine analytic with educative influence; and even with the majority, occasions now and then arise in which the physician is bound to take up the position of teacher and mentor. But it must always be done with great caution, and the patient should be educated to liberate and fulfill his own nature, not to resemble ourselves [p. 165].

Similarly, Freud (1937) alluded to the difficulties of analyzing that group of patients who required character, as opposed to so-called therapeutic, analysis. The termination in these cases was not particularly satisfying or clear-cut, and, even though its goals were modest, the results of the treatment were limited and tenuous at best (p. 250). It was held that in their analyses these patients required what was elsewhere called *Nacherziehung,* a belated attempt to complete their upbringing in an effort to promote a reasonable level of maturity. The presence of more and more of these patients, as opposed to psychoneurotic ones, on analytic couches led to the postulation of a so-called widening scope for the application of psychoanalysis. The intrusion of the analyst's personality in the form of educational and exhortative efforts was often deemed necessary to help such patients overcome their immature, fixed character traits: for example, their unreasonable demandingness, their oversensitivity to slights, their tendency to deify the analyst, and, subsequently, their intense rage when he was found to be only human and imperfect.

However, these sorts of interventions have always been less than satisfactory for psychoanalysts, for it is the examination and resolution of the transference, not its manipulation, that is fundamental for psychoanalysis as opposed to other psychotherapies. The work of Kohut opened the door to the resolution of this problem.

Kohut was led in his discoveries by a patient's insistence that he put aside his preconceptions and listen to her. Miss F, whose case is reported in *The Analysis of the Self* (Kohut, 1971), stubbornly refused to go along with Kohut's classical interpretation of her immature behavior as indicative of resistance to sexual and aggressive feelings in the transference. In doing so, she catalyzed his recognition that she was unconsciously attempting to recreate in the treatment a very different and earlier period of development. Kohut eventually recognized that Miss F was not transferring to him the ambivalent love that a child mobilizes toward the parent of the opposite sex during the period of the oedipal conflict. Rather, she was manifesting a much earlier attitude, namely, the need to have the parent respond not as an identifiable individual but simply as a need-fulfilling extension of the child—a genie to her Aladdin, so to speak. Once Kohut was able to accept his patient's wish to merge with him and in doing so to eliminate him as an individual with feelings and an existence of his own, he ceased to think of himself as necessarily an object of either her love or her anger. He was now sufficiently freed from theoretical preconceptions to let himself resonate empathically with the content and tone of what the patient was saying. Her associations, memories, and feelings and the reconstructions generated by them led Kohut to realize that she was expressing very different concerns from the ones he had assumed she was expressing. When, at the opportune moment, he showed her these needs from early childhood, that is, to be echoed in her significance and to be found worthwhile, the patient felt understood. Associative clarification and elaboration followed, and the transference deepened. What had been a stalemated analysis now moved forward to an essentially satisfactory conclusion.

Kohut's continued investigation of aspects of the transference other than the oedipal led him, over a period of years, to a concept of development that expanded and supplemented the one postulated on the basis of the analysis of the classic psychoneurotic patient. He realized that his patients were transferring to him their need for a structured, cohesive, and stable sense of self. They could not themselves fulfill this need for validation of their existence and worthwhileness because of the less than optimal response to such needs during their formative years. These patients seemed to relate to the analyst in one of two ways, behaving either as if they were fused with the analyst, who then had no independent existence, or raising him to God-like status and attributing to him all virtues, knowledge, and power, in which they then wished to share. If the analyst did not regard these attitudes as artifacts to be eliminated, and avoided confronting the patient with their supposedly unrealistic nature, they developed into the narcissistic or selfobject transference on which the analysis of these heretofore often unanalyzable patients is based. Kohut has taught that rather than repeating the conflict of the oedipal period in the transference, these patients repeat the longing and disappointments that accompanied an unsuccessful attempt to establish a workable experience of the self—hence the label "self psychology" that is now attached to his discoveries[2] (Basch, 1981).

Kohut distilled three basic needs from early development: (1) to have one's competent performance validated and approved; (2) to be protected and supported at times of stress or tension that is beyond the competence of the infant or child to manage satisfactorily; and (3) to be acknowledged by one's kin as a fellow being. When these needs go significantly unmet or are otherwise misunderstood, they are eventually reactivated in a therapeutic relationship. Kohut refers to these repetitions respectively as the mirroring, idealizing, and alter ego transferences. In the mirror transference, the patient seeks to be validated by the therapist's approval; in the idealizing transference, he looks upon the therapist as an admired and powerful helper who will protect him and from whom he can gain strength; in the alter ego transference, the patient seeks the comfort that kinship, "being like," has to offer (Basch, 1988)

The Mirror Transference

As the experiments of Papousek (1969) and other infant researchers have demonstrated, nothing is as reinforcing for a baby as to

---

[2]The practical or clinical consequences of looking at analytic patients' development from the viewpoint of the whole range of self development have been detailed in Kohut (1971, 1977, 1978, 1984), Strozier (1985), Elson (1987), and Goldberg (1978, 1988). Kohut (1979) reported the analysis and reanalysis of a patient whose first treatment antedated the discovery of the selfobject transferences while the second was informed by them. Kohut and Wolf (1978) have written a summary of the principles of self psychology, and Wolf (1988) has provided an excellent introduction to the field.

establish a contingent relationship between his behavior and what is happening in the environment. It is especially important for infants and children to have an appropriate affective response from their parents as they seek to establish competence in communication and in autonomous behavior (Basch, 1988). The mirror transference shows that the patient had experienced difficulties in being validated in his attempts to achieve mastery.

The Idealizing Transference

The unrequited longing to be strengthened and protected when necessary by an alliance with an admired, powerful figure gives rise to the idealizing transference. The contentment, safety, and reassurance conveyed to the infant and small child when he is tenderly but firmly enveloped by or carried in his parents' arms forms the basis for this reaction. It is a need to be united with someone one looks up to and who can lend one the inspiration, strength, and whatever else it takes to maintain the stability of the self-system when one is endangered, frustrated, or in search of meaning.

The Alter Ego Transference

The need for a response acknowledging a bond of sameness or kinship between the participants in a therapeutic relationship is what is called an alter ego transference. This phenomenon was at first seen as a part of the mirroring process, but Kohut (1984) later drew a distinction between the two (see also Detrick, 1986). His reason for doing so was that he concluded that the alter ego transference answers a basic human need, the need to have one's humanness, one's kinship or sameness with others of the species, quietly acknowledged. It is understandable why the alter ego transference was initially subsumed under the mirror transference since the validation of an infant's or child's worth, the pleased and proud recognition of his accomplishments, also happens to meet the youngster's need to have his belonging to the group affirmed. However, there are situations in everyday life when the strengthening of the self comes about not through the calming effect of joining with the greater power of the ideal, nor through the mirroring that attests to competence and achievement, but through being quietly sustained by another in whose presence one feels accepted.

It should be emphasized that although the description of the transference has been changed by Kohut, its management has not.

There is no role playing by the analyst in a misguided attempt to provide the patient with a meaningful experience over and above the analytic one. It is the analyst's outlook that is different as a result of Kohut's addition to clinical theory. The analyst no longer finds himself impelled to interfere actively with the development of the mirroring or the idealizing transference, either through premature and inexact interpretation or by pointing out external rather than psychic reality to the patient (Basch, 1988)

Whereas Freud gave us a theoretical framework that prepared us for the onslaught of the sexualized transference of the psychoneurotic so that we were prepared to recognize its beginnings and to tolerate its unfolding, this was not the case for the impact of other selfobject transferences. Idealizations are no more directed at the analyst as a person than are another patient's attempts at seducing him. Though it might seem otherwise, it is not easy to sit still and think about the unconscious meaning of what the patient is saying when you feel the discomfort of being assigned importance you do not have, of having virtues attributed to you that you do not possess, and of being extolled for powers, especially therapeutic ones, that imply demands you cannot possibly meet. The urge to set the patient straight or to insist that he harbors negative feelings behind his fulsome praise is very strong. As with the oedipal transference, only a theory that takes us beyond the affective impact of the patient's needs makes us sufficiently independent of the immediate meaning of what he says. Such a theory promotes the proper equidistant stance that allows us to experience the transfer of feelings without having to defend ourselves against them. Only under those circumstances can a patient, tentatively and bit by bit, bring out his childhood longings and fears and in their recapitulation with the analyst let them be clarified and eventually interpreted.

Similarly, Kohut's clinical generalizations based on his experience with the so-called mirror transferences prepare us to deal objectively with patients' grandiosity and need for merger with the analyst. Here we find our individuality painfully vitiated at the hands of a patient bent on recreating some phase of the objectless condition of infancy and childhood when others only existed in so far as they were used as means to an end. Once understood for what it represents, a patient's need to be mirrored (an evocative term describing a child's need to have his potential for individuality and significance empathically validated) can be met with an analytic response as the transference unfolds. No role playing with or indulgence of the patient is called for. It is sufficient that the patient feel understood, not misunderstood. Miss F felt mirrored, that is to say, understood, once her analyst stopped insisting that she must be evading her true feelings for him and focused his interpretations or reconstructions on her transference need for a selfobject experience that confirmed her presence and her activities rather than demanding, as her mother had, that he be the center of her interest. Then she could make progress in her analysis.

The criterion for establishing whether or not one is doing psychoanalysis is whether or not the patient's cure or improvement depends primarily on his pathology being brought into the transference to the analyst; the transference is interpreted so as to enhance the patient's understanding of himself and worked through to the point where the formerly malfunctioning structures have been restored or the defective structures strengthened so that the patient is able to lead a productive life. Judged by the criteria I have set forth, Kohut's contribution is in complete harmony with classical Freudian analysis. Indeed, it has made it possible once more to draw a definitive line between psychoanalysis and psychotherapy. Now that *Nacherziehung,* the belated maturing of patients with, for example, narcissistic personality disorders, can be attained in the traditional manner through transference analysis, we can truly claim that the scope of psychoanalysis has been widened. It is for this reason that I object to a division that is often made between the analysis of psychoneuroses or psychoneurotic character disorders and the analyses of earlier selfobject disorders. This schism implies that there is something essentially different in the psychoanalytic management or understanding of these two groups of patients. I believe that my examination of Kohut's work in the framework of psychoanalytic theory has established that no such difference exists (Basch, 1981).

KOHUT AND METAPSYCHOLOGY

The implications of Kohut's work are as important for the explanatory theory of psychoanalysis, the so-called metapsychology, as they are for psychoanalytic practice. Kohut's retrospective reconstructions, based on observations made in the analysis of adult patients, corroborate and complement in many respects what is now known about early mental development (Basch, 1977). Infant research has shown that babies seek stimulation rather than avoid it and that thought is not a product of speech. These findings agree with Kohut's concept of the self as dependent on reasonably empathic communication between the baby and its parents. Only a theory recognizing that infancy is a period of learning in which the baby lays down nonverbal memory traces that shape its problem-solving techniques can account for the lifelong influence of infantile experience on character formation. Piaget (Piaget and Inhelder, 1969) has shown not only that the learning process is one of simple accretion, but that superficially similar events are interpreted differently depending on the phase of cognitive development that has been reached by the experiencing person. Kohut's recognition that how patients relate in the selfobject transference reflects the domain of their development in which empathic communication failed is in keeping with the hierarchical concept of cognitive maturation. The oedipal phase with its potential conflicts, is only one phase of development, reflecting the child's newly acquired ability for symbolic abstraction and concrete operations. It is a mistake to see all developmental problems in these particular terms. The communication between infants and their caretakers cannot be explained by what is essentially a closed-system concept in which the goal is the discharge of instinctually derived psychic energy. An open system that permits error-correcting feedback and feedforward must be postulated to account for the complexities of maturation that are evident from the very first. Both motivation and its intensity can be accounted for by the vicissitudes of affective life, rather than by instinct and psychic energy—affect being understood as an inherited set of automatic and autonomic behavior patterns that serve as the basis for communication and cognition from the beginning to the end of life (Basch, 1976b, 1988).

Kohut's work refutes those who would say that Freud's method is circular, a self-fulfilling prophecy that always turns up what it expects to find. Potentially, there are other aspects of development that, just like selfobject transference, are always there to be studied and only await the application of Freud's method by a talented analyst whose background and whose capacity for self-analysis are such that he can make the necessary connections between what he is experiencing in the analytic situation and what its implications are for the larger theory of human development to which psychoanalytic theory belongs.

The necessity for revisions in psychoanalytic theory has been evident for some time, but analysts have been reluctant to accept them, preferring to isolate themselves from other sciences rather than risk what they felt might be damaging to their clinical work. Kohut's discovery of the broad range and scope of the transference is the first systematic exposition from within psychoanalysis that clearly demonstrates on the basis of clinical material the need to make the changes briefly sketched here. It should be emphasized that none of these revisions of metapsychology alters the significance of Freud's *clinical* discoveries in any way. What has changed is that what we can learn about development from the study of neurotic pathology is no longer paradigmatic for all of mental life. The oedipal phase and its vicissitudes form one aspect of maturation, and its importance is not diminished by the fact that it now fits into the larger schema for the evolution of character that is implicit in Kohut's concept of self-development.

In terms of epistemology and formation of scientific theory, it should be clear that Kohut has set psychoanalytic theory back on the track that it left so many years ago. The psychoanalytic method uncovers data regarding the meaning of human behavior, its motivation. Psychoanalysis alone can never generate a general psychology, as Freud believed it would. On the other hand, general psychology needs an investigative method that will clarify unconscious motivation. In the past, the confusion about the nature of psychoanalytic theory has made it difficult, indeed impossible, for even those psychologists who appreciate the clinical achievements of psychoanalysis to coordinate what psychoanalysis has to offer with other aspects of their discipline. A psychoanalytic theory of motivation and meaning based on selfobject transferences is capable of probing the affective significance of relationships in any given domain of development insofar as they are recreated in the transference of a particular patient. The accumulation of such data should prove very useful in the investigation of human behavior on all levels.

CONCLUSION

Kohut's work has not yet been integrated by the psychoanalytic establishment. There are those who feel that self psychology deviates from and represents a threat to psychoanalysis. I believe that these critics fear self psychology because they have failed to make a rigorous distinction between the data of free association, the laws or clinical generalizations that can be abstracted from them, and the hypotheses from other fields adduced to explain them (Basch, 1973). Only the first two are directly related to the psychoanalytic method. The last, the explanatory theory, belongs to a different universe of discourse, and changes in these theories have nothing to do with the validity of psychoanalytic propositions. Kohut, by indirectly throwing new light on infancy and early childhood through psychoanalytic reconstructions, necessarily calls into question the exclusivity and centrality of the instincts and the Oedipus complex as explanatory hypotheses by demonstrating that the vicissitudes in the development of the concept of self are more complex than we had suspected.

Self psychology is not a separate or new form of psychotherapy but is very much an extension of and a corrective for traditional psychoanalytic practice. It is a mistake to think of comparing Freud's and Kohut's work as if they represented fundamentally different positions. Kohut was able to take Freud's clinical discoveries to their logical conclusion and, through his emphasis on the primacy of empathy and introspection for psychoanalysis, advance Freud's work in ways that had not been possible before. That Kohut's contributions underscore the inadequacy of using 19th-century biology in the form of Freud's instinct theory to explain psychoanalytic findings is all to the good, but nothing new—that the instinct theory and the explanations based on it have no scientific standing has been known for years (Basch, 1975a).

As more analysts come to appreciate Kohut's extension of the transference first in their own analyses and then in the analyses of their patients, the now existing dichotomy in psychoanalytic thinking will disappear. Self psychology will be seen as the evolutionary successor to ego psychology, much as ego psychology succeeded id psychology. And Kohut will be recognized and honored for what he certainly always thought he was: a contributor to Freudian psychoanalysis.

REFERENCES

Andersson, O. (1962), *Studies in the Prehistory of Psychoanalysis.* Stockholm: Svenska Bokforlaget/Norstedts.

Basch, M.F. (1973), Psychoanalysis and theory formation. *The Annual of Psychoanalysis,* 1:39–52. New York: Quadrangle/New York Times Books.

——— (1975a), Toward a theory that encompasses depression: A revision of existing causal hypotheses in psychoanalysis. In: *Depression and Human Existence,* ed. E.J. Anthony & T. Benedek. Boston: Little, Brown, pp. 485–534.

_____ (1975b), Perception, consciousness, and Freud's "Project." *The Annual of Psychoanalysis,* 3:3–19. New York: International Universities Press.

_____ (1976a), Theory formation in Chapter VII: A critique. *J. Amer. Psychoanal. Assn.,* 24:61–100.

_____ (1976b), The concept of affect: A re-examination. *J. Amer. Psychoanal. Assn.,* 24:759–777.

_____ (1977), Developmental psychology and explanatory theory in psychoanalysis. *The Annual of Psychoanalysis,* 5:229–263. New York: International Universities Press.

_____ (1981), Selfobject disorders and psychoanalytic theory: A historical perspective. *J. Amer. Psychoanal. Assn.,* 29:337–351.

_____ (1983a), Some theoretical and methodological implications of self psychology. In: *The Future of Psychoanalysis,* ed. A. Goldberg. New York: International Universities Press, pp. 431–442.

_____ (1983b), The concept of self: An operational definition. In: *Developmental Approaches to the Self,* ed. B. Lee & G. Noam. New York: Plenum Press, pp. 7–58.

_____ (1988), *Understanding Psychotherapy: The Science Behind the Art.* New York: Basic Books.

Breuer, J. & Freud, S. (1893–1895), Studies on hysteria. *Standard Edition,* 2. London: Hogarth Press, 1955.

Detrick, D.W. (1986), Alterego phenomena and the alterego transferences: Some further considerations. In: *Progress in Self Psychology,* Vol. 2, ed. A. Goldberg. New York: Guilford Press, pp. 299–304.

Elson, M. ed. (1987), *The Kohut Seminars.* New York: Norton.

Freud, S. (1888), Preface to the translation of Bernheim's "*Suggestion.*" *Standard Edition,* 1:75–87. London: Hogarth Press, 1966.

_____ (1891), *On Aphasia,* tr. E. Stengel. New York: International Universities Press, 1953.

_____ (1895a), Project for a scientific psychology. *Standard Edition,* 1:281–397. London: Hogarth Press, 1966.

_____ (1895b), On the grounds for detaching a particular syndrome from neurasthenia under the description "anxiety neurosis." *Standard Edition,* 3:87–117. London: Hogarth Press, 1962.

_____ (1900), The interpretation of dreams. *Standard Edition,* 4 & 5. London: Hogarth Press, 1958.

_____ (1914), On narcissism: An introduction. *Standard Edition,* 14:67–102. London: Hogarth Press, 1957.

_____ (1915a), The unconscious. *Standard Edition,* 14:159–204. London: Hogarth Press, 1957.

_____ (1915b), Instincts and their vicissitudes. *Standard Edition,* 14:117–140. London: Hogarth Press, 1957.

_____ (1919), Lines of advance in psycho-analytic therapy. *Standard Edition,* 17:157–168. London: Hogarth Press, 1955.

_____ (1923), The ego and the id. *Standard Edition,* 19:3–66. London:

Hogarth Press, 1961.

——— (1933), New introductory lectures on psycho-analysis. *Standard Edition,* 22. London: Hogarth Press, 1964.

——— (1937), Analysis Terminable and Interminable. *Standard Edition,* 23:209–253. London: Hogarth Press, 1964.

——— (1940), An outline of psycho-analysis. *Standard Edition,* 23:141–207. London: Hogarth Press, 1964.

Goldberg, A., ed. (1978), *The Psychology of the Self.* New York: International Universities Press.

——— (1988), *A Fresh Look at Psychoanalysis.* Hillsdale, NJ: The Analytic Press.

Jones, E. (1953), *The Life and Work of Sigmund Freud,* Vol. 1. New York: Basic Books.

Kohut, H. (1959), Introspection, empathy and psychoanalysis. *J. Amer. Psycho-Anal. Assn.,* 7:459–483.

——— (1971), *The Analysis of the Self.* New York: International Universities Press.

——— (1977), *The Restoration of the Self.* New York: International Universities Press.

——— (1978), *The Search for the Self,* ed. P.H. Ornstein. New York: International Universities Press.

——— (1979), The two analyses of Mr. Z. *Internat. J. Psycho-Anal.,* 60:3–27.

——— (1984), *How Does Analysis Cure?* ed. A. Goldberg & P. E. Stepansky. Chicago: University of Chicago Press.

——— & Wolf, E.S. (1978), The disorders of the self and their treatment: An outline. *Internat. J. Psycho-Anal.,* 59:413–425.

Langer, S. K. (1942), *Philosophy in a New Key.* Cambridge, MA: Harvard University Press.

Papousek, H. (1969), Individual variability in learned responses in human infants. In: *Brain and Early Behavior,* ed. R. J. Robinson. New York: Academic Press, pp. 251–266.

Piaget, J. & Inhelder, B. (1969), *The Psychology of the Child.* New York: Basic Books.

Strozier, C. B., ed. (1985), *Self Psychology and the Humanities.* New York: Norton.

Wolf, E.S. (1988), *Treating the Self.* New York: Guiford Press.

2

Kohut and Jung
A Comparison of Theory and Therapy

LIONEL CORBETT

While clearly maintaining its own identity, the Jungian analytic community has been profoundly influenced by theorists of other schools, of whom Heinz Kohut is currently of particular importance because of various intriguing points of contact between his writing and that of Jung. Both of their positions have been viewed as "metaphysical," and Kohut too is seen as a defector who "opens the door to a strange and enchanted land of make-believe" (Hanley and Masson, 1976).

As Samuels (1985) has shown, the historical reality is that Jung anticipated many modern developments within psychoanalysis, including some aspects of self psychology. Samuels quotes Roazen: "Few responsible figures in psychoanalysis would be disturbed today if an analyst were to present views identical to Jung's in 1913" (p. 9). It is significant that Kohut's position is close to that of Jung on many of the issues that led to the Freud-Jung break in 1913, such as their mutual deemphasis of drive-defense psychology and a purely oedipal theory of neurosis.

Various factors make it difficult to compare the therapeutic approaches of Jung and Kohut. There is no single or formal Jungian method of therapy, although there are typical therapeutic attitudes. These have never firmly been codified, because to do so would contravene a fundamental point of agreement within the field: although there exists a core corpus of literature and concepts, the personality and level of psychological development of the individual practitioner remain the most important therapeutic factor (Jung, 1966a, p. 78; 1976, p. 439). Furthermore, Jung's work stretches over a period of more than 50 years and consequently contains a variety of changing views and emphasis. Many beginnings were made but not developed, or development proceeded in different directions in the hands of his successors. This lack of homogeneity complicates comparative studies, but nevertheless various areas of comparison may be delineated.

THE CONCEPTS OF THE SELF IN KOHUT AND JUNG

Both Kohut and Jung stress the overriding importance of the self as a supraordinate intrapsychic structure. Their descriptions of the nature of the self sometimes overlap but also differ in many important ways. A brief summary of the two concepts follows; fuller discussions have been provided elsewhere (Jacoby, 1981; Schwartz-Salant, 1982; Redfearn, 1983; Samuels, 1985; Corbett and Kugler, 1989;).

Both authors state that the self cannot be fully described. Kohut (1977) refers to its cognitive impenetrability; only its "introspectively or empathically perceived psychological manifestations are open to us" (p. 311). Jung (1966b) also refers to the self as an "unknowable essence" that transcends our powers of comprehension. For Kohut (1977) the self is "the way a person experiences himself as himself" (p. xv), a permanent mental structure consisting of feelings, memories, and behaviors that are subjectively experienced as being continuous in time and as being "me." The self is also a "felt center of independent initiative," and an "independent recipient of impressions"—the center of the individual's psychological universe (p. xv), and not simply a representation. Jung uses the term in ways that cannot be described in a unitary manner. For him, the self is not developed by accretion out of the internalization of selfobject relationships but is the a priori ordering, structure-giving principle within the psyche. Kohut's description of man's goal as "the realization, through his actions, of the blueprint for his life that had been laid down in his nuclear self" (p. 133) is similar to Jung's (1968a) concept of individuation as meaning the unfolding of the self throughout life in an attempt to realize the potential wholeness of the personality. The maturation of factors, such as

Kohut's nuclear determinants, or blueprint, into a cohesive structure is implied within this process.

The self for Jung (1971) is also the totality of the psyche, both unconscious and conscious. The self is seen as purposive, acting as an organizing center that tries to maintain the integrity of the personality by maintaining intrapsychic homeostasis. Jung (1969) believed that the personality operates according to fundamental morphogenetic laws, which he termed "archetypes." Archetypes govern perception, and affective experience, especially as they influence the formation of complexes, which develop around a particular archetypal (core) issue. The archetypes are the individual components or manifestations of the self; they determine particular intrapsychic structures: Kohut's innate grandiosity and need for an idealizing selfobject, two such components, meet the definition of what is archetypal because they organize psychic reality and produce typically human needs and patterns of behavior. Jung's self is the preexistent matrix of consciousness from which the ego, or individually differentiated consciousness, arises. The ego is that aspect of the self which is experienced as personal and self-reflexive. It is the felt center of consciousness, while the self is the center of the total psyche (Jung, 1966b, 1968a). The implication is of a "deeper" center than can be consciously experienced, one that acts as a psychological center of gravity (Jung, 1966b). Ideally, the ego and the self are in a dialectical relationship with each other—the "ego-self axis," which is based on the attempt of the conscious personality to respond to the manifestations of the unconscious. Without ego consciousness, the self cannot realize itself in the world; and without the self, the ego has no depth or source of meaning and integration. The ego stands to the self as the moved to the mover (Jung, 1969b) and through the process of individuation, as consciousness of the self increases, the ego increasingly experiences itself as the object of a supraordinate subject (Jung, 1966b).

One metaphorical comparison between the two self concepts is found in the analogy of the personality as a dynamic sculpture, in which Jung's self corresponds to the wire armature onto which the clay of Kohut's self must be attached to finish the work. Without the armature, the clay has no support or adequate form; without the clay, the armature remains lifeless and lacking in specificity. The metaphor requires that specific qualities and quantities of the clay be understood as differentially attracted to specific parts of the armature, because Jung believed that we become involved with people in the world who correspond to our essential nature. As

Redfearn (1983) put it, in development "one can only introject what one is in the first place" (p. 99). The unconscious, form-determining (archetypal) components of the personality, and the complexes of ideation and affect that form around them seem to act like inductive magnets for certain events and affects to which they correspond (Jung, 1960, 1969c). The result is that the "inner" psychic predisposition of the individual and his "outer" world become one and the same, joined within an interactive field. Unconscious aspects of the self are therefore experienced as "outer," according to Jung, so that we "happen to ourselves." Some aspects of the self are consequently experienced only within relationships, which are faithful mirrors of intrapsychic dynamics. (This concept of Jung's links his notion of the self with Kohut's concept of the selfobject.)

The self and its a priori (archetypal) categories represent Jung's fundamental ontological ground. These factors cannot be reduced to any simpler phenomenon, and for Jung they are certainly not reduceable to an epiphenomenon of brain. The multiplicity of usages within Jung's position leads to the paradox that the self is at the same time the center of the psyche, its source of integration, and also the totality. While it is the matrix of personal awareness, the experience of the self is also the goal of the development of consciousness.[1]

According to Jung, the self depicts its own processes within the psyche by the production of specific imagery, in dreams and fantasy and is thus an experience-near concept when felt as immanent through such symbols, but is also experience-distant when used as a theoretical concept. Kohut pays no particular attention to symbolic experiences of the self (except in relation to self-state dreams), but

---

[1]According to Jung, the self and the archetypal level of the unconscious seem to behave autonomously, or objectively from the point of view of consciousness. Because Jung grants ontological primacy to this level of the psyche, his psychology is widely criticized as too religious or too romantic. I suspect that this criticism may be defensive, because of the felt power of archetypal pressures such as archaic selfobject needs, which are intense but poorly articulated. Jung (1966a) writes that he hopes not to "arouse the prejudice that I regard the unconscious as something personal. The unconscious consists of natural processes that lie outside the sphere of the human personality" (p. 234). He suggests that when these processes behave autonomously, we must admit their superior force, which has led people to characterize and personify them as "divine," because they are a "force as real as hunger and the fear of death" (Ibid p. 239). Because such unconscious organizing processes are not purely individual or personal, but are found generally, Jung initially referred to them as "collective," and later as the "objective" unconscious. Kohut's archaic grandiosity and idealized parent imago are "collective" in this sense.

these are of considerable importance to Jung. For him, symbols of the self typically range from the most abstract to the most human, depending on which aspect of the totality of the self needs to be stressed. The particular content of a self-symbol found in a patient's imagery is determined by whatever is being ignored by ego consciousness, because such experience of the self is a homeostatic attempt to correct for a one-sided or incomplete conscious attitude. According to Jung (1968b, 1971) typical symbols that mediate the intrapsychic experience of the self are (a) geometric figures suggesting symmetry, wholeness, and completion, such as the circle or square; (b) figures that are idealized or transcendent, such as royalty or saviour figures; (c) figures representing the union of opposites, since the self is a complex of opposites with a paradoxical, antinomial character. Kohut's self is also structured as a pair of opposites, in the sense that grandiosity implies that the greatest value lies within the person, whereas idealization locates this value within another person. However, for Jung, many other pairs of intrapsychic opposites can also be found within the self. Thus, in dreams, the self may be represented by a king and queen, a marriage pair, an elderly person with a child, a hermaphrodite, or any image of unity that transcends or includes opposites. The full appreciation of such symbolic experience in analysis is thought to supply what is required by consciousness to enhance the growth and wholeness of the personality. In a sense, therefore, Jung's conception of the symbol is similar to Kohut's conception of the selfobject—both provide missing structure. This is possible because the symbol is derived from, and is the best possible expression of, an archetypal content of the psyche (Jung, 1967). It is a short step to suggest that sometimes the self will produce an intrapsychic symbol, or, given the opportunity, a particular form of relationship, in its attempt to achieve the integration of the personality.

According to Jung (1968), the self has also been projected onto whatever is the cultural image of the divine. The self functions as an intrapsychic god image, symbolizing whatever is of the highest value to the individual. Jung (1969a, b) is clear, although widely misunderstood, that the existence of this psychological phenomenon has no bearing on the existence of a metaphysical, extrapsychic god. Hence Jung sees the phenomenology of the self expressed in religious systems, mythology, art and literature, as well as secular "religions" such as science, political beliefs, money, psychological schools of thought, and so on. Jung paid so much attention to symbol systems outside psychology because he felt that depth psychology needed an outside system of reference with which to compare itself. This is why, for instance, he studied alchemy—he saw that tradition as an opportunity to study a very old record of the structure and dynamics of the psyche in projected form. Thus, the alchemical "gold" made out of lead was, in reality, the alchemist's attempt to experience the self, as he struggled to emerge from his initial psychological state of chaos and depression. Alchemical texts are therefore seen as symbolic representations of unconscious processes projected onto the operation of the laboratory.

Unlike Jung's stress on the intrapsychic experience of the self via the image or symbol, Kohut's concept of the selfobject implies that selfhood is most fully experienced within a relationship that provides for the person what is otherwise missing. However, this apparent dichotomy must not be upheld too rigidly. Kohut stresses that the selfobject is an intrapsychic phenomena, not simply an interpersonal process, whereas Jung is aware that the self may be experienced between two persons. Jung is sometimes hard to understand because of his use of alchemical imagery and metaphors to depict clinical situations. Thus, his major work on the transference describes the experience of the self in the relationship as a *coniunctio,* or conjunction, an alchemical term for the union of opposite principles, the goal of their work, which was depicted symbolically in certain of the alchemical literature as a couple in the act of coitus. Using this metaphor, Jung suggests that within the transference dyad both participants typically experience a variety of opposites, such as consciousness and the unconscious, the contrasexual components of the personality, and conflictual elements within the patient's psyche. The self as an integrated whole is the epitome of the union of such opposites, which is one of the goals of therapy (Jung, 1966a). Jung suggests that at the core of the transference phenomena is a factor he calls "kinship libido," or the seeking of human connection: "relationship to the self is at once relationship to our fellow man, and no one can be related to the latter until he is related to himself" (p. 234). In other words, "inner structure must be created and then led back toward kinship and relationship with others" (Schwartz-Salant, 1982, p. 24).

When Kohut (1977) writes that "our transient individuality also possesses a significance that extends beyond the borders of our life" (p. 180) and describes "cosmic narcissism," which transcends the boundaries of the individual (Kohut, 1966), he seems to be referring to the phenomenon that Jung describes as the transpersonal or transcendant aspects of the self (Jung 1968(a) p. 182).

Gordon (1980) notes how Kohut, while discussing Kafka and O'Neill, emphasized man's search for wholeness and meaning, which is close to Jung's association of the experience of the self with the discovery of meaning. According to Jung (1969b) only meaning liberates; neurosis can be understood as the suffering of a soul that has not discovered its meaning, and the doctor has to help find the "meaning that quickens" (p. 330).

THE ORIGIN AND DEVELOPMENT OF THE SELF

Samuels (1985) points out that Kohut's self is created during development and forms at a specific point in time; this idea seems antithetical to Jung's concept of an a priori self. The use of the same term to indicate very different, but possibly equally necessary, concepts is responsible for some of this confusion. Samuels compares Kohut's theory of a self that coalesces from smaller units with the work of the Jungian writer Fordham (1976, 1985). Fordham's theory of "deintegration" described the baby as possessing an initially integrated self-unit (in Jung's sense), which unfolds or deintegrates because of the interaction of its innate organizing ability with the environment. This two-fold theory encompasses both concepts; Kohut's two poles would represent deintegrates of Jung's self.

Theories of the self that require an innate "blueprint" (Kohut, 1977) are problematic because they produce an infinite regression: they presuppose a designer of the blueprint or an agent more complex than the phenomenon to be explained. Kohut's blueprint includes two primary needs, for mirroring and idealizing. Either these originate in brain mechanisms, in which case they must be structured through yet another, genetic, blueprint, or he must assume a psychic organizing principle independent of the physiological structures that embody mental processes (Yates, 1984). Such a principle is implied by Jung's position about how the self self-organizes; Kohut's own position is not clear, but some current self psychologists reduce his blueprint to a more ontologically primary brain mechanism. This reduction inevitably regresses the problem onto organic systems without accounting for *their* structurality. It does not account for the manner in which macroscopic psychic regularities emerge out of microscopic chemical or physiological events, such that the psychological regularities exhibit autonomy and sovereignty. Psychological events are ordered lawfully, in ways that are independent of the laws of physiology (Kugler and Turvey, 1987). In response to this issue, Jung (1969c) postulates the existence of "archetypes," which are self-organizing intrapsychic principles. He therefore begs the question of morphogenesis but at least keeps the self within the realm of discourse of psychology and attempts to account for the intentionality of the psyche without appealing to extrapsychic structural principles. Jung's self, with its archetypal components, represents his attempt to delineate the lawfulness of the psyche; the poles of Kohut's self are similarly fundamental and could be conceived of as components of Jung's self. In this way, the two concepts are highly compatible. Jung's self is the principle by which Kohut's self organizes.

THE IMPORTANCE OF INTRAPSYCHIC SPLITTING

Both Jung and Kohut stress the importance of intrapsychic splitting. Kohut (1971) makes a major distinction between vertical and horizontal splits. In the former case, intrapsychic material is not repressed, but its emotional significance is ignored. Such disavowal leads to the coexistence of intrapsychic contents that do not communicate with each other. This emphasis is similar to Jung's (1969a) fundamental theory of neurosis, which concerns the inherent dissociability (splitting tendency) of the psyche, and the autonomy of the resultant split off "complexes," or clusters of associated images, feelings, ideas, and associations, that can potentially behave like "splinter-psyches," conscious to varying degrees and more or less in harmony with the larger personality. Complexes are structural units within the psyche, which develop as a result of the interaction of childhood experiences with the innate (archetypal) disposition of the individual. They are not necessarily pathogenic, and are based on a group of memories with a common feeling-tone (Jung, 1960). The complex may form around any archetypal, that is, structurally important, component of the psyche; the Oedipus complex is considered to be only one of many such archetypal possibilities. Kohut's use of the term disavowal to refer to the maintenance of split-off, archaic selfobject relationships, is in keeping with Jung's use of the term complex, since early selfobject needs are of archetypal importance within the personality and form complexes in Jung's sense.

Jung regarded the ego (which in his work is synonymous with personal consciousness, or the experience of individual identity) as that complex which is hierarchically dominant within the personality, but related to others, with which it may coexist peacefully or conflictually, with varying degrees of consciousness. Jung's view of the importance of splitting is similar to Kohut's description of the intrapsychic barrier which does not allow the psyche's "right hand" (the reality ego, with its low self-esteem) to know what the "left hand" (the grandiose, split-off self) is doing (Kohut, 1971). Kohut's "vertical split" describes two contradictory feeling states, so that there exist, side by side, "cohesive personality attitudes with different goal structures, different pleasure aims, different moral and aesthetic values" (p. 183). This formulation is similar to Jung's notion of the complex. Jung (1969a) attempted to explain the origin of splitting as derived from "the apparent impossibility of affirming the whole of one's nature" (p. 98) because of the painful contents of the complex. Situations in which people say "I don't know what came over me," or similar figures of speech, are examples of the temporary overwhelming of normal, conscious behavior by a complex that has developed a degree of autonomy such that it is at that moment not integrated into the totality of the self. The autonomy of the complex would be exemplified by the acting out of a perversion, related, for instance, to the sexualization of a pathologic selfobject need. In terms of Freud's structural theory, each complex might contain components of id, ego, and superego but is structurally more complex than such a formulation. Freud eventually discarded the term complex in favor of the idea of conflict between intrapsychic agencies, except when he referred to the Oedipus complex, but its use persisted with more general application within analytical psychology.

Jung (1969b) refers to neurosis as the result of inner cleavage, resulting in different aspects of the personality operating in opposition to one another. For Jung, this leads to the problem of how to reconcile oneself with one's own nature. He thought that the tension produced within the personality by complexes with opposing ideation and affect is an essential part of human life and development, providing a certain dynamism to the personality, and is not necessarily negative as long as such internal oppositions remain related within the totality of the personality. Jung (1969a) describes psychopathology as caused by internal splitting due to the excessive intensity of the emotional differences between such fragments, so that the experience of the internal unity of the personality is lost.

This is a notion similar to Kohut's concept of a cohesive self, which is able to contain internal tension without fragmentation; for Kohut, manifestations of "conflict," or the appearance of raw affect or drive, can be seen to be secondary to the fact that there are areas of the self in which it is incompletely established. Thus, both self psychology and Jungian psychology place much less stress on conflict as it was understood in classical psychoanalysis.

Kohut (1977) refers to a patient whose personality disturbance was marked by a vertical split in his personality. One fragment was characterized by a sense of superiority and messianic identification; this resulted from a merger with his mother, who had idealized him and encouraged his grandiosity. In Jung's terms, these contents represent a split-off complex, unintegrated with the rest of the personality. He is particularly concerned with the need to achieve the wholeness of the personality, which requires the integration of material split off from the totality of the person's self, and Kohut's approach is remarkably similar. In the case of Mr. X, he focused on "breaking down the barrier that maintained the vertical split" in the patient's personality. This allowed his patient to experience aspects of his authentic self that were deprived, rather than only the self-experience of arrogance, which "did not emanate from an independent self but from a self that was an appendage to the self of his mother" (p. 211). Later, Kohut's analytic work focused on uncovering this horizontally repressed (unconscious) material that underlay the patient's conscious self-experience, leading to a more authentic sense of identity.

Hearing this case material, a Jungian would use different language but describe a similar therapeutic task. The patient's grandiosity would be seen as an unintegrated complex. This pathology would be seen as partly purposeful, in the sense that neurotic difficulties are seen as attempts to consciously incorporate the neglected side of the personality (Jung, 1966b). When the patient was relating to others based on this material, he would be described as behaving within a "persona" identification. The persona is that functional complex which acts as a mask the person wears to relate to the outer world, for reasons of social and often narcissistic adaptation (Jung, 1966c). In this kind of case, the persona becomes pathologically defensive because it developed in response to mother's needs. Those aspects of the patient's personality of which he is unconscious are termed the "shadow" in Jung's (1968b) work. Therapy partly consists of becoming conscious of the shadow and the attempted integration (not rerepression) of the shadow, which in this case includes the patient's grandiosity, including material that is horizontally split (repressed).

THE IDEA OF WHOLENESS IN JUNG AND KOHUT

Kohut (1984) emphasizes the total personality of the patient. He writes that this is "an intrinsic constituent of the overall stance of the self psychologist" (pp. 126–127). He prefers to see the patient in overview before assessing individual psychic mechanisms such as defenses and resistances; "it is not the parts that explain the meaning and significance of the whole, but the whole that explains the meaning and significance of the parts" (p. 127).

This position is strikingly similar to a guiding principle of Jung's (1966a, 1969a)—the concept of the totality of the psyche, which he began to articulate soon after his break with Freud in 1913 (Jung 1969(a) p. 88; Jung 1966(a) p. 138). All psychological phenomena are seen as parts of a whole, because of an integrating or centering tendency within the psyche, which is, in fact, the self, or the core of the personality. He regarded ego consciousness as a limited component of a much greater totality. The ego is only a partial, and often developmentally distorted, realization of the total or true personality, which he describes as the self. Jung's stress on the inevitable one-sidedness of ego development, and the suffering this produces, is similar to Kohut's understanding of "tragic man's" suffering his incompleteness. Perhaps the major difference here is one of emphasis. For Jung, the self exists as an a priori source of wholeness, which acts as an inner authority and seems to press for conscious recognition, unfolding, and integration; while for Kohut, wholeness is achieved only by virtue of relationships. However, Kohut does postulate an innate program, and Jung is clear that the self in potentia needs human contact to become actualized in the world.

Kohut's concept of the self allows psychoanalysis to consider the whole person, just as Jung was concerned with neurosis in terms of the total personality rather than as a conflict between individual agencies of the mind. He believed that neurotic suffering is only approachable in terms of the "distorted totality of the human being" (Jung, 1966a, p. 89). The concept of wholeness has always been fundamental to Jungian psychology, since wholeness is associated with the experience of the self, which is a central concern within analytical psychology. One of the meanings of Jung's concept of individuation is the gradual realization in life of the potential wholeness of the personality—the urge toward individuation is thought to include an inherent striving for completeness as a kind of theoretical goal for the personality. Many Jungian writers equate healing with the attainment of wholeness; the common etymology of "heal" and "whole" is often indicated (see Gordon, 1979). Gordon, a contemporary Jungian analyst has distinguished between cure, which involves ego development, and healing, which is a "process in the service of the whole personality towards ever greater and more complex wholeness" (p. 216).

THE TRANSFORMATIONS OF NARCISSISM

Kalsched (1979) has pointed out that the first metapsychological debate about the origin of narcissism began in the context of the conflict between Freud and Jung. Freud's (1914) paper "On Narcissism" was a direct response to Jung's (1912) "Symbols of Transformation", which challenged Freud's ideas about incest and the libido theory. The issue of narcissism is thus a watershed issue in the history of psychology. It is therefore particularly interesting that this topic also provides a major parting of the ways for Kohut and Freud.

Certain similarities can be found in the concepts of libido found in the work of Jung and Kohut. In his early work, Kohut (1971) referred to "narcissistic libido" in a manner that distinguished it from object-instinctual libido. Like Jung, he did not see libido as purely sexual. Eventually, when he too abandoned the drive-defense model of psychopathology, Kohut had no further need for the term "narcissistic libido," because he no longer understood narcissism as the attachment of libido to the self, which is a formulation in terms of instinct theory. Kohut described the therapeutic transformations of archaic narcissism into areas such as improved relationships, enhanced self-esteem, creativity, humor, wisdom, and so on.

One of the major causes of the Freud-Jung rift was their disagreement about the concept of libido. Jung disagreed with the idea that psychic energy was based purely on sexuality. Instead, he conceived of libido as a neutral energy or intentionality, which could express itself in many different ways. Jung did not use the term energy in a mechanical sense, but to refer either to differences in the intensity of psychological experiences or to subjective evaluations of their quality and value. Like Kohut, Jung (1967) stressed the transformations of libido, pointing out that the same abstract form of energy might express itself in any form of psychological activity, such as creativity, affect, intellectual work, or spirituality. Both Jung and Kohut, therefore, described broad and essentially psychological theories about narcissism, distinct from the biological flavor of Freud's original concept.

THE IMPORTANCE OF THE PATIENT'S SUBJECTIVITY

Kohut (1971) stressed the importance of empathic attunement to the patient's affective state, or the "perception of complex psychological configurations" (p. 300). In fact, he defined the essence of psychoanalysis as the analyst's "protracted empathic immersion" in the patient's material, which is the starting point for all subsequent theory building. He defined empathy as "vicarious introspection," and as the "essence-creating first step," which lies "outside the realm of causal sequences," which we are unable to account for with "our present means of logical or psychological explanation" (p. 302). Kohut was aware that this attitude exposed him to criticisms of being unscientific and "quasi-religious or mystical." He held that rather than repudiate the primacy of empathy on these grounds, one should strive for both conceptual clarity in its definition and also carefully applied standards of research and practice.

These comments of Kohut are remarkably similar to Jung's (1914), insistence that all investigation of psychological processes was grounded in subjectivity and could not be considered scientific in the causal, reductive sense. He was opposed to the idea of psychic determinism and pointed out that Freud's method stressed causal explanation and the attempt to explain what is unknown in terms of what is known. He insisted that any attempt at the objective analysis of the subjective world of another person would be inadequate, just as we could not understand works of art in this way. Jung (1960) wrote, "If we want to understand anything psychological, we must bear in mind that all knowledge is subjectively conditioned" (p. 182). "The subjective can only be understood and judged subjectively . . ." (p. 187). Jung emphasizes the need to grasp the subjective meaning of the patient's material, or of a work of art, suggesting that we should try to discern the goal and meaning of the work, and understand it "in and through ourselves." Or, he suggests, when we study the delusions of a patient like Schreber, we should ask, "What is the goal the patient tried to reach through the creation of his system?" (p. 186). It is fundamental to try to understand how the patient (or artist) is trying to express (or redeem) himself. Jung refers to this as a "constructive" attitude, which although it is capable of analyzing, does not reduce (p. 187). It is unfortunate that Jung was uses the word "constructive" here. He does not mean the attempt to reconstruct the patient's developmental history, which he terms reductive analysis; rather he wishes to convey the idea of looking toward the future development of the personality, which he describes as a "synthetic" approach. Different patients require reductive or synthetic work to different degrees. In the attempt to understand the meaning of the patient's imagery, the Jungian approach includes the possibility that it points forward in time, as well as referring to the here and now or the past, and is therefore not always fully understandable in terms of the patient's developmental history.

Jung says that "analysis" in this context means the attempt to break down the material into typical intrapsychic components and find parallels and analogies to it in other systems of thought in order to discover typical natural formations. This is the basis of his hermeneutics, which tries to discover the "typical ways in which humans invest their world and their existence with psychic significance" (Steele, 1982). Because he believed that the psyche depicts its own process imagistically and that fundamental intrapsychic images are not reduceable, Jung sought to amplify their meaning by the search for analogy and metaphor, as an aid in understanding symbol and image. The search for such generalizable phenomena led Jung into studies of other symbol systems, such as religion and mythology, so that the fate of being labeled unscientific, which Kohut was concerned about, actually befell Jung. However, if Jung was correct in stressing the irreducible and unique, but definitely patterned, quality of human subjectivity, and if self psychology also continues to stress the importance of such data, then Jung's hermeneutical method is also applicable to self psychology. The data gathered through the process of empathy still require ordering, and it is unlikely that the symbolic contents of the patient's unconscious will all be reduceable to manifestations of the transference.

Steele (1982) points out that one of the major differences between Freud and Jung lay in their concept of what is real. Jung (1969a) believed that we live in a world of psychic images. "Far from being a material world, this is a psychic world, which allows us to make only indirect and hypothetical inferences about the real nature of matter" (p. 384). The only reality is the reality of the psyche. By contrast, Freud's (1933) view was more materialistic and empirical, holding that there is a "real external world we call 'truth' " (p. 170). Jung is clearly closer to Kohut's (1977) view that the subject matter of psychoanalysis is "that aspect of the world that is defined by the introspective stance of the observer" (p. 303). They appear to differ, however, in that Kohut (1984) uses empathy to "experience the inner life of another while simultaneously retaining the stance of an objective observer" (p. 175), whereas Jung (1976) would not allow the therapist to conceive of himself as objective: "Never forget that the analysis of a patient analyzes yourself, as you are just as much in it as he is" (p. 439). In a passage that sounds similar to Kohut, Jung (1969b) also writes:

> If the doctor wants to guide another, or even accompany him a step of the way, he must *feel* with that person's psyche. He never feels it when he passes judgement. Whether he puts his judgments into words, or keeps them to himself, makes not the slightest difference. To take the opposite position, and to agree with the patient offhand, is also of no use, but estranges him as much as condemnation. Feeling comes only through unprejudiced objectivity. This sounds almost like a scientific precept, and it could be confused with a purely intellectual, abstract attitude of mind. But what I mean is something quite different. It is a human quality—a kind of deep respect for the facts, for the man who suffers from them, and for the riddle of such a man's life [p. 338].

The phrase "unprejudiced objectivity" seems to be close to Kohut's (1980) notion of empathy as being "value neutral" and "in essence neutral and objective. . . . not in its essence subjective" (p. 483).

TRANSFERENCE AND THE THERAPEUTIC INTERACTION

Kohut's view of the narcissistic transferences is fundamental to his psychology. This concept bears certain important points of comparison with Jung's writing about the transference. Jung (1966a) distinguished between those aspects of the transference which are "archetypal" from those which are "personal." Archetypal here refers to the experience within the treatment of fundamental intrapsychic organizing principles, or the deepest levels of psychological structure, common to the human psyche in general; whereas personal refers to the reexperiencing of the specific contents of the individual's early relationship within the therapy. These two forms of the transference cannot always be clearly distinguished, because the archetype provides the potential form for experiences that are given individual content by the person's actual experiences with his parents. For example, in the course of a mother transference, the patient may attribute qualities to the therapist that were not present in the patient's mother, but that belong to the mother archetype, or the psychological predisposition to be, and to experience, a mother. The practical importance of this concept is that even if the patient's mother was negative, the intrapsychic potential for a positive experience also exists and can become active in the treatment, because the archetype contains the potential for both poles (Jung, 1969c). Hence the potential for healing exists if access can be gained to the positive pole within the treatment relationship. The successful establishment of the needed mirroring or idealizing transference in such a situation would be seen as the actualization of this healing potential through the therapist's capacity to stimulate and "hold" the positive side.

If Kohut is correct in believing that the need for mirroring and idealizing selfobjects is as psychologically fundamental as is the physiological need for oxygen and nutrients, then by definition these represent archetypal laws within the psyche. Kohut's two transferences would in principle be archetypally based, but their particular contents would be personal in the sense that the specific circumstances of the individual's early selfobject milieu would color their presentation. Jungian theory would predict that since there are other archetypal forms within the psyche, other fundamental forms of the transference remain to be elucidated.[2] The archetypes are seen by Jung as unconscious regulators of psychic life that attempt to redress psychic imbalances. The unconscious is considered to interact with consciousness in a compensatory way, which leads to intrapsychic self-regulation or homeostasis (Jung, 1966a). Kohut's stress on the appearance of important (but unconscious) components of the patient's self within the transference is understandable

[2]From within self psychology, Stolorow and Lachmann (1980) have in fact arrived at a definition of transference as the operation of primary organizational principles within the transference. This is another way of saying that transference has an archetypal basis.

within this theoretical framework, since the transference the patient needs emerges as a compensation attempting to restore wholeness. Jung (1969a) wrote that the transference must be understood in terms of its purpose, which is ultimately the process of individuation. Kohut explains in detail how this occurs—his notion of the unfolding of the self's nuclear blueprint in the context of the transference is a similar concept. For Jung, the progressive assimilation of unconscious contents into consciousness was crucially important. He used the somewhat misleading term "transcendant function" to describe this process of uniting or bridging the two and felt that the analyst had to carry this capacity for the patient until he was able to do it alone. In this sense, Kohut's description of the analyst's selfobject function for the patient is similar—the analyst is a bridge to the patient's unconscious deficit, reproduced in the transference, until the patient no longer needs him for this purpose.

Jung would see a transference as archetypal if it was depicted in ways that were not simply based on the actual life experience of the patient, but instead the therapist appeared in the patient's imagery in such forms as magician, witch, demon, redeeming messiah, or some other more than human entity. (These may all be forms of the idealizing transference, or they may represent individual categories). Such an extremely archaic, and distorted, image of the therapist provides the clue that more than personal material is being experienced. Seeing the therapist in such a light means that the patient is projecting mythological, rather than purely personal, material (Jung, 1966b). For example, when the therapist is idealized, he may appear to be omniscient to a superhuman extent. It is as if the subjective experience of fundamental structural needs within the relationship produces a larger-than-life quality—Jung refers to this as the "numinous" property of the archetype, which when activated has a powerful and attractive quality. Jungian theory would explain the intensity of Kohut's narcissistic transferences in terms of their archetypal, rather than purely personal, origin. Via the unconscious force of the archetype, the analyst is the medium by which the patient is able to experience what is nonego within himself.

In his discussion of a case involving such a transference, Jung (1966b) wrote, "What would be the good of explaining. . . . I am not in the least sinister, nor am I an evil magician. That would leave the patient quite cold, for she knows that just as well as I do" (p. 91). He went on to say that the doctor then has to accept the patient's need for the particular transference, without trying to interpret it away and must acknowledge himself as representing an archetypal image. Jung regards these as impersonal determinants within the psyche that behave in an autonomous way. (That is, they are not under the control of consciousness). Exactly like the need for mirroring or idealizing, they emerge in the treatment because they are significant factors within the patient's psyche that need conscious recognition and attention.

Archetypal transference images appear in dreams or fantasy (unless the patient is psychotic) and may be extremely positive as well as negative; their appearance in positive form may indicate the beginning of healing within the relationship. For example, Jung reported a case of what he described as an archetypal transference that, in Kohut's terms, was clearly based on an idealization by the patient. Jung appeared in the patient's dreams either as supernaturally large, or extremely old, occasionally resembling her father, as in a dream in which her father (therapist) appeared as an enormous giant who held her in his arms and rocked her like a little child. Although the patient knew intellectually that she saw Jung as a semidivine father-lover and could distinguish this image from reality, and despite the fact that this had been repeatedly discussed in the treatment, the transference obstinately refused to resolve. Jung asked what the purpose of this obstinancy was, (rather than understanding it as a resistance), because the intensity of the transference gave him the impression of a "vital instinct." By amplifying the dream's specific imagery in its mythological context, he eventually understood the situation as representing the patient's deep need to "free a vision of God," or a reaching out for a God projected onto the prosaic figure of the doctor. In psychological terms, the patient was experiencing the self in her dreams in the form of the analyst as a superhuman figure. Eventually, the transference resolved itself, and the patient developed an important relationship outside of therapy. Jung understood her dreams, which for a while continued to swell the doctor to "ever vaster proportions," as self-representations of unconscious developments within the patient, which allowed her psyche gradually to grow out of the personal tie to him. In other words, he allowed the natural history of the idealization to continue until the patient no longer needed him to meet that need. Jung felt that this process was guided by a "transpersonal control point" within her psyche. This is a confusing choice of words, but he is referring to the tendency of the self to guide the development of the personality autonomously toward its natural unfolding, in a manner which is not directed by conscious intent. What Jung refers to as the self includes just this self-organizing property of the psyche.[3]

The idealizing parent imago has an archetypal correspondence—that of the mythic image of Great Mother or Father. The child can be seen to relate to his mother as if she were the mother goddess of mythology. In the transference, this idealization is repeated; Jung refers to such archetypal transferences as the result of the projection of the self onto the therapist. The mirror transference can also be seen as archetypal, in the sense that, rather than projecting the self onto the therapist, the patient is reexperiencing the intense need for his inner experience of the self to be recognized by another person. Archetypally, this corresponds to two possible intrapsychic configurations, which I believe are distinguishable clinically. One is the appearance in dreams or fantasy of the mythic image of the divine child (for example, Jesus, Krishna) who is joyful and full of wonderous future potential, but helpless at the moment although he commands recognition. The other represents what is referred to in analytical psychology as an ego-self merger. Here these terms are used in a highly specific sense, referring to the ego as an island of discreet consciousness, which has not fully differentiated itself out of the self as the totality of the psyche, both conscious and unconscious. In infancy, the child's experiences itself as incompletely differentiated from mother; self and other seem to be part of the same self, so that the child experiences itself as powerful. As the child's ego (individual awareness) develops, it has to free itself from this merger with a felt totality into a sense of discreet identity, no longer immersed in the original state of unconscious fusion that is accompanied by the sensation of omnipotence.

Adequate mirroring of the child's joyful experience of itself, as described by Kohut (1971), leads to the process of ego-self differentiation. If this process does not occur during childhood, the archetypal pressure for individuation, which in Jung's psychology means the full development of individual consciousness, leads to a mirror transference so that the original need can be met. This

---

[3]The idea that the psyche is ordered and predisposed to unfold in particular ways is analogous to similar concepts in the work of Chomsky (1980) with regard to language, and Piaget and Inhelder (1969) in regard to cognitive development. Kohut (1977) writes that one of the major functions of the analyst is to provide the correct environment for the patient, whose psyche will then correct itself. This view is close to Jung's (1966a) view of the psyche as constantly trying to maintain homeostasis.

pressure from the self for mirroring illustrates Jung's idea of the "purposive" nature of the psyche, which aims for a final goal. Kohut's idea of the constructive purpose of the narcissistic transferences is also forward looking and cannot be understood only as a reexperiencing of childhood needs. Both theorists suggest that unrealized potentials within the personality emerge in the transference and are necessary for the full development of the individual.

In his discussion of archetypal transferences, Plaut (1956) points out some of their countertransference dangers to the analyst, in particular the need to accept the image projected by the patient without either becoming inflated (grandiose) or rejecting the patient. His discussion is reminiscent of Kohut's (1971) later and much more detailed discussion of the effects on the analyst of the idealizing and mirror transferences. Kohut (1977) describes how the analyst's psyche is "engaged in depth" during treatment, responding from the "deepest layers of the analyst's unconscious . . ." (p. 251). He regards this as a sine qua non for the process. Kohut (1984) recognizes the inadequacy of the traditional idea of the analyst as a neutral blank screen, as if a purely cognitive or objective view of the patient were possible. Rather, he (Kohut, 1971) indicates how the analyst's own personality structure and narcissistic needs become important factors in the treatment.

Jung (1966a) too reacted against the idea of the analyst as a neutral observer. In a very early appreciation of the importance of countertransference, he insisted that therapy is a dialectic, reciprocal interaction between two psychic systems. However, Jung seemed to go further than Kohut in stressing the importance of the analyst's personality and the mutual influence that occurs in treatment. Jung used the metaphor of a chemical reaction, suggesting that if change were to occur, both participants would be transformed, because their behavior is so mutually interactive. Kohut notes that although the analyst participates in the narcissistic transferences in very important ways, only rarely does the analyst's personality affect the choice between equally valid ways of restoring a patient's defective self. Kohut is less sure than Jung about the influence the analyst's personality has on the analysand. Kohut (1977) prefers to allow the patient find his own solution to his difficulties without gross identification with the analyst. Kohut's attitude can be compared with such comments of Jung's (1966a) as: "In any effective psychological treatment the doctor is bound to influence the patient; but this influence can only take place if the patient has a reciprocal influence on the doctor. You can exert no influence if you are not susceptible to influence" (p. 71). He goes on to describe how the analyst can become profoundly affected by the patient's illness. Kohut's writing therefore suggests a clearer sense of boundary between analyst and patient. His attitude is that if the analyst behaves properly and does not intefere because of his own needs, the transference the patient needs will emerge and can be resolved without too much distortion of the development of the patient's nuclear self. Jung also wants the analyst to pay attention to his own narcissistic defenses and needs, as he indicates in the following passage, which sounds like a Jungian version of Kohut's remarks on the effects on the analyst of the patient's narcissistic transference:

> We could say, without too much exaggeration, that a good half of every treatment that probes at all deeply consists in the doctor's examining himself, for only what he can put right in himself can he hope to put right in the patient. It is no loss, either, if he feels that the patient is hitting him, or even scoring off him: it is his own hurt that gives the measure of his power to heal. This, and nothing else, is the meaning of the Greek myth of the wounded physician [p. 71].

However, Kohut would probably feel that Jung (1976) goes too far in this direction asserting that the transference reveals "in a pitiless light what the healing agent really is: it is the degree to which the analyst himself can cope with his own psychic problems" (p. 493). Jung is probably referring to the fact that a patient's resistance may occasionally be justified, and the analyst then has to analyze himself to resolve the situation before treatment can proceed.

Kohut's emphasis on the importance of allowing a transference to develop gradually without any interference from the analyst is reminiscent of a comment of Jung that we must be careful not to impose on the patient or do anything contrary to his nature. Letting things happen in the psyche, a form of action through nonaction, became a key principle for him. Jung (1967b) was afraid that otherwise: "Consciousness is forever interfering, helping, correcting and negating, and never leaving the simple growth of the psychic processes in peace" (p. 16).

CONCLUSION

When Jung (1966a) wrote about the patients who came to consult him, he described people in the second half of life whose previous therapy had not been completely successful. Typically, they had no specific or easily defined neurotic symptoms, but rather complained of a vague sense of emptiness and meaninglessness in their life, which made them feel aimless. In retrospect, it is clear that these patients suffered from narcissistic character pathology, with self-defects in Kohut's sense. Kohut looked to the transference relationship to repair such a defect, after it was reconstellated in the therapy, because the patient's intrapsychic life is created in his selfobject experience—indeed, they are synonymous. Jung's approach was to encourage the patient to gain access to the depths of his own psyche by paying careful attention to his dreams, fantasies, and imaginal life. Jung believed that because of the psyche's innate tendency toward wholeness, which can be achieved by the gradual assimilation by consciousness of the products of the unconscious, his patients would heal by establishing a dialogue with the unconscious. In his psychology, the unconscious is granted ontological reality and is treated as if it were a source of awareness other than ego consciousness. The function of the therapist is to help mediate between consciousness and the unconscious by assisting in the amplification and interpretation of the patient's imagery, until the patient no longer needs the therapist for this purpose. Thus the patient's deficit is filled in from the unconscious, via the understanding of the symbol.

At first sight, it seems that this is a therapeutic method different from that of Kohut, but the major difference in practice is one of emphasis. Jung was well aware of the importance of the transference, and that the relationship with the therapist would often determine the content of the patient's imagery, so that work on this material inevitably includes work on the relationship. In fact, although much of Jung's writing is concerned with the elucidation of complex intrapsychic material derived from dreams and fantasy, it is clear that he knew of the powerful influence and importance of the relationship in determining the content of the patient's material: "With regard to your patient, it is quite correct that her dreams are occasioned by you. . . . In the deepest sense we all dream not out of ourselves, but out of what lies between us and the other" (Jung, 1973). If the self is truly the totality of consciousness, there cannot be any essential difference between the introspective experience of our inner life as it is depicted by the unconscious in our dreams and imagination, and the experience of ourselves in relationships. The "inner" and the "outer" must be a function of each other. Thus, Kohut's method of empathic immersion in the patient's experience of the relationship, when carried to its logical conclusion, must also lead the therapist to pay careful attention to the patient's intrapsychic imagery, especially as this depicts the details of the transference. What is of archetypal—that is, organizational and structural—importance to the personality will emerge in both situations. It is therefore suggested that although Jung and Kohut seem to approach the psyche from different vantage points, with different theories of cure, the simultaneous application of their ideas not only is possible, but leads to the finding that their approaches are mutually enhancing rather than exclusive.

REFERENCES

Chomsky, N. (1980), *Rules and Representations.* New York: Columbia University Press.

Corbett, L. & Kugler, P. (1989), The self in Jung and Kohut. *Dimensions of Self Experience: Progress in Self Psychology,* Vol. 5, ed. A. Goldberg. Hillsdale, NJ: The Analytic Press, pp.189–208.

Fordham, M. (1976), *The Self and Autism.* London: Heinemann.

——— (1985), *Explorations into the Self.* New York: Academic Press.

Freud, S. (1914), On narcissism: An introduction. *Standard Edition,* 14:73, 102, London: Hogarth Press, 1957.

——— (1933), New introductory lectures on psycho-analysis. *Standard Edition,* 20: 5–182. London: Hogarth Press, 1964.

Gordon, R. (1979), Reflections on curing and healing. *J. Anal Psychol,* 24:207–219.

——— (1980), Narcissism and the self. *J. Anal. Psychol,* 25:247–264.

Hanley, C. & Masson, J. (1976), A critical examination of the new narcissism. *Internat. J. Psycho Anal.* 57:49–66.

Jacoby, M. (1981), Reflections on Heintz Kohut's concepts of narcissism. *J. Anal. Psychol,* 26:107–110.

Jung, C.G. (1960), The psychogenesis of mental disease. In: *The Collected Works of C.G. Jung,* Vol. 3, ed. H. Read, M. Fordham & G. Adler (trans. R. Hull). Princeton, NJ: Princeton University Press/Bollingen Series XX.

——— (1966a), The practice of psychotherapy. In: *The Collected Works of C.G. Jung,* Vol. 16, ed. H. Read, M. Fordham & G. Adler (trans. R. Hull). Princeton, NJ: Princeton University Press/Bollingen Series XX.

——— (1966b), Two essays on analytical psychology. In: *The Collected Works of C.G. Jung,* Vol. 7, ed. H. Read, M. Fordham & G. Adler (trans. R. Hull). Princeton, NJ: Princeton University Press/Bollingen Series XX.

_____ (1967a), Symbols of transformation. In: *The Collected Works of C.G. Jung,* Vol. 5, ed. H. Read, M. Fordham & G. Adler (trans. R. Hull). Princeton, NJ: Princeton University Press/Bollingen Series XX.

_____ (1967b), Alchemical studies. In: *The Collected Works of C.G. Jung,* Vol. 13, ed. H. Read, M. Fordham & G. Adler (trans. R. Hull). Princeton, NJ: Princeton University Press/Bollingen Series XX.

_____ (1968a), Psychology and alchemy. In: *The Collected Works of C.G. Jung,* Vol. 12, ed. H. Read, M. Fordham & G. Adler (trans. R. Hull). Princeton, NJ: Princeton University Press/Bollingen Series XX.

_____ (1968b), Aion: Researches into the phenomenology of the self. In: *The Collected Works of C.G. Jung,* Vol. 9ii, ed. H. Read, M. Fordham & G. Adler (trans. R. Hull). Princeton, NJ: Princeton University Press/Bollingen Series XX.

_____ (1969a), The structure and dynamics of the psyche. In: *The Collected Works of C.G. Jung,* Vol. 8, ed. H. Read, M. Fordham & G. Adler (trans. R. Hull). Princeton, NJ: Princeton University Press/Bollingen Series XX.

_____ (1969b), Psychology and religion: West and East. In: *The Collected Works of C.G. Jung,* Vol. 11, ed. H. Read, M. Fordham & G. Adler (trans. R. Hull). Princeton, NJ: Princeton University Press/Bollingen Series XX.

_____ (1969c), The archetypes and the collective unconscious. In: *The Collected Works of C.G. Jung,* Vol. 9i, ed. H. Read, M. Fordham & G. Adler (trans. R. Hull). Princeton, NJ: Princeton University Press/Bollingen Series XX.

_____ (1971), Psychological types. In: *The Collected Works of C.G. Jung,* Vol. 6, ed. H. Read, M. Fordham & G. Adler (trans. R. Hull). Princeton, NJ: Princeton University Press/Bollingen Series XX.

_____ (1973), *Letters, Vol. I,* ed. G. Adler (trans. R.F.C. Hull). Princeton, NJ: Princeton University Press.

_____ (1976), The symbolic life: Miscellaneous writings. In: *The Collected Works of C.G. Jung,* Vol. 18, ed. H. Read, M. Fordham & G. Adler (trans. R. Hull). Princeton, NJ: Princeton University Press/Bollingen Series XX.

Kalshed, D.E. (1979), Narcissism and the search for interiority. Unpublished thesis presented to the C.G. Jung Institute of New York.

Kohut, H. (1966), Forms and transformations of narcissism. *J. Amer. Psychoanal. Assn.,* 14:243–272.

_____ (1971), *The Analysis of the Self.* New York: International Universities Press.

_____ (1977), *The Restoration of the Self.* New York: International Universities Press.

_____ (1984), *How Does Analysis Cure?* ed. A. Goldberg & P.E. Stepansky. Chicago: University of Chicago Press.

Kugler, P.N. & Turvey, M. (1987). *Information, Natural Law and the Self Assembly of Rhythmic Movements.* Hillsdale, NJ: Lawrence Erlbaum Associates, pp. 405–423.

Piaget, J. & Inhelder, B.(1969). *The Psychology of the Child.* New York: Basic Books.

Plaut, A. (1956). The transference in analytical psychology. In: *Techniques in Jungian Analysis,* ed. M. Fordham. London: Heinemann, 1974, pp. 152–160.

Redfearn, J.W.T. (1983), Ego and self terminology. *J. Anal. Psychol.,* 28:91–106.

Roazen, P. (1976), *Freud and His Followers.* New York: Knopf.

Samuels, A. (1985), *Jung and the Post-Jungians.* London: Routledge & Kegan Paul.

Schwartz-Salant, N. (1982), *Narcissism and Character Transformation.* Toronto: Inner City.

Steele, R.S. (1982), *Freud and Jung Conflicts of Interpretation.* London: Routledge & Kegan Paul.

Stolorow, R. & Lachmann, F. (1980), *Psychoanalysis and Developmental Arrests.* New York: International Universities Press.

Yates, F.E. & Kugler, P.N. (1984). Signs, singularities and significance: A physical model for semniotics. *Semniotica,* 52:49–77.

3

Adler, Kohut, and the Idea of a Psychoanalytic Research Tradition

Paul E. Stepansky

Michael Polanyi (1958), who, among contemporary philosophers of science, has addressed himself most profoundly to the "intellectual passions" that fuel scientific discovery, provides us with a compelling statement on the "logical gap" that separates the protagonists in a scientific controversy. I quote him at length because his remarks capture, with uncanny timeliness, the tenor of the ongoing controversy in psychoanalysis between the proponents and opponents of Heinz Kohut's self psychology:

> . . . scientific controversies never lie altogether within science. For when a new system of thought concerning a whole class of alleged facts is at issue, the question will be whether it should be accepted or rejected in principle, and those who reject it on such comprehensive grounds will inevitably regard it as altogether incompetent and unsound. . . . The two conflicting systems of thought are separated by a logical gap, in the same sense as a problem is separated from the discovery which solves the problem. Formal operations relying on *one* framework of interpretation cannot demonstrate a proposition to persons who

Previously published in *The Annual of Psychoanalysis,* 11:51–74, 1983. Reprinted with minor changes with the kind permission of The Chicago Institute for Psychoanalysis.

> rely on *another* framework. Its advocates may not even succeed in getting a hearing from these, since they must first teach them a new language, and no one can learn a new language unless he first trusts that it means something. . . . Proponents of a new system can convince their audience only by first winning their intellectual sympathy for a doctrine they have not yet grasped. Those who listen sympathetically will discover for themselves what they would otherwise never have understood. Such an acceptance is a heuristic process, a self-modifying act, and to this extent a conversion. It produces disciples forming a school, the members of which are separated for the time being by a logical gap from those outside it. They think differently, speak a different language, live in a different world, and at least one of the two schools is excluded to this extent for the time being (whether rightly or wrongly) from the community of science [pp. 150–151].

But Polanyi's fatalistic posture on the radical incommensurability of competing scientific systems does not blind him to the productive necessity of just such controversies in the history of science. "Our appreciation of scientific value," he goes on to state,

> has developed historically from the outcome of such controversies, much as our sense of justice has taken shape from the outcome of judicial decisions through past centuries. . . . ultimately, all past mental strife can be interpreted today only in the light of what we ourselves decide to be the outcome and lesson of this history. And we have to take this decision within the context of contemporary controversies which perhaps challenge these lessons afresh and raise in their turn quite novel questions of principle. The lesson of history is what we ourselves accept as such [p. 158].

It is with Polanyi's strictures in mind that I approach the comparison between Kohut and Alfred Adler, the earliest exemplar of "dissidence" in psychoanalysis. My attempt to explicate the "outcome and lesson" of Adler's dissidence in 1911 as it bears on Kohut's self psychology as it developed in the 1970s will ultimately have a paradoxical effect: I will show that certain formal comparabilities between Adler's self psychology and Kohut's self psychology may belie a striking incommensurability between the "dissident" status of their respective theories. My intention in undertaking this comparative analysis is to goad analysts to reflect more critically on the historical meaning of dissent in their profession. It is not enough to take the early defections from Freud as a secure referent—a paradigm—for adjudging the dissident implications of ongoing innovations in theory and practice. To the contrary, it is recent innovations deriving from a contemporary perspective on analysis that should induce analysts to reconsider the first generation of psychoanalytic dissidents with new critical awareness of the historical evolution of their profession over nine decades.

I

Consider the critique of classical analysis embodied in Adler's summary lectures before the Vienna Psychoanalytic Society in the winter of 1911. Here, on the eve of his rupture with Freud, Adler rejected the analytic concept of ego instincts as "redundant and empty," arguing that these instincts should be viewed not as rigidified and discrete, but as part of an expansive outlook (*Einstellung*) directed toward the environment. For Adler (1911b), this dynamic concept of the ego was tantamount to a striving for significance, for power, for dominance, all of which he equated with the cultural valuation of the "masculine" (pp. 104–105).

In accord with his view of ego development as inherently expansive and assertive, Adler rejected the idea of primary instinctual aggression. In fact, as early as 1908, in his paper on "The Aggressive Drive in Life and Neurosis," Adler had confronted the Vienna group with a remarkably nonpsychoanalytic perspective on the drives. Elaborating certain presuppositions about the nature of organ activity spelled out in his monograph on organ inferiority of 1907, Adler assigned a separate "drive" to each organ and proceeded to identify drive satisfaction with primary organ activity. Within this schema, "aggression" was construed as the energy field that potentiated individual organ performance. By this analysis, aggression was not an "instinctual" drive, but an aspect of the "psychological super-structure" that directed organ activity. Adler (1908) called it "a superordinated psychological field connecting the drives" (p. 28). Aggression, for Adler, thereby inhered in organs; any behavioral aggression existing apart from the healthy activity of organ systems was a secondary, derived phenomena. This kind of secondary "destructive" aggression ensued when an organ system was subject to frustration; it embodied the unfinished excitation (*unerledigte Erregung*) that afflicted the individual whose organ drives were denied satisfaction.

In a paper of 1909, "On Neurotic Disposition: A Contribution both to the Etiology of Neurosis and the Question of the Choice of Neurosis," Adler elaborated this perspective further, equating the unfinished excitation of the malfunctioning organ with a kind of organic "oversensitivity" (*Überempfindlichkeit*). "Oversensitive" organs were organs unable to function normally and thereby release the normal quota of aggression inhering in their healthy functioning. With organs that were inferior and hence oversensitive, the dammed-up aggression inhering in organ activity was displaced to general behavior and released in antisocial ways; unreleased organ aggression, in other words, became the basis for characterologically destructive aggression.

Adler's estimation of the ego as inherently expansive and assertive in accord with a governing masculine principle, teamed with his conception of the drives as corresponding with the normal aggressive potential of various organ systems, led to his reassessment of libido and infantile sexuality from the standpoint of the masculine protest. This reassessment was premised on the assumption that only the sexual "organ" could be generative of genuine sexuality. To the extent that sexuality assumed a broader connection with drive life, this reflected the ability of different inferior organ systems to appropriate the sexual factor on behalf of their own "psychical compensations." In less arcane phraseology, Adler's (1911a) point was simply that sexual constitution could be cultivated in response to the compensatory needs of different types of organ inferiorities (pp. 94–95).

The masculine protest provided an evaluative paradigm for understanding infantile sexuality by providing a referent against which the interpersonal significance of sexuality could be appraised. Precociously stimulated sexuality, for Adler, entered into neurosis because it represented a type of safeguard or security device (*Sicherung*) through which the neurotically predisposed child could mitigate his feeling of inferiority and achieve adequate self-esteem or "self feeling" (*Persönlichkeitsgefühl*).[1] To the extent that libidinal

[1]The term *Persönlichkeitgefühl,* a central article in Adler's post-Freudian writings, first appears in *The Nervous Character* of 1912, the full-scale explication of Adler's "system" that was the logical outcome of his summary lectures before the Vienna Psychoanalytic Society (see Stepansky, 1983, pp. 151ff.). Adler's various English translators have carelessly and inconsistently rendered the term "individuality-feeling," "self-esteem," or "feeling or personality," effectively obscuring its technical importance as an organizing concept of Adler's psychology. In the context of this presentation, I feel entirely comfortable with the translation "self feeling" as a

expressiveness subserved "self feeling," Adler argued that the libido of the neurotic was "inauthentic"; it subserved ulterior interpersonal aims promoting self-esteem—that is, a viable self feeling.

In accounting for neurotic development in the child, Adler did not invoke a notion of unempathic mothering per se, but he did single out the quality of the child's adaptation to his family environment, in particular, the "affective values" (*Gefühlswerte*) adhering to the child's first adaptations to the significant persons of his environment. When these values were negative, when the child's feelings toward the parents reflected insecurity, timidity, and defiance instead of security and love, the child felt "inferior" and resorted to neurotic safeguards to ward off his sense of worthlessness (1911b, p. 106).

From this development perspective on neurosogenesis, there followed Adler's more pointed commentary on the Freudian drives and the Oedipus complex. As Adler saw it, Freud's drives were in reality derivative phenomena that functioned as compensatory attempts to ward off the inferiority (i.e., the lack of self feeling) occasioned by deficient early parenting. Defiance and obedience—in a more contemporary idiom, aggressiveness and passive compliance—were the principal safeguarding tendencies that determined the manifestations of drive life. When appropriated by the child whose attachment to his parents was characterized by negative affective values, these reactive characterological formations blossomed into protective strategies designed to "modify, change, suppress, or excite every drive impulse to such an extent that anything that manifests itself as a veritable drive can be understood only from this point of view" (1911, p. 106).

The reappraisal of the Oedipus complex was the logical outcome of Adler's reassessment of the drives. Since sexual precocity functioned as part of a "defiant" safeguarding tendency designed to restore masculine "self feeling," it stood to reason that

---

contemporary expression of Adler's intended meaning. The essential point, of course, is that Adler's understanding of psychological development and the neurotic process in 1911–1912 pointed to a state of "self" or "person" that transcended the framework and the terminology of an "ego" psychology. (This contrasts with my earlier decision [Stepansky, 1983] to translate the term "ego feeling.") Significantly, the term *Ich* does not appear in Adler's writings, although Freud, of course, was pejoratively to identify Adler's work with "ego psychology" (*Ichpsychologie*) both in the Vienna Society debates of 1911 (Nunberg and Federn, 1974, p. 147) and, subsequently, in "On the History of the Psycho-Analytic Movement" (Freud, 1914, pp. 52, 55).

mere recognition of the libidinal component of the Oedipus complex frequently did not lead to therapeutic improvement. Hence Adler's (1911b) plaint: "I have seen plenty of patients who are sufficiently knowledgeable about their Oedipus complexes without feeling any better" (pp. 113–114). Only when the Oedipus complex was understood as "a small part of the overpowering neurotic dynamic, a stage of the masculine protest," did it become "instructive in its context" (p. 114). The precise route by which aggressiveness toward one parent and sexual possessiveness toward the other subserved a sense of masculine self feeling was spelled out by Adler in a paper of 1910 written for the *Zentralblatt für Psychoanalyse.* In a "Contribution to the Theory of Resistance," he explained that oedipal rivalry and jealousy in the young child were essentially unrelated to normal *sexual* development. Instead, these emotions corresponded to the fact that, already in the first year of life, the neurotically predisposed infant operated according to a standard of masculine possessiveness that led him to seize hold of persons who satisfied his needs and to experience jealousy toward those objects that would frustrate this "desire to possess" (*Besitzenwollen*). The Oedipus complex did no more than mark the appearance of the child's strategies for safeguarding his parental "possessions":

> The oedipal forms of experience, which Freud has described in the clearest and most unequivocal way, have in themselves no driving energy. They successfully function as a [developmental] landmark and they succeed in obtaining [clinical] recognition because they depict striking manifestations of the dynamics of neurosis, and furthermore because they can be construed without further consideration as a momento or a means of expression understood within the framework of the masculine protest [Adler, 1910, p. 218].

II

Heinz Kohut, I would argue, effected a comparable reassessment of classical drive theory from the standpoint of his psychology of the self "in the broad sense." For Kohut, as for Adler, the epigenetic principle of self development, understood holistically, leads to a reconceptualization of clinical data that have long been taken to support classical drive theory. Like Adler, Kohut sought to supplant a conceptual focus on discrete ego instincts operating inside a mental apparatus with a self that is inherently assertive and expansive in obtaining nurturance (i.e., selfobject sustenance) and whose ultimate vitality and cohesiveness account for mental health.

Although Kohut's theory of self development takes as its obvious point of departure certain inductions that followed the psychoanalytic treatment of patients with severe narcissistic disorders (1971), the broadening estimation of the role of narcissistic vulnerability in human development that bridges Kohut's transition from a psychology of narcissism to the psychology of the self has a significant Adlerian referent. In "Thoughts on Narcissism and Narcissistic Rage" (1972), an important transitional essay that retains the language but not the delimited psychopathological focus of *The Analysis of the Self* (1971), Kohut undertook to resuscitate Adler's notion of "organ inferiority" by refracting this concept from the standpoint of a narcissistic energetics. For Kohut, the "inferior organ" regained its status as a valid object of analytic focus when reconceptualized as a reservoir of the "archaic narcissistic cathexis of the child's body-self." The pathogenic implications of such cathectic investment in a defective organ were environmentally determined; they derived from a mother's failure to provide confirming "mirroring" responses to the child who was victimized by such a bodily defect. When this occurred, the child's narcissistic cathexis of his inferior organ became frozen at the level of archaic-grandiose goals, split off from the reality ego that normally tempered and eventually transformed archaic narcissism. When the grandiose-exhibitionistic claims associated with archaic narcissism broke through the repression barrier, the organ-inferior child was flooded with a sense of shame and with "narcissistic rage" (1972, pp. 628–632).

The reconceptualization of instinctual aggression as "narcissistic rage"—i.e., as a reactive aggression deriving from the archaic claims of a "grandiose self" and the archaic demands placed on idealized "selfobjects" (1972, pp. 643–645)—paves the way for the more radical reassessment of aggression—and of classical drive theory in general—effected in *The Restoration of the Self* (1977). From his developmental assumptions about the "assertive" quality of healthy self development, Kohut, paralleling Adler in certain respects, posits that the child's destructive aggressiveness is not an expression of primary instinctuality, but a regression product, a fragment of the healthy assertiveness of the nuclear self. Kohut's destructive aggression, like Adler's "defiance," functions as a pathological means of regaining viable "self feeling"—it is a self "safeguard" activated under conditions in which the self has not elicited the type of empathic parenting that issues in a cohesive nuclear self—or, adopting Adler's terminology, in adequate "self feeling" (pp. 114–119).

In a comparably Adlerian way, Kohut expands the new perspective on aggression into a radical reinterpretation of drive psychology in general. In accord with the presuppositions of a psychology of the self, the sexual drive derivatives are no longer to be conceptualized as primary constellations; they are instead "disintegration products" that reflect the childhood failure to elicit a degree of empathic responsiveness that can subserve the expansive, confirmatory needs of the self. Drive fixations reflect the "feebleness of the self" (p. 81); it is the self-selfobject failures of early life that lead to the "defensive" stimulation of erogenous zones along with the pleasure aims associated with them (pp. 74–81). Comparably, the perversions are reconceptualized as disintegration products in which the self deprived of empathic parenting attempts to regain a lost self-selfobject merger by pathological means (e.g., by sadistic fantasies that constitute a pathological attempt to regain possession of an idealized omnipotent selfobject).

In line with an ostensibly Adlerian estimation of both aggression and the sexual drive derivatives, the self-psychological approach to the experiential content of the Oedipus complex has become increasingly Adlerian in its consideration of oedipal dynamics from the standpoint of the requirements of burgeoning selfhood. In *The Restoration of the Self* (1977), Kohut was content merely to pose rhetorically the possibility that self-psychological stress on the intrinsically positive aspects of the oedipal period might entail "a different perception of the very content of the child's oedipal experiences" (p. 246). Over the next four years, Kohut apparently answered this question to his own satisfaction, and he subsequently differentiated a pathological Oedipus complex from a healthy oedipal stage; the latter, in accord with the presentation in *The Restoration of the Self,* was conceptualized as a joyfully experienced stage of self development in which the child derives enhanced self-esteem from parental selfobject validation of the developmental achievement betokened by phase-appropriate forms of oedipal expressiveness (pp. 228ff.). The Oedipus complex, on the other hand, became a pathological distortion of healthy self development that acquired meaning as a "means of expression" (in Adler's terms) for an oedipal self whose phase-appropriate "vigor and assertiveness" (p. 230) had not elicited parental confirmation. The following passage from "Selected Problems of Self Psychological

Theory," one of Kohut's final essays, highlights the quasi-Adlerian import of differentiating a healthy oedipal stage from a pathological Oedipus complex:

> . . . the failures of the oedipal selfobjects . . . transform the normal upsurge of affectionateness and assertiveness—essential attributes of the proud and joyful oedipal self—into the pathological and pathogenic drives, which we traditionally viewed as the manifestations of the final stage of normal infantile sexuality. Suffice it to say that, as with "preoedipal" infantile sexuality and destructive aggression, we consider the infantile sexuality and hostile-destructive aggression of the oedipal phase (i.e., the Oedipus complex) to be disintegration products. As such, they supervene only after the selfobjects have failed to respond to the primary affectionateness and assertiveness of the oedipal-phase self with fondness and pride because they have, on the basis of their own psychopathology, experienced (preconsciously) these emotions of their oedipal child as sexually stimulating and aggressively threatening [1981, p. 390; cf. 1984, pp. 22ff.].

III

The comparable import of Adlerian theory and contemporary self psychology on classical drive theory points to a meaningful historical question: If, following Freud's critical estimation of Adler's work in 1911, we consider Adler a "dissident," must we not consider Kohut a "dissident" as well? Conversely, if we find Kohut's work compatible with psychoanalysis—if self psychology "in the broad sense" embodies a theoretical advance mandated by important clinical discoveries, are we not entitled to defend the psychoanalytic status of Adler's work from the same clinical vantage point? Kohut has explicitly appealed to the therapeutic effectiveness of self psychology relative to classical theory in defending the central *psychoanalytic* import of his theories (Kohut, 1979). But it was Adler who continually invoked the perspective of clinical relevance throughout his dialogue with the Freudians: "I have seen plenty of patients who are sufficiently knowledgeable about their Oedipus complexes without feeling any better." If Kohut's self psychology is entitled to retain the "psychoanalytic" appellation, why not the self psychology posited by the masculine protest?

My historical viewpoint in approaching these issues leads me to pose the following question: Was psychoanalysis the same thing for Kohut in 1981 as it was for Adler in 1911? Or, in somewhat different terms, did the psychoanalytic tradition against which the admissibility of Adler's and Kohut's theories must be appraised remain unchanged in 70 years?

In the remaining portion of this essay, I will address these questions by invoking a key distinction between "theories" and "research traditions" that Laudan has elaborated in *Progress and its Problems* (1977). In a significant continuation of a methodological and historical debate initiated by Kuhn's (1962) theory of scientific "paradigms" and Lakatos's (1970) theory of "research programmes," Laudan has offered a persuasive reassessment of the epistemological status of "global theories" in scientific progress. He has differentiated between global theories or "research traditions" and the more delimited theories that fall within, and collectively exemplify, such traditions, in the following way: A research tradition is characterized only by certain metaphysical and methodological commitments, i.e., it specifies certain modes of procedure which constitute legitimate methods of inquiry within the tradition in question. Research traditions such as Darwinism, Cartesian physics, Newtonian physics, and quantum theory are thereby understood as providing a set of guidelines for the development of specific theories conforming with the metaphysical and methodological requirements of the tradition. Such guidelines constitute an ontology that specifies, in a general way, the type of fundamental entities existing in the domain within which the research tradition is conceptually situated. The ontological guidelines posited by Cartesian physics, to take but one illustrative example, posit that only matter and minds exist; other substances (e.g., mixed mind and matter) have no ontological status within the research tradition. Comparably, the Cartesian stricture that particles of matter only interact by contact means that physical theories presupposing any type of action-at-a-distance necessarily exist outside the Cartesian research tradition (Laudan, 1977, p. 79).

Laudan points out that many theories within an evolving research tradition will be mutually inconsistent rivals, precisely because some of these theories will represent attempts to improve earlier theories within the framework of the tradition. It is unexceptional, then, that the Cartesian research tradition, to return to our example, should generate optical theories positing that light travels faster in optically denser media and opposing theories maintaining the very opposite; both kinds of theories conform to the ontological guidelines integral to Cartesianism (p. 85).

To repeat and summarize, a research tradition only specifies a general ontology for nature and a general method for solving natural problems within a given natural domain. A theory falling within a research tradition, on the other hand, articulates a very specific ontology and a number of specific and testable laws about nature.

Laudan's distinction between discrete theories and the broader research traditions that encompass them provides a useful conceptual framework for critically estimating the dissident implications of the theories of Adler and Kohut. I would argue that when Adler broke from Freud in 1911 he was deviating from specific clinical theories with delimited experiential content. For all intents and purposes, libido theory and the Oedipus complex *were* psychoanalysis in 1911. No superordinate psychoanalytic research tradition existed to which Adler could appeal to justify the psychoanalytic admissibility of his perspective, just as no community of analysts existed who embodied this research tradition and to whom Adler could appeal. The fact is that Adler's work was ultimately appraised as nonanalytic by a community of one: Freud. This is tantamount to saying that psychoanalysis in 1911 did not entail methodological commitments that transcended the basic content of Freud's early clinical discoveries; it was not a question of studying psychopathology from the standpoint of a psychoanalytic "method" that could be divorced from the content of these clinical theories. In 1911, Freud clearly believed that acceptance of the clinical theories encompassing his early discoveries was always at issue in the attribution of a specifically "psychoanalytic" identity (cf. Stepansky, 1983, pp. 202–205).

This stress on clinical content as the proving ground for psychoanalytic affiliation highlights the political concerns that were paramount during the early years of the psychoanalytic movement. By 1910, in the aftermath of the Nuremberg Congress that heralded the birth of the International Psychoanalytic Association, Freud's intensifying preoccupation with the politicization of analysis had this consequence: It led him to view any Vienna Society member who rejected the content of clinical theory as jeopardizing the unity of the psychoanalytic front and thereby impeding the political institutionalization of the movement (Stepansky, 1983, chapter 5). Despite the internal consistency of Adler's views for the entire tenure of his involvement with the psychoanalytic group, it was only in 1911 that Freud negatively reassessed the viability of his continuing affiliation with analysis. Only in the aftermath of Nuremberg, in other words, did Freud become convinced that Adler's reformulation of the clinical *content* of analysis, as determined by libido *theory,* jeopardized the political unity of the movement.

The interpenetration of Freud's estimation of clinical theory with his political sensitivity to the public image of the movement is highlighted by the eroding estimation of Adler that he confided to Jung. As early as December 19, 1909, Freud gauged his unhappiness with Adler's work, along with his incipient apprehensiveness about the direction of Jung's own theorizing, in these revealing terms:

> Thus far, it is true, I have concentrated on the repressed material, because it is new and unknown; I have been a Cato championing the *causa victa:* I hope I have not forgotten that there is also a *victrix.* Adler's psychology takes account only of the repressive factor; consequently he describes "sensitivity," this attitude of the ego in opposition to the libido, as the fundamental condition of neurosis. And now I find you taking the same line and using almost the same word: i.e., by concentrating on the ego, which I have not adequately studied, you run the risk of neglecting the libido, to which I have done full justice [McGuire, 1974, pp. 277–278].

A year later, Freud was more explicit in addressing the growing Adlerian liability from the standpoint of Adler's rejection of the clinical theories:

> The crux of the matter—and that is what really alarms me—is that he [Adler] minimizes the sexual drive and our opponents will soon be able to speak of an experienced psychoanalyst whose conclusions are radically different from ours. Naturally in my attitude toward him I am torn between my conviction that all this is lopsided and harmful and my fear of being regarded as an intolerant old man who holds the young men down . . . [p. 376].

By March of 1911, Freud was frankly adament in protesting the politically deleterious impact of Adler's work on the cause: ". . . we inside our circle really ought to come to a decision about Adler, before he is held up to us by outsiders" (p. 409).

IV

It is noteworthy that, almost seven decades after Adler's reinterpretation of libido theory eventuated in his rupture with Freud, Kohut should espouse a self psychology incorporating key elements of the Adlerian critique. But the seeming comparability of self psychology with certain assumptions of Adlerian theory masks an underlying incommensurability: Kohut understands analysis to be a research tradition (in Laudan's sense) that is radically discontinuous with the content of specific clinical theories—Freud's included. For Kohut, analysis as a research tradition encompasses no more than the specific methodology appropriate to the subject matter of a "depth psychology"; the ontology of psychoanalysis reduces to the product of a depth-psychological investigation employing a suitably "psychoanalytic" method of inquiry. Kohut has consistently defined this methodology in terms of introspection and empathy (1959; 1971, pp. 300–307; 1977, pp. 302–312; 1980, pp. 482–489; 1984, pp. 174–175). This methodological perspective, in turn, accounts for Kohut's frequent use of "psychoanalytic" as an adjective, as in his recurrent references to a "psychoanalytic depth psychology" and to "psychoanalytic self psychology." Psychoanalysis, from this vantage point, refers to "the domain of the psychology of complex mental states," whereas this "domain" is adequately defined "when we say that it is that aspect of reality that is accessible via introspection and empathy" (1980, p. 488). Empathy, in turn, becomes a "data-gathering operation," a "value-neutral tool of depth-psychological observation" (pp. 487, 484). Construed in this way, empathy is to be scrupulously differentiated from the clinical results to which the empathic operation leads (p. 485).

It follows from this perspective that Kohut understands Freud's enduring legacy to generations of analysts to be neither the content of clinical theory nor the viewpoints of metapsychology, but the introspective-empathic method of investigating depth-psychological phenomena. Historically, Kohut (1980) traces analysis to "the investigation of the field that had been opened by Breuer's and Anna O's discovery" (p. 488). The encounter between Breuer and Anna O is "the mutation that opened the door to the new field of introspective-empathic depth psychology (psychoanalysis)" (1977, p. 301). Breuer and Freud are "par excellence pioneers in the *scientific* use of introspection and empathy" (Kohut, 1959, p. 211). Here are the terms in which Kohut (1981) enjoins his colleagues to adopt his operational perspective on analysis:

> I believe . . . that analysts should realize that it is not specific theories that define their science, but the field of investigation (the inner life of man) as defined by their basic observational stance (introspection and empathy). The contributions of both Newton and Planck, although based on completely different orienting theories, constitute physics because the field of observation (the inanimate world) and the scientist's basic attitude toward it (extrospection) remain unchanged. And the same should hold true for psychoanalysis, a science that is defined not by the specific theories formulated by Freud's ordering mind, however awe-inspiring the depth and breadth of his life work, but by the good fortune—the genius of the moment, one might say—of Breuer's and Anna O's seminal encounter. It is the basic psychoanalytic situation, in other words, the situation of someone reporting his inner life while another empathically listens to the report in order to be able to explain it, that defines analysis and not the particular theory or ordering principle that the listener employs [p. 409].

In a way that is entirely consistent with this viewpoint, Kohut has held, from early in his work, that the primary articles of psychoanalytic technique are of only secondary importance in defining analysis. Consider the early methodological statement, "Introspection, Empathy, and Psychoanalysis" (1959), where he relegated free association and the analysis of resistance to the status of "specific refinements" of introspection. The unquestionable value of these refinements in psychoanalytic observation, Kohut noted, did not "contradict the recognition that free association and resistance analysis are to be considered as auxiliary instruments, employed in the service of the introspective and empathic method of observation" (p. 211; see also 1977, p. 303).

Following Laudan, then, we might say that Kohut sees psychoanalysis as tantamount to a methodological commitment to the centrality of introspective-empathic data-gathering in the scientific study of depth-psychological contents; the particular theories that encapsulate such contents are essentially incidental to the methodology that constitutes the research tradition yielding all such theories. It follows that anything that emerges from a suitably scientific introspective-empathic investigation is, per se, "psychoanalytic."

From the standpoint of the history of psychoanalysis, Kohut's conception of self psychology as a new psychoanalytic "theory" falling within a more broadly gauged psychoanalytic "research tradition" certainly seems plausible, assuming one accepts the adequacy of Kohut's definition of the research tradition itself. I would submit that, historically, there is no a priori reason for rejecting out of hand his equation of this research tradition with a depth-psychological methodology that is independent of the clinical theories and metapsychological constructs handed down by Freud. Research traditions, as Laudan (1977, pp. 95–100) has persuasively shown, are themselves "*historical* creatures" that evolve not only with respect to specific theories which have formerly occupied a place of honor within the tradition (e.g., the Oedipus complex), but in relation to certain core elements of the tradition. From Kohut's standpoint, one would of course point to the status of intrapsychic conflict in nuclear psychopathology, the clinical status of narcissistic formations as pathological, and the equation of mental health with the relinquishment of narcissistic attachments and the commensurate growth of object-libidinal ties as formerly "core" assumptions that have undergone substantial modification if not outright abandonment at the hands of self-psychological theory.

The obvious question to be asked at this juncture is whether Kohut has abandoned certain elements of the psychoanalytic research tradition that are sacrosanct and cannot be rejected without repudiating the tradition itself. But this question is itself historical: What is taken to embody the unrejectable core of a given research tradition changes over time. In 1911, libido theory was unquestionably part of the unrejectable core of analysis; by the 1970s, this may no longer have been the case. The historical disjunction at issue is highlighted by considering the substantive grounds for Freud's repudiation of Adler in 1911. To suggest that certain aspects of Freud's critique of Adler in 1911 apply to Kohut's self psychology of the 1970s may be true enough, but may also represent an historically trivial observation. To the extent that psychoanalysis evolved over the course of 70 years, the epistemological centrality of Freud's criticisms of Adler may be open to question.

Consider Freud's commentary on Adler's summary lectures before the Vienna Psychoanalytic Society in the winter of 1911. Freud submitted that Adler's viewpoint was to be criticized because of its antisexual tendency and its tendency "directed against the value of detail and against the phenomenology of the neuroses" (Nunberg and Federn, 1974, p. 146). Adler's representation of neurosis was more specifically faulted because it was "seen from the standpoint of the ego and thought about from the standpoint of the ego, as the neurosis appears to the ego. This is ego psychology, deepened by the knowledge of the psychology of the unconscious" (p. 147). On behalf of the psychoanalytic community, Freud adjudged the damaging political implications of Adler's viewpoint in a way that blatantly incorporated a public referent into the definition of analysis: "by adopting the new terms [i.e., the terms of the masculine protest], we would have to suffer the loss of those terms that indicate our program and which have established our connection with the great cultural circles. The [concepts of] *suppression of instinct* and *overcoming resistance* have aroused the interest of all alert and educated people" (p. 147). Freud continued his criticism by referring to the deleterious psychological implications of Adler's viewpoint for the community of analysts: "instead of the psychology of the libido, of sexuality, it offers general psychology. It will, therefore, make use of the latent resistances that are still alive in every psychoanalyst, in order to make its influence felt. Consequently, this doctrine will at first do harm to the development of psychoanalysis; on the other hand, as far as psychoanalytic findings are concerned, it will remain sterile" (p. 147).

V

The verdict that Kohut's self psychology is ultimately a "psychoanalytic" self psychology must be an historical verdict, i.e., it must proceed from an assumption that the unrejectable core of analysis has changed eight decades after Freud's disavowal of Adler. To concede the importance of such change is effectively to concede the irrelevance of Freud's criticisms of Adler as they may in fact apply to Kohut. I believe a strong case can be made that such a change has occurred over the past eight decades, and that it is largely the result of the impact of ego psychology. Psychoanalysis by the 1970s openly aspired to the status of a "general psychology," and this aspiration, in turn, can no longer be summarily equated with "resistance" to the theory of infantile sexuality. Correspondingly, in the aftermath of the contributions of Anna Freud, Heinz Hartmann, Ernst Kris, and Rudolph Loewenstein, it no longer seems reasonable to reject as nonanalytic an "ego psychology deepened by the knowledge of the psychology of the unconscious"—the very formulation Freud invoked to underscore the incompatibility of Adler's viewpoint with analysis.

Kohut's perspective on Hartmann is noteworthy in this context and is worthy of special mention. Kohut sees Hartmann's interest in the problem of adaptation and his hypotheses of the conflict-free sphere in the ego and of the ego's primary and secondary autonomy as enlarging the domain of analysis beyond the parameters of a "conflict psychology," thereby paving the way for a self psychology that broadens the meaning of adaptation beyond the workings of a "mental apparatus"—the metaphor that Hartmann, of course, retains. Kohut (1980) expressed his indebtedness to Hartmann in these revealing terms:

> I am grateful to Hartmann because his work gave me the courage to move further along the road that his acknowledgment of the legitimacy of analytic interest in healthy functions had opened. And even though I know from many personal discussions with him that he could not have accepted the "psychology of the self in the broad sense" with which we are now working, I am very happy that he still read the manuscript of my *Analysis of the Self* (1971) and gave it his approval [pp. 544–545].

I submit that Kohut's desire to record self psychology's Hartmannian lineage should not be taken lightly by analysts because it points to the historicity of self psychology within a psychoanalytic research tradition. The fact that Hartmann, by Kohut's own admission, could not accept self psychology "in the broad sense" is in itself unexceptional; the transmission of any research tradition from one generation to the next always entails the possibility—even the likelihood—of a reinterpretation that introduces wholly novel elements into the tradition and thereby modifies it. Such intergenerational modification is customary within the history of science and has been discussed by Polanyi (1946, p. 58), among others. I would add, in passing, that in recent years the legacy of ego psychology has itself been confounded by the ongoing critique of metapsychology within psychoanalysis (e.g., the work of George Klein, Robert Holt, Roy Schafer, and John Gedo). Influential critics of the metapsychological commitments retained by ego psychology now constitute a theoretically influential segment of the psychoanalytic community that must ultimately appraise the psychoanalytic admissibility of Kohut's formulations.

I believe my presentation has to this point made clear the conceptual vantage point from which I approach self psychology. I believe a central issue regarding Kohut is not the clinical utility of his self-psychological categories, but the epistemological self-sufficiency of his understanding of psychoanalysis as a research tradition. It seems to me that we can reject both the content of significant portions of clinical theory and the language of metapsychology as constitutive of analysis and still question whether Kohut has adequately defined the psychoanalytic enterprise when he boils it down to a depth-psychological operation relying on introspection and empathy.

In presenting his operational perspective on psychoanalysis, Kohut, in his later years, stressed the fact that the analyst's employment of empathy must be "scientific" (1980, pp. 483ff.). But how do we know that empathy is being employed scientifically in the psychoanalytic setting? We presumably know that the analyst uses empathy "scientifically" when he obtains empathically derived data that, in accordance with his understanding of psychoanalytic theory, can be "ordered" into explanations and interpretations that are therapeutically efficacious. But what exactly is the relationship between empathically derived data and the explanatory theories through which these data are ordered in accounting for the therapeutic impact of particular interpretations, explanations, and reconstructions? To the extent that both empathically "accurate" data and theoretically "accurate" ordering principles are implicated in optimally therapeutic interpretations, the positive effect of such interpretations must be taken to confirm both the accuracy of the empathic data-gathering that precedes interpretation and the validity of the ordering principles that make the act of interpretation possible. This amounts to the claim that for psychoanalysis, as for other sciences, only theory complexes—not individual theories—are subject to empirical tests (Duhem, 1954). In the case of analysis, the theory complex that is invoked whenever interpretations prove successful is comprised of both the (empathic) methodology that accounts for objective understanding and the ordering principles that provide the basis for interpretation. An adequate definition of psychoanalysis as a research tradition must incorporate both dimensions of the psychoanalytic process. In Laudan's terms, it must provide not only a methodology, but an ontology that circumscribes the nature of theories that fall within the research tradition.

I have no difficulty with Kohut's claim that psychoanalytic data can be *gathered* via a neutral observational process relying on empathy. But the ordering process that issues in interpretations, explanations, and reconstructions cannot be neutral. One "orders" data according to existing theoretical commitments; "ordering" is a theory-laden operation. In psychoanalysis, or in any other science for that matter, what is it about "accurate" data that ensures either the truth-value or the problem-solving effectiveness of the theoretical principles according to which data are ordered? I submit that one cannot adequately define a scientific research tradition without commenting systematically on the ontology underlying the particular ordering principles—the theories—that organize data and provide the basis for deductive explanation. Research traditions cannot be defined solely on the basis of the precision with which they "obtain" the data that fall within their respective domains. Thus, to differentiate the "scientific" empathy that issues from psychoanalytic training and experience from empathy in its "popular" connotations (Kohut, 1980, pp. 483ff.) is really to do no more than reiterate that, within a given scientific domain, one can obtain "data" with varying degrees of precision. But is psychoanalysis fully constituted by virtue of its ability to collect data that are empathically "accurate"? I think rather that it becomes a scientific research tradition when its empathically derived data are "ordered" according to theoretically sound principles that derive from a specifiable ontology. Empathically accurate data may be a precondition for the interpretations that flow from these principles, but, to repeat, the data cannot be constitutive of either the truth-value or the clinical efficacy of interpretations that are inherently theory-laden. To this extent, I do not believe a "neutral" empathic operation can be meaningfully characterized as "scientific" (though it certainly may be characterized as "scientifically precise") as the term "scientific" is conventionally used.

I believe I have circumscribed the key dimension in which Kohut's perspective on psychoanalysis as a research tradition is still wanting: He neglected to provide an epistemological basis for imputing "scientific" status to explanations and interpretations that proceed not from a data-gathering operation, however precise and objective, but from an ordering operation that presupposes an ontology and derivable theoretical commitments. In short, Kohut (1977) was content to define psychoanalysis by delimiting the field of psychoanalytic observation (p. 306; 1984, pp. 174–175); he never addressed the psychoanalytic research tradition from the standpoint of how the analyst's empathic observations issue in what Thomä and Kächele (1975) in a related context, term "a reliable knowledge of the psychically alien" (p. 55). By presupposing rather than critically elucidating the "scientific" status of the analyst's nonempathic "ordering" of his data (Kohut, 1980, pp. 483-484)—by simply taking for granted the existence of consensually validated "scientific standards" that safeguard the employment of empathy in psychoanalytic research and therapy (Kohut, 1977, p. 305)—Kohut's perspective on the psychoanalytic research tradition provides no basis for ascribing validity to clinical theories that are the necessary condition for the dynamic and genetic interpretations that proceed from empathic data-gathering. To this extent, Kohut neglected to comment definitionally on the manner in which an empathic data-gathering operation is necessarily related to explanatory theories "from which one could derive recommendations for actions that have the power to change behavior" (Thomä and Kächele, 1975, p. 55). To be sure, the developmental psychology and theory of therapy that constitute self psychology *do* provide a cogent account of the therapeutic efficacy of self-psychological psychoanalysis, but Kohut explicitly dissociated his definition of psychoanalysis as a broadly gauged research tradition from the content of self psychology. To the extent that he could envision the possibility of a future in which the presently indispensable concepts of transference and resistance would be irrelevant to analysts (1977, p. 308), he would have had to concede, by the same rationale, the possibility of an even more distant future in which the key explanatory concepts of self psychology—the selfobject, transmuting internalization, and so forth—would be equally irrelevant. But the psychoanalytic research tradition, anchored in empathic data-gathering, would live on, and the question of defining this research tradition would remain.

It is certainly a reasonable first step to approach the significance of psychoanalytic theories from the standpoint of their "correlation" with the empathic data-gathering process (Kohut, 1977, p. 303), but I am not convinced that the mere fact of a correlation is adequate to identify the distinctively "psychoanalytic" features of psychoanalytic theories. To underscore the incompleteness of Kohut's operational approach to the psychoanalytic research tradition, let us briefly consider the work of Wilhelm Dilthey, the nineteenth-century psychologist-philosopher who defined all the cultural sciences (*Geisteswissenschaften*) from the standpoint of an "empathic" methodology that closely approximates Kohut's definition of psychoanalysis (see Hodges, 1944, 1952).

Dilthey argued that our knowledge of the cultural sciences is diametrically opposed to our knowledge of the natural sciences because we can only know physical objects as mere appearances, whereas we enter into human beings via sympathetic insight (*verstehen*) based on the identity between ourselves and what we study. This identity comes about through the power of mental expressions to evoke the same expression in the subject as in the object of study, enabling the subject to relive the object's experience as part of his own mental history. Dilthey termed this reproduced image of someone else's mental experience in ourselves the *Nachbild* (literally, the afterimage), and he believed the central role of the *Nachbild* in achieving sympathetic insight made psychology central to all the cultural sciences (Hodges, 1944, pp. 11–19). In his *Ideas Concerning a Descriptive and Analytic Psychology* (Dilthey, 1894), he went so far as to define the cultural sciences from the standpoint of a veritable "self psychology," holding that mental life was not reducible to sensations, feelings, or instincts, but to a total reaction of the whole self to the situations confronting it. The "self," for Dilthey as for Kohut, encompassed cognitive, affective, and conative elements, and it was the unity of the self that imparted a structural teleological unity to the successive actions of the individual. Dilthey's simple teleology was directed toward the happiness of the individual; Kohut's clinically sophisticated variant points to the cohesiveness and productive vitality of a self that has achieved sustenance from the archaic selfobjects of infancy and continues to derive strength from empathic relatedness to the "mature" selfobjects of later life.

In adopting this outlook, Dilthey was taking issue with the neo-Kantian distinction, popular in his day, between "nomothetic" natural sciences (i.e., generalizing, law-governed sciences) and "idiographic" cultural sciences (i.e., sciences confined to the study of the individual via descriptive and comparative methods). Indeed, Dilthey's "understanding psychology" took as its essential province the very cultural and historical concerns that Kohut (1975a, b) ultimately identified with a broadened self psychology. Dilthey believed the ultimate goal of understanding psychology was not the analysis of the individual self, but a more ranging consideration of the relationship of the individual to the cultural realm that was the most profound product of the *verstehen* operation. For Dilthey, *all* the cultural sciences shared a common foundation in psychology—not a "scientific" psychology modeled on the natural sciences, but a "realistic" psychology whose task was the study of the structures by which the various functions of the human mind were organized (Holborn, 1950). As a philosopher of history, he commended to the historian a hermeneutic approach that relied on a "trained intuitive insight" able to decipher the inner aims and motivations of the preeminently creative individuals of different historical epochs (Kluback, 1956, pp. 59ff.).

Dilthey, like Kohut, was taken to task by contemporaries who rejected both the methodological preconceptions and the expansive claims of his "self psychology." He was criticized by the neo-Kantians (e.g., Windelband, Rickert) who chided him for trying to separate psychology from the "extrospective" natural sciences, but also by contemporary psychologists like Ebbinghaus who took issue with the claim that "introspection" could reveal the deep-seated unity of mental life (Hodges, 1952, pp. 211–213).

Given the consistency with which Dilthey undertook to make an introspective-empathic psychology the scientific basis for work in the cultural sciences, are we justified in claiming that he theorized within, or at least significantly anticipated, a distinctively "psychoanalytic" research tradition? If not, what exactly is it that separates Dilthey from Freud and *his* particular utilization of a scientific introspective-empathic psychology?[2]

In posing these questions, I am not rejecting Kohut's operational perspective on psychoanalysis, but only suggesting that it has yielded a definition of analysis which, in its failure to address itself to the ontology of psychoanalytic theories, is epistemologically incomplete. Moreover, I am not sure that "among the sciences that inquire into the nature of man, psychoanalysis . . . is the *only one*

---

[2]This, of course, is the very question with which Hartmann (1927) grappled in attempting to *dissociate* psychoanalysis from Dilthey's "understanding" psychology (p. 373ff.). Hartmann's critique of Dilthey and Jaspers is highly suggestive of the vantage point from which he might have criticized Kohut's later equation of psychoanalysis with introspective-empathic observation. See, in particular, Hartmann's critical reply to Jasper's claim that empathic understanding "leads us . . . right into the mental connections themselves" (pp. 379ff.).

Hartmann's vigorous defense of psychoanalysis as an "explanatory" psychology rooted in the methods of the natural sciences renders still more interesting the matter of his "approval" of *The Analysis of the Self.* We should bear in mind, of course, that Kohut's consideration of empathy in this work is virtually a postscript to his elucidation of the narcissistic transferences and, as such, falls far short of the position he would adumbrate in *The Restoration of the Self* and later essays. In *The Analysis of the Self,* Kohut does not claim that the employment of scientific empathy encompasses a "psychoanalytic" research tradition, but is content to follow Hartmann (1927) in stressing that empathy can *only* be a data-collecting process: "The scientific psychologist, in general, and the psychoanalyst in particular, not only must have free access to empathic understanding; they must also be able to relinquish the empathic attitude. If they cannot be empathic, they cannot observe and collect the data which they need; if they cannot step beyond empathy, they cannot set up hypotheses and theories, and thus, ultimately, cannot achieve explanations" (Kohut, 1971, p. 303).

that, in its essential activities, combines empathy, employed with scientific rigor in order to gather the data of human experience, with experience-near and experience-distant theorizing, employed with equal scientific rigor in order to fit the observed data into a context of broader meaning and significance" (Kohut, 1977, pp. 302–303; emphasis added). Much remains to be clarified in the attempt to differentiate an introspective-empathic psychology that is distinctively "psychoanalytic" from the work of a whole succession of *verstehen* exemplars who espoused preanalytic introspective-empathic methodologies with equally scientific claims. Dilthey's work is certainly significant in this regard, but Max Weber's explanatory sociology also comes readily to mind. In his protracted grappling with the nineteenth-century *verstehen* tradition in German scholarship, Weber clearly differentiated between the internal meaning and the empirical-causal explanation of social action. As he saw it, the former dimension of sociological understanding was not only conceptually prior, but necessarily proceeded from an "imaginative reconstruction" of the aims and inner intentions of historical actors resulting from the scientific employment of the *verstehen* operation (see Weber, 1949).

My conclusion, regrettably but perhaps predictably, is that I am unable to offer a definitive verdict on the psychoanalytic status of Kohut's self psychology. On the one hand, I believe such a verdict must await a more substantive statement by Kohut's coworkers on the ontology of the psychoanalytic domain within which the analyst's empathic data-gathering is situated. But I would decline to offer a verdict in any event. The job of deciding what body of theory legitimately falls within the psychoanalytic research tradition, of reaffirming the enduring scientific value of psychoanalysis within the context of contemporary controversies that challenge historical lessons afresh and raise "quite novel questions of principle"—to return to Polanyi's formulation—ultimately falls to the community of analysts whose "lived experience"—to borrow the leitmotif of John Dewey's later philosophy—falls within the psychoanalytic research tradition itself. In this essay, with the aid of the analogy of Adler, I have undertaken only a skeletal clarification of the historical issues that bear on the question of dissidence. In the context of this discussion, I have argued for the hypothetical admissibility of self-psychological theories within a broadly construed psychoanalytic research tradition, but I have questioned the adequacy of Kohut's definition of the psychoanalytic research tradition within which his self-psychological theories are to be situated.

In closing, I enjoin analysts to undertake a fruitful dialogue that ranges beyond the clinical utility of self-psychological concepts to the basic issues of epistemology and methodology that are the enriching legacy of Kohut's theorizing. I believe such a dialogue, taking as its referent the relationship between theories and research traditions in the history of science, offers the prospect of bridging the logical gap that threatens to separate irremediably the proponents and opponents of self psychology, joining analysts who increasingly seem to "speak a different language" and "live in a different world"—as Polanyi puts it—in common scientific endeavor.

REFERENCES

Adler, A. (1907), *Study of Organ Inferiority and Its Psychical Compensation.* trans. S. E. Jelliffe. New York: Nervous and Mental Disease Pub., 1917._____ (1908), Der Aggressionstrieb im Leben und in der Neurose. In: *Heilen und Bilden: Aerztlich-paedagogische Arbeiten des Vereins fuer Individualpsychologie,* ed. A. Adler & C. Furtmueller. Munich: Ernst Reinhardt, 1914, pp. 23–32.

_____ (1909), Ueber neurotische Disposition: Zugleich ein Beitrag zur Aetiologie und zur Frage der Neurosenwahl. *Jahrbuch fuer Psychoanalytische Forschungen,* 1:526–545.

_____ (1910), Beitrag zur Lehre vom Widerstand, *Zentralblatt fuer Psychoanalyse,* 1:214–219.

_____ (1911a), Zur Kritik der Freudschen Sexualtheorie der Nervositaet: I. Die Rolle der Sexualitaet in der Neurose. In: *Heilen und Bilden: Aerztlich-paedagogische Arbeiten des Vereins fuer Individualpsychologie,* ed. A. Adler & C. Furtmueller. Munich: Ernst Reinhardt, 1914, pp. 94–103.

_____ (1911b), Zur Kritik der Freudschen Sexualtheorie der Nervositaet: II. "Verdraengung" und "Maennlicher Protest"; Ihre Rolle und Bedeutung fuer die neurotische Dynamik. In: *Heilen un Bilden: Aerztlich-paedagogische Arbeiten des Vereins fuer Individualpsychologie,* ed. A. Adler & C. Furtmueller. Munich: Ernst Reinhardt, 1914, pp. 103–114.

_____ (1912), *Ueber den Nervoesen Charakter: Grundzuege einer vergleichenden Individual-Psychologie und Psychotherapie.* Wiesbaden: J. F. Bergmann.

Dilthey, W. (1894), Ideen über eine beschreibende und zergliedernde Psychologie. In: *Gesammelte Schriften,* Vol. 5 Leipzig: Teubner, 1964.

Duhem, P. (1954), *The Aim and Structure of Physical Theory.* Princeton, NJ: Princeton University Press.

Freud, S. (1914), On the history of the psycho-analytic movement. *Standard Edition,* 14:7–66. London: Hogarth Press, 1957.

Hartmann, H. (1927), Understanding and explanation. In: *Essays on Ego Psychology.* New York: International Universities Press, 1964, pp. 369–403.

Hodges, H. (1944), *Wilhelm Dilthey.* London: Routledge & Kegan Paul, 1969.

——— (1952), *The Philosophy of Wilhelm Dilthey.* London: Routledge & Kegan Paul.

Holborn, H. (1950), Wilhelm Dilthey and the critique of historical reason. *J. Hist. Ideas,* 11:93–118.

Kluback, W. (1956), *Wilhelm Dilthey's Philosophy of History.* New York: Columbia University Press.

Kohut, H. (1959), Introspection, empathy, and psychoanalysis: An examination of the relationship between mode of observation and theory. In: *The Search for the Self,* Vol. 1, ed. P. Ornstein. New York: International Universities Press, 1978, pp. 205–232.

——— (1971), *The Analysis of the Self.* New York: International Universities Press.

——— (1972), Thoughts on narcissism and narcissistic rage. In: *The Search for the Self,* Vol. 2, ed. P. Ornstein. New York: International Universities Press, 1978, pp. 615–658.

——— (1975a), The future of psychoanalysis. In: *The Search for the Self,* Vol. 2, ed. P. Ornstein. New York: International Universities Press, 1978, pp. 663–684.

——— (1975b), The psychoanalyst in the community of scholars. In: *The Search for the Self,* Vol. 2, ed. P. Ornstein. New York: International Universities Press, 1978, pp. 685–724.

——— (1977), *The Restoration of the Self.* New York: International Universities Press.

——— (1979), The two analyses of Mr. Z. *Internat. J. Psycho-Anal.,* 60:3–27.

——— (1980), Reflections on *Advances in Self Psychology.* In: *Advances in Self Psychology,* ed. A. Goldberg. New York: International Universities Press, pp. 473–554.

——— (1981), Selected problems of self psychological theory. In: *Reflections on Self Psychology,* ed. J. Lichtenberg & S. Kaplan. Hillsdale, NJ: The Analytic Press, 1983, pp. 387–416.

——— (1984), *How Does Analysis Cure?* ed. A. Goldberg and P. E. Stepansky. Chicago: University of Chicago Press.

Kuhn, T. (1962), *The Structure of Scientific Revolutions.* Chicago: University of Chicago Press.

Lakatos, I. (1970), Falsification and the methodology of scientific research programmes. In: *Criticism and the Growth of Knowledge,* ed. I. Lakatos and A. Musgrave. London: Cambridge University Press, pp. 91–196.

Laudan, L. (1977), *Progress and its Problems.* Berkeley: University of California Press.

McGuire, W., ed. (1974), *The Freud/Jung Letters,* trans. R. Manheim & R.F.C. Hull. Princeton, NJ: Princeton University Press.

Nunberg, H. & Federn, E., ed. (1974), *Minutes of the Vienna Psychoanalytic Society,* Vol. 3, trans. M. Nunberg. New York: International Universities Press.

Polanyi, M. (1946), *Science, Faith and Society.* Chicago: University of Chicago Press, 1964.

_____ (1958), *Personal Knowledge.* New York: Harper & Row, 1964.

Stepansky, P. (1983), *In Freud's Shadow: Adler in Context.* Hillsdale, NJ: The Analytic Press.

Thomä, H. & Kächele, H. (1975), Problems of metascience and methodology in clinical psychoanalytic research. *The Annual of Psychoanalysis,* 3:49–119. New York: International Universities Press.

Weber, M. (1949), *The Methodology of the Social Sciences,* trans. E. Shils & H. Finch. New York: Free Press.

4

Otto Rank and Self Psychology

ESTHER MENAKER

The creative products of human endeavor as they are expressed in culture evolve in response to the needs of the times. This is also true of psychological theories, whose particular orientation is in large part a reflection of sociopsychological conditions. In Freud's time, the repressive nature of social and sexual mores dictated values that called for excessive emotional restraint, especially in the realm of sexuality. The result for many persons was psychological conflict so severe that it was expressed in neurotic symptoms whose origin remained unknown, since the socially unacceptable emotion was relegated to the unconscious. The discovery of the dynamic unconscious—that is, that the repressive social influences of the outer world were internalized, came into conflict with instinctual wishes and caused repression within the person's psychic life—was Freud's great achievement. It led to an explanation of the life of the mind in terms of conflict between the gratification of drives and the dictates of ego and superego and was referred to as a conflict psychology.

Certainly times have changes since Freud's discovery. Sexual repression is not the social problem of the moment—although it could so become again if lethal venereal diseases such as AIDS continue to be uncontrollable. For many reasons—population explosion, technological advances, loss of religious belief, rapidity of communication, to name only a few—the major sociopsychological problems of our time are quite different. The present-day population suffers primarily from a sense of alienation, from a loss of meaningfulness in life, from disillusionment and an absence of faith in themselves and others. People are depressed, and the psychological help they require is not in the resolution of conflict but rather in affirmation in a new relationship that will make good an emotional loss or fill a void created in the course of development by lack of emotional sustenance. The problems of today cry out for a psychology of relationship and of the self in the context of relationship. These contemporary psychological needs have created a niche in the evolution of psychological theory and therapy that in the psychoanalytic world is filled by interpersonal theory and self psychology. While traditional psychoanalysis developed ego theory as an aspect of a structural conception of personality, there was little concern either for the genesis of the self as representing the total personality or for an in-depth study of the person's experience of self and of how such experience influenced the total life of the person—his or her thoughts, feelings, and behavior.

Even in the early days of psychoanalysis, however, there was an outstanding exception to the predominant orientation among psychoanalysts. This was the orientation of Otto Rank, who early in his career focused his thinking on phenomena that were manifestations of the sense of self: creativity, guilt, and anxiety. For Rank, human psychology was primarily a self psychology, the dynamics of which had their origins in the familial setting but were also strongly subject to social and cultural influences. Relative to the breadth, depth, and uniqueness of his contributions to psychological understanding, Rank is little known, rarely read, often misunderstood and misinterpreted, and insufficiently appreciated. His theories, which emphasized the development of an expressive and autonomous self, led inevitably to a rift with Freud. When one considers that Freud once said to Jung, "Promise me that you will never abandon the sexual theory," (Jung, 1963, p. 150) it is little wonder that Rank's departure from classical theory led to an acrimonius separation between the two men.

Rank, who in his early years was mainly self-educated, was first introduced to Freud through extensive reading. Psychoanalytic theory appealed to him, for he thought that it offered an explanation for the creativity of the artistic personality, a subject that had always interested him. He was, in fact, inspired by Freudian theory to make a psychoanalytic creative effort of his own. At the age of 21, he (Rank, 1907) wrote a treatise entitled "The Artist" (*Der Künstler*). It was a psychoanalytic explanation of the artist's creative urge, which at that time Rank grasped in true Freudian fashion as the sublimation of sexual impulses. Yet despite his early commitment to Freudian doctrine, Rank went beyond it. He was aware of the creative thrust of his own personality; and although he thought of himself as an artist in the broadest sense, he was aware that creativity had a more general meaning for all human beings, in fact for life itself. Much later in his career, when he wrote *Art and Artist* (Rank, 1932) an expression of the same interest that inspired him to write *Der Künstler,* he said: "Creativeness lies equally at the root of artistic production and of life experience" (p. 38). Whereas for Freud the drives were primary for an understanding of human psychology, for Rank it was creativity that stood at the center of personality development. The artist must appoint himself or herself as artist before fashioning the product of the creative impulse. That is to say, the self-definition of artist must precede the appearance of the work. According to Rank, this is a spontaneous manifestation of the creative impulse, but the creative work that follows has an important volitional aspect. It is at this point in his awareness of the origin and importance of the self-image that Rank's understanding of and concern with processes of the self emerges. Rank is less concerned with the origins and formation of the self in the familial matrix and the effect on its subsequent functioning (as Kohut is) than with the process of its expression, expressiveness, and the emotions that are thereby aroused. Although Rank began theorizing on the self through introspection about himself, his observations about his patients, and then about the artist, he very quickly came to understand that the need and drive toward self-definition was universal for all human beings, in fact, for all living organisms (rf. Langer, 1967).

Self-definition, while not always entirely conscious, is for the most part the aware aspect of individuation. Early in his career Rank was concerned with processes of individuation, especially from the point of view of separation. It was in his search for a paradigm for anxiety that he concluded that the loss entailed by separation was responsible for the origins of anxiety. With this in mind he wrote the *Trauma of Birth* (Rank, 1929), for which, unfortunately, he is best known. I say unfortunately because the book deals in a very literal, physical sense with the first separation experienced as one enters the world: the parting from the mother. Initially Rank had a very literal conception of the relationship between birth and anxiety: the more difficult the birth, the greater the traumatic experience and thus the greater the fear to be mastered. The origin of neurosis, which had a direct quantitative relationship to the anxiety experienced, lay in the birth experience. The imprint of this experience becomes the prototype for all future experiences of separation, with their attendant anxiety. Both Rank and Freud arrived at this theory almost concurrently.[1] However, in his later writings Rank went beyond the view of birth as a paradigm for anxiety to a metaphysical understanding of birth as the human psychological process of growth toward individuation. This process itself is anxiety producing. The oneness with the womb, in which there is no responsibility even for one's physical survival is lost, to be replaced by responsibility for one's separate existence and survival. The growth toward increasing autonomy throughout life is both feared and wished for. It is by way of his metaphoric conception of birth as individuation that Rank becomes a self psychologist.

Rank, like Freud, seldom uses the term "self." He speaks more often of ego, a legacy of his Freudian background, but thinks of ego not in structural, but in functional, terms. The self is not an entity for Rank but a conscious awareness of a way of being—not a static state, but one that strives constantly to give expression to its unique, individual character. This relentless striving manifests itself in the function of the will, a term that is practically absent in Freud's writings and in those of other psychoanalytic theorists.

It is significant that the study of the expression of the will, a commonly observed phenomenon, has been ignored in psychoanalytic thinking. This omission is a measure of the deterministic, materialistic reductionism of the scientific ethos of the historical period in which psychoanalysis originated. But Rank transcended the limitations of the hyperrationalism of the late 19th and early 20th centuries by introducing the will principle into human psychology in opposition to a principle of strict deterministic causality. It is because of the uniqueness of each individual—his or her self—that the expressions of the will cannot be universalized and cannot therefore be predicted. For Rank it is not the drives that are primary in human psychology but the striving for individuation, which finds expression in the manifestations of the individual will. In Rank's (1945) words, the self is the "temporal representative of the cosmic primal force . . . the strength of this force represented in the individual we call the will" (p. 212). The cosmic primal force is not

[1]Freud (1926) credits Rank with the theory that places the birth experience at the core of anxiety.

a mystical power, but the energic nature of the universe, especially the living universe:

> This force manifests itself in the human (because of consciousness and self-consciousness) not solely in adaptation to environment, but in psychological interchange between inner and outer reality which can result in a *freely chosen* modification of either or both. It is such action which Rank calls creative as distinguished from adaptive, and which he comprehends as *will phenomena*" [Menaker, 1982, p. 43, italics added].

Such expression of the will is the most characteristic manifestation of the self.

In developmental terms, the earliest expression of will begins as counterwill, as opposition to the will of another, primarily the mother. This is the familiar negativism of the small child, the two- to four-year-old. This normal aspect of the development of an autonomous self is essential for the separation of generations by which social progress is achieved. However, since the separation draws its strength from opposition, which is inevitably expressive of hostility toward the "other," a certain amount of guilt results. Rank's profound insight into the nature of existential guilt forces us to accept the inevitable paradox that the emergence of "self" is always at the expense of another self, because it begins by separation, which in human experience is felt by the "other" as hostility. It is because of our beginnings in the oneness of the mother-child dyad, and the profound attachment that results, as well as our capacity for empathic identification with the one we leave as we grow apart, that the development of the self leads to guilt. Ironically, the more delineated and creative this self is, the greater the guilt, for so much greater is the separateness of the self. It would follow, then, that the creative artist, whose self is more sharply defined and expressed than that of most people, is particularly vulnerable to the feeling of guilt. After the completion of each creative work, the artist may be overwhelmed with guilt, which must be expiated through new creative endeavors. Thus, the separateness of the self invites creative expression, which engenders guilt, for which the artist atones by the creation of new works.

It is interesting at this point to contemplate some differences and similarities in thinking between the founder of self psychology, Heinz Kohut, and that of Otto Rank. Rank began his psychological studies by exploring creativity and anxiety and their role in the processes of separation and individuation. Kohut's interest in the psychology of the self began with pathology, with disturbances that he described as narcissistic personality disorders. From the history of these patients and from their reactions in the transference, he deduced that their deficits in emotional nourishment for the establishment of a cohesive self resulted in extremely low self-esteem, with consequent difficulty in establishing satisfactory relationships with others. The self-structure of these patients was never fully integrated; consequently their ability to love was seriously impaired. Kohut was keenly aware that in the therapeutic situation insight alone was not curative for these patients. They required the opportunity to experience, at the hands of the analyst, the parental affirmation they had missed as they were growing up. The self-structure was rebuilt, as it were, through the internalization of the analyst's positive attitude toward and acceptance of them. In the development of Kohut's thinking, one gains the clear impression that he came to believe that a reparative process of this sort was needed in the treatment of most people who came for help for emotional difficulties and that the seemingly greater need for persons with narcissistic personality disorders was only one of degree.

An important similarity in Kohut's and Rank's views of the development of personality and its aberrations is the conception of the primacy of self development as the driving force motivating human action and expressiveness. Human beings do not seek primarily the gratification of drives, although they do that also; it is the structuring of a cohesive, autonomous self and the freedom to express one's independent will that are the hallmarks of human striving. While Kohut speaks of "self" and Rank of "will" (a function of the self), they both view failures in the successful development of self or of inhibition in the ability to will primarily as products of parental failure—again, not in their ability to gratify instinctual needs, but in the failure to affirm the very person of the child. Kohut (1977) called this a parental (initially on the part of the mother) failure in positive mirroring, or subsequently, a failure (generally on the father's part) to provide an opportunity for idealization. Rank (1945) saw the cause of inhibition in a parental failure to affirm and accept the child's separate and individual will. In the course of growth and development, the indispensability of affirmation is clear in the psychology of both thinkers. For Kohut, a normal sense of worth requires affirmation; for Rank, the ability to will freely depends on affirmation.

It is affirmation from the world of the human environment, generally from parents, that makes possible the separation from those very people to whom the child is attached. And it is the ability to bring separation to a relatively felicitous conclusion that furthers the process of individuation, a process that characterizes all living things. Susanne Langer characterizes this process in the following profound statement:

> To trace the development of mind from the earliest forms of life that we can determine, through primitive acts which may have vague psychical moments, to more certain mental acts, and finally the human level of "mind," requires a more fertile concept than "individual," "self," or even "organism"; not a categorial concept but a *functional* one, whereby entities of various categories may be defined and related. The most promising operational principle for this purpose is the principle of *individuation.* It is exemplified everywhere in animate nature, in processes that eventuate in the existence of self-identical organisms. . . .
>
> Under widely varying conditions, this ubiquitous process may give rise to equally varying kinds of individuality, from the physical self-identity of the metabolizing cell to the intangible but impressive individuality of an exceptional human being [quoted in Menaker, 1982, p. 30].

While Langer has chosen the term individuation because of its functional nature to describe the striving for the formation of a specific and separate identity, the term self has persisted in the world of psychoanalytic psychology. In some sense it represents a reaction to the Freudian emphasis on drives as the primary motivators of human behavior; the term self-psychology emphasizes the primacy of the self in human development and thus differenciates itself from a psychology of conflict—conflict between impulse gratification and the censoring super-ego or ego-ideal. However, the term self has come under criticism from some psychoanalytic quarters because it is thought to be a reification of an aspect of personality that does not exist as a real and separate entity. The same criticism was leveled at Freud's concept of ego, which derived from his structural model of personality. To my mind, neither criticism is fully justified. In Freud's case, the terms are admittedly aspects of a model and the reality of the entities is metaphorical.

The use of the term self is descriptive of a subjective experience. One has a sense of self, an awareness of one's own person. But this is not an ever-present awareness, for we usually take the sense of self, which we associate with our everyday being, for granted. It is when an event occurs that disturbs the particular sense of being we are used to, and in fact creates disharmony with our usual sense of self, that we become aware of our ongoing "self-image." I am reminded of a situation in which a very anxious woman revealed precisely this kind of incongruity between the accepted sense of self and the experience of herself in a traumatic situation. As a very elderly woman, lying near death in the hospital and having complete knowledge of her situation, she, who throughout her lifetime knew herself as an exceedingly anxious person, said, "I'm surprised at myself; I don't seem to be afraid at all."

The question of how we become aware of our self-image in the context of the juxaposition of two discrepant self-images is relevant to Rank's theory about the creation of personality, which is tantamount to the evolution of an awareness of self.

It is through introspection that we experience and acquire a sense of our own selves. Rank was aware that the capacity for introspection was not always equally developed and that it changed and evolved gradually under the influence of culture, specifically through the *Weltanschauung* of a given historical epoch. Rank is unusual among psychoanalysts, and certainly among the early ones, in that his background in, knowledge of, and interest in the products of culture—myths, religious beliefs, values, social structures, art, and literature—alerted him to the fact that there is a reciprocal relationship between the individual and the culture in which he or she is embedded. While individuals create the products of culture—especially uniquely creative individuals—the culture inevitably molds the character, reactions, and viewpoints of the individuals. It is through such interaction between culture and individuals that social evolution takes place and that consequently changes occur in society as well as within individuals (Menaker and Menaker, 1965). One of the things that depends in some measure on culture for its specific character is the nature of the sense of self. It can change as the culture changes. This sense of self is a highly unique phenomenon for each individual and yet has a general character that can be defined as a type for a specific society or time in history.

Speaking of our Western culture, Rank (1958) places the time at which a profound change in a philosophy of life occurred, and thus a consequent change in the human psychological type, at the beginning of the Christian era. The old world of antiquity was disintegrating at this time, and the standards for social conduct were being modified from a communal code for behavior to a more individualistic one. The individual carried more responsibility for his own actions and his destiny than had previously been the case. Rank refers to the new psychological type of human being as the "inspirational" type, because the average individual was inspired "to live up to a plane spiritually much higher than he could possibly aspire to in reality" (p. 144). Ranks refers to the attempt to effect a change in personality that would approach the inspired ideal as a change in world outlook based on a "therapeutic ideology."

The emergence of the idea that through faith and one's own efforts one can effect a change in personality is a new development in the psychological history of humankind. By implication, a change in personality means an awareness of difference between an earlier sense of self and a newer, changed self-image. According to Rank, before the advent of Jesus the self-conception and the world view of the average person within the Jewish world was based on the Messianic hope for salvation. Rank emphasizes the change in world view that is expressed with the onset of Christian belief: "[I]nstead of a realistic deliverance through the Messiah an inner experience and change in the individual self was the salvation" (p. 149). The possibility of change through an inner experience—in fact, the awareness of an inner experience itself—was testified to by Paul's conversion on the way to Damascus. This experience caused him to become the most ardent disciple of Jesus after having been an enemy of the followers of Jesus. We can only guess at the psychodynamics of Paul's experience of the vision of Jesus, which turned him away from his destructive intentions as he set out on his journey to identify instead with Jesus' own mission. What is important for us in terms of self psychology is that Paul, through his identity with the Christ ("It is no longer I who live, but Christ who lives in me" *Gal.* 2.20 *RSV*), acquired a new self and subsequently preached the possibility of a similar change for others. The centrality in the early Christian church of the experience of baptism as *rebirth,* as the casting off of the "old Adam" and entering into a new life, provides support for Rank's interpretation.

It is the juxtaposition of two differing self-experiences that elicits the awareness both of self and of the possibility of change. Rank's use of Paul's experience of conversion and change, cast in the religious terms that expressed the central concerns at the time of Jesus, illustrates the influence of cultural pressure in bringing about an altered self conception. While the *content* of the self-experience is historically determined, as a process such change in the sense of self and in world outlook is equally applicable today and is in fact an aspect of a sociopsychological process that is ongoing in every historical period throughout time.

In our modern epoch, it is Freud's discovery that through introspection it is possible to uncover and understand aspects of personality that were formerly hidden and to effect change by forging the causal link between what is in awareness (consciousness) and what remains repressed (unconscious). The causality resides, according to Freud, in childhood experience, especially sexual experience. Psychoanalytic treatment was thus geared to uncovering repressed childhood memories; and change, which in Freud's time referred primarily to the elimination of neurotic symptomatology, was brought about by the lifting of repression. However sketchy or schematic this description of Freudian psychoanalysis may be, it is noteworthy that the stated goal of treatment omits any reference to the self or to changes in the person's sense of self. It is Rank's special contribution to a philosophy of therapy that he emphasized the uniqueness of the individual and saw as a major function of psychological treatment the fostering of growth of the self and its free expression in the creative will. The central problem for most persons seeking treatment was an inhibition in the ability to will. "Willing" was excessively guilt producing for many patients because it represented self-assertion, which was associated with separation from the "other"—which separation was experienced as a hostile act. Parental failure to affirm the child's will resulted in an inhibition of will and therefore limited self-expressiveness. The therapist's task was to make good this deficit for the patient through acts of affirmation. Here we see a similarity to Kohut's (1984) conception of therapy, wherein the therapist must offer himself or herself as a selfobject—a source or nurturance for the building of self through internalizations—to the patient in order to repair the developmental deficits caused by parental failure to affirm the child's self.

It is both Rank's and Kohut's emphasis on the core of the personality—the self—that differentiates them so clearly from Freud. Although Rank (1945) developed a psychology of the will as an expression of self rather than of the self per se, both he and Kohut (1977) departed from Freud's drive theory, which held that the primary motivating force in human psychology is the drives. For Rank and Kohut, the self (Rank referred to ego) is primary. Current infant research seems to confirm them. In studies of very young infants (Demos, 1987) the tendency—one might almost say striving, since the organism seems to move out to master the environment—to differentiate the outside world from what one must inevitably call a rudimentary sense of self is apparent.

To facilitate and foster the growth and cohesive development of the self in the treatment situation by opening a new experience to the persons seeking therapy is the aim of both Rank and Kohut. Such a view, which is informed by a belief in the human capacity for growth and change, has its eye on the possibilities of the future. While acknowledging the influences of the past on a person's life in the present, the primary emphasis is on the potentiality for new development.

This raises the interesting issue of Rank's position on transference phenomena in the therapeutic situation. Unlike Freud, whose thinking is almost overwhelmed by an awareness of the power of the repetition compulsion in the course of living, and especially in the transference phenomena as they appear in analysis, Rank is cognizant of the opportunity analysis offers for a new experience. While in the treatment he would not ignore the appearance of the patient's projections onto the person of the analyst as derivatives of the past, he was aware that insight into this transference phenomenon was not the source of cure or change. It was, in fact, an interference with progress, as was the set-up of the analysis itself with the use of the couch, the darkened room, and the relatively inactive yet authoritative analyst. The analytic situation in reality, therefore, tended to duplicate the childhood situation of the patient vis-à-vis his or her parents. To create the opportunity for a new experience with a new type of authority figure for the patient, the therapist must neutralize the deleterious effects of the transference, as well as of the reality of the analytic situation, by actively offering affirmation of the patient's will. Such affirmation is akin to the philosophy of therapy in the self-psychological mode, in which the therapist, hoping to set in motion the development of a cohesive self and a balanced sense of self-esteem for the patient, especially in the case of narcissistic personality disorders, offers himself or herself as an affirming selfobject, that is, someone with whom the patient can identify and whom the patient can internalize.

Both Rank and Kohut were intrigued by the psychodynamics of the creative personality. In fact, Rank's interest in psychology began, as noted earlier, with an attempt to understand the personality of the artist. He concluded that the artist, owing to innate talents and abilities, was an especially expressive and productive exemplar of the creative potential that resides in everyone. For most people, the awareness of the creativity involved in the gradual structuring of the self is less clear than in the case of the artist, who appoints himself or herself as artist. What bears on Rank's historical relationship to self psychology is his perception that the structuring of the self is a creative process.

Creativity—which is at the heart of Rank's psychology (see Menaker, 1982, ch. 3)—is the human being's response to the fear of separation, especially the fear of the final separation, death. In the face of the finitude of life, the creative impulse makes a bid for immortality in three major ways: through procreation, through an idealization with a group ideal of which the individual feels himself or herself a part, or—for the artist or scientist—through the creation of a concretely expressed work. The artist's works are manifestations of unique creative will and are therefore statements of the separate self. Rank (1945) speculates, and it seems a valid speculation (one which in a slightly different form also occurred to Kohut, 1984), that the act of making a statement of one's unique and separate self is experienced with some guilt because separation implies a pulling away from some "other" and is therefore often felt as a hostile act. The creative product is an atonement for this guilt, but since by its very nature it too is a manifestation of the unique and separate self, more guilt is generated. This guilt in turn must be expiated. Hence the creative person is under a perpetual mandate to keep on creating. It is the price for the self-definition and measure of immortality that is bought through the works of the creative will.

Kohut, although he does not speak of the guilt caused by the creative expressions of the self, is keenly aware of the loneliness that the creative person of genius suffers in the face of his or her own innovations. He (Kohut, 1985) writes:

> A genius, frightened by the boldness of his pioneering discoveries and yearning to relieve his loneliness, creates for himself the figment of a vastly overestimated figure on whom he leans temporarily but whom he discards (i.e. from whom he has withdrawn his idealization) after his essential work has been achieved. During the transference of creativity itself, the genius projects his own mental powers onto someone else. He assigns his discoveries temporarily to that other person and feels humble toward and dependent upon this idealized protector, mentor and judge, who is in essence his own creation [p. 7].

Kohut calls this defensive maneuver of projection a "transference of creativity." Why, if not for guilt, would a person fear to carry the responsibility for his or her own creativity? Rank appears to have been right in perceiving the cost of expressing an unusually unique self.

More than 50 years before Heinz Kohut began to organize his thoughts into what came to be known as self psychology, Otto Rank was excommunicated from the psychoanalytic movement for his profound understanding of the ways of the self. I have tried to weave in and out of the thought-paths of these two great thinkers, showing their deviation from Freudian drive theory and following the points on which they converge and those on which they differ. Although Rank's theories about the will and the self were all but lost because he was so far ahead of his time, it is good to see a revival of some of his concerns in the current work of self psychologists.

REFERENCES

Demos, E.V. (1987), The central role of affect in infancy, presented to American Psychological Association, Division 39, Section III. New York.

Freud, S. (1917), Introductory lectures on psychoanalysis, *Standard Edition,* 16. London; Hogarth Press, 1963.

_____ (1926), Inhibition, symptom, and anxiety, *Standard Edition,* 20: 87–172. London:Hogarth Press, 1959

_____ (1940), An outline of psycho-analysis, *Standard Edition,* 23:144–207. London:Hogarth Press, 1964

Jung, C.G. (1963), *Memories, Dreams, Reflections.* New York, Pantheon.

Kohut, H. (1977), *The Restoration of the Self.* New York: International Universities Press.

_____ (1984), *How Does Analysis Cure?* ed. A. Goldberg and P.E. Stepansky. Chicago: University of Chicago Press.

_____ (1985), *Self Psychology and the Humanities.* New York: Norton.

Langer, S. (1967), *Mind: An Essay on Human Feeling.* Baltimore: Johns Hopkins University Press.

Menaker, E. (1982), *Otto Rank: A Rediscovered Legacy.* New York: Columbia University Press.

_____ & Menaker, W. (1965), *Ego in Evolution.* New York: Grove Press.

Rank, O. (1907), *Der Künstler.* Vienna: Hugo Heller.

_____ (1932), *Art and Artist.* New York: Knopf.

_____ (1945), *Will Therapy and Truth and Reality.* New York: Knopf.

_____ (1958), *Beyond Psychology.* New York: Dover Press.

_____ (1929), *The Trauma of Birth.* London: Routledge & Kegan Paul.

5

Ferenczi's Contributions to the Evolution of a Self Psychology Framework in Psychoanalysis

ARNOLD WM. RACHMAN

The major aim of this chapter is to outline the pioneering clinical and theoretical work of Sandor Ferenczi and demonstrate its relevance as a precursor to self psychology. Several authors, both within and outside of the self psychology movement, have pointed out that psychoanalysts and psychotherapists who preceded Kohut laid the foundations for self psychology (Stolorow, 1976; Cohler, 1980; Basch, 1984; Chessick, 1985; Kahn, 1985; Bollas, 1986). Elsewhere (Rachman, 1988) I introduced the notion that Ferenczi was the originator of the empathic method in psychoanalysis. It is appropriate now to expand this perspective and add Ferenczi to the list of psychoanalytic thinkers who pioneered an alternate form of psychoanalysis that anticipated many aspects of the self psychology framework. In this regard, there are several basic concepts that bear comparison between Ferenczi and Kohut: (1) the role of empathy in psychoanalysis; (2) The selfobject transference; (3) reintroduction of the trauma theory; and (4) revision of the resistance model.

I wish to express my gratitude to Marc Wayne, M.S., C.S.W., for his scholarly and empathic critique of this manuscript.

THE ROLE OF EMPATHY

Ferenczi's approach to psychoanalysis was a function of his personality as well as of his intellect and clinical capacity. His predominant personal qualities were enthusiasm, warmth, tenderness, giving, optimism, and compassion. The full array of these qualities, plus their intensity, encouraged in others the feelings of trust, openness, understanding, and empathy.

It was a special blend of Ferenczi's family background, his warm and vibrant personality, his interpersonal skills, and his active, searching intellect that moved him toward an empathic method of psychoanalysis. Ferenczi's family background has been chronicled (Balint, 1949; Barande, 1972; Bergman and Hartman, 1976; Sauborin, 1985). He identified with the revolutionary spirit of his father, whom he idolized, and had an intensely ambivalent relationship with his mother. New evidence has been uncovered from the voluminous Freud/Ferenczi correspondence that verifies a view of maternal deprivation. Ferenczi wrote to Freud on October 13, 1912 that he was the ". . . son of an 'otherwise harsh mother' . . . (Simitis-Grubrich, 1986, p. 274). He was, then, a man who had experienced empathic failures as a child. He turned the emotional awareness of his own "traumatic" childhood into a gift to his patients by developing his personal empathy into clinical empathy, thereby empathizing with their sense of deprivation and trauma.

Ferenczi's interest in empathy began with his technical recommendations for changing the emotional atmosphere of an analytic session. His keen powers of clinical observation allowed him to become the first analyst to employ nonverbal cues to interpret unconscious processes (Ferenczi, 1919a, 1920, 1924b, 1925). He began to observe and concern himself with the nature of resistances to the analyst's interventions.

> I recall, for instance, an uneducated, apparently quite simple patient who brought forward objections to an interpretation of mine, which it was my immediate impulse to reject; but on reflection, **not I, but the patient, turned out to be right,** and the result of his intervention was a much better general understanding of the matter we were dealing with [Ferenczi, 1928, p. 941].

From such empathic interchanges, Ferenczi reached the following conclusion, which ushered the use of tact, or empathy, into psychoanalytic practice: "I have come to the conclusion that it is above all a question of psychological tact whether one should tell the patient some particular thing. But what is 'tact' It is the capacity for empathy" (p. 89)

Ferenczi's observations lead to the clinical recommendation that, to reduce the resistances, one should present any interpretation in a tactful manner. What Ferenczi was suggesting was that empathic awareness, concern, and compassion were important in relating to an analysand.

Ferenczi's new method also was a call to analysts to be more empathic and flexible about accepting patients for analysis. In his growing experience as "the analyst of difficult cases," he used his new method to work successfully with patients whom other analysts had either terminated prematurely or found unanalyzable, or whose problems persisted after years of Freudian therapy. He urged analysts to follow "the rule of empathy," to understand patients who act out their feelings of rejection by being "bad patients." When an analyst has "an excessive degree of antipathy," he said, they should strive for empathic understanding. That is to say, patients who trigger negative feelings in an analyst do so "because the unconscious aim of intolerable behavior is often to be sent away. Also, . . . dropping the patient . . . would be merely leaving him in the lurch . . ." (p. 95).

Ferenczi felt the empathic method he was proposing was crucial for understanding the clinical work of psychoanalysis: "One gradually becomes aware how immensely complicated the mental work demanded from the analysts is . . . One might say that his mind swings continuously between empathy, self-observation and making judgements" (p. 96).

Several published sources provide examples of Ferenczi's empathic functioning as an analyst. There are Ferenczi's first case of psychoanalytic therapy (Ferenczi, 1919a), what I (Rachman, 1976) have termed Ferenczi's "Case of the Female Croatian Musician" (Ferenczi, 1920); the "Grandpa Encounter" in Ferenczi's discovery of the language of empathy (Ferenczi, 1931); and Thompson's (1964) report of "The Case of The Slovenly Soldier".

Freud's response to Ferenczi's introduction of empathy was positive and congratulatory. In a letter dated January 4, 1928, Freud wrote:

> Dear Friend:
>
> Your accompanying production ["Elasticity of Psychoan-

> alytic Technique"] displays that judicious maturity you have acquired of late years, in respect of which no one approaches you. The title is excellent and deserves a wider provenance. . . . The only criticism I have of your paper is that it is not three times larger and divided into three parts. There is no doubt that you have much more to say on similar lines, and it would be very beneficial to have it [Jones, 1953, p. 241].

Freud realized that he needed Ferenczi's clinical genius to further develop the technique of psychoanalysis. His own attempts at technical recommendations produced a negative atmosphere. Analysts felt constrained to experiment, or modify Freudian methods. By 1928, Freud's suggestions became taboos in analytic behavior, rather than flexible guidelines. Freud admitted this in this same letter (Jones, 1953, p. 241). (For a fuller treatment of this matter see Rachman, 1988).

After the publication of the "Elasticity Paper" in 1928, Ferenczi devoted the rest of his clinical career to the development of his empathic method, from 1928 until his death on May 22, 1933. The empathic method was noted in a series of three significant papers (Ferenczi, 1930, 1931, 1933), a clinical diary (Ferenczi, 1932); and the latter portion of the Freud/Ferenczi correspondence (unpublished—portions available in French and German).

The elaboration of his empathic method involved changes in the process of an analytic session (Ferenczi, 1930); development of an empathic communication with an analysand (Ferenczi, 1931); focus on the analyst's contribution to empathic failures (Ferenczi, 1928, 1932, 1933); the development of psychopathology based on empathic defects in childhood (Ferenczi, 1932, 1933). The sections to follow touch upon many of these issues.

Toward the end of his clinical career, Ferenczi was totally absorbed in his empathic method, attempting both to understand and to respond to the needs of the narcissistic and borderline cases (Ferenczi, 1932). His thinking and technical experiments can be viewed as opening up the vista of empathy within the psychoanalytic framework. But he realized he had only begun the process and that the generations of analysts to follow would need to continue his pioneering efforts (Ferenczi, 1928). The concept of empathy did receive some attention in the years to follow (Levy, 1985; Rachman and Wayne, 1986). It was not, however, until Kohut's work evolved that empathy was to receive the same attention as an essential variable in the analytic process that it originally received from Ferenczi.

It is clear that Ferenczi (1928) realized that others who followed his lead, like Kohut, would open wide the doors of empathic research for all psychoanalysis:

> My principal aim in writing this paper was to rob "tact" of its mystical character. I agree, that I have only broached the subject and have by no means said the last word about it. . . . The process of empathy and assessment will obviously take place, not in the unconscious, but at the pre-conscious level of the well-analyzed analyst's mind [p. 100]

When Kohut (1984) reintroduced empathy in psychoanalysis and expanded upon the contributions of Ferenczi and others, he did show some awareness that the concept had a history: "Although self psychology must not claim that it has provided psychoanalysis with a new kind of empathy, it can claim that it has supplied analysis with new theories which broaden and deepen the field of empathic perception" (p. 175).

Kohut fulfilled every fantasy that Ferenczi may have had about the importance of empathy for psychoanalysis. He outlined the far-reaching conceptualization of empathy to expand its boundaries in four basic ways: (1) as the principal mode of observation in psychoanalysis (Kohut, 1959, 1971, 1977, 1978, 1984); (2) as the significant emotional experience in the psychoanalytic situation (Kohut, 1975, 1984) (3) as the significant ingredient that bonds human beings (Kohut, 1975, 1977); (4) and as a force for good in the interaction of groups, whether collegial, political, or national (Kohut, 1971, 1975, 1978).

THE SELFOBJECT TRANSFERENCES

Many consider Kohut's discovery of the selfobject transferences to be his single most important contribution to psychoanalysis (Gedo, 1986). Kohut's description of the various configurations of selfobject and their working through should be consulted (Kohut, 1971, 1977, 1984).

These transferences—the mirror transference, the twinship transference, and the idealizing transference—emerge naturally in a self psychology analysis of patients with narcissistic personality disorder. Inherent in this idea is the "spontaneous emergence" of selfobject transference and the "proper conduct" of their analyses

(Ornstein, 1978). These transferences are not defensively regressive in nature, as the object-instinctual conflicts of traditional psychoanalysis have been characterized. The differences that exist between Kohut's view of selfobject transferences and traditional view of object-instinctual transferences are based on the differences in the notion of the development of pathology.

The curative function of the selfobject transferences is to foster self-cohesion. The analyst is internalized through "transmuting internalizations." Bit by bit, the person acquires psychic structure, when the clinician empathizes with the developmental strivings that were not acknowledged in childhood by parental figures. Through the positive experience of the analytic selfobject acquired through continued empathic interaction, the various fragmented self-images coalesce around the stable introject of the analyst.

By virtue of the splitting that occurred during childhood, the selfobject transference allows cohesion of the split-off fragments of the self. Splitting (or more specifically, lack of integration) is overcome, not by its interpretation as a defense, but because the self is strengthened by the empathy and understanding of the analyst. In the self psychology model, one interprets what the patient needs to maintain rather than what he is defensively warding off (Stolorow and Lachmann, 1980). This approach is in contrast to the traditional one, in which interpretation is a means of uncovering the defense that wards off sexual and aggressive wishes.

Ferenczi believed, as did Kohut, that the analyst needed to function as a corrective selfobject, so to speak. But in the humanistic method he pioneered, Ferenczi assumed the role of the empathic parent, rather than interpreting the need for one. He appeared to gratify the mirroring selfobject need in the here-and-now of the analytic situation. In an interaction where Ferenczi was attempting to understand the childhood failures in empathic parenting, he role-played a responsive grandfather (Ferenczi, 1931, p. 129). In fulfilling the role of the empathic parental figure, Ferenczi attempted to correct the emotional deficits caused by the narcissistic wounds of childhood. The use of the analyst as a corrective selfobject was put to its most flexible application in Ferenczi's "Grand Experiment" (Balint, 1968) and his last clinical cases as reported in his clinical diary (Ferenczi, 1932).

The apparent difference between the self psychology and the humanistic analytic approaches is that Kohut espoused the interpretation of the selfobject need. He offered an empathic explanation of how the need is necessary for the patient's self cohesion and self esteem. Yet, in his last work, Kohut (1984) began to talk about the corrective emotional component in the selfobject transference.

TRAUMA THEORY

Ferenczi's clinical innovations, especially his later work, introduced a revolution in psychoanalysis (Ferenczi, 1928, 1930, 1931, 1932, 1933). Among these works was his last clinical presentation (Ferenczi, 1933), which was the inaugural presentation at the 12th International Psychoanalytic Congress in Wiesbaden, Germany, on September 4, 1932. Controversy surrounded this paper both before it was written and when it was presented:

> Their response to the paper was uniformly negative. These senior analysts, the "bearers of the ring," were of the opinion that views such as those expressed in the paper should not be circulated more widely than was absolutely necessary, that the dissemination of such views constituted a danger to society [Masson, 1984, pp. 150–151].

That paper raised enormous issues of a professional, personal, and social nature for psychoanalysis, for Ferenczi, and for the psychoanalytic community. It solidified the new method of humanistic psychoanalysis; reintroduced the seduction hypothesis; encouraged professional acceptance of sexual abuse of children by parents and parental surrogates; introduced the concept that analysts should retraumatize their patients in Freudian therapy; and precipitated the final disruption of Ferenczi's relationship with Freud and the analytic community.

There are those who consider Kohut's work as encompassing a similar significant event in the history of psychoanalysis:

> . . . we now have enough compelling "analytic" clinical data that necessitate Kohut's a revision of the classical paradigm to incorporate Kohut's findings into what might well turn to be a contribution toward a unified theory of the psychoanalytic treatment process. Freud changed the paradigm of the Psychoanalytic treatment process with his *The Ego and The Id* (1923). Kohut's *The Analysis of the Self* (1971) might turn out to be a landmark of no lesser significance [Ornstein, 1974, pp. 127–128].

When Freud abandoned the seduction hypothesis and introduced the Oedipus complex as an alternative explanation for the report of childhood sexual experiences, psychoanalysis shifted its focus from the interpersonal to the intrapsychic sphere. What is more, the actual incidence of sexual experiences between children and parents (or other adults) became neglected.

The reason for Freud's abandonment of the seduction hypothesis has been the subject of much debate within psychoanalysis. Jones (1953) saw the event as an intellectual advance and suggested that Freud's self-analysis was the decisive factor. Others have both concurred with this view and elaborated upon it (Schur, 1972; Anzieu, 1975, Sulloway, 1979). Masson (1984) attacked the established view, suggesting the shift from seduction to oedipal fantasy was a "loss of courage" for Freud in the face of professional opposition (p. 134). Krull (1986) also viewed the shift as a retrogressive step and emphasized its personal importance as "a creative solution" to Freud's ambivalent feelings for his father (p. 88).

Ferenczi's reintroduction of the seduction hypothesis was based on his clinical work with narcissistic, borderline, and psychotic patients, in whom he observed a high incidence of childhood sexual seduction and emotional trauma. At the time, Ferenczi wished these ideas to be integrated into Freudian psychoanalysis (Gedo, 1976, 1986). He was always ambivalent about his deviations from Freud and never seemed to realize how far afield he had deviated or that he was founding an alternative view (Thompson, 1944; Rachman, in press). We now have new evidence demonstrating that Ferenczi's later clinical behavior and thinking were clearly different from Freud's (Ferenczi, 1932; Sylwan, 1984; Dupont, 1985; Sabourin, 1985).

Ferenczi challenged the traditional notion of both Freudian psychoanalysis and the culture at that time that the report of sexual abuse was the fantasy of the child and therefore was unreliable (an idea that is still held by many). Ferenczi's empathic plea for the reality of child abuse and its pathological effect on adult functioning can be outlined in the following way:

1. The child is traumatized by the adult (parent or parental surrogate) when the adult seduces the child sexually.
2. The child wanted "tenderness" not "sexual passion."
3. The adult is not really showing love or tenderness to the child but is aggressing against the child, intruding adult sexual

needs onto the innocent longings of a child for love and parental tenderness.

4. The child is "tongue-tied," confusing sexuality for love, but cannot speak of the confusion.
5. The child cannot refuse the sexual advances of the adult because he or she feels helpless and paralyzed by fear and needs "tenderness." "The child brings to bear instead a pathogenic defense mechanism," identification with the aggressor (Ferenczi, 1933, p. 162), which Ferenczi was the first to name (Masson, 1984, p. 148).
6. Besides identification with the aggressor, a host of pathological defenses can develop to cope with the seduction experience, for example, dissociation, depression, schizoid withdrawal, blunted affect, and splitting.
7. "These children feel physically and morally helpless, their personalities are not sufficiently consolidated in order to be able to protest, even if only in thought, for the overpowering force and authority of the adult makes them dumb and can rob them of their senses" (Ferenczi, 1933, p. 162).
8. "The same anxiety, however, if it reaches a certain maximum, compels them to subordinate themselves like *automata* to the will of the aggressor, to divine each one of his desires . . ." (Ferenczi, 1933, p. 162).
9. "As a defense the child sinks into a dream or trance state in which it is easier to misperceive the quality of the aggression.
10. "The child's need to deny altogether what has happened, severely loosens her hold on reality" (Masson, 1984, p. 149).
11. "The guilt that the patent ought to feel but does not is then introjected by the child (the act is perceived as wrong, but there is nobody else to take responsibility for it except the child victim)" (Masson, 1984, pp. 148–149).
12. ". . . The patent who denies what he has done, or denies its harmful effect, often becomes physically abusive toward the child (projecting the wickedness onto the child).
13. "A seduction is generally followed by violence, suggesting to the child a connection between sexuality and violence, with disastrous effects on the child's ability to love later in life" (Masson, 1984, p. 149).
14. The childhood pathology lays the groundwork for adult perversions, disturbed object relations, lack of trust, special need of empathy, and the establishment of a narcissistic or

borderline adaptation. Ferenczi was suggesting that sexual abuse in childhood plays a significant role in the development of severe narcissistic, borderline or psychotic conditions.

Empathic Failure as Trauma

Perhaps no analyst has ever spoken so empathically in behalf of abused children and their adult traumatized selves as Ferenczi. It would be comforting to dismiss these conclusions about the sexual seduction of children as a function of a different era, where puritanical values forced covert sexual activity within families. But the evidence mounts regarding the incidence of sexual abuse of children in contemporary society (Burgess et al., 1978; Groth and Birnbaum, 1979; Rush, 1980; James and Masjleti, 1983).

Ferenczi also opened the door for psychoanalysis to consider emotional abuse as trauma. Although he focused on sexual seduction as the etiology of adult psychopathology, he had been previously developing the notion of empathic failure in the early mother-child relationship as a primary source of emotional disturbance (Ferenczi, 1928, 1930, 1931, 1932; Rachman and Wayne, 1986; Rachman, (in preparation).

Ferenczi pioneered several techniques to guard against the retraumatization of the analysand, to create a corrective emotional experience, and to maintain an empathic milieu for treatment: a) analysis of countertransference to "rock bottom"; b) the development of "mutual analysis"; c) a fuller analysis of the analyst; periodic return to analysis; d) therapist self-disclosure (Ferenczi, 1933; Rachman, 1977). Some of these technical methods (for example, therapist self-disclosure, mutual analysis) continue to be seen as controversial and risky (Dupont, 1985, 1988).

Ferenczi was the first analyst to identify the traumatic aspects of the psychoanalytic situation (Rachman, 1977). It was a remarkable observation because it meant the complete willingness to examine his own responsiveness, or lack of it, without concern for a loss of status in the relationship. In addition he pioneered an emotional openness to severe criticism by the analysand, risked navigating transference reactions with difficult patients (which places an enormous emotional strain on the analyst), and was willing to respond in novel and uncharted ways to provide an empathic milieu.

Ferenczi (1933) identified a "confusion of tongues in parents" caused by what he called the "professional hypocrisy" of the analyst.

The unstated and unexplored negative feelings and thoughts by the analyst toward the patient creates an emotional atmosphere of insecurity and ungenuine contact, which leaves patients confused, feeling bad about themselves, and eventually traumatized by the neurotic interaction with the analyst:

> Something had been left unsaid in the relation between physician and patient, something insincere and its frank discussion freed, so to speak, the tongue-tied patient; the admission of the analyst's error produced confidence in his patient. It would almost seem to be of advantage to commit blunders in order to admit afterwards the fault to the patient (p. 159).

According to Ferenczi, the Freudian analytic situation recreated the original trauma for an analysand who had suffered childhood abuse. The deliberate "restrained coolness," "professional hypocrisy," the focus on the patient's criticisms of the analyst as resistance, the clinical facade behind which an analyst hides from a genuine interpersonal encounter, all contribute to producing a ungenuine and therapeutically limited experience. Ferenczi alienated the entire analytic community by contending that the traditional analytic stance was akin to "reproducing the original childhood trauma":

> The analytical situation (i.e. the restrained coolness) the professional hypocrisy and hidden behind it but never revealed—a dislike of the patient which, nevertheless, he felt in all his being—such a situation was not essentially different from that which in his childhood had let to the illness. . . . When, in addition to the strain caused by this analytical situation, we imposed on the patient the further burden reproducing the original trauma, we created a situation that was indeed unbearable (pp. 159–160).

Kohut (1968, 1971) makes many references to trauma in his self psychology: the concept of "narcissistic tramata"; psychopathology results from an unwholesome family interaction, where the parents fail to affirm the child's worth or traumatically disillusion him about their own worth (Kohut and Wolf, 1978; a traumatized analysand "turns back from his reliance on empathy" (Kohut, 1984, p. 66). Kohut (1971) is clear that emotional disturbance is related to trauma, that is, "disturbances in the relationship with the idealized object:

> 1. Very early disturbances in the relationship with the idealized object appear to lead to a general structural weakness . . . a personality thus afflicted suffers from a diffuse narcissistic vulnerability.
>
> 2. Later yet still preoedipal traumatic disturbances in the relationship with the idealized object (or, again, especially, a traumatic disappointment in it) may interfere with the (preoedipal) establishment of the drive-controlling, drive-channeling and drive-neutralizing basic fabric of the psychic apparatus . . . [p. 47].

It is the trauma of interpersonal relations with parents to which Kohut is referring; even in the most intense pathology: "As I have stressed repeatedly, in the vast majority of even the most severe narcissistic personality disturbances, it is the child's reaction to the parent rather than to gross traumatic events in the early biography which accounts for the narcissistic fixations" (p. 82).

Trauma in the "idealized parent imago" has two significant selfobject aspects; one relating to paternal, the other to maternal: ". . . a preoedipal or oedipal traumatic disappointment of a son in his father . . . may rest on the deeper basis of an early, inexpressible disappointment in the idealized mother which may have been due to the unreliability of her empathy and her depressed moods, or may be related to her physical illnesses, or her absence or death" (p. 53).

Kohut also talks about the "susceptibility" to the trauma: "The susceptibility to the trauma is, in turn, due to the interaction of congenital structural weaknesses with experiences which antedate the specific pathogenic trauma" (p. 52). The "essential genetic trauma" is also "grounded in the parents psychopathology, in particular in the parents own narcissistic fixations" (p. 79).

Kohut demonstrated his continued adherence to a trauma theory when, during the latter part of his career, analysts began to label self psychology a supportive therapy. In a surprising response to what is usually "the kiss of death" criticism in psychoanalysis, to wit, labeling a method "a corrective emotional experience," Kohut (1984) defended his method as follows:

> If an ill-desposed critic now gleefully told me that I have finally shown my true colors and . . . demonstrated that I both believe in the curative effect of the "corrective emotional experience" and equate such an experience with analysis, I could only reply: so be it. To my mind, the concept of a "corrective emotional experience" is valuable as long as, in referring to it, we point to

> but a single aspect of the multifaceted body of the psychoanalytic cure [p. 78].

Kohut was also clear that both the analyst's interpretations in the form of empathic responses and his selfobject function in the analytic relationship inherently correct the traumatic childhood experience:

> . . . the more accurately your theories correspond to the psychic realities that underlie our patient's disturbances, the closer our interpretations will come to providing for the patient, in an adult setting and in an adult form, the optimal frustrations that were not forthcoming from the imperfect selfobject responses of early life. Should an ill-disposed critic again claim gleefully that he has caught me redhanded, that once more I have openly admitted that "horrible dictu"—we are indeed providing "corrective emotional experiences" for our patients, I could only reply once more with "so be it!" [p. 153].

It has become fashionable in traditional analytic circles to use the label of corrective emotional experience to denounce any alternate framework as "not psychoanalysis." But Kohut realized that Franz Alexander's (1933; Alexander and French, 1946) concept, derived from Ferenczi's relaxation therapy, was relevant because the empathic failures of childhood need to be ameliorated in the psychoanalytic situation:

> The analyst's protracted and consistent endeavor to understand his patient leads to two results that are analogous to the outcome of normal childhood development: (1) his occasional failures, constituting optimal frustrations, lead to the building up of self structure, while (2) his on the whole adequately maintained understanding leads to the patient's increasing realization that, contrary to his experiences in childhood, the sustaining echo of empathic resonance is indeed available in this world [Kohut, 1984, pp. 77–78].

The corrective emotional experience is a valuable method and concept that has been distorted by traditionalists to denote supportive and cathartic methods without insight. But, as more humanistically oriented analysts have pointed out, "the emotional experience in the transference lends conviction to, and is the necessary underpinning of insight. Having thus reached some stability, this insight elects new, more up-to-date and reality-oriented solutions to old conflicts" (Balint, Ornstein, and Balint, 1964).

Psychoanalytic self psychology, as described by Kohut, is also concerned about the retraumatization of the analysand in the psychoanalytic situation. Kohut, like Ferenczi, struggled with his own clinical functioning in arriving at this theoretical understanding. In one vignette he described the crucial moments of interaction in dealing with a borderline condition, when continued empathic resonance prevented retraumatization. This patient developed self-fragmentation symptoms in response to Kohut's transference interpretations:

> . . . he had indeed felt overwhelmed by the traumatizations to which he was now exposed by virtue of his expanding activities, and he continued to react with prolonged intense suffering as a result of remaining broadly engaged with the world. What I had not seen, however, was that the patient had felt additionally traumatized by feeling that all these explanations on my part came only from the outside: that I did not fully feel what he felt, that I gave him words but not real understanding, and that I thereby repeated the essential trauma of his early life [Kohut, 1984, p. 182].

It seems likely that this case, although not fully explicated by Kohut, was the "insight provoking case" that crystallized his ideas about a "psychoanalytic psychology of self" (Kohut, 1984, p. 182). He became aware that the only avenue to developing a selfobject transference was to proceed along the lines of what I have already mentioned, Ferenczi's self-analysis of "professional hypocrisy." Kohut's struggle emerges from between the lines and parallels the more explicit emotional encounter Ferenczi (1932) described. "To hammer away at the analysand's transference distortions brings no result; it only confirms the analysand's conviction that the analyst is as dogmatic, as utterly sure of himself, as walled off in the self-righteousness of a distorted view as the pathogenic parents (or other selfobject) had been" (Kohut, 1984, p. 182).

Kohut, like Ferenczi, realized that the key to the treatment process was the analyst's willingness and capacity for countertransference analysis, the analyst's avenue for personal and professional growth:

> The task that the analyst faces . . . is largely one of self-scrutiny. . . . Only the analyst's continuing sincere acceptance

> of the patient's reproaches as (psychologically) realistic, followed by a prolonged (and ultimately successful) attempt to look into himself and remove the inner barriers that stand in the way of his empathic grasp of the patient, ultimately have a chance to turn the tide [p. 182].

These are truly remarkable statements from a psychoanalyst who was called "Mr. Psychoanalysis" in the 1970s. Kohut was aware of how radical a departure he had come to by the 1980s, and he was willing to accept it. He now, I believe, moved into the same orbit as Ferenczi: "and if some of my colleagues will say at this juncture that this is not analysis—so be it. My inclination is to respond with the old adage that they should get out of the kitchen if they cannot stand the heat" (pp. 182–183).

REVISION OF THE "RESISTANCE MODEL"

Ferenczi pioneered the reformulation of the resistance model in psychoanalytic therapy in an attempt to understand the expressions of intense negative affect, verbal attacks, continual exclamations of dissatisfaction, resentment, and protestations of rejection and hurt that were part of the clinical work with difficult cases.

Ferenczi's clinical experience with narcissistic and borderline conditions was very similar to Kohut's. However, there was a significant difference. Ferenczi had pioneered an experimental motif for analytic therapy prior to his empathic method. In developing his active method, Ferenczi had already realized that the analyst could not evoke a resistance model if he wished to reach neurotic patients who showed obsessive and phobic symptoms (Ferenczi, 1919a, b, 1920, 1924a, b).

When he became "the analyst of difficult cases," the need to deal with resistance in an empathic way became even more evident and Ferenczi was prepared to meet the challenge. He had an unfailing belief in himself, in the growth potential of the individual, and in the curative power of psychoanalysis: "I have refused to accept such verdicts as that a patient's resistance was unconquerable, or that his narcissism prevented our penetrating any further, or the sheer fatalistic acquiescence in the so-called 'drying up' of a case" (Ferenczi, 1931, pp. 128–129).

Ferenczi's willingness to view the analytic situation as a two-person experience, as well as his genuine sense of personal humility, moved him to examine his own functioning when there was a resistant interaction: "Is it always the patient's resistance that is the case of the failure? Is it not rather our own convenience, which disdains to adapt itself, even in technique, to the idiosyncrasies of the individual?" (pp. 128–129).

The basic innovations that Ferenczi's abandonment of the resistance model encouraged were the acceptance of the analysand's manifest behavior in the analytic situation, acknowledging the analysand's internal frame of reference, and the development of the analyst's use of empathy. When Ferenczi applied these insights about resistance to new case material, he discovered that the results were salutary. Using his relaxation therapy, he pioneered a change from the austere, authoritarian atmosphere of a traditional psychoanalytic session to a more interactive, emotional spontaneous, empathic one (Ferenczi, 1930). This produced a change in the associative process:

> . . . so I urged the patient to deeper relaxation and more complete surrender to the impressions, tendencies, and emotions, which quite spontaneously arose in him. Now the freer the process of association actually became, the more naive (one might say, the more childish) did the patient become in his speech and his other modes of expressing himself [Ferenczi, 1931, pp. 128–129].

In the analysis of Miss F, Kohut (1968, 1971) observed the manifestation of resistance that needed to be understood from within a new framework. He described how the patient would become violently angry and accusatory if he went a single step beyond what she had verbalized. The moment of insight was described as follows:

> . . . the crucial recognition that the patient demanded a specific response to her communications and she completely rejected any other . . . after a prolonged period of ignorance and misunderstanding during which . . . was inclined to argue with the patient about the correctness of . . . interpretations and to suspect the presence of stubborn, hidden resistances" [Kohut, 1968, pp. 108–109].

Ornstein (1978) described the "creative leap" that Kohut was able to take when he could examine his own "inner resistances" (and not the patient's), enabling him to develop a different attitude and response, for example, the capacity to empathize with the childhood reality that drove the patient to reenact them in the analytic session.

Resistance interpretation based on transference fantasies at an oedipal level would totally disavow Miss F's need for an empathic selfobject in the form of her analyst. Kohut (1968) needed to fulfill the specific role of: "an archaic object that would be nothing more than the embodiment of a psychological function that the patient's psyche could not yet perform for itself: to respond empathically to her narcissistic sustenance through approval, mirroring, and echoing" (p. 109).

Ornstein (1978) reported his own overcoming of the temptation to resort to a resistance to oedipal material interpretation in a supervisory experience with Kohut. Kohut helped the analyst to overcome a stalemate by encouraging his awareness of an empathic failure.

The analysis of Miss F was a pivotal experience for redefining the concept of resistance in psychoanalysis. Kohut viewed the anger, whining, and complaining in the transference not as a regressive defense against instinctual wishes, but as an expression of a developmental need. He was able to view Miss F as reactivating the state of frightened child who needed reassurance. Lacking the internal resources to provide it for herself, she was asking the analyst to do so. When Kohut responded in a more empathic way, by clarifying what she needed and empathizing with the distress she experienced in not getting it, she improved.

There are some who feel Kohut's greatest contribution to psychoanalysis was his reformation of the resistance model: "Among these lasting accomplishments, I would rank highest Kohut's challenge to psychoanalysis not to seek alibis—above all, never to blame patients!—when analytic efforts fails as a consequence of the contemporary limitations of knowledge" (Gedo, 1986, p. 127).

Thus, one of the most salient expressions of both Ferenczi's and Kohut's empathic focus was that their behavior, in all of its subtleties, affected the self-experience of the analysand. Consequently, they were able to appreciate the analysand's subjective, restless, motivating resistances, and to convey these understandings to them more empathically.

Kohut's emphasis on the empathic bond, selfobject transferences, a two-person psychology, and the curative elements in the relationship has returned psychoanalysis, or at least provided an alternative, to those of us who wish to continue the humanistic tradition that Ferenczi pioneered. Psychoanalysis has taught us how identifications with lost objects of our past continue to enrich our personalities and influence our current motivations and actions. I believe this is also true with regard to earlier theoretical contributions and the subtle and silent ways they are woven into our current psychoanalytic theories, continuing to enrich and further them. In demonstrating the relationship between the theories of Ferenczi and Kohut I have tried to show how Ferenczi's seminal contributions to clinical work and, especially, the critical importance of empathic functioning, began the tradition of humanistic analysis continued by Kohut.

REFERENCES

Alexander, F. (1933), On Ferenczi's relaxation principle. *Internat. J. Psycho-Anal.,* 14:183–192.

_____ & French, T. M. (1946), *Psychoanalytic Therapy.* New York: Ronald Press.

Anzieu, D. (1975), *L'auto-analyse de Freud et la decouverte de la Psychanalyse.* Vol. I. Paris: Presses Universitaires De France.

Balint, M. (1949), Sandor Ferenczi: Obit 1933. *Internat. J. Psycho-Anal.,* 30 (4).

_____ (1968), *The Basic Fault.* London: Tavistock.

_____ Ornstein, P. H. & Balint, E. (1964), *Focal Psychotherapy.* London: Lippincott, 1972.

Barande, I. (1972), *Sandor Ferenczi* Paris: Payot.

Basch, M. F. (1984), The selfobject theory of motivation and the history of psychoanalysis. In: *Kohut's Legacy,* ed. P.E. Stepansky & A. Goldberg. Hillsdale, NJ: The Analytic Press, pp. 3–41.

Bergman, M.S. & Hartman, F.R., ed. (1976), *The Evolution of Psychoanalytic Technique.* New York: Basic.

Bollas, C. (1986), Who does self psychology cure? *Psychoanal. Inq.,* 6:429–435.

Burgess, A.W., Groth, N.A., Holmstrom, L.L. & Sgyoi, S.S. (1978), *Sexual Assault of Children and Adolescents.* Lexington, MA: D.C. Heath.

Chessick, R.D. (1985), *Psychology of the Self and the Treatment of Narcissism.* New York: Aronson.

Cohler, B.J. (1980), Developmental perspectives on the Psychology of the self in early childhood. In: *Advances in Self Psychology*, ed. A. Goldberg. New York: International Universities Press, pp. 69–115.

Dupont, J. (1985), *Ferenczi's Journal Clinique: Janvier–Octobre 1932.* Paris: Payot.

_____ (1988), Ferenczi's "madness." *Contemp. Psychoanal.,* 24:250–261.

Ferenczi, S. (1919a), Technical difficulties in the analysis of a case of hysteria: Including observations on larval forms of onanism and onanistic equivalents. In: *Further Contributions to the Theory and Technique of Psychoanalysis,* Vol. 2, ed. J. Rickman. London: Hogarth Press, 1950, pp. 189–197.

_____ (1919b), On influencing of the patient in psycho-analysis. In: *Further Contributions to the Theory and Technique of Psychoanalysis,* Vol. 2, ed. J. Rickman. London: Hogarth Press, 1950, pp. 198–217.

_____ (1920), The further development of the active therapy in psychoanalysis. In: *Further Contributions to the Theory and Technique of Psychoanalysis,* Vol. 2, ed. J. Rickman. London: Hogarth Press, 1950, pp. 198–217. 1950.

_____ (1924a), *Thalassa: A Theory of Genitality.* New York: Psychoanalytic Quarterly, 1938.

_____ (1924b), On forced phantasies: Activity in the association technique. In: *Further Contributions to the Theory and Technique of Psychoanalysis,* Vol. 2, ed. J. Rickman. London: Hogarth Press, 1950, pp. 68–77.

_____ (1925), Psycho-Analysis of sexual habits. In: *Further Contributions to the Theory and Technique of Psychoanalysis,* Vol. 2, ed. J. Rickman. London: Hogarth Press, 1950, pp. 259–297.

_____ (1928), The elasticity of Psychoanalytic technique. In: *Final Contributions to the Problems and Methods of Psychoanalysis,* Vol. 3, ed. M. Balint. New York: Basic, 1955, pp. 87–102.

_____ (1930), The principle of relaxation and neo-catharsis. In: *Final Contributions to the Problems and Methods of Psychoanalysis,* Vol. 3, ed. M. Balint New York: Basic, 1955, pp. 108–125.

_____ (1931), Child Analysis in the Analysis of Adults. In: *Final Contributions to the Problems and Methods of Psychoanalysis,* Vol. 3, ed. M. Balint. New York: Basic, 1955, pp. 126–142.

_____ (1932), *Ferenczi's Clinical Diary,* ed. J. Dupont. Cambridge, MA: Harvard University Press, 1988.

_____ (1933), The confusion of tongues between adults and children: The language of tenderness and of passion. In: *Final Contributions to the Problems and Methods of Psychoanalysis,* Vol. 3, ed. M. Balint. New York: Basic, 1955, pp. 156–167.

Gedo, J.E. (1976), The wise baby "reconsidered." *Psychological Issues,* Monogr. 34/35, pp. 357–378.

_____ (1986), *Conceptual Issues in Psychoanalysis.* Hillsdale, NJ: The Analytic Press.

Groth, N.A. & Birnbaum, J.H. (1979), *Men Who Rape.* New York: Plenum Press.

James, B. & Nasjleti, M. (1983). *Treating Sexually Abused Children and Their Families.* Palo Alto, CA: Consulting Psychologists Press.

Jones, E. (1953). *The Life and Work of Sigmund Freud,* Vol. 1. New York: Basic.

Kahn, E. (1985), Heinz Kohut and Carl Rogers: A timely comparison. *Amer. Psychol.,* 40:893–904.

Kohut, H. (1959), Introspection, empathy and psychoanalysis: An examination of the relationship between mode of observation and theory. In. *The Search For The Self,* ed. P. Ornstein. New York: International Universities Press, 1978, pp. 205–232.

_____ (1968), The psychoanalytic treatment of narcissistic personalty disorders: Outline of a systematic approach. *The Psychoanalytic Study of the Child,* 23:86–113. New York: International Universities Press.

_____ (1971), *The Analysis of the Self.* New York: International Universities Press.

_____ (1975), The psychoanalyst in the community of scholars. In: *The Search For The Self,* ed. P. Ornstein. New York: International Universities Press, 1978, pp. 685–724.

_____ (1977), *The Restoration of the Self.* International Universities Press.

Kohut, H. (1978). *The Search for the Self,* ed. P. Ornstein. New York: International Universities Press.

_____ (1984). *How Does Analysis Cure?* ed. A. Goldberg & P.E. Stepansky. Chicago: University of Chicago Press.

_____ Wolf, E. (1978), The disorders of the self and their treatment: An outline. *Internat. J. Psycho-Anal.,* 59:413–425.

Krull, M. (1986), *Freud and His Father.* New York: Norton.

Levy, S.T. (1985), Empathy and psychoanalytic technique. *J. Amer. Psychoanal. Assn.,* 2:353–378.

Masson, J.M. (1984), *The Assault on Truth.* New York: Farrar, Straus & Giroux.

Ornstein, P.H. (1974), On narcissism: Beyond the introduction—highlights of Heinz Kohut's contributions to the psychoanalytic treatment of narcissistic personality disorders. *The Annual of Psychoanalysis,* 2:107–129. New York: International Universities Press.

_____ (1978), The evolution of Heinz Kohut's psychoanalytic psychology of the self. In: *The Search for the Self,* ed. P. Ornstein. New York International Universities Press, pp. 1–106.

Rachman, A.W. (1976). The first "encounter" session: Ferenczi's case of the female Croatian musician. Presented at annual meeting of the American Group Psychotherapy Association Conference, New Orleans, LA, February.

_____ (1977), Self-disclosure, self-analysis, and self-actualization for the group psychotherapist. In: *Group Therapy, 1977,* ed. L.R. Wolberg. New York: Stratton Intercontinental Medical.

_____ (1988), The rule of empathy: Sandor Ferenczi's pioneering contributions to the empathic method in psychoanalysis. *J. Amer. Acad. Psychoanal.,* 16:1–27.

_____ (in press). Confusion of tongues: The Ferenczian metaphor for childhood seduction and emotional trauma. *J. Amer. Acad. Psychoanal.*

_____ (in preparation), *Sandor Ferenczi: The Psychoanalyst of Tenderness and Passion.*

—— Wayne, M. (1986), The emergence of the concept of empathy in psychoanalysis: From Ferenczi to Kohut. Seminar, Society for the Advancement of Self Psychology, New York City, September 27.

Rush, F. (1980), *The Best Kept Secret.* New York: McGraw Hill.

Sabourin, P. (1985), *Ferenczi: Paladin Et Grand Vizir Secret.* Paris: Editions Universitaires.

Schur, M. (1972), *Freud: Living and Dying.* New York: International Universities Press.

Simitis-Grubrich, I. (1986), Six letters of Sigmund Freud and Sandor Ferenczi on the interrelationship of psychoanalytic theory and technique. *Internat. Rev. Psycho-Anal.,* 13:259–277.

Stolorow, R. (1976), Psychoanalytic reflections on client-centered therapy in the light of modern conceptions of Narcissism. *Psychother. Theory Res. Prac.,* 13:26–29.

—— & Lachmann, F. (1980), *Psychoanalysis of Developmental Arrests.* New York: International Universities Press.

Sylwan, B. (1984), An untoward event. *Confrontation,* 12:101–122.

Sulloway, F. (1979), *Freud: Biologist of the Mind.* New York: Basic.

Thompson, C. (1944), Ferenczi's contribution to Psychoanalysis. *Psychiat.,* 7:245–252.

—— (1964), Ferenczi's relaxation method. In: *Interpersonal Psychoanalysis,* ed. M. R. Green. New York: Basic, pp. 67–71.

6

Karen Horney's Theory of Self

HENRY A. PAUL

This chapter examines some of the main contributions of the psychoanalytic pioneer Karen Horney, with special emphasis on her concepts of self and briefly compares them with self psychology of Heinz Kohut. Horney's contributions to psychoanalysis can be best understood if viewed in a historical context. Thus, after a brief survey of some of the major trends in the evolution of psychoanalysis, the development of Horney's ideas will be reviewed, including her final theoretical exposition of a theory of self. It will become evident that the evolution of her ideas was remarkably parallel to that of psychoanalysis as a whole. In fact, some of her main contributions actually foreshadowed and antedated developments of recent times.

For the sake of simplicity—given the shortcomings of categorization and the fallacy of neat divisions—psychoanalytic evolution will be discussed in terms of three familiar phases: 1) the drive, or id, psychology phase; 2) the ego psychology phase, with the associated object relations movement; and 3) the self psychology phase.

THE EVOLUTION OF PSYCHOANALYSIS

The Drive Psychology Phase

Meissner (1985) offers an excellent review of classical psychoanalytic concepts. He points out the the drive psychology phase began with Freud about a hundred years ago. Freud, working in Europe in the late 19th century and influenced strongly by the prevalent natural science atmosphere, introduced his early ideas on the basis of biological and physiologic principles. His early works are heavily imbued with neurologic and energic concepts. This trend in his work never totally disappeared. From the beginning of this first phase until the early 1920s, the beginning of the next phase, Freud and other classical analysts continued to define and expand a host of concepts: unconscious mental functioning, psychic determinism, conflict psychology, dream psychology, instinctual energy theories, mental topography, sexual repression, psychosexual developmental phases, narcissism, aggression, anxiety, thought processes, and treatment methods. All of these concepts were intertwined with instinctual drives.

The Ego Psychology Phase

But in the early 1920s, with the introduction of the tripartite structure of the mind, psychoanalysis began to shift emphasis to the ego and its functions—the ego psychology phase. Prior to this time, the ego had been touched on, but now it became established as a special structure of the mind. At first it was formulated as weak and passive but soon came to viewed as a powerful structure of control, regulation, integration, and adaptation. This last function, adaptation, necessitated a shift in psychoanalytic interest from internal mental functioning to external reality. The outside world, especially the world of interpersonal relations became a focus of psychoanalytic scrutiny. Although the classical psychoanalytic movement had considered so-called objects from the earliest time, it had mostly been in fragmented drive-oriented fashion. Now the external object became the center of interest and with it came the growth of the object relations movement.

Just as Anna Freud (1966) and Heinz Hartmann (1964) are closely associated with the ego psychology phase, Melanie Klein is considered by many to have formally introduced the object relations movement. As Guntrip (1971) points out, it was her work with children that shed light on the area of conflicting feelings towards others and self. Although she strongly considered herself part of the classical movement, her elaboration of the ideas of projection, reintrojection of instincts, and internalized object relations set the stage for the object relations movement. She established a link between the ego and object relations and showed how instincts became transformed into internal objects.

Views of the ego changed as well. Fairbairn (1954) stressed the centrality of the ego even at birth. He saw it as the center of all psychic functioning. As well, the view of aggression as secondary to frustration, rather than as a primary instinct, was becoming popular. The idea of a divided ego secondary to psychic trauma was also introduced.

Further developments in the ego-object-relations movement continue in some form even in modern times by such pioneers as Erikson (1964), Jacobson (see Tuttman, Kaye, and Zimmerman, 1981), and Winicott (1965), to mention only a few. The serious psychoanalytic historian studying the evolution of the ego psychology and the object relations phase might easily be confused by the confluence of many trends in this phase, which took hold in the 1920s and 1930s and persists until the present.

The Self Psychology Phase

The self psychology phase, which has received the most concentrated attention in the last 20 years, may seem even more confusing and vague. Part of this confusion seems to come from the translation of the German word *Ich,* used by Freud, into the English word *ego* rather than self. The word ego seemed to be more impersonal, mechanistic, and structural than the word self, which usually connotes a personal, subjective experience. This translation is often offered as the main reason for the persistence of the conflict between those who see the self as an ego subfunction and those who see it as the whole person, interacting with others. Some, like Kernberg (1975), feel that the self is part of the ego, while others, such as Erikson (1964) and Spiegel (1959), try to tie it in some way to the tripartite structure. Others, such as Kohut ((1977), elevate the the self to a position of so-called supraordinance over the tripartite mental structure, although still tied to this classical paradigm.

Functional definitions of the self seem more inclusive and less decisive than those of the ego. These include the self as a source of personal actions and autonomous strivings. Also the self is often viewed as the center of personal values and characteristics and the source of creativity, virtue, and freedom.

The Self Psychology Phase

The who and when of the self psychology phase is also open to question. Some point to early pioneers such as Adler (Ansbacher and Ansbacher,1956) and Jung (Whitmont,1967) as the first to focus on the self. Others point to the so-called post- or neo-Freudians, including the culturalists and existentialists. Some even say that the work of Kohut (1971) marks the beginning of the phase. The most recent work on the self comes from the field of infant research, notably the developmental line introduced by Stern (1985), in which the development of the various senses of self, beginning in infancy, are tied in with social experience and relatedness.

In summary, at first predominantly biological, physiological, neurological, and mechanistic, psychoanalysis has evolved to include the personal, subjective experience of the self and others. Interest shifted from the internal workings of the mind to internal and external relations, with a focus on the ego, interpersonal relations, and the boundary between self and others both in the family and in the world at large. Along with this shift, interest in culture, sociology, and anthropology became evident. Now, finally, the self occupies center stage.

KAREN HORNEY

What about the contributions of Karen Horney? Symonds and Symonds (1985) have reviewed her life and work. Karen Horney lived from 1885 to 1952. She was born in Berlin and came to the United States in 1932, after completing her medical training, training analysis, and deep involvement in the classical Berlin Psychoanalytic Institute. In 1934 she came to New York City. In 1941 she founded the Association for the Advancement of Psychoanalysis and shortly thereafter the American Institute for Psychoanalysis, of which she was the Dean until her death. She wrote 76 scientific papers and five books, and edited and contributed to a sixth. The bulk of her work occurred in the three decades of the 1920s, 30s, and 40s.

Horney worked during a time of very active evolution in psychoanalysis. At first she was a Freudian analyst (for approximately the first 15 years of her professional life). Her own interest shifted to the ego, character structure and object relations, and finally the self. As her ideas grew, so did her emphasis on the growth of the individual. This growth orientation lies at the heart of her work. It describes her personal odyssey as well, from faithful classicist, to questioner, to modifier, to developer of a radically revised, fully psychoanalytic viewpoint. Her movement toward self transcends the still active polarization in psychoanalysis between the classicists, who stress the centrality of structural conflict, and the self psychologists. I (Paul,1985) have addressed this issue in detail, and Rendon (1986) discussed it within a philosophical framework.

Horney's earliest papers, published in the 1920s and 1930s, focused on women (Horney,1966). But in these papers we see the beginning of her conception of the neurotic process as a whole. She questioned the classical views about women. She felt that prevailing social conditions contributed in great measure to womens' self-evaluation. This idea contrasted sharply to the classical, instinct-oriented view. We see here the beginning of her deemphasis of the instinct theory, a deemphasis she was to develop fully later. In this early period we also see Horney questioning the intellectual and obsessive focus on childhood events as the only determinants of character structure. She felt that all of life affects us and the focus should be on the ongoing life process as well as childhood. In this early period we also see the beginning of her holistic-dynamic orientation as she began to stress the mutual interaction of individual and society, internal experience and external reality, and the present and the past. By the mid-1930s Horney was already well known for emphasizing the effects of the culture on the family, which in turn affects the young child. These effects would help to mold the evolving sense of identity of the growing individual.

Through the 1920s and 1930s Horney was a leader in a psychoanalysis evolving toward ego psychology and object relations. This trend included the study of the cultural determinants of the neurotic process, and Horney eventually revised the premises on which most psychoanalytic theory stood, a revision more radical than most psychoanalytic theoreticians. Before examining this movement I would like to examine, briefly, the cultural interests of Horney.

I have often heard Horney referred to as the originator, or one of the main figures, of the cultural school of psychoanalysis. This designation is especially interesting inasmuch as she is best known for her work on the intrapsychic aspects of neurosis. Her early concentration on the interpersonal and cultural realms actually did represent a new and decisive shift in focus for psychoanalysis. Her interest in these, though, was short. They became integrated into her later works, which were more encompassing and focused on the intrapsychic. Fortunately some of Horney's predecessors have extended her work in this area, for example, Symonds (1983) with her prolific work on women and the culture.

As Portnoy (1974) points out, Horney discussed four major areas in regard to the culture. First, she pointed out that cultures vary as to what they consider either healthy or ill. Thus, a culture must be understood if the individual is to be understood. This axiom is one of the earliest examples of what is known today as folk psychiatry, ethnopsychiatry, or transcultural psychiatry with links to cultural relativism and anthropology.

Second, Horney (1939) felt that our society emphasized competitiveness, destructive rivalry, suspiciousness, and begrudging envy in both the economic and social areas, making people feel a degree of helplessness, hostility, and insecurity. A third neurotic force in the culture was the composite of inherent inconsistencies, such as the well-known divergence between the quest for success at all costs and the mandate that we treat each other with brotherly love. Cultural conflicts often confuse people and also become the anlages of inner psychological conflicts. Fourth, Horney felt that cultural ideals often become those of the neurotic person. The latter three neurotogenic forces affect all of us but more the neurotic person, especially in childhood because of parental susceptibility. Horney felt that the neurotic person was actually the "stepchild" of the culture.

In *The Neurotic Personality of Our Time,* Horney (1937) wrote about these cultural issues and her ideas regarding interpersonal relations as generators of neurosis and the interpersonal relations of the neurotic individual. She not only discussed the relationship between the culture and its effect on more intimate interpersonal relations, but also tried to define neurosis. The early definition was that neurosis was a psychic disturbance, with fears, defenses, and attempts at compromise solutions, all of which deviated from the culturally accepted pattern. She focused on parentally-induced hostility in the child, the need to repress this hostility due to fear of its interpersonal consequences, and the repression being a main source of anxiety. In addition, the child elaborates retaliatory fears, which further induce anxiety. Attempts to gain reassurance against this anxiety by devising various interpersonal strategies, such as trying to gain affection, submitting, trying to exert power, or withdrawing from people, lead to more anxiety, as they often conflict with each other and with people in the environment. This Basic Hostility of the child who will be a neurotic adult, if unrelieved, eventually becomes generalized to the world and through various defensive rearrangements becomes a character attitude called Basic Anxiety—a feeling of isolation and helplessness in a world perceived as potentially hostile. Basic Anxiety is the soil from which an entire character neurosis would grow. This theory of anxiety is essentially different from Kohut's, whose theory of anxiety and, for that matter, whose theory of psychological development, is tied to his concept of the self-selfobject unit.

Horney's ideas regarding the cultural determinants of anxiety, hostility, and psychic conflict, and the idea of vicious cycles as the main fuel for neurotic development, would remain in one form or another throughout her work.

In this early work one will also find a detailed account of object relations as they exist in the areas of affection-seeking, sexuality, jealousy, feelings of rejection, power striving, masochism, and suffering. These descriptions are as valuable today as they were then and are excellent examples of conflict-centered viscissitudes of everyday life engendered by neurotic anxiety. These subjects are described and explained on a here-and-now basis without resort to highly questionable (and recently disproven) "developmental hypotheses." These phenomena are seen each day in our practices. Horney's persistent focus on the conflicts present in the current character structure is a hallmark of her work, and she felt that this focus is what, in fact, helped the patient grow.

This reasoning is clearly shown in her next publication, *New Ways in Psychoanalysis* (Horney, 1939). This book signals her official shift away from the basic premises on which Freudian theory rests. It was a logical extension of her shift in focus to the interpersonal and cultural. Specifically, she questioned the biological, constitutional, dualistic, mechanistic-evolutionistic premises of classical theory. She did feel, though, that certain fundamentals of Freudian thinking should be retained in any system that was considered psychoanalytic. These were the concepts of psychic determinism and the unconscious, and the idea that emotions were the driving forces of our behavior. She stated that these fundamentals are the "constructive . . . and imperishable values Freud has given to psychology and psychiatry" (p.18). In addition, she felt that the concepts of transference, resistance, free association, the importance of childhood events, anxiety and its role in neurosis, the role of psychic conflict, and dreams were also fundamentals that should be retained by psychoanalysis.

By abandoning the specific Freudian premises just alluded

to—something modern self-theorists have not done—the issue of the self begins to take hold in Horney's ideas.

Prior to 1939, the specific concept or use of the word self was not a focus in Horney's ideas. In *Neurotic Personality of Our Time* (Horney, 1937), the concept of the self was mentioned in describing neurotic self-evaluation. In the same work, the self was seen as threatened by the emergence of hostility; it was weakened by basic anxiety; it was the object of love, as in self-love; it was used in reference to inferiority, as in the lowering of oneself; it was casually mentioned in relation to ambitious strivings and fears of disapproval; and it was mentioned in regard to vicious cycles versus lucky cycles. Finally it was given a somewhat larger role when neurotic suffering, submersion in misery, masochism, and the abandonment of the self were discussed.

Horney seems not to have been particularly interested in defining a specific concept of self yet. From the beginning, implicit in her writing was that a self was present.

But in 1939, in *New Ways in Psychoanalysis,* a decided shift took place in this regard. When discussing the effects of changing the classical premises, Horney stated, "We have to search anew for the environmental factors responsible for creating neurotic conflicts. Thus, disturbances in human relations become the crucial factor in the genesis of neurosis" (p.9). She went on to introduce a decidedly new concept:

> Neuroses thus represent a peculiar kind of struggle for life under difficult conditions. Their very essence consists in disturbances in relation to the self and conflicts arising on these grounds. The shift in emphasis as to factors considered relevant in neurosis enlarges considerably the tasks of psychoanalytical therapy. The aim of treatment then is not to help the patient gain mastery over his instincts but to lessen his anxiety to such an extent that he can dispense with his neurotic trends. Beyond this aim there looms an entirely new therapeutic goal, which is to restore the individual to himself, to help him regain his spontaneity and find his center of gravity in himself [p. 11].

Linked to these concepts Horney introduced what would be her basic premise from then on. She stated that alienation is at the root of neurotic development. She had already described alienation from others as the generator of neurotic development and now described alienation from the self as being the result and perpetuating principle of further neurotic elaboration. The self she now described was referred to as the "spontaneous individual self" (p.9) At this time this self had as its most salient characteristic, genuineness. It was a self that was both spontaneous and elemental; it could not be further analyzed into instinctual components.

By this time Horney had given rough outline to her theory of neurosis. She had already stated that disturbed human relations resulted in basic anxiety. Neurotic trends were developed in an attempt to gain reassurance, and these often conflicted with each other and caused more anxiety. Over and above these, a disturbance of greater significance was taking place—alienation from others had led to alienation from self. The idea of a "spontaneous individual self" was introduced. In the same work, the idea of defensive self-aggrandizement was discussed. This was the forerunner of her other well-known concept, the idealized image (Horney, 1946). Horney's self psychology was now introduced.

Around this time, 1939, trouble reached a peak for Horney in the New York Psychoanalytic Society, where she had been an active teacher and training analyst (Symonds and Symonds, 1985). Her abandonment of the instinct theory and substitution of a view of the ongoingness of a dynamic theory aroused great hostility and dissension. Her theories were condemned, and she was criticized personally for her own "instinctual life." Eventually she was disqualified as instructor and training analyst. She resigned in May 1940. She and several colleagues, among whom were Thompson, Robins, Ephron, and Kelman, decided to start a new psychoanalytic group—the Association for the Advancement of Psychoanalysis—and soon thereafter the educational arm called the American Institute for Psychoanalysis. Unfortunately, Horney was ostracized from the American Psychoanalytic Association as well.

Although the basic elements of her theory were in place, Horney's theory was still disorganized, not yet unified (Rubins, 1978). Enlargements and revisions were to take place. Rubins has reviewed the development of Horney's theory in excellent fashion. Much of what follows is an elaboration of his great effort.

Self Analysis (Horney, 1942) is considered the first revision. Not only were neurotic trends expanded to include ten separate categories, but associated with each trend was a set of "needs, behaviors, values, feelings towards self, inhibitions, demands on others, secondary conflicts etc." (Rubins, 1978, p. 279). This enlargement, along with a focus on realization of one's potential, foreshadowed the next two revisions, in 1946 and 1950.

In 1946, *Our Inner Conflicts* was published. This work also centered on neurotic trends, but now they were grouped into three well-known categories: moving toward, against, and away from people. These trends were a response to basic anxiety and were thus driven behaviors, infexible and pervasive. They were qualitatively different from normal, free, healthy movements toward, against, and away from others. As they became compulsive, they conflicted with each other and constituted what was called the Basic Conflict. Immediate attempts to solve this conflict were activated: attempts to repress all but one of the trends, movement away from involvement with people altogether; the development of an idealized image of oneself; and externalization of various aspects of the inner conflict experience. The idealized image formation was the most important of the solutions for the further development of her theory. This defensively evolved picture of oneself was unconscious, unrealistic, static, and ideationally fixed. It served as substitute for real confidence and pride. It gave the anxious person a feeling of being better than others. It gave a person a feeling of meaningfulness. Horney pointed out that people vary as to whether they feel that they are their idealized images or are the opposite of these images (the despised image), or whether they feel in constant struggle to be the idealized image. The focus here was on idealization on one hand and devaluation of what Horney called the real or actual self on the other.

By 1946 Horney had introduced the concepts of the idealized and the despised image and the still not completely clear concept of the real self (the term actual self was also used but is not germane to this discussion). In *Our Inner Conflicts* she also talked about other character traits by which one attempted to achieve artificial harmony in the face of conflict and the overall consequences of the unresolved conflicted state.

The subtitle of *Our Inner Conflicts* was, importantly, "A Constructive Theory of Neurosis." This highlighted Horney's idea of growth. She felt that neurotic conflicts could be outgrown as anxiety lessened, and people could change by assuming more responsibility for their lives and gaining inner independence, increased spontaneity, and wholeheartedness. This idea was an extension of the "spontaneous individual self" of 1939 and foreshadowed her final treatise, in 1950, where her contribution to self psychology finally blossomed.

As Rubins (1978) has pointed out, Horney's (1950) final theoretical revision, *Neurosis and Human Growth* embodied all that came before it and also introduced a new integration. It is here that her self psychology really took form. The most important difference between this work and her earlier ones was the emphasis she gave to the real self. It was more systematized here. Finally given central position in her psychology, it was defined as a "central inner force common to all human beings and yet unique in each which is the deep source of growth" (p.17). Growth meant free, healthy development in accordance with the potential of one's "generic and individual nature" (p.17). The central, inner force was really a conglomeration of such constructive forces as clarity, the ability to tap one's resources, the strength of one's will power, special gifts and talents, expressiveness, the ability to relate to others with spontaneity, and the development of personal values and aims in life. All of these factors urges each of us toward self-realization. Thus, the real self is a process or movement or directed growth orientation that in the final analysis is not truly analyzable. It is fluid, natural, and unique. The ultimate goal of psychoanalysis for Horney now became the identification, support, nurturance, and liberation of these constructive forces in each person. This final placement of the real self at the heart of her theory places her self psychology on a high level of optimism with regard to the tragedy of neurosis. As Horney stated regarding her basic philosophy, "With all the cognizance of the tragic element in neurosis it is an optimistic one" (p.17), by which she meant, like Albert Scweitzer, "world and life affirming".

The real self is present in each of us, but to the degree that we have become neurotic we have shifted our energies away from self-realization toward what Horney called actualization of the idealized image. Neurosis was now seen as a "special form of human development antithetical to healthy growth" (Horney, 1950, p.13). This special form of development had alienation from the real self as the central neurotic process.

The idealized image changed somewhat in this final revision. Before, it had been one of four attempts at conflict solution. Now it was given much more significance. Anxiety had given birth to this image in childhood. According to Horney, as development proceeds, the person slowly begins to identify with this image. The idealized image becomes an idealized self and self-idealization becomes the center of the search for glory. This comprehensive neurotic solution, the search for glory, lends a feeling of integration and identity to its bearer. It signifies the outcome of early neurotic development and signals its continuation as it stimulates further alienation and the drive toward actualization of the idealized image. The search for glory with self idealization at its core is comprehensive, for it also contains the drive for perfection, neurotic ambitiousness, and the drive for vindictive triumph.

If the neurotic process is viewed chronologically, the introduction of the search for glory signifies a major shift from the interpersonal to the intrapsychic phase of neurotic development (Portnoy, 1974). It usually takes hold in late adolescence or early adulthood. The early basic anxiety caused by alienation from others causes a split, predominantly in ways of relating (conflicting neurotic trends), which lead to a search for unity and safety. When these solutions fail, the center of gravity shifts even more to the outside, alienation increases, dividedness is perpetuated, and a firm sense of identity is further derailed. Helplessness and vulnerability increase. Now this final shift holds out the illusion of final integration. It really represents the abandonment of the soul—alienation from the real self.

Horney's self psychology is further elaborated in her description of the neurotic process. The search for glory leads to further neurotic functions. Self-idealization demands certain treatment from the outside world. These demands, or feelings of entitlement, are called neurotic "claims" (Horney, 1950). Horney described them as unrealistic, egocentric, vindictive, and only minimally conscious. When the outside world does not comply, rage, righteousness, self-pity, abused feelings, intense envy, depression, somatization, and other syptoms may ensue. Self-idealization also leads to demands on oneself-"the shoulds" (Horney, 1950)—by which the person attempts to mold himself into the perfect, idealized self. Pretenses and façades grow. Some of these demands are externalized, leading to critical attitudes toward others or to the fear of criticism from others. According to Portnoy (1974), the shoulds are the most destructive of the neurotic phenomena, for they sap spontaneity and stimulate alienation.

The idealized image assumes great importance because it has become invested with neurotic pride. This type of pride is spurious and easily hurt. Since it is counterfeit and illusional, it actually increases vulnerability. Whenever the person catches true glimpse of his imperfect self either consciously or, more commonly, unconsciously, he experiences intense shame. If others hurt his pride, the major experience is humiliation. Derivatives of these two very powerful feelings are intense anxiety, depression, rage, psychosis, and psychosomatic reactions. Commonly called to the rescue are narcotizing measures, including the compulsive use of alcohol, drugs, food, and sex. To the degree that we are neurotic, we are always on guard to avoid any situation that might lead to hurt pride. Pride restoring measures such as revenge, loss of interest in an event, denial, and humor are constantly being called upon as well.

This attempt to actualize the pride-invested grandiose illusional self is, of course, doomed to failure. This failure constantly generates contempt for all the aspects of oneself that are not idealized. This self-hate generates a despised image—the flip side of the idealized image. Horney called neurotic pride and self-hate the pride system. As I have outlined elsewhere (Paul, 1985), it is the pride system that constitutes the core of Horney's self psychology. The neurotic process leads a person to a dual identification—both with the idealized self and with the despised self. This conflict in self-experience calls forth further neurotic solutions.

According to Horney (1950), compartmentalization of these two self-experiences leads to alternating self-evaluations, erratic behavior, and mood fluctuations. Streamlining, which is similar to attempting to supress one image entirely, results in either an expansive character solution (initiated by identification with the idealized image and its supportive structures) or a self-effacing character solutions (stemming from a predominant identification with the despised image). Or there may be an attempt to withdraw entirely from this conflict by the act of resignation. These three solutions are the well-known character types of Horney's theory.

There is a major difference between resignation and all the strategies that go with it, on one hand, and both streamlining and comparmentalization, on the other. Resignation implies a withdrawal from activity and from others, while either of the other two solutions in one way or another keeps people more in touch with more aspects of both self and other. Although further clarifying work is necessary in this area, there is the tempting possibility that Horney's theory may yield a comprehensive understanding of the schizophrenic versus the affective illness diathesis that we know exists. The autism and withdrawal of the schizophrenic might be the end of a spectrum of resignation, while the mania and depression of affective illness might be related to unleashed total identification with either the idealized or the despised image.

I would like to emphasize that the neurotic selves that Horney described—the idealized and despised selves—are static, growth-retarding structures, but are not primitive or archaic. They are essentially the result, and not the cause, of neurotic development.

The whole shift away from the real self to actualization of the idealized self, with development of the pride system and other solutions, is part of the central alienating process. Horney (1950) compared this shift to the devil's pact:

> There is a human being in psychic or spiritual distress. There is a temptation presented in some symbol of an evil principle: the devil, the sorcerer, witches, the serpent (in the story of Adam and Eve), the antique dealer (in Balzac's *Magic Skin*), the cynical Lord Henry Wotton (in Oscar Wilde's *The Picture of Dorian Gray*). Then there are the promises of not only a miraculous riddance of the distress but of the possession of infinite powers. And it is a testimony of true greatness when one person can resist the temptation, as the Christ's temptation shows. Finally, there is the price to pay, which (presented in various forms) is the loss of the soul (Adam and Eve lose innocence of their feelings) its surrender to the forces of evil: "All these I will give thee if thou will fall down and worship me," says Satan to Christ. The price may be psychic torment in this life (as in the Magic Skin) or the torment of Hell. In the Devil and Daniel Webster we have the beautifully realized symbol of the shriveled souls collected by the devil [p. 375].

She states that in her theory the parallel is that "an individual in psychic distress arrogates to himself infinite powers, losing his soul and suffering the torments of his self hate" (p. 376).

In conclusion the following can be said of Horney's theory:

1. It is coherent and unified (Rubins, 1978).
2. It is holistic in the sense that Rubins (1978) points out. Horney emphasized the intrapsychic phenomena as they occur in a context. Cultural; interpersonal and intrapsychic; mental, emotional, and somatic; past and present, all are closely interwoven. The boundaries between subject and object and external and internal are often blurred.
3. It is a dynamic theory. The dynamics of movement and forces supercede the importance of description and typologies.
4. It use a systems approach, as described by Rubins (1978). Primary, secondary, and tertiary conflicts become the rule. Complexity and profundity increase in each theoretical revision.
5. It is a theory that evolved and that concerns itself with

evolution—of the real self and of the neurotic process. Thus, Horney's is a truly developmental theory in contrast to the theories spuriously known as developmental.

6. It is essentially a theory of self. To quote Horney, "The neurotic process . . . is a problem of self. It is the process of abandoning the real self for an idealized one; of trying to actualize this pseudoself instead of our given human potentials; of a destructive warfare between two selves; of allaying this warfare the best, or at any rate the only way we can; and finally by having our constructive forces mobilized by life or by therapy of finding our real selves [p. 371]."
7. Her focus on self was one of the earliest in psychoanalysis. I think, in fact, that it was the earliest systematized self psychology in psychoanalysis. Horney's focus on omnipotence and devaluation, the expression of contrasting self-evaluations in the analytic relationship, and her ability to transcend the polarities of conflict versus deficit, structural conflicts versus the self, all antedate the current emphasis on these subjects by at least 20 years.

HORNEY AND KOHUT: COMPARISONS AND CONTRASTS

It is interesting to compare and contrast a few of Horney's and Kohut's concepts, some of which I have covered elsewhere (Paul, 1985).

Both Horney and Kohut considered the etiology of neurosis to be mainly within a broadly defined child-parent relational dysfunction. But Horney, having radically departed from the classical paradigm, came to see neurosis as emanating from the resultant anxiety of child-parent problems; whereas Kohut, still linked to classical concepts, saw fixation and regression as major constituents of neurosogenesis.

Both Horney and Kohut felt that each person potentially possessed a growth-oriented self and that liberation or nurturance of, or attendance to, this self was essential for recovery during treatment. But while Horney's real self was seen as a central inner conglomeration of constructive forces, Kohut's nuclear self was a bipolar structure related to specific developmental lines and specific transference developments.

Both Horney and Kohut describe acute and chronic dysequilibrium reactions. While Horney sees these reactions as a result of hurt neurotic pride or a frustrated claim, Kohut conceptualizes them as regressive nacissistic swings.

Both authors see the full blown oedipal complex as secondary to another psychic event: Horney, as secondary to basic hostility and competitiveness within the nuclear family, along with possible sexual stimulation; Kohut, as a disintegration product of a damaged supraordinate self-structure.

While both Horney and Kohut focus on growth of a self (real, nuclear) in treatment, Horneyan treatment emphasizes analysis of current character structure and the analyst-patient relationship, undermining of the pride system, and assumption of responsibility by the patient for real self development. In Kohutian treatment, strengthening of the nuclear self seems secondary to the analysis and the relinquishing of archaic psychic structures as they are revealed in the transference.

Finally, both Horney and Kohut stress mental health as a goal of treatment. But while Horneyan treatment has curious and hopeful searching for the constructive forces of the real self as its major tool, a Kohutian therapy attempts to redirect libido from archaic psychic structures and, through a process called transmuting internalization, emerge with a stronger and more dominant nuclear self. Thus, health, in a Kohutian, system represents essentially a change in dynamic patterns of mental energy; whereas Horney felt that healthy functioning was actually antithetical to neurotic functioning.

REFERENCES

Ansbacher, H. & Ansbacher R. (1956), *The Individual Psychology of Alfred Adler.* New York: Harper & Row.

Erikson, E. (1964), *Childhood and Society.* New York: Norton.

Fairbairn, W. (1954), New York: *An Object Relations Theory of the Personality.* Basic Books.

Freud, A. (1966), *The Ego and the Mechanisms of Defence.* New York:International Universities Press.

Guntrip, H. (1971), *Psychoanalytic Theory, Treatment and the Self.* New York, Basic Books.

Hartmann, H. (1964), *Essays on Ego Psychology.* New York:International Universities Press.

Horney, K. (1937), *The Neurotic Personality of Our Time.* New York:Norton.

_____ (1939), *New Ways in Psychoanalysis.* New York:Norton.

_____ (1942), *Self Analysis.* New York:Norton.
_____ (1946), *Our Inner Conflicts.* New York:Norton.
_____ (1950), *Neurosis and Human Growth.* New York:Norton.
_____ (1966), *Feminine Psychology,* H. Kelman, ed. New York:Norton.
Kernberg, O. (1975), *Borderline Conditions and Pathological Narcissism.* New York:Aronson.
Kohut, H. (1971), *The Analysis of the Self.* New York:International Universities Press.
_____ (1977), *The Restoration of the Self.* New York:International Universities Press.
Meissner, W. (1985), Theories of personality and psychopathology:Classical psychoanalysis. In: *Comprehensive Textbook of Psychiatry,* ed. H. Kaplan & B. Sadock. Baltimore, MD:Williams & Wilkins, pp. 337-418.
Paul, H. (1985), Current psychoanalytic paradigm controversy:A Horneyan perspective. *Amer. J.* Psychoanal., 45:221-233.
Portnoy, I. (1974), The school of Karen Horney. In:*The American Handbook of Psychiatry,* 2nd edition, ed. S. Arieti. New York:Basic Books, pp. 862-876.
Rendon, M. (1986), Philosophical paradigms in psychoanalysis. *J. Amer. Acad. Psychoanal.,* 14:495-505.
Rubins, J. (1978), *Karen Horney—Gentle Rebel of Psychoanalysis.* New York: Dial Press.
Spiegel, L. (1959), The self, the sense of self and perception. *The Psychoanalytic Study of the Child,* 14:81-112. New York: International Universities Press.
Stern, D. (1985), *The Interpersonal World of the Infant.* New York:Basic Books.
Symonds, A. (1983), Emotional conflicts of the career woman. *Amer. J. Psychoanal.,* 43:21-37.
Symonds, A. & Symonds, M.(1985), Theories of personality and psychopathology:Cultural and interpersonal psychoanalysis—Karen Horney. In:*Comprehensive Textbook of Psychiatry,* 4th ed., ed. H. Kaplan B. Sadock. Baltimore, MD:Williams & Wilkins, pp. 419-426.
Tuttman S., Kaye, C. & Zimmerman, ed. (1981), *Object and Self.* New York:International Universities Press.
Whitmont, E. (1967), Carl Jung. In:*Comprehensive Textbook of Psychiatry,* 1st ed., ed. A. Freedman & H. Kaplan. Baltimore, MD: pp. 366-372.
Winnicott, D.W..(1965), *The Maturational Processes and the Facilitating Environment.* New York:International Universities Press.

Part II

Existential-Humanistic Thinkers

7

Narcissism and Nihilism
Kohut and Kierkegaard on the Modern Self

JANE RUBIN

In 1846, Soren Kierkegaard contrasted human relationships in the modern age with those in earlier ages. In a striking passage, Kierkegaard (1846) described modern relationships as follows:

> A father no longer curses his son in anger, using all his parental authority, nor does a son defy his father, a conflict which might end in the inwardness of forgiveness; on the contrary, their relationship is irreproachable, for it is really in process of ceasing to exist, since they are no longer related to one another within the relationship; in fact it has become a problem in which the two partners observe each other as in a game, instead of having any relation to each other, and they note down each other's remarks instead of showing a firm devotion [pp. 44–45].

As this passage indicates, Kierkegaard believed that in the modern age detachment had replaced commitment in human relationships. Thus, talk about "relationships" increases in proportion to the loss of committed relationships in the modern world:

> More and more people renounce the quiet and modest tasks of life, that are so important and pleasing to God, in order to achieve something greater; in order to think over the relationships of life in a higher relationship till in the end the whole generation has become a representation, who represent . . . it

> is difficult to say *who;* and who think about these relationships . . . for *whose* sake it is not easy to discover [p. 45].

One hundred and thirty years later, Kohut (1977) arrived at a strikingly similar diagnosis of the modern condition. In comparing the patients who entered analysis in Freud's time with those who do so in our own, Kohut noted that complaints of definite symptoms such as hysteria and obsessional neurosis had been replaced by complaints of what he called "empty depression." Like Kierkegaard, Kohut theorized that this change was the result of profound changes in our culture. In Freud's time, according to Kohut, the emotional relationships between parents and children were overly close. In our time, they seem to have become overly distant. Thus, if the psychological problems of Freud's time were the emotionally overcharged results of the repression of libidinal conflicts and of the defenses against these conflicts, the problems of our time are the results of an "emotional void":

> The environment which used to be experienced as threateningly close, is now experienced more and more as threateningly distant; where children were formerly *over*stimulated by the emotional (including the erotic) life of their parents, they are now often *under*stimulated; where formerly the child's eroticism aimed at pleasure gain and led to internal conflict because of parental prohibitions and the rivalries of the oedipal constellation, many children now seek the effect of erotic stimulation in order to relieve loneliness, in order to fill an emotional void [p. 271].

These diagnoses of the modern condition sound strikingly similar. And yet, as similar as their analyses appear to be, Kierkegaard and Kohut are describing two very different problems. Kierkegaard's problem, which he calls the problem of "leveling" (Kierkegaard, 1846), is what we would more commonly call the problem of nihilism. Kohut's problem, as is well known, is the problem of narcissism, or, more accurately, of narcissistic personality disorders. For all of their superficial similarities, narcissism and nihilism are profoundly different problems.

In spite of their differences, however, both of these diagnoses of the modern condition seem to be accurate descriptions of contemporary reality. This puts us in a very difficult position. On one hand, it is very difficult to see how these two positions can be reconciled; on the other hand, it is very difficult to abandon either one of them. This quandary is unavoidable because the two positions represent the two traditions that have shaped our understanding of what it is to be a self in our culture. Kierkegaard's position, as is well known, claims to be Christian. As I have argued elsewhere (Rubin, 1984), it is a secularized version of Christian insights about what it is to be a human being. Kohut's (1977) position, on the other hand, is the latest incarnation of what Kierkegaard (1985b) calls the Socratic position, which is the understanding of the self that we inherit from Greek philosophy. Because both of these traditions have made us who we are, we are unable to abandon them even as we are unable to harmonize them.

I have no proposal for reconciling these two traditions. I can only articulate the differences between them so that we might recognize what is at stake for our understanding of what it is to be a self in modern culture in the contest between these two competing visions.

NARCISSISM AND NIHILISM

If we were to instantiate in a concrete example Kierkegaard's understanding of what it means to live in a leveled culture, I believe that it would look something like this. The prototypical contemporary man sits in front of the television set. He gossips about the latest scandals in the religious or political worlds but does not make any religious or political commitments of his own. He does not really care about anything, although he is very skilled at creating the illusion that he cares.

If we were to instantiate Kohut's understanding of narcissism in a concrete example, it would look very different. The problem with Kohut's patient is not that she does not really care about anything. The problem is that she does not have the self-confidence to pursue what she cares about in a satisfying manner. Thus, with Kohut, we can imagine the person in front of the TV as someone who has come home from work early, turned on the TV, and started drinking. She is depressed and anxious about her inability to get her work done. Her inability to work is confusing to her because she is doing work she genuinely cares about. She tries to calm her anxiety with the alcohol and to overcome her feelings of depression with the tv.

What we have here, then, is a contrast between two descriptions of the problems of the modern self. This contrast can be articulated as follows. In Kierkegaard, the problem is one of leveling versus differentiation. In Kohut, the problem is one of cohesion versus fragmentation.

As I remarked earlier, Kierkegaard (1846) calls the nihilism of the present-age "leveling." He defines leveling as the weakening of what he calls qualitative distinctions. The weakening of the distinction between fathers and sons, which Kierkegaard describes in the passage quoted at the beginning of this chapter, is one example of the leveling of a qualitative distinction. In the same passage, Kierkegaard also describes the leveling of such distinctions as those between kings and subjects and teachers and students.

It is important to emphasize at the outset that Kierkegaard's choice of examples to describe the leveling of qualitative distinctions is not the expression of political or social conservatism. Kierkegaard is not calling for a return to monarchy or the patriarchal family. On the contrary, he praises revolutions that overthrow the old, qualitative distinctions and establish new ones in their place. Kierkegaard's own project is not to restore the social hierarchies of the past but to demonstrate that in modern society the possibility of a life that expresses qualitative distinctions is equally open to everyone (see Rubin, 1984).

Kierkegaard does not criticize the present age because it weakens traditional qualitative distinctions; he criticizes it because it weakens all qualitative distinctions. In this respect, the present age is no more revolutionary than it is reactionary. We can best understand this analysis of the present age and why Kierkegaard calls the weakening of qualitative distinctions "leveling" if we examine one of his examples of leveling, the leveling of the distinction between teachers and students. In the same passage in which he describes the relationship between fathers and sons, Kierkegaard (1846) says:

> A disobedient youth is no longer in fear of his schoolmaster—the relation is rather one of indifference in which schoolmaster and pupil discuss how a good school should be run. To go to school no longer means to be in fear of the master, or merely to learn, but rather implies being interested in the problem of education [p. 45].

The argument that lies behind this passage seems to be that in a traditional culture, the distinction between teacher and student is a qualitative, not a quantitative, one. The difference between a teacher and a student is not that the teacher knows more than the student. On the contrary, the student may know more about all kinds of things—cartoon shows, baseball cards, comic books. The difference between a teacher and a student is, rather, that the teacher knows the difference between what is and what is not important to know. The teacher knows the distinction between serious and trivial literature, between science and superstition, and so on.

Kierkegaard contends that qualitative distinctions can be maintained only by commitment to the practices that embody them. Thus, the distinction between serious and trivial literature can be maintained only by teachers who are committed to teaching serious literature. Kierkegaard further contends that it is precisely this kind of commitment, which he terms "passion," that has been progressively weakened in modern culture. It has been replaced by the kind of detached reflection Kierkegaard describes in the passages I have quoted.

The end result of this replacement of passion by reflection is the situation Kierkegaard calls levelling. If there are no qualitative distinctions—between serious and trivial literature, between science and superstition—everything has been reduced to the same level. This creates two related problems for the modern person. First, no particular practices can make any difference to her. Second, she cannot have a differentiated world.

These two problems are related, for Kierkegaard, in the following way. The commitments Kierkegaard is interested in defending are what I want to call world-defining commitments. A world-defining commitment not only makes a difference to me; it also tells me what difference everything else in my life makes to me. For example, if teaching is a world-defining commitment for me, everything else in my life will be subordinate to it. It is important to note that Kierkegaard is not endorsing a kind of monomaniacal asceticism here. His point is not that once I become committed to teaching I will never go to a baseball game or read *Sports Illustrated* again. His point is, rather, that if my commitment to teaching and my interest in sports come into conflict—if, for example, an education bill will be defeated in the legislature if teachers do not lobby on the day I have tickets to the seventh game of the World Series—it is clear that my commitment to teaching overrides my desire to go to the game. Kierkegaard's (1846) therapeutic goal, then, if we wish to call it that, is to enable people to move from a situation of leveling to one of differentiation by enabling people to make world-defining commitments.

For Kohut (1977), in contrast, the therapeutic goal of the treatment of patients with narcisstic personality disorders can best be described as enabling them to overcome fragmentation and achieve cohesion. Because people with narcissistic personality disorders lack confidence in their ambitions or ideals, they engage in addictive or other pursuits aimed at making them feel alive or feel calm. These pursuits become substitutes for the kinds of activities and relationships that, for a healthy self, would be sources of adult mirroring or expressions of adult ideals. But, as inadequate substitutes for appropriate selfobjects, they drag the patients away from their adult activities and relationships and weaken the ability to pursue them. Thus, the narcissistic personality is a fragmented self, part adult with adult selfobjects and part archaic with archaic selfobjects.

The first contrast between Kierkegaard and Kohut's analyses of the problems of the modern self, then, is the contrast between an analysis of the problem in terms of leveling versus differentiation and an analysis of the problem in terms of fragmentation versus cohesion. There is a second issue, however, that also divides Kierkegaard and Kohut. For Kierkegaard, this issue is one of identity. One way of understanding Kierkegaard's analysis of the weakening of qualitative distinctions is as a description of people who are indifferent. Another, related, way of reading it is as a description of people who have no identity.

According to Kierkegaard (1980b, 1985a) a world-defining commitment is a commitment that gives me my identity. This can best be understood if we understand the difference between losing a world-defining commitment and losing the possibility of engaging in some other, non-world-defining activity. To return to the baseball example, if I must forfeit the opportunity to attend the seventh game of the World Series, I will undoubtedly experience extreme disappointment. But if I lose the possibility of ever teaching again, I will experience grief. The difference between the two experiences, according to Kierkegaard (1985a), is the following: In the first case, I have lost the possibility of participating in an activity within my world. In the second case, I have lost the commitment that defines my world. But a commitment that defines my world defines my self. I would no longer be the person I am now if I lost the possibility of teaching. I would still be the same person, albeit a sadder one, if I could not attend the seventh game of the World Series.

It is precisely the anxiety about the vulnerability of world-defining commitments that, according to Kierkegaard, contributes to the leveling of qualitative distinctions in the present age. People do not identify themselves unconditionally with any particular practices. Instead, they are always keeping their options open. If they should happen to lose a job or a lover, they simply go on to another one. They have not lost their world or their identity for the simple reason that they have no world and no identity to lose. Kierkegaard would presumably endorse Bob Dylan's description of the passionless contemporary person: "When you ain't got nothing/ You've got nothing to lose."

For Kohut (1977) in contrast, the problem is not that modern people do not have real identities. They do have ambitions and ideals that are recognizably their own.[1] However, because of the selfobject failures they have experienced in the past, they are unable to develop these ambitions and ideals consistently and coherently. Instead, they tend to get stuck in archaic identities that may have been serviceable in childhood but are no longer so in adulthood. Thus, while for Kierkegaard the problem with people in our culture is that they are always keeping their options open and refusing to allow themselves to be identified with anything, for Kohut people are stuck in archaic identities. One goal of psychotherapy is to get development moving again.

Finally, Kierkegaard and Kohut hold contrasting views about how modern people experience their own life histories. Kierkegaard (1985b) argues that one result of having a specific commitment that defines what counts as significant and insignificant for me is that it tells me which events in my past and future make a difference to me. Thus, if I am committed to being a political activist, I will see the significant events in my past as the ones that led up to my making this commitment. Similarly, I will know that the significant

---

[1]Kohut himself does not use the term "identity" to refer to a person's nuclear ambitions and ideals. This seems to be because he wants to differentiate his concept of the self from the Eriksonian concept of identity. My use of the term identity in this context is not intended to foist upon Kohut a term with which he was uncomfortable but simply to make the comparison with Kierkegaard clearer. For Kohut's discussion of the limitations of Erikson's concept of identity, see Elson (1987, pp. 222–227). Kohut himself defines identity as "the point of convergence between the developed self . . . and the sociocultural position of the individual (Ornstein, pp. 471–472).

events in my future will be the ones that are related to my carrying out of this commitment. Because people do not have significant commitments, according to Kierkegaard, their lives are characterized by a kind of temporal leveling. Every moment of their lives is equally significant and thus equally insignificant.

For Kohut, on the other hand, the temporality of narcissistic personality disorders is not a leveled temporality. Instead, it is one in which the significance of the past overshadows the significance of the present and the future. A second goal of psychotherapy is to help the patient to be able to experience the present and the future as something other than repetitions of the past.

THE NUCLEAR SELF AND THE EXISTENTIAL SELF

Such, then, are Kierkegaard and Kohut's contrasting descriptions of the problems of the modern self. As I have argued, these contrasting descriptions derive from two very different views of what it is to be a self. To understand these differing diagnoses of our current condition, then, we must understand the views of the self that lie behind them.

Before describing these views, however, I must add a few qualifying comments. First, all of Kierkegaard's voluminous work deals in one way or another with the question of what it is to be a self. It is impossible to summarize Kierkegaard's views on the subject effectively in a few pages. It would be counterproductive, as well, to introduce in this essay the technical terminology that Kierkegaard uses to describe the self (see Kierkegaard, 1980a, pp. 13–14, 29–74; see also, Rubin 1984). Thus, for the purposes of this chapter, I want to lay out aspects of Kierkegaard's view of the self in very general terms in order to highlight the contrasts between his view and the view of self psychology. I hope this brief summary will be a stimulus for self psychologists and those interested in self psychology to investigate Kierkegaard's work in greater depth.

Second, Kierkegaard does not have one view of the self but four. According to Kierkegaard, people do not have a self simply by virtue of being human. If they are to have one, they must take a leap into what Kierkegaard calls a "sphere of existence." There are four of these spheres—the aesthetic, the ethical, Religiousness A, and Religiousness B—and people go through them in this order. Each sphere defines what it is to be a self in a way that is incommensurable with the definitions of each of the other spheres. Thus, the aesthetic sphere makes the pursuit of enjoyment definitive of what is to be a self; the ethical sphere makes choice definitive; Religiousness A proposes a self-definition that it calls "self-annihilation before God."

The Aesthetic Sphere

According to Kierkegaard (1980b), each of the first three spheres of existence defines the self in a way that makes the kind of life the sphere proposes unliveable. For example, the aesthetic sphere proposes that the answer to the leveling of the present age is to commit myself to some sort of immediate enjoyment. The idea here is that nothing could be more opposed to the passionlessness of the present age than immediate enjoyment. If I throw myself unconditionally into enjoyment, I will have overcome leveling because everything in my life will get its significance or insignificance in relation to what I am committed to enjoying. If I am committed to skiing, everything in my life will get its significance in relation to my life on the slopes. If I am committed to eating gourmet food, everything in my life will get its significance in relation to my search for the perfect restaurant, and so on.

The problem with the immediate aesthethic, according to Kierkegaard, is that immediate enjoyment is extremely vulnerable. If I break my leg or develop chronic gastroenteritis, I can no longer ski or be a gourmand. Insofar as this is the case, my attempt to overcome leveling will fail. Furthermore, that this kind of vulnerability is built into any attempt to make immediate enjoyment world defining means that the immediate aesthetic cannot provide a stable way of life. To put it in Kierkegaard's language, the immediate aesthetic life is a life of despair. When I acknowledge the vulnerability of immediate enjoyment, I recognize that as a permanent commitment my way of life is unliveable, that it has always been unliveable, and that it will always be unliveable (Kierkegaard, 1944b, pp. 184–198; Rubin.)

The first response to the despair of the immediate aesthetic is what Kierkegaard calls the reflective aesthetic. The reflective aesthetic claims that I can overcome the vulnerability of the immediate aesthetic while preserving the enjoyment if I simply transfer the enjoyment from reality to fantasy. Instead of skiing on the slopes, I ski in my head. The problem here, Kierkegaard thinks, is that when fantasied satisfaction is not merely a temporary substitute for real satisfaction but is the permanent replacement for real satisfaction, it is no longer enjoyable. Insofar as I do not want to fulfill any of my fantasies because all attempts at fulfillment are inherently vulnerable, one fantasy is as satisfying—or as dissatisfying—as any another. Thus, the person in the reflective aesthetic is invulnerable but his life is completely levelled (Kierkegaard, 1944a; Rubin.)

The Ethical Sphere

The ethical sphere is a direct response to the despair of the reflective aesthetic. The person in the ethical sphere argues that I can venture out of fantasy and back into reality once I realize that what makes something significant or insignificant is not whether I enjoy it or not but whether I choose to make it significant or insignificant. According to the ethical sphere, once I am clear about what my desires are, so that I am no longer driven by them, I can decide which ones I want to express in my life and choose a social role that allows me to do so. Thus, if I decide that my desire to play music is what is important to me, I will choose to be a musician. If I decide that my athletic talent is what is important to me, I will choose to be an athlete, and so on.

The problem here, according to Kierkegaard, is that when choice is world defining, it is impossible to have any standards for making particular choices, since these standards too must be objects of choice. Once it is up to me to give everything significance, the significance I give is completely arbitrary. Thus, ethical choice can never get off the ground. This means that, like the reflective aesthetic, the ethical sphere fails to overcome levelling. Instead, it is another form of despair. (Kierkegaard, 1944b; Rubin.)

Religiousness A

Religiousness A is a response to the breakdown of the ethical sphere. According to Religiousness A, the way to overcome the arbitrariness of the ethical is to return to the aesthetic idea that my desires are the foundations of my commitments. However, Religiousness A modifies the aesthetic in such a way as to be able to claim that it has achieved invulnerability at the same time that it has overcome levelling.

The claim of Religiousness A is that if I commit myself to satisfying my desires but remain absolutely indifferent to whether or not they are actually satisfied, I will overcome leveling while achieving invulnerability. For example, I may commit myself to the attempt to satisfy my desire to be a professional athlete; this will be my world-defining commitment. However, I will be absolutely indifferent to winning or losing in competition. Indeed, I will be completely indifferent even to suffering a career-ending injury. If I am severely injured, I will simply have a new world-defining commitment—going through rehabilitation, learning new job skills, and so on.

Not surprisingly, Kierkegaard finds this solution to the problems of the present age to be as unworkable as those of the aesthetic and ethical spheres. His argument is that having a desire always involves having an interest in its satisfaction. It simply makes no sense to say that I have a desire to be a professional athlete but am abolutely indifferent as to whether I will ever be one or not. Insofar as Religiousness A proposes absolute indifference to the satisfaction of my desires as a way of achieving invulnerability, it eliminates the possibility of my having the very desires that allow me to overcome leveling. (Kierkegaard, 1958; Rubin, 1984, chapter V; Dreyfus and Rubin, 1987)

This is a trememdously oversimplified account of Kierkegaard's spheres of existence. Among other things, it leaves out of account Kierkegaard's views about how people in each sphere cover up the despair of their sphere—a view that leads Kierkegaard to describe the spheres and their contradictions not directly, as I have done here, but through the use of a method he terms "indirect discourse" and by using pseudonymous authors for his works. However, this necessarily sketchy presentation of the lower spheres provides the background for discussing the highest sphere of existence, Religiousness B.

Religiousness B

According to Kierkegaard, the lower spheres all fail for a similar reason. They all try to make a formal capacity—imagination or choice or absolute indifference to the satisfaction of desire—the basis of commitment. In contrast to these spheres, Religiousness B claims that a human being becomes a self only by "relating itself to another" (Kierkegaard, 1980b, pp. 13–14). A human being can come to have a commitment that gives her a self only by modeling herself after another person who has such a commitment and is a self. Kierkegaard (1941) calls this person a "paradigm" (p. 109).[2]

Kierkegaard emphasizes that the relationship between an individual and her paradigm is an indirect one. Just as a Kuhnian scientist does not directly copy the research of her paradigm but engages in work that bears a family resemblance to it (Kuhn, 1970), so the Kierkegaardian individual does not necessarily copy the commitment of her paradigm but makes a commitment that resembles it indirectly.

For those conversant with self psychology, Kierkegaard's discussion of the role of paradigms in the creation of the self may have a decidedly familiar ring. The idea that I need another person in order to become a self sounds similar, if not identical, to the Kohutian emphasis on the role of selfobjects in the constitution of the self. The Kierkegaardian emphasis on the indirect nature of the resemblance between the individual in Religiousness B and her paradigm only seems to reinforce this sense of familiarity. When Kohut (1984) describes a patient's relationship to a therapist, he compares it to the body's ingestion of protein. Just as the body transforms protein in the process of assimilating it, so a patient does not simply take over the gross functions of the therapist but assimilates and transforms them as they become part of her own self.

Despite these seeming similarities, however, there is a major difference between a Kohutian therapist and a Kierkegaardian paradigm. According to Kohut, the patient takes over from the therapist such psychological functions as calming and soothing. She does not take over the content of her therapist's ambitions and ideals. According to Kierkegaard, a person in Religiousness B imitates her paradigm's concrete commitment. Thus, a Kierkegaardian paradigm has a kind of authority for the person in Religiousness B that a Kohutian therapist can never have. Or, to state the matter in psychoanalytic terms, Kohut would probably be inclined to say that the kind of authority that a Kierkegaardian paradigm has for the person in Religiousness B is a sign of an unresolved idealizing transference.

This difference between Kierkegaardian paradigms and Ko-

[2]Kierkegaard argues that Jesus is the paradigm after which the self must model itself. All other paradigms are "derived" from Jesus or are "minor" paradigms. I (Rubin, 1984) argue, in contrast, that Kierkegaard's arguments for this position violate his own logic and that any individual in Religiousness B can be a paradigm.

hutian selfobjects allows us to understand the major difference between Kierkegaard and Kohut's views of the self. In Kohut, a self is defined by ambitions and ideals, and a correlated set of skills and talents, which are internal to it. External commitments are expressions of the self. Thus, if I am committed to being a painter, my being a painter is an expression of preexisting ambitions and ideals. Perhaps when I was young I received the greatest praise from my parents for my artistic productions. Or perhaps when my parents failed to give me adequate mirroring, I began to idealize my art teacher and tried to become like her. In either case, my commitment as an adult to being a painter is an expression of preexisting ambitions and ideals.

For Kierkegaard, in contrast, the commitment I get from modeling myself after a paradigm is not an expression of myself. Instead, my imitation of a paradigm gives me a self for the first time. On this view, I may have had no artistic ambitions or ideals in the past at all. Only subsequent to my recognizing a committed artist and attempting to model myself after her does my art teacher become important to me. She receives her importance retroactive to my commitment.

To state this contrast in the sharpest possible terms, it is no accident that Kohut (1977) referred to the goal of self psychology as the *restoration* of the self. In self psychology, a therapist can help to restore the self because there is already a self there to be restored. For Kierkegaard, the self does not have to be restored, but created. The self of the individual in Religiousness B is what Kierkegaard, (1985a) calls "a new creation" (p. 70).

As may already be clear from this initial contrast and as Kierkegaard (1985b) argues, the best way to understand the difference between these two views is as a difference in views about the temporal nature of the self. In Kohut, the "nuclear self"—a person's basic ambitions and ideals—is consolidated in childhood. Kohut (1977) argues that ambitions are generally consolidated in early childhood, while ideals are consolidated in later childhood. Thus, what I am committed to in the present and what I will be committed to in the future are expressions of what has been important to me all along.

This is not a kind of crude determinism, of course. It does not mean that a person who becomes a political activist was necessarily a red diaper baby whose parents applauded him when he sang the Internationale at age two and who included him in their political activities at an early age. This person could have grown up in a conservative or an apolitical household. But something in his upbringing led him to develop his current commitments.

For Kierkegaard, a self is not something I have always had. I have not always been committed to being a professor. I made that commitment at a particular moment in time. However, once I made it, it told me what was important to me in my past and what would be important to me in my future. On this view, before I committed myself to becoming a professor, I may have had no intellectual interests at all. However, upon recognizing the possibility of taking up such a commitment, I found that events in my past that were of no significance to me suddenly became significant. For example, a teacher who meant nothing to me at the time I knew her suddenly became important to me. Similarly, according to Kierkegaard, before I became a professor, my future did not include the possibility of an intellectual life. Now that I have made that commitment, however, I know that from now until the end of my life I will be committed to this vocation.

KIERKEGAARD VERSUS KOHUT

Kierkegaard's contention that a paradigm gives a person's past its significance has a very important consequence for any attempt to arbitrate between Kierkegaard and Kohut's views of the self. If a paradigm gives a person's past its significance, the person can never use her past to provide a rational justification for her acceptance of her paradigm.

This consequence is one of the factors in Kierkegaard's (1985a) referring to the self in Religiousness B not just as a "new creation" but as a new creation "on the strength of the absurd" (p. 70). While there are objective criteria for excluding individual candidates for paradigms, there are no objective criteria for including them. The complete argument for this is too complicated to enter into here.[3] But the fact that I can never use my past to legitimate my acceptance of a particular paradigm is one example of Kierkegaard's view that Religiousness B cannot be rationally justified.

It is precisely in respect to the possibilities of rational justification—or, at least, of rational discussion—that Kohut's view of the

[3]For an analysis of Kierkegaard's position on this issue, see Rubin, 1984.

itself seems to be more plausible than Kierkegaard's. It simply seems to make more sense to say that my present commitments get their significance from my past than to say that they give my past its significance. Furthermore, the role of another person in helping me to become a fully functioning self makes more sense on the selfobject model than on the paradigm model. It makes more sense to say that a person develops a selfobject transference because of significant relationships in her past that continue to color her self-understanding in the present than to say that her paradigm for her present commitments gives her past its significance. Thus, it is tempting to dismiss Kierkegaard's view of the self altogether.

In this concluding section I want to present some of what I take to be Kierkegaard's arguments that his view of the self should be taken seriously despite its lack of rational justification. I do so not to refute Kohut's view, but simply to demonstrate once again that we are faced here with a conflicting set of intuitions about the nature of the self.

The first set of arguments in favor of Kierkegaard's position, not surprisingly, has to do with temporality. The first of these arguments concerns the relationship between the present and the past. For Kierkegaard, the idea that a Religiousness B commitment can give retroactive significance to the past is of crucial importance, because it frees Religiousness B from determinism while saving it from arbitrariness. Events in the past do not cause me to have the commitment I have. Rather, the commitment I have gives me an interpretation of the events in my past. At the same time, my commitment has to make sense of the events in *my* past, not someone else's. It seems clear that not every object of commitment has this ability.

These two points are summed up in Kierkegaard's (1980b) claim that a person who is a self has what he calls "essential contingency" (p. 33). No fact or set of facts about me determines which commitment will define me. In this sense, all facts about me are contingent. But particular facts about me become essential to me through my commitment. They could not become essential to me if they were not contingent facts about *me* in the first place.

A second argument in favor of his view of the self, which is related in some ways to his argument against determinism, is an argument about the nature of human equality. As a Christian, Kierkegaard is committed to the belief that all human beings are equal before God. In Kierkegaardian terms, this means that all human beings, with the exception of those who are severely mentally impaired, are equally capable of going through the spheres of existence and arriving at Religiousness B.

Insofar as Kierkegaard excludes the severely impaired from the possibility of going through the spheres of existence, he is, of course, in agreement with Kohut. Kohut knows that not all personality disorders are analyzable and that therefore not everyone can have a fully functioning self. The disagreement arises, rather, about the people who can go through the spheres of existence or who can become fully functioning selves. For Kohut, the ability to become a fully functioning self is always a matter of degree. Presumably, those who have had better selfobjects or better therapy will stand a better chance than those who have not. For Kierkegaard, in contrast, a person's capacity to go through the spheres can never be a question of degree. My ability to go through the spheres is identical to my willingness to go through the spheres, and willingness knows no degrees. I am either willing or not, and whether I am is up to me.

The connection between this argument and Kierkegaard's argument against determinism is clear. No circumstance in my past can be so powerful as to prevent me from being able to go through the spheres. But the emphasis of this argument is different. Kierkegaard claims that the undeniable differences in people's past experiences make no difference when it comes to being able to become a self. Quantitative differences—of more or less empathy, more or less mirroring, and so on—make no qualitative difference. The spheres of existence are equally open to everyone.

Kierkegaard, then, can advance at least two reasons for accepting his position: it avoids determinism, and it allows for human equality. In addition to providing these arguments for his position, Kierkegaard also spells out several basic contrasts between his position and the Socratic position. While these contrasts are not arguments for Kierkegaard's position, they do help to sharpen the differences between Kierkegaard and Kohut and are thus worth discussing briefly.

The first major contrast involves differing views about individual responsibility for becoming a fully functioning self. Related to this contrast are two different views about the reasons that people resist becoming fully functioning selves. In Kierkegaard's view, people resist Religiousness B commitments for two reasons: because these commitments cannot be rationally justified and because they are vulnerable. Because he sees individuals as responsible for their resistance, it is not surprising that Kierkegaard uses the traditional Christian term for it. He calls it "sin."

For Kohut, in contrast, individuals are not ultimately responsible for their failure to become fully functioning selves. The failure to have optimally frustrating selfobjects cannot be the responsibility of the person who does not have them.

Closely related to these differing views about responsibility are differing views about the kind of vulnerability that keeps people from becoming selves. For Kohut (1977), vulnerability is essentially related to the past. The person who has a self-disorder is someone who has been traumatized by selfobjects in the past. She resists getting involved in certain kinds of relationships or situations because of a fear of repeating the original trauma.

For Kierkegaard, vulnerability is essentially related to the future. People resist Religiousness B because they resist becoming committed to something they might lose. If my commitment to being a painter or a political activist gives my life significance and gives me my identity, to lose that commitment is to lose my world and myself. Thus, I am highly motivated to resist the possibility of Religiousness B.

One way of understanding these two differing accounts of vulnerability is to see how they involve differing accounts of anxiety. Whereas Kohut's anxiety is psychological, Kierkegaard's is existential. For Kohut, anxiety essentially refers to the past and to a specific emotional situation that I do not want to repeat. For Kierkegaard, anxiety essentially refers to the future. Not only am I anxious that I might lose whatever commitment I get, but because I cannot know what Religiousness B or any sphere of existence is like before I have taken the leap into it, my anxiety is not anxiety about a specific situation. Rather, as Kierkegaard (1980a) argues, it is anxiety about nothing: ". . . the whole actuality of knowledge projects itself in anxiety as the enormous nothing of ignorance" (p. 44).

Perhaps the clearest contrast between Kierkegaard and Kohut, however, is not in their accounts of why people resist becoming fully functioning selves or of the anxiety which accompanies that resistance. Rather, it is in their descriptions of the individuals who successfully overcome their resistance. Interestingly enough, this comparison also involves a difference in the status of anxiety.

Kierkegaard (1985a) contrasts the Knight of Faith, who is in Religiousness B, with the "tragic hero." Abraham is an example of the first; Agamemnon is an example of the second. One of the major differences between the two is that, while Agamemnon maintains a kind of heroic calm in his sacrifice of Iphegenia, Abraham is in fear and trembling at the prospect of sacrificing Isaac. The reason for the difference in emotional demeanor is that the tragic hero can rationally justify his actions. The god's demand for the sacrifice of Iphegenia is essential to the maintenance of Athens. Abraham, in contrast, has no rational justification for his commitment. It is a private command from God to him alone.

If we remove the mythological element from both of these stories, we can more easily recognize the major contrast between Kierkegaard and Kohut. Again, in Kierkegaard, that I have no rational justification for my commitment in Religiousness B means that I am always in anxiety, in "fear and trembling." Unperturbed calm seems to belong only to the character whom Kierkegaard refers to as the Knight of Resignation—the person who lives in memory or hope rather than for a concrete commitment.

In contrast, Kohut's description of the tragic hero is a kind of psychologized version of Kierkegaard's story of the tragic hero. According to Kohut (1985) the hero is calm not because she has a rational justification for her action but because her action fulfills her nuclear program. While Abraham, according to Kierkegaard, necessarily appears crazy to the people around him, one of the three things that distinguish a Kohutian hero or heroine from a psychotic is "generally at the time when the ultimate heroic decision has been reached and the agonizing consequences have to be faced, the suffusion of the personality with a profound sense of inner peace and serenity" (pp. 15–16).

As I argued at the beginning of this chapter, it is tempting to try to harmonize Kierkegaard's and Kohut's views of the self. We may be tempted to think, for example, that Kohut can provide us with the psychology of Kierkegaard's spheres of existence. Perhaps self psychology can tell us something about why people in the different spheres become blocked in their capacity to act on the ambitions and ideals which characterize their sphere. For example, self psychology might tell us why a person in the aesthetic sphere is unable to realize her ambitions and ideals of enjoyment or why the person in the ethical sphere is unable to realize her ambitions and ideals of autonomous choice.

This strategy, however, will not work. If Kohut's view of the self is correct, there cannot be Kierkegaardian spheres of existence. The idea that there are spheres of existence is premised on the view that human beings are self-defining. Thus, on this view, even if human beings could be said to have a preexisting set of ambitions and ideals, these ambitions and ideals could not be said to make a human being a self. This is clearest in the case of the ethical sphere, in which a person has to choose which of her ambitions and ideals are important to her. The premise of the ethical sphere is that nothing just *is* important to a person. Or, rather, insofar as it is, that person has not freely chosen herself. While Kierkegaard rejects the ethical notion of radical choice as incoherent, the idea that no one always already has a self—that, if you will, there is no such thing as a nuclear *self*—carries over, as I have just argued, into Kierkegaard's understanding of Religiousness B.

Thus, we are left with two conflicting sets of intuitions about what it is to be a self. The question of whether there exists some third position that would allow us to dissolve this conflict rather than resolve it lies beyond the scope of this essay. Understanding the nature of the conflict, however, may allow us to understand better the issues of self-understanding and self-definition in modern culture.

REFERENCES

Dreyfus, H. L. & Rubin, J. (1987), You can't get something for nothing: Kierkegaard and Heidegger on how not to overcome nihilism. *Inquiry,* 30:33–75.

Elson, M., ed. (1987), *The Kohut Seminars on Self Psychology and Psychotherapy with Adolescents and Young Adults.* New York: Norton.

Kierkegaard, S. (1846), *The Present Age,* trans. A. Dru. New York: Harper & Row, 1962.

_____ (1941), *Training In Christianity,* trans. W. Lowrie. Princeton, NJ: Princeton University Press.

_____ (1944a), *Either/Or, Volume I,* trans. D. F. Swenson & L. M. Swenson. Princeton, NJ:Princeton University Press.

_____ (1944b), *Either/Or, Volume II,* trans, W. Lowrie. Princeton, NJ:Princeton University Press.

_____ (1958), *Edifying Discourses,* trans. D. F. & L. M. Swenson. New York:Harper & Row.

_____ (1980a), *The Concept of Anxiety,* trans. R. Thomte. Princeton, NJ:Princeton University Press.

_____ (1980b), *The Sickness Unto Death,* trans. H. V. Hong & E. H. Hong. Princeton, NJ:Princeton University Press.

_____ (1985a), *Fear and Trembling,* trans. A. Hannay. Middlesex, Eng.: Penguin.

_____ (1985b), *Philosophical Fragments,* trans. H.V. Hong & E.H. Hong. Princeton, NJ:Princeton University Press.

Kohut, H. (1977), *The Restoration of the Self.* New York:International Universities Press.

_____ (1984), *How Does Analysis Cure?* ed. A. Goldberg & P. E. Stepansky. Chicago, IL: University of Chicago Press.

_____ (1985), *Self Psychology and the Humanities,* ed. C. B. Strozier. New York:Norton.

Kuhn, T. (1970), *The Structure of Scientific Revolutions.* Chicago, IL:University of Chicago Press.

Ornstein, P. H., ed. (1978), *The Search for the Self.* New York: International Universities Press.

Rubin, J. (1984), Too much of nothing: Modern culture, the self and salvation in Kierkgaard's thought. Unpublished doctoral dissertation, University of California, Berkeley.

8

Kohut and Husserl
The Empathic Bond

MARILYN NISSIM-SABAT

Empathy, as Kohut (1984) emphasized, has always been a feature of psychoanalytic practice. For Kohut, however, empathy became the central concept of psychoanalysis. Indeed, both illness and health are self-psychologically conceptualized in terms of empathy: psychopathology is said to originate in empathic failures on the part of the child's primary caretakers, whereas the capacity for empathy for oneself and others is viewed as the most significant indicator of psychic health (Kohut, 1984). While some commentators have criticized these aspects of Kohut's thought, others (Gedo, 1986) have reserved their principal objections for Kohut's (1980) global claims that (1) empathy defines the psychoanalytic field and (2) that empathy, as practiced by the analyst in the clinical setting, is a *scientific* method of investigation. These considerations give rise to a crucially important question: can Kohut's most global claims regarding the role of empathy in psychoanalysis be understood and justified exclusively within the context of self psychology? That is, is self psychology self-sufficient? And, if it is not, what additional foundation is required?[1]

Kohut himself did not think that self psychology is self-

Though the present essay stands on its own, it is also a continuation of the work begun in Nissim-Sabat (1986).

sufficient. This is shown by his (Kohut, 1981a, 1984) frequent references to the observer-dependent aspect of the contemporary, or postmodern, scientific paradigm (represented by quantum physics) as a means of grounding the scientific status of empathy. Kohut (1973b) believed also that it is necessary to maintain and strengthen the view that psychoanalysis is a science. He was aware that psychoanalysis must be viewed in relation to science in general and to its history and philosophy. Though Kohut (1980, 1981b) appealed to the contemporary paradigm of natural science to justify the scientific status of psychoanalysis, he believed that self psychology is not a natural science, like physics, but a different kind of science, one related to the humanistic disciplines.

Kohut (1973b) placed great emphasis on the relatedness of self psychology to the humanistic disciplines. Indeed, he viewed self psychology as a new scientific paradigm for these disciplines. However, although highly suggestive, Kohut's writings do not provide the conceptual foundation for the development of self psychology as such a paradigm. Does this mean that no such paradigm can be constructed and, consequently, that this project should be abandoned? I contend that (1) *abandoning this project would be equivalent to abandoning self psychology;* and (2) *that when elaborated within the framework of phenomenology, Kohut's concept of empathy is such a paradigm.* Justification for these contentions will emerge as I demonstrate and interpret the "empathic bond"[1] between Kohut and Husserl as a conceptual homology between self psychology and Husserlian phenomenology. As we shall see, Kohut's global claim that empathy defines the psychoanalytic field cannot be adequately justified by appealing, as he did, to the postmodern scientific paradigm. This can be accomplished, however, by placing self psychology within the framework of Husserlian phenomenology.

It is well known that Husserl (1936) viewed phenomenology as the only philosophical standpoint that could provide philosophical foundations for science in general and, most important, for the humanistic disciplines in particular. The great emphasis he (Husserl, 1950) placed on empathy, *Einfühlung,* in the context of his attempts to establish phenomenological foundations for the experi-

[1]Of course, the phrase "the empathic bond" was used by Kohut. In the present context, as in the title of this essay, my use of ths phrase is a deliberate *double entendre;* that is, this is a study of the empathic bond *between* psychoanalysis and phenomenology, as wall as a study of the nature of the empathic bond as such.

ence of others as other *persons,* a point to which we will return, is also well known. Less appreciated is that Husserl (1936) viewed psychology as the "decisive field" (p.203) of phenomenological investigation, that he viewed empathy as defining that field (Husserl, 1952a, pp. 162–169; b, pp. 191–204), and that he wrote many pages of description and interpretation of empathic experience (Husserl, 1952a, b).

Disclosing the homology between phenomenology and self psychology will show that, in asserting that empathy defines the field of psychoanalysis, Kohut manifested the logic of his own insights; that is, in order to be adequate, any explanatory account of empathy as concept and as experiential actuality requires (1) that empathy be grasped as defining the psychoanalytic field; (2) that when empathy is grasped as the psychoanalytic field, that field is grasped as a self-sufficient domain; and (3) that this move provides the foundation for construing psychoanalysis as the scientific paradigm for the humanistic disciplines.

Kohut's global claims regarding empathy were mirrored in various definitions of it and explanations of related ideas, which he expressed throughout his writings. His (Kohut, 1959) best known, and justifiably emphasized, definition is that empathy is "vicarious introspection" (p. 209). This definition has its exact counterpart, as we shall see, in Husserl's writings regarding empathy. However, the most telling aspect of the homology between self psychology and phenomenology, and, I believe, the most illuminating and moving aspect of Kohut's thought, can be found in passages in his work in which he extends empathy beyond "vicarious introspection." One of the most expressive of such discussions is the following (Kohut, 1973a):

> From the beginning of life, it is empathy, the psychological extension of an understanding human environment, that protects the infant from the encroachment of the inorganic world. And it is human empathy, as we mirror and confirm the other and as the other confirms and mirrors us, that buttresses an enclave of human meaning—of hate, love, triumph, and defeat—within a universe of senseless spaces and crazily racing stars. And, finally, it is with our last glance that we can yet retain, in the reflected melancholy of our parting, a sense of continuing life, of the survival of essential human sameness, and thus protection against the fallacy of pairing finiteness and death with meaninglessness and despair. . . . I will stress once more that our unashamed commitment to the survival of

> human life, the commitment to contribute our share to the preservation of the vitality of fulfilling human life, is not only compatible with scientific rigor, but that scientific rigor is indeed indispensable [p. 682].

This beautifully written, moving passage resonates with rich empathy for all of us, human beings whose lives will enact a common denouement. A striking aspect of Kohut's thought here is his conviction that an authentically empathic appreciation of our shared humanness, one that gives rise to a commitment to preserve "fulfilling human life," requires scientific rigor. This conviction, which finds the existence of an essential human sameness to be intimately bound up with the possibility of a scientific psychology, is the essence of phenomenology as understood by Husserl. Kohut's emphasis on empathy as both constitutive and protective of our "shared human sameness" is closely paralleled in Husserl's (1950) constitutive analyses of our experience of others as *persons* and of our embeddedness in the *Lebenswelt,* the "life world," of shared meaning that bodies forth from the ground of essential human sameness (Husserl, 1936). This essential human sameness, explicated by both Kohut and Husserl in terms of an alterego psychic structure, is what makes for the possibility of a scientific psychology that is paradigmatic for the human sciences. That is, the essential human sameness is the locus of regularities that it is the task of science to discover. Later in this essay, these most significant aspects of the empathic bond between phenomenology and self psychology will be discussed. First, however, it is necessary to lay the foundations.

FOUNDATIONS

Phenomenology, Science, and Empathy

We begin with the following question: given that Kohut believed that the self-psychological conception of empathy is scientifically paradigmatic for the human sciences, how is it that he entertained the idea that postmodern natural science, the science of the quantum, could, and should, be adduced to establish the scientific credentials of self psychology? That is, why did Kohut believe that the scientific status of psychoanalysis must be justified through appeal to natural science? The significance of this question here is that the empathic bond between self psychology and phenomenology will not come into view until it is shown that the empathic field, the object of investigation of both of these disciplines, is conceptually and actually independent of any other domain, that is, *until the empathic field is conceptualized as a self-sufficient domain.* Unless it is so conceptualized, all regularities discovered within it are subject to dissolution through reduction to a material or other ontological foundation with which they may not correspond one to one. Since natural science presupposes the ontological priority of *its* object of investigation, the physical world, it is necessary to show that the empathic field cannot be conceptualized, as Kohut thought, as deriving its scientific status from a presumed relation to natural science, that is, as if it were reducible to natural science, physics for example. Rather, it must be shown that the empathic field does not depend on the natural scientific object of investigation, because, if it does, then it cannot be a self-sufficient object of investigation. Since phenomenology suspends ontological presuppositions, the homology necessary to establish self psychology's status as a science is between self psychology and phenomenology. That is to say, *the empathic field is, as we shall see, just that object of investigation which comes into view when all ontological presuppositions are put out of play.*

Kohut is not the only theoretician who seeks to link self psychology and quantum physics. Toulmin (1986b) claims that with quantum physics positivism has finally been overcome, thus making possible for the first time a synthesis between natural science and the humanistic disciplines, self psychology in particular.

Toulmin claims, however, that Kohut had positivistic presuppositions in the form of Kohut's belief in empiricism and factuality with regard to psychic reality. Toulmin suggests, therefore, that if self psychology would understand itself as phenomenological, a genuine synthesis with postmodern science could occur because the phenomenological standpoint rules out positivism in psychology, just as postmodern science, he claims, rules it out with respect to the physical world. Were this the case, all talk of empiricism and factuality in the psychic domain would be obviated. Toulmin thus implies that not only self psychology, but phenomenology as well, is compatible with postmodern science. As I will show, Toulmin is incorrect in holding (1) that quantum physics overcomes positivism; (2) that phenomenology and self psychology are compatible with the postmodern scientific paradigm; and (3) that phenomenology rules out empiricism and factuality in the psychic domain. I will show that the empathic bond between self psychology and phenomenology is precisely Kohut's empathic field and Husserl's *Lebenswelt*, and I will argue that they represent the same self-sufficient domain of scientific investigation as conceptualized psychoanalytically and philosophically, respectively.

For Kohut, the scientific status of psychoanalysis was grounded in empathy as method and field of investigation. He saw similarities between empathy and that aspect of the postmodern scientific paradigm according to which the observer cannot be separated from the observed. As we shall see, the dependence of the observed on the observer is more adequately explained within the phenomenological attitude than within the natural scientific attitude.

Kohut (1984) claimed that reality has two aspects, "introspective" and "extrospective" (p. 32): psychoanalysis is the science of reality in its introspective aspect, and natural science is the science of reality in its extrospective aspect. Here it is necessary to elaborate and interpret implications of this distinction that Kohut did not elaborate, but that, I believe, are implicit in his viewpoint. Accordingly we ask, what characterizes the "extrospective" or natural scientific object of investigation? Most important, the natural world is viewed as a *self-sufficient whole.* This is the basis for the principle of the uniformity of nature, a principle that is a necessary presupposition for all science. Unless nature is uniform—unless regularities can be discovered that enable us to expand the scope of the known—science is not possible. In this regard, Kohut's claim that empathy defines the psychoanalytic object of investigation means that the empathic field, reality in its introspective aspect, is conceived as a self-sufficient whole, just as is reality in its extrospective aspect, and is therefore construed as a proper object of scientific investigation. Thus, if psychoanalysis is a science, *then its object of investigation must be grasped as a self-sufficient whole.* How, then, are we to understand the notion of the empathic field as a self-sufficient whole? It is here that the conceptual homology between self psychology and phenomenology is most revealing.

Phenomenology can be described as *radical* empiricism. Radical empiricism is to be contrasted with empiricism in the positivist sense. Positivist empiricism is related to the psychic act in and through which the natural scientific object of investigation is given. This act, physicalist reduction, is an act of abstraction from the whole of experience whereby the experienced world is viewed as (that is, reduced to) those quantifiable and measurable properties given through sensory data. The material world as the object of investigation of natural science is construed either as nothing but sensory data (Mach), or as all that which gives rise to sense data, that is, as everything that exists prior to, and thus independently of, the knowing subject. According to Einstein (1957), it is "the scientist's faith" (p. 248) that the world exists independently of consciousness and is a self-sufficient whole. Einstein thus recognized that the independent existence of the world is undemonstrable.

Radical empiricism, on the other hand, grasps the experienced world, or *Lebenswelt,* as a self-sufficient whole prior to any abstractive acts, any ontological commitments, as to the existence or nonexistence of the world independently of consciousness (Husserl, 1936). Husserl (1913) expressed the sense of phenomenology as radical empiricism when he formulated the act in and through which the phenomenological object of investigation is given: the phenomenological "*epoche*" or "reduction" (p. 61). The phenomenological reduction is a psychic act such that all judgments as to the ontological status of the world are suspended, or put out of play, and the world, including oneself and other persons, is investigated just as it gives itself to the experiencing subject. Positivist empiricism is not radical empiricism because it abstracts from the world as actually experienced and begins nonempirically, with the presupposition that the world exists independently of any consciousness of it.

In relation to classical physics, positivism posited the existence of matter independent of consciousness. In its more recent manifestation, for example, Mach, positivism turned from objectivism to subjectivism by denying the independent existence of the external world and asserting that only sensory data exist. Objectivism and subjectivism in this context are but two sides of the same act of abstraction from the whole of experience. Grasping that it is in principle impossible to *know* whether or not the external world exists independently of consciousness, the phenomenologist suspends judgment regarding its ontological status, and, in so doing, discovers that the world is still given just as it is, along with other persons, and that it retains its character as "objective", as "external", "there for everyone". The world as so construed is the *Lebenswelt.*

The *Lebenswelt* is properly described as an empathic field in that it is intersubjectively constituted and disclosed in and through a decision to investigate the world "on its own terms"—just as it gives itself when all ontological commitments, all indemonstrable presuppositions, are suspended. Most important, this act of suspending presuppositions does not commit one to the view that the world either *does* or *does not* exist independently of consciousness. Husserl (1913) used the term "constitution" to designate the relation between consciousness and the world prior to all ontological commitments, and the relation is thus termed "constitutive."

For the sake of clarity, it is appropriate at this point to discuss the phenomenological concept of consciousness. Husserl's works contain numerous references to psychoanalysis, to the unconscious, and to the dynamic nature of the psyche, for example, in the following :

> We must mention here also the entire domain of *associations and habits*. . . . A singular element in such domains is motivated from out of a dark realm; *it has its "psychic reasons" which lead us to ask: how did I get to this,* what brought me to this? The fact that one can raise such questions characterizes all motivation in general. The "motives" are often deeply hidden and are to be brought to light by "psychoanalysis". A thought may "remind" me of other thoughts and it may call me back to a past event in recollection, etc. In some cases this can be perceived. In most cases, however, motivation is in consciousness but it does not come into relief. It is unnoticed or not noticeable ("unconscious") [Husserl, 1952a, pp. 222–223; 1952b, pp. 268–269].

It is clear from this passage that the term "consciousness" meant to Husserl just *psychic,* including the unconscious.

As a self-sufficient whole, the *Lebenswelt,* the empathic field, can be investigated empirically, *through experience and experience alone.* Facts regarding the *Lebenswelt* can be uncovered and grasped in their true contingency, their relativity to the *Lebenswelt* itself. Thus, if self psychology is phenomenological, then it is also scientific in the phenomenological, rather than natural scientific, sense, a sense that allows for empiricism—radical empiricism—and factuality—the discovery of regularities—in relation to the *Lebenswelt,* its proper object of investigation. In addition, the relativity of empirical findings to the *Lebenswelt,* the empathic field, indicates that phenomenology is a hermeneutic discipline, a theory of interpretation. This indicates further that science, as an endeavor to discover regularities, and hermeneutics, as a theory and praxis of interpretation, are not, as they are often held to be, incompatible.

Thus, Toulmin's (1986b) claim that Kohut's use of empiricism and factuality means that Kohut had not transcended positivism misunderstands Kohut's standpoint and is not correct. Toulmin failed to follow through on his insight that self psychology is phenomenological in the Husserlian sense. On the contrary, Kohut's insistence on the scientific status of psychoanalysis, his claim that empathy defines the field of psychoanalysis, and his use of empiricism and factuality all show the inner bond between psychoanalysis and phenomenology.

Self Psychology, Phenomenology, Positivism, Postmodern Science

We must now turn to the task of explicating the basis for my claim that phenomenology, and thus self psychology, is incompatible with the postmodern scientific paradigm, that is, that postmodern science has not moved beyond positivism.

Natural science seeks knowledge of nature. It seeks to know what is, what actually exists. This is called reality. However, natural science does not view as reality the immediate experience of human beings *qua experience,* as a totality with nothing left out, *and this is just as true within the postmodern scientific paradigm as it was for modern science.*

Those who look to the new scientific paradigm to justify the scientific status of the humanistic disciplines often cite the aspect of quantum physics according to which the observed is dependent on the observer. This seems to suggest that objectivity in the classical sense, that is existence of the world independent of the observer, is unattainable and that therefore a discipline can be scientific and successfully obtain new knowledge even if investigator and object of investigation are inseparable, as is the case in all of the humanistic disciplines. However, one salient question is seldom discussed: *how is the observer construed, that is, what is the nature of the observer, within this new scientific paradigm?* This problem is the source of considerable controversy within physics itself.

According to an interpretation of quantum mechanics prevalent among scientists (Rae, 1981), nature is conceived just as surely in purely quantitative terms as in classical physics. The relation between the macro world of perceived objects and the micro world of quantum effects is merely quantitative: the macro world is larger. One issue is whether or not a human consciousness is required as the observer. For some physicists, an instrument serves just as well as a human being, as long as the wave function collapses: the measurement is made and the information is registered.

Other physicists, for example Wigner (Rae, 1981), offer another interpretation of the dependence of observations on the observer, one that is perhaps most suggestive to those working in the humanistic disciplines. According to this interpretation, a human observer is necessary, for, by observing, and thus recording, the quantum effect, the observer *determines* that effect as an irreversible event. This means that there are irreversible events in nature and the knowing subject is the record of those events. Nevertheless, the events in question occur in purely physical systems, systems composed exclusively of quantifiable entities, for natural science does not include nonquantifiable effects. Even though Wigner maintains that consciousness is different from the physical, material world (see Wolf, 1981), the effect of consciousness on that world is nevertheless purely material; it is quantifiable. This rules out what Kohut (1984) referred to as the "introspective," as contrasted with the "extrospective," aspect of reality.[2]

As we have just seen, the nature and role of the observer is a controversial issue in contemporary physics.[3] That the interpretation of quantum mechanics is scientifically controversial means in itself that the phenomenon of observer dependence ought not to be used as justification for claims regarding the nature and methodology of the humanistic disciplines. Moreover, an examination of the nature of the controversy indicates that, since all of the rival interpretations exclude the *Lebenswelt,* none of them is relevant to the humanistic disciplines. It seems that those who have sought to use the observer-dependent aspect of quantum physics as an explanatory tool in other fields have failed to investigate the concept of consciousness presupposed by physics. Most important, one must ask whether or not it is ever meaningful to use the natural scientific world view as a basis for conceptualizing the scientific status of the humanistic disciplines. From the point of view of phenomenology, it is not meaningful (Husserl, 1936). Natural science, including the science of the quantum, necessarily presupposes an act of abstraction from experience as a totality, as the *Lebenswelt,* the empathic field. Unless this abstractive act is performed, the material world as object of scientific investigation cannot be conceived. Human experience in the most immediate sense, however, prior to any abstractive acts and ontological presuppositions, includes phe-

---

[2] Keller (1985) presents a psychoanalytically informed critique of the problem of the dependence of the observed on the observer in quantum physics.

[3] My research in the interpretation of quantum physics has been assisted by Dr. Charles Nissim-Sabat, Chair, Department of Physics, Northeastern Illinois University.

nomena that are given qualitatively and that, as such, are inexpressible in purely quantitative terms. In fact, experience itself, *qua* experience, is not quantifiable.

Given that natural science's object of investigation is constituted through an act of abstraction from the *Lebenswelt,* it follows that the radical separateness of subject and object of investigation, — the subject-object split — is built into it. For the subject-object split to be obviated or transcended, subject and object must be grasped in their essential relatedness, as necessarily implying one another. Natural science, on the other hand, seeks to conceive objectivity independently of subjectivity and thus inevitably splits what is given intrinsically as one whole: experience itself, the empathic field, the *Lebenswelt.*

Phenomenology and Self Psychology

I stated earlier that the project of interpreting Kohut's conception of psychoanalysis as a new paradigm for the humanistic disciplines should not be abandoned. Kohut's conception of empathy as method and field of psychoanalysis suggested to him the paradigmatic status of self psychology. We now see that, contrary to Kohut, since it too presupposes the subject-object split and thus rules out empathy, the postmodern scientific paradigm cannot help to found self psychology as the new paradigm for the humanistic disciplines. However, this can be accomplished when self psychology is understood as a phenomenological discipline because the subject-object split is obviated when the empathic field is understood to be the *Lebenswelt* (Husserl, 1936).

The *Lebenswelt,* as we have seen, is the life world, the world as given in experience as a whole, and it comes into view when all abstractive acts and all ontological presuppositions are suspended within the attitude of the phenomenological reduction. Husserl (1913) referred to the constitutive relationship between experiencing subject and experienced object as the noetic (subject pole) — noematic (object pole) relation. The noema is constituted in and through noetic acts. Though the emphasis is on the *activity* of consciousness, consciousness does not create its objects *ab nuovo.* The phenomenological concept of consciousness is intentionality: consciousness is consciousness-of; there is no consciousness without an object. Therefore, consciousness does not create its objects. Neither does the noetic-noematic relation rest upon a presupposition of the existence of the world independently of consciousness. Rather

(Husserl, 1948), consciousness *constitutes* its objects: they come into view *in and through the history of sense sedimented in consciousness;* they are constituted in and through their meaning for the subject, and this meaning is both subjectively and intersubjectively constituted. If Kohut had been aware of the phenomenological sense of the constitutive relation between the mind and its objects, he would not have appealed to the phenomenon of the dependence of the observed on the "observer" in quantum mechanics in order to establish the scientific status of self psychology. The noetic-noematic relation both obviates the subject-object split and provides a sure foundation for the scientific investigation of phenomena occurring within the empathic field.

In this regard, phenomenology offers a solution to the problem regarding the conception of self-selfobject relationships indicated by Kohut (1984):

> If, as is indeed the case, we claim that the concepts of a self and of a selfobject refer to inner experiences, that they are not part of physical reality but of psychological reality, observable only via introspection and empathy, how then can we speak of relationships between them as if we were dealing with actors on the stage of external reality? [p. 50]

Since Kohut believed that relations between a self and its selfobjects can not properly be spoken of as if they were relations between "actors on the stage of external reality," he asks this question merely rhetorically. However, Kohut did not explain with philosophical clarity and precision why this is the case. That is, Kohut did not explain how it is that the selfobject, a psychic structure, a structure of the "introspective", not of the "extrospective", world, can refer to another person.

The phenomenological explanation is as follows: the phrase "actors on the stage of external reality" implies not just that other persons are involved, but that these persons are construed as existing independently, ontologically, of the subject interacting with them. But the natural scientific attitude toward external reality—that it exists independently of consciousness—does not appear. That attitude, with its presuppositions, is suspended within the empathic field, the *Lebenswelt.* But reality, an objective world, does appear. This is a phenomenological factum, given self-evidentially when the phenomenological reduction is performed (Husserl, 1950): *neither the existence nor the experience of reality, including the existence of other persons, depends on ontological presuppositions.*

Thus, an insight that is by now axiomatic within psychoanalysis (Sandler and Rosenblatt, 1962; Leowald, 1976), that the "objectivity" of physical objects is constituted not before, but *after* others are experienced as other persons, can now be phenomenologically grounded. That is, for human beings, psychic, intersubjective reality, the *Lebenswelt,* is primary reality. Physical objects cannot be experienced as objective, as "there for everyone," until intersubjectivity is constituted, until others are *constituted* as other persons. Thus, within the phenomenological framework of suspension of all ontological commitments, the objectivity of physical objects is grasped as a constituted sense that does not require ontological presuppositions. What it does require is the prior constitutiuon of other persons as persons. Nor do we experience other persons *qua* persons as if they existed absolutely independently of ourselves. To do so would be to experience them as purely quantitative entities, as natural scientific objects of investigation, "actors on the stage of external reality." In conclusion, then, the selfobject ("noema") is the other person for the self ("noesis"), and the relation between them is constitutive in the phenomenological sense. Most important, these findings represent aspects of the "essential human sameness" referred to by Kohut as a core concept in self psychology and as the object of investigation of psychoanalytic science.

Conclusion

As we have seen, positivism is inseparable from the postmodern scientific paradigm. How, then, can it be overcome? The answer to this question, I believe, is that positivism can be overcome through an empiricism far more radical than that of natural science. Further, when Kohut talked of empiricism and factuality, when he refused to grant to natural science the sole warrant to these concepts and their concomitant terms, he was not, as Toulmin (1986a, b) argued, infected with positivism; rather, he remained faithful to his discovery that the empathic field is a proper object for scientific investigation and that psychoanalysis is the science that investigates it. To put the point most strongly and, I think, most accurately, *Kohut discovered that the concept of empathy is meaningless unless empathy defines the psychoanalytic field.* Unless empathy defines the psychoanalytic field, unless it is the *Lebenswelt,* empathy cannot be unambiguously conceptualized. In phenomenological terms, its existence-sense cannot be explicated. For this reason I maintain, as I indicated earlier, that abandoning the view that empathy defines the psychoanalytic field would be equivalent to abandoning self psychology. Moreover, since the empathic field is the *Lebenswelt,* in defining the object of psychoanalytic investigation as the empathic field, Kohut came close to discovering the phenomenological reduction.

THE EMPATHIC BOND: ALTEREGO IN KOHUT AND HUSSERL

As discussed earlier, the essence of both self psychology and phenomenology is the construal that empathy and science mutually imply one another. Science is the search for regularities, and empathy is the method that, like all scientific methods, defines, or brings into view, its field of investigation—the empathic field, or *Lebenswelt.* As a self-sufficient field of investigation, the empathic field exhibits regularities, and these are in the form of aspects of the essential human sameness. In elaborating and concretizing the conceptual homology between phenomenology and self psychology, it is pertinent now to explore the notion of human sameness implicit in each.

Kohut (1959) provided a clear explanation of the meaning of empathy defined as "vicarious introspection":

> Let us consider a simple example. We see a person who is unusually tall. It is not to be disputed that this person's unusual size is an important fact for our psychological assessment—without introspection and empathy, however, his size remains simply a physical attribute. Only when we think ourselves into his place, only when we, by vicarious introspection, begin to feel his unusual size as if it were our own and thus revive inner experiences in which we had been unusual or conspicuous, only then do we begin to appreciate the meaning that the unusual size may have for this person and only then have we observed a psychological fact [p. 207].

An important feature of this description is the importance Kohut attached to revealing the nature of empathy by differentiating empathic experience from experience of the world, including the human body, as merely physical. This indicates that the empathic field is the *Lebenswelt* in the phenomenological sense. Empathy occurs only when one feels the feelings of the other person as if they were one's own, and this occurs when we relive analogous experiences, when, that is, we become acutely aware of our sameness: "only then have we observed a psychological fact." Thus, a psychological fact is an experiential regularity where experience is construed as a self-sufficient domain of investigation: the domain of meaning, not matter.[4]

Let us compare Kohut's description of empathy with the following statement by Husserl in which he describes how we experience the personalities of other people:

> I understand the thinking and the actions of someone else according to my own habitual manners of comportment and motivations, but all judgments of the other do not come about according to the external style of his life so to speak, that is abstracted from experience. For, in this case, I do not penetrate into the inner sphere of the motivations and I can not have a vivid representation of them. But I do learn to see into the inner sphere of another, and I do come to know the person himself inwardly: the motivational subject who comes to the fore when I represent to myself the other ego as motivated in such a manner. . . . [Husserl, 1952a, p. 273; 1952b, p. 329].
>
> I gain these motivations by placing myself into his situation, into his level of education and early development, etc., and in so doing, I must "join in" with them; not only do I empathize myself into his thinking, feeling, and acting, but I must follow them and his motives become my quasi-motives which, however, motivate insightfully in the mode of intuitively self-fulfilling empathy [Husserl, 1952a, p. 275; 1952b, p. 331].

Husserl thus defined empathy as vicarious introspection exactly as Kohut had: as an experience of sameness. Additionally, this passage introduces the characteristic Husserlian use of the concept of motivation (Nissim-Sabat, 1977). For Husserl, and, I think, for Kohut as well, empathy—vicarious introspection—is precisely awareness of the motivational structure of the other person's experience. Though in this context the concept of motivation implies transindividual regularities, it has no positivist connotations, as if it were a type of naturalistic causation. Rather, within the framework of phenomenology, motivational regularities are transindividual in that they represent the core sameness in and through which we are all humans amongst humans.

[4]There are in Kohut's writings numerous instances in which he manifests unequivocally that he views the world as the *Lebenswelt* in the phenomenological sense. Two such instances are: 1) his discussion of Goethe's theory of color as contrasted with the natural scientific theory (Kohut, 1973b), and 2) his discussion of the experience of size (Kohut, 1981b).

Another important aspect of the confluence of ideas regarding empathy in the thought of Husserl and Kohut is that both held that activation of the capacity for empathy is a developmental task; that is, both maintained that in the history of a given psyche, there is a time when the capacity for empathy is not yet activated. Furthermore, for both, the activation of the capacity for empathy is mediated by an alter ego phenomenon, that is, a perception of sameness. According to Kohut (1984), the alterego line of development indicates a pervasive need for the feeling of being a "human among humans":

> . . . we do encounter important self-affirming and self-maintaining experiences in early childhood [which] . . . I associate . . . with archaic alter-ego relationships. . . .
>
> Some of the most painful feelings to which man is exposed . . . relate to the sense of not being human. The awareness of such a central distortion in the personality stems . . . from the absence of *human* humans in the environment of the small child. The mere presence of people in a child's surroundings—their voices and body odors, the emotions they express . . . creates . . . a sense of belonging and participating that cannot be explained in terms of a mirroring response or a merger with ideals. . . . These aspects of our basic alikeness are signposts of the human world that we need without knowing we need them so long as they are available to us [p.200].

Thus, infants do not experience themselves as humans at birth. Rather, the sense of humanness, the capacity to feel oneself to be the same as other persons, is a developmental achievement that depends on the infant's empathic caretakers, "human humans." The *comportment of the caretakers in relation to the infant* facilitates or hinders the formation of the self-selfobject relation. Moreover, as we shall see, the alterego self-selfobject relation is the earliest, most archaic form of human interrelatedness.

Detrick (1985) has explored and emphasized the crucial significance of this aspect of Kohut's thinking. In the course of discussing experiences of aloneness reported by some patients, Detrick remarks, "Although this can be understood as a severe disturbance in mirroring or idealizing needs, I think this kind of aloneness is primarily a function of a more basic, more primitive disturbance, a disturbance in the capacity to experience oneself as a human being surrounded by other human beings (p. 250). Detrick then goes on to explain how alterego needs—the need to feel oneself to be a "human among humans"—and empathy are interrelated:

> Kohut saw the interpretive process . . . as having two aspects . . . The understanding phase can be seen primarily as an aspect of one of the alterego needs, the alterego need for sameness. After all, is not the empathic process, at its core, the finding and experiencing of sameness in another individual's experience? . . . The second interpretive phase is the explaining phase. . . . This explanatory phase can be conceived of as giving the person a particular cognitive tool. By this I mean that they are given a . . . language by which to describe first to others and then to themselves, both what they are experiencing and why. . . . the alterego self-selfobject relationship is at the center of both phases of the interpretive process. In this sense I think that the alterego selfobject relationships are more fundamental than either the mirroring or the idealizing. . . . it is the experience of empathy or sameness that then allows for the remobilization of the split-off or defended against mirroring and idealizing wishes [p. 251].

In this passage, Detrick (1) emphasizes the crucial role of the experience of sameness in the psychological development of human beings, (2) explains that empathy is just such an experience of sameness, and (3) shows that empathic experience is mediated by the alter ego self-selfobject relation. The question then naturally arises: since the experience of another psychic life is never direct, but only "vicarious," how can we establish that the sameness we experience is a *sameness,* that is, an experience of another person, rather than a modality of ourselves? In other words, how does Husserl show that the other as other *person* is constituted as an *alter*-ego phenomenon? In explicating this point, I can do no better than to refer to the work of Ricoeur. Ricoeur (1986) summarizes Husserl's constitutive analysis of the origin of our awareness of others as other persons and shows the relatedness of Husserl's analysis to Kohut's views:

> Even though I cannot live the experiences of another subject, I can at least transport myself into this subject's consciousness and grasp its experience as analogous to my own. This is possible thanks to a *Paarung,* a pairing, at the level of the lived body, a lived body that feels its affinity for the lived body of the other by a sort of consonance. This *Paarung* . . . is not just bodily and emotional, it is also mental. I perceive the other person as a subject who perceives me. . . . Through empathy, I can imagine what I would feel if I inhabited that body over there that is the here of the other person. . . . The analytic

> counterpart of the analogical grasping of the other is the self-selfobject relation, where the very word *self* is redoubled. . . . I can see an even closer kinship between what Husserl calls *Paarung* and what Kohut calls attunement or consonance [p. 451–452].

To fully understand this material, the following point must be made explicit: a phenomenological analysis is quite similar to the kind of analysis to which Kohut (1959) referred as "operational." Phenomenology, like self psychology, makes no pretense to *possessing* truth, only to *seeking* it. Immediate experience is its point of departure: Given this, phenomenology seeks to understand what must be the case if, for example, one's experience includes experiences of other persons. Phenomenology's acknowledgment that we often do have experiences of other persons does not imply that phenomenology presupposes what it claims to demonstrate: that solipsism is false. It does mean that the experience of other persons is given as such, just as what it is; otherwise, we could not even discuss it. What is required is a constitutive analysis of the givenness of other persons in our experience. That is, although the experience of others is a given, we do not uncritically assume that we grasp, without further ado, the sense, the meaning, of the experience of other persons. Rather, the constitutive sources of this sense, its origin in experience, can and must be explicated. Thus, the experience of others as persons can neither be demonstrated in an impossible sense, as if it could be the object of investigation of positivist science, nor, as in some hermeneutic standpoints, presupposed as an unanalyzable fiat.

Husserl's (1950) phenomenological explication of the origin of the alter ego-self relation shows that our experience of others as other persons is constituted in the following manner: prior to the formation of any ontological commitments, an originally egocentric subject "constitutes" another as another *person.* This constitutive act is accomplished in and through an experience of a perceptual analogy between one's own and another's body, and between one's own and another's actions. When the ego pairs itself in this way with the other acting, perceptually analogous animate organism, the ego simultaneously becomes aware of itself and of the existence of other selves. Most important, the awareness of the otherness of the other person is constituted in and through experience and does not exist prior to experience. From the point of view of phenomenology, and, I maintain, within Kohut's "operational" stance, to seek any other kind of confirmation of the experience of others as other persons is not only to presuppose an ontology, but also to reduce persons to objects. Thus, for Husserl as for Kohut, the activation of empathy requires an encounter with "human humans," persons whose comportment enables, rather than repels, a twinning, an experience of sameness.

Ricoeur (1986) discusses the parallel conceptualization of the origin of the alterego self-selfobject structure by Kohut:

> As we have seen, in his last work Kohut distinguishes twinship transference from mirroring and idealizing transference. This is what corresponds to the alter ego in Husserl, to the extent that the support given by a selfobject is neither that of fusion nor that of idealization, but rather a relation of resemblance that makes the other person similar to me [p. 452–453].

Thus, for both Husserl and Kohut, the capacity for empathy is activated as an alter ego self-selfobject experience. Moreover, for both, the capacity for empathy is a capacity to experience another person's motives and affect as one's own, as alter-ego phenomena.

ETHICS AND EMPATHY, PHENOMENOLOGY AND SCIENCE

Kohut did not believe, as do positivists, that science is, could, or ought to be "value free." "There is", he stated (Kohut, 1981b), "no science of man that is thinkable without some value system behind it" (p.261). What Kohut objected to in Freud was precisely Freud's view that science is value free. Freud's system was "moralistic"—unethical—because its creator refused to recognize the moral stance inherent in it. For Kohut, to be ethical was to acknowledge the values inherent in one's standpoint so that others could evaluate them, and to be open to the possibility of alterations, originating in oneself or in one's culture, in one's hierarchy of values. Moreover, Kohut's (1981a) statement that "every human activity has to be seen as embedded into a hierarchy of values" (p. 221) is an excellent description of the *Lebenswelt.* Within the phenomenological perspective, what is most important is to gain awareness and understanding of the values by which one is motivated in order to make a critique and change what is not beneficial. For this ethic, knowledge as an end in itself is neither desirable nor possible. Yet, why did Toulmin

(1986b) claim that Kohut believed that science is value free in the positivist sense? The reason, I believe, is that Toulmin does not understand the role of empathy in Kohut's thought.

Referring to Piaget's concept of egocentricity, Toulmin (1986b) writes:

> Putting Piaget and Kohut together, we obtain a view of personality development that is restricted to neither the cognitive nor the affective aspect of experience. On both levels, the developing child can be seen as faced with the same basic task: that of recognizing, and coming to live happily with the recognition that each of us shares the world with other human beings who view it from different standpoints and have different hopes, feelings, and satisfactions . . . few of us fail to decenter our perceptual worlds . . . . But many of us find it harder to decenter our affective lives, and continue throughout life expecting others to have the same attitudes, goals, and ambitions we have ourselves [p. 471].

That Toulmin misconstrues the meaning of self psychology can be seen by comparing this statement with the following description by Detrick (1985) of the experience of one of his patients:

> The experience of sameness symbolized by the sculpture and the mold allowed for the transmission of information, learning in a fundamental sense that is experienced by a child as coming from the benign empathic parent. Mr. X then went on to add that one could never become a person, a real person, if one had never had early in life this kind of experience of sameness. It was only through the experience of empathy, or to use his word, "resonance", that one could eventually allow oneself to become different [p. 247].

Thus, in his statement Toulmin focuses on the awareness of differences as a precondition for health, whereas Detrick and his patient focus on the experience of sameness. One might argue that the two statements do not conflict in that they refer to different stages and different problems: Toulmin refers to the necessity of overcoming grandiosity and idealization, whereas Detrick refers to the formation, on a more primitive level, of the alter ego self-selfobject relation. However, Detrick has shown that the experience of sameness is a precondition for overcoming pathological forms of grandiosity. Like all those who privilege the natural scientific world view, Toulmin cannot conceptualize an essential human sameness, constituted in and through experience, that is irreducible to the natural scientific object of investigation and is, at the same time, the foundation for a science of psychoanalysis, that is, a science of empathy.

It is for this reason, I maintain, that Toulmin (1986b) attempts to place self psychology within the framework of the Kantian ethics of respect for persons. This too is misguided, because the notorious, ahistorical formalism of Kantian ethics clashes sharply with the Husserlian and Kohutian emphasis on the historical and developmental concreteness of human experience. There is no doubt that human beings are ends of themselves, as Kant maintained. This formulation, however, does not help us to understand the psychic concreteness of human interrelatedness. In the quest for a constitutive foundation for the intersubjective domain, for the *Lebenswelt,* the Kantian (Kant, 1785) ethic of respect for persons, even if we accept this value, provides no basis for mediating human separateness and differences.

Phenomenology does not deny that human beings are separate from one another. Toulmin's (1986b) statement that "for phenomenologists . . . the separateness of different people's minds is not axiomatic, but is an artifact of life experience" and that for them "the idea of 'shared' mental lives has nothing paradoxical about it" (p. 476) is misleading. Husserl (1936) affirmed the separateness of human beings from one another when he recognized that each person is a separate stream of inner time and internal time consciousness. Husserl (1936, 1950) was extremely clear in explicating the point that one person cannot experience the consciousness of another person in an unmediated fashion, for then there would not be different persons at all, nor would there be experiences of empathy. The *Lebenswelt,* the surrounding world of life, is indeed constituted intersubjectively (Husserl, 1936). But, intersubjectivity requires that there be separate subjects.

Toulmin's (1986) essential aim is to show that the postmodern scientific paradigm enables the reconstitution of "natural theology," a world view that prevailed before being undermined by modern science and the dualistic-materialistic philosophy associated with it. According to Toulmin, a rebirth of natural theology, potentiated by the postmodern scientific paradigm, can reverse the damage done by positivism and enable us to experience once more our oneness with all of nature.

It seems to me that, given his view of the postmodern

paradigm, Toulmin seeks to pair natural scientific, reductive materialism with a point of view (natural theology) such that there is no essential human sameness; there are, rather, essential differences mediated by that which is the transcendent source of all creation and which does not accord to the human a sameness of its own, different from that of the nonhuman world (Toulmin, 1986a).

Yet, as we have seen, Kohut (1973a) conceptualized the essential human sameness as just that which protects humanity against the "fallacy of pairing finiteness and death with meaninglessness and despair" and which is the source of "the commitment to contribute our share to the vitality of fulfilling human life." And, Kohut emphasized, to do this, "scientific rigor is indeed indispensable." But what would be the source of equating finiteness and death with meaninglessness and despair? The source of this, as Kohut indicated, would be to think that there is no empathy, no *Lebenswelt,* that we are just the same as the rest of the universe, no different from "a universe of senseless spaces and crazily racing stars" (p. 682).

The stars have endured for a very long time. And how will human life endure? If we take as our whole purpose mere survival, humanity, which is not among the enduring stars, may perish. If it does, it will be because physical extinction was preceded by psychic extinction. But if we take as our purpose the achievement and sustenance of "vitally fulfilling life," we will endure. For Kohut and Husserl, self psychology and phenomenology, empathy and empathy alone grounds survival and is the wellspring of human vitality and fulfillment.

REFERENCES

Detrick, D. W, (1985), Alterego phenomena and alterego transferences. In: *Progress in Self Psychology,* Vol. 1, ed. A. Goldberg. New York: Guilford Press, pp. 240–256.

Einstein, A, (1957), *Albert Einstein,* ed. P. A. Schlipp. New York: Tudor Press.

Gedo, J. E. (1986), *Conceptual Issues in Psychoanalysis.* Hillsdale, NJ: The Analytic Press.

Husserl, E. (1913), *Ideas Pertaining to a Pure Phenomenology and to a Phenomenological Philosophy,* Vol. 1, trans. F. Kersten. Hague: Nijhoff, 1982.

_____ (1936), *The Crisis of European Sciences and Transcendental Phenomenology,* trans. D. Carr. Evanston, IL: Northwestern University Press, 1970.

_____ (1948), *Experience and Judgement,* rev. & ed. L. Landgrebe (trans. J. S. Churchill & K. Ameriks). Evanston, IL: Northwestern University

Press, 1973.
_____ (1950), *Cartesian Meditations,* trans. D. Cairns. Hague: Nijhoff, 1960.
_____ (1952a), *Ideen Su Einer Reinen Phaenomenologie Und Phaenomenologischen Philosophie, Zweites Buch.* Hague: Nijhoff.
_____ (1952b), *Ideas Pertaining to a Pure Phenomenology and to a Phenomenological Philosophy.* Vol. 2, trans. M. Frings, ed. M. Nissim-Sabat, 1980. Unpublished.
Kant, I. (1785), *Foundations of the Metaphysic of Morals,* trans. L. W. Beck. Indianopolis: Bobbs-Merrill, 1969.
Keller, E. F. (1985), *Gender and Science.* New Haven, CT: Yale University Press.
Kohut, H. (1959), Introspection, empathy, and psychoanalysis. In: *The Search for the Self.* Vol. 2, ed. P. H. Ornstein. New York: International Universities Press, 1978, pp. 205–233.
_____ (1973a), The future of psychoanalysis. In: *The Search for the Self,* Vol. 2, ed. P. H. Ornstein. New York: International Universities Press, 1978, pp. 685–724.
_____ (1973b), The psychoanalyst in the community of scholars. In: *The Search for the Self,* Vol. 2,ed. P. H. Ornstein. New York: International Universities Press, 1978, pp.685–724
_____ (1980), Reflections on advances in self psychology. In: *Advances in Self Psychology,* ed. A. Goldberg. New York: International Universities Press, 1980, pp.473–554.
_____ (1981a), The psychoanalyst and the historian. In: *Self Psychology and the Humanities,* ed. C. B. Strozier. New York: Norton, 1985, pp. 215–223.
_____ (1981b), The continuity of the self. In: *Self Psychology and the Humanities,* ed. C. B. Strozier. New York: Norton 1985, pp. 232-243.
_____ (1981c), Religion, ethics, values. In: *Self Psychology and the Humanities,* ed. C. B. Strozier. New York: Norton 1985, pp 261–262.
_____ (1984), *How Does Analysis Cure?* ed. A. Goldberg & P. E. Stepansky. Chicago: University of Chicago Press.
_____ Leowald, H. W. (1976), Perspectives on memory. In: *Psychology versus Metapsychology,* ed. M. M. Gill & P. S. Holzman. New York: International Universities Press.
Nissim-Sabat, M. (1977), Edmund Husserl's theory of motivation. Doctoral dissertation, De Paul University. *Dissertations Abstracts International,* v. 37, no. 9. University Microfilms no. 77–428.
_____ (1986), Psychoanalysis and phenomenology: A new synthesis. *Psychoanal. Rev.,* 73:437–458.
Rae, A. I. M. (1981), *Quantum Mechanics.* New York: Wiley.
Ricoeur, P. (1986), The self in psychoanalysis and in phenomenological philosophy. *Psychoanal. Inq.* 6:437–458.
Sandler, J. & Rosenblatt, B. (1962), The concept of the representational world. *The Psychoanalytic Study of the Child,* 17:128–145. New York:

International Universities Press.
Toulmin, S. (1986a), *The Return to Cosmology.* Berkeley: University of California Press.
_____ (1986b), Self psychology as a "postmodern" science. *Psychoanal. Inq.*, 6:459–477.
Wolf, F. A. (1981), *Taking the Quantum Leap.* San Francisco: Harper.

9

On Maurice Merleau-Ponty and the Psychology of the Self

ROBERT J. MASEK

Angelo Hesnard (1960), a leading French psychoanalyst, once argued that Freud's discoveries had burst the boundaries of established philosophies and stood as an anomaly with respect to their ability to faithfully contain both the insights of psychoanalysis and its own self understanding. Freud's novel view of disorder, his discovery of the unconscious, the peculiar nature of psychological life as a theatre of *meaning*—showing twists and turns through symbolizations, condensations, and displacements, along with other defenses—require, says Hesnard, a "new philosophy" capable of assimilating these discoveries and clarifying their existential and clinical significance. Toward this end, Hesnard sought help from his colleague, the philosopher Maurice Merleau-Ponty. For 25 years Merleau-Ponty had maintained a dialogue between his phenomenology and psychoanalysis, until his untimely death in 1961 at the age of 55. While the scope of his writings went far beyond psychoanalysis into science, philosophy, psychology, sociology, history, language, art, and political theory, Merleau-Ponty appeared never to tire of returning to the question of how psychoanalysis could be revised through a recasting of its philosophical foundations. In turn, psychoanalytic insights drawn concretely from a therapeutic praxis would, he believed, greatly enrich his philosophical clarification of human existence by expanding the philosophical understanding of the nonrational currents of our psychological life, the nature of relationships to other people, and the role they play in our ongoing behavior and self development. Merleau-Ponty (1960) often spoke of a convergence of purpose and complementarity of insights in the relationship between phenomenology and psychoanalysis. I will detail what some of the similarities and differences between these two approaches are later, when I compare self psychology with Merleau-Ponty's phenomenology. For now, let us simply say that Merleau-Ponty was no stranger to psychoanalysis; his work sponsors valuable outlines for a regrounding of psychoanalysis into a truly human scientific activity.

Kohut's self psychology, however, poses a special challenge to Merleau-Ponty's thinking. First of all, Merleau-Ponty knew and wrote about Freud's psychoanalysis. In contrast, contemporary self psychology has been seen as a vivid departure from this tradition, as well as from its successor in ego psychology. In short, self psychology expresses an important paradigm change for what may now be considered mainstream psychoanalysis (Atwood and Stolorow, 1984; Schwaber, 1979; Masek, 1986, 1987). As a new paradigm, self psychology has shown itself to be capable of assimilating and understanding old phenomena in a new way, *and* of including new phenomena originally expressive of a psychology of the self. All this is consistent with how Kohut (1984), in his last work, came to reassess the relationship of self psychology to its predecessors, especially ego psychology. Here, he abandoned the conservative appraisal advanced earlier in *The Analysis of the Self* (1971), that ego psychology and self psychology have a side-by-side complementarity to one another. In this view, ego-psychological metapsychology and treatment are appropriate to the range of classical drive/defense disorders, while the approach of self psychology aims at an understanding and treatment of self disorders. However, by the time Kohut (1984) was writing *How Does Analysis Cure*?, some 13 years later, his views on the relationship of self psychology to its predecessors achieved considerable expansion and transformation. He critiques his earlier viewpoint by characterizing it as a narrow appraisal of self psychology, written at a time when he was attempting ". . . to pour new wine into old bottles . . ." (p. 114), that is, to fit the often unique data of self psychology into mainstream metapsychology. By 1977, however, he had come to appreciate in self psychology an originality that could no longer be contained by established metapsychology. As he put it,

> . . . I came to the decision that I would have to reformulate the old theories decisively and that I required a terminology that

> was in harmony with the new interpretations of the clinical data that I had presented . . . [pp.114–115].

From this point on, Kohut speaks of the *superordinate* position of self psychology with respect to mainstream psychoanalysis. He concretely showed how this was so in his dual analysis of Mr. Z (Kohut, 1977, 1984). With respect to its predecessors, self psychology is capable of understanding and assimilating the data of ego and drive/defense psychologies, but the latter cannot do justice to the original data of self psychology. All this is at the heart of what Kuhn (1970) means by a paradigm change. When this occurs, old things are seen in a new light, and novel phenomena are appreciated and understood as original discoveries not possible through the preceeding paradigm.

If all this is so, then does Merleau-Ponty's phenomenology have anything new to say in a comparative dialogue with self psychology? Let us remember that the psychoanalysis that he knew and wrote about was drive/defense psychoanalysis, a moral psychology of "Guilty Man" (Kohut, 1977). Can Merleau-Ponty's phenomenology do justice to Kohut's clarification of "Tragic Man," for whom developmentally acquired *innocences*, rather than self deceptions, more faithfully describe many contemporary variations of disorder and health? Further, given the innovations and refinements of self psychology, its transformed way of seeing and altered metapsychology, does self psychology, like its predecessors, continue to need the "new philosophy" of which Hesnard spoke?

Our answers are in the affirmative to all these questions. My own reading of these issues is that what Merleau-Ponty had to say about Freud's psychoanalysis has implications for *all* of psychoanalysis, including self psychology (Masek, 1980). Second, I believe that Kohut's self psychology lends specific and concrete form to many of Merleau-Ponty's philosophical concepts, thereby enriching that philosophy in its consideration of many features of human existence. Finally, and perhaps most importantly, I will show that Merleau-Ponty's thought can, indeed, provide a *needed*, new philosophical foundation for self psychology. Throughout his writings, Kohut struggled with the problem of a philosophical foundation for self psychology. Like Freud's, his clinical discoveries often far outdistanced his ability to provide a metapsychological foundation that would faithfully ground and give understanding to those exciting discoveries drawn from practice. While Kohut, I believe, recognized many of the problems in this project and sketched out tentative solutions; the revision of a new philosophical foundation for self psychology is a project still to be completed. In summary, Merleau-Ponty's phenomenology and self psychology show a reciprocal need for one another.

Let me introduce psychoanalytic readers to Merleau-Ponty by first admitting that, among philosophers, he is probably less well known than Martin Heidegger to readers who are familiar with phenomenological revisions of psychoanalysis. Heidegger's (1927) *Being and Time* is perhaps the best known philosophical inspiration for variations of phenomenological psychoanalysis, beginning with the seminal work done by Binswanger (1975) and the later work of Boss (1957) and May (1958). *Being and Time* is an *ontological* position on the essence of human existence, in terms of its structures of Being. From this work, psychological scholars have drawn implications for a phenomenological psychoanalysis, a psychoanalysis regrounded on a philosophy of human, rather than natural scientific, existence. In contrast, Merleau-Ponty's work is especially relevant to a revision of psychoanalysis because, as a philosopher, he insisted on first moving through and clarifying the *epistemological* basis of psychology as a human science before he ever arrived at an ontology. Put differently, he saw a phenomenological interrogation of how we actually live our relations in the world through perceptual consciousness to be propadeutic to any ontological statement. Ontology presupposes perception in his view, and the chronology of his publications testifies to this route. In these respects, I have always believed that the psychology of Merleau-Ponty is more originally direct, sensitive to an empirical grounding in human science, and more expansive than those derived psychologies that pull from Heidegger as a basis for reformulating psychoanalysis. Nevertheless, Merleau-Ponty's thought is less well known to the analytic community at large.

MERLEAU-PONTY AND SELF PSYCHOLOGY: COMPARISONS AND CONTRASTS

Merleau-Ponty (1945) has suggested that phenomenology existed and was practiced as "a manner or style of thinking" long before it became formally recognized as a coherent philosophy (p. viii). Freud's psychoanalysis was one such place where Merleau-Ponty saw this style of thought at work. In saying this, he was also very careful not to see phenomenology and psychoanalysis as synonymous. Instead, he suggested that they show a convergence of purpose and complementarity of insights in how they follow their respective interests. Both, he says, aim at uncovering a more primordial "latency" in our lived existence—the unreflected, denied, inchoate, or ambiguous moments, which we *live out* but do not articulately *know* (Merleau-Ponty, 1960, p. 87). Freud's psychoanalysis, of course, does this by an interrogation of the unconscious, through an uncovering and analysis of this latency in the patient's associations, transference, resistance, dreams, and symptoms. Phenomenology, in turn, discovers its latencies by making visible our prereflective, actually lived through, concrete relations in the *Lebenswelt.* The aim here is to reflect systematically the inherent meanings and essential structure of those relations *in their own terms,* as they appear experientially, apart from the unexamined assumptions, personal prejudices, and privileged interpretations that make up the taken-for-granted "natural attitude" of everyday life. In this respect, Merleau-Ponty saw phenomenology and psychoanalysis converging in a common mission: to reflect the depths or, better still, the richness of our everyday life, and to restore those meanings to our understanding of self, other people, and the world.

Were Merleau-Ponty alive today, and writing, this time, about self psychology, I doubt that he would see the same convergences that he proposed with respect to Freud's psychoanalysis. One could, I suppose, maintain that these similarities are still applicable with respect to the relations between Merleau-Ponty's phenomenology and self psychology. But I see two problems with this. First, self psychology is not a psychology of the repressed, even though its interpretations take up the unreflected life of the patient in both the *understanding* and the *explaining* processes of the therapy (see Kohut, 1984, pp. 173–191). Second, if one maintains that "reflecting the unreflected" is the convergence, then self psychology would be indistinguishable from many other of the verbal therapies, for most verbal therapies address some version of the unreflected through what a therapist reflects in a patient's unrecognized life (Masek, 1984).

No, we must find new grounds more faithful to the specific nature of self psychology if we are to see its points of correspondence with Merleau-Ponty's thought. In the spirit of phenomenology, I have sought those grounds in an examination of the situation of self psychology—that is, in its origins, intentions, original clinical reflections, and self-understanding. One fundamental point of convergence, containing other overlapping similarities, emerged from this examination: *the centrality of perception.* Centering on this theme, then, our comparison between self psychology and Merleau-Ponty's phenomenology is meant to be fundamental and exemplary, rather than wide ranging and comprehensive.

CONVERGING THEMES IN MERLEAU-PONTY

Situating Merleau-Ponty Within Phenomenological Psychoanalysis

Traditionally trained analysts, originally drawn to a phenomenological approach, were motivated by an empirical intention. They sought a new, more certain basis in evidence, one that could faithfully reflect the nature of human phenomena and serve as a ground for the approach, theory, methods, and practice of psychoanalysis. They found that basis first in continental, phenomenological thought, in the projects of Husserl (1936) and Heidegger (1927) to clarify distinctly human existence by mirroring faithfully how it is first actually lived. From this point on, the *Lebenswelt* assumes the role of primary data in psychoanalysis through this theme: if we want to understand more clearly the concrete actions and experiences of our patients, then we must first recover and make explicit the individualized nature of their worlds, for both everyday action and experience presuppose the lived world. Stated clinically, psychological disorders first reflect a more fundamental deformation in the ontic dimensions of a person's existence, for example, the lived spatial and temporal contours of their existence. Thus, the expansiveness of manic patients directly reflects a more fundamental expansion in the lived space afforded to them—where the possibilities for thought and action are not constricted by genuine obstacles. In contrast, depressive styles disclose a constriction in the temporal horizons of the lives of those patients. Here, moral recriminations over the past eclipse the present and the future, thus making understandable the vegetative gravity of depression, its indifference to life beyond the present. The pathology here is a past that, by drawing its very life from the present and the future, refuses to be simply past. Recognizing all this, van den Berg (1972) says that, fundamentally, pathology is first a disorder of these and other dimensions of the patient's lived world, that *the patient's world is ill.* Accordingly, the move to a phenomenological approach, with its focus on the *Lebenswelt,* assumed central importance for psychoanalysts desiring greater clarity and certainty about their work.

How does Merleau-Ponty's phenomenology allow us to make contact with the life-world of our patients, so that we may make known the unnoticed foundation for understanding their concrete thoughts and actions? Access to the life-world means ultimately returning to the patient's perceptual relations, as those were lived spontaneously and often without explicit awareness. This is Merleau-Ponty's thesis of the *primacy of perceptual consciousness.* But this return is only possible by first challenging the apparent, conventional meanings of the patient's experience through the use of a procedure called the phenomenological reduction. Let me explain what this means. As we move through everyday life, we take for granted the way the world appears to us. We neither doubt the existence of that world, nor challenge the typical meanings that its objects and situations have for us. All this is taken for granted in the interest of carrying out our practical and theoretical motives, goals, and specific interests. But this world is already clothed and prearranged through presuppositions, institutionalized meanings, and stock interpretations derived from our cultural, social, educational, and personal experience, and this clothing already covers and objectifies the life-world, as a map preorders the landscape so that we may efficiently move through its terrain. From Husserl (1936) on, phenomenologists have referred to this as the "natural attitude," indicating our spontaneous, habitual, socialized orientation to daily life. Now, the problem that Husserl raises is how this attitude has come insidiously to replace our original, prereflective contact with things, such that their intrinsic meanings have become obscured if not lost. In his last work, Husserl (1936/1970) designated this a crisis in understanding, a problem in the very nature of the rationality that we bring to bear in understanding our cultural, social, scientific, and personal existence. Hence, scientific experience, and more specifically psychoanalysis, is bound up with this problem, for the natural attitude diffuses throughout perceptual experience as a whole. Knowing this problem, May (1967) asks how we can be sure that we are truly grasping the realities of our patients' lives, apart from our own unacknowledged assumptions, preferred orientations, and time-worn explanations. This problem includes, yet goes far beyond, the usual definition of countertransference.

In Merleau-Ponty's phenomenology, the phenomenological reduction is a systematic means for answering that question. First, as a general principle, Merleau-Ponty's reduction reveals a structure that expresses directly the person's uninterrupted presence—within-the-world *etre-au-monde.* These relations are first lived through what

Husserl (1936) called a *functioning intentionality,* and precede distinctions between real-unreal, objective-subjective, fact-opinion, or what Merleau-Ponty (1942) referred to as the "classical prejudices" of materialism and intellectualism, which explain person-world relations by reducing them to the action of the person *or* the world. Further, unlike Husserl, whose phenomenological reduction sees intentionality as the linking of specific noetic acts of consciousness to specific object, noematic presences, Merleau-Ponty (1964) discovers in our intentional relations an interrupted screening of our lived relations, available to the perceptually engaged subject. Seen this way, intentionally is perception, and perception is ". . . the theatre of all being . . ." as we directly inhabit it by being-in-the-world (p. 55).

The reduction is a two-phase, double reflection on what initially appeared through perceptual consciousness to a particular person as he or she lived through an actual situation (Merleau-Ponty, 1945). The first phase is a described inventory of the person's *phenomenal field.* The task is to describe, from within an attitude of open acceptance and wonder, what appears to perceptual consciousness apart from preconceptions, scientific characterizations, or preferred personal and social meanings. This first reflection is a move to recover the life-world as it was actually experienced and allows one to discover the individualized meanings of phenomena. The phenomenal field, however, is not self-contained or autonomous, is not like a photograph, which freezes the perceived world apart from its dynamic changes in lived time and space. What was immediately experienced radiates out to both past and future horizons of meaning, into the *transcendental field.* A second reflection, therefore, is required, which focuses on the extensions of phenomenal givens into not immediately experienced horizons and which makes explicit the concrete conditions that led to their origins in the relations *between* person and world. Accordingly, in principle, the reduction seeks to clarify questions about the individualized meaning of phenomena as well as their origins in the concretely experienced world. A rough analogy to this, I believe, is present in the intention, not necessarily the realization, of the psychoanalytic project to follow out unbiasedly an analysand's free associations from manifest to latent meanings (the descriptive question) and to discover the origins of those meanings in the life of that person (the genetic question). Too often, however, the presuppositions brought forward by psychoanalytic orientations compromise an unbiased execution of these operations.

In summary, the reduction reveals the world as "already there" for reflection to take up, such that the person now *knows* what has been experienced. Saying the world is already there does not imply a materialist vision that preexistent, fully constructed objects exist external to the subject and simply await perceptual illumination. No, the already-there quality (*Dasein*) of these relations denotes a person's lived bodily engagement with things, an inseparable union of person and world being lived out within dynamic alterations of lived time and space. This is the life-world, or as Merleau-Ponty (1945) prefers, *existence.* It is both anterior to and the condition for all reflected knowledge and is neutral with respect to its origins in person *or* world. Hence, human existence can only be described, not explained, through a reflective inventory of our prereflective life, of what we have actually lived through perceptually. The reduction is the royal road for this project yet is necessarily incomplete—"The most important lesson which the reduction teaches us is the impossibility of a complete reduction" (Merleau-Ponty, 1945, p. xiv). Assumptions and unseen perspectives always remain to some degree, for like perception itself, the reduction performs its inventory finitely within the dynamic flow of lived time and space. Seen this way, perception is the fundamental grounding of all knowledge, the precursor of all scientific, social, and personal ideas.

DISCUSSION

Self psychology and Merleau-Ponty's phenomenology converge on the necessity to read and understand what appears in its own right, apart from unexamined assumptions and established orientations. Further, each of these orientations recommends a return to nascent perception as the means to accomplish this project. But two important differences also exist between these two approaches and caution us from seeing them as synonymous with each other on this point.

First, how one systematically knows and sets aside philosophical, psychoanalytic, and social assumptions about the phenomena remains unclear in self psychology. We do know that, since Freud, psychoanalysis has shown a strong capability for handling those *personal* perspectives in a therapist's life, as they may prefigure his or her perception of the clinical data. Psychoanalysis accomplishes this through an examination of the countertransference in clinical supervision. But Kohut (1977, 1984) is equally sensitive to other sources that may compromise an empathic reading of phenomena. How can these be made explicit and set aside? Here I believe the work of Merleau-Ponty, and phenomenological psychology in general, can enrich the practice of self psychology and facilitate a greater realization of its stated intentions. Giorgi (1970), for example, has drawn out the implications of Merleau-Ponty's thought and framed them into a new, human scientific approach for psychology, in general, and the 25-year history of American phenomenological psychology has shown the effectiveness of a phenomenological approach for very specific and often diverse psychological phenomena. Accordingly, self psychology could profit greatly from an intimate dialogue on this point and, as I will show, on other issues as well.

The second point surrounds the degree to which fidelity to clinical phenomena is accomplished, given Kohut's (1977) stated recommendations for accomplishing this intention. I believe that his metapsychological theory does not always reflect accurately the intentions or practice of self psychology. Kohut (1977, 1984) brought forward the most liberal intellectual means at his disposal in struggling to depict what goes on in practice; nevertheless, a more radical characterization of the analyst's return to nascent perception is required if the intentions and practice of self psychology are to be in concert with its reflected theory. All this, I believe, rests on how observation is understood in analytic work. Let me expand on this.

One can argue strongly for the originality of self psychology, including its very starting point, the discovery of the self-selfobject structure (Masek, 1986, 1987). Especially toward the end of his work, Kohut (1984) came to see how original concepts and terms must be utilized to reflect both the originality of the phenomena discovered and the resulting alterations performed in analytic practice. Hence, I believe he adopted a variation of an *eclectic* position, in contrast to mainstream psychoanalysis, where observation is guided by aximoatic assumptions through which the observed is filtered, understood, and explained. We know that he wished to avoid the "empiricide" resulting from the latter and insisted on experience-near reflections in the understanding phase of therapeutic interventions. Accordingly, Kohut (1984) proposed this characterization of observation:

> [W]e must admit that strictly speaking, there can be no observation without theory. The number of explanatory configurations available to an analyst, in other words, will influ-

> ence the scope of his observations vis-a-vis a given patient. And if he is able to compare the explanatory power of a number of different configurations by *postponing* a definitive commitment either to a specific one of them or to a specific combination of them, he will ultimately be best able to explain to the analysand those experiential configurations mobilized in the therapeutic situation that are most relevant to his psychopathology [p. 96, italics added].

The point is also made earlier in the same source: The analyst must avoid seeing the patient through pregiven appraoches "*until* he has more accurately grasped the essence of the patient's need and can convey his understanding to the patient via a more correct interpretation" (p. 67; italics added). In short, a two-step process proceeds first through the analyst's observation of the events wherein empathic perception is maximized by a postponement of assumptive and theoretical commitments. This empathic-understanding phase is also supported by the longstanding psychoanalytic commitment, since Freud (1900, p. 620) to suspend consideration of *conventional reality* and to stay closely with the meanings expressed through the patient's first-person report of their *psychic realities.* Nevertheless, Kohut acknowledges the impossibility of suspending all influences, for, in his view, there can be no observation without theory. Now, once this understanding step has been accomplished, and assuming a developmental readiness of the patient to tolerate the experienced distance of explanatory formulations by the analyst, structural-genetic interventions drawing from pregiven theories may be employed. All this is so even when the interpretation is incorrect with respect to a self-psychological position. For example, Kohut (1984, pp. 97–98) showed this in his discussion of the Freudian and Kleinian interpretations of a case discussed by a South American colleague. Strictly speaking, then, fidelity to clinical phenomena is crucial to the understanding phase but not necessarily the explaining phase of self psychology, where an analyst may use many means at his disposal to express an understanding of the patient (Kohut, 1977).

Two problems accrue from this variation of eclecticism, which would be approached differently from a phenomenological psychoanalysis inspired by Merleau-Ponty. First, Merleau-Ponty would propose a more radical program for recovering lived experience than that advanced by Kohut. This phenomenology would be critical of Kohut's belief that observation without theory is impossible, although Merleau-Ponty would affirm Kohut's recognition that an *absolute* purity of perception is impossible, if one seeks to suspend *all* presuppositions or arrive at an exhaustive finality in the analyst's perception of events.

With respect to the reduction, Merleau-Ponty would consent to the inevitability of implicit horizons of interest that guide the analyst's empathic perception of events. He would point out that the analyst always occupies a finite perspective on the perceived, which, in turn reveals itself in profiles (*Abschattungen*) unfolding over time to the observer. All this is in contrast to positivism, which holds that objects present themselves as fully complete to perception—as though seen from everywhere and nowhere at the same time, without standpoint, perspective, or mutability depending on context. Instead, for Merleau-Ponty, what reveals itself phenomenally stands out figurally from the backdrop of lived existence in general, as ground in the Gestalt psychological sense is not explicitly visible in itself but nonetheless is always copresent as context giving all figures their dimensionality and depth of meaning. This is why Merleau-Ponty always speaks of the necessary incompleteness of the reduction. Situated, mutable moments of perceiving, what Husserl (1936) called the appearances, always unfold their significance over time in a growth toward clarity (*Erfullung*), and this takes place within implicit, contextualizing horizons that necessarily limit what we experience. Merleau-Ponty would have us appreciate both the clarity and the obscurity that perceiving has in its hold on the world. As he once said, "Nothing is more difficult than to know precisely *what we see*" (Merleau-Ponty, 1945, p. 58). Hence, what is true of perceiving is also true of the phenomenological reduction: some perspectives of what we experience at a point in time *necessarily* escape us and require the passage of time and later reflection, or the viewpoints of other people, for us to achieve greater clarity about their essential nature. Submerged assumptions, unseen perspectives of what we individually witness, and relative degrees of clarity and ambiguity are the rule, if we seek to clarify the perceived world as it presents itself. All these limits are inherent in perceiving. Given this, Merleau-Ponty would acknowledge the impossibility of a "complete" reduction on these grounds but would not consent to the inevitable presence of pregiven theory in nascent perceiving. Kohut's views on empathic observation would be seen as not radical enough in the light of his aim to remain true to the patient's experience, and I believe that other phenomenological psychologists would agree on this point.

This problem diffuses over into the self psychologist's movement from the understanding phase to the explanatory phase. Explanation is an altered mode of conveying to the patient that he or she is understood. Whereas therapeutic intervention centers on coinciding with the patient's first-person point of view, through affirming and clarifying it, explanation, while still remaining empathic, invites the patient to experience and take up the analyst's third-person point of view available through dynamic and genetic interpretations. Here, Kohut (1977) opens the door to the use of pregiven insights and theories, including self-psychological ones, which will contribute to the patient's understanding. Kohut's (1984) criterion of selection appears to be that these resources be drawn from other than a drive/defense outlook, and focus on the patient's self (pp. 97–98). Now, the problem is that these pregiven insights and theories contain their own presuppositions, both philosophical and otherwise, which may not be faithful to the nature of those phenomena originally read in the descriptive, understanding phase of the analyst's work. Hence, explanations may take on an empirically alienated status with respect to the primary, understood data, and diverge from both the intentions and practice of self psychology. I believe many specific instances of this problem occur, but I will concentrate on a more fundamental depiction by focusing on the question of how, for example, primitive, archaic, self-selfobject structures come to be constituted and lived out in the transference and everyday life situations. Let me make this point by tracing Kohut's movement from the descriptive to the explanatory phases to arrive at the issue of constitution.

The return to naive, empathic perceiving led Kohut (1984) to discover an original typology of patients' modes of relatedness to the analyst—mirroring idealizing, and twinship—and to characterize these modes within a fundamental concept, the self-selfobject bond, an indivisible union that originally and faithfully describes the patient's relationship to the analyst. At this level, Kohut (1984) is fundamentally descriptive, laying out *how* that relatedness appears and who it is that he as a person would have to be for the patient to be relating in these terms. But in the overall project to understand and restore the patient, the understanding-empathic phase is but one perspective on the patient, the other two being the dynamic and the genetic perspectives. These latter two take up the task of showing how enfeebled structures give rise to compensatory and defensive relations where features of other people, things, and situations become chronicly used as selfobjects, which provide missing functions in the patient's relations whereby an *equilibrium* is achieved in self-other relations, including the esteem one holds for oneself. In turn, the genetic perspective explores how these structures arose and were formed in the concrete relations between parent and child over time. All this is necessary in providing the understanding a patient needs and in facilitating the patient's willingness to appropriate and embody needed features of the analyst's overall presence as their (the patient's) own.

Here I believe Merleau-Ponty would be in accord with Kohut's intentions and his appreciation of what needs to be covered for understanding and change to occur. In self psychology Merleau-Ponty would likewise appreciate a commitment to remain faithful to how things are; he would support the foundational centrality of perceiving in self psychology and affirm its role in empirically grounding therapeutic action and self-understanding. He would respect Kohut's struggle to define metapsychological concepts in a language that faithfully depicts how these events were actually lived by the participants in psychotherapy. Above all, he would share Kohut's discovery that our individual lives are always self-transcendent, seen through the self-selfobject bond, which is an imperfect analogue to Merleau-Ponty's understanding of intentionality. But he would sharply take issue with Kohut's explanatory account of how these relations become constituted in therapy and everyday life.

Merleau-Ponty would see Kohut, in the explanatory phase, as abandoning direct experience as his guide by going outside it to explain it. Here, explanation abandons its therapeutic role—to expand understanding—and, instead, takes on a role indigenous to the early natural sciences: to explain causally the existence of something. Hence, Kohut (1971, 1977, 1984; Kohut and Wolfe, 1978) explains self-selfobject transferences as the result of developmentally archaic "selfobject representations," expressed by a self conceived from within the person. This philosophy runs throughout Kohut's mature thought.

In all this Merleau-Ponty would detect a philosophy, a manner of thinking, that has inhabited psychoanalysis from its first expressions in Freud's (1900) Kantian account of transference, projection, displacement, and the like, through contemporary self psychology. This way of thinking stems from an idealist-intellectualist tradition in philosophy and explains the constitution of our perceptual life by recourse to the projection of representations and memories already existent in the mind. In practice such thinking would say: if I notice the elliptical form in the presence of a dining plate, it is because my consciousness already contained this form and put it there (Merleau-Ponty, 1945).

Explanations drawn from this philosophy appear incapable of assimilating the peculiar manner through which concrete clinical phenomena are lived out and known in the analytic dialogue. For example, if selfobject representations constitute the transference and other phenomena, then how can we understand what analysts already know in practice: that their patients do not live out their transferences indiscriminately. They are lived out in some moments not all, with some people not all. In short, some situations become "preferred" (Merleau-Ponty, 1942) as occasions through which transference and other clinical events show themselves. Now, this implicit philosophy of self psychology cannot help us understand this exquisitely situated, differential expression of the transference because this philosophy cannot discriminate when from when-not. With this in mind, Merleau-Ponty would echo what we earlier presented as Hesnard's (1960) remarks about Freud's psychoanalysis: that it bursts the seams of traditional philosophies and requires a new one, more faithful to the events lived through in analysis.

Merleau-Ponty's own analysis would not take recourse in factors outside perceptual experience, nor would he approach the existence of phenomena through their explanation in the manner that I have criticized. He would tell us that if we really look, and allow ourselves to see, then we will find not an omnipotent subject, who constitutes the meaning of the events undergone in his experience, but a person inseparably immersed in situations that disclose varying meanings for him, that distinguish themselves as being the same or different from each other, and that contextualize the appearance of variations in forms of his behavior. Accordingly, understanding the constitution and variable expression of clinical behaviors means first taking radical recourse to faithfully reflecting the patient's world, as it appears in its own terms, as ground for that person's action.

For Merleau-Ponty, this means a radicality in our commitment to perceptual consciousness in both its *phenomenal* and *transcendental* moments, a commitment more radical than Kohut and his successors allow. This is so because we are originally dealing with relations and their meaningful structure unfolded over time, with forms of behavior and their lived contexts, not events and their isolated causes; and this would hold true with respect to our genetic questions, where the answer is already contained in the temporality of perceptual relations, not outside them.

I also believe that Kohut was aware of many of these problems, and the spirit of his work was to overcome them. For example, he (Kohut, 1984) wrote, "We need an orientation that acknowledges the analyst's influence, *in principle,* as an intrinsically human presence, not his influence via countertransference" (p. 37). Here Kohut recognizes that the analyst's presence presents the patient with many possibilities of meaning, which often go beyond conventional clinical foci in the analytic situation, but which nonetheless coconstitute the patient's behavior in it. While recognizing the significance of the analyst's presence, Merleau-Ponty would have us extend this openness to the meanings of the analytic situation, in general, as Barton (1974) has done. Likewise, in practice, Kohut takes partial recourse in the transcendental field in his recognition that selfobject transferences and resistances are situated in, and a reply by the patient to, the relationship—rather than being determined by drives, introjects, or internal object relations outside this context. He knows, in short, that self psychology can be understood only from within the contexts, undivided forms of behavior, and relations that are immanent in actual practice. But, for lack of an alternative philosophy of these relations, he innocently opens the door to borrowed theory and explanations outside the field of perception. Perhaps this is why Wertz (1985), for example, can rightly criticize features of self psychology's explanations while affirming its origniality of insights and direction in practice.

In conclusion, these problems have consequences for the consistency of self psychology—for its commitment to stay faithful to direct experience as evidence, for its use of empathic understanding as a ground for therapeutic effectiveness, and for the role of empathic perception as foundation for self-psychological theorizing and practice. Merleau-Ponty would concur with all these aims, but he would call for a more radical commitment to perception in the style that I have emphasized.

REFERENCES

Atwood, G. & Stolorow, R. D. (1984), *Structures of Subjectivity.* Hillsdale, NJ: The Analytic Press.

Barton, A. (1974), *Three Worlds of Therapy.* Palo Alto, CA: National Press Books.

Binswanger, L. (1975), *Being in the World,* ed./trans. J. Needleman. London: Souvenir Press.

Boss, M. (1957), *Psychoanalysis and Daseinanalysis.* New York: Basic Books, 1963.

Freud, S. (1900), The interpretation of dreams. *Standard Edition,* 5. London: Hogarth Press, 1956.

Giorgi, A. (1970), *Psychology as a Human Science.* New York: Harper & Row.

Heidegger, M. (1927), *Being and Time,* trans. J. Macquarrie & E. Robinson. New York: Harper & Row, 1962.

Hesnard, A. (1960), *L'Oeuvre de Freud et son importance pour le monde moderne.* Paris: Payot.

Husserl, E. (1936), *The Crisis of European Sciences and Transcendental Phenomenology.* Evanston IL: Northwestern University Press, 1970.

Kohut, H. (1971), *The Analysis of the Self.* New York: International Universities Press.

_____ (1977), *The Restoration of the Self.* New York: International Universities Press.

_____ (1984), *How Does Analysis Cure?* ed. A. Goldberg& P.E. Stepansky-.Chicago: University of Chicago Press.

_____ & Wolfe, E. (1978), The disorders of the self and their treatment: An outline. *Internat. J. Psycho-Anal.,* 59: 413–426.

Kuhn, T. (1970), *The Structure of Scientific Revolutions.* Chicago: University of Chicago Press.

Masek, R. J. (1980), The problem of approach in a psychology of the unconscious. Unpublished doctoral dissertation, University of Regina (Canada), *Diss. Abst. Internat.,* 42, 812 B.

_____ (1984), Phenomenology of the unconscious. In: *Exploring the Lived World,* ed. C. Aanstoos. Atlanta, GA: Darby Press, pp. 49–64.

_____ (1986), Self psychology as psychology: The revision of Heinz Kohut. *Theoret. Philosoph. Psychol.,* 6: 22–30.

_____ (1987), Reading psychoanalytic developments contextually: A reply to Bocknek on Kohut. *Theoret. Philosoph. Psychol.,* 7: 43–48.

May, R. (1958), The origins and significance of the existential movement in psychology. In: *Existence,* ed. R. May, E. Angel & H. F. Ellenberger. New York: Basic Books, pp. 3–36.

_____ (1967), On the phenomenological basis of psychotherapy. In: *Readings in Existential Phenomenology,* ed. N. Lawrence & D. O'Connor. Englewood Cliffs, NJ: Prentice Hall, pp. 365–376.

Merleau-Ponty, M. (1945), *The Phenomenology of Perception,* trans. C. Smith. New York: Humanities Press, 1962.

_____ (1942), *The Structure of Behavior,* trans. A. L. Fisher. Boston, MA: Beacon Press, 1963.

_____ (1964), Phenomenology and the sciences of man. In: *The Primacy of Perception,* ed. J. M. Edie (trans. J. Wild). Evanston, IL: Northwestern University Press, pp. 43–95.

_____ (1960), "Phenomenology and psychoanalysis," preface to Hesnard's *L'Oeuvre de Freud.* In: *The Essential Writings of Merleau-Ponty,* ed & trans. A. L. Fisher. New York: Harcourt Brace, pp. 81–87, 1969.

Schwaber, E. (1979), On the "self" within the matrix of analytic theory: Some clinical reflections and reconsiderations. *Internat. J. Psycho-Anal.*, 60: 467–479.

van den Berg, J. H. (1972), *A Different Existence.* Pittsburgh, PA: Duquesne University Press.

Wertz, F. J. (1985), Review of *Structures of Subjectivity. J. Phenomenol. Psychol.*, 16:95–107.

10

Psychoanalytic Phenomenology and the Thinking of Martin Heidegger and Jean-Paul Sartre

George E. Atwood

The significance of the existential philosophical systems of Martin Heidegger and Jean-Paul Sartre for psychoanalysis arises out of their concern with the nature of man as an experiencing being, situated in a world constituted by human purposes and meanings. The ideas and proposals of these philosophers pertain to the deepest level of our assumptions regarding subjectivity and thus are of profound relevance to any discipline focusing on the genesis and patterning of experience.

Two goals may be achieved through a critical discussion of existential thought from the vantage point of psychoanalytic phenomenology and self psychology. First, such a discussion can help to bring the philosophical assumptions underlying psychoanalytic studies more clearly into view. Second, the exploration offers an opportunity to illuminate the experiences of personal selfhood that lie at the origin of the philosophers' works. Progress on this latter task provides a partial context for discerning the particularization of scope associated with the philosophical formulations and thus for determining the limits of their applicability as foundational constructs for psychoanalysis and other human sciences.

The material that follows is organized into three sections. In the first, I offer a preliminary comparison of psychoanalytic phenomenology[1] with existential-phenomenological thought. The second section presents a detailed discussion of Heidegger's and Sartre's principal ideas regarding human nature and human subjectivity, together with reflections on the psychobiographical context of these ideas. The final section is devoted to a brief consideration of the nature and limitations of the contribution of philosophical phenomenology to psychoanalysis.

PSYCHOANALYTIC PHENOMENOLOGY AND EXISTENTIAL-PHENOMENOLOGICAL THOUGHT

Psychoanalytic phenomenology, understood as a discipline occupied with the illumination of meanings in personal experience and conduct, takes for its point of departure the concept of an experiencing subject. This means that at the deepest level of our theoretical constructions we are operating within a sphere of subjectivity, abjuring assumptions that reduce experience to a material substrate. This is in contrast to a theoretical position that would assign ontological priority to physical matter and interpret human consciousness as a secondary expression of material events. The development of knowledge in the sciences of material nature involves the organizing and interconnecting of human observations, which are experiences. Materialist schools of psychological thought, on the other hand, are based on a doctrine that *reifies* the concepts of natural science and then interprets consciousness as an epiphenomenal manifestation of those reifications.

The idea that an authentic science of human experience requires its own unique assumptions and methods and cannot rely on emulating the sciences of nature forms a central tenet of the existential-phenomenological movement. I am in agreement with this tenet, and especially with the phenomenological critique of the

[1]In speaking of psychoanalytic phenomenology I shall be referring to the framework of psychoanalytic ideas elaborated by Atwood and Stolorow (1984) and Stolorow, Brandchaft, and Atwood (1987). This framework, emphasizing the perspective of intersubjectivity, was profoundly influenced by Kohut's works (1971, 1977, 1984) and embraces his most central ideas. It nevertheless has other roots as well, including the hermeneutic tradition in the human sciences, structuralism, certain contemporary reformulations of psychoanalytic theory arising out of the critique of metapsychology (Klein, 1976; Schafer, 1976), and a series of studies of the subjective origins of theories of personality (Stolorow and Atwood, 1979).

doctrines of consciousness that descend from Lockean empiricism. Such doctrines rest on a view of man as the passive receptor of discrete, elemental impressions from the external world, an idea that body and mind are separate yet causally connected entities, and an interpretation of the nature of consciousness as a quasi-spatial container. These assumptions and metaphors involve a projection *into* experience of the qualities of material objects *of* experience and reflect a failure to confront the attributes of subjectivity in its own distinctive terms.

Although psychoanalytic phenomenology joins with the existential-phenomenological movement in affirming the need for an autonomous science of experience, there is one fundamental difference between the psychoanalytic approach and the phenomenological systems elaborated within philosophy. Psychoanalytic phenomenology is guided by observations conducted in the dialogue of the psychoanalytic situation, observations always made as part of an inquiry into the experiential world of a particular person. The phenomenological investigations of philosophers, by contrast, have traditionally relied on solitary reflection and have inevitably defocused the individualization of a world in the quest for knowledge of subjectivity in universal terms.

Correlated with the methodological isolation of philosophical phenomenology is a portrayal of relationships to others as intrinsically alienating affairs that threaten to take the person away from his own most essential, authentic nature. This negative philosophy of interpersonal life is also in contrast to psychoanalytic phenomenology and self psychology, wherein the relationship to the other is viewed as the sustaining matrix of personal selfhood at every stage of the life cycle. Although analysts are intimately familiar with those classes of interpersonal bonds that alienate and estrange a person from himself, they do not regard such effects as inevitable features of one's engagement with other persons. This difference of vision, mirrored by contrasting investigatory stances and methods, presents in my view the chief reason for the inadequacy of Heidegger's and Sartre's thought as a foundation for psychoanalysis.

HEIDEGGER AND SARTRE

I shall now turn to a specific discussion of the existential-phenomenological systems presented in Heidegger's (1927) *Being and Time* and Sartre's (1943) *Being and Nothingness*. These systems represent proposals for the understanding of human existence and human experience. I shall use a critical evaluation of these proposals to render the assumptions underlying psychoanalytic phenomenology more explicit. (see Atwood and Stolorow, 1984).

Martin Heidegger

Heidegger's contributions were made in the context of his lifelong quest for understanding of the meaning of being. Unlike his mentor, Edmund Husserl, whose central fascination was with the knowing subject or ego, Heidegger explored the problem of unveiling the nature of being as such. His magnum opus, *Being and Time* (1927), is an attempt to prepare the way for an understanding of being in general by clarifying the nature of a particular being—Man. Heidegger's analyses deal with the ontology of the person and are therefore relevant to a discussion of philosophical assumptions underlying psychoanalysis as a human science.

Heidegger refers to the mode of being belonging to the human individual as *Dasein* (being-there). He justifies the selection of Dasein as the proper approach to universal ontology by noting that there is a special relationship between the question of being and Dasein's essential nature.

> Dasein is an entity which does not just occur among other entities. Rather it is . . . distinguished by the fact that, in its very Being, that Being is an *issue* for it [p. 32].
>
> Dasein always understands itself in terms of a possibility of itself: to be itself or not itself [p. 33].

Concern with the issue of being defines both the sovereign theme of *Being and Time* and also the central distinguishing characteristic of Dasein. Heidegger's book displays an interesting relationship to itself in this connection: its portrait of man is a microcosm of the work itself, a sketch-in-miniature mirroring the concerns that motivate the philosophy as a whole. The inquiry into the nature of being, by defining Man as an entity for whom being is an issue, posits its own ontological motivation as an essential trait of being human.

The issue of being is a deeply problematic one in the world of Heidegger's thought, for at the heart of Dasein's nature lies a tendency to interpret its own being on the model of objects other than itself: "Dasein gets its ontological understanding of itself in the first instance from those entities which it itself is *not* but which it encounters "within" its world, and from the Being which they possess" (p. 85).

It is inherent in Dasein, according to Heidegger, to have a mistaken self-conception, to envision itself as something that in actuality it is not. In noting this self-estrangement, he claims to have identified one of Man's deepest ontological attributes: "The kind of Being which belongs to Dasein is . . . such that, in understanding its Being, it has a tendency to do so in terms of that entity toward which it comports itself proximally—in terms of the 'world' " (p. 86).

Substantial portions of *Being and Time* are devoted to explicating the attributes of Dasein in such a manner as to sharply distinguish it from the kinds of entities encountered in its world. Heidegger uses the term "existentialia" to refer to these attributes, differentiating them from the properties possessed by objects, which he calls "categories." His analysis thus runs in a direction counter to Dasein's inclination to fall back on its world and interpret itself in terms of that world. *Being and Time* circles reflexively on itself, in that the questioning of Dasein's being is itself explicitly taken as one of Dasein's modes of being. This book may therefore be understood as an effort *by* the particular Dasein embodied in Heidegger the person to distinguish itself from the world and assemble a representation of its own separate selfhood. We thus catch a glimpse here of a dominant form of Heidegger's own personal selfhood experience, an experience characterized by estrangement, vulnerability to the defining influences of the external milieu, and efforts to differentiate and separate from the milieu.[2]

The existentialia discussed by Heidegger form a system of interlocking "ontological structural concepts" referring to the a priori foundation of human existence. He arrives at these through an analysis of Dasein as it is seen in its concrete actuality or everyday-

---

[2]Heidegger's mentor, Edmund Husserl, was also a person in whom the isolated exploration of the nature of man's experiencing was associated with a vulnerability to becoming swept away from himself in falling under the influence of other people. One can discern the imprint of this vulnerability, and of Husserl's solution to it of withdrawal and disengagement, in the doctrine of the transcendental reduction (see the discussion of Husserl in Atwood and Stolorow, 1984, chapter 1). Sartre as well was haunted by a lifelong struggle with a feeling of inner nothingness and a tendency to become engulfed in other persons' perceptions and definitions of him. A recognition that this common context of personal subjectivity lies at the origin of the great phenomenological systems has significance from the perspective of the psychology of knowledge.

ness. The general term under which the existentialia fall is "being-in-the-world," where the hyphenation emphasizes the presence of an indissociable unity. This unity is meant to undercut the split between subject and object that has been traditional in Western philosophical thought. Being-in-the-world is characterized primarily in terms of that which it is not. Being-in-the-world is *not* the mode of being of entities other than Dasein; being-in is *not* a matter of one thing being inside another in physical space; and the world of being-in-the-world is *not* itself any kind of entity analogous to those Dasein encounters in its daily life. The worldhood of the world consists in its being the irreducible context that makes it possible for entities to show themselves and be encountered. The world is thus actually a property of Dasein's being, which is said to "have" a world.

Dasein is ontologically related to other entities by the attitude of care (*Sorge*). This kind of relatedness, involving human concern and meaning, is of an order altogether different from the mode of relatedness or interaction shown by things. Heidegger discusses two specific ways in which nonhuman objects are experienced: readiness-to-hand (*Zuhandenheit*) and presence-to-hand (*Vorhandenheit*). The former of these refers, broadly speaking, to man's relationship to tools or instruments, that is, objects encountered as subordinate means to reach intended goals. The latter pertains to objects seen in a way detached from pragmatic activity and refers to the mode of theoretical contemplation.

Being-in-the-world also involves what Heidegger calls "thrownness" (*Geworfenheit*), meaning that Dasein finds itself in circumstances, in a time and a place not entirely of its own choosing, delivered over to a situation that possesses an enveloping "thereness" or facticity. The world into which Dasein has been thrown includes not just the kinds of entities encountered as ready-to-hand and present-to-hand; also given as a constitutive element of the human situation is the existence of other Daseins. In Heidegger's thought, there is no isolated "I," or ego, such as the one which appears in Husserl's (1936) analysis of transcendental subjectivity. Being-in-the-world is inherently and indissociably a being-with-others. The attribute of being-with is described as another of the existentialia, and Heidegger again takes care to distinguish this characteristic from the kind of co-existence possessed by things in the realm of the present-at-hand.

> The phenomenological assertion that "Dasein is essentially Being-with" has an existential-ontological meaning. It does not

> seek to establish ontically that factically I am not present-at-hand alone, and that others of my kind occur. . . . Being-with is an existential characteristic of Dasein even when factically no Other is present-at-hand or perceived. Even Dasein's Being-alone is Being-with in the world. The Other can be missing only *in* and *for* a Being-with [pp. 156–157].

Being-with-Others is presented as a dimension of being-in-the-world, which has the property of alienating Dasein from its own true self. This is because Dasein's concern for others supposedly includes a constant care about how one differs from them. Such care disturbs being-with-one-another and gives rise to a tendency to become like others, to allow them to define who and what one should be.

> Dasein, as everyday Being-with-one-another, stands in *subjection* to Others. It itself is not; its Being has been taken away by the Others. Dasein's everyday possibilities of Being are for the others to dispose of as they please. . . . Being-with-one-another dissolves one's own Dasein completely into the kind of Being of "the Others" [p. 164].

The Others to whom one's autonomy is surrendered are collectively known as "the they" (*das Man*). The responsibility of defending one's independent selfhood is a heavy burden according to Heidegger, and Dasein therefore turns to the anonomous social milieu for the guiding directives of life. "The they" to which Dasein turns brings forth the self of everydayness, the "they-self" (*das Man-Selbst*), which is sharply distinguished from the so-called "authentic self." Heidegger claims that the constancy of identity experienced in ordinary social life is a manifestation of the dictatorship of "the they," which create an enduring they-self in collusion with Dasein's inauthenticity and failure to stand by its own deepest possibilities. The existential movement of becoming absorbed and lost in the publicness of "the they" is known as "falling" (*Verfallen*), and is described as the dominant state of being which belongs to man.

> [Falling into inauthenticity] amounts to a quite distinctive kind of Being-in-the-world—the kind which is completely fascinated by the "world" and by the Dasein-with of Others in "the they." Not-being-its-self functions as a *positive* possibility of that entity which, in its essential concern, is absorbed in a world. This kind of not-Being has to be conceived as that kind of Being

> which is closest to Dasein and in which Dasein maintains itself for the most part [p. 220].

In falling, Dasein falls away from itself into a state of groundless floating. This state is a tranquilizing one, for fallenness into the world has the sanction of "the they" and gives the appearance of being a secure and genuine mode of existence. But this drifting along is actually a drifting toward self-alienation in which one's ownmost potentialities and concerns become hidden and lost.

Falling may also be characterized as a fleeing, where the flight is from Dasein's own authentic nature as being-in-the-world. Heidegger introduces the concept of *anxiety* at this point to refer to the state of mind underlying falling. Anxiety is the opposite of the tranquilization of "the they"; it is the existential mood that individualizes Dasein and frees it for the realization of its most essential possibilities. Closely related to anxiety is the "uncanniness" (Unheimlichkeit) of authentic being, a sense of not-being-at-home, which Heidegger claims accompanies Dasein's union with its own deepest self. Falling numbs Dasein to the uncanniness of authentic selfhood, replacing anxiety with the tranquilized familiarity of everydayness. At the same time this uncanniness of being, which is escaped through embracing the they-self, is existentially a more fundamental attribute of Dasein's constitution.

Heidegger continues his explication of the a priori structure of human existence by taking up the relationship between authenticity and death as possibilities of Dasein's being. Dasein is wholly itself, according to his analysis, only when there is nothing left outstanding for it to be, only at its end, in death. An intimate bond is said to connect the reality of death as an existentially constitutive element of Dasein with the possibility of Dasein achieving a full and deep-ranging authenticity. This is because death is the one thing in one's possession that cannot be taken away: "No one can take the Other's dying away from him. . . . Dying is something that every Dasein itself must take upon itself at the time. By its very essence, death is in every case mine, in so far as it 'is' at all" (p. 294).

Heidegger's ontological descriptions show that he regards death as having the power to dissolve the they-self and liberate Dasein in its fullest authenticity.

> With death, Dasein stands before itself in its ownmost potentiality-for-Being. . . . If Dasein stands there before itself as this

> possibility, it has been fully assigned to its ownmost potentiality-for-Being. When it stands before itself in this way, all its relations to any other Dasein have been undone. This ownmost non-relational possibility is at the same time the uttermost one [p. 294].
>
> [In being-toward-death] it can become manifest to Dasein that in this distinctive possibility of its own self, it has been wrenched away from "the they" [p. 307].

Of course, it is possible for death to be incorporated into the superficial talk of "the they," in which case the individual's anxiety at confronting the inevitability of coming to an end is replaced with tranquilizing formulae such as, "Death certainly comes, but not right away" (p. 302). Such a formula, embraced in falling, defers the reality of death and covers up what is central in an authentic view of death's certainty—"that it is possible at any moment" (p. 302). Heidegger stresses again and again that death, by virtue of being a property of Dasein that cannot be appropriated by other Daseins, enables one to individualize himself and stake a claim to his ownmost being. By passionately seizing upon the inevitability of death, Dasein secures the foundation for living its life in an authentic and autonomous way.

> When, by anticipation, one becomes free *for* one's own death, one is liberated form lostness in ["the they"] and one is liberated in such a way that *for the first time* one can authentically understand and choose among the factical possibilities lying ahead of that possibility which is death [p. 308, italics added].

It is testimony to the extraordinary difficulty experienced by Dasein in existing authentically that it must resort to consciousness of death as a means for tearing free from others. In my view this reflects again the very precarious nature of Heidegger's sense of his own personal being and the impossibility of establishing and consolidating that sense through relationships with other people. Indeed, it often seems that Heidegger, in searching for a grounding of his own authentic selfhood, has seized upon the very precariousness of his self-experience as the ground and essence of his own true nature.

In the world of Heidegger's thought, the individual's relationship to his ownmost being or self is radically in question. In this context, his litany of the existentialia may be viewed as an effort by the specific Dasein personified in Heidegger himself to move away from alienation and falling and toward a representation of its own individual selfhood. Specifically, by identifying the supposed structural constituents of human existence and projecting these elements into the ontological foundation of human nature, this Dasein seeks to replace a sense of groundless floating with a picture of its own deepest roots. It is difficult to escape the impression of a certain emptiness in the results of this effort; one learns much more about what Dasein *is not* than about what it *is*. It sometimes even appears that the most essential positive characteristic of Dasein is the tendency to attribute to itself characteristics which in reality it does not possess.

The very existence of *Being and Time,* however, points to the presence in Dasein's essential nature of a countervailing tendency to throw off the disguises of falling. Heidegger labels the primordial inclination of Dasein to restore itself to itself "the call of conscience." Conscience is said to issue a call that pushes "the they" into insignificance and summons the self to its ownmost possibility of being-itself. This call comes forth from that same existential location which Dasein in falling seeks to escape, namely, the uncanniness of individualized being-in-the-world.

> Conscience manifests itself as the call of care; the caller is Dasein, which in its thrownness (in its Being-already-in) is anxious about its potentiality-for-Being. . . . Dasein is falling into "the they" . . . and it is summoned out of this falling by the appeal [p. 322].

The task of assessing the significance of Heidegger's *Being and Time* confronts the psychoanalytic theorist with a dilemma. This work is in the first place an investigation in ontology, aiming at clarifying the meaning of being as such. The question of the meaning of being, as I understand it, does not enter the field of concern of psychoanalysis, even at the level of pretheoretical assumptions. The analyst takes it for granted that man *is* and, further, that the nature of man's being can be studied productively without considering the problem of being in general. At the same time, psychoanalytic research is obviously not a philosophically neutral activity. It is based on premises about its subject matter, and these premises guide and delimit the investigations it undertakes.

There are at least two general ways in which the philosophical commitments of psychoanalytic phenomenology resemble those of Heidegger's existential analytic of Dasein. First, both inquiries begin with a conception of man as an experiencing being, situated in a world involving human purposes and meanings. Second, the contemporary analyst recognizes that man's interpretation of himself in terms of categories applying to material objects in his world effectively prevents his understanding of himself *as man.*

A divergence between Heidegger's analysis and the psychoanalytic approach appears, however, when we come to consider the finer details of the ontological characterization of Dasein. Heidegger singles out as a pivotal fact of human nature man's tendency to view himself, mistakenly, in terms of that which he is not. Human beings have, as one of their existential possibilities, the possibility of being depersonalized and estranged from their own nature. Such an estrangement indeed is exemplified in the objectifying images of man's nature that have dominated the human sciences in the 20th Century. But to locate this alienation in man's ontological constitution makes it something that must be presupposed by every inquiry into human life. Such a postulate unnaturally magnifies the significance of this one human possibility to the exclusion of all others, and confers upon the resulting vision of mankind a very specific, limiting focus. It is not the problem of being as such that interests the analyst, but rather the problem of understanding the varied forms of the *individual experience of being.* The elucidation of this experience takes place on an empirical plane, in studies of specific personal worlds and their development.

Heideggers' *Being and Time* cries out to be read from a psychobiographical as well as a philosophical perspective. Such a reading unveils a contribution of this work as a fascinating descriptive study of human self-estrangement. The ontology of Dasein may then be understood as a *symbol* of an anguished struggle for individuality and grounded authenticity in a world where one is in perpetual danger of absorption in the pressures and influences of the social milieu.

Jean-Paul Sartre

A phenomenological system bearing a resemblance to that of Heidegger appears in the philosophy of Jean-Paul Sartre. This system, which presents an ontology of consciousness, is developed most fully in the central work, *Being and Nothingness* (1943). The nature of consciousness, according to Sartre, is radically different from the nature of objects. Consciousness is a mode of being that exists *for* itself, whereas an object exists only *in* itself. The world of human existence is thus divided into two distinct and nonoverlapping regions: *being-for-itself* and *being-in-itself.* Being-for-itself is characterized by Sartre as composed of pure nonbeing, or nothingness. This is in contrast to being-in-itself, which is understood as a fullness or plenitude of being. No description of the for-itself is possible within the Sartrean framework except in terms of that which is not, namely, in-itself. The nothingness that constitutes the nature of consciousness is a matter of literal negativity and insufficiency, subsisting in the midst of the fullness of the world of things. Moreover, it is inherent in consciousness to be aware of its nature as incompleteness and nothingness.

> Consciousness is a being, the nature of which is to be conscious of the nothingness of its being [p. 86].
>
> The pure event by which human reality rises as a presence in the world is apprehended by itself as its own lack. In its coming into existence human reality grasps itself as an incomplete being [p. 139].

What is missing in the for-itself is a substantial foundation that would give it the positive characteristics of self-identity and permanence possessed by objects in the world of the in-itself.

Sartre writes that being-in-itself simply "is what it is," whereas being-for-itself "is what it is not and is not what it is." This formula is meant to emphasize that consciousness does not coincide with itself in the same manner that an object does. Whatever particular role or identity is assumed by a person, this identity is never identical to the person who has assumed it. For example, if a man is a cafe waiter, he is not a waiter in the same way a table is a table. He is being a waiter "in the mode of not being one." Human consciousness does not possess any features that would give it self-identity. "What the for-itself lacks is the self—or itself as in-itself. . . . The missing in-itself is pure absence" (p. 138). Not only does Sartre's philosophy make a sharp distinction between the for-itself and the in-itself, it portrays the for-itself as itself engaged in this same sharply differentiating activity. "The for-itself is perpetually determining itself not to be the in-itself and against the in-itself" (p. 134).

The concept of consciousness as a species of nonbeing is intimately tied to the Sartrean doctrine of man's *freedom.* Consciousness is regarded as a perpetual spontaneity, radically free in the sense that it determines itself at every instant and is never determined by anything external to itself. The objects constituting the realm of being-in-itself are subject to external causation, whereas consciousness is *no-thing;* it has no permanent features, no substantiality, and no casual dependence on things. It is in this context that one may understand the famous existentialist formula: "Existence precedes essence." If the for-itself had an essence or preexisting nature defining it and remaining constant throughout its vicissitudes, it would thereby join the world of things and become subject to the laws that govern the world of things. But it has no determinate nature or essence except the one it freely chooses, and each of its choices is vulnerable to overthrow and tranformation from one moment to the next. Man is thus separated from himself as he was and as he will be; stability and continuity through time are properties not of consciousness but of objects.

Sartre's emphasis on the radical freedom of consciousness is an expression of his more general tendency always to stress the differences between the for-itself and the in-itself. This differentiating, separating trend, however, is actually just one side of a dialectical struggle in which the for-itself is engaged; for man's recognition of his nothingness and his freedom does not lie peacefully upon him. A clear awareness of freedom means an acknowledgment that one is the absolute creator of himself and his destiny. The extraordinary responsibility implied by this role is felt as *anguish,* and a longing arises in consciousness to escape from freedom into the secure solidity and self-identity possessed by things in the world of the in-itself.

> [F]reedom, which manifests itself through anguish, is characterized by a constantly renewed obligation to remake the *self* which designates the free being [p. 73].
>
> We flee from anguish by attempting to apprehend ourselves . . . as a *thing* [p. 82].
>
> Everything takes place . . . as if our essential and immediate behavior with respect to anguish is flight . . . to fill the void which encircles us, to re-establish the links between past and present, between present and future . . . [We thereby seek] the absolute positivity of being-in-itself [pp. 78–79].

The flight from anguish through embracing the illusion of being thing-like Sartre calls *bad faith.* In the attitude of bad faith, the heavy burden of human freedom is lifted as man pretends to possess a determinate nature that he can hold responsible for who he is. The problem with the attempt to appropriate to the for-itself the positive attributes of the in-itself is that, were this project to succeed, the for-itself would be extinguished. A person can genuinely escape freedom—the ever-renewed responsibility for defining who he is—only in death. Consciousness is, therefore, trapped in an irresolvable contradiction: It is an insufficiency seeking to complete itself by adopting the permanence and substantiality of things, but its efforts in this direction are blocked by the grim fact that being permanent and substantial would also mean becoming inert and dead. "The being of human reality is suffering because it [can] not attain the in-itself without losing the for-itself. Human reality is therefore by nature an unhappy consciousness with no possibility of surpassing its unhappy state" (p. 140).

Being-for-itself moves in two directions with respect to the in-itself. It differentiates itself from things by affirming its freedom and acknowledging its nothingness, and it attempts to identify itself with things by fleeing from anguish and engaging in acts of bad faith. This to-and-fro movement between being and nonbeing lends a tragic dimension to human existence. Its goal is to achieve a state that actually is impossible, namely, a transcendent fusion of the spontaneity of consciousness with the substantiality and permanence of objects.

> [This state would be] the impossible synthesis of the for-itself and in-itself; it would be its own foundation not as nothingness but as being and would preserve within it the necessary translucency of consciousness along with the coincidence with itself [self-identity] of being-in-itself [p. 134].

It is my impression that Sartre's writings contain a hidden attempt to achieve the "impossible synthesis" of being-for-itself and being-in-itself. This attempt appears in the reification of the concept of nothingness, that is, the transformation of the absence of the attributes of a thing into a literal gap or insufficiency in the universe, a hole in the fabric of the world presented as man's true nature. The conception of the for-itself as an *actual lack of being* places consciousness on the same factual plane of reality occupied by the tangible substances of the in-itself. The doctrine of the radical freedom of the subject may be interpreted as an elaboration of this conflict-reducing reification. In a striking contradiction of his thesis that man has no essence that precedes his existence, Sartre posits freedom as the *essential* feature of human consciousness. By visualizing man's nothingness as freedom, he changes a supposed lack of definition and temporal continuity into a permanent, positive characteristic of human nature. This change has the added effect of conferring upon consciousness an enduring self-identity.

A third category of being is also extensively described by Sartre, and is of utmost significance in understanding and evaluating his conception of the human situation. This is the category of *being-for-others.* The for-itself, in its apprehension of other persons, regards them as objects in its experiential field. The subjective consciousness belonging to a a person can never be directly known except by the person himself; what it is *for itself* is radically different from what it is *for others.* In addition, consciousness cannot directly know the self that it is for-the-Other, because this self comes into being only as the object of the other's awareness: "I am incapable of apprehending for myself the self which I am for the Other, just as I am incapable of apprehending on the basis of the *Other-as-object* which appears to me, what the Other is for himself" (p. 327).

The consequences of the "objectness" of being-for-others include a severe threat to the continued life of the for-itself as an autonomous center of freedom. When a person comes under the gaze of another, he grasps the other as a freedom that constitutes a world of meanings and possibilities around itself. This understanding may then extend to a sudden recognition that he is himself in the process of being articulated within the structures of that alien world, which threatens to displace his own and absorb him into pure objectness. He senses a foreign outline being imposed upon his nothingness, and without knowing what this outline is he feels himself being stripped of his subjectivity and transformed into an object: "[O]nce more the in-itself closes in upon the for-itself. . . . I have an outside, I have a *nature*" (p. 352). When one is made the object of the other's look, an "internal haemorrhage" occurs in one's subjective world, which then flows in the direction of the other's freedom. Sartre describes this relationship of one consciousness to another as analogous to slavery.

> I am a slave [to the other] to the degree that my being is dependent at the center of a freedom which is not mine and which is the very condition of my being . . . insofar as I am the instrument of possibilities which are not my possibilities, whose pure presence beyond my being I cannot even glimpse, and

> which deny my transcendence in order to constitute me as a means to ends of which I am ignorant—*I am in danger.* This danger is not an accident but the permanent structure of my being-for-others (p. 358).

It is worth remarking that Sartre finds in this endangerment of being-for-itself a "permanent structure," that is, a tenuous yet enduring way in which personal consciousness does achieve its longed-for state of self-identity.

The response of being-for-itself to the threat of reduction to the status of an object in being-for-others is to deny the freedom of the other by reducing *him* to an object. "The objectivation of the Other . . . is a defense on the part of my being which, precisely by conferring on the Other a being-for-me, frees me from my being-for-the-Other" (p. 359).

The loss of freedom and the imprisonment of subjectivity in being-for-others is vividly symbolized by the image of damnation in Sartre's play *No Exit* (1946). Here the principal characters are condemned for eternity to know themselves only through the frozen images they have of one another's odious lives. Human relationships are thus pictured as never-ending battles between competing subjectivities struggling to strip each other of freedom and reduce each other to objects.

Deep insight into the personal background of this image of interpersonal life can be gained from a reading of Sartre's autobiographical fragment, *The Words* (1964). This book, devoted to his early years, contains rich descriptions of a childhood dominated by Sartre's experiences of being superfluous to others, inauthentic in his conduct, and devoid of content within himself. One gains the overpowering impression from these descriptions that Sartre's personal sense of nothingness was rooted in severe empathic voids in his relationships with early caregivers. One also sees how closely his later descriptions of the various struggles of being-for-itself mirror his lifelong efforts to avoid enslavement by others and establish a sense of his own autonomous identity. (See Atwood, 1983, for a detailed discussion of the psychobiographical context and meaning of Sartre's ideas.)

In the theoretical world of Jean-Paul Sartre, the subjective being of the individual is perpetually threatened by the objectivating, engulfing power of alien consciousness. This image of interpersonal life is one in which the person is constantly being absorbed into roles with which he cannot truly identify. His treatment of social relationships does not include the possibility of being empathically understood in such a manner that one's sense of self is mirrored and enhanced rather than ensnared and degraded. This omission is of great significance, for once the experience of such empathy is introduced into the structure of being-for-others, the tensions and conflicts that plague the for-itself undergo a complete transformation. Social life ceases to be a battleground of competing subjectivities locked in a life-and-death struggle to annihilate one another. The relationship to the other becomes instead a realm of experience in which one's personal selfhood can rest secure, indeed, in which it can be powerfully affirmed.

Psychoanalytic methods and ideas could never arise out of Sartre's ontology of consciousness, because psychoanalysis is a science of the intersubjective, grounded in empathic dialogue between two persons. The analyst presupposes that he *can* apprehend what he is for-his-patient and also what his patient is for-himself; it is further assumed that this understanding can develop in a collaborative endeavor posing no intrinsic threat to the self-definitions of the persons involved. In a psychotherapeutic relationship patterned consistently on the principles of *Being and Nothingness,* by contrast, the analyst could encounter his patient only as the carrier of an alien and hostile world, a dangerous enemy to be neutralized through reduction to the status of an object.[3]

I would also take exception to the notion of freedom developed in Sartre's philosophy. The problem with this idea is that it elevates a specific attribute of self-experience to an ontological level of man's being, making it something that must be assumed to be present at the heart of every person's world. The doctrine of the radical freedom of the subject renders Sartre's framework incapable of adequately describing and accounting for human situations in which this experience is not the central one. Moveover, by locating spontaneity and autonomy in the very essence of consciousness, his thought deters the pursuit of questions about the developmental origins and vicissitudes of the experience of personal freedom. The study of such questions is an important part of the psychoanalytic quest for understanding of the genesis of human selfhood.

Sartre's writings nevertheless contain a significant contribution

---

[3]Perhaps this is one of the functions of objectifying metapsychological and diagnostic formulations in clinical practice: to create distance from the patient and thereby protect the clinician from being swept into the vortex of the patient's subjective world.

to psychoanalytic knowledge. The philosopher Charles Hanly (1979) hints at the nature of this contribution with his interesting suggesting that Sartre's theory of consciousness applies more clearly to the psychological disorder known as the "as-if personality" than to human subjectivity in general. *Being and Nothingness* may be read as a richly elaborated phenomenology of those subjective states in which a lack of full consolidation of the structure of self-experience results in the problem of self-definition becoming the person's central preoccupation.

PHILOSOPHICAL PHENOMENOLOGY AND PSYCHOANALYSIS

The phenomenological systems reviewed here are proposals concerning the assumptions underlying the study of human experience. These proposals have in common an emphasis on differentiating between the properties of material objects in the world of experience and the properties of subjectivity itself. This same emphasis has been of growing importance in recent psychoanalytic thought, specifically in the critique of Freudian metapsychology. It seems to me that this agreement establishes the possibility of an integration of phenomenological insight into psychoanalysis. In the past there were two main obstacles to such integration. The first of these was the commitment of analysts to a vision of their field modeled on the image of the natural sciences. This commitment is enshrined in the metaphorical language of classical metapsychology, which pictures mental life in terms of forces, energies, mechanisms, and a reign of causal determinism. The second obstacle was an insufficiently critical attitude toward the phenomenological philosophers themselves. Many exceptional thinkers have tried to restructure the assumptions of psychoanalysis along existential-phenomenological lines (e.g., Binswanger, 1963; Boss, 1963, 1979; May, Angel, and Ellenberger, 1958). I am in sympathy with such reformulations, insofar as their aim has been to free the phenomenological knowledge of psychoanalysis from its procrustean bed of mechanism and determinism. Limiting the success of so-called existential analysis, however, has been its tendency to import uncritically into psychoanalytic theory philosophical concepts and categories not genuinely grounded in clinical observation. To introduce Heidegger's or Sartre's ontology in place of Freud's assumptions, for example, appears to me of questionable value in advancing psychoanalytic knowledge as a whole. Especially problematic in the philosophers' portrayals of human existence are their visions of social life as intrinsically alienating the individual from his own authentic self. This negative picture of the interpersonal dimension of existence is not just a detail of the philosophical systems, which could perhaps be modified. The picture radiates throughout the systems, conferring upon them much of their distinctive structure and content.

REFERENCES

Atwood, G. E. (1983), The pursuit of being in the life and thought of Jean-Paul Sartre. *Psychoanal. Rev.,* 70:143–162

_____ & Stolorow, R. D. *Structures of Subjectivity.* Hillsdale, NJ. The Analytic Press.

Binswanger, L. (1963), *Being-in-the-*World. New York: Basic Books.

_____ Boss, M (1963), *Psychoanalysis and Daseinsanalysis.* New York: Basic Books.

(1979), *Existential Foundations of Medicine and Psychology.* New York: Aronson.

Hanly, C. (1979), *Psychoanalysis and Existentialism.* New York: International Universities Press.

Heidegger, M. (1927), *Being and Time.* New York: Harper & Row, 1962

Husserl, E. (1936), *The Crisis of European Sciences and Transcendental Phenomenology.* Evanston, IL: Northwestern University Press, 1970.

Klein, G. (1976), *Psychoanalytic Theory.* New York: International Universities Press.

Kohut, H. (1971), *The Analysis of the Self.* New York: International Universities Press.

_____ (1977), *The Restoration of the Self.* New York: International Universities Press.

_____ (1984), *How Does Analysis Cure?* ed. A. Goldberg & P. E. Stepansky. Chicago IL: University of Chicago Press.

May, R., Angel, E. & Ellenberger, H. (1958), *Existence.* New York: Basic Books.

Sartre, J.-P. (1943), *Being and Nothingness.* New York: Washington Square Press, 1966.

_____ (1946), *No Exit.* New York: Knopf, 1947.

_____ (1964), *The Words.* New York: Braziller.

Schafer, R. (1976), *A New Language for Psychoanalysis.* New Haven, CT: Yale University Press.

Stolorow, R. D. & Atwood, G. E. (1979), *Faces in a Cloud.* New York: Aronson.

_____ Brandchaft, B. & Atwood, G. E. (1987), *Psychoanalytic Treatment.* Hillsdale, NJ: The Analytic Press.

11

Carl Rogers and Heinz Kohut
On the Importance of Valuing the Self

EDWIN KAHN

I have studied the similiarities and differences between the work of Heinz Kohut and Carl Rogers with the aim of developing a constructive collaboration between the two theorists (Kahn, 1985, in press). I contend that some of Kohut's essential discoveries, especially those related to the therapeutic "ambience," were preceded by those of Rogers. Moreover, recent attempts to further separate Kohut's work from its classical psychoanalytic origins (Stolorow, 1986) have brought the therapeutic approach of self psychology even closer to Roger's client-centered approach. It is true that Kohut's therapeutic goal of strengthening the self by way of the self's belated maturation in the psychotherapeutic relationship has gone an important step beyond Rogers's therapeutic goal of congruence, which seems identical to Freud's aim of making what was unconscious conscious (Kahn, 1985, in press). Also, Kohut's theorizing has provided extraordinarily helpful explanations for a person's "maladaptive" or "unwholesome" behaviors, explanations that Rogers's approach lacks. On the other hand, Rogers's long-time stress on the primacy of the human, genuine quality of the therapist-patient interaction is an attitude that analytic self psychology is accepting more and more.

SUMMARY OF ROGERS'S VIEWS

The basic philosophical assumption of client-centered therapy is that there is an "actualizing tendency" present in the human organism; that is, the organism has "a tendency to grow, to develop, to realize its full potential" (Rogers, 1986, p. 127). The fact that an infant will "learn painfully to walk when crawling would meet the same needs more comfortably" (Rogers, 1959, p. 196) is one illustration of this actualizing tendency. Rogers felt that a specific nurturing climate, consisting of three conditions, is necessary for this actualizing tendency to fully reveal itself. The first condition is a prizing of, acceptance of, or a nonpossessive caring for the other, what Rogers often referred to as an "unconditional positive regard." Rogers (1980) said.

> When the therapist is experiencing a positive, acceptant attitude toward whatever the client *is* at that moment, therapeutic movement or change is more likely to occur. . . . [T]he therapist is willing for the client to be whatever immediate feeling is going on . . . the therapist prizes the client in a total rather than a conditional way [p. 116].

A second facilitative aspect of the relationship is an empathic understanding of the other.

> When functioning best, the therapist is so much inside the private world of the other that he or she can clarify not only the meanings of which the client is aware but even those just below the level of awareness. . . . This kind of sensitive, active listening is exceeding rare in our lives. We think we listen, but very rarely do we listen with real understanding, true empathy [p. 116].

The third condition, according to Rogers, is that the therapist be with the client in a real, genuine, and human way. "The more the therapist is himself or herself in the relationship, putting up no professional front or personal facade, the greater is the likelihood that the client will change and grow in a constructive manner" (p. 115). According to Rogers (in Kirschenbaum, 1979, pp. 200–201), these three attitudes constitute the necessary and sufficient conditions for personality growth. Rogers also distinguished client-centered therapy from the "person-centered approach," the latter referring to the application of the same assumptions and attitudes outside of the therapeutic situation, in, for example, the family, education, business, and—an area that occupied him considerably prior to his death—international relations.

In a classic article, Rogers (1959) detailed his theory of personality adjustment. He distinguished between the experience of the "self" and "organismic experience." Self-experience consists of the perception of the characteristics of the "I" or "me" that exists in consciousness or awareness, while organismic experience is what a person is actually feeling at a gut level. Adjustment, in Roger's view, is associated with being congruent. Congruence occurs when all experiences in one's organism are accessible to the self or awareness. When a person experiences unconditional positive regard, empathy, and genuineness from others, then the self of that person will have access to all experiences, because the person knows that no matter what he or she thinks or feels, he or she will be valued and understood. This ability to experience in awareness all organismic experiences constitutes congruence.

Incongruence, which is associated with maladjustment, occurs when a person is treated with "conditional love," or what Rogers called "conditions of worth." In this situation, certain experiences of the person are disapproved of by others, such as parents, and these disapproved experiences become inaccessible to the self—they are either denied or distorted in awareness. Thus, incongruence is associated with the defensive denial or distortion of organismic experiences. In client-centered therapy, the therapist provides unconditional positive regard and empathy, while being genuine and real. In such a facilitative atmosphere, the client no longer has to defend against the previously disapproved of experiences; these experiences are now accepted and understood by the therapist. Therefore, gradually, all experiences gain accessibility to awareness or self, and, as a result, the person becomes congruent and adjusted. Also, Rogers believed that by receiving unconditional positive regard the person would gain increased "positive self regard," becoming able to accept himself or herself more completely. Rogers often stressed that interpretations are not necessary in the process of widening awareness (see Interpretations, and the Medical Model, this chapter). Because of the actualizing tendency, all that isnecessary is the nurturing climate of acceptance, empathy, and genuineness.

THE SELFOBJECT AND TRADITIONAL POSITIVE AND NEGATIVE TRANSFERENCES

For some time I was perplexed about the issue of selfobject transferences, as described by Kohut (1977, 1984), and how they differed from traditional positive and negative transferences. Let's assume that a person enters therapy, who, throughout his development, was frequently criticized by his parents. It is reasonable to predict that he would also expect to be criticized in the therapy situation, and this expectation would clearly constitute a transference. But, what if because of the delightful, newly experienced empathic attunement of the therapist, the patient begins to idealize the therapist. Does this idealization properly constitute a "transference"? After all his parents were critical and rarely gave him the opportunity to idealize them. Is he "transferring" onto the therapist feelings he had toward important people in his early development, or, rather, is the therapist giving him the opportunity to express an *inborn idealizing need* that he only rarely had the opportunity to express before?

Kohut, in the early phase of his work on self psychology, did *not* refer to these archaic psychological needs as transferences. In his seminal paper on introspection, empathy, and psychoanalysis, Kohut (1959) said, when describing addicts.

> their addiction must not, however, be confused with transference: the therapist is not a screen for the projection of existing psychological structure; he is a substitute for it . . . the patient now really needs the support, the soothing of the therapist. His dependence cannot be analyzed or reduced by insight; it must be recognized and acknowledged [p. 225].

Thus, Kohut's position in this early paper is that the patient really needs the support and soothing of the therapist, and that analysis is not necessary.

Later, after formulating the concepts of idealizing and mirroring transferences, Kohut (1971) still questioned whether these were legitimate transferences. He wrote:

> In the specific regression which takes place in the analysis of such patients the analysand becomes addicted to the analyst or to the analytic procedure, and—although in the metapsychological sense of the word, the term transference may not be fully

> correct here—one might say that the transferencelike condition which establishes itself in such analyses is indeed the reinstatement of an archaic condition [p. 46].

And elsewhere in that work he said, "Here I shall bypass taking sides concerning the decision whether the narcissistic transferences are transferences in the strict metapsychological sense of the word" (p. 205). Although in self psychology transference continues to be the accepted term for the expression of these inborn psychological needs, the question may still be asked whether it is the most accurate or most helpful term to use.

From Kohut's and Rogers's work, it may be hypothesized that, instead of Freudian innate sex and aggressive instincts, the young child is born with *innate psychological needs*, or selfobject needs, such as the need to be mirrored, be listened to, be cared about, be understood, be treated with positive regard, be treated genuinely, have someone to idealize as a source of calming strength, and the like. The two traditional categories of transference, then, may be conceptualized as follows:

Negative transferences, which are *completely learned* from unempathic parental responsiveness. Anger and hostility are the natural responses to the lack of empathy in early development, and this anger and hostility is intrapsychically available to be expressed toward the therapist when he or she, in some inevitable, minor way, is unempathic or is just naturally carrying out the analytic procedure by setting time limits, collecting fees, or having relatively more power (Rogers, 1977) in the therapeutic relationship. These negative transferences, then, do not stem from any inborn need, such as an innate aggressive drive; rather, they are completely learned from the empathic failures of the past. It is important to note that anger and hostility occur as responses to lapses of empathy in all human relationships (see, for example, Rogers, 1977, pp. 133–134); what distinguishes the negative transference in the therapeutic situation is the excessive intensity or duration of the reaction. Moreover, negative transferences do not come out of the blue; they are usually set off by some stimulus. When the therapist is attuned to the patient and the patient's needs, the patient is unlikely to react angrily. Another complicating factor is that a patient's excessively hostile reaction may not only be explained by transferred anger, but also be attributed to the immaturity of the patient's self; that is, as a result of arrested development the self is unable to control or modulate its annoyance at empathic failures. At some point in therapy, these negative transferences may become suitable for analysis; that is, their origins from childhood deficits in empathy can be usefully explored.

Positive transferences, which originate from the *inborn* selfobject needs of the person. As noted, it may be assumed that there are innate psychological needs in the young child, such as the need to be mirrored, be treated with positive regard, be treated genuinely, be understood, be consistently cared about, have someone to idealize, and so on. Positive transferences probably originate from these *inborn psychological needs,* which have been either optimally satisfied (as in reasonably healthy development) or insufficiently or inconsistently satisfied (as in developmental arrest). Selfobject needs probably have not been responded to optimally during the development of patients who enter psychotherapy. These needs have been occasionally, or at least partially, satisfied in the past, and this inconsistent attunement provides the basis for the positive transference; it is very likely, however, that important empathic failures have occurred. In the therapeutic relationship, the selfobject needs are responded to in a more consistent way than ever before. This optimal responsiveness (Bacal, 1985; Miller, 1985; Terman, 1986) to the selfobject needs of the patient elicits the positive transference. Again, the basis for the positive transference is the occasions in the past when the patient received an appropriate response to his or her inborn selfobject needs, for example, the need to be understood and accepted. It may be that the genetic interpretations of the analyst are to some extent effective because they too contribute to satisfying these inborn needs.

In conclusion, the most essential element for the therapeutic growth of the person may be the therapist's consistently caring and understanding attitude, his or her real presence in the life of the patient (Rogers, 1986), so that the patient's *inborn psychological needs,* which, up to the present, have not been adequately responded to, can at long last be optimally satisfied. The needs that require satisfaction probably include those that Kohut (1984) and Rogers (1959) wrote about—the need to be mirrored, to be treated with empathic understanding, to be treated with positive regard, treated genuinely, to be consistently cared about, and to have someone to idealize as a source of calming strength. The designation selfobject transference may be inadvertently misleading, since the term implies that these needs can be removed through "analysis" or "insight," when, in fact, what the needs may require is an optimal responsiveness (Bacal, 1985).

ON THE IMPORTANCE OF BOTH THE "REAL" AND THE "TRANSFERENCE" RELATIONSHIP*

John M. Shlien (1987), a modern client-centered theorist, has argued that the concept of transference is, for the most part, a fiction and that often the concept is used by therapists as a defense mechanism "to protect themselves from the consequences of their own behavior" (p. 15). Shlien presented a fascinating appraisal of Breuer's interaction with Anna O. He noted that given the circumstances of their relationship—a lonely young woman and a respected, somewhat older physician, who visited her daily, fed her, allowed her to hold his hands when she could not see, and even took her for carriage rides with his daughter—it is not surprising that she developed erotic feelings. Shlien also felt that so-called negative transferences are often precipitated by misunderstandings of the patient of which the therapist is unaware. Shlien believed that it is only understanding that heals, and he distinguished between understanding in "real life in ordinary relations and equally real life in therapy," and said that in real life outside of therapy "we do not devote the considerable or sometimes near-consuming effort to understand fully" (p. 45). Rogers (1987), in agreement with Shlien, said, "When the therapist's understanding is accurate and his acceptance is genuine, when there are no interpretations given and no evaluations made, 'transference' attitudes tend to dissolve, and the feelings are directed toward their true object" (pp. 186–187).

Before we proceed further, several terms should be defined. Gill (1982) noted that there has been some confusion about the concept of transference in the analytic literature. Some analytic investigators restrict the use of transference (and countertransference) to "the distortion of a realistic patient-analyst relationship by additions from past unconscious and repressed object relations" (A. Freud, quoted in Gill, 1982, p. 12). This definition involves only the transferring of material that is inappropriate to the present, such as negative and erotic feelings. According to Gill, Freud, however, included in the transference not only the repetition of the repressed material that is inappropriate to the present, but also conscious and

*Portions of this section originally appeared in the *Person-Centered Review* (1987), 2:471–475.

appropriate elements, such as the friendly feelings that make up the unobjectionable positive transference and that do not require analysis.

Self psychology has stressed the importance of the analyst as a real person in the relationship, that is, as a person who serves important selfobject functions for the patient. Despite this emphasis on the analyst as a real person in the relationship, Kohut (1984) maintained that "self psychology does not advocate a change in the essence of analytic technique. The transferences are allowed to unfold and their analysis . . . occupies, now as before, the center of the analyst's attention" (p. 208). More recently, Stolorow (1986), in his critique of Kohut's work, said "the analysis of transference . . . produces the greatest yields in both maximizing our therapeutic effectiveness and advancing our psychoanalytic theories" (p. 401). However, I wonder, in partial agreement with Shlien, whether the transference is the primary therapeutic vehicle. Or, rather, is the primary therapeutic vehicle the real empathic relationship between two people?

In an ideal therapeutic moment, a therapist will understand his or her patient optimally, as part of a real, genuine human interaction (Rogers, 1951). The therapist will be willing to supply information about himself or herself so that the patient may be willing to do likewise. Wolf (1983) said, "The analyst may reveal that he or she is ignorant or clumsy in attempting to understand the analysand, or perhaps, the analyst's own selfobject needs may seek some surcease in the psychoanalytic situation, even at times using the patient as a selfobject" (p. 500). In such a context the patient may gain "courage from these self-revelations of the analyst to know that the analyst does not need to feed on the patient to achieve cohesion and harmony" pp. 500–501). Surely each of the two participants in the process is transferring experiences and feelings from the past into the present, and these experiences and feelings, from one perspective, constitute "transferences." These transferences are certainly readily apparent in the therapeutic situation, as when one patient may idealize, while another devalues the same therapist. However, when the empathic interaction is ongoing and real, there is no need to explain or account for the transferred material from the past. As a matter of fact, considering a genuine interaction as the medium for the transference is both distancing and distracting (Rogers, 1986, pp. 132–133). Focusing on the transference diverts attention from the constructive human interaction of the moment, which may be the most important facilitator of growth (Rogers, 1951, 1959,

1986), when growth is defined as the maturation of the patient's self (Kohut, 1971, 1977, 1984).

INTERPRETATIONS AND THE MEDICAL MODEL

Kohut (1984) said, "Self psychology is at one with the technical principle that interpretation in general, and the interpretation of transference in particular, is the major instrumentality of therapeutic psychoanalysis" (p. 210). Rogers (1986) was critical of Kohut's self psychology because Kohut felt that the analyst rather than the patient was responsible for movement in therapy, that the analyst cures by giving interpretations and explanations. This approach, Rogers thought, was a reflection of the medical model, which assumes that the analyst as the doctor, and not the client, is the one with the expertise to cure the illness. In the Rogerian approach, with empathic understanding alone clients can discover their own answers and are responsible for the improvement in therapy. Rogers's belief that clients know more about themselves than do their therapists is valid, and, as a matter of fact, Kohut (1984) in a very moving way, acknowledged this philosophy as well. He said:

> If there is one lesson that I have learned during my life as an analyst, it is the lesson that what my patients tell me is likely to be true—that many times when I believed that I was right and my patients were wrong, it turned out, though often only after a prolonged search, that *my* rightness was superficial whereas *their* rightness was profound (pp. 93–94).

It appears, then, that Rogers, before Kohut and without going through a prolonged search, recognized the profundity of the patient's self-understanding.

Rogers, however, may have gone to an unnecessary extreme in avoiding interpretations entirely. From the insights of many psychoanalytic thinkers, therapists have a variety of explanations that can further a person's growth by reducing guilt and providing enhanced self-understanding. For example, Kohut's insights have helped therapists demonstrate to patients that their "mirroring," "idealizing," and other dependency needs are appropriate to have; that these needs were never fully responded to in childhood, and therefore they persist in their demand for satisfaction during adulthood. Kohut's insights have also permitted therapists and patients to understand that excessive aggressiveness, compulsive sexuality, or other behavioral excesses serve important functions; for example, these behaviors may stimulate a self that has become depleted because of the empathic failures of the past. These, as well as many other psychoanalytic insights, can be tentatively and empathically communicated to patients so as to help them better understand themselves.

However, interpretations may serve only as an important ancillary, a supplement to the genuine, empathic attitude of the therapist. Miller (1985), sounding very much like Rogers, said:

> The stressing of interpretation is an ancient tradition in analysis, a tradition that has been perpetuated through the passing of analytic generations, without, in my opinion, open-minded reexamination based upon empirical data. It is possible that if one attempted to maintain an empathic resonance with one's patient, in so far as possible continuously to maintain the mutual efforts at understanding the patient's inner state, that this might be the most productive way to promote increasing self-awareness and maximum therapeutic effectiveness.

Such empathic attunement encourages growth within the therapy session and may stimulate advances outside of therapy as well. There may be a reluctance in the analytic literature to acknowledge that events in a person's life, such as successes and even tragedies, can promote maturation of the self. One patient commented that important progress in her development during therapy had occurred after significant successes in her life. The therapeutic environment, according to her, provided the understanding support that she needed to undertake and succeed in these challenges. Another patient experienced significant growth after recovering from an acute illness that he had experienced as life threatening. He said that he had recognized during this illness how alone each person is in life and that awareness had had a profound maturational effect on him. He felt that he was now able to make some of the necessary compromises in life that he had never been able to make before. Maturation of the self may also occur after therapy terminates, when the person feels more independent and self-sufficient. Kohut (1984) said of several of his patients whose primary symptom was a creative block that "in each case . . . the reactivation of creative ability was reached indirectly and only after the passage of some time following the termination of treatment" (p. 218n). That *in each case* a fuller success in life was achieved only after therapy ended seems worthy of further investigation.

IS "ANALYSIS" THE PRIMARY TASK?

Just as self psychology had to move away from the medical-biological assumptions of Freud to psychological assumptions, it may also have to move away from the mechanistic, physical science notion that the primary function of the therapist is to "analyze" the psyche. Optimally satisfying the unmet needs of the patient may be the more important function of the self psychologist. Guntrip (1971) said that "analysis [is] a name appropriate enough to the investigation of a material object, but not very appropriate to the sympathetic healing study of a person whose wholeness is in jeopardy" (p. 93). In describing a patient he had helped, Guntrip (1971) said, "This is not analytic therapy; it is personal relationship therapy" (p. 183).

The Personal Questions of the Patient

The technique of psychoanalysis may be overly analytical when patients ask such personal questions as "Are you married?" or "Where are you going on your vacation?" or "What kind of car do you own?" The classical analytical response to such a personal question would be, "What do you imagine?" a response based on the belief that important transference information can come from the patient's fantasies about the analyst's life. Perhaps useful information can be obtained from such inquiries, but after this information is discussed, is any purpose served by refusing to answer the question? In normal interpersonal relations answers to inoffensive personal questions are freely given, and, in this respect, I wonder whether the therapeutic relationship should differ from a relationship in life. Withholding relatively innocuous information may have the effect of treating the patient as a subordinate rather than as an equal. Rogers (1977) noted that therapists have to guard against exerting unnecessary power in their relationships with patients. Rogers (1985, 1986) also believed that being openly oneself in the therapeutic relationship may be the factor that contributes most to healing.

Role Playing, Gratification and Analytic Neutrality

Basch (1984), in describing Kohut's neutrality, said:

> Nor did he . . . directly gratify wishes by role playing the good, understanding parent or friend that these patients so desperately needed. . . . In this way Kohut continued to use his capacity for empathy in the interest of interpretation and never fell into the error of neglecting the rule of abstinence [p. 23].

And Ornstein (1978) said:

> The mobilization of the selfobject transferences and their working through is accomplished here without the use of "parameters," that is, without any active interventions or deliberate transference gratifications beyond the empathic acceptance and ultimate interpretation of the patient's archaic experiences [pp. 73–74].

Rogers (1985, 1986,) would strongly disagree with those comments since he felt that the human qualities of the therapist were most healing. Kohut (1984) too, by acknowledging the importance of providing a "corrective emotional experience" (p. 70), implies that playing the role of the "good parent" may sometimes be appropriate. For example, on one occasion, Kohut (1984), deeply concerned about his analysand's dangerous driving, called him "a complete idiot" (p. 74) and went on for a couple of minutes to express concern "about certain aspects of his behavior, especially his potentially destructive and self-destructive outbursts of reckless driving (pp. 74–75)." The caring tone in Kohut's response had an important effect on the patient, and this human concern, which Rogers stressed, is, I maintain, like that of the "good parent" the patient never consistently had.

Another case cited by Kohut illustrates, I believe, the therapeutic value of need gratification. Kohut (1984) was discussing "anal-retentive erotism" as one of several types of resistance characteristic of classical analysis. The patient, a middle-aged lawyer, brought up the topic of anality fairly often, as it had been discussed by his previous senior analyst. The former analyst had on several occasions used such words as "first you are holding back for all you're worth . . . but then you are making a b-i-i-i-g production" (p.

145), which "was purportedly manifested in the interrupted and then overly abundant flow of associative material that the patient 'produced' in the analysis" (p. 124). Kohut (1984) said:

> The patient realized that it was the comfortable warmth that the former analyst exuded whenever he discussed the anal theme with the patient that had a simply magical effect on him—not because of the content of the analyst's interpretations but because of the tone of voice he adopted at such times, one that communicated aliveness, enjoyment of life, deep emotionality, and vitality. . . . It was at such moments that the patient's deepest need elicited an inadvertent response . . . in view of the joyless atmosphere of the patient's childhood that I described earlier [p. 145].

Clearly, then, in this situation of primary therapeutic value was the satisfaction of an unmet need, and not the analytic content of the transference interpretation.

Miller (1985) provided an interesting explanation for the analytic reluctance to gratify the patient.

> The principal question that concerns me is why optimal gratification or optimally positive therapeutic experiences has not been more fully studied so far. Political considerations are undoubtedly of importance. Also analysts and therapists tend to be almost phobic about gratification or optimal positive experience. An important reason for this may lie in a strong unconscious apprehensiveness. Our work does expose us to regressive pulls of wishes to merge, identify with, seek comfort with, have erotic experience with, dominate, be dominated by our patients, and this may compel us to seek distance from the patient, and we often utilize austerity and abstinence as tools for this purpose.

Miller's explanation, that neutrality protects the analyst from the very highly charged emotional relationships of therapy, seems accurate.

I would like to suggest an additional explanation, which may add somewhat to the understanding of this phenomenon. I think that the detached attitude of classical analysis, as exemplified by the restraint advocated for transference analysis, may, in part, be a reflection of traditional sex-role stereotypes. Thus, the attitude of the neutral, interpreting observer may have evolved from the masculine ideal of detached objectivity. The reluctance in classical psychoanalysis to be genuine and caring, to provide gratification or unconditional positive regard, and to experience love as the patient is helped (Maddi, 1987, p. 174, depicted such love) may emanate from the association of these qualities with weakness, softness, and femininity. Perhaps the analyst's resistance to accepting the vital importance of these more emotional qualities in facilitating change reflects at least to some extent, the male's reluctance to deal with his more caring, feminine self.

The neutral attitude of the analyst seems contrary to Kohut's (1984) hypothesized third constituent of the self—the need to be with another alike person, a human among humans. Rogers (1985), in a conference on The Evolution of Psychotherapy, responded to a question from the audience about what the profession of psychotherapy had learned over the past 100 years. Rogers thought about the answer for several moments and then said, "I don't know what the profession has learned, I really don't. I've learned to be more human in the relationship, but I am not sure that that's the direction the profession is going." Rogers (1986) noted, approvingly, the therapeutic approach of Milton Erickson, where "he sometimes took individuals into his home, or used pets, or told of his own life—doing whatever would keep him in close personal touch" (p. 132). Kohut, by recognizing the importance of responding to a person's selfobject needs, helped free classical psychoanalysis from its defensive overemphasis on abstinence and neutrality. However, Kohut (1984), himself, had to overcome some resistance to being involved in a more caring way with his patients. He said that owing to self psychology "I have come to feel freer and, without guilt and misgivings, to show analysands my deep involvement and concern via the warmth of my voice, the words that I choose, and other similarly subtle means" (p. 221n). It is remarkable that Kohut first had to shed guilt and misgivings before being able to show deep involvement and warmth toward the persons he sought to help.

REFERENCES

Bacal, H. A. (1985), Optimal responsiveness and the therapeutic process. In: *Progress in Self Psychology, Vol. 1,* ed. A. Goldberg. New York: Guilford Press, pp. 202–227.

Basch, M. F. (1984), Selfobjects and selfobject transference: Theoretical implications. In: *Kohut's Legacy,* ed. P. E. Stepansky & A. Goldberg. Hillsdale, NJ: The Analytic Press, pp. 21–41.

Gill, M. M. (1982), *Analysis of Transference, Vol. 1.* New York: International Universities Press.

Guntrip H. (1971), *Psychoanalytic Theory, Therapy, and the Self.* New York: Basic Books.

Kahn, E. (1985), Heinz Kohut and Carl Rogers: A timely comparison. *Amer. Psychol.*, 40:893–904.

_____ (in press), Heinz Kohut and Carl Rogers: A constructive collaboration psychotherapy.

Kirschenbaum, H. (1979), *On Becoming Carl Rogers.* New York: Delta.

Kohut, H. (1959), Introspection, empathy, and psychoanalysis: An examination of the relationship between mode of observation and theory. In: *The Search for the Self, Vol. 1,* ed. P. H. Ornstein. New York: International Universities Press, 1978, pp. 205–232.

_____ (1971), *The Analysis of the Self.* New York: International Universities Press.

_____ (1977), *The Restoration of the Self.* New York: International Universities Press.

_____ (1984), *How Does Analysis Cure?* ed. A. Goldberg & P. E. Stepansky. Chicago: University of Chicago Press.

Maddi, S. R. (1987), On the importance of the present: Reactions to John Shlien's article. *Person-Centered Rev.* 2:171–181.

Miller, J. P. (1985), Introductory address. Presented at the Eighth Annual Conference on the Psychology of the Self, New York, October.

Ornstein, P. H. (1978), Introduction: The evolution of Heinz Kohut's psychoanalytic psychology of the self. In: *The Search for the Self, Vol. 1,* ed. P. H. Ornstein. New York: International Universities Press, pp. 1–106.

Rogers, C. R. (1951), *Client-Centered therapy.* Boston: Houghton Mifflin.

_____ (1959), A theory of therapy, personality, and interpersonal relationships, as developed in the client-centered framework. In: *Psychology: A Study of a Science, Vol. 3,* ed. S. Koch. New York: McGraw-Hill, pp. 184–256.

_____ (1977), *Carl Rogers on Personal Power.* New York: Delta.

_____ (1980), *A way of Being.* Boston: Houghton Mifflin.

_____ (1985), Conversation hour. Conducted at the Evolution of Psychotherapy Conference, Phoenix, AZ, December.

_____ (1986), Rogers, Kohut, and Erickson: A personal perspective on some similarities and differences. *Person-Centered Rev.,* 1:125–140.

Rogers, C. R. (1987), Comment on Shlien's article "A countertheory of transference." *Person-Centered Rev.,* 2:182–188.

Shlien, J. M. (1987), A countertheory of transference. *Person-Centered Rev.,* 2:15–49.

Stolorow, R. D. (1986), Critical reflections on the theory of self psychology: An inside view. *Psychoanal. Inq.,* 6:387–402.

Terman, D. M. (1986), Optimum frustration, structuralization, and the therapeutic process: A model whose time has passed. Presented at

Ninth Annual Conference on the Psychology of the Self, San Diego, CA, October.

Wolf, E. S. (1983), Concluding statement. In: *The Future of Psychoanalysis,* ed. A. Goldberg. New York: International Universities Press, pp. 495–505.

Part III

English Object Relations Theorists

12

Klein, Balint, and Fairbairn

A Self-Psychological Perspective

BERNARD BRANDCHAFT

Psychoanalysis in North America is undergoing a period of profound turbulence. The recognition grows that the concepts of traditional psychoanalysis fail to encompass fundamental forms of developmental psychopathology not envisaged by the founders of our science or by their followers, who established psychoanalysis in the new world and became its first teachers. Influenced by the work of Heinz Kohut and his followers, this reexamination has stimulated an interest in an earlier set of divergences that began in the period from 1930 to 1965, mainly in Great Britain—object relations theory, from which development American psychoanalysts had largely been insulated. Both self psychology and object relations theory can be seen as facets of a more broadly based psychoanalytic tradition: a neverending, laborious effort, beginning with Freud's first searching attempts, to generate concepts emanating from closer observation of hitherto unavailable or little-appreciated dimensions of subjective experience and representing more encompassing truths. In this chapter we will consider the contributions of British object relations theorists Melanie Klein, Michael Balint, and W.R.D. Fairbairn in the light of the evolution of self psychology.

An earlier version of this paper appeared in *Progress in Self Psychology,* Vol. 2 (1986) ed. A. Goldberg. New York: Guilford Press, p. 245–272.

Space limitations preclude a similar consideration of Donald Winnicott, one of the most important of the British object relations theorists; the reader is referred to (Brandchaft, 1986).

MELANIE KLEIN

Although the term "object relations theory" first arose as an attempt to set apart the work of such writers as Balint, Fairbairn, and Winnicott from that of Melanie Klein and her followers, there is little doubt that she was a towering influence on each. Nor is there any doubt that her work has "contributed to a change in the psychoanalytic approach to the understanding of the mind" and specifically "in shifting the focus from economic, physical considerations to the importance of object relationships as fundamental determinants of the personality" (Segal, 1979, p. 161) Once she and her colleagues (1952) had succeeded in bringing about this shift in focus, the question of what constitutes the fundamental nature of the tie to objects began to occupy the attention of psychoanalysts and continues to the present day. She maintained that the archaic tie was foundational when she concluded from her psychoanalytic investigation and treatment of small children that the basic structures of normal and pathological development were laid down in earliest infancy. She thereby signaled her departure from Freud and the theory of the centrality for development of the oedipal conflict of the fourth and fifth year. She emphasized the significance of deeper configurations, states of mind, and affects than those that had been uncovered by Freud's revolutionary discoveries (Klein, 1950, pp. 386–390). Her example and her teaching influenced a generation of psychoanalysts outside the United States in the conviction that the key to understanding and amelioration of basic psychological disorders lay in the activation, observation, understanding, and explanation of archaic transference configurations, together with their displacements and disavowals, as entities in their own right and not simply as evasions of or regressions from too intense an oedipal rivalry. The key to understanding the disorders of development being thought to lay in the vicissitudes of the infant's experience of its objects and the structures laid down as a consequence, its world of "internal objects," the detailed nature of the infant's ties to its objects became the object of Klein's and her followers' scrutiny. Differences in the observations of this tie as it reveals itself in psychoanalytic transferences and subsequent differences in theoretical constructs is at the very heart of the differences among the various object relations theorists and are also central to the distinctness of Kohut's contributions.

Klein's contributions stemmed from the observations she made in adapting the methods of psychoanalytic investigation and treatment of small children, the youngest aged 2 3/4 years. Since the method of free association was foreclosed with young patients, she hit upon the idea of using the child's play with appropriate toys as the key to its conscious and unconscious preoccupations, concerns, and strivings (Klein, 1954, pp. 23–39). She recognized that the child's play was an enactment of its phantasies and that the key to its psychological development lay in the understanding of how its phantasy life had come to be structured in its own particular way. From the beginning, she was impressed with the intensity of the anxiety of even the youngest child, by the child's propensity to fear the cruelest of punishments, and by the child's savage feelings of guilt. She attempted at all times in her work with children to maintain the posture of a neutral, if interested, observer of the events unfolding before her, limiting herself to interpretations in the transference of the anxieties and defenses that she believed she observed. Klein (1961) wrote:

> The psychoanalytic procedure consists in selecting the most urgent aspects of the material and interpreting them with precision. The patient's reactions and subsequent associations amount to further material, which has to be analyzed on the same principals. . . . I was determined not to modify my technique and to interpret in the usual way even deep anxiety situations as they came up and the corresponding defences [pp. 13].

Klein recognized that "the assessment and interpretation of the patient's material by the analyst are based upon a coherent framework of theory" (p. 12). The central theoretical assumptions that guided her observations and understandings were those that Freud (1920) had arrived at and that Abraham (1948) her analyst and teacher, had elaborated. Specifically, she was influenced by the dual instinct theory that the struggle between libidinal and aggressive instincts and their derivatives determined the nature and course of the child's ties to his objects and underlay the development of its psychological structures. She became convinced in the course of her work that the child's development was from the beginning influenced by the necessity of its immature ego to deal with the death instinct and with the intolerable anxiety of annihilation stemming from it. She observed that her small patients experienced anxieties of being treated with far greater severity and cruelty than she felt the parents had ever administered and, in the transference, certainly harsher than she was capable of. She explained this disparity by attributing it to the operation of archaic and violent mechanisms of defense against instinctual forces that came into operation long before repression. Among Klein's earliest patients was one, Erna, "who had phantasies of being cruelly persecuted by her mother and considered every step in her education, every frustration, and even every amusement her mother enjoyed as a persecution and punishment. She had frightening phantasies of a 'robber woman' who would take everything out of her" (see Segal, 1979, p. 48).

From repetitive material of this kind, together with the phantasies of rage expressed by the children, Klein began to construct a picture of the child's internal world. Central to her thesis, throughout the many changes in it that were to take place, was "a basic and largely unchallenged assumption that has pervaded psychoanalytic thought since its inception . . . the existence of an 'objective reality' that can be known by the analyst and eventually by the patient" (Stolorow, Brandchaft, and Atwood, 1987, p. 4). The idea of one "objective reality," and the concomitant explanations as defensive denials and distortions applied to subjective experience that run counter to it, is at the heart of Klein's reconstructions of infantile object ties and is the determining factor in her interpretive stance.

> The essential difference between infantile and mature object relations is that whereas the adult conceives of the object existing independantly of himself, for the infant it always refers in some way to himself. It exists only by virtue of its function for the infant. . . . Whilst in reality the infant is utterly helpless and depends for the maintenance of his life completely on the mother . . . in phantasy he assumes an omnipotent position to his objects. They belong to him, are part of him, live only through and for him—he confirms his prenatal oneness with his mother [Klein et al., 1952, p. 142].

The child protects itself from the beginning against the threat of the death instinct, she hypothesized, partly by projecting it into its object (originally a part object), the breast, and by converting another part of it into the aggressions she observed. At the same time, the infant, by way of splitting mechanisms, deals with its pleasurable, "good" experiences similarly by projecting part of its libido into an ideal object and retaining the rest to establish and maintain a loving relationship with this ideal object. Concurrent with these projective mechanisms, the child's relationship with its objects is also marked by processes of introjection. These are motivated by the child's primary developmental task of acquiring, keeping inside, and identifying with the ideal object experienced as life giving and protective and keeping outside the bad object and those parts of the self harboring the destructive instincts. These defensive operations of the ego, splitting and projective identification, together with the products of introjective processes, constitute the phantasy life of the small child and dominate its early development. In this way, the child gradually builds up an internal world of ideal and persecutory objects split off and kept widely apart from one another that color and distort his perception of his "real" objects.

From these observations and constructs, Klein described the development of a superego of a much more archaic character then that described by Freud, and regarded it as being influenced more by the child's own instinctual drives than by the real parents. The child's intense fears of its objects and its own savage reproaches against itself, she maintained, were to be explained partly by the "talion law," an intrapsychic law of an innate connection between aggression and retaliation, partly by projection into external objects and their subsequent introjection and, in a later development, by projection into its internal objects.

During the course of her work, Klein et al. (1952) came to advance the thesis that the developmental process centered on the establishment of two organizations of experience, which she called the *paranoid-schizoid* and the *depressive* positions. The central conflict in the first of these stages, between life and death instincts, becomes a struggle between the libidinal good self, identified and allied with the ideal object, and the objects experienced as persecutory. The leading anxiety is that of persecution. Hunger and frustration are felt as persecution, while good experiences sustain and reinforce the phantasy of an ideal object.

Rather late in the development of her ideas about defense mechanisms, Klein introduced the concept of projective identification. It is an attempt to explain both the patient's discrepant and unidimensional ("all-good" or "all-bad") experience of the analyst in certain situations and the appearance within the analyst of an alien and intrusive experience of himself. Here, not only impulses but parts of the self, or even the whole self, are described as being projected into an object. The aims can be manifold: getting rid of unwanted parts of the self, control of the object, avoiding separation or avoiding conflict. Under the influence of the growing maturation and integrative tendencies of the ego, further development becomes organized in the depressive position. The infant's capacity to bring destructive and loving parts of the self into closer alignment increases and, with the reduction of splitting and projective identification, the infant is better able to experience the hated object, the one that frustrates, as the same as the loved object, the one who gives and cares. In this way, with the increasing acceptance of his ownership of his own destructiveness, the infant is able to empathize with the objects of his hatred, to pine for them, and fully to experience the intense affects that characterize the depressive position—mourning and loss, guilt and also love and gratitude. Gradually, in various ways, the child gains confidence in its ability to modify its expectations and its disappointments and hatred and to restore and repair its objects (damaged or destroyed in its "omnipotent" phantasy) and its relationship to them.

These structural configurations, the paranoid-schizoid and depressive positions, were, it should be emphasized, conceived of as innate and invariant patternings of normal infancy. They were believed to be determined constitutionally and only their intensity or fixation affected by the contribution of the parents. Klein held fast to the conviction that, in their revival in the analytic situation, the structural configuration and the intense affective components of fear, rage, and guilt were part of a persisting and basic pathological character structure. Any investigation of the patient's experience of the contribution of the analyst and her adherence to her "coherent framework of theory" as codetermining was aborted by the doctrinal belief that such assertions simply constituted "further material which again has to be analyzed on the same principles" (Klein, 1961, p. 12).

It was ideas of this sort that Bion (1980), one of Klein's most distinguished students, later addressed:

> I suggest that we cannot be sure that these theories, which are so convenient and which make us—both as individuals and as a group—feel better because they appear to make an inroad into this enormous area of ignorance, are therefore final. One would like to say "thus far and no further," but if one carries on this same procedure then one is back again in contact with this vast area of ignorance [p. 30].

A major and continuing product of this conceptual scaffolding is the position of central importance that "envy" came to hold late in

Klein's career (Klein, 1957). In these formulations, primitive envy is clinically the clearest derivative of the constitutionally rooted death or destructive instinct. Other forms of hatred are directed toward objects experienced as persecutory and bad, but envy is directed toward objects that have been experienced as good. Here, Klein held, the infant wants to spoil and destroy the breast precisely because it contains the goodness that the infant needs and because he cannot tolerate that it is outside his control. Envy counteracts the splitting of objects into good and bad, which Klein holds is a normal and necessary developmental phase permitting eventual integration and resolution via the mourning and reparative processes of the *depressive position.* In the phantasied envious destruction of the goodness of object, the infant (and later the patient so motivated) also destroys his own hope with a corresponding increase in terror and the persecutory cycle.

Undoubtedly these inferences were drawn from observations of difficult patients who were unable to gain anything positive from the persistent and dedicated attempts of their analysts' applying Klein's own "coherent framework of theory" and who were therefore manifesting a therapeutic dead end similar to that which Freud's attempts to apply his own basic concepts, however repeatedly revised, had encountered in the "negative therapeutic reaction."

A detailed critique of Kleinian metapsychology from a self-psychological perspective is beyond the scope of this chapter. Nonetheless, it may be possible to illuminate a few of the more important theoretical differences and the basis in observation in which they are rooted. The most fundamental difference lies in the understanding of the nature of the infant's archaic tie to his objects and of the motivational priorities and complex mental states that are experienced within it. Klein's observations were widely divergent from her patients' own experience of the cruelty of their objects. This discrepancy was explained by theories of distortion, and the therapeutic task that ensued was to win the patients' cooperation in understanding their experiences as the analyst understood them and thereby to reduce the conflictful elements in the patients' relationship to their objects and within themselves.

Since Klein's propositions were first advanced the guiding assumption of a "hierarchically ordered two-reality view" has come under increasing question. Schwaber (1988) for example, argues persuasively against the idea of transference as distortion on the grounds that the reality "known" by the analyst is more objectively true than the reality experienced by the patient (p. 383).

Elsewhere (Stolorow, Brandchaft, and Atwood, 1987) this point is specifically addressed.

> A fundamental assumption that has guided our work is that the only reality relevant and accessible to psychoanalytic inquiry (that is, to empathy and introspection) is "subjective reality"—that of the patient, that of the analyst, and the psychological field created by the interplay between the two. From this perspective, the concept of an objective reality is an instance of the ubiquitous psychological process that we have termed "concretization"—the symbolic transformation of configurations of subjective experience into events and entities that are believed to be objectively perceived and known (Atwood and Stolorow, 1984) "Attributions of objective reality," in other words, are "concretizations of subjective truth." Analysts' invoking the concept of objective reality, along with its corollary concept of distortion, obscures the subjective reality encoded in the patient's productions, which is precisely what psychoanalytic investigation should seek to illuminate [p. 4–5].

A different view of the developmental process than that described by Klein, with radically different understandings and implications for the therapeutic bond holds

> That both psychological development and pathogenesis are best conceptualized in terms of the specific intersubjective contexts that shape the developmental process and that facilitate or obstruct the child's negotiation of critical developmental tasks and successful passage through developmental phases. The observational focus is the evolving psychological field constituted by the interplay between the differently organized subjectivities of child and caretakers.
>
> This observational stance is, in our view, a fundamental methodological requirement for investigating changes occurring within the subjective world of any party within the developmental system. We stress, as Sander (1975) also stresses in regard to his studies of infants, that this stance is different from the more traditional psychoanalytic one in that the questions asked, the route of discovery, the window into the unconscious and to ontogeny, and the understandings that become possible are all different [Atwood and Stolorow, 1984, pg. 65–66].

This position is in accord with Winnicott's (1965) statement that "there is no such thing as an infant" (p. 39), by which he meant that infant and maternal care together form an indivisible unit.

The understanding of development and the psychoanalytic situation as profoundly intersubjective in nature, namely, the product of the intersection of differently organized subjective worlds, led to an interest in the further exploration of the patient's subjective reality from *a stance within* rather than outside that perspective.

> Rather than being viewed as a distortion to be modified, it (the transference) is seen as a perception to be recognized and articulated, in the hope that it will facilitate a deeper entry into the patient's inner world. . . . We will, to be sure, still need to check the patient's perception and view of reality against our own, but this is primarily to maintain vigilance against the superimposition of our view, which may be conveniently rationalized as our theoretical stance [Schwaber, 1983, pp. 274–275].

Schwaber goes on to suggest that the emphasis then shifts to the influence, often to a profound extent, of the observer on the observed, of the patient's perception of the analyst, and to the meanings assigned to those perceptions. Understood in this way, the emergence of some affect state, such as a feeling of persecution, or presenting phantasy, such as of having injured or destroyed the mother or the analyst, or a defensive stance, such as withdrawal, may be "seen as a vital clue to a silent or as yet undefined perception of the analyst and to the relationship between that perception and the nature of the patient's response" (p. 275). We have written of the extent to which such discrepant affect states contain

> encoded and encapsulated memories of past traumatic experiences. Thus the acceptance of the perceptual validity of the patient's subjective experience permits a retracing of the history of the patient's world and an access to the invariant ("prereflective unconscious") organizing principles that have become established and which have come to shape his attitudes towards himself and his world. [Stolorow, Brandchaft, and Atwood, 1987, pp. 12–13].

In this way a milieu is created in which a patient can become aware of his own role "as a constitutive subject in elaborating his personal reality" and basic processes set in motion to transform the nature of his experience.

Kohut's observations of the analytic experience led to a

heightened awareness of and sensitivity to the constitutive role played by the analyst and expecially by her "coherent framework of theory." He came to see the role of the analyst and the stance he adopts, which determines what he does and does not, what he says or refrains from saying, as an immanent force *in principle* and not simply as a factor of occasional and intrusive countertransferences (Kohut, 1984, p. 37). Distinctive archaic transferences developed as Kohut abandoned interpreting as defensive material similar to that described by Klein and sought to understand the evolving tie from a vantage point strictly within the patient's subjective experience. Observations of the archaic world of self- and object experience, strikingly similar to those described by Heimann (1952), led him to a radically different view. The child's experience of objects as "belonging to him," part of a self just beginning to emerge, and not yet recognized as a center of independant initiative but "living only through him and for him" were not defensive against a painful recognition of the "reality" of a dependance on objects or part objects perceived from the outside, Kohut's findings indicate. Its experience did not derive from the operation of a primitive defense of "omnipotent denial." Instead, these were manifestations of a normal phase of development of the self in its relationships to objects centered on the functions they provided, which were essential to his psychological survival and growth. These "selfobject" experiences were the necessary precursor to the child's acquiring these functions as part of his own equipment, and they were expected by him with the same certainty that he expected the environment to provide the oxygen he breathes (Kohut, 1971, pp. 90–91).

Kohut then reconstructed a phase of development that took place before differentiating processes had become consolidated. From them might emerge as developmental achievements such differentiating accomplishments as the recognition of self and objects as distinct and independent centers of achievement and empathy for the experience of an object whose needs and hurts are as important to that other as one's own are to oneself. The primary tie to objects was conceptualized by Kohut (1971, 1977, 1984) in his description of the "selfobject" dimension of experience. The supraordinate area of development was toward self cohesion and resilience. Subsequent development was marked by increasing self-differentiation and the laying down of an intrinsic design of goals and ideals. The developmental line of relationship to selfobjects, lasting throughout one's lifetime, lay in the maturational transformation from archaic to mature selfobject experiences. The primary disorders we are called upon to treat, Kohut (1984, p. 22–25, 207–210) asserted, are not those associated with the vicissitudes of a primal destructiveness, love and concern, or guilt. Rather, they are derailments within a milieu of selfobjects, of one or another facet of the normal development of the self.

Kohut (1971, pp. 212–214) addressed directly, and again from a stance within the patient's subjective experience, the problem of infantile destructiveness, the vicissitudes of which formed a basic part of the "coherent framework of theory" by which Klein organized and interpreted her observations, a theoretical framework she maintained resolutely in the face of her patients' reactions to this perspective on their experiences.

Elemental aggression, Kohut (1977) wrote, must be distinguished by the role it plays from the beginning "in the service of the establishment of a rudimentary self" and later in its maintenance. "Nondestructive aggressiveness" is an important affect in the delimitation of self from object, and it arises whenever "nontraumatic delays in the empathic responses" of the object are experienced. It does not develop out of primitive destructiveness but has its own developmental line from primitive to mature forms of nondestructive assertiveness, in which developmental line it is subordinated to but necessary for the performance of tasks. In its primitive as well as its most developed form, nondestructive aggressiveness subsides as soon as the goals that are striven for are reached or are altered. "If, however, the phase-appropriate need for omnipotent control over the self-object had been chronically and traumatically frustrated in childhood, then chronic narcissistic rage, with all its deleterious consequences, will be established" (p. 121) Destructiveness and its ideational component, the conviction of an inimical environment (Klein's "paranoid position") are not innate, primary psychological givens, but however well entrenched are "failures of traumatic degree in the . . . responsiveness of the self-object vis-à-vis a self the child is beginning to experience, at least in its first, hazy outlines" (p. 121).

A detailed explication of the clinical observations of archaic transferences that led Kohut to conclude that Klein was in error in equating mental health with the attainment of the specific early developmental psychological task of the capacity for post-paranoid-depressive object love is set forth in his last work (Kohut,

1984). Reports of clinical cases illustrating some of the differences herein discussed are contained in papers by the present author (Brandchaft, 1983; Brandchaft and Stolorow, 1984).

MICHAEL BALINT

Michael Balint's career was overshadowed by that of Melanie Klein, as was his influence in psychoanalysis. As he recounts (Balint, 1953), he began his studies in Budapest, where she had already become an outstanding teacher, much admired by him. Later he was instrumental in sponsoring and supporting her when she came to London.

It is impossible in a short review to give Balint's work, much of it the result of collaboration with his wife, Alice, the credit it deserves for the originality, courage, and creativeness that distinguished his efforts. For a more comprehensive summation, the reader is referred to Khan (1969). A half century ago, Balint began a systematic reappraisal of accepted psychoanalytic theories. To this effort he brought clinical observations and formulated theoretical concepts that were to differentiate them clearly from both the classical tradition of the Viennese and the Kleinian school then becoming established in London. In a series of papers, Balint (1953, chs, 3, 5, 8, and 9) anticipated the methodological principle that was to be spelled out explicitly some 30 years later by Kohut, that the empathic-introspective mode of observation defines and limits the domain of psychoanalytic inquiry. No penetration by analytic technique, he asserted, reveals a psychological configuration that is not object related (p. 59); all so-called autoerotic expressions are revealed in analysis "as consolations for or defiance against, objects which had been lost or led the child into severe conflicts" (p. 59). From these observations he argued cogently against the concept of primary narcissism, an objectless state from which object ties arose secondarily, and against regarding narcissistic pathology as a regression from or defense against object relations at an oedipal level, as classical analysts maintained, or excessive sadism or envy in preoedipal part-object relations, as put forward by the Kleinians. Rather, he proposed, such narcissism is always a protection against an excessively frustrating object. "If the world does not love me enough, I have to love and gratify myself" (p. 63). He took issue with Freudians' (Freud, 1920) emphasis on the destructive instincts and their purported appearance in the form of negative analytic transferences stressed in clinical work of the Kleinians. Klein et al., 1952; Rosenfeld, 1971; Joseph, 1982).

Thus, as early as 1930, Balint, with a growing body of colleagues, approached a type of disorder that had hitherto not been systematically studied as a psychoanalytic entity in its own right and that was later to emerge in Kohut's classifications, first as narcissistic personality and behavior disorders (Kohut, 1971, 1977) and later in a broader concept of self disorders (Kohut, 1984). Balint departed from psychoanalysts who, following Abraham (1948), viewed narcissistic phenomenology as a "resistance" to analysis, the strength of which had become the leading criterion of unanalyzability (Balint, 1968, p. 133–134, 159–181).

By listening to the accounts of his patients without attempting to fit those accounts into existing metapsychological concepts, Balint became convinced that the illness of these patients was largely the result of early environmental factors in their life. In an early and seminal observation (Balint, 1953), by no means sufficiently appreciated even today, he argued against the notion of defensive mechanisms as arising strictly from instinctual forces, as conceptualized by Abraham (1948) and Klein et al. (1952). All those defects of development which we group under the collective name "the repressed," Balint (1953) wrote, "were originally forced into that state by external influences . . . that is to say, there is no repression without reality, without an object relation" (p. 196). Balint went on to delineate further the nature of pathogenic environmental influences on development by recognizing that particularly noxious was the use of the child to satisfy a parent's unconscious needs. Thus he anticipated Kohut's investigations into the nature of pathological self-selfobject ties.

In his clinical work, Balint described what others, and especially Kleinian analysts, regarded as the essence of the infantile psychological organization:

> loss of security, the feeling of being worthless, despair, deeply bitter disappointment, feelings [of mistrust]. Mixed with these came, venomous aggression, wildest sadistic phantasies . . . the most cunning tortures and humiliations for the analyst. Then again fear of retaliation . . . contriteness, for one had spoilt forever the hope of being loved by the analyst . . . [p. 97].

Balint noted, however, that these reactions invariably ensued when his patients expected, and often demanded, "certain primitive gratifications from their analysts or others in their environment" and when the analyst "stuck strictly to the rule of analytic passivity" (p. 97). In these observations it is clear that Balint was adhering tc the principle that Sander (1975) characterized as representing "a major turning point in developmental research" (p. 147). They had grasped and embraced the perspective that organization of behavior and intrapsychic experience are not to be viewed as the property of the individual but rather as part of a system of differently organized subjective universes.

From repeated and painstaking observations Balint was led to reconsider the role of the analyst in the psychoanalytic process and to conclude that analyzability itself and the results of analysis were as much the product of the analyst's understanding and the concepts he used (determined to a greater or lesser extent also by his own unconscious needs) as they were attributable to the disorders of his patients. How similar is this observation to Kohut's (1984):

> The theories held by the observer influence not only what he sees when he scrutinizes the psychoanalytic process and its results—but, and par excellence, how he evaluates what he sees, what he deems to be central and significant and what he dismisses as peripheral, insignificant or trite. To be specific; it is clear that a psychology —traditional psychoanalysis—that explains man in terms of a psychic apparatus that processes drives and, during therapy, focuses predominantly on the flaws of conflict solution of psychic macrostructures (id, ego, superego) will see the essence of the analytic process and the essence of cure in a different light from a psychology—the psychoanalytic psychology of the self—that explains man in terms of a self that is sustained by a milieu of selfobjects and, during therapy, ultimately focuses not on the flawed functional results of the faulty structures of the self (i.e., not on the mishandled drive as the fons and origo of psychopathology) but on the defects and distortions of the microstructures of the self [p. 41].

Such ideas of Balint's were received with little more enthusiasm in Great Britain than they would be when they were similarly proposed in America by Kohut (1971, 1977, 1984). Nonetheless Balint (1953, pp. 210–211) insisted that the then predominant psychoanalytic emphasis on the role of pathological superego formation was misplaced and that it overlooked and distorted the period of development before such structures could be formed and the more inclusive (intersubjective) system in which that development had taken place. Balint argued forcefully that "orthodoxies and factional rigidities in the psychoanalytic movement [create a] bias in our technique especially where training analyses [are concerned]," and he persistently maintained that in such analyses "perhaps dependence and superego pedagogy plays the operative role and goes against a creative and independent discovery of self and one's own mind" (Khan, 1969, p. 239).

Balint's (1953, 1968) core theoretical constructs were: (1) "the basic fault"; 2) primary or primitive object love; and (3) a scheme of developmental progression from passive primitive object love to interdependent mature love. His distinctive contribution to technique was "the new beginning."

If patients are permitted to regress in the psychoanalytic situation, Balint (1968) found, the area of "basic fault" will become exposed. Such regression frequently is interfered with by the analyst's "irresistable urge to organize their patient's complaints into an illness" (p. 108) The characteristics of the basic fault are that it is exclusively dyadic, not triadic; the relationship is not oedipal; and it is not motivated by conflict. In this experience, in which feelings of deadness and emptiness may be strong, the patient feels there is a "fault within him" that must be repaired and that this fault was brought about because someone failed him. Balint noted that this experience is accompanied by great anxiety and a "desperate demand that this time the analyst must not fail him" (p. 21).

The therapeutic relationship that then ensues is "very primitive and peculiar, different from those usually observed between adults" (p. 23). In these passages, Balint established his own position on the all-important question of the essential nature of the primitive object tie. Only wishes and needs of one of the parties matters and must be attended to; the other counts only insofar as he gratifies or frustrates; his own interests, wishes and needs do not exist. Clearly, Balint was observing the same phenomenology as Kohut (1971) described three years later, when he developed his concept of the selfobject. Kohut recognized the essential pathology (the "basic fault") here as a defect in the cohesiveness of the self and the "peculiar" relationship as one in which the patient was attempting to revive with the analyst a period of development of the self at which it had been arrested. In this experience for Kohut as well as Balint, the analyst was not perceived subjectively as separate but rather as a part of the patient's self-experience. This object relationship was, according to Kohut (1977), characterized not by the analyst's gratifying or frustrating the desires and needs of the patient, but by his being looked to for his unquestioned and unquestionable provision of essential functions that the patient could not provide for himself. Within the actuating matrix of the psychoanalytic situation, Kohut (1971) proposed, the archaic needs that appear are those necessary for narcissistic sustenance, that is, the need for mirroring and the need to merge with an ideal, not provided for in childhood. The reactivation of these needs signals an incomplete structuralization of the self, with the result that the patient reacts to narcissistic injury with temporary break-up, enfeeblement, or disharmony. Kohut (1984) emphasized "the essential importance of such patients reexperiencing and working through the lethargies, depressions and rages of early life via the reactivation and analysis of their archaic traumatic self-selfobject relationships in the transference" (p. 5).

Thus the goal of analysis for Kohut is the reestablishment of the interrupted developmental process, and the sine qua non of psychological health, or "cure," is that which leads to the structural completeness of the self (p. 7).

For Balint (1968), the "basic fault" represented an arrest in development but not in the course of the organization and structuralization of self-experience. His developmental scheme was expressed in the second core construct, that of "primary object love." The aim of human striving," Balint wrote, "is to establish or reestablish an all-embracing harmony with one's environment, to be able to live in peace" (p. 69).

He described primary object love as follows:

> This form of love works according to principle; what is good for me, is right for you, i.e., it does not recognize any difference between one's own interests and the interests of the object; it assumes as a matter fact that the partner's desires are identical with one's own. Claims of the object which go beyond this harmony are intolerable, and call forth anxiety and aggression [p. 100].

Balint objected strongly to the then current psychoanalytic practice of taking the more flagrant manifestations of this object relation as evidence of "oral greed." That, he wrote was a subjective impression in adultomorphic language. In this peculiar form of love proper, timely satisfaction of all needs was crucially important because of the infant's (or patient's) almost absolute dependence on the object. In it, he observed (Balint, 1953), again anticipating

Kohut, the object must be simply taken for granted, very much as the adult take the supply of air for granted. In this state, "hate is the last remnant, the denial of and the defense against the primitive object love (or the dependent archaic love)" (p. 148). Under analysis, hate always reveals itself as a derivative of frustrated love.

The central aspect of the Balints' developmental scheme was the progression in object love from a primary, dependent, passive, archaic object relation to a mature, interdependent form of love. Beginning with a stage in development in which subject and object are felt to be indistinguishable, the "work of conquest" transforms the object relationship to one of "mutuality," in which the object can no longer be taken for granted. The object's own independent and interdependent needs must be recognized and respected. One comes to realize that "our needs have become too varied, complicated and specialized, so that we can no longer expect automatic satisfaction by our objects; we must be able to bear the depression caused by this realization; and we must accept that we have to give something to our object" (Balint, 1968, p. 146) in order for the object to be a "co-operative partner." The Balints insisted that the development and transformation of object relation in an infant from primitive to mature requires optimal caretaking.

Familiarity with the psychoanalytic setting in the Balints' Great Britain makes it easy to understand their central concern with the failure to recognize and appreciate the infant's inherent capacity for love. In an historical era when psychoanalysts were becoming increasingly transfixed upon the infant's presumptive sadism and in which patients' presumptive "destructive instincts" had come to occupy the focus of therapeutic endeavor, the restoration of balance through an emphasis on "basic archaic object love" made good sense and would be likely to produce better results.

The theory of man's primal destructiveness, one dimension of self- and object experience, in its time illuminated some important aspects of human experience. Fidelity to this theory continues today, however, and constitutes an article of faith, an analytic pledge of allegiance that is relatively unaffected, sad to say, by the work of Balint, Winnicott, and Fairbairn, all of whom addressed this point with intelligence and vision. Perhaps the explanation for its persistence now is more a practical than a theoretical matter. Theories of innate destructiveness, which have explained a succession of clinical entities from purported infantile sadism, to negative transference, to moral masochism and unconscious guilt, to more contemporary explanatory theories of "highly pathological (and destructive) grandiose self" continue to serve a useful if dubious purpose. For those who believe and apply them in the consulting room, they delineate where the problem lies whenever an analysis is not proceeding as favorably as might be hoped. However, from today's vantage point it does not seem that the errors of excessive weighting of archaic destructive forces are correctable by insistence on the primacy of the infant's archaic love, or as Balint (1968, p. 65) proposed, that behind the rage of a narcissistically injured patient lies his love. Kohut (1984) has enabled us to recognize as central the more salient factors of a defective, weakened self. When an infant (or patient) in distress is relentlessly exposed to an insufficiently attuned selfobject, assertiveness as a signal will proceed to chronic, unreflecting, and relentless rage. In acknowledging the truly significant contributions of Balint, pioneer in his own historical era and setting, we should also acknowledge the theoretical and clinical gulf that divides Kohut's psychology from that of Balint.

Balint's success in actuating the emergence in analysis of regressed and archaic states was an historic achievement. His (Balint, 1968) description of what is required from the analyst to expose the experience of "basic fault" and engage it therapeutically toward a "new beginning" is the work of an empathic clinician. However his innovative concepts did not carry him a sufficient distance to maintain an analytic procedure with which to bring about the transformations he sought. Instead, for example, he openly proposed that there is, at certain points in the analytic procedure, an indispensable role for the analyst to lend himself to the patient's reactivated needs for physical contact, such as holding a hand.[1] Whatever merits or flaws might have been assigned to such a course, it reflected an abandonment of the analytic procedure and therefore imposed a limitation on the experiences being concretely communicated and responded to in the request for physical responses. It derailed inquiry into experiences of discrepant affect states that arise from the actively experienced selfobject failure that needs for physical contact frequently reflect, for instance when the patient feels the analyst to be hopelessly distant and untouched. It thus bypasses the therapeutic potentialities inherent in the procedures Kohut was later to described in the concepts of "optimal frustration" and "transmuting internalization."

[1]Balint (1963) found that only about one patient in five responded favorably to this procedure. He acknowledged that further experience was necessary in this area.

Kohut's (1971, 1978) concept of the selfobject and selfobject transferences made possible an extension of the analytic procedure beyond these limits. With these constructs, it becomes possible to broaden our understanding of contexts of subjective experience in which urgent needs for connectedness may arise and become concretized. In addition, Kohut's concepts have led us to appreciate that the basic fault includes not only severe narcissistic injury, but inevitably also failures on the part of important caretakers to become attuned to the discrepant affect states resulting from such injuries and so to assist in the process of healing. The implications of these findings for analysis are profound and include an appreciation of the expanded potential for the analytic procedure. Balint was forced to relinquish not only classical concepts, but important elements of psychoanalytic investigatory processes in favor of direct responses and exhortations to abandon narcissistic object relations for a seemingly more mature "co-operative partnership." Such educational efforts contribute in his own way to result by "compliance," the very danger that Balint recognized in classical and Kleinian efforts and that he strove so valiently to avoid.

W.R.D. FAIRBAIRN

The work of W.R.D. Fairbairn was summarized in a review by Winnicott and Khan (1953). Guntrip (1968) integrated Fairbairn's work with that of Winnicott and refined and advanced it. Bacal (1984) has written on the relationship of self psychology to the work of Fairbairn, as well as an integration of the works of object relations theorists Suttie, Balint, Fairbairn, Winnicott, and Guntrip with that of Kohut. The interested reader may wish to consult this latter reference as a comprehensive auxiliary to this chapter.

In his preface to Fairbairn's *An Object Relations Theory of the Personality,* Jones (1954) wrote:

> Instead of starting as Freud did, from the stimulation of the nervous system proceeding from excitation of various erotogenous zones and internal tension arising from gonadic activity, Dr. Fairbairn starts at the centre of the personality, the ego, and depicts its strivings and difficulties in its endeavor to reach an object where it might find support. All this constitutes a fresh approach in psycho-analysis which should lead to much fruitful discussion [p. v].

Fairbairn's focus on schizoid factors in the personality arose directly in relation to Melanie Klein's crucial concepts of the "paranoid position" and defensive splitting of ego and objects in earliest childhood. For Fairbairn, only the exploration of schizoid states could yield the deepest understanding of the origins and foundations of the human personality: "The fundamental schizoid phenomenon is the presence of splits in the ego and . . . the basic position in the psyche is invariably a schizoid position" (p. 8). Although Fairbairn accepted Klein and her colleagues' (1952) view that the splitting of the ego occurred in response to conflicts between aggressive and libidinal relationships, he nonetheless emphasized, as did Balint (1953, 1968) and Winnicott (1965) the contribution to arrests in development and continuing pathogenic effects of persisting internal ties to unsatisfactory caretakers. The schizoid condition, he maintained, is the outcome of an unsatisfactory mother-infant relationship, determined by the failure on the part of the mother "to convince her child by spontaneous and genuine expressions of affection that she loves him as a person" (p. 13).

Balint visualized as central in the developmental process the progression from primary to mature love; Fairbairn's (1954) counterpart conceptualization was that infantile immature dependence, based on primary identification (by which he meant an attachment to an object not yet differentiated), was gradually abandoned in favor of adult or mature dependence based upon differentiation of object from the self. Like Balint, Fairbairn regarded as crucial to development the infant's acceptance of "reality" and its "abandonment" of archaic object strivings.

Fairbairn's position, which appears sometimes contradictory and often confusing in his earlier work is set forth more coherently in a paper written near the close of his career (Fairbairn, 1958). There he affirmed that his "chief conscious psychoanalytic interest now lies in promoting a more adequate formulation of psychoanalytic theory" (p. 376). He argued passionately against the tendency to regard existing psychoanalytic theory as objective truth. In this Fairbairn anticipated the subsequent focus on "relativism" that has been described earlier in this discussion.

> Scientific truth is simply explanatory truth; and the picture of reality provided by science is an intellectual construct . . . an attempt to describe the various phenomena of the universe, in as coherent and systematic a manner as the limitations of human intelligence permit, by means of the formulation of

> general laws by inductive inference under conditions of maximum emotional detachment and objectivity on the part of the scientific observer. A special difficulty arises in respect to psychological science for subjective aspects of phenomena are the most important data being studied and these can only be understood in terms of the subjective experience of the psychologist himself. He therefore is necessarily involved in the difficult task of adopting as detached and objective an attitude as possible to his own experience as to that of those whom he observes [pp. 376–377].

Fairbairn characterized his theoretical position as comprising four main conceptual formulations: (1) a theory of dynamic psychic structure, (2) a theory to the effect that libidinal activity is inherently and primarily object-seeking, (3) a theory of development not of zonal dominance but of the quality of dependence, and (4) a theory of the personality in terms of internal object relationships.

In his attempt to find his way to a new theory of endopsychic structure that would address the clinical phenomenology of the schizoid condition, Fairbairn (1954) described a self split into three egos, (1) a central ego (the "I"), (2) a libidinal ego, and (3) an aggressive persecutory ego, which he first called "the internal saboteur," a term later discarded in favor of "antilibidinal ego." "Subsequent experience" he wrote, "has led me to regard this classification as having a universal application" (p. 101). These ego structures, he believed, arise from an original, inherent, and unitary ego that becomes split in all cases during the earliest phases of development, and each has its own characteristic internal object relationship. The central ego is related to objects in the outer world. It is ambivalent in its attitude toward its objects, and this leads to an inner world in which unconscious split relationships exist between ego and an "exciting" and a "rejecting object." The antilibidinal ego is identified with the rejecting object and is therefore arrayed against the "libidinal ego" in its attachment to "exciting" objects. The antilibidinal ego represents the structuralization of attitudes of contempt and hatred for the object-seeking libidinal self, developed in part by identification with parental attitudes toward infantile needs as signs of "weakness" and in part as a reaction to the vulnerability to rejection posed by object-related needs.

Fairbairn's clinical experience, reflected in these concepts, made him especially critical of the requirement of traditional analysts that the analysand should possess a relatively mature, strong, and unmodified ego. He could not understand what would induce such an person, if one there were, to seek psychoanalytic treatment. People, he maintained, seek psychoanalytic treatment because they have come to recognize that they are suffering. Even a psychoanalytic candidate's interest in psychoanalysis "must be regarded as ultimately springing from a desire, largely unconscious perhaps, to resolve his own conflicts" (1958, p. 375). Fairbairn was equally critical of the notion that an average patient is interested in the undertaking of a scientific exploration of his personality. Where such a condition exists, he maintained, it reflects obsessional or schizoid personality defenses and formidable resistances against emotional involvement, a phenomenon to be investigated, not a motivation to be credited as primary. He considered this justification by analysts to be an apologia for their lack of therapeutic results.

Fairbairn's (1958) passionate commitment to the reestablishment of psychoanalysis as the most advanced psychological treatment led him to reconsider clinical assumptions that had also become regarded as ultimate truths.

> It becomes obvious, therefore, that from a therapeutic standpoint, interpretation is not enough, and it would appear to follow that the relationship existing between the patient and the analyst in the psychoanalytic situation serves purposes additional to that of providing a setting for the interpretation of transference phenomena [p. 377].

The disabilities of patients arose, Fairbairn held, not from the distortion of early experiences with objects, but "from the effects of unsatisfactory and unsatisfying object-relationships experienced in early life and perpetuated in an exaggerated form in inner reality" (p. 377). Therefore, only the actual relationship between analyst and patient as persons could constitute a new reality and thus an indispensable therapeutic factor. Only such a relationship could provide a means of correcting distorted internal relationships and also provide the patient with the opportunity, foreclosed in his childhood, "to undergo a process of emotional development in the setting of an actual relationship with a reliable and beneficent parental figure" (p. 377). He maintained that although such an actual relationship is difficult to reconcile with a psychology of "impulse," it is compatible with a psychology of object relations and dynamic structure.

Fairbairn never fully detailed what he had in mind with this recommendation. He himself abandoned the use of the couch "to great advantage, in my opinion," because he considered that "the stock arguments in favor of couch technique are now rationalizations" (p. 378). He suggested that rigid adherence to the details of the classical psychoanalytic technique, as standardized by Freud, is liable to defensive exploitation in the interests of the analyst and at the expense of the patient, "and certainly any tendency to treat the classic technique as sacrosanct raises the suspicion that an element of such defensive exploitation is at work" (p. 379). Theoretical or clinical purism, he insisted, "resolves itself simply into an apotheosis of the method at the expense of the aims which the method is intended to serve" (p. 379). In a succinct passage Fairbairn wrote, "In recent years I have shed enough sophistication to enable me to ask myself repeatedly such naive questions as, "if the patient does not make satisfactory progress under analysis, how far is this due to some defect in the psychoanalytic method?" (p. 379).

Much of what Fairbairn wrote is as refreshing and stimulating today as it was 40 years ago. But as revolutionary as Fairbairn's approach was in 1950, it seems now an important but limited link in a continuing evolutionary process within psychoanalysis.

The fundamental nature of the tie to objects remains unclear in Fairbairn's writings, and he seemed never fully to separate himself from the influence of Klein's thinking that the crucial events of infancy surround conflicts aroused by gratifying and frustrating experiences with objects. Sometimes it appears in his view that the need for objects is per se the central motivational force, and the ego, or self, is psychologically significant only insofar as it is able to progress from archaic dependence to mature interdependance. Although he came to recognize and describe a fundamental need for objects so as not to "break down," thus approaching Kohut's (1971, 1977) concept of selfobject, his (Fairbairn, 1954) reconstruction of infantile development has as its central focus the events presumed to flow from the infant's total dependence on its maternal objects. The ties to archaic objects are those in which such dependency needs are either gratified or frustrated, and whether needs are gratified or frustrated determines whether the object is experienced as good or bad; it also determines the subsequent pathological structuralizations that occur. The awareness of a complex self-structure with its own developmental program and of the need for object ties in the functional service of this fundamental area of development as primary motivational forces is still at some distance in Fairbairn's conceptualizations.

Fairbairn's concepts therefore fail to engage the central psychopathology of the fragile cohesiveness and precarious boundary formation that lie behind defensive schizoid barriers in therapeutic transferences. For Fairbairn (1954), the goal of analysis was to heal "splits in the ego" in order to develop the capability for object relations, not to establish an object relation in order to consolidate a nuclear self so that its own intrinsic developmental design, including the achievement of mature, interdependent love relations, can evolve. Kohut (1984) demonstrated how pathological defenses such as Fairbairn's "internal saboteur" are unwittingly reinforced by analysts' failures to appreciate that schizoid defenses are fundamentally in the service of self-preservation. "Successful self preservation" Kohut (1984) wrote, "is not only compatible with the full flowering of investment in object: it is, for many individuals, though significantly not for all, a precondition for 'object love' " (p. 143).

Fairbairn's (1954) investigations led him to focus analytically on the internal object relations of his patients. These involved "obstinate attachments" to exciting or frustrating objects that embody the child's hopes for parental acceptance. The attachments also serve as a protection against the childhood terrors of total aloneness if disengagement occurs, although they necessitate a repetitive withdrawal from engagements in the real world. The vicissitudes of these attachments, together with their affective components, are sketched out in some detail in Fairbairn's work. He saw the "antilibidinal ego" as the preeminent source of resistance to the emergence of "dependency" needs in analysis, along with the reluctance of patients to relinquish ties to their frustrating objects. He came to regard these factors as the source of intransigent resistance in psychoanalysis and his own "negative therapeutic reactions."

In my own experience, this stance has often been perceived by patients as critical of protective aspects of their own self-organization or of cherished values that persist as a consequence of failures in the processes of differentiation of self from other experience in this area. Consequently the analyst is experienced as a frustrated and frustrating archaic selfobject, and the path is opened to an intensification of the existing unconscious, invariant principles that pattern the patient's experience of himself and his world.

Fairbairn (1958) was intensely dissatisfied with the quality of emotional experience available in a psychoanalytic procedure in which the analyst regarded himself as a dispassionate and objective observer of events occurring within the psychic apparatus of the patient and as a screen for the projection of previously installed images. He recognized that such a posture could itself reflect schizoid characteristics by analysts who feared emotional involvement and who in any case contributed to schizoid encapsulation in patients. His understanding led him to attempt to alter the experience through concretized changes in the analytic procedure. Kohut (1984) addressed the same problem in the following way.

> In harmony with the popular saying that "half truth is the worst enemy of the truth," the half truth of Freud's early experience-distant formulations about libido regression and fixation allowed analysts to protect themselves against empathic immersion in the analysand's diseased self and prevented them from arriving at the experience-near formulations of self psychology that are relevant to the psychic miseries of our time. Specifically, the availability of the classical theory of fixation and regression . . . has been able to cover up the fact that one of the most important clusters of human psychic disturbance remained deemphasized. . . . The security that these claims have provided for us has up to now, prevented us from perceiving what many of our patients have been trying to tell us for a long time; that the issues they are facing cannot be joined in earnest as long as our theories dictate an ultimate focus either on the drives, genital or pregenital, as the biological bedrock of our personalities, or on the ego, mature or infantile, as the central organ of a mental apparatus that mediates between biological drives and the curbs imposed upon them by reality [pp. 221–222].

Kohut's understanding led him to a deepening immersion into his patients' subjective experience. He came to recognize that the analyst's presence or absence, what he did or did not do, and especially his attitudes as reflected in his theories played a constitutive role in the analysis. Investigating and understanding this aspect of the patient's subjective experience, always from a stance within the framework of that experience, occupied a central role in his therapeutic process. In the maintenance of an experience-near psychoanalytic stance, Kohut found the possibilities for the "new relationship" that Fairbairn, like Balint, sought by other means.

CONCLUSION

Aside from the broadened and increased precision of our theories and clinical observations, what lessons can be learned from the innovations that have been described? It is to be hoped, surely, that it will be apparent that every analyst—indeed psychoanalysis itself—can develop only in an environment in which the widest diversity is encouraged. The encouragement of such diversity provides the firmest link to a tradition that illuminates and frees, just as the most precious of parenthoods provides the security and wisdom to enable each child to the experiences that will free the creativity that particular child needs to determine truly along what course his own unique interests lie. It is the parents' insistence that the child follow a parentally determined path that shackles the development of the child or turns it into a hollow victory for the parents. The object relations theorists and Kohut together made it possible for succeeding generations of psychoanalysts to see more than had before been visible. They shared the determination to continue the tradition of Freud not by the celebration and reaffirmation necessarily of his concepts but of his ideals. They had in common a passionate commitment to stretch themselves, to expand man's understanding of his experience and be better able to heal what is damaged and change and revitalize what has become stagnant. Perhaps the most significant of the many facets of their commonality in this continuing quest and of their legacy is expressed in the following quotations:

> Suppose we were really steadfast, one would wonder what was the matter with us. Time passes, we grow older, and if our ideas remain the same there must be something wrong [Bion, 1980, p. 37].

> Even the most convincing conclusions seemingly self-evident beyond question, may ultimately come into serious question [Kohut, 1984, p. 57].

REFERENCES

Abraham, K. (1948), *Selected Papers.* London: Hogarth Press.

Atwood G. & Stolorow R. (1984), *Structures of Subjectivity.* Hillsdale, NJ: The Analytic Press.

Bacal, H. (1984), British object relations theories and self psycholoy. Presented at the 7th Annual Self Psychology Conference, Toronto, Ontario, October 20.

Balint, M. (1953), *Primary Object Love and Psycho-Analytic Technique.* New

York: Liveright.
_____ (1968), *The Basic Fault.* London: Tavistock.
Bion, W. (1980). In: *Bion in New York and Sao Paolo.* Perthshire, Scotland: Clunie Press.
Brandchaft, B. (1983), The negativism of the negative therapeutic reaction and the psychology of the self. In: *The Future of Psychoanalysis,* ed. A. Goldberg. New York: International Universities Press, pp. 327-362.
_____ (1986), British object relations theory and self psychology. In: *Progress in Self Psychology,* Vol. 1, ed. A. Goldberg. New York Guilford Press.
_____ & Stolorow, R. (1984), The borderline concept: Pathological character or iatrogenic myth? In: *Empathy II,* ed. J. Lichtenberg, M. Bornstein & D. Silver. Hillsdale, NJ: The Analytic Press, pp. 333–357.
Fairbairn, W.R.D. (1954), *An Object Relations Theory of the Personality.* New York: Bane.
_____ (1958), On the nature and aims of psychoanalytic treatment. *Internat. J. Psycho-Anal.,* 39:374–386.
Freud, S. (1920), Beyond the pleasure principle. *Standard Edition.* 18:7–64. London: Hogarth Press, 1955.
Guntrip, H. (1968), *Schizoid Phenomena, Object Relations and the Self.* London: Hogarth Press.
Jones, E. (1954), Preface. In: *An Object Relations Theory of the Personality,* by W.R.D. Fairbairn. New York: Basic Books.
Joseph, B. (1982) Addiction to Near-Death. *Internat. J. Psycho-Anal.,* 63:449–56.
Khan, M. (1969). On the clinical provision of frustrations, recognitions and failures in the analytic situation: An essay on Dr. Michael Balint's researches on the theory of psychoanalytic technique. *Internat. J. Psycho-Anal.,* 50:237–248.
Klein, M. (1950) *Contributions to Psychoanalysis 1921–1945.* London: Hogarth Press.
_____ (1954), *The Psychoanalysis of Children.* London: Hogarth Press.
_____ (1957), *Envy and Gratitude.* Boston: Delacorte Press, 1975.
_____ (1961), *Narrative of a Child Analysis.* New York: Basic Books.
_____ Heimann P., Isaacs, S. & Riviere J. (1952), *Developments in Psychoanalysis.* London: Hogarth Press.
Kohut, H. (1971), *The Analysis of the Self.* New York: International Universities Press.
_____ (1977), *The Restoration of the Self.* New York: International Universities Press.
_____ (1984) *How Does Analysis Cure?* ed. A. Goldberg & P. E. Stepansky. Chicago: University of Chicago Press.
Rosenfeld, H. (1971) A clinical approach to the psychoanalytic theory of the life and death instincts. *Internat. J. Psycho-Anal.* 52:169–78.
Sander, L. (1975), Infant and caretaking environment: Investigation and conceptualization of adaptive behavior in a system of increasing

complexity. In: *Explorations in Child Psychiatry,* ed. E. Anthony. New York: Premium Press, pp. 129–166.

Schwaber, E. (1983), Construction, reconstruction and the mode of clinical attunement. In: *The Future of Psychoanalysis,* ed. A. Goldberg. New York: International Universities Press, pp. 273–292.

Segal, H. (1979), *Klein.* Glascow: William Collins & Son.

Stolorow, R., Brandchaft, B. & Atwood, G. (1987), *Psychoanalytic Treatment.* Hillsdale, NJ: The Analytic Press.

Winnicott, D.W. (1965), *The Maturation Processes and the Facilitating Environment.* London: Hogarth Press.

Winnicott, D.W. & Khan, M. (1953), Review of *Psycho-Analytic Studies of the Personality* by W.R.D. Fairbairn. *Internat. J. Psycho-Anal.,* 4:329–333.

13

Winnicott and Self Psychology

Remarkable Reflections

HOWARD A. BACAL

Unlike Freud's or Klein's work, Winnicott's never became identified as a school of psychoanalytic thought,[1] nor did he ever propose that his ideas constituted a comprehensive theory of object-relations.[2] Yet the spread of his influence on the understanding of early child development and its application to common clinical issues in psychoanalytic and psychotherapeutic practice is really quite remarkable.

Winnicott's ideas are, however, largely unsystematized, and his exposition of them sometimes makes their differences from classical and Kleinian theory unclear. While this undoubtedly contributes to their richness and lengthens the reach of their creative power, it also tends to produce a sense of theoretical inconsistency and inconclusiveness. We must assume that Kohut had some familiarity with Winnicott's ideas, but it is perhaps for these reasons that he chose not to build on them, despite their evident similarity to his own. Elsewhere I (Bacal, 1987) have outlined the similarities between certain British object relations theorists and self

[1]Melanie Klein's work, of course, did become identified as "Kleinian psychoanalysis" and is referred to as the English School.

[2]As Modell (1983) notes, "[Winnicott] was a psychoanalytic revolutionary without the temperament or personality with which to make a revolution" (p. 112).

psychology,[3] of whom Winnicott is a prime example; this theme will be expanded in a forthcoming book (Bacal and Newman, in press). There are so many concepts in Winnicott's work that anticipate those later elaborated in self psychology that it is remarkable that Kohut did not consider Winnicott as a source for the development of his theories. From this perspective, Modell's (1985) assertion that "Kohut's contribution could be viewed as an extension of Winnicott's work" (p. 98) is understandable. In this chapter, I shall discuss a number of ideas introduced by Winnicott and show how they have been conceptualized by self psychology. In certain instances, these conceptualizations extend and render more precise Winnicott's formulations; in others, the richness of Winnicott's understanding surpasses and could enhance self-psychological theory. I shall also indicate areas of significant divergence between their perspectives.

Winnicott's focus on the environmental factors contributing to the psychological development of the infant and on the central role that the mothering figure plays in this development provides a thrust and tone to his theorizing that distinguishes it sharply from Freudian psychoanalysis. Although Melanie Klein had some influence on his early thinking, this did not prevail. Klein and Winnicott both underscored the significance of object relations and indicated its importance for self-development. For Klein, however, the nature of the object relation and the development of the self derive ultimately from the quality and degree of the instinctual charge. For Winnicott, they are determined primarily by the responsiveness of the object: The nature of the caring functions of the maternal figure and her symbolic representatives ultimately determines the quality of the child's development. A now famous, apparently off-the-cuff remark that Winnicott (1960a) made at a meeting of the British Psycho-Analytical Society (around 1940) expresses the essence of his perspective. He said, "There is no such thing as an infant. What [I meant], of course, [was] that whenever one finds an infant one finds maternal care, and without maternal care there would be no infant . . . the infant and the maternal care together form a unit" (p. 39). This unit, which consists of the infant in relation to a maternal *subjective object,* closely resembles the archaic self-selfobject unit later elaborated by Kohut (1971, 1977).

---

[3]Self psychology is a body of theory in which the experience of the relationship between the self and its selfobjects is regarded as essential for self development. Thus, *selfobject theory,* as it is more appropriately called, can be regarded as an object relations theory in which *selfobject* relations are central (Bacal, in press a).

There is, in fact, compelling evidence that Winnicott understood the idea of early selfobject functioning in much the same sense as Kohut did, but did not, so to speak, organize the idea so precisely. The caring functions of the mother are facilitated by the infant's capacity to experience her as a *subjective object* (Winnicott, 1962a, p. 57). For Winnicott (1971a) the subjective object was "the first object, the object *not yet repudiated as a not-me phenomenon*" (p. 80), that is, an object that is experienced as an extension of the self. Winnicott indicated that this form of object relating, which he compares with primary identification, is an essential precondition for the development of the sense of self. Winnicott's concept of the subjective object is very similar to Kohut's initial view of the selfobject insofar as the latter is also conceived of as being experienced as an extension of the self. The term "selfobject" as currently used in self psychology, is a shorthand for the experience of functions provided by an object that is felt to sustain, enhance, or restore the sense of self, but the question of the degree of distinctness with which it is experienced by the self has not been clearly explicated. Kohut initially considered the *selfobject* to be synonymous with the object of primary identification; that is, it is *always* experienced as contiguous with the self. While this situation may in theory prevail in earliest infancy[4] (and later become manifest in analysis in certain kinds of regressions, or as a developmental arrest), it is hardly, if at all, an aspect of the experience of more mature self-selfobject relationships. The quality of the infant's experience of the subjective object, however—in effect, of the infant's early holding environment—*is* that of a merger. In other words, it is comparable to Kohut's *archaic* self-selfobject relationship. Although Winnicott did not conceptualize the subjective object (as Kohut did the selfobject) as the experience of being provided the essential functions that affect the sense of self, he gave extensive indirect expression to this in his understanding of the self-sustaining and growth-enhancing functions of the early maternal environment in his ideas of the ordinary devoted mother (Winnicott, 1966), the good-enough mother (Winnicott, 1960b), the holding environment (Winnicott, 1960a), and the mirroring func-

[4]Winnicott (1962b) asserted that there was a peried in early infancy "in which it is not possible to describe an infant without describing the mother whom the infant has not yet become able to separate from a self" (p. 177). However, some developmental psychologists, such as Stern (1985), doubt the existence of an undifferentiated phase in development.

tion of the mother's face (Winnicott, 1971b). We have already alluded to Winnicott's (1958) paradox that "the experience of being alone in the presence of someone" constitutes the basis of "the capacity to be alone" (p. 36). He also asserted that this comes about as "the ego-supportive environment is [gradually] introjected and built into the individual's personality . . ." (p. 36). Here Winnicott is unmistakably indicating the importance of assimilating what self psychologists call *selfobject functions* for maturation and for the development of psychological strength. For both Winnicott and Kohut, the infant's "weakness" is largely nullified by the mother's care and support. Winnicott called this relationship *ego-relatedness* (p. 33), which characterizes the *holding environment* (Winnicott, 1960a). The equivalent of *ego-relatedness* in self psychology is the experience of a *selfobject relationship* that is appropriate to the sustenance and development of the infant's self, and the functions of a *holding environment* are reflected in those of *archaic selfobject functioning.*

The holding environment is Winnicott's (1960a) term for the overall technique of good-enough mothering of the infant, the provision of which is determined by the mother's ability to empathize with her baby's needs.[5] The mother's ability to meet the needs of her very young infant derives from a state of *primary maternal preoccupation* (Winnicott, 1956) which, as Winnicott described it, can be understood as a state of enhanced maternal empathy. At this time, when the infant is maximally dependent, his world must be maximally adaptive to his needs. In this very early phase of life, if the mother fails to adapt adequately or if she intrudes substantially with her own needs (impingement), the infant's reaction breaks up his "going-on-being". If *reactions to impingement* becomes a characteristic pattern in his life, it will seriously interfere with the integration of his self (Winnicott, 1963b). Holding, for Winnicott, is "the basis for what gradually becomes a self-experiencing being" (quoted in Davis and Wallbridge, 1981, p. 99). If, as I contend, optimal responsiveness to the infant's selfobject needs is synonymous with holding, self psychologists share the identical perspective on early self-development as Winnicott. In effect, when pondering the beginnings of the nuclear self, Kohut (1977) recognized that the most primitive function of the selfobject is its "deeply-anchored

[5]Winnicott (1963b) stresses the importance of the quality of the mother's physical holding of her infant, which must entail an identification with the baby that he compares with the function of the primary substances described by Balint (1968); see also Bacal and Newman (in press).

responsiveness" to the infant from the beginning, and postulated that the baby's rudimentary self may arise at the point where, in a state of mutual empathic merger, the potentialities of the baby and the selfobject's expectations of him converge (pp. 99–100).

While Winnicott did not explicitly formulate the notion of the *self* as a supraordinate organizing concept for understanding the individual, his predominant area of interest was unquestionably the healthy and the pathological development of what is regarded as the self in self psychology today. Winnicott, however, in contrast to self psychology, which addresses self-development throughout the life cycle, focused on the developing self of the *infant.* Winnicott believed that the sense of self develops out of unordered, formless activity or play, but only if the environment reflects it back, and that one truly discovers oneself only in the process of being creative. Winnicott was particularly interested in distinguishing between what he called the true self and the false self. The true self develops in an adequately empathic and caring maternal environment, but in the absence of such an environment a false self evolves to protect the true self from adverse maternal influence. The true self is first present at the inception of primitive mental organization simply as "the summation of sensori-motor aliveness" (Winnicott, 1960b, p. 149). It then becomes the psychological sense of the several ways in which a particular person experiences himself as being both alive and real, if you like, authentic. In effect, Winnicott regards the true self as equivalent to psychic reality. Its essence, and its distinction from the notion of false self, is exemplified by the actor who can be himself and also act rather than someone who is "completely at a loss when not in a role, and when not being appreciated or applauded . . ." (p. 150). The applause is experienced as the acknowledgment of the person's existence, which the false self cannot feel. The experience of personal acknowledgment is essentially what both Winnicott and Kohut (1979, personal communication) mean by the idea of being *mirrored* (Winnicott, 1971b). It is not *grandiosity* that the child needs confirmed, but a recognition of his uniqueness, of his creative capacity, that is, of his true self. Kohut (1979, personal communication) realized that terms such as *archaic grandiosity* and *healthy grandiosity* do not really do justice to this meaning, but by then self psychology was stuck with them.

Winnicott has suggested that the very core of the self in a healthy person remains isolated from the outside world, that this core is never influenced by external reality, and that the primitive-defenses that the infant erects in reaction to traumatic experiences are, above all, intended to prevent this core from being found, altered, or even communicated with. Guntrip (1968) repudiated this 20 years ago, as would self psychology today, and for similar reasons. Guntrip cited this view of Winnicott's as inconsistent with the latter's central concept of a basic ego-relatedness, that is, that in health, no one is isolated internally, even if one is alone. In effect, Winnicott asserted that the capacity to be alone (in external reality) depends on one's sense of never being alone (internally). Similarly, self psychology recognizes that the availability of the selfobject is a necessary condition for the self to maintain its cohesiveness and strength in the face of separation.

Winnicott's account of the development of the true self in contrast to the development of the false self is closely reflected in Kohut's conception of the healthy development of the self in contrast to its unhealthy development. Winnicott (1960b) regards the cohesion of the early self as depending on "the fact that the mother holds the infant, sometimes physically, and all the time figuratively" (p. 145). The good-enough mother, or the ordinary devoted mother (Winnicott, 1966), enables the true self to become a reality by meeting the omnipotence of the infant and giving it meaning (Winnicott, 1960b). Winnicott's phrase, "meeting the omnipotence of the infant" conveys a meaning very similar to Kohut's notion of the mother's mirroring the infant's "archaic grandiosity," but neither describes the situation adequately. The essence of both could be more clearly conveyed by expressing it partly in Winnicott's and partly in current self psychology language: the good-enough mother functions as a selfobject for the infant insofar as he experiences her as validating his creative gesture as his own and giving it meaning. Although this statement may be difficult for some self psychologists to accept, Kohut might have arrived at it himself if he had integrated the valid aspects of Winnicott's work with his own creative contributions.

The self-psychological idea of the enfeeblement or fragmentation of the self as a reaction to selfobject failure could be enriched by the addition of Winnicott's idea of the false self, which is a reaction to environmental failure and is not necessarily weak or fragmented; it has compromised its genuineness by complying with environmental demands as an adaptation to selfobject shortfall.

The infant matures by moving out of a world of subjective objects, where he is *relating,* in a merged state, to the enriching mutual *usage* that comes from recognizing objects outside himself and outside his omnipotent control. For Winnicott, the "term 'maturational process' refers [not only] to the evolution of the . . . self, [but also] includes the whole story of the id, of instincts and their vicissitudes, and of defenses in the ego relative to instinct" (p. 85). Thus, Winnicott (1963a) formulated the idea of two mothers for the infant, corresponding to two aspects of infant care—the object-mother and the environment-mother: "The environment-mother . . . receives all that can be called affection and sensuous coexistence; it is the object-mother who becomes the target for excited experience backed by crude instinct-tension" (pp. 75–76). The integration in the child's mind of the split between the "two mothers" into one person comes about through two experiences: of good-enough mothering and of his experience of his mother's survival of his phantasied as well as actual attacks on her over time (Winnicott, 1954–55, p. 267). Winnicott thus regards destructiveness not only as a reaction to frustration, but also as a primary instinct whose discharge plays a crucial role in the maturation process. Winnicott speaks of a stage of *preruth,* where the infant is not aware of his ruthless destructive intent toward the mother;[6] he is not angry, or hating, but is simply expressing himself and releasing instinctual tension toward the object. If the mother is an adequate caretaker, the infant comes to experience concern for her as he becomes aware of his aggression toward her. However, "If there is not good-enough mothering, then the result is chaos rather than talion dread and a splitting of the objects into 'good' and 'bad' "[7] (Winnicott, 1962b, p. 177). The shift from this kind of ruthlessness to *ruth,* or concern, occurs gradually over the period between 5 and 15 months and corresponds with the period labeled by Klein (1952) as the *depressive position.* However, the normal infant, according to Winnicott (1954–55) does not pass through a stage of depression. He thus regarded Melanie Klein's term, *depressive position,* as "a bad name for a normal process" and suggested that it be regarded as "the stage of concern" (p. 265). He also disagreed with Klein's view that a baby envies the breast. He thought, rather, that the baby's impulse to attack and destroy is not only "pre-ruth," not only not angry, but that, most important, the result is that the mother is felt to survive the attack. Thus, Winnicott emphasized the developmental significance of destructiveness for

[6]Winnicott notes that patients in regression can look back and realize that they were ruthless then (Winnicott, 1954–55).

[7]It was Winnicott's (1962b) opinion that Klein paid lip service to the importance of the environmental factor.

the infant: because the object survives and does not retaliate, reject, or moralize, she can be used. She can now be experienced as existing external to the infant in her own right, as separate and permanent, and thus useable. In Winnicott's (1971c) words, "In this way, a world of shared reality is created which the subject can use and which can feed back other-than-me substance into the subject" (p. 94). For Winnicott, this change in the relationship between self and object is a precondition for *the ability to empathize.* That is, while the ability to stand in someone else's shoes necessitates a blurring between the "me" and the "not-me," it also requires a "different-from-me" understanding and this kind of understanding also comes with the growing ability to experience objects as separate from the self (Davis and Wallbridge, 1981).

Winnicott's view that the object becomes useable because it survives the infant's destructiveness, and that the infant develops a capacity for concern for the object as he becomes aware of his destructive intent, would be untenable to self psychologists, for they reject the idea of a primary destructiveness. From the perspective of self psychology, concern reflects a capacity to provide a mature selfobject function for another person—to become involved and to interest oneself in another[8]—an inherent capacity that develops as a result of one's experience of optimal selfobject responsiveness.

THE NATURE AND FUNCTION OF ILLUSION

Winnicott is undoubtedly best known for his concept of the *transitional object,* which he defines as "the first not-Me possession" (Winnicott, 1951, p. 229). The transitional object, which belongs to the infant but is not experienced as part of himself, should be distinguished from the subjective object (discussed earlier), which is experienced as part of the self. Transitional objects and transitional phenomena are experienced—unchallenged by adults as to their reality, their importance, or who created them—in an intermediate area, a potential space, located somewhere between the infant and the world outside him.

The child normally becomes particularly attached to one of a variety of, usually soft, objects, such as a blanket or a cloth animal,

[8]Definition of *concern, Collins English Dictionary,* p. 312.

which seems to have a special importance and even a kind of real existence of its own. However, while transitional objects and transitional phenomena (such as a repertoire of songs at bedtime) symbolize both the baby and the mother, their importance is not as symbols but as early stages of the infant's use of *illusion*. Winnicott regards the capacity for illusion as of the greatest importance for healthy development. In these early stages of life, "there is no interchange between the mother and the infant. Psychologically, the infant takes from a breast that is part of the infant, and the mother gives milk to an infant that is part of herself" (p. 239). One might say that the transitional object and transitional phenomena concretize illusion, which Winnicott characterizes as "an intermediate area of *experiencing,* to which inner reality and external life both contribute. It is an area . . . that shall exist as a resting-place for the individual engaged in the perpetual human task of keeping inner and outer reality separate yet interrelated" (p. 230). It is not the object or the phenomenon that are transitional. They represent the infant's transitional state with respect to his merger with the mother and his relation to her as external and separate[9] (Winnicott, 1971d).

The self-psychological concept of the *selfobject* also implies Winnicott's understanding of transitional objects[10] as constituting the experiencing of illusion. In effect, the "selfobject experience" depends partly on the capacity for illusion and partly on the quality of the presentation of the object that is experienced as fulfilling selfobject functions. Neither alone constitutes a substantive basis for the development of a strong and vital self. Elsewhere, I (Bacal, 1981, 1985, in press b) have described the vulnerability of patients whose selfobject experience is essentially a *fantasy selfobject* experience, an experience created almost totally out of the capacity for illusion in a nuclear environment that barely functioned in ways that gave substance to the satisfaction of selfobject needs. In these instances, the patient is peculiarly vulnerable to stresses that strain his capacity for illusion. Winnicott believes that the child's capacity for illusion is dependent on the mother's "good-enough" early

[9]This is part of Winnicott's addition to his original version of the paper, "Transitional Objects and Transitional Phenomena" (1951) published in the *International Journal of Psychoanalysis* in 1953, and reprinted in his *Collected Papers* in 1958.

[10]From the point of view of self-psychological theory, transitional objects would intelligibly be regarded as transitional *selfobjects* insofar as they are experienced as providing selfobject functions.

adaptation to his needs. In other words, the infant's experience of the responsive mother's archaic selfobject function gives him the sense that there is an external reality that corresponds to his own capacity to create. In time, the importance of the transitional object fades, but the capacity for illusion remains as the basis for playing, creativity, and the appreciation of culture. We would like to suggest that, throughout life, the personal meaning of the interpersonal relationship, or object relationship, *always* depends to some extent on illusion, and that, while the stability of illusion depends upon experiences of optimal responsiveness, its existence is inherent in the human organism (Bacal, in press b).

FURTHER COMPARISONS BETWEEN WINNICOTT AND SELF PSYCHOLOGY

Although Winnicott (1960b) explicitly stated that he was not referring to the satisfaction of instincts when he refers to the meeting of infant needs, his view was that "id-satisfaction" [is] a very important *strengthener* of the ego, or of the True self (p. 141, italics added). Winnicott also stressed, however, that it is only when the infant's self gains strength that instinctual demands become experienced as part of the self, rather than felt to come from outside, and that when the infant's self is not yet strong enough to include them, id excitements themselves can be traumatic and will, in any case, have no meaning.

Self psychology regards lustful appetites as an expression of a healthy self; but insofar as it otherwise concerns itself with "the instincts," its focus is on the emergence of isolated drives as disintegration products of a fragmenting self consequent upon selfobject failure and as comprising an attempt at restitution of the self and its relatedness to the selfobject. Winnicott's idea that id satisfaction can, under certain conditions, strengthen the self and, under others, be traumatic would be a clinically valuable addition to self-psychological theory and practice.[11]

Winnicott, like Kohut,(1977) attributes, without blame, the false self, or pathological self-development, to varying degrees and kinds of environmental failure (Winnicott, 1962a); but, unlike Kohut, Winnicott regards the very early maternal environment as

[11]The implications of Winnicott's work for therapy, in particular as it articulates with self psychology, are elaborated more fully in Bacal and Newman (in press).

overshadowing in importance any other factors. This focus on *primitive* object relations characterizes the work of all the British object relations theorists and was, in part, a reaction to the emphasis by classical analysts that significant emotional problems centered almost wholly on the oedipal situation. The systematic development of the idea that the self's strength and the fulfilment of its potential depend on its experience of phase-appropriately responsive selfobjects *from birth to death* is the unique contribution of Heinz Kohut. Yet, Winnicott (1963b) had very much that kind of thing in mind when he wrote of the developmental shift from the *absolute dependence* of the infant to the stage of *relative dependence.* This shift is characterized by adaptation of the infant to the gradual, manageable failure of adaptation of the mother to the infant. The stage that Winnicott calls *towards independence,* which extends through adolescence and adulthood "where local society is a sample of the self's personal world as well as being a sample of truly external phenomena" (p. 91) is a stage in which the individual can do without actual care because he has introjected the memories of care and has developed confidence in the environment (Winnicott, 1960a). That is, the mother, whose close adaptation to her infant's needs—an adaptation necessary for his healthy development early on—will be able to increasingly fail as the infant's mind becomes able "to allow for failures in adaptation. In this way, the [infant's] mind is allied to the mother and takes over part of her function" (Winnicott quoted in Davis and Wallbridge, 1981, p. 53). Here, Winnicott has succinctly stated the importance of "optimal responsiveness" (Bacal, 1985) as well as the usefulness of inevitable, nontraumatic frustration ("optimal frustration"[12]) for psychological development. He has also virtually defined the selfobject experience and its transmuting internalization into self-substance in a way that hardly differs from the essence of the process described by Kohut (1984). However, while Winnicott discussed the importance of these ideas for the maturational process, Kohut built a systematic theoretical model around them.

REFERENCES

Bacal, H.A. (1981), Notes on some therapeutic challenges in the analysis of severely regressed patients. *Psychoanal. Inq.* 1:29–56.

---

[12]The validity of the concept of "optimal frustration" has recently come into question (Bacal, 1985, 1988; Terman, 1988).

_____ (1985), Optimal responsiveness and the therapeutic process. In: *Progress in Self Psychology, Vol. 1,* ed. A. Goldberg, New York: Guilford Press, pp. 202–226.

_____ (1987), British object-relations theorists and self psychology: Some critical reflections. *Internat J. Psycho-Anal.,* 68:81–98.

_____ (1988), Reflections on "optimum frustration." In: *Learning from Kohut,* ed. A. Goldberg. Hillsdale, NJ: The Analytic Press, pp. 127–131.

_____ (in press a), Does an object relations theory exist in self psychology? *Psychoanal. Inq.*

_____ (in press b), The elements of a corrective selfobject experience. *Psychoanal. Inq.*

_____ & Newman, K. M. (in press), *Theories of Object Relations.* New York: Columbia University Press.

Balint, M. (1968), *The Basic Fault.* London: Tavistock.

Collins English Dictionary (1979), London: William Collins Sons.

Davis, M. & Wallbridge, W. (1981), *Boundary and Space.* New York: Brunner/Mazel

Guntrip, H. (1968), *Schizoid Phenomena, Object-Relations and the Self.* London: Hogarth Press.

Klein, M. (1952), Some theoretical conclusions regarding the emotional life of the infant. In: *Developments in Psycho-Analysis,* by M. Klein, P. Heimann, S. Isaacs, & J. Riviere. London: Hogarth Press, 1970, pp. 198–236.

Kohut, H. (1971). *The Analysis of The Self.* New York: International Universities Press.

_____ (1977), *The Restoration of the Self.* New York. International Universities Press.

_____ (1984), *How Does Analysis Cure?* ed. A. Goldberg & P. E. Stepansky. Chicago: University of Chicago Press.

Modell, A. (1983), Review of *Boundary and Space.* by M. Davis & D. Wallbridge. *Internat. J. Psycho-Anal.,* 64:111–112.

_____ (1985), Object relations theory. In: *Models of the Mind,* ed. A. Rothstein. New York: International Universities Press, pp. 85–100.

Stern, D. (1985), *The Interpersonal World of the Infant.* New York: Basic Books.

Terman, D. (1988) Optimum frustration: Structuralization and The therapeutic process. In: *Learning from Kohut,* ed. A. Goldberg. Hillsdale, NJ: The Analytic Press, pp. 113–125.

Winnicott, D. W. (1951), Transitional objects and transitional phenomena. In: *D. W. Winnicott, Collected Papers.* London: Tavistock, 1958, pp. 229–242.

_____ (1954–55), The depressive position in normal emotional development. In: *D. W. Winnicott, Collected Papers.* London: Tavistock, 1958, pp. 262–277.

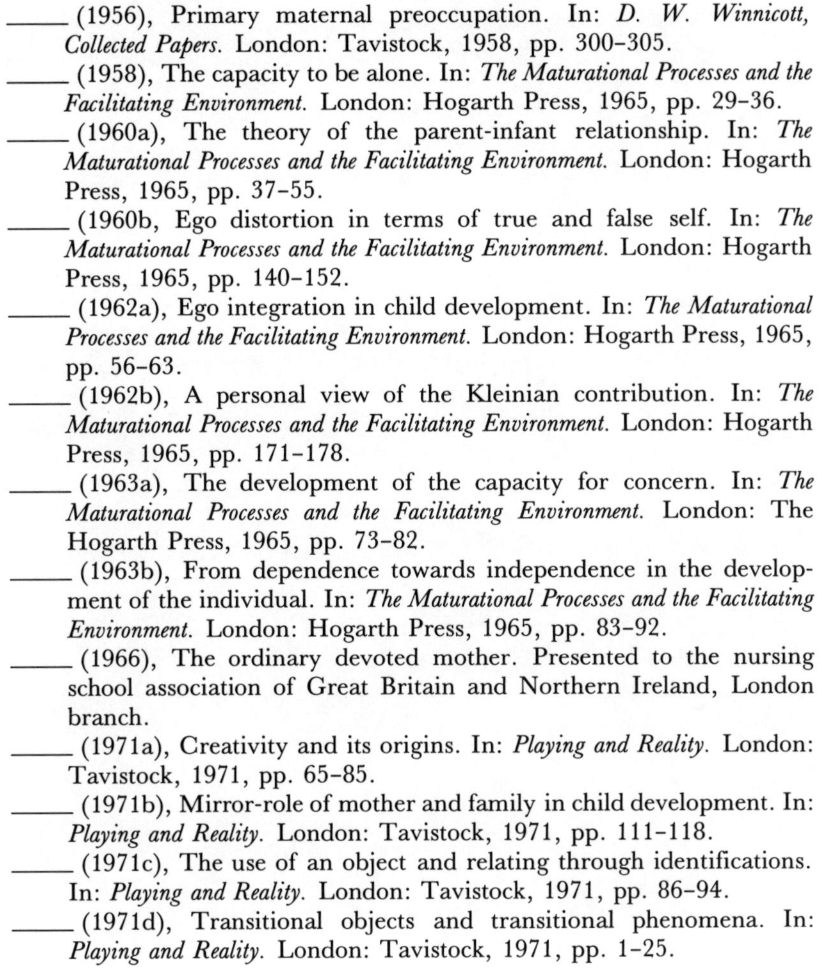

_____ (1956), Primary maternal preoccupation. In: *D. W. Winnicott, Collected Papers.* London: Tavistock, 1958, pp. 300–305.

_____ (1958), The capacity to be alone. In: *The Maturational Processes and the Facilitating Environment.* London: Hogarth Press, 1965, pp. 29–36.

_____ (1960a), The theory of the parent-infant relationship. In: *The Maturational Processes and the Facilitating Environment.* London: Hogarth Press, 1965, pp. 37–55.

_____ (1960b, Ego distortion in terms of true and false self. In: *The Maturational Processes and the Facilitating Environment.* London: Hogarth Press, 1965, pp. 140–152.

_____ (1962a), Ego integration in child development. In: *The Maturational Processes and the Facilitating Environment.* London: Hogarth Press, 1965, pp. 56–63.

_____ (1962b), A personal view of the Kleinian contribution. In: *The Maturational Processes and the Facilitating Environment.* London: Hogarth Press, 1965, pp. 171–178.

_____ (1963a), The development of the capacity for concern. In: *The Maturational Processes and the Facilitating Environment.* London: The Hogarth Press, 1965, pp. 73–82.

_____ (1963b), From dependence towards independence in the development of the individual. In: *The Maturational Processes and the Facilitating Environment.* London: Hogarth Press, 1965, pp. 83–92.

_____ (1966), The ordinary devoted mother. Presented to the nursing school association of Great Britain and Northern Ireland, London branch.

_____ (1971a), Creativity and its origins. In: *Playing and Reality.* London: Tavistock, 1971, pp. 65–85.

_____ (1971b), Mirror-role of mother and family in child development. In: *Playing and Reality.* London: Tavistock, 1971, pp. 111–118.

_____ (1971c), The use of an object and relating through identifications. In: *Playing and Reality.* London: Tavistock, 1971, pp. 86–94.

_____ (1971d), Transitional objects and transitional phenomena. In: *Playing and Reality.* London: Tavistock, 1971, pp. 1–25.

Part IV

Contemporary Contributions

14

Interpersonal Psychoanalysis and Self Psychology
A Clinical Comparison

Philip M. Bromberg

"I dance naked in my apartment," she confessed. "Sometimes I even do it with abandon." My air conditioner slightly muffled the last hesitant syllable as she spoke, turning what my patient had just said into an image so unexpectedly comic that I, equally unexpectedly, heard myself responding with a laugh, "You do it with a band? Are *they* naked too?" This was a woman who until that moment seemed to possess no available sense of identity other than that of a grimly pitiful misfit, without humor but ever ready to be laughed at, and ostensibly incapable of experiencing a difference between being seen as zany and being seen as ridiculous.

In fact, she burst into laughter so deep and so "abandoned" that tears rolled "nakedly" down her cheeks. Had I first thought about my response and weighed the risk, I doubt if I would have (or could have) chosen that path. Was it a "technical error" that luckily turned out well? A merciful rescue from a serious breach in empathy? Or was I perhaps more empathically attuned than I recognized? Was I allowing my unconscious to guide me to an aspect of her that could emerge only in response to an authentic reaction to it? Or was it just countertransference, plain and simple? Perhaps I was unconsciously disguising with humor my disclaimed reciprocation of her emerging sexual transference, and if so, might not her "abandoned" laughter have been the laughter of relief at having been spared the further scrutiny of the "genuine" analytic response she anticipated? For an interpersonal analyst the answers to questions like these are not derived a priori from one's theoretical assumptions or metapsychology. They are arrived at with the patient in a mutual exploration of the event as it was enacted on both sides, and it is through this process of exploration that interpretations can find a context in which to be formulated, and the work progresses.

In making an evaluative assessment of an alternative school of analytic thought, it is always heartening to discover some support from within that school itself. I can imagine no more eloquent or candid a summation of the main theme of my critique than the following statement made, not by an interpersonalist, but by Schwaber (1983), and it is with her observation that I would like to begin. Kohut, she asserts, has in his later work

> betrayed the position that it is the correctness of the theory rather than how we use our theory which was of the foremost importance. In assigning this status to theory and arguing for a more "correct" view of man, by implication, he placed the analyst in the position of arbiter of which is the more "correct" and which the more "distorted" view [p. 381].

It is no secret that the primary reader to whom Kohut (1971, 1977) addressed his most powerful and persuasive arguments is the "classical" psychoanalyst—the analyst who systematically interprets into the patient's pathological narcissism and unmasks its disregard of reality and of others. Amazingly little effort has been expended by self psychologists in surveying the broader landscape of analytic thought to discover and acknowledge those who advanced similar ideas before Kohut, so as to distinguish those areas where Kohut's formulations are indeed original from those in which his departure from Freudian metapsychology echoes and often draws upon similar revisions that preceded them. In this regard, interpersonal psychoanalysis (and object relational theories) have tended to be ignored by Kohut rather than credited and challenged. In his seminal work on narcissism, Kohut (1966) in one broad stroke of the brush rejects the assumption that narcissism is basically pathological, postulates a developmental line of mature narcissism, and exiles object relational theories (and, by implication, interpersonal theory) to "social psychology." He here establishes the importance of the *function* of the object in contrast to its representational qualities, paving the way for his 1971 monograph, in which he makes the sharp distinction between a selfobject and a real object. In the invention of the idea of a selfobject, Kohut hit upon a brilliant strategy that, as Ghent (1986) puts it, "at once did away with the focus on the real object, . . . retained the focus of psychoanalysis as a one-person psychology[1] [and] avoided the taint of in any way being associated with interpersonal theory" (p. 35). In contrasting interpersonal psychoanalysis with self psychology, it must therefore be kept in mind that for Kohut, the "selfobject" is also a "strategic object."

THE INTERPERSONAL LISTENING STANCE

In a recent dialogue between Arnold Goldberg and me, a pair of contrasting statements were made that I hope might place the basic distinction between the interpersonal and self-psychological positions into high relief and set the stage for its exploration in greater detail.

> An interpersonal position takes as axiomatic that growth of self occurs through dyadic interchange rather than through what the patient receives in some "correct" way. . . . For an interpersonal analyst, the empathic mode of observing is *not* designed to discourage an observational stance in the patient nor are confrontations systematically avoided as "failures" in empathy. . . . For characterological growth to occur the patient must be able to see himself through the eyes of the analyst as an ongoing aspect of feeling himself validated and understood in the terms he sees himself [Bromberg, 1986, p. 382].

> Self psychology struggles hard not to be an interpersonal psychology not only because it wishes to avoid the social psychological connotations of the phrase but also because it wishes to minimize the input of the analyst into the mix. . . . It is not minimized merely to keep the field pure so much as to allow a thwarted development to unfold. Since self psychology is so pre-eminently a developmental psychology, it is based on the idea of a developmental program (one that may be innate or pre-wired if you wish) that will reconstitute itself under certain conditions [Goldberg, 1986, p. 387].

---

[1]Gill (1984) presents a thoughtful and lucid argument for taking the two-person view seriously in the context of the classical view of analytic technique and for reconceptualizing the nature of the interpersonal interaction between patient and analyst.

Different analysts not only conceptualize differently, they also listen differently. Although an analyst's theoretical allegiance certainly plays some role in the latter, I believe there is much more to it than that. Once we have settled into our "normal" stance with someone, how do we frame what we hear as going on? Is it going on in the patient's life? In the patient's psyche? Is it going on between ourselves and the patient? Do we see these kinds of distinctions as clinically relevant? If so, do we see them as blending, as shifting from one to the other, or as one always framing the rest? If the latter, which one frames our most basic listening stance? Finally, how does the way we listen to process versus content inform what we personally believe is a "legitimate" analytic situation and what we think is therapeutic?

In an article on the journals of Princess Marie Bonaparte (Goleman, 1985), a number of excerpts were quoted in which Bonaparte records comments allegedly made by Freud, among which is the following parable:

> A European comes to Japan and sends for a Japanese tree expert to have a garden planted. On the first day, the gardener sat on a bench all day long and did not do anything. On the second day, it was the same. And the same on the third, fourth, and fifth day—all week long. Then the European asked: When are you going to get started on the garden? "When I have taken in the scenery." It is the same with analysis. One first has to take in the scenery of every new psyche [p. C2].

Freud (1912) described the appropriate stance for the analyst "taking in the scenery" as one that

> consists simply in not directing one's notice to anything in particular and in maintaining the same "evenly suspended attention" . . . in the face of all one hears. . . . Or to put it purely in terms of technique: "He should simply listen and not bother about whether he is keeping anything in mind" (pp. 111–112).

Translated into our everyday work with patients, Freud's definition remains a one word guideline, as valid now as it was then, that directs everything we do. The word is *listen.* But what do we listen to? What constitutes the "scenery" that we are taking in? Historically, the conception of the analyst listening to the patient as if he were observing scenery has made two important shifts, the second of which is still in progress. The first, which was more or less initiated in 1923 with Freud's publication of *The Ego and the Id,* became the foundation of analytic technique based on Freud's structural theory—the shift from observing a descriptive unconscious (that is, static "scenery") to observing a dynamic unconscious whereby the analyst is listening to an implied (but one-sided) interaction between the patient's psyche and the analyst's presence as a fantasy object of projected imagery.

The second shift ultimately led to the development of different camps within the Freudian model and to the revision or abandonment of the classical model by others. Probably the single most powerful set of ideas that has shaped this frame of reference has been the work of the interpersonal school of psychoanalysis and the influence of Harry Stack Sullivan (1940, 1953, 1954) in particular. The model is of a field of observation framed by the *real* (not implied) interaction between the two participants. It rejects the idea of an analytic situation divided into two components; "how to listen" and "what to do" (that is, "technique"). *The analyst's participation is seen as an ongoing element in the field of observation and inseparable from it.* What the analyst must be trying to listen to in his basic stance includes the immediate and residual effects of his own participation.

From this perspective, transference is not simply something that *has* happened, which the analyst then interprets to the patient. In its most vivid form, transference is what is being enacted *while* the analyst concentrates on making the transference interpretation. The interpersonal analyst's frame of reference is optimally structured to hear these moments and make clinically appropriate use of them. In this regard, technique is something the analytic candidate learns not from a supervisor, but from his patient. Countertransference, therefore, is, in its broadest meaning, "the natural, role-responsive, necessary *complement or counterpart* to the transference of the patient, or to his style of relatedness" (Epstein and Feiner, 1979, p. 12). The awareness and use of it requires that the analyst disembed himself from the immediate context that is framing his experience and broaden his perspective to one that now includes observing his own participation as well as the patient's. It requires, in other words, a shift from the stance of full participation to that of participant observer. By full participation I mean whatever was commanding focal involvement; it could be an involvement with one's own interpretive efforts, or with the details of the patient's life, or with one's empathic relatedness—or it could even be an involvement in exploring some aspect of the analytic interaction. Regardless of which it may be, it is the shift to observing oneself as part of the immediate field that is the critical element and is what permits participant observation its exquisitely refined use of the here-and-now as the flexible frame of reference for a multilevel listening stance. Its therapeutic benefit is fundamentally a characterological enrichment of *perceptiveness,* which then enhances self-understanding, self-acceptance, and human relatedness.

Let me give an example of what I mean by drawing upon a paper from the classical analytic literature, entitled *"China" as a Symbol for Vagina* (Gray, 1985). This is a brief report of an analytic turning point that was achieved through understanding a specific dream in the treatment of a female scientist who was unable to achieve vaginal orgasm in her marriage and who was unable to publish her research under her own name, but permitted her immediate supervisor to present it as if it were his own. The dream was as follows: "I was preparing to give a dinner party with my husband. I was setting the table and I went to the cabinet where my party dishes are stored. I found they were all broken. It was frightening. I woke up and I found my period had begun. I was bleeding profusely" (p. 620).

The author traces the patient's associations to the dream and states that

> the dream confirmed to the patient her continuing, unconsciously held belief that her female organ, which was represented by the highly condensed symbol of her wedding china, had been permanently damaged. . . . Through the analysis of the dream, we discovered a path that led to the source of the patient's neurosis. . . . Eventually, over the long course of the psychoanalysis, we were able to reconstruct an early experience which formed a basis for the patient's symptoms. . . . She became the docile, compliant, helpful, and definitely asexual little girl who was content to wait for permission to be a woman at some later time. This was symbolized by her hope of receiving some family china as a gift. The feminine oedipal nature of the core neurotic conflict was unequivocally communicated in the symbolic equation, china = vagina [pp. 622–623].

What is of interest here is the nature of the listening stance and to what in the work the author attributes the cure, not whether I agree with the metapsychology. Gray's explanation for the cure is that the analytic work led to a reconstruction of the early experience that resulted in the neurosis, and that it was *the integration of the reconstruction* that led to the conflict resolution and to analytic growth. The here-and-now relational process—the *act* of psychoanalysis itself—is seen by the author as simply the medium through which the "genuine" analytic material—the symbolic equation, "china = vagina"—could emerge from the buried past and is thus framed by and listened to for its derivative content.

My point, also made by Levenson (1983), is "not to say that the traditionalists are not interested in the present or that interpersonalists are not interested in the past; but for the former, the past is impacted on the present. For the latter, the past and present lie on an experiential continuum" (p. 68). What is going on must coexist with what has gone on. For an interpersonal analyst, the first must frame the field of perception for the second to make its contribution.

As an interpersonal analyst, I am no more able to listen to a session the way Gray does than I was able to read her paper from that frame of reference. It is simply built into my listening stance to widen my perspective to include the ongoing participation of the analyst, regardless of what the analyst may be doing at the moment (including writing a paper). So as I read Gray's paper, my thoughts went as follows:

Observing customary procedure, Gray would have undoubtedly obtained permission from the patient to publish this material and, I would guess, would have waited until the analysis was terminated successfully. If so, that would make the finding, "china = vagina" itself a piece of "successful research" that the patient and analyst did together, and was then published under the analyst's name. The patient, however, would no longer be the same "docile, compliant, helpful little girl" who formerly granted the permission (to her supervisor) out of neurosis, but someone who could now grant it maturely, with free choice. My reading of the paper was thus framed by my observation of what seemed to me a remarkable posttermination scenario between patient and analyst that embodies the same issues that brought the patient into treatment in the first place. What particularly caught my attention was that the termination occurred without being commented upon by the author even if only as evidence supporting a successful analytic outcome, citing a significant difference in the way the patient had dealt with the analyst's request as compared to the way she formerly dealt with her supervisor. Why, as an interpersonalist, would I find this omission so noteworthy? Because it is only through the act of living that a person comes to be understood. In a psychoanalysis, patients do not reveal their unconscious fantasies to the analyst. They *are* their unconscious fantasies and live them with the analyst through the *act* of psychoanalysis. A symbolic equation such as "china = vagina" is not located in the patient's psyche as "content." It is lived by the patient as process within the space framed by the interrelated acts of two people.

The interpersonal listening stance, however, no more reveals the ultimate truth than does any other. Analysts of all persuasions have historically embraced schools of thought that turn useful formulations into "truths" that then limit their own natural evolution. The most obvious case in point, the classical Freudian school, has found itself entrenched in this position largely because of its militant insistence on enshrining *psychic reality* as the one source of clinical truth. With regard to interpersonal psychoanalysis, Sullivan's opposite emphasis on *observable reality* is itself vulnerable to the same fault but nevertheless has remained remarkably flexible, because the intrapsychic has always been an intrinsic aspect of the interpersonal perspective. But in the midst of the debate between the proponents of reality as framed by the patient's intrapsychic world and those who frame it by the interpersonal field, a new perspective has emerged out of the former tradition, with its own reality that defines the analytic situation: the *empathic/introspective* listening stance of self psychology. Since the defining element of this stance is its dedication to full empathic responsiveness to the patient's subjective experience, I think it appropriate to turn now to the issue of empathy and empathic communication.

THE INTERPERSONAL NATURE OF EMPATHIC COMMUNICATION

It seems to me that the most critical clinical difference between the interpersonal and the self-psychological models is in an attitude toward the process of analytic treatment that has always distinguished the interpersonal tradition from all others. I refer to its fundamental commitment to the process being shaped by who the specific individual is as a human being rather than by its theoretical assumptions, thus making it an approach rather than a technique.[2]

---

[2]See Bromberg (1983) for an elaboration of the "approach" versus "technique" distinction, with specific regard to the treatment of narcissistic disorders.

It would therefore be antithetical to interpersonal analysis to consider any analytic stance—including the empathic/introspective stance of self psychology—as facilitative to all patients. We see human personality development and change as located within a relational context and not as "prewired." To an interpersonalist, the latter conception misses the crucial point of what is analytic—the need to find out who the patient is rather than believing you know in advance what he needs, be it conflict resolution or reconnection to his selfobjects. The interpersonal approach by its very nature engages in an ongoing struggle, or dialectic, with the very issue that self psychology sees as resolved by the "correct" analytic stance. We see this struggle as the heart of the work itself and as the act that embodies the very growth that we are hoping to bring about in the patient.

Barrett-Lennard (1981), in an empirical study on the interactive nature of empathy, points out that the effects of the therapist's empathy depend on characteristics of both patient and therapist and may be a function of unique differences in perceptual, cognitive, and even personality styles. For different patients, what feels empathic involves components that might be predominantly cognitive or affective, or sharing, or supportive, and so on. Kohut's (1971) original findings, which were derived from a relatively homogeneous patient sample possessing a certain personality configuration (which he called narcissistic personality disorder) were highly responsive to the stance he described. But then to generalize the "truth" of this stance to all patients and build a developmental theory upon it is, in my view, precisely the same error made by the classical analysts. It casts the process of therapeutic relatedness into a mold that is mechanistic and causal. "In this view, intentions to direct the experience in advance, that is in prescribed roles-if unexplored -however well intentioned, whether to correct, inform, repair, or restore, will only lead to obfuscation and falsification of the analytic process . . ." (Held-Weiss, 1984, p. 355).

Interpersonal psychoanalysis is based on a field theory paradigm. Each person is shaping the responsiveness of the other, including empathic responsiveness. There is no suggestion of an empathic therapist operating on a patient in need of empathy. Rather, the model is of an open system, changing, developing, enriching itself through a process of interpenetration. Barrett-Lennard (1981, p. 94) reports something very close to this in his empirical description of the cyclical stages of empathy. The patient's perception of the therapist's empathy is followed not only by the patient's further capacity for self expression (Kohut's, 1977, "self as independent center of initiative") but by an interpersonal process in which this increased self-expression includes feedback by the patient that signals the extent to which he feels understood. This, in turn, has an impact on the therapist's affective state, mood, and frame of reference, which then shape the quality of his further efforts (and limitations) in empathically communicating with his patient. Thus, depending on the individual empathic style of a patient, the manner in which empathy is communicated by the therapist will be differentially effective.

For example, a patient reports a dream in which she has asked me to serve her breakfast and I willingly agree. She expected "natural-grain" health food but got something that was too sweet, as if it were sugar coated. The dream followed a session in which I had acknowledged that her difficulty in feeling comfortable about revealing her current state of panic and loneliness was increased by my having responded to a previous panic without realizing the shame she was experiencing in showing those feelings to me. She left that session saying that she felt better in one way by my having said this but also felt "weird" in another way. Her associations to the dream led to an image of me in the previous session as not wanting to see how angry she was at me underneath her panic and of my trying, as her father had, to cajole her away from her anger by giving her a "sugar-coated" gift. Further exploration of our respective experiences during the previous hour (as well as in the current moment), confirmed some degree of accuracy to her perception of me. This allowed her to become vividly aware of how attached she was to her unconscious fear that I, like her father, could not tolerate seeing myself as I really was and that if she had revealed her perception that my "empathic response" was partly self-serving, it would have destroyed the security of mutual protectiveness upon which her core identity had long been based.

Sullivan's manner of communicating his empathic understanding was built into the process of analytic inquiry. It was not contained in a prescribed mode of interacting designed to convey empathic contact. The interpersonal method of participant observation is, consequently, more intrinsically flexible in adapting to the individual empathic styles of a broad range of patients than is *any* one-person psychology, including self psychology. Empathy is inherently interpersonal. In psychoanalysis, its cyclical nature is built into participant observation. As part of the pursuit of an analytic inquiry, the analyst is monitoring (resonating with) the patient's experience of feeling understood or not feeling understood, resulting in a progressive development of intersubjective attunement that is the heart of the growth process referred to by Sullivan (1940, 1953) as *consensual validation.*[3] "Do I understand correctly that . . . ?" "How do you mean that?" "Am I to understand that . . . ?" Analytic inquiry is not simply a means of obtaining factual information; it is not data collection in the obvious meaning of the phrase. It is an interpenetrating involvement with both the there-and-then (the obscure details of the patient's narrative and history) and the here-and-now (the analysis of the analysis). Is inquiry into unreported details, for example, making the patient feel empathically abandoned? Does he experience the analyst's need for more—the analyst's need to question—as equivalent to being robbed of his own experience and meaning? Is he becoming increasingly anxious or depressed? These kinds of questions are continually alive in the interpersonal multilevel listening stance. There is no need for a concept such as optimal failure in empathy because the analytic process is an ongoing dialectic between empathy and anxiety (see Bromberg, 1980b) and between responsiveness to the patient's state of mind and the elucidation of external events. It is this dialectic that I find most lacking in the clinical technique of self psychology and that I hold to be its most serious limitation. Consider, in this light, a statement made by Ricoeur (1986) in a paper otherwise highly supportive of Kohut's major contribution to psychoanalysis:

> For a mature narcissism to emerge from an archaic one, the self has to discover, at the price of inevitable blows, that it is not the omnipotent self that is reactivated by mirroring transference. . . . We have already seen that the self always needs the support of a selfobject that helps it to maintain its cohesion. . . . What needs to be added now is that a certain degree of disillusionment about oneself, *of deception as regards others,* needs to be integrated into the self's education [pp. 446–447, italics added].

EXPLORATION AND INTERPRETATION

To add the dimension pointed out by Ricoeur, self psychology faces a barrier that is quite substantial, though not necessarily insur-

[3]For a more detailed exploration of Sullivan's concept of "consensual validation" as it relates to empathy and intersubjective attunement, see Bromberg (1980a).

mountable. The trouble, as I see it, is that the empathic/introspective stance is in its own but opposite way as unnecessarily one dimensional as that of the school of thought it departed from—the classical inferential stance that positions the analyst *outside* of the patient's subjective world. The self-psychological stance focuses in the opposing direction, only on what the patient needs from the analyst, or, how it feels to be the subject *rather* than the target of the patient's needs and demands. From an interpersonal standpoint, a self psychologist is thus required to function as if he were an interpersonal analyst who is deaf in one ear. This same limitation is I think what Modell (1986) had in mind when he said that "there is a dark side of empathy which Kohut does not adequately acknowledge. The analyst who is constantly empathic may seriously inhibit the patient's own creative powers" (p. 375). The analyst is locked into the closed-ended position of attributing his "failures in empathy" to a presumed (but unstated) deficiency in himself, as though he himself should require nothing from the patient other than what he gets, in order to use his own capacity for empathy, and should be able continually to meet the patient's need for empathic responsiveness regardless of what the patient himself brings to the relationship. The analyst is implying (without saying it) that unlike the patient, he, for better or for worse, in effect exists as a real person in a real relationship *now,* while the patient can only hope to exist *later* through the analyst's humanly imperfect ability to relate empathically to him.

So the most an analyst is allowed to reveal of himself from the empathic/introspective stance is a kind of quasi-apology for having failed to be sufficiently empathic and a rectification of the "imperfection" by admitting it (even if the admission is only by implication). The patient thus has little opportunity to deal with his feelings about his analyst's empathic stance as ongoing analytic material without breaching the analyst's own interpretive context of meaning. Ornstein and Ornstein (1980), for example, report a clinical vignette in which the turning point hinged on the fact that the analyst

> finally said [to the patient] on further reflection that his earlier attempt . . . rightly created the feeling in her that he was by-passing or minimizing the patient's current reactions. . . . It was important to her—the analyst was now able to say—that this time someone should understand *exactly how she felt;* only then could her feelings be validated and made acceptable and thereby real for her [p. 209, italics added].

Is not the process through which the analyst "failed" in his earlier attempt richer than simply the fact of the failure itself? Did the failure have nothing to do with the patient as she existed that is worth considering as part of the interpretive context? Reflect on what Friedman (1986) has to say about this issue:

> If the analyst could see only maturational inevitabilities, he would lose the ordinary social sense of what the patient is *doing* to him. If a patient is mean, envious, degrading, competitive, angry, or seductive, the analyst must be able to feel the act *as* mean, envious, competing, degrading, etc., in order to *recognize* it as such, before he considers its use to the patient's equilibrium. How is one to perceive the particulars of interaction if not by the ordinary, only semi-empathic sensitivities of everyday life? We may approach a holistic view in composing a eulogy. But in the live moment, we think of people as attracted and attracting, lustful, fantasying, envious, appeasing, flattering, combative, scornful, dangerous, evil, as well as admiring, admirable, useful, and using, etc. These ordinary perceptions and attributions must be felt by an analyst as well [p. 346].

What Friedman is saying is not simply that a self psychologist overlooks who the patient is as a real person. He is saying that the stance interferes with the patient's ability to exist fully as he is, with the analyst. Self psychology remains embedded in a mode of intervention that it inherited from classical analysis, the unalloyed process of interpretation. The difference is that what is interpreted is focused on an explication of the selfobject transferences rather than on an explication of the patient's unconscious motives. In both cases, however, some aspect of the patient must be sacrificed to the interpretive context of meaning and is lost to the living act of the analytic process itself. In the Ornstein and Ornstein (1980) clinical vignette, for example, the actual transaction between patient and analyst that led to the analyst's earlier "failure" is interpreted away, and along with it, the potential for empathically shared use of the analyst's "ordinary social sense" of what the patient is doing to him.

An interpersonal analyst's mode of listening allows him optimally to widen his perspective so that both his own countertransferential response and his empathic sensitivity to the patient's state of mind are incorporated by him as inseparable elements in a single relational matrix. As a participant observer, he is free to use himself within this field to explore with the patient their respective experiences of whatever transaction has occurred (or is occurring) rather than having to make a choice as to the "correct" stance from which to interpret it. It is not that an interpretation might not be offered. It is simply that there is no great investment in its power per se or a conception of it as being mutative in and of itself. An interpretation is not seen as containing a "reality" that is more accurate than the patient's own, but rather as a formulation coming from the analyst's experience of the patient, to which the patient will have some response that becomes, in turn, more grist for the mill. The content of an interpretation is a moment in an analytic process; the analytic process is not the raw material for a "correct" formulation of content or the cause of an "optimal failure in empathy".

The interpersonal stance is an empathically implemented, two-sided look at both participant's roles; it inherently allows the analyst to make statements about what he sees in the patient that the classically derived interpretive stance of self psychology cannot accommodate. The focus is not on what a person lacks internally (a developmental deficit), but on what he does with that which he already has and on what sorts of fixed, concrete patterns constitute his world of interpersonal mental representation. Past parental failures in empathy are indeed explicated where relevant, but always in the context of elucidating how the patient's resulting character development has led to ways of being in which he manages to evoke those same types of responses in others (including the analyst) and how he has become "geared" to the familiarity and security of these fixed patterns of relatedness even though he desperately wants to be released from them.

For the patient to be able to look into his own nature through the analytic process, the context must permit him not to feel continually blamed for being who he is. It is not easy, however, to maintain a "nonadversarial approach to character analysis" (Schafer, 1983, p. 152) from an interpretive analytic posture; and interpretations made *outside* of the nonadversarial context are always experienced by the patient as parental acts of attribution and fail in their purpose. Participant observation inherently provides the needed context. It allows the patient to look at himself and at what he is doing to the analyst without having to surrender his own perspective. The context of *exploration,* unlike that of interpretation, is not trying to get the patient to "own" the analyst's construction of reality. It is not an attempt to get the patient to accept the analyst's image of him, but rather to let him know how the analyst is experiencing him. Because the patient's own "truth" is less at risk in this approach he is able to live more fully who he is in the analysis and allow most aspects of himself to find their place in a broader configuration of interpersonal reality that was shaped by the perspectives of both parties.

Nonetheless, it is undeniable that self psychology has made an outstanding contribution to clinical psychoanalysis. Its listening stance, focused on the patient's subjective experience and state of mind as the primary data base, came out of Kohut's work with patients he called narcissistic disorders and out of his recognition that something in his stance allowed these people to grow beyond where they were stuck developmentally. Showing them what they were "really like" only made them worse. The accuracy of these observations and the power with which he formulated them has left an indelible impression on analysts of all theoretical persuasions. So whether or not an analyst adopts the self psychology paradigm as his "truth," there must be a central dimension of this same element in whatever model informs his clinical work, including, of course, the interpersonal. Levenson (1983), speaking from an interpersonal position, accurately asserts that "the cardinal question for the patient may not be "what does it mean?" but "what's going on around here?" (p. ix). With certain patients, however, this stance can prove to be as unadaptive as any other if simply applied as a technique. Its ongoing effects must be scrutinized by the analyst in order to monitor how any particular patient is experiencing it and is able or unable to make use of it. As I have elaborated more fully elsewhere (Bromberg, 1983), there are patients who need to *not* see "what's going on around here" for a long initial period of an analysis. They need the analyst to adapt his own interpersonal style to their inability to work in the transference and focus on the here-and-now without feeling lost, artificial, or abandoned empathically. Consider, for example, the following situation:

A patient has a dream in which the analyst, undisguised, and with an earnest manner and a genuinely warm smile, throws into the patient's lap a plastic bag containing a small, two-headed monster. The patient is terrified because she knows she is expected to open the bag, but she can't tell the analyst how frightened she is because the monster will just get larger. As an interpersonal analyst I would (if I were aware enough at the moment) hear the dream at several levels: first, as an expression of the current state of the patient's internal object world; second, as a statement of her more characterological level of self-development. Third, I would hear the dream in its expressive function as a channel of communication to the analyst about something he is doing with the patient that the patient is not benefiting from (to say the least), but that the analyst believes is good for the patient. The patient cannot consciously formulate any of this, much less communicate, without the likelihood (probably accurate) that telling the analyst will just make the problem grow larger. How is it possible for the analyst to go anywhere near the dream in his usual style without enacting it?

I do not know what I would do. I would probably just have to see how it felt *not* to do what I might typically do and see what comes out of that. I hear one level of the dream as a message that the approach of "exploring what is happening between us" is being experienced by the patient as empathically unadaptive and is gradually changing an otherwise positive (though perhaps overly intense) analytic stance into a monstrosity, without the analyst's being aware of it. At the level of technique, I would try to use the dream as if it were supervision and would try to modify my natural stance in some way that would not feel like a sudden retaliative withdrawal, but without trying to communicate what I think is going on or asking the patient what *she* thinks is going on. The likelihood, however, is that none of this would "work." I would probably end up mystifying the patient, and consequently another dream might be in produced in which I appear equally naive but in which further information is communicated as to what I was failing to perceive the last time. I suspect that gradually, being led by the patient, things would become clearer for both of us, and the analytic work would move along. As Witenberg (1987) has aptly put it, "A theory which is devised to explain clinical phenomena should also be a source of questions for clinical experience. Hopefully, relevant questions will eventually give us relevant answers" (p. 194).

REFERENCES

Barrett-Lennard, G.T. (1981), The empathy cycle: Refinement of a nuclear concept. *J. Counsel. Psychol.*, 28:91–100.

Bromberg, P.M. (1980a), Sullivan's concept of consensual validation and the therapeutic action of psychoanalysis. *Contemp. Psychoanal.*, 16: 237–248.

_____ (1980b), Empathy, anxiety and reality: A view from the bridge. *Contemp. Psychoanal.*, 16:223–236.

_____ (1983), The mirror and the mask: On narcissism and psychoanalytic growth. In: *Essential Papers on Narcissism,* ed. A. P. Morrison. New York: New York University Press, pp. 438–466.

_____ (1986), Discussion of "The Wishy-Washy Personality" by Arnold Goldberg. *Contemp. Psychoanal.,* 22:374–387.

Epstein, L. & Feiner, A. H. (1979), *Countertransference.* New York: Aronson.

Freud, S. (1912), Recommendations to physicians practicing psychoanalysis. *Standard Edition,* 12:109–120. London: Hogarth Press, 1961.

_____ (1923), The ego and the id. *Standard Edition,* 19:12–59. London: Hogarth Press, 1961.

Friedman, L. (1986), Kohut's testament. *Psychoanal. Inq.,* 6:321–347.

Ghent, E. (1986), Credo. Presented at a scientific meeting of the New York University Postdoctoral Program in Psychoanalysis, December.

Gill, M.M. (1984), Psychoanalysis and psychotherapy: A revision. *Internat. Rev. Psycho-Anal.,* 11:161–179.

Goldberg, A. (1986), Reply to Philip M. Bromberg's discussion of "The Wishy-Washy Personality" by Arnold Goldberg. *Contemp. Psychoanal.,* 22:387–388.

Goleman, D. (1985), Freud's mind: New details revealed in documents. *The New York Times,* November 12, pp. C1–C3.

Gray, S.H. (1985), "China" as a symbol for vagina. *Psychoanal. Quart.,* 54:620–623.

Held-Weiss, R. (1984), The interpersonal tradition and its development: Some implications for training. *Contemp. Psychoanal.,* 20:344–362.

Kohut, H. (1966), Forms and transformations of narcissism. *J. Amer. Psychoanal. Assn.,* 14:243–272.

_____ (1971), *The Analysis of the Self.* New York: International Universities Press.

_____ (1977), *The Restoration of the Self.* New York: International Universities Press.

Levenson, E. (1983), *The Ambiguity of Change.* New York: Basic Books.

Modell, A. (1986), The missing elements in Kohut's cure. *Psychoanal. Inq.,* 6:367–385.

Ornstein, P.H. & Ornstein, A. (1980), Formulating interpretations in clinical psychoanalysis. *Internat. J. Psycho-Anal.,* 61:203–211.

Ricoeur, P. (1986), The self in psychoanalysis and in phenomenological philosophy. *Psychoanal. Inq.,* 6:437–458.

Schafer, R. (1983), *The Analytic Attitude.* New York: Basic Books.

Schwaber, E. (1983), Psychoanalytic listening and psychic reality. *Internat. Rev. Psycho-Anal.,* 10:379–392.

Sullivan, H.S. (1940), *Conceptions of Modern Psychiatry.* New York: Norton.

_____ (1953), *The Interpersonal Theory of Psychiatry.* New York: Norton.

_____ (1954), *The Psychiatric Interview.* New York: Norton.

Witenberg, E.G. (1987), Clinical innovations and theoretical controversy. *Contemp. Psychoanal.,* 23:183–197.

15

Conflict and Deficit Models of Psychopathology
A Unificatory Point of View

HELEN K. GEDIMAN

Conflict and deficit psychopathology must be understood within a broad, multiaxial psychoanalytic context. The structural model alone cannot fruitfully be compared and contrasted with the deficit model in the psychology of the self as put forth in the works of Kohut and his followers. To attempt that comparison, one would need to assume that the structural model per se is superordinate, all-inclusive, or able to embrace all relevant other points of view. I cannot make that assumption any more than I can view a "structure" of self as superordinate to the traditionally designated structures, id, ego, and superego (see Richards, 1981, 1982). If one's theoretical approach to psychoanalytic material is perspectival—and I believe mine is—then one must look at the value for integrating conflict and deficit models, of multiple points of view. Only then can we hear multiple themes in the clinical material we listen to and observe, themes that in the past have been obscured by unidimensional theoretical perspectives. And only then can we engage in timely shifts in technique geared to the material that emerges. New views on old and new perspectives permit new ways of grasping and of applying psychoanalytic interpretations insightfully. The position I am developing is not uniquely mine, nor is it held by all Freudian psychoanalysts. It derives from Freud's (1915) idea that any psychical process can be described from various points of view, in which case we speak of a metapsychological presentation. Freud's multiaxial position was expanded by Gill (1963) and is, I believe, still, to this day, the better model for understanding the complex relationships of conflict and deficit than the structural point of view alone. In its attempts at parsimoniously explaining everything, the structural point of view alone runs the risk of collapsing important distinctions that a metapsychological presentation—as Freud originally conceived it, broadly, though not so specifically as to include such anachronisms as the original ideas about cathexis and excitations—does not do.

Important aspects of self psychology may be incorporated into the psychoanalytic corpus as a whole. That corpus, that body of knowledge recognized as psychoanalytic, would have to include not only the structural model of classical psychoanalysis, but also the topographical, economic, genetic, dynamic, adaptive, developmental, and environmental points of view as well. This expanded scope of metapsychological viewpoints would, in addition, have to address those real clinical phenomena formerly designated by the rubric "actual neuroses" (see Rangell, 1968; Gediman, 1984). That is, it would acknowledge the importance of stimulus regulation and the antecedents and sequelae of generalized tension states of all kinds: sexual and aggressive, preoedipally and oedipally linked. It would also have to deal with psychic trauma, carefully sorting out the contributions to psychic reality of not just fantasies, but also material reality and historical truth. It would take particular note of the way in which fantasy makes use of real, traumatic historical occurrences, such as seductions, abuses, and failures in maternal empathic attunement; and it would note how real traumatic abuse, say, affects all areas of psychic functioning, including but not limited to fantasy formation. That is, an inclusive, perspectival psychoanalytic point of view requires an appreciation of the various admixtures of fantasy and reality and centers on a concept of psychic reality that includes intrapsychic representation of real interpersonal events (Gediman, 1987). And here is where the psychology of the self also enters into what the reader will by now recognize as a unificatory effort at integrating multiple points of view dealing with multiple aspects of human psychic functioning.

The self states that Kohut (1977, 1984) has succeeded in *recalling* to our attention are, I believe, embedded in the very clinical phenomena that receded from psychoanalytic illumination when specific but inadequate theories relating to actual neuroses and psychic trauma were abandoned in favor of newer developments in psychoanalytic theory. An attempted integration of the deficit and conflict models within a general psychoanalytic theory would reflect, in my view, a resurrection of aspects of all these worthy viewpoints which the structural model, when conceived in isolation from the rest, has cast into relative oblivion. The spotlight is once again on these neglected phenomena and their pathological manifestations. And it is to Kohut that all psychoanalysts owe a special debt of gratitude, for it is he who in large measure revived their importance through his selective emphases on both the clinical manifestations themselves, and on the timely shifts in technique that, to my mind, may be included within the basic treatment model, for dealing with them psychotherapeutically.

Kohut (1971) distinguished nonspecific as well as specific narcissistic forces, particularly defenses and resistances. Nonspecific narcissistic phenomena accompany all forms of anxiety, the frustration of instinctual drives, and the frustration, particularly, of oedipal wishes. Here narcissistic injury may be secondary to a core neurotic conflict. Specific, primary narcissistic pathology, on the other hand, relates, said Kohut, to a specific genetic trauma: the insufficient mirroring or traumatic withdrawal of phase-appropriate mirroring of the child's self. This position feels right, clinically, and is consistent with classical psychoanalytic theory, even though one might identify other pathogens in the development of narcissistic disorders, such as mutual derailments in attunement which may or may not relate to mirroring. What feels wrong, clinically, is a tendency to polarization. Kohut (1974) once again implied two separate, mutually exclusive groups of individuals. The first he called "Guilty Man," people suffering primarily from structural conflicts and compromise formations constituting the neuroses. The second he called "Tragic Man," those suffering primarily from developmental conflicts involving pathology of the self, mainly the narcissistic personality disorders. These groups correspond to Kohut's two paradigmatic forms of psychopathology: nuclear oedipal pathology that is hidden by a broad cover of narcissistic disturbance; and narcissistic disorders that are hidden by seemingly oedipal pathology.

I believe that both mainstream psychoanalytic theory and Kohut's self psychology have suffered from a tendency to polarization. At the same time, many integrative efforts, such as the one I am attempting, have been made. There are two paradigmatic forms of psychopathology that seem to apply in certain cases, but there is a broad spectrum in between and overlapping as well. Therefore, they do not require us to *split* mankind, as Kohut (1971, 1977) appears to have done, in order to understand and treat them. Rather, their existence dictates a shift in emphasis, technically, to deal with different facets of psychopathology in individuals, as well as in different people. We should speak, rather, of the pleasure-seeking Guilty Man *sector* and the shame-prone Tragic Man *sector,* a position implied in Kohut's (1971) earlier work but abandoned in favor of his so-called cohesive theory of the self (Kohut, 1977), which, ironically, implies a false split, a "vertical split," whereas the abandoned position was more true to phenomenological reality. Both phenomena, the neurotic and the narcissistic, and their underlying intrapsychic, prestructural and preoedipal and oedipal conflicts may be seen as essential features of all patients, granted in varying degrees.

Since all patients, neurotic or otherwise, are shame prone, especially in treatment, all interpretations of unconscious or ego-alien material inevitably provoke narcissistic resistances against all psychoanalytic interpretations because the very discovery of unconscious processes dethrones, as Freud's work implies, man's narcissism, and such resistances do not necessarily confirm the correctness of the analyst's interpretation of conflicts in the area of object-instinctual drives. Similar ideas have been proposed by Sandler and Sandler (1983, 1984, 1987), who claim that a universal content in the "present unconscious" of *every* person is the presence of feelings of shame, embarrassment, and humiliation. They believe that the second censorship of the *topographical* model, that between the systems Conscious and Preconscious, has as its fundamental orientation the avoidance of or resistance to these feelings. Sandler and Sandler, unlike Kohut, do not propose a new theory to account for shame resistances; rather, they revive the importance of some of the metaphors of the topographical model, integrating that approach with the structural point of view. But it was at the heart of Kohut's (1977) technical recommendations that the unspecifically as well as the specifically narcissistic resistances require empathy from the analyst, who must show the patient that he or she understands the feeling of shame and helplessness and lack of omniscience at a sudden revelation over which the patient has no conscious control. I believe that these resistances are amenable to interpretation as well as requiring empathy in a uniquely important way. Kohut had therewith added centrality to these issues by raising the consciousness of all practicing analysts to the emphasis that this kind of empathy must be accorded. It is here, in the attention that is being paid to shame proneness in our daily clinical analytic work, that the potential for rapprochement between Kohut's self psychology and new developments in conflict models is to be found.

THE PROBLEM OF ANNIHILATION ANXIETY: A TEST CASE

In 1983, I (Gediman, 1983) took the phenomenon "annihilation anxiety" as a test case to try to document the views on the unfortunate polarization of people that the conflict and deficit models, when viewed as mutually exclusive, could lead to. I turn once again to a consideration of annihilation anxiety, for the various ways in which it has been conceptualized can tell us much about comparing and contrasting self psychology with a conflict model, which subsumes the multiple points of view of a broadly conceived perspectival psychoanalytic approach.

Annihilation anxiety has been described in the psychoanalytic literature variously as fear of the ego's own dissolution, fear of fragmentation of the self, fear of unreality of the self, and the disintegration products of narcissistic trauma. It also covers the range of "existential anxieties." Kohut (1977) believed that the primary anxiety of the oedipal child was not castration anxiety, but what Kohut viewed as a more basic anxiety, "disintegration anxiety," a fear of psychological death, a fear of loss of the human self, deriving from the "loss of the self-cohesion-maintaining responses of the empathic subject . . ." (Kohut, 1984, p. 19). It is referred to, in the structural model, as the overwhelming of the ego, or the "dread of the strength of the instincts" (Freud, 1923; A. Freud, 1937).

There is something about the subjective experience of annihilation anxiety that is at the heart of what I regard as a major polarization in psychoanalytic theory today: the deficit versus the conflict model. Perhaps one reason for the polarization is the failure to understand that the rubric annihilation anxiety conceals multiple referents in its various meanings: a manifest experiential content, traumatic intrusions of stimulation, the anticipation of psychically traumatic helplessness. It could be said that the deficit model of Kohut's self psychology has been employed largely to account for psychopathology associated with the *conscious* experience of annihilation or disintegration anxiety and its associated manifest content.

For Kohut and his followers, annihilation anxiety has been regarded as an archaic, "prestructural" prototype of the more familiar poststructural anxiety developments. They would see its manifestation in adults as a unique anxiety *form.* In fact, Kohut (1984) states that none of the "forms" of anxiety described by Freud are equivalent to the basic experience of psychological disintegration posited by self psychology. Kohut is not quite right in assuming that Freud referred to "forms" of anxiety. And the conflict model, as understood today, has generally regarded all anxieties, including those with the manifest content of annihilation fears, not as four separate forms, but as relating to the four prototypical *danger situations* of childhood: loss of the object, loss of the object's love, castration, and loss of the superego's love and approval. In viewing annihilation anxiety as a class of anxiety experience different from what is subsumed under the traditional danger situations, Kohut (1977) states, "Whatever the trigger that ushered in or reinforced the progressive dissolution of the self, the emphasis of the experience lies . . . on the precarious state of the self and not on the factors that may have set the process of disintegration into motion . . . (p. 102).

The nucleus of the patient's annihilation anxiety, according to Kohut, and to Stolorow and Lachmann (1980), is his experience that his *self is undergoing an ominous change.* This postulation of annihilation anxiety as a fifth and transcendental danger situation is one that self psychologists regard as requiring a so-called complemental deficit model or theory.

In looking at some interrelations of conflict and deficit, in an attempt to integrate the two models, I would say that one nonpolarizing way of looking at the problem is not to forget Freud's (1923) view that the experience of the anticipation of traumatic intensity of excessive stimulation and the corresponding feeling of psychic helplessness as a narcissistic catastrophe underlies *all* the danger situations. And these situations, when there has been a history of psychic trauma, tend to be repeated in the present, constituting a trauma in their own right, called variously, depending on whether we are speaking conceptually or in terms of experiential states, the overwhelming of the ego, the fear of disintegration of the self, annihilation anxiety. This dread becomes potentiated whenever instinctual drives or narcissistic tensions associated with it involve an accumulation of need tensions beyond the assimilating capacity of the individual. Waelder (1960) made a similar point in explaining that need tensions could lead to narcissistic catastrophe in anybody when they take on the meaning of the four great dangers that, for the very young child, can be all-around catastrophes.

Narcissistic catastrophe, then, as manifest content or latent fantasy of self-annihilation, as traumatic state, or as susceptibility to traumatic states, is not fruitfully conceived as a separate anxiety form or a fifth prototypical danger situation. Rather, it refers to the vulnerability of the psychic structure, of the person, in the face of undischarged accumulated need tensions in situations of psychic helplessness (Freud, 1926). The unconscious or the manifest experiential content known as annihilation anxiety refers to powerful affects, that is, the quantitative intensification of anxiety, associated with representations of all four of the traditional danger situations. That the emphasis in *understanding* the process shifts to what Kohut (1978) describes as the threat to the cohesive, integrative psychic structure, to the sense of self, does not, to my way of thinking, in any way reduce the importance of the danger situations that trigger this threat; for in order to master the traumatic *sequelae* of the vulnerability, or the belief that one is vulnerable, one must know what potentiates it. Whatever its various and consistent unconscious or manifest experiential qualities, annihilation anxiety does also signify a psychoeconomic state, or, as Kohut (1984) said, a self state, to which I shall return shortly. These hallmark phenomena of accumulated undischarged psychic tensions lend a certain experiential quality, such as feelings of unreality and dissolution anxiety, *whether or not these feelings are also neurotic compromise formations.*

My reconciliatory position contains two basic assumptions. (1) Both narcissistic and neurotic manifestations of anxiety, in the broadest sense, are implicated in conflict and compromise formation, although these manifestations may differ with respect to the relative preponderance of preoedipal or oedipal conflicts. (2) Both narcissistic and neurotic annihilation anxieties reflect a certain degree of traumatic excitability, deriving either from traumatic failures in empathy and any other trauma or from other factors, such as rigid defenses, which could be held responsible for unusual drive intensities or which, metapsychologically, could be characterized as a flooding of the psychic apparatus, an overwhelming of the ego. Note here that the formulations are both structural and psychoeconomic, as well as genetic and developmental-environmental. The structural point of view alone will not suffice, just as the psychoeconomic point of view did not suffice when Freud (1923, 1926) attempted to integrate the psychoeconomic theory of the traumatic and actual neuroses (the first anxiety theory) with that of signal anxiety in the psychoneuroses. His second anxiety theory did accomplish that integration. Thus, Freud's "problem" of anxiety was analogous, I believe, to the problem of integrating the deficit and conflict models with respect to annihilation anxiety: both may be resolved through a unificatory approach embracing multiple viewpoints.

Whether the traumatic excitability of annihilation anxiety was originally conflict free (as deriving from a low neonatal stimulus barrier) or deriving from preoedipal conflicts between the child and his environment (as in the mother's failure as "protective shield" or "holding environment" [Winnicott, 1958] or as in the fear of annihilation during the "rapprochement crisis"), it may play a part in the development and content of the intrapsychic conflict, for the psychoeconomic state of excessive excitability is *capable of being psychically represented,* or being given experiential content. A patient's experiential descriptions of intense anxiety may be just that; or they may be used defensively or in the service of resistance. For example, a patient may claim the fantasy content or the affective state generally subsumed under annihilation anxiety defensively, as in "I feel annihilated by your interpretations," a claim with which the analyst often colludes by modifying his analytic stance, unreflectively. Such presentations are not always insusceptible to motivational analysis.

These ideas are not original to me but may be traced back to the work of Freud (1926) and particularly to Jones (1927, 1929, 1936) in his work on "aphanisis," which he conceived as a dread of the ultimate danger situation of total annihilation of the capacity for sexual gratification, Jones said that the fear of a permanent extinction of this capacity is a primal trauma underlying all the neuroses as well as psychotic states and is expressed by different contents in different conditions. For example, the manifest content of the dread of aphanisis among obsessionals is the fear of loss of the personality. In hysterics, the dread takes the form of being overcome by sadistic excitement. The phenomenon was also referred to by Anna Freud (1937) in her discussion of instinctual anxiety, as the ego's fear of its own extinction when there are excessive instinctual accessions. Winnicott (1958) advanced similar ideas about "extinction" anxieties produced by a lack of id tension following orgastic discharge after intercourse. Melanie Klein's (1975a, b) views on psychotic anxieties and a "psychotic core" in everyone's personality makeup are also relevant. The phenomenology discussed by Klein does not seem too different from that emphasized by Kohut. But in my view, a new theory, a different model is not so much required as is a resurrection of certain aspects of the psychoeconomic and other points of view and their integration with the structural.

Thus, in distinction to self psychology, a contemporary conflict model, along with its coordinate other viewpoints within mainstream psychoanalysis, maintains that annihilation anxiety is not "contentless," is not simply the accumulated, undischarged psychic tensions of the actual and traumatic neuroses. The so-called conflict theorists would understand fears of annihilation or disintegration as a content experienced *manifestly,* and often described *metaphorically,* by patients and theorists alike in such terms as splitting, vulnerability, fragmentation, dissolution, disintegration, and fragmentation of the self. These, I maintain, are the subjective side, the experience of what is explained by the theoretical constructs of either id-ego or narcissistic tensions of extreme degree. In my view, these phenomena, as I stated before, do not warrant a new conceptualization of a different form of anxiety; but, understood as self states, they do warrant special attention and specific therapeutic stances such as those proposed by Kohut and his followers.

Thus, the value of calling attention to what has variously been called annihilation or disintegration anxieties lies, I believe, not in investigating whether those clinical phenomena can best be accounted for by a conflict or by a deficit model, but rather in focusing on important aspects of the clinical phenomena themselves. Bach (1985) has referred explicitly to narcissistic states of consciousness, a form of an altered self-state that may be appreciated on its own terms. Transitory modifications in technique that address altered states therapeutically need in no fundamental way contradict the traditional approach to conflict resolution through the basic model of psychoanalytic treatment. Subjective states of extreme anxiety, dissolution, disintegration, annihilation may indeed require noninterpretive interventions and interventions that are variants of holding or soothing, but so too do other "momentary" occurrences in the course of psychoanalytic treatment. But that is not all that altered ego states require, for they may serve multiple functions as compromise formations, which are attempts at conflict resolution as traditionally understood. That is, a self-image, as fragmented, may serve id wishes, for example, of anal explosive pleasure; may serve superego needs for punishment for forbidden gratifications of sexual and aggressive wishes; and may serve defensive purposes as well, for one's focus of attention on an altered state of consciousness within oneself may protect from knowing how angry or enraged one may be toward an important person upon whom one is dependent. Ultimately, it should be possible to interpret all of these aspects of an altered state of consciousness, of a self-state, in a way that results in a more successful compromise formation than one that eventuated in such painful subjective experiences. Attention to conflict alone, or to deficit aspects alone, is inadequate. What we attend to is the patient's psychic reality.

Freud's (1926) first anxiety theory, a purely psychoeconomic one, revolved around the traumatic state as responsible for anxiety. Freud's second theory focused on the traumatic anxiety that all four danger situations signaled—a portent of the original state of psychic helplessness that, for Freud, was not conflict based, but that loomed significantly as a component of intrapsychic conflict *as soon as the person was capable, developmentally speaking, of investing helplessness with varied representational content.* Thus, traumatic states are interpretable in the terms they take on of the patient's psychic reality. The flooded or overwhelmed psyche, the quantitative factor, that featured so prominently in Freud's first anxiety theory is essentially that which Kohut (1977) identifies as the contentless mental state of annihilation anxiety. But, as I have been attempting to show, these accessions themselves are not devoid of psychic content.

The original, mechanistic view of the actual neuroses ignored the importance of both conflict and objects toward whom accumulated need tensions were directed. Similarly, a pure deficit model of self psychology ignores the role of conflict and the object of instinctual drives. It does not, for example, refer, as Freud (1914) in effect did, to how even a selfobject may also be an object of sexual or aggressive instinctual drives. The build-up of sexual and aggressive tensions in the traumatic experiential state of psychic helplessness implies, in essence, an object relations point of view. An aggressive or libidinal drive derivative, especially when traumatically intense, requires an object not only for its satisfaction, but for the reduction of trauma. An object, as understood in the evolving context of psychoanalysis, does more than gratify a need associated with an instinctual drive. The object, or "other," also reduces trauma by affirming the person's reality sense, thereby restoring a state of well-being and self-continuity. This is important because a prototypical outcome of traumas of seduction, or of failures in maternal empathy, is, in addition to chaotic self-states, an alteration in the sense of reality. Therapeutic care addresses the functioning of the ego *and* the restoration of the self. It also may provide libidinal gratification. The principle of multiple function is hereby applicable to the effects of technique. The presence or absence of the object, the degree and quality of the object's availability, thus play an important role not only in the continuation or the lessening of the trauma, but in the mental content, the psychic representations of the annihilation anxiety experience.

One reason why annihilation anxiety poses a problem is that attempts to understand it lead to a common conceptual error committed by analyst and analysand alike, as in what I (Gediman, 1983) have called "the fallacy of parallel importations." This error occurs when the analyst offers metaphor as concrete, and the conceptual is confused with the clinical level of thinking for both analyst and patient. Reed (1985, 1987) made a similar point in recognizing, in the tendency of self psychology to draw parallels between the restoration of the self and the restoration of meaning, a tendency to concretize understanding, to "transform it into substance." She also found this tendency to be responsible for the confusion, in self psychology, between theoretical language and language in the clinical process. Despite his call for clearer conceptualization of psychic structure, Kohut often used the kind of metaphorical language that reflects a mixing of conceptual levels (see Grossman, 1982). Thus, when Kohut (1971) talked of penis envy in girls, or of fellatio, or of perversions generally, as a need to fill in a structural defect, he was, as Slap and Levine (1978) have pointed out, using "hybrid concepts," and implying, as in the case of girls, that the fantasy of being defective is based on a reality. When Kohut said that children who do not acquire internal structure because of sudden narcissistic trauma from a lifelong object hunger, he was correct clinically and developmentally. However, when he said that these children intensely search for objects who may serve as a substitute for the missing segments of psychic structure, he confounded metapsychological constructs with clinical phenomenology, despite his disclaimer that self as superordinate structure is just a metaphor. Grossman and Stewart (1976) present cases where "penis envy" is concretized as metaphor by both analyst and analysand in a similar manner. The authors argue that penis envy, whether inferred or interpreted as unconscious wish, or stated openly as experiential content during analysis by the patient, must be treated like the manifest content of a dream. It is not to be regarded as an ultimate irreducible truth, impenetrable to further analysis. I believe, analogously, that *we also must not regard as "bedrock" or not further analyzable* such clinical contents as reported or inferred experiences of self-dissolution, annihilation anxiety, and feelings of unreality.

Slap and Levine (1978) adopt a similar point of view, arguing that Kohut's central concern that narcissistic psychopathology is caused by the patient's realistic perception of deficiencies in ego structure exemplifies a trend of using metapsychological terms as though they refer not to abstractions but to substantial entities that the patient can perceive directly. This reification of metapsychology thus gives apparent reality to patients'—and, I would add, analysts'—fantasies.

CONFLICT, DEFICIT, AND THERAPEUTIC TECHNIQUE

One reason for choosing the subject of annihilation anxiety as a test case for the type of analysis I (Gediman, 1983) proposed was that it seems to lend itself both to therapeutic interventions aimed at addressing "deficit" and to interpretations addressing conflicts and compromise formations for a broad range of cases. Like Wallerstein (1985), I believe that the same kinds of psychotherapeutic interventions employed in self psychology can be found in classical analysis as well. To this end, I discussed annihilation anxiety in two "pure" and two "mixed" neurotic and narcissistic cases, trying to account for it by showing how traditional psychoeconomic formulations can be used conjointly with structural and dynamic formulations for a given patient without adopting a bipolar schema, such as Kohut's (1984), for diagnosing and therefore treating the narcissistic and neurotic disorders.

Narcissistic and self-states, and their potentially disorganizing feelings of helplessness, require analytic efforts to provide the patient with a means of representing, symbolically, the underlying perverbal trauma and its currently associated affect. But offering empathic understanding as a substitute for interpreting conflicted wishes, say for exceptional entitlement, could reflect a nonneutral collusion by the analyst with only one side of a complex conflict. These narcissistic tensions and their underlying conflicts in cases of the more narcissistic patients require interpretation, just as interpretation of conflicts is required in the case of the more neurotic patients.

I believe that in accounting for structural, dynamic, *and* psychoeconomic aspects of mental events, in this instance annihilation anxiety, conflict theorists can explain their therapeutic strategy differently from the way Kohut did when he evoked the principles of self psychology as guidelines for technique. Kohut would, I believe, have seen disintegration anxieties as a component of neurotic symptom formation only rarely, but often as simply an accurate, endopsychic perception of the self. Kohut (1984) also said that often the four familiar anxiety danger situations are but the patient's attempts to give a circumscribed content to a deeper, unnameable dread, experienced when the patient feels that his or her self is becoming enfeebled or disintegrating. This may, of course, happen. However, I believe that if one continues to explore analytically and avoids "incomplete" interpretations, one need not necessarily be strengthening defenses against danger anxieties. Even when material expressing conscious castration concerns, for example, is being used defensively against the deepest annihilation fears, perhaps a psychotic core of the personality, it does not follow that the genesis of that defense for a given patient and its manifestations are to be ignored or discounted. But before we can deepen our interpretive attempts, we must succeed in our aim of the eventual expansion of the patient's contextual understanding of his or her subjective reaction. For this treatment phase, the analyst's attempts are not necessarily interpretive, but aim to help the patient represent symbolically, through reconstruction, the early, preverbal, precognitive, preoedipal trauma (for example, seduction, abuse, failures in maternal empathy) that resulted in susceptibility to traumatically tinged self-states, which may be experienced as annihilation anxiety—as though the self were disintegrating. Only then, when there is the possibility of investing later revivals and revisions of early states with representational content, will interpretive attempts be meaningful.

Like Brenner (1976, 1979), I believe that even when ego deficit is present, it, like any other mental phenomenon, may play a part in compromise formation once it is invested with meaning or representational content by the patient. Unlike Brenner, I do not regard such deficits as are manifest, say, in altered self-states as simply another compromise formation. We owe Kohut a debt of gratitude for raising our consciousness to an empathic appreciation of altered self-states as clinically important above and beyond the functions they serve in compromises. I regard these states, when encountered in the analytic situation, as requiring shifts in technique, although I do not see these shifts as an alternative to the basic psychoanalytic treatment model. Rather, they expand and enrich its contextual applicability.

I believe that therapeutic strategy must assume the presence of conflict whether or not some degree of deficit is also present. To do otherwise would risk questionable reinforcement of deficit feelings and possibly a consolidation of narcissistic defenses, both at the expense of insight and conflict resolution. When the dissolution of the self metaphor is contained in interpretations that the analyst offers to narcissistic patients, the patients often respond narcissistically, with any of a number of narcissistic "entitlement" fantasies. Of the two narcissistic patients whom I studied in connection with annihilation anxiety, one felt entitled to restore his self-esteem by holding his creditors at bay and recklessly spend money in pathological esteem-building ways. The second felt entitled to resist analytic interpretations because, he in effect claimed, he deserved self-restoration by a symbiotic, orally fulfilling, noninterpretive restorative stance on the part of his analyst. If the analyst were to neglect latent content and the role of conflict in the kind of incomplete, one-sided interpretations aimed only at addressing developmental arrests, he or she could produce an iatrogenic effect in helping along the patient's expectation of being treated either as defective or as an exception. However, once aware of the potential effect of the use of metaphor, the analyst can deal with the consequences, analytically.

Self psychology has tended to regard shame resistances as noninterpretable. One hears a case made for avoiding too much interpretation of aggression or sadism as instinctually gratifying, because the patient then internalizes a self-image as too hostile, too sadistic. Resistances to such interpretations are taken, in self psychology, not so much as indications of unconscious conflicts but as self-dystonic feelings of shame. The aggression and sadism are then presumed to be only expressions of narcissistic rage, or the disintegration products of a damaged-feeling self resulting from the analyst's failures of empathy in the attempts to link such rage with instinctual gratification. There is no doubt that we frequently observe narcissistic rage when a patient feels misunderstood by an analyst believed to be unempathic. However, consistent with Sandler and Sandler's (1983, 1984, 1987) revival of the metaphors of the topographical point of view, I contend that the shame resistances at the more "superficial" level of censorship between the systems Conscious and Preconscious are also subject to interpretation, just as the resistances between the systems Preconscious and Unconscious are customarily interpreted in all conflict and compromise formation analysis.

The analyst must sometimes address the material in a *sequence* that assumes that compromise formation and conflict is more likely than ego deficit. By sequential analysis, I do not mean literally that at any given moment we would not choose to address transitory disorganization and chaotic self-feeling empathically and by offering some representational contents, perhaps by reconstruction of the past, for understanding its genetic roots, in preference to interpretation—which often has to await diminution of traumatic excitability. The patient's momentary state with regard to relative panic or serenity would dictate flexibility in the tactics of our timing, in order to avoid an early crystallization of narcissistic entitlement resistances. But sometimes, as in the case of Mr. Z (Kohut, 1979), the "deficit" issues must be addressed before meaningful work on conflict can proceed.

By sequence, then, I am referring to an overall strategy and its related hypotheses and assumptions—it is a sequence of thinking through the problem of technique. I am not attempting to offer specific technical recommendations closely correlated with any cohesive theoretical framework, but only to suggest the way we must think of working when we do not rigidly dichotomize our patients into the clearly conflicted and the clearly developmentally arrested. In fact, the purpose of this chapter is to show that prescribing one treatment strategy for one "type," another for another type, prematurely attempts to settle an issue by precategorizing individuals rather than by developing a unificatory, multiaxial, psychoanalytic theoretical context which can guide our understanding and treatment of all psychic disorders.

CONCLUSION

In attempting to bring together the conflict and deficit models, I draw attention once again to the issue of false polarities. The false polarities deficit and conflict are paralleled by other false polarities: reality *or* fantasy; historical truth *or* psychic reality. Rather than think of polarities, we might think of two series, complemental series, as Freud (1905) called them, that overlap considerably, conceptually speaking. According to Freud, the complemental series paradigm holds that the diminishing intensity of constitutional and predispositional drive factors is balanced by the increasing intensity of environmental and accidental factors and vice versa. Restated in this conflict and deficit context, the complemental series paradigm holds that when there has been severe early trauma and subsequent deficit, external influences are more prominently involved in pathogenesis, relative to the strength of the drives and subsequent conflict than they are in the absence of early trauma and subsequent deficit, and vice versa.

REFERENCES

Bach, S. (1985), *Narcissistic States and the Therapeutic Process*. New York: Aronson.

Brenner, C. (1976), *Psychoanalytic Technique and Psychic Conflict*. New York: International Universities Press.

_____ (1979), The components of psychic conflict and its consequences in mental life. *Psychoanal. Quart.*, 48:547–567.

Freud, A. (1937), *The Ego and the Mechanisms of Defense*. New York: International Universities Press, 1946.

Freud, S. (1905), Three essays on the theory of sexuality. *Standard Edition*, 7:120–245. London: Hogarth Press, 1953.

_____ (1914), On narcissism: An introduction. *Standard Edition*, 14:73–102. London: Hogarth Press, 1957.

_____ (1915), The unconscious. *Standard Edition*, 14:166–204. London: Hogarth Press, 1957.

_____ (1923), The ego and the id. *Standard Edition*, 19:12–59. London: Hogarth Press, 1961.

_____ (1926), Inhibitions, symptoms and anxiety. *Standard Edition*, 20:87–172. London: Hogarth Press, 1959.

Gediman, H. K. (1983), Annihilation anxiety: the experience of deficit in neurotic compromise formation. *Internat. J. Psycho-Anal.*, 64:59–70.

_____ (1984), Actual neurosis and psychoneurosis. *Internat. J. Psycho-Anal.*, 65:191–202.

_____ (1987), Seduction trauma: Complemental intrapsychic and interpersonal perspectives on fantasy and reality. Presented at meeting of the New York Freudian Society, December.

Gill, M. M. (1963), Topography and systems in psychoanalytic theory. *Psychological Issues*, Monogr. 10. New York: International Universities Press.

Grossman, W. I. (1982), The self as fantasy: Fantasy as theory. *J. Amer. Psychoanal. Assn.*, 30:919–938.

_____ & Stewart, W. A. (1976), Penis envy: From childhood wish to developmental metaphor. *J. Amer. Psychoanal. Assn.*, 24, Supplement: 193–212.

Jones, E. ed. (1927), The early development of female sexuality. In: *Papers on Psychoanalysis*. Boston, MA: Beacon Press, 1961, pp. 438–451.

_____ (1929), Fear, guilt and hate. In: *Papers on Psychoanalysis*. Boston, MA: Beacon Press, 1961, pp. 304–319.

_____ (1936), Love and morality. In: *Papers on Psychoanalysis*. Boston, MA:

Beacon Press, 1961, pp. 196–200.

Klein, M. (1975a). *Envy and Gratitude and Other Works.* New York: Delacorte Press/Seymour Lawrence.

_____ (1975b). *Love, Guilt and Reparation and Other Works.* New York: Delacorte Press/Seymour Lawrence.

Kohut, H. (1971), *The Analysis of the Self.* New York: International Universitities Press.

_____ (1977), *The Restoration of the Self.* New York: International Universities Press.

_____ (1978), *The Search for the Self,* ed. P. Ornstein. New York: International Universities Press.

_____ (1979), The two analyses of Mr. Z. *Internat. J. Psycho-Anal.,* 60:3–27.

_____ (1984), *How Does Analysis Cure?* ed. A. Goldberg & P. E. Stepansky. Chicago, IL: University of Chicago Press.

Rangell, L. (1968), A further attempt to resolve the problem of anxiety. *J. Amer. Psychoanal. Assn.,* 16:371–404.

Reed, G. S. (1985), Psychoanalysis, psychoanalysis appropriated, psychoanalysis applied. *J. Amer. Psychoanal. Assn.,* 30:939–958.

_____ (1987), Rules of clinical understanding in classical psychoanalysis and self psychology: A comparison. *J. Amer. Psychoanal. Assn.,* 35:421–446.

Richards, A. (1981), Self theory, conflict theory, and the problem of hypochondriasis. *The Psychoanalytic Study of the Child,* 36:319–337. New Haven, CT: Yale University Press.

_____ (1982), The superordinate self in psychoanalytic theory and in the self psychologies. *J. Amer. Psychoanal. Assn.,* 30:939–958.

Sandler, J. & Sandler, A-M. (1983), The "second censorship," the "three box model" and some technical implications. *Internat. J. Psycho-Anal.,* 64:413–425.

_____ &_____ (1984), The past unconscious, the present unconscious, and interpretation of the transference. *Psychoanal. Inq.,* 4:367–399.

_____ &_____ (1987), The past unconscious, the present unconscious, and the vicissitudes of guilt. *Internat. J. Psycho-Anal.,* 68:331–341.

Slap, J. W. & Levine, F. T. (1978), On hybrid concepts in psychoanalysis. *Psychoanal. Quart.,* 47:499–523.

Stolorow, R. & Lachmann, F. (1980), *Psychoanalysis of Developmental Arrests.* New York: International Universities Press.

Waelder, R. (1960), *The Basic Theory of Psychoanalysis.* New York: Schocken, 1971.

Wallerstein, R. (1985), How does self psychology differ in practice? *Internat. J. Psycho-Anal.,* 66:391–404.

Winnicott, D. W. (1958), The capacity to be alone. In: *The Maturational Processes and the Facilitating Environment.* New York: International Universities Press, 1965, pp. 29–36.

16

Masterson and Kohut
Comparison and Contrast

Ralph Klein

In the history of the study of the personality disorders, the work of James Masterson stands in the mainstream of developmental, object relations theory. Moreover, it represents the purest application of developmental, object relations theory to guide the clinician in working with the spectrum of personality disorders.

Masterson's theoretical contributions emanate from and also enhance the work of Melanie Klein, W.R.D. Fairbairn, D.W. Winnicott, and Margaret Mahler. His work concerning the identification and treatment of the borderline personality disorder in adolescents and adults began in the 1960s. By this time, theorists had produced an extensive body of knowledge regarding the identification of preoedipal conflicts and structures.

Melanie Klein (1932, 1946, 1948, 1957) had first opened up the world of the infant and young child for exploration. The representational world—the world of fantasy and imagination, of wonderful and terrible tales and stories—became the focus of much of the work of Klein and of her followers. In addition, she first described the tools utilized for organizing the primitive, yet complicated, internal world of objects—splitting, projection, and projective identification.

Following Klein, Fairbairn (1952) extensively contributed to the systematic description of the organization of the internal world of the preoedipal child by introducing the notion of internalized relational units. These units consist of object- and self-representations linked in a stable, affect-dominated manner and compete with, and drain energy from, the healthy ego's focus on adaptation to external realities.

Winnicott (1958, 1965) conceptualized a dynamic description and narrative of the role of the "good enough" caretaker or "facilitating environment" in the developmental process. His emphasis on the relationship between mother and infant helped to expand the study of early object relations into the systematic study of that relationship.

Thus, when Masterson began his work with disturbed adolescents, object relations theory had already provided a blueprint for understanding preoedipal conflicts. Yet there seemed to Masterson to be a crucial missing piece. What was lacking was a way of integrating the previous observations into a comprehensive system of understanding the psychopathology and the treatment of character disorders. At the same time that Masterson was attempting to understand and treat the troubled adolescent, Kernberg (1975, 1980, 1984) was making similar observations and attempting to develop treatment strategies for the adult character (borderline) disorder.

However, in his work during this period, Kernberg linked his model of the development of the psychopathology of characterological (borderline) organization to the model of development proposed by Melanie Klein (1932), which emphasized the motivational primacy of constitutionally determined drive derivatives and their pathological elaboration.

For Masterson, it was not Klein, but Mahler who provided the key to the missing piece. Mahler (1968; Mahler, Pine, and Bergman, 1975) provided a systematic, affective developmental theory of normal development that explained the role of the mother-infant relationship in the genesis and evolution of the intrapsychic structural organization of the preoedipal child.

The affective developmental theory of Mahler (1968) revolved around the concept of separation-individuation and filled in the developmental period (essentially from 6 months to 24 months), which previous theorists had left unclear. Separation-individuation successfully clarified the developmental progression between the primitive paranoid-schizoid and the depressive positions of Klein, between the period of immature dependence and mature dependence of Fairbairn (1952) and between the period about which Winnicott (1965) wrote:

> Gradually the need for the actual mother (in health) becomes fierce and truly terrible, so that mothers do really hate to leave their children, and they sacrifice a great deal rather than cause distress and indeed produce hatred and disillusionment during this phase of special need. This phase could be said to last from (roughly) six months to two years [p. 88].

By carefully scrutinizing these early months and years of life, Mahler (Mahler, Pine, and Bergman, 1975) was able to describe the child's successful progression from relatively unintegrated, fragmented experiences to more integrated, cohesive experiences of self- and object constancy.

Masterson (1972) was now able to integrate the descriptive phenomenon of the borderline patient (adolescent or adult) and the stable, intrapsychic structure of the preoedipal relational units proposed by Fairbairn (1952) and elaborated by Kernberg (1966) with the failures in parental support for mastering the tasks and challenges of separation-individuation. The genesis and evolution of the psychopathology of the borderline personality disorder were defined and described by Masterson as pathological distortions in the parent-child relationship involving those functions and capacities of the primary caretaker(s) that were necessary to facilitate the child's movement from one developmental phase to the next through separation-individuation.

To the extent that these pathological distortions in the parent-child relationship resulted from the parents' or caretakers' pathological projections and depersonifications (and not from constitutional, or temperamental, factors or accidents of fate), Masterson's model could provide the clinician with important clues about what had gone wrong in the developmental process and, perhaps more significantly, point the way toward a treatment approach.

In fact, Masterson (1981) proposed a new dynamic paradigm—the borderline triad—to describe the nature of the interaction between the pathological relational units (split object relations units) of the borderline patient. Paralleling the model for neurotic conflict (which could be defined as: conflict leads to anxiety, which leads to defense), the borderline triad was defined as: the attempt at separation-individuation leads to an abandonment depression, which leads to defense. Just as the concept of neurotic conflict anchors the work with the neurotic patient, so the concept of the borderline triad anchors the work with the borderline patient.

The concept of an abandonment depression cannot be easily

described. It is the primary manifestation of a developmental arrest. It is a barrier on the normal developmental pathway that must be overcome and cleared away, or else the normal developmental route cannot be followed. Normal developmental functions and capacities will be interferred with and impaired, and pathological detours instituted.

For Masterson (1989), the concept of a personality disorder necessarily involves a developmental arrest associated with an underlying abandonment depression. This concept is applicable to all personality disorders, not just the borderline personality. What varies among the personality disorders is the specific nature—form and content—of the pathological relational units and the nature of the underlying abandonment depression.

The goal of long-term psychotherapy for any personality disorder, then, is the removal of the barrier to the development of those functions and capacities associated with the successful mastery of separation-individuation. The abandonment depression, ideally, must be worked through. In other words, the conditions which brought about its existence must be uncovered in memory and relived in feeling.

In his most recently published works, Masterson (1985, 1988; Masterson and Klein, 1989) has focused increasingly on the concept of the "self." This concentration is in part a response to issues raised by psychology of the self theorists such as Heinz Kohut and has directed clinical attention to areas that were left underdeveloped and out of the main focus of the work of most object relations theorists.

While Mahler (1968) always emphasized that the process of separation-individuation, as the principle conceptual organizer of preoedipal personality development, identified two distinct, but interrelated, developmental tracks—separation and individuation—she highlighted in her clinical work the process of separation—the ways in which the self is differentiated from and maturely attached to the object on the way to mature object representations and libidinal object constancy.

As I view it, the study of the developmental progress on the way to libidinal self-constancy (individuation) was at the center of Kohut's work. It was Kohut (1971, 1977, 1984) who was primarily responsible for "flipping the coin" from the side of separation and attachment to the side of individuation. In so doing, he turned attention to the development of the self-regulating, autonomous functions and capacities of the self and away from the primacy of the capacities associated with object relatedness. In so doing, he turned from the motivational primacy of object relationships to the motivational primacy of the self-organization.

Masterson's (1985) new emphasis on the "real self" integrates the constructs of developmental, object relations theory (with its emphasis on separation and mature attachment) with the constructs of the psychology of the self (with its emphasis on individuation, autonomy, and self-regulation).

Masterson's concept of the "real self" denotes basically healthy personality development, with an associated stable, integrated, triadic intrapsychic structure. It encompasses the capacities for separation, mature attachment, individuation, and autonomy. It includes the experience of the self maturely related with others and comfortably self-regulating without others. It is this entire area of identity that Masterson puts under the clinical microscope and examines throughout the life cycle. The child at birth can be described as a reservoir of potential, a repository of functions and capacities, all of which exist *in statu nascendi*. The "real self" will develop if the double tracks of separation and individuation are successfully negotiated by the person.

I believe that the concept of separation-individuation already includes those ideas basic to the "psychology of the self." Therefore, a "self psychology" that competes with or replaces a "psychology" or theory of object needs and relationships is unnecessary and confusing.

This argument that separation-individuation theory already incorporates the ideas inherent in the psychology of the self rests with Mahler's (1968) assertion that "the parallel line of development is the child's growing awareness of his functioning independently of, and separately from, the hitherto symbiotically fused external part of his ego—the mother. This line centers, perhaps, more around the child's developing object representations." (p. 221). Simply stated, the line of separation leads to the establishment of integrated and differentiated object representations. For it is only when one is truly separate from another person that the one is able to know the other as an independent source of feelings, thoughts, wishes, and initiative. Separateness—the full awareness of two independent centers—promotes the person's wish to build and rebuild an interpersonal world of relationships.

Separateness defines the limit of person's illusion of omnipotence and omnipotent control. The experience of separateness makes the person more tolerant and willing to share, emphathize, commit, and work toward intimacy. The concept of separation is thus deeply imbedded in the need for object relationships and is necessary for the achievement of mature object relationships with whole objects experienced as stable and continuous over time and in the face of changing emotional valences. Separation as a "precondition" for attachment, or even experiences of "merger" or "fusion," has been extensively described by Stern (1985).

Developmentally, separation-individuation theory suggests that separateness involves two different tasks. First, the self (internal reality) must be differentiated from the object (external reality). This is a commonly held, albeit retrospective and pathomorphic, idea of symbiosis—a depolarization across the self/nonself barrier. Failure to achieve this "separation" results in all sorts of psychotic manifestations, including infantile autism and symbiotic psychosis (Mahler, 1968).

Second, and most important for understanding normal development, the self-representation must be differentiated from the object representation. This is a totally internal process involving the representational world and reflects Mahler's use of the term "symbiosis" as a purely intrapsychic phenomenon and as a blurring of maternal and self mental representations. Defined in this manner, Mahler (1968) noted, "the mutual cueing between infant and mother is the most important requisite for normal symbiosis" (p. 34). Since it is hard to imagine how mutual cueing could take place between a fused self and object, Mahler's notion of "symbiosis" is clearly revealed as an intrapsychic phenomenon referable to an affective state of intent, and not a cognitive phenomenon that violates the boundary between self and the object world.

Kohut, and self psychology more generally, helped to clarify this confusion by describing the stage of relative undifferentiation (blurring) of self- and object representations as the stage of immature selfobjects during which the selfobject functions as a critical component of the self organization. Stern (1985) describes how the infant at this stage relates to the other as a "self-regulating other"—one that helps the infant to manage the subjectively, affectively, and cognitively perceived world.

Whether described in terms of intrapsychic symbiosis, immature selfobjects, or self-regulating others, the infant's ability to separate out fantasies, wishes, ideas, and experiences of what he is like and contains as a person (self-representation) is only gradually differentiated from the infant's fantasies, wishes, ideas, and experiences of others and what he believes others are like and contain as people (object representations). In normal development such a differentiation is achieved during, and is part of the definition of, rapprochement (Mahler) or the "subjective self" (Stern), which is characterized by the child's having achieved a "theory of separate minds."

Maintaining the central relational primacy of the concept of the selfobject, as self psychology does, is a pathomorphic error. The idea of selfobjects after the phase-appropriate early stages of separation-individuation adds nothing to our understanding of object needs in normal development while blurring fundamental distinctions between psychological and psychopathological processes.

Beyond this theoretical objection to continuation and prolongation of the notion of selfobjects is the clinical phenomenon that results. Within the framework of developmental, object relations theory, separation and mature attachment—expressed by the ability to love—has always been a focus of therapeutic concern. Where is this the focus of attention in the work of self theorists? Where is this basic need for relationship (object seeking, attaching, need, and transferences) given primary importance? Nowhere. Selfobject relationships continue to be important, but the need for selfobjects is a secondary or derivative one. They either stabilize autonomous capacities or continue to exist as auxillary structures to fill in for those defects or failures in the person's ability to achieve totally autonomous, "perfect" self-regulation. Attachment to selfobjects is pursued (or simply exists) because ultimately human beings are not perfect and can never achieve perfection. Would the perfect, and perfectly self-regulating human being, according to self psychology, quietly going about the task of creative self-expression, have need for anyone—except those who can admire, mirror, and reflect that person's creativity or self-sufficiency. In the theoretical and clinical writings of the self theorists and therapists rarely is the object (as distinct from the selfobject) valued for itself.

The second track of individuation is related to, but separate from, the track of separation. In Mahler's (1968) words this line of development "is the toddler's rapidly progressing individuation, which is brought about by the evolution and expansion of the autonomous ego functions. These center around the child's developing self-concept" (p. 221). In short, if the track of separation in on the way to libidinal object constancy, then the track of individuation in on the way to libidinal self-constancy. The functions that Masterson (1985) has described related to this track all involve the ability for mature self-regulation and autonomy: self-acknowledgment, self-activation, self-assertion, self-direction, spontaneity of affect and action (similar to Winnicott's, 1965, "spontaneous gesture"), self-esteem regulation, and creativity. Again, in simple language, this track perhaps emphasized the person's capacity "to work." Here Kohut made, I believe, his second important contribution to understanding normal developmental processes. The concept of "transmuting internalizations" (Kohut, 1971) provided a missing piece to understanding fully the nature by which the child "takes in," assimilates, and accommodates functions and capacities of the parent (such as self-soothing). This gradual internalization of function, as opposed to mood, expectation, or characteristic, fleshes out the concept of mature autonomy and self-regulation.

If one were to attempt to highlight the differences between the developmental, self- and object relations theory of normal development, and the psychology of the self, it is perhaps with the difference in the meaning of the terms "real self" and "nuclear self" that such differences can be best demonstrated. For these two concepts really point out the basically different view of the nature of man that underlies the clinical approaches of Masterson and of Kohut.

The term nuclear self, as I understand it, refers to the capacity to acknowledge and give appropriate weight to one's own individuative needs, ambitions, goals, wishes, talents, and skills separate from the impingement of the needs, wishes, and actions of others. This concept is close to Winnicott's concept of the "true self". Winnicott (1965), however, qualified some of his comments about the private and deeply personal nature of the true self in order to acknowledge that, to be truly healthy, a person has to exist in some harmonious alliance with the environment:

> Maturity of the human being is a term that implies not only personal growth but also socialization. Let us say that in health, which is almost synonymous with maturity, the adult is able to identify with society without too great a sacrifice of personal spontaneity. . . . Independence is never absolute. The healthy individual does not become isolated, but becomes related to the environment in such as way that the individual and the environment can be said to be interdependent [pp. 83–84].

Self psychology, it seems to me, fails to acknowledge this fact. In his efforts to stress the value of normal healthy narcissism and to remove the concept of narcissism from its devalued position in the past, Kohut essentially went to the other extreme and equated narcissism with creativity, autonomy and spontaneity. He then set these at the pinnacle of human values—above love, sharing, "community," and intimacy.

PSYCHOPATHOLOGY OF THE SELF

In describing the psychopathology of the self, there is a great deal of agreement between Masterson and Kohut at least as regards the therapeutic engagement and the initial stages of treatment of the narcissistic personality disorder. However, the basic disagreements regarding normal developmental processes and formulations ultimately creates problems and, in some instances, irreconcilable differences.

For Kohut (1977) development essentially proceeds from immature selfobjects to mature selfobjects and from relative dependence to relative independence. This developmental pathway has no need for a separation-individuation phase. It requires only that intrapsychic structures achieve "cohesiveness" in order to be treatable (or analyzable). By cohesiveness, Kohut (1971) is essentially reiterating, in different language, the need for differentiation of self (internal reality) and object (external reality). In other words, Kohut insists that his patient not be psychotic (schizophrenic) or vulnerable to psychotic decompensations (borderline) or irreversible fragmentation (schizoid). For Kohut, depolarization or dedifferentiation of self- and object representations is neither psychotic (clinically) or a "stage" to grow out of (developmentally). It is simply a line of development that undergoes maturation or, when interferred with, pathological distortion and malformation.

In the realm of the personality (narcissistic) disorders, pathology was the result of failure in one subsystem of development—specifically failure of phase-appropriate support for, and acknowledgment of, the illusion of omnipotence and omnipotent control; failure of phase-appropriate disillusionment and the bringing of such fantasies into accord with reality; failure in providing a phase-appropriate, encouraging receptacle for idealizing projections that supports the child's efforts at "borrowing" from the caretaker's perceived omnipotence, and failure of phase-appropriate disillusionment of the fantasy of parental omnipotence.

For Masterson (1981) the clinical description of the psychopathology of the self as described by Kohut is informed and clinically invaluable. However, Masterson's concept of the personality structure, and the genesis and evolution of the personality disorders, is far broader. Masterson (1972, 1976) defines the borderline personality disorder as mired (arrested) in the rapprochement subphase of separation-individuation. Self- and object representations are fully differentiated, and the child is exposed to the full impact of his helpless dependency on his caretakers. The child must now effect various mechanisms to deal with this state of perceived helpless dependency. How the child negotiates this period depends on various factors: constitutional, especially temperamental, features; accidents of fate; and the special quality and nature of the various projections and depersonifications of the caretakers (nurture). Parental support for meeting the tasks and challenges of rapprochement (increasing employment of autonomous functions and abilities in the two areas of task mastery and social competence) is an absolute necessity.

The "good enough parent" at this time must be able to subordinate his or her own needs (expressed as conscious and unconscious projections and depersonifications) in favor of the ability to acknowledge, tolerate and encourage the individual needs, wishes, feelings, and actions of a separate, though narcissistically invested, other.

For Masterson (Masterson and Klein, 1989) there is a range of maladaptive, inappropriate, and self-defeating projections and depersonifications that the "not good enough parent" may activate and an equally broad range of behaviors that the patient will attempt in order to deal with external reality.

In fact, though the pathological parental projections and depersonifications may certainly involve excessive, inadequate or phase-inappropriate idealizing or mirroring requests or responses, they are far more likely to take the form of regressive and infantile projections that maintain the child in a relatively dependent state and therefore emotionally available for the caretaker's self-stability and cohesiveness of identity. It is Masterson's clinical experience that such a pattern of reward for regression and withdrawal for individuation is widely prevalent—at least in patient populations—and accounts for the clinical experience that finds borderline patients to outnumber narcissistic patients in hospital and clinic populations.

Since maintaining the distinction between borderline and the narcissistic personality disorders is so fundamental to developmental, object relations theory, it is worth clarifying in some additional detail the differing intrapsychic structural relational units to be found in the borderline, the exhibitionistic narcissistic disorder, and the closet narcissistic patient.

Masterson has clearly tested in many clinical situations the hypothesis that rather than receiving support for individual self-assertion and activation and nonsupport for regression—patterns that promote healthy personality development—the borderline patient has received support for regressive, infantile, dependent, and compliant behaviors. As a matter of fact, individuative, self-assertive behavior has been grossly or subtly discouraged, criticized or attacked. This support for maladaptive behavior underlies the pathologically split object relations units of the borderline personality disorder.

In other instances, the patterns of depersonification revolve around continuous, pervasive, and phase-inappropriate maintenance of idealizing and grandiose projections that support achievement, assertion, activation, and accomplishment that is not directed by the real self but by the false (defensive) self. The child reacts to the idealizing projections rather than experiencing his self-expression as a spontaneous part of an emerging real self-identity. The working model of relatedness being described here as intrinsic to the manifest, exhibitionistic, grandiose, narcissistic disorder can be expressed in the following way: "I am perfect (special), but I need you to affirm this (specialness)."

Masterson (1981, 1988) has also pointed out that the child whose primary caretaker and narcissistic supplier has himself or herself an exhibitionistic, narcissistic disorder may require not a receptacle for idealizing projections but, rather, a mirror for his or her own grandiose self. In this case, the working model of relatedness for the child can better be expressed in the following way: "You are perfect (omnipotent), and I can be a part of (share in) your power (specialness)." The child here may likely develop a closet nacissistic disorder. The child must idealize the object and then feel special by "basking in the glow" of that object. In this way, the mirroring needs of the child's grandiose self are met, albeit indirectly.

A closet narcissistic disorder may also develop (Masterson, 1988) as a result of an initial idealization followed later in childhood by a severe attack on the child's grandiosity by the parent, which forces the grandiosity "underground." In either case, patients with closet narcissistic disorder may look anything but narcissistic to the world while maintaining a hidden core of grandiose and omnipotent fantasies. At times, the closet narcissistic disorder may take unusual forms. These patients may not only be inhibited and retiring, but may assume such manifestations as being the "perfect martyr" or a "modern day Job."

Though this disorder may at first be confused with a higher level, clinging, borderline disorder, the nature of the underlying self-representation will eventually clarify the diagnostic picture. The patient with a closet narcissistic disorder establishes the idealizing transference in order to feel "special" or like the "chosen one," whereas the borderline patient uses the clinging, compliant relationship to feel like the one "cared for."

The distinctions between the borderline and narcissistic personality disorders are of more than just theoretical importance. These fundamental distinctions have to be maintained because to do otherwise would sacrifice therapeutic efficacy. A dimensional approach to the personality disorders that maintains the fundamental distinction between the borderline and the narcissistic disorders (as well as the schizoid and the antisocial) is clinically necessary.

DIMENSIONS OF DIFFERENCE BETWEEN BORDERLINE AND NARCISSISTIC DISORDERS

Phase of Developmental Arrest

While it has been generally accepted that developmental arrest in the borderline patient occurs during the rapprochement subphase of separation-individuation, there is much confusion about the comparable phase at which arrest occurs in the narcissistic disorder. Certainly Kohut's (1971) developmental model for maturation of selfobjects permits the placing of the developmental arrest at any point prior to the intrapsychic ascendency of the oedipal complex, perhaps as late as the fifth or sixth year of life.

Masterson (1981) has, on the other hand, been consistently troubled by his need to place the arrest prior to rapprochement, at a time when infantile grandiosity and the illusion of omnipotence still holds sway over the developing child. He argues that this placement is necessary because the narcissistic patient does not seem to experience the rapprochment crisis; and because the narcissistic disorder demonstrates fused self- and object representations whereas the borderline patient has separate, but pathologically split and malignantly transformed, intrapsychic relational units. Nevertheless, to place the arrest earlier would seem to violate, according to Masterson, a basic tenet of object relations theory—that ego functions mature in parallel with the maturation of intrapsychic structure. This leaves Masterson in a quandary.

There are several avenues of solution. Clinically it is arguable whether the narcissistic disorder or the borderline disorder suffers more from profound disturbances in object relationships. Developmentally, the quandary is a spurious one, created by the continued dual use of the term symbiosis as discussed previously to represent both undifferentiated internal and external objects as well as undifferentiated internal self- and internal object representations. The early rapprochement child still has relatively undifferentiated self- and object representations. In other words, the child may clearly recognize mother's separate existence, but may still feel that her wishes and needs are similar to, if not almost identical with, his own. Only further growth through separation-individuation will gradually make it clear that this similarity of aims is less and less the case. The persistence of undifferentiated self- and object representations (also referred to as selfobjects or fused self- and object representations) is not psychotic, there is no breakdown of the boundary between subjective and objective reality. When the narcissistic patient speaks about another person as though the other person were a body part, the patient is making an affective, not a cognitive, statement.

Therefore, that the narcissistic patient does not seem to experience the rapprochement crisis is because of relative efficiency and ubiquitousness of the narcissistic defense and the fact that the essential parental projection or depersonification is different for the narcissistic disorder than for the borderline. The narcissistic child is essentially given the message, "You can grow but you can not separate." In other words, the patient may achieve stature, success, and supplies appropriate to his age or stage in life, but he is not free to separate self- and object representations—to be "different." Self- and object representations must remain undifferentiated to provide the patient with either an unending source of mirroring responses or a ready avenue for idealizing projections. It is the narcissistic patient who has the most difficulty with "separation stress," that is, in accepting that others have their own separate minds—thoughts, feelings, and needs separate from those of the patient. These differences are perceived by the narcissistic patient as an injury, an assault, or an unbearable disappointment.

The borderline patient is given a different message: You can separate (self- and object representations) but you cannot grow. In other words, you can have your own feelings and thoughts (often self-defeating and destructive) as long as you do not use them to support your own need to grow. The borderline patient can feel different and separate (and often does feel exquisitely "different") as long as he remains infantile and regressed, dependent and compliant.

Nature of the Transferencelike Structures

The narcissistic patient, as described by Kohut (1971) must spontaneously establish one of a variety of mirroring or idealizing transferences. In other words, the patient with narcissistic disorder must view the other as an extension of his or her own grandiose, exhibitionistic self or as the desired and desirable, omnipotent, idealized object. Should the real person (in actual, external reality) fail to react as the narcissistic patient expects, on the basis of his stable view of what other people should be like, the narcissistic patient will either deny that external reality by withdrawing, devaluing, or attacking it, or attempt to coerce actual reality to correspond to his illusion of reality by manipulating, controlling, or defeating it.

The borderline personality, as described by Masterson (1981) must of necessity spontaneously establish (or project) a rewarding object relations unit or a withdrawing object relational unit. That is, the borderline patient must view the other as either like the internalized "good" caretaker, rewarding infantile, regressive, compliant, dependent, and phase-inappropriate maladaptive and immature behaviors; or like the internalized "bad" object; frustrating, nongratifying, critical, cruel, uncaring, or abandoning; whenever the patient acts in a self-interested, directed, or assertive manner.

The nature of these relational units are quite specific and easily differentiated. Moreover, they are stable, predictable, and not interchangeable.

Different Therapeutic Interventions

Differences in the structure of narcissistic and borderline disorders are manifested by response to different interventions. In the analyst's work to establish the therapeutic alliance with the borderline patient, confrontation alone provides the the crucial tool for answering the borderline patient's fundamental, and initial, questions: Do you understand what I need? Can I trust you to believe that I can be responsible for my life, my feelings, my thoughts, my actions?

For the borderline patient, only confrontation can answer these questions successfully and move the patient from his chronic state of regressive, self-destructive, or compliant defense into genuine individuation. In work with the borderline patient, confrontation—in whatever form it is expressed—fundamentally says: "My expectation is that you will contain your infantile, maladaptive, and self-destructive tendencies and behave in a healthy, adaptive, and self-interested manner. When you don't, I will be curious, concerned, and surprised."

While confrontation is essential to work with the borderline patient, it is anathema to the narcissistic disorder. The narcissistic defense is ubiquitous. Since the intrapsychic structure involves what has been previously described as relatively undifferentiated self- and object representations, the patient cannot acknowledge the thoughts, feelings, or wishes of others as separate without feeling that his narcissistic defense is being punctured like a balloon and traumatically deflated.

Kohut was the first to emphasize the importance of the therapist's acknowledging as accurately and empathically as possible the narcissistic patient's sensitivity and vulnerability to narcissistic injury. With the narcissistic patient, the therapist builds a therapeutic alliance by responding empathically—tolerating, acknowledging, and encouraging the patient's unique self-expression—and by interpreting the patient's responses to failures in mirroring (disappointment, contempt, devaluation, rage, manipulation) as self-protection and defense from vulnerability to narcissistic injury. In this manner alone, also according to Masterson (1981, 1988), can affect and defense ultimately be linked, thereby permitting the possibility of working through to take place.

Working Through

There is a fundamental difference in the concept of working through in the work of Kohut and Masterson. In my view, for Kohut (1971) the essence of the curative process in psychotherapy is to provide the "missing" psychic structure—to permit the grandiose self to emerge, be acknowledged, and gradually be brought into accord with external reality without loss of spontaneity, aliveness of affect, or creative potential. Psychotherapy provides a receptacle for the patient's idealizing projections and then permit the omnipotent and magical object to be gradually brought into accord with actual reality. These idealized, but realistic, self- and object representations, with their associated functions and capacities, are internalized into the intrapsychic world as permanent, stable, mood-regulating structures through the gradual process of transmuting internalizations. The end result is a stable, cohesive, realistic—but creative—self-identity.

For Masterson (1981, 1985), in contrast, the essence of the work in treating the personality disorders is the working through of the abandonment depression, the fundamental roadblock on the developmental pathway, which underlies all the disorders of the self. The abandonment depression, and the powerful and pathological affects of which it is composed, results when the child is forced to relinquish his own development of a "real self" in order to concentrate on reacting to the needs, deprivations, wishes, impingements, and projections of his caretakers.

While the specific affects that constitute the abandonment depression will change among the personality disorders, the process of working through is fundamentally similar. The key feature of working through involves reexperiencing the memories and the feelings associated with the original abandonment. Only in this way can the abandonment depression be removed as the obstacle blocking the pathway of the patient's development of a "real self."

CONCLUSION

Normal personality development is a pathway from unevoked potential to "real self" actualization. The ability of any person to manifest his or her full potential as a human being involves mature separation, attachment, autonomy, and individuation—a kaleidoscope of functions, abilities, talents, and relationships—all of which create a unique mosaic for each person.

The psychology of the self adds to and refines existing constructs, especially in expanding our knowledge of the role of selfobjects in early development and in describing the process of (transmuting) internalization of functions and capacities which had heretofore been only vaguely defined. The psychopathology of the self—the description and treatment of narcissistic personality disorders—is also a valuable addition to clinical practice in allowing the therapist inroads into the treatment of a sector of personality disorganization that has seemed inaccessible. Beyond this, however, the psychology of the self adds only needless confusion and creates controversy where none is necessary.

REFERENCES

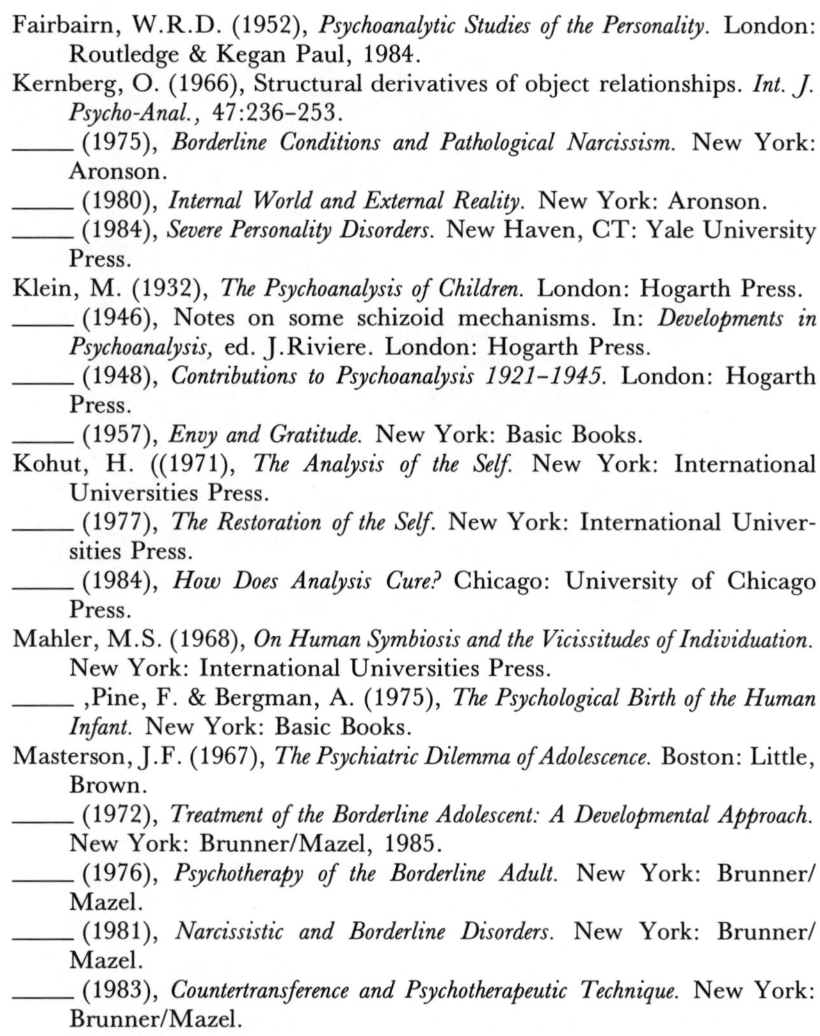

Fairbairn, W.R.D. (1952), *Psychoanalytic Studies of the Personality.* London: Routledge & Kegan Paul, 1984.

Kernberg, O. (1966), Structural derivatives of object relationships. *Int. J. Psycho-Anal.,* 47:236–253.

_____ (1975), *Borderline Conditions and Pathological Narcissism.* New York: Aronson.

_____ (1980), *Internal World and External Reality.* New York: Aronson.

_____ (1984), *Severe Personality Disorders.* New Haven, CT: Yale University Press.

Klein, M. (1932), *The Psychoanalysis of Children.* London: Hogarth Press.

_____ (1946), Notes on some schizoid mechanisms. In: *Developments in Psychoanalysis,* ed. J.Riviere. London: Hogarth Press.

_____ (1948), *Contributions to Psychoanalysis 1921–1945.* London: Hogarth Press.

_____ (1957), *Envy and Gratitude.* New York: Basic Books.

Kohut, H. ((1971), *The Analysis of the Self.* New York: International Universities Press.

_____ (1977), *The Restoration of the Self.* New York: International Universities Press.

_____ (1984), *How Does Analysis Cure?* Chicago: University of Chicago Press.

Mahler, M.S. (1968), *On Human Symbiosis and the Vicissitudes of Individuation.* New York: International Universities Press.

_____ ,Pine, F. & Bergman, A. (1975), *The Psychological Birth of the Human Infant.* New York: Basic Books.

Masterson, J.F. (1967), *The Psychiatric Dilemma of Adolescence.* Boston: Little, Brown.

_____ (1972), *Treatment of the Borderline Adolescent: A Developmental Approach.* New York: Brunner/Mazel, 1985.

_____ (1976), *Psychotherapy of the Borderline Adult.* New York: Brunner/Mazel.

_____ (1981), *Narcissistic and Borderline Disorders.* New York: Brunner/Mazel.

_____ (1983), *Countertransference and Psychotherapeutic Technique.* New York: Brunner/Mazel.

_____ (1985), *The Real Self: A Developmental, Self, and Object Relations Approach.* New York: Brunner/Mazel.

_____ (1988), *The Search for the Real Self.* New York: Free Press.

_____ & Klein, R. (1989), ed. *Psychotherapy of the Disorders of the Self.* New York: Brunner/Mazel.

Stern, D. (1985), *The Interpersonal World of the Infant.* New York: Basic Books.

Winnicott, D.W. (1958), *Collected Papers.* London: Tavistock.

_____ (1965), *The Maturational Processes and the Facilitating Environment.* New York: International Universities Press.

17

Kohut and Kernberg
A Critical Comparison

SALMAN AKHTAR

In a paper that is now considered a psychoanalytic classic, Stone (1954) discussed the "widening scope" of indications for psychoanalysis. He offered profound clinical insights regarding the rule of abstinence, resemblance as a necessary condition for transference development, variable degrees of deprivation in the analytic situation, modifications of technique with borderline cases, and, finally, legitimate transference gratifications to prevent undesirable severe regressions in sicker patients. Stone emphasized the need for detailed history taking and of carefully observing the patient's reactions to the examiner during the assessment of analyzability. He stated that psychoanalytic treatment should be supported by painstaking diagnosis and should not be used for "trivial or incipient or reactive illness, or in persons with feeble personality resources" (p. 593). However, he also emphasized that

> psychoanalysis may legitimately be invoked, and indeed *should* be invoked, for many very ill people, of good personality resources, who are probably inaccessible to cure by other methods, who are willing to accept the long travail of analysis,

---

The author thanks Selma Kramer, M.D., Henri Parens, M.D. and Sydney Pulver, M.D. for their helpful suggestions on an earlier version of this paper.

> without guarantees of success. There is always a possibility of helping, where all other measures fail. With the progressive understanding of the actions of psychotherapeutic admixtures or of large-scale "parameters" in the psychoanalytic method, now so largely intuitive in their application, we can hope such successes will be more frequent [pp. 593–594, italics added].

Since the publication of Stone's paper in 1954, many outstanding psychoanalysts have enriched our understanding of this widening scope of psychoanalysis. Two investigators who are the most prominent, most theoretically influential, and, in some ways, the most controversial in this group are Kohut and Kernberg. Together, they have provided the much-needed rejuvinating stimulus to American psychoanalysis that had begun to experience "a dimunition of scientific productivity and a loss of intellectual excitement" (Cooper, 1983, p. 4). Both have occupied prominent positions in the American and international psychoanalytic organizations. Both are regarded as enthusiastic teachers and charismatic lecturers. Both have presented significant emendations of classical theory and in doing so have gathered followers and opponents. Both have been, at various times, viewed as having fostered cultlike social phenomena within the scientific community of psychoanalysts and other mental health professionals (Calef and Weinshel, 1979; Cooper, 1988). Both have addressed matters of central concern to the British object relations theorists. Both have, therefore, directly or indirectly, spurred the current American interest in examining the contributions of Klein, Fairbairn, Winnicott, Guntrip, Balint, and others. Both have made contributions that extend beyond the restricted clinical domain. Both have written about aspects of "normal" psychology. Kohut has written of appreciation of music (1950, 1957) creativity (1976), humor (1971, 1977), group psychology (1976), charisma (1976), and wisdom (1971); Kernberg, of mature love (1976), aging (1977a), leadership patterns (1978a, 1980), regression in groups and organizations (1978a, 1980). Finally, both have stimulated work in applied psychoanalysis especially in the psychoanalytic study of sociopolitical conflicts (GAP report, 1978; Volkan, 1980, 1986; Zonis, 1980).

Despite these remarkable similarities, fundamental differences exist in the depth psychologies of Kohut and Kernberg. These differences are evident in their views on personality development, origins of psychopathology, and the nature of curative factors in psychoanalysis. The degree of their allegiance to general psychiatry is not the same, and they occupy different positions vis-à-vis "mainstream" psychoanalysis. In addition, they display a markedly different attitude toward the theoretical contributions of others. These three areas of difference—relationship to psychiatry, regard for others' contributions, and proximity to the classical theory—are amply exemplified (see Akhtar and Thomson, 1982) in their writings on narcissistic personality disorder.

RELATIONSHIP TO GENERAL PSYCHIATRY

When 138 national psychiatric experts were asked (Strauss, Yager, and Strauss, 1984) to identify the top ten publications during 1970–1980 that they regarded to be "seminal or of lasting value," their list included Kohut's two monographs (1971, 1977) and Kernberg's two collections of papers (1975a, 1976). As the article reporting this opinion survey was entitled "The Cutting Edge in Psychiatry" and as it appeared in the foremost psychiatric journal of the country, it is tempting to assume that Kohut and Kernberg have a similarly close relationship to psychiatry and the impact of their work on the field of general psychiatry is comparable. A closer inspection of their respective contributions, however, reveals the contrary.

Kohut (1971) specifically disavows "the traditional medical aim of achieving a diagnosis in which a disease entity is identified by clusters of recurring manifestations" (pp. 15–16). He (Kohut, 1982) declares his theory and the methods emanating from it to be "psychology through and through" (p. 399). Kohut maintains the traditional psychoanalytic caution about psychiatric nosology. In the case of narcissistic personality disorder, for instance, he (Kohut, 1971) emphasizes that "the crucial diagnostic criterion is based not only on the evaluation of the presenting symptomatology or even of the life history, but on the nature of the spontaneously developing transference" (p. 23). He places great emphasis on the analyst's empathic immersion in his patients' subjectivity and his self psychology is devoted, almost in its entirety, to the elucidation of the narcissistic transferences and their ontognetic antecedents in faulty parental empathy.

Kohut expresses much trepidation regarding psychoanalytic characterology as well. When he does describe various types of narcissistic personalities (Kohut and Wolf, 1978), he uses labels that differ from customary psychiatric terminology. He does not attempt to correlate the merger-hungry and contact-shunning types, for instance, with borderline and schizoid personality disorders respectively, thus missing an opportunity for his nosological eloquence to have a psychiatric counterpart. Moreover, Kohut is visibly less interested in the more severe end of the narcissistic-borderline spectrum. And, on the only occasion in his three monographs that he does mention medication (Kohut, 1984, p. 215), Kohut regards its mode of action as predominantly through its symbolic meanings to the patient.

Kohut's participation in the forums and publications of academic psychiatry is also minimal. A quick glance at the indexes of the *American Journal of Psychiatry* and *Archives of General Psychiatry* reveals no contribution from Kohut over the last 30 years (1951–1981) of his professional life. Finally, though Kohut was an enthusiastic teacher and an outstanding lecturer, he seldom participated in the annual APA conventions and similar major psychiatric conferences (Paul Fink, personal communication).

In contrast, Kernberg has maintained a close affiliation with academic psychiatry. He is among the contributors (Kernberg, 1975b) to the widely read *Comprehensive Textbook of Psychiatry-II* (Freedman, Kaplan, and Sadock, 1975). He editorially participated in the *American Psychiatric Association's 1982 Annual Review* (Grinspoon, 1982) of psychiatry. His work, often in the form of collaborative participation in empirical research, has appeared in major psychiatric journals, for example, *Archives of General Psychiatry* (Koenigsberg, Kernberg, and Schomer, 1983), *Journal of Nervous and Mental Disease* (Kernberg et al., 1981), and the *American Journal of Psychiatry* (Selzer, Koenigsberg, and Kernberg, 1987). In addition, Kernberg has frequently presented his ideas at the yearly APA conventions. He is a frequent examiner for the American Board of Psychiatry and Neurology. He reviews papers for the *American Journal of Psychiatry* and recently published a book review (Kernberg, 1988) in that journal.

Kernberg's clinical concerns also overlap with those of general psychiatrists: borderline personality organization (Kernberg, 1967); clinical features of narcissistic personality disorder (Kernberg, 1974); normal psychology of aging (Kernberg, 1977a); diagnosis, prognosis and intensive treatment of schizophrenic patients (Kernberg, 1977b); distinctions between adolescent identity crisis and borderline identity diffusion (Kernberg, 1978b); refinement of diagnostic interviewing techniques (Kernberg, 1981); supportive psychotherapy (Kernberg, 1982); hospital management of patients with severe character pathology (Kernberg, 1976, 1984); evaluation and management of chronically suicidal patients (Kernberg, 1984); and the establishment of initial therapeutic contract with borderline patients (Selzer, Koenigsberg, and Kernberg, 1987).

Kernberg's nosologic terminology frequently matches customary psychiatric language. When he uses a term differently from its current psychiatric usage, he clarifies his stance. This is manifest in his distinguishing between "hysterical" and "histrionic" personalities (Kernberg, 1985); even his adopting the "histrionic" label for what he would have earlier (Kernberg, 1967) referred to as "infantile" personality is accommodation to the mainstream psychiatric nosology. On the other hand, he unhesitatingly points out omissions of entities he deems valid, for example, hypomanic (Akhtar, 1988a) and as-if (Deutsch, 1942) personalities, from the current "official" psychiatric classification. Rather than summarily ignoring DSM-III (American Psychiatric Association, 1980) a document with pervasive impact on general psychiatry, Kernberg (1984) critically evaluates it. Finally, Kernberg includes psychotropic medications, and even ECT, as valid treatment modalities, the effect of which he does not readily reduce to their symbolically encoded significance alone.

The degree to which Kohut's and Kernberg's work has been assimilated by general psychiatrists also varies. Kohut's self psychology has been the subject of a lead article (Baker and Baker, 1987) in the official APA journal. Kernberg's work has not warranted such *en bloc* introduction, perhaps because it has already become more diffusely assimilated. Blashfield and McElroy (1987), for instance, report that Kernberg is the second most frequently cited author, and the most frequently cited psychoanalyst, in the current psychiatric literature on personality disorders.

In summary, Kohut and Kernberg seem to occupy considerably different positions vis-à-vis mainstream academic psychiatry. Kohut has little to do with the forums, perspectives, terminology, and preoccupations of general psychiatry whereas Kernberg is intimately involved with all these aspects. A brief digression, however, is necessary before discussing whether this difference has affected the psychoanalytic aspect of Kohut's and Kernberg's work. The relationship between academic psychiatry and psychoanalysis has been, since Freud's day, a confusing and ambiguous one. Freud's alienation from academic medicine and its complex historical reasons have been amply documented (Jones, 1953). Less well remembered is Freud's (1919) recommendation that psychoanalysis should play a prominent role in medical school curricula. He stated that teaching psychoanalysis to medical students would impress upon them "the significance of mental factors in the different vital functions as well as in illnesses and their treatment" and would afford them "a preparation for the study of psychiatry" (pp. 171–172). Although Freud emphasized that such a didactic curriculum would not equip general psychiatrists to practice clinical psychoanalysis, he believed an important purpose would still be served if they learned "something *about* psychoanalysis and something *from* it" (p. 173).

Since Freud made his comments much literature has accumulated underscoring the importance of psychoanalysts' involvement in academic psychiatry (Potter and Klein, 1951; Gitelson, 1962; A. Freud, 1966; Meissner, 1976; Strassman et al., 1976; Altshuler, 1979). Most authors agree that a continued involvement of psychoanalysts in academic psychiatry is indeed desirable.[1] Analysts provide a balanced ambience in the departments of psychiatry and, in their teaching role, serve as significant professional ego ideals for psychiatric residents. Such involvement positively influences the latter's applying for psychoanalytic training (Strassman et al., 1976). Even the residents who choose nonanalytic careers find it valuable to be exposed to teachers who can help them connect their patients' manifest symptomatology with its underlying unconscious motivations. This involvement enhances their capacity for clinical understanding and wins informed friends for psychoanalysis within psychiatry at large. These considerations have acquired even greater importance in the current climate of narrow biological overenthusiasm in psychiatry and the dwindling candidate pool for psychoanalytic training. Active involvement with psychiatric departments does pose challenging demands for psychoanalysts, but the potential impact they thus have on future professionals may outweigh the sacrifices and hardships involved.

Another question that has received less attention, however, needs to be answered before one wholeheartedly endorses continued psychiatric involvement on the psychoanalyst's part. This question pertains to the impact a general psychiatric involvement has on the psychoanalyst's analytic work ego.[2] On one hand, it can be argued

---

[1]This is not to deny that significant practical barriers may exist for a practicing psychoanalyst to establish or maintain an academic career in psychiatry. That these barriers come from both the analytic institutes and the medical schools is recognized by many prominent psychoanalysts (Altshuler, 1979).

[2]The lively and informative dialogue between Charles Brenner and Robert

that the ideal for which a psychoanalyst should strive is exclusive dedication to psychoanalytic practice and teaching. Such focused immersion, the argument continues, is the best way to sharpen one's analytic work ego, avoid nosological superficialities, strengthen theoretical rigor, and maintain professional identity as a psychoanalyst. On the other hand, it can be argued that seeing a large number of patients, providing consultation to people with varying degrees and types of psychopathology, interacting with medical colleagues, and remaining open to challenges to psychoanalysis from newer developments in psychiatry may widen the psychoanalyst's perspective. Whether such a broadening of perspective strengthens or weakens the analyst's analytic identity would then depend on a complex set of factors, which may range beyond merely his psychiatric involvement. These factors may include, among others, the genuineness of his interest in psychoanalysis to begin with, his maintenance of an analytic practice, and, above all, his self-analyzing capacity.

Returning from this digression specifically to Kohut and Kernberg, one would think that if involvement in psychiatry were indeed detrimental to an analyst's dedication to psychoanalysis, Kernberg would suffer more. Kohut's work will deepen its anchor in psychoanalytic theory, and Kernberg's approach will loosen its moorings, become detached from depth psychology. Actually, the opposite seems to be the case. However, before discussing their positions vis-à-vis classical theory and technique, I will highlight their attitude toward the significant, related contributions of other psychoanalysts.

REGARD FOR THE THEORETICAL CONTRIBUTIONS OF PREDECESSORS AND CONTEMPORARIES

Kohut has been repeatedly criticized for not acknowledging antecedent theoretical ideas that are reflected in his self psychology (Stein, 1979; Rothstein, 1980; Bacal, 1987). I myself have earlier (Akhtar, 1988b) elaborated this tendency in Kohut's writings. He implies originality in presenting ideas that clearly existed in earlier literature. For instance, in emphasizing the powerful impact of

---

Michels during the 1987 fall meetings of the American Psychoanalytic Association in New York sharply elucidated the two sides of this argument.

maternal care on the developing psychic structure of the child, Kohut disregards Freud's deep awareness of this matter. Not only did Freud (1923) recognize the significance of the real nature of early objects to the development of ego, he (Freud, 1940) explicitly emphasized the "mother's importance, unique, without parallel, established unalterably for a whole lifetime as the first and strongest love-object and as the prototype of all later love relations—for both sexes" (p. 188). Kohut does not acknowledge Freud's profound statement. He also ignores Hartmann (1939, 1952), who had further highlighted the complex interplay of instinctual drives and early object relationships underlying ego development. Even more striking in this context is Kohut's stance toward Mahler's work. In his first monograph, Kohut (1971) condemns Mahler with faint praise and then dismisses her developmental observations as belonging in a sociobiological framework outside "the core area of psychoanalytic metapsychology" (p. 219). In his second monograph (Kohut, 1977), the acknowledgment of Mahler's work is limited to the mention of her name in the book's preface. The entire body of research on separation-individuation (Mahler, 1968, 1972; Mahler, Pine, and Bergman, 1975) is thus ignored, and so is its careful elaboration of the importance of the "optimal emotional availability" (Mahler, 1972, p. 410) of the mother to her growing infant.

Kohut's disregard of earlier contributions is even more evident when it comes to British object-relations theorists: Fairbairn, Winnicott, Guntrip, and Balint. Fairbairn is not widely read in this country, and under different circumstances his omission might have gone unnoticed. Kohut's conceptual debt to Fairbairn, however, is greater than can be comfortably denied. Robbins (1980), in a paper suggesting that the current Kernberg-Kohut controversy is an outgrowth of the earlier Klein-Fairbairn schism, lists the similarities between Fairbairn and Kohut. Both underemphasize the pleasure principle and instinctual drives, especially inborn aggression. Both regard a pristine, whole self to exist from the beginning, and both view its growth to depend more on satisfactory objects relations than on libidinal gratification. Both believe that disappointments in the primary object lead to regressive autoerotic fragmentation and drive supremacy. Both view regression a separate pathway, not a reversal of developmental steps previously taken. Moreover, as Bacal (1987) points out, Kohut's (1977) description of "self-state dreams" (p. 109)—dreams that are not wish fulfillments but straightforward depictions of the current psychological condition of the self—is a near replica of Fairbairn's (1944) earlier concept of "state-of-affairs dreams." In view of these remarkable similarities, it is disturbing to note the absence of Fairbairn's (1952) work from all three Kohut monographs (1971, 1977, 1984).

Winnicott receives a similar treatment. His concepts of "true" and "false" selves (Winnicott, 1960) closely parallel Kohut's notions (1977) of the joyful "nuclear self" and the "compensatory structures" elaborated to mask defects in the self. Winnicott suggests that the "false self" is a caretaker of the withdrawn "true self" and that it searches for optimal human circumstances in which the latter may come into its own. Kohut attributes a similar function to drive activity in general; drives are enlisted in an attempt to bring about a selfobject relationship that would repair the injured self. Both Winnicott (1965) and Kohut (1977) see psychopathology as a result of environmental failure. Both emphasize the "holding," rather than psychosexual gratification, aspect of the maternal care. Even the mirror metaphor popularized by Kohut was mentioned earlier by Winnicott. Winnicott (1967) describes the role mother plays in mirroring the child's self to him and the deleterious effects of chronically deficient mirroring on the child's growing personality. Finally, Kohut (1977) suggests that the mother not only needs to enthusiastically reflect her growing child's grandiosity, but also to gradually shift her responsiveness to increasingly age-specific tasks and skills. Winnicott (1953) similarly states that the "mother's main task (next to providing opportunity for illusion) is disillusionment" (p. 95; parenthesis author's). Despite these overlaps in their outlook, Kohut makes no mention of Winnicott except in an inconsequential footnote in his 1971 monograph.

Guntrip is not even mentioned though there are many similarities (Bacal, 1987) between his and Kohut's views. Guntrip's (1969) description of the fundamental human anxiety as the fear of the loss of ego itself is akin to Kohut's (1977) later description of the "disintegration anxiety" (p. 104) or the feared anticipation of the breakup of the self. Guntrip, like Kohut, speaks of the self as the most meaningful psychic constellation. Moreover, both of them suggest that instinctual conflicts are themselves defenses against more basic, self-related anxieties. Finally, Guntrip's theory of therapy, with its emphasis upon regrowth of the personal self, is strikingly similar to Kohut's view in this regard.

Kohut's attitude toward Balint is a curious one. In his 1971 monograph, he dissociated himself from Balint's views. He stated that he wished to "remain faithful to the classical formulation" of primary narcissism and could not impute to "the very young child

. . . the capacity for even rudimentary forms of object-love" (p. 220). Kohut was thus criticizing Balint's (1937) concept of "primary love." However, as Bacal (1987) has convincingly argued, "primary love" is not really an object-instinctual concept at all and is in essence similar to Kohut's (1977) own later formulation of infantile selfobject tie. One therefore expected that, in his second monograph, Kohut would reassess Balint and discuss what now appeared to be a great similarity between their ontogenetic formulations. He does not do so.

Kohut also ignores those contemporary investigators who present evidence contradictory to his theses. Certain aspects of Mahler's work and the object relations theories of Jacobson (1964) and Kernberg (1975a, 1976) belong in this category of omissions. Finally, Kohut makes little effort to correlate his developmental scheme with the data of infant observational research. He barely mentions Spitz (1965) and completely ignores Bergmann and Escalona (1949), Lustman (1956), Thomas et al. (1963), Thomas, Chess and Birch (1968), Emde, Graensbauer, and Harmon (1976), and Stern (1976) to name just a few. Some of this data could put to considerable test the purely environmental view of the development of self and its psychopathology as espoused by Kohut and his followers.

Kernberg's theoretical formulations and suggested treatment techniques have also had their share of critical evaluation and disagreements (Atkin, 1975; Holzman, 1976; Calef and Weinshel, 1979; Klein and Tribich, 1981; Segal, 1981). While many of Kernberg's critics disagree with his interpretation of earlier literature, not one has suggested that he does not pay enough attention to others' contributions. Calef and Weinshel (1979), even in their pervasive disagreement with Kernberg, acknowledge that he has attempted to incorporate the views of "object relations theory, Kleinian theory, ego psychology theory, the developmental approach, Bionian theory, and probably others as well" (p. 473). Brenner (1976a) states that Kernberg, as compared with other object relations theorists is "the most scientifically conscientious." Klein and Tribich (1981), while sharply questioning some of Kernberg's interpretations of the earlier literature, implicitly acknowledge that he has extensively cited Freud, Hartmann, Jacobson, Fairbairn, Guntrip, Bowlby, and Winnicott, among others. The only omission they locate is of Balint. However, their review does not include Kernberg's 1980 book, which does refer to Balint's contributions in a meaningful way.

Kernberg (1980) openly acknowledges his conceptual gratitude to his predecessors. He states that "some of Fairbairn's ideas have contributed to my own thinking"[3] (p. 68) and that Jacobson's work (1964) has had a "profound influence" (p. 85) on his theoretical formulations. This willingness to acknowledge important others while maintaining a thoughtful distance is evident in Kernberg's having provided detailed, separate evaluations of Klein's, Fairbairn's, and Jacobson's theoretical achievements. Moreover, he has attempted to correlate his own reconstructive hypotheses with Mahler's developmental theory (Kernberg, 1980) and his metapsychological formulations regarding instincts and affects with new findings in such fields as ethology, neurophysiology, general learning theory, and psychophysiology of affect (Kernberg, 1976). It therefore appears that when it comes to others' contributions, Kernberg shows much greater acknowledgement and gratitude than does Kohut. Ironically, Kernberg (1975a) even acknowledges that he has borrowed the term "grandiose self" from Kohut, although he uses it with a different etiological formulation. This brings us to a comparison of their respective positions regarding classical psychoanalysis.

RELATIONSHIP TO MAINSTREAM PSYCHOANALYSIS

Kohut's involvement with classical psychoanalysis can be divided into three phases: the "classical" phase, the "transitional" phase, and the "radical" phase. In the first phase, he operated within the bounds of the classical theory. His technique was directed by its framework, and he made significant contributions (Kohut and Levarie, 1950; Kohut, 1957, 1964) from within this perspective. Kohut was recognized as an outstanding teacher and clinician. He vigorously participated in the activities of the American Psychoanalytic Association and was elected its President in 1964. Then, he gradually began to question the theory and technique of classical psychoanalysis. A transitional phase of his theory building followed, culmi-

[3]Fairbairn has influenced Kohut and Kernberg in different ways. Kohut (1977) has elaborated on Fairbairn's (1952) environmental or "external" emphasis, that is, the actual role of early caretakers, minimization of the pleasure principle, a view of aggression as only a reaction to frustration and, consideration of drives and the Oedipus complex as strategies for maintaining a cohesive self. Kernberg (1975a, 1976, 1980) on the other hand, has been more influenced by Fairbairn's (1944, 1952) endopsychic or "internal" focus, that is, the early dyadic internalizations, mechanism of splitting and the necessary coexistence of self- and object representations in early internalizations.

nating in the publication of his 1971 monograph. The innovations introduced there by Kohut were still, though with already palpable conceptual discomfort, within the framework of classical drive theory. The concept of "narcissistic libido" (Kohut, 1971), for instance, was, on one hand, an accommodation to the classical drive model and, on the other, a significant departure from it. It invokes such concepts as narcissism, libido, and cathexis and quantitative, economic factors, while at the same time bifurcating Freud's libido theory into two independent developmental lines, one leading to object love and the other to healthy self-regard. This transitional phase constituted what Kohut (1977) later referred to as "psychology of the self in the narrow sense of the term" (p. 207). It regarded self as a content of the mental apparatus, that is, as mental representations within the id, ego, and superego. This phase was followed by the final, "radical" phase, in which Kohut proposed the self psychology in its "broad sense" (p. 207), that is, in a sense that views the self as a superordinate constellation with the drives and defenses of its constituents. With this shift, Kohut's language also underwent a noticeable change. What he had earlier (Kohut, 1971) termed grandiose self, idealized parent imago, transmuting internalization, and narcissistic transferences now (Kohut, 1977) became nuclear goals, nuclear ambitions, selective inclusion, and selfobject transferences. Narcissism became synonymous with self; the tripartite structure was discarded; and, as Rothstein (1980) points out, "analysis" (Kohut, 1971) became "restoration" (Kohut, 1977). The tone of his last paper (Kohut, 1982), with pervasive first-person beginnings, poignant feelings of his having struggled more or less alone, haughty dismissal of the influential theoretician Hartmann, portrayal of instinctual drive as a "vague and insipid biological concept" (p. 401), and a desire for "decisive scientific action" (p. 398), befits more a pioneer of a new school rather than a major collaborator with psychoanalysis.[4] Kohut's break with classical theory here is clearly in sight. "Self psychology has freed itself from the distorted view of psychological man espoused by traditional analysis" (Kohut, 1982, p. 402).[5]

[4]The prose of this paper has an almost uncanny and, given its contents, ironical resemblance to Freud's style of writing.

[5]Five years before this triumphant declaration, Kohut (1977) had reproached Schafer, whose theoretical contributions he praised, for not taking into account "the need for gradualness in theory change if the psychoanalytic 'group self' is to be preserved" (p. 85). Could it be that Kohut was, at the same time, restraining his own pioneering spirit?

Kernberg's relationship with mainstream psychoanalysis is less surgically divisible into phases, although it appears that he has followed an opposite trajectory than has Kohut. Initially, he was regarded as somewhat of an "outsider"[6] who was presenting a "loose theoretical amalgam [which] does conceptual violence both to the old theory and the new product" (Calef and Weinshel, 1979, p. 473). His theory was criticized for glossing over thought processes in psychic life (Holzman, 1976). His nosological clarifications were regarded as unrealistically precise (Segal, 1981), "atomistic distinctions" (Calef and Weinshel, 1979 p. 477). He was seen as blurring the distinction between psychoanalysis and psychotherapy, overemphasizing the role of pregenital factors, especially pregenital aggression, and giving undue importance to "the *real* activity and care of the early introjected objects *in toto,* particularly the mother" (Calef and Weinshel, 1979, p. 488).[7] With passage of time, which diluted the impact of his introducing some Kleinian concepts into the mainstream theory, and also with Kernberg's (1975b, 1979, 1980) thorough presentations of his agreements and disagreements with his predecessors and contemporaries, as well as with his increasing attention to the complex interplay of drives, affects, ego capacities, and maturational factors in early structure formation (Kernberg, 1976, 1985), he came to be regarded as more of an "insider." Kernberg is now the associate editor of the *Journal of American Psychoanalytic Association* and is regarded highly by prominent mainstream psychoanalysts.[8] Indeed, "there is probably no psychoana-

---

[6]Kernberg's having been trained in Chile and thus not having "grown" in the organized American psychoanalysis may also have facilitated this impression.

[7]Kernberg's harshest critics (Klein and Tribich, 1981), on the other hand, state that "his object-relations theory is essentially oblivious to the infant's external world" (p. 31). How can these two diametrically opposed interpretations of Kernberg's position be reconciled? In my opinion, while Kernberg's focus is on endopsychic structures, he overlooks neither the constitutional nor the environmental roots of their development and distortion in health and psychopathology. Two quotations from his ample elaboration of this matter illustrate my point. Writing about pregenital aggression, Kernberg (1976) states that "the inborn determinants of economic factors (that is, the intensity of the affective, behavioral, and other neurophysiological components which enter into aggressively determined internalized object relations, and general affective and cognitive thresholds) *together with* environmental influences crucially contribute to the organization of the aggressive drive" (p. 118, italics added). Or, "excessive aggression may stem *both* from a constitutionally determined intensity of aggressive drives or from severe early frustration" (Kernberg, 1975a, p. 28, italics added).

[8]A similar reconcilliatory stance towards the later-day Kohut also is already in evidence (Wallerstein, 1983; Bach, 1985; Pine, 1985; Bacal, 1987). This is not only

lytic author more widely read or quoted in the world today" (Wallerstein, 1986, p. 711) both within and outside of specifically psychoanalytic circles, than Kernberg. Wallerstein (1986) believes that Kernberg's secure eminence in this regard is, in part, because he

> has not encouraged a revisionist movement in the sense of a new "school" or new (and different) overall psychology for psychoanalysis, nor has one developed in the sense, for example, that Kohut's self psychology has become a new psychology confronting psychoanalysis with a different overall mental paradigm. Kernberg has unswervingly seen his contribution as squarely within edifice of classical psychoanalysis, trying to integrate two of its major emphases, the American ego-psychological and the British object-relational, within one coherent schema to be sure, but in that sense only additive and synthesizing, not divisive or cultish. And here history seems to have borne him out and allayed the concern expressed seven years ago by Calef and Weinshel [p. 714].

It is with such a historical backdrop that a comparison of Kohut's and Kernberg's respective positions regarding major concepts of classical psychoanalysis is most useful. Such a comparison should ideally include their respective views on a variety of theoretical and technical matters. Since such an all-encompassing review is not possible here, I will select only two matters to compare the views of Kohut and Kernberg. These include the concept of conflict and oedipus complex. I will discuss their technical contributions in the section on narcissistic personality.

Conflict

Intrapsychic conflict is central to the structural model of the mind and psychoanalysis has prototypically been a psychology of conflict. In Kris's (1947) famous aphoristic definition, the subject matter of psychoanalysis is nothing but "human behavior viewed as conflict" (p. 6). Brenner (1976b, 1982) provides a more current, detailed statement of the same fundamental theme, and there remains a broad consensus among psychoanalysts that the concept of conflict

---

a reflection on the contemporary vulnerability of the psychoanalytic profession which can ill afford further splits within its ranks but, on the positive side, shows a spirit of greater flexibility and maturation within psychoanalytic theorizing.

is basic to the understanding and treatment of psychopathology. The inevitability, even desirability, of frustration and conflict in the maturation and development of the self are also views peacefully adhered to by most analysts.

In contrast, Kohut's self psychology proposes that, under optimal circumstances, the origins of the self are free of conflict.[9] Moreover, Kohut (Kohut and Wolf, 1978) suggests that the "primary disturbances of the self," including psychoses, borderline states, narcissistic behavior disorders, and narcissistic personality disorders, are not manifestations of intrapsychic conflict but of a state of psychological deficit. Such a stance, besides causing a major rupture in the historical continuity of the psychoanalytic emphasis on conflict from Freud to Brenner, also leaves many of Kohut's own clinical observations unexplained. For instance, is there no potential conflict between grandiose and idealizing aspirations? Do the grandiose beliefs about the self not contradict the more realistic, conscious assessments of the self? Does the patient not experience any tension between his narcissistic wishes and his later acquired moral prohibitions? If the "contact-shunning personalities" (Kohut and Wolf, 1978) avoid social interaction out of fear of their intense longings, then are their need for others and their avoidance of them not in conflict with each other?[10] One possible reason for the negation of conflict by Kohut's self psychology may be that the term "conflict" is being extremely narrowly defined. Almost exclusively

[9]Among Kohut's followers, Tolpin (1980) makes this point most emphatically. She distinguishes "Mahler's baby" from "Kohut's baby" (p. 51) and suggests that while Mahler viewed conflict to be inherent in psychic development and growth of the child, Kohut proposed that, given optimal parental responsiveness, the growing child is internally conflict-free. In this view, any conflict experienced during development is already pathological. Clearly, this position is fundamentally different from the traditional psychoanalytic viewpoint in which Mahler's theory is deeply anchored.

[10]Such a clarifying attempt can be derided as phenomenological hair-splitting and taking the word "conflict" too literally. It could appear to ignore that psychoanalytic thought has been moving in the direction of a more object relations type of theory in keeping with our greater understanding of the initial dyad and its many reverberations, and that there is, as a consequence, a kind of political conservative vs. progressive aspect to the "conflict"-"deficit" debate. "Conflict" has come to stand for oedipal, neurotic conflict and not an internal psychic struggle alone, while "deficit" implies preoedipal or dyadic, while not excluding the existence of intrapsychic struggle of forces. It should therefore be emphasized that the choice here to sharply define the term "conflict" is purposive and not based on ignorance of the unfortunate, political buzz-word significance of the term.

(Kohut, 1977, pp. 132, 260), an intrapsychic conflict is equated with a structural or intersystemic conflict. This overlooks other varieties of intrapsychic conflicts. There is intrasystemic conflict (A. Freud, 1965) between different instinctual tendencies or conflicted ego impulses or contradictory identifications in the superego. There is also object-relations conflict (Dorpat, 1976), which involves a less differentiated psychic structure that is antecedent to id-ego-superego differentiation. The subject with an object-relations conflict experiences the conflict as being between his own wishes and his internalized representations of another person's values. This is in contrast to a person with a structural conflict, where the subject experiences both vectors of the quandary as belonging to his own self. This manner of conceptualizing various types of intrapsychic conflict is consonant with the hierarchical model of mind proposed by Gedo and Goldberg (1973). Their design allows for a tripartite model at a higher developmental level and an object-relations model at a lower developmental level. This view is also supported by Greenspan's (1977) correlation of "internal object constancy" (Mahler et al., 1968) with structural conflicts and lack of such constancy with object relations conflicts.

Kohut, however, insists on a conflict-deficit dichotomy. This "puzzling and . . . fundamentally unhelpful" (Wallerstein, 1983) dichotomy has led to the creation of the reified psychological postulates of the "Tragic Man" and the "Guilty Man" (Kohut, 1977). "Tragic Man" is a person with a psychological deficit, who is struggling to maintain cohesion of his fragmenting self and "Guilty Man" refers to one battling with his prohibited sexual and aggressive longings. This dichotomy, however, leads to an artificial separation of preoedipal and oedipal development. I have suggested elsewhere (Akhtar, 1984) that the Tragic Man is no less guilty than Guilty man; the Tragic Man's guilt emanates from his pregenital sadism toward the parental objects and from a sense of having taken too much from the mother and depleted her. Similarly, Guilty Man is no less tragic than Tragic man insofar as the source of his guilt are his incestuous and patricidal fantasies (but not acts), wishes that emanated from within him with the unfolding of a constitutional blueprint beyond his control, and a family structure not of his chosing. What is more tragic than to punish oneself for one's own thoughts? The artificial dichotomy of the Tragic Man and the Guilty Man oversimplifies human experience, ignores genetic spirality, overlooks the "principle of multiple function" (Waelder,

1930), and produces unnecessary and unfortunate duplicity in psychoanalytic technique.

In contrast to Kohut, Kernberg does not posit a deficit-conflict dichotomy. He regards the classical structural neuroses to be a symptomatic counterpart of the "higher level" character organization where "defensive operations against unconscious *conflicts* center on repression" (Kernberg, 1976, p. 143, italics added). On the "lower level" (Kernberg, 1970) too, that is, among people in the borderline range of psychopathology, Kernberg sees the compromised ego capacities to be the result of an intrasystemic conflict. This is the conflict of ambivalence whereby predominantly aggressively derived self- and object representations are defensively kept apart from libidinally derived self- and object representations in order to protect a safe ego core and to avoid the anxiety emanating from the potential destruction of any internalized goodness. Such conditions, according to Kernberg (1976), are characterized by a "pathological condensation of pregenital and genital *conflicts* with predominance of pregenital aggression" (p. 146, italics added). Also, in accordance with classical psychoanalytic perspective, Kernberg regards intrapsychic conflict to be a necessary and inevitable aspect of mental life and not merely an unfortunate byproduct of faulty parental responsiveness to the growing child. However, it is simplistic to leave things at this level alone. The fact remains that conflict, defined as the dynamic struggle of internal forces, is clearly evident in Kohut's descriptions of patients; and deficit, defined as inadequacy of libidinal internalizations, is implicit in Kernberg's portrayal of severe character pathology. This is not surprising. Indeed this is to be expected since

> in the flow and flux of analytic clinical material we are always in the world of "both/and." We deal constantly, and in turn, both with the oedipal where there is a coherent self, and the preoedipal, where there may not yet be; with defensive regressions and with developmental arrests; with defensive transferences and defensive resistances and with recreations of earlier traumatic and traumatized states [Wallerstein, 1983, p. 31].

Since this is true, what is all the fuss about? I believe that it has to do with whether intrapsychic conflict is seen as primary and hence causative of whatever "deficits" or "defects" might exist in a given psychic structure or whether a primary deficit model is proposed that pushes intrapsychic conflict aside, rendering it only an epiphenomenon. Kernberg's views belong in the first category, and Kohut's in the second. The former fits in better with out usual understanding of psychoanalytic theory and practice.

Oedipus Complex

During his "classical" phase, Kohut accepted the traditional view of the nature and significance of the oedipus complex. In his "transitional" phase, too, Kohut retained a significant place for oedipal conflicts, though he separated narcissistic libido from object libido and assigned narcissistic issues a parallel, equal importance. In a clinically astute observation Kohut (1971) emphasized that

> following relationships may exist between the phallic-oedipal structures in which the child's wounded narcissism plays only a secondary role, and the narcissistic structures (phallic and prephallic) which are the leading pathogenic determinants of a narcissistic transference. (1) Either (a) the narcissistic or (b) the object-transference pathology is clearly predominant; (2) a dominant narcissistic fixation coexists with an important object-transference pathology; (3) a manifestly narcissistic disorder hides a nuclear oedipal conflict; and (4) a narcissistic personality disorder is covered by manifestly oedipal structures [pp. 154–155].

Kohut suggested that late in the analysis of even the narcissistic pathology, an oedipal situation may emerge that "must be dealt with analytically as in the case of a typical primary transference neurosis" (p. 155). Later, Kohut (1977) added that such oedipal constellations were a result of a consolidation of the self never before achieved. They were therefore "new, . . . not a transference repetition" (p. 228). Reconstructing from the joy of his patients in arriving at such an experience, Kohut portrayed the childhood oedipal phase itself in a glowing manner. However, this positive emphasis led Kohut to locate the origin of oedipal conflict differently from classical theory. The conflict does not originate in the child's stimulating, contradictory and unrealistic strivings themselves. It results from unempathic parents who see the constituents of the child's oedipal aspirations in isolation and therefore cause their intensification. A second departure from classical theory was Kohut's related proposal that "the oedipus complex of classical analysis that we take to be a ubiquitous human experience is . . . already the manifestation of a pathological development" (p. 246). Moreover, with his progressive move toward self psychology, Kohut's view of the Oedipus complex became increasingly "sanitized." Little mention is found in his writings of penis, vagina, urinary stream pleasure, infantile theories of childbirth, penis envy, primal scene, castration fears, and the like. Most important, Kohut's approach to the oedipal phase does not genuinely recognize the triadic, as against dyadic, nature of relationships typical of this phase. Even the Odysseus myth, which Kohut (1982) finally proposed as the centerpiece of his theory and by which he wished to replace the centrality of oedipus complex, is essentially a dyadic parable.

Kernberg, in contrast, recognizes the Oedipus complex to be a landmark developmental event. Although his interest is clearly in the "prehistory of the oedipus complex" (Freud, 1925), Kernberg does not question the essential nature of the conflict as portrayed by classical psychoanalysis. His classification of character pathology (Kernberg, 1970) includes a category of "higher level" organization displaying solely or predominantly oedipal-phase conflicts. This group of disorders, including hysterical, obsessional, and some depressive-masochistic personalities, is seen by Kernberg as ego-syntonic counterpart to the respective, classical symptom neuroses. Kernberg (1978b, 1980) discusses the vicissitudes of oedipal resurgence during adolescence and during middle age. Finally, in his descriptions of borderline and narcissistic characters, Kernberg (1967, 1975a) emphasizes the pathognomonic condensation of oedipal and preoedipal conflicts under the overriding influence of pregenital aggression. He points out that intense oedipal strivings may prematurely develop in a child to deny frustrated oral dependent needs. Kernberg emphasizes that such development powerfully reinforces oedipal fears by pregenital fears of the mother. Under these circumstances, a positive Oedipus complex is seriously interfered with. Adult sexuality is then characterized by either sexualized dependency or prominent negative oedipal trends. These manifest in greedy promiscuity and orally derived homosexuality among men and, among women, in an intensified penis envy, flight into promiscuity to deny penis envy, or a sexualized search for the gratification of oral needs from an idealized mother leading to homosexuality. Obviously, the differences Kohut and Kernberg have in their views of the Oedipus complex reflect their overall positions vis-à-vis classical psychoanalysis. These differences are further manifested in their approach to narcissistic personality disorder.

VIEWS ON NARCISSISTIC PERSONALITY

Phenomenology

Kohut (1971) emphasizes that the diagnosis of narcissistic personality depends less on observable behavior than on the spontaneously evolving mirror and idealizing transferences during the psychoanalytic treatment of such patients. However, he does acknowledge that a person with a narcissistic personality disorder frequently presents the following clinical features:

> (1) in the sexual sphere: perverse fantasies, lack of interest in sex; (2) in the social sphere: work inhibitions, inability to form and maintain significant relationships, delinquent activities; (3) in his manifest personality features: lack of humor, lack of empathy for other people's needs and feelings, lack of a sense of proportion, tendency towards attacks of uncontrolled rage, pathological lying; and (4) in the psychosomatic sphere: hypochondriacal preoccupations with physical and mental health, vegetative disturbances in various organ systems [Kohut, 1971, p. 23].

Although profoundly angry reactions had been associated with narcissistic personality by many earlier observers (For example, Reich, 1933; Nemiah, 1961), Kohut (1972) describes such a tendency in eloquent detail. The central features of "narcissistic rage" are the need for revenge—the undoing of hurt by whatever means—and a compulsion in this pursuit, with utter disregard for reasonable limits. The irrationality of this vengeful attitude is frightening because reasoning is not only intact but sharpened. Another affective feature, in the description of which Kohut anticipated Grunberger (1975), Bach (1977), and Svrakic (1985), involves the narcissistic person's tendency toward hypomanic exaltation. Kohut portrayed it as an anxious excitement, sometimes associated with trancelike ecstasy and near-religious feelings of transcendence. This emotion is often precipitated by favorable occurrences in reality that stir up the narcissist's as yet untamed exhibitionism and flood his psyche with archaic grandiosity.

Finally, Kohut (Kohut and Wolf, 1978) described five types of narcissistic personalities: (a) *mirror-hungry personalities,* who are impelled to display themselves and to seek other's admiration to combat their inner sense of worthlessness, (b) *ideal-hungry personalities,* who chronically search others whom they can admire for their power and prestige and from whom they can draw emotional sustenence, (c) *alter-ego personalities,* who need a relationship with someone who conforms to their own values and thus confirms their inner reality, (d) *merger-hungry personalities,* who seek to control others in an enactment of their need for inner structure, and (e) *contact-shunning personalities,* who avoid social contact out of a fear of intensity of their need for attachment and love. While this classification is didactically appealing, it leaves many questions open. First, Kohut and Wolf (1978), after describing the first three of these narcissistic types, make a puzzling and unexplained turnabout and state that "they should, in general, not be considered as forms of psychopathology but rather as variants of the normal human personality" (p. 422). Second, whether these are to be considered separate types or facets of a unitary syndrome remains unsettled at this particular time. After all, what actuarial data exist to support subclassification within a syndrome that itself remains disputed and unsettled for many pratitioners in the field? Third, Kohut and Wolf (1978) do not comment on the fact that their "merger-hungry" and "contact-shunning" types overlap borderline and schizoid personalities respectively and thus miss an opportunity for psychoanalytic-psychiatric linkage. Finally, while they state that the relationships established by mirror-hungry, ideal-hungry, and alter-ego hungry do not last long, they do not address the issue of aggression, which spoils these initially blissful unions.

Kernberg (1975a, 1976) portrays people with narcissistic personality disorder as displaying excessive self-absorption, intense ambition, grandiosity, overdependence on tributes from others, and an unremitting need for power, brilliance, and beauty. He emphasizes the pathology of the inner worlds of such persons. This manifests in their shallow emotional life, defective empathy, inability to love, and a peculiar inability to experience sadness and mournful longing when facing separation and loss. Kernberg also points out that the narcissistic person lacks genuine sublimations; his work is in the service of exhibitionism and self-esteem regulation, done in order to receive praise. In addition, there are associated superego defects and a tendency toward corruptibility and cutting ethical corners.

Kernberg's description of narcissistic personality differs from that of Kohut in four ways. First, he emphasizes the paranoid substrate of the syndrome and hence regards mistrust, hunger, rage, and guilt about this rage (Kernberg, 1975a) to be the basic cause of the self-inflation and not merely reactive phenomena, as Kohut proposes. Second, he gives a special place to the chronic envy that underlies the narcissistic person's seeming scorn for others. Indeed, Kernberg considers defenses against such envy particularly devaluation, omnipotent control and narcissistic withdrawal, a major aspect of the clinical picture of narcissistic personality disorder. Third, Kernberg, in his usual attitude of rapproachement with general psychiatry, provides a diagnosis of narcissistic personality that differentiates it from other personality disorders. Among these he includes borderline and antisocial personalities on one hand, and obsessional and hysterical personalities on the other hand. Finally, unlike Kohut, Kernberg does not attribute the middle-aged narcissist's denial of his age-specific limitations and his envy of younger generations to a failure in achieving his true destiny. Instead, he suggests that this deterioration of the narcissist's internal world is yet another step in the repeating cycles of "wants, temporary idealizations, greedy incorporation, and disappearance of supplies by spoiling, disappointing, and devaluation" (Kernberg, 1980, p. 138).

Pathogenesis and Metapsychology

Kohut (1971) sees narcissistic disorder, or the primary disturbance of the self (Kohut, 1977), as originating in faulty parental empathy with the growing child. The disorder is regarded as a developmental arrest in which archaic grandiosity and the need for idealization have failed to be subsumed under phase-specific, mature psychic functioning. Deficient maternal mirroring and traumatic ruptures of parental idealizations lead to a failure of "transmuting internalization" (Kohut, 1971). The resulting clinical picture depends on the extent to which these structures are experientially felt, repressed, split off, or acted out.

In his theoretically "transitional" phase (Kohut, 1971) separated narcissism from the developmental line of drive-based object relations. He saw oedipal issues, and the structural neuroses consequent upon them, as having a sequential relation to the narcissistic sector and its pathology. However, such a separation left theoretical loopholes. Greenberg and Mitchell (1983) point out, for instance, that Kohut's distinction between narcissistic disorders and structural neuroses stemming from instinctual conflicts

> seems fundamentally contradicted by Kohut's formulations concerning the development of self. If drives are disintegration products reflecting a breakdown of primary relational configurations, how can 'structural neuroses' contain at one and the same time no self pathology and conflicts concerning drives, which by definition reflect severe self pathology?" [p. 359]

In his "radical" phase, that is, in the development of self psychology in its broad sense, Kohut (1977) maintained his essential thesis that the disorder is a result of deficient parental empathy. However, this time Kohut attempted a more far-reaching revision of classical metapsychology. He totally minimized the significance of instinctual drives and, as described earlier, placed the Oedipus complex in a context completely different from its classical view.

The problem with Kohut's view of the genesis of the narcissistic personality disorder is its undue, single-minded emphasis on one etiological factor, namely, deficient maternal empathy. Indeed, Kohut (1977) proposes that the mothers of these patients suffer from a specific "pathogenic personality disorder"[11] (p. 189). However, if this is true, why do all children of the same mother not have narcissistic personalities? Even in the realm of parental influence, Kohut's self psychology does not do justice to "the spectrum of mothering and fathering experiences by patients who have narcissistic disorders" (Rothstein, 1980 p. 431). Almost totally ignored are the role that patient's gender, birth order, special endowments, parental overvaluation and the child's own primary process distortions of the real objects play in the genesis of the disorder.

Kernberg, on the other hand, does not propose a separate line of development of narcissism. He sees the narcissistic personality not as a form of developmental arrest, but as a specific pathological formation to begin with. Kernberg posits that narcissistic patients do not suffer from an absence of certain structures in the ego and superego, but the presence of pathological primitive structures. He

[11]Not only is this reminiscent (Wallerstein, 1983) of the now disproven "schizophrenogenic mother" concept, it also reveals a curious contradiction in Kohut's approach to nosology. On one hand, he hesitates to diagnose patients from their symptoms and histories alone; on the other hand, he "diagnoses" their mothers from second-hand data!

differentiates the normal narcissism of children, which he believes retains a realistic quality, from the early development of pathological narcissism, which creates fantastically grandiose fantasies (Kernberg, 1975a). Kernberg believes that narcissistic patients were treated by their parents in a cold, even spiteful, but nonetheless "special" manner. In addition, the quality of their early introjections was altered by age-specific misperceptions as well as by paranoid distortions of parental figures due to their own aggression toward their parents. Using Kohut's term with a different structural formulation, Kernberg proposes that the "grandiose self" is formed by a fusion of aspects of the real self, the idealized self, and an idealized object representation. Associated with such fusion, which permits a greater overall cohesion than is evidenced in borderline pathology, is the disowning through splitting of the needy-hungry self-representations, the depriving object representations, and the rage, envy, and fear that bind them together.

Such a state of affairs, Kernberg further posits, leads to a condensation of preoedipal and oedipal conflicts under the overriding influence of pregenital, especially oral, aggression. This has deleterious effects on the oedipal experience[12] and on the salutary identifications that, under ordinary circumstances, should follow from its resolution. These effects include intense castration anxiety, on one hand, and an orally derived greedy promiscuity and perverse tendencies on the other.

In summary, the differences between Kohut's and Kernberg's views of narcissism involve: (1) its separateness versus necessary relationship with object relations, (2) a developmental-arrest versus a pathological-formation view of the grandiose self, (3) the reactive versus the fundamental substrate view of aggression, and (4) the relative importance of the Oedipus complex in pathological narcissism. These differences effect the treatment techniques suggested by Kohut and by Kernberg.

Treatment Technique

The treatment of the narcissistic personality proposed by Kohut is psychoanalysis. However, his version of psychoanalysis is clearly different from that which is commonly understood. Kohut's (1971,

[12]That narcissistic pathology may result from predominantly oedipal conflicts is held neither by Kernberg nor by Kohut. However, other investigators (Spruiell, 1975; Rothstein, 1979) do hint at such a possibility.

1977) approach aims at permitting the full-blown development of narcissistic transferences with the activation of either unfulfilled mirroring or idealizing selfobject needs. The implication is that such transference itself completes a halted development. A second suggested step is to interpret to the patient that his grandiosity or idealizing needs were once phase appropriate and that it was lack of environmental provision that led them to persist as such. The patient's rage, if it erupts in the treatment, is interpreted as an understandable response to the (inevitable) empathic failures of the analyst. Such an experience is reconstructed backwards to similar experiences caused by faulty parental empathy during childhood. The entire approach is anchored in the analyst's empathic immersion in his patient's subjective experience, which is regarded as a replica of the patient's childhood experience. Kohut (1984) summarized his view of the curative factors in psychoanalysis when he stated that

> psychoanalysis cures by the laying down of psychic structure. And how does this accretion of psychological structure take place? The most general self psychological answer to this . . . question is also simple: psychological structure is laid down (a) via optimal frustration and (b) in consequence of optimal frustration, via transmuting internalization. . . . A good analysis, we believe, leads to a cure only by its employment, in countless repetitions, of the basic therapeutic unit of understanding and explaining, that is, via interpretation, the analyst's only active function in the analytic process [pp. 98, 209].

Despite this statement about interpretation, a reading of Kohut's (1977) second monograph leaves one with the impression that the treatment he proposes differs from traditional psychoanalysis in significant ways. There is an overemphasis on the reparative function of the analyst and the role of empathy. In the usual understanding of analytic work, empathy is a prerequisite, and not a replacement, for interpretation. Moreover, there are limits to empathically derived knowledge (Wallerstein, 1983). I have elsewhere (Akhtar, 1984) summarized the potentially problematic consequences of overemphasis on empathy. These include (1) overvaluation of the person of the analyst, (2) erroneous data emanating from the subjectivity of the analyst and not the patient's material, (3) a shift in responsibility for therapeutic difficulties from patient's intrapsychic resistances to the countertransference of the analyst,

(4) a negation of the limits of empathically derived knowledge, and (5) in a totally empathic atmosphere, the splitting off of aggression and its discharge outside the treatment hours.

There are other differences in Kohut's technique and traditional psychoanalysis. Drive-related fantasies are regarded as regressive products of a fragmenting self. The unity of self-knowledge and cure is denied. Dreams are often interpreted on a manifest level with little need for associative material. Negative transference is viewed as a result of countertransference blocks. Reconstructions often are linear, with an implied absolute parallelism between the transference recapitulations and childhood experience, taking no account of unconscious memory distortion in this regard.

Kernberg (1976), on the other hand, emphasizes that narcissistic transferences are multilayered structures, which include in them early wishes, defenses, real experiences, and unconscious distortions of them. He states that the

> patient's disappointments in the analyst reveal not only fantasied—or real—frustrations in the transference: they *also* reveal dramatically the total devaluation of the transference object for the slightest reason and, thus, the intense overwhelming nature of the aggression against the object. . . . "Disappointment reactions" in these cases reflect conflicts about aggression *as well as* libidinal strivings. . . . The narcissistic transference, in other words, first activates past defenses against deeper relationships with the parents, and only then the real past relationships with them [p. 263, italics added].

Kernberg's view is in greater accordance with the "principle of multiple function" (Waelder, 1930), and, in its regard for the complex, multifactorial nature of transference manifestations, is more consonant with the usual analytic approach. He agrees with Kohut that most narcissistic patients should be treated by psychoanalysis and that it is important to permit a full development of their transferences. However, he does not regard their rage reactions as reactive to analyst's empathic failure. Indeed, he proposes a full exploration, interpretation and working-through of negative transference to be the only way to diminish patient's envy and resolve his pathological grandiose self. Kernberg (1976) also suggests that the positive (libidinal) aspects of the patient's experience should also be addressed since

> focusing on such remnants as exist of a capacity for love and object investment, and for realistic appreciation of the analyst's

> efforts, prevents an almost exclusive focus on the latent negative transference, which can be misinterpreted by the patient as the psychoanalyst's conviction is that the patient is "all bad" [p. 263].

Kernberg also regards the analysis of oedipal issues as an important second step in the treatment, which by the time these issues occupy the center stage should proceed in a fashion increasingly closer to the standard classical analysis of a neurotic patient. Finally, Kernberg does not suggest a different technique of dream interpretation and regards empathy as only a tool, not a replacement for interpretation and working-through.

SUMMARY AND CONCLUSIONS

This comparison of Kohut and Kernberg reveals important similarities and yet profound differences between them. Among their similarities are their influential positions in the field of psychoanalysis, their rejuvenating stimulus to psychoanalytic theorizing, their enrichment of our understanding of patients who belong in the "widening scope" (Stone, 1954) of psychoanalysis, the interest they have stimulated in the study of British object relations theorists, the psychoanalytic studies of sociopolitical process they have spurred, and their enhancement of our technical skills, especially in the psychoanalytic treatment of narcissistic characters. Their differences are no less numerous or impressive. Kohut rejects the medical model of diagnosis and regards general psychiatry as a potential threat to psychoanalysis; Kernberg maintains a close affiliation with the language, preoccupations, and organized forums of general psychiatry. Kohut ignores others' contributions even though his own contributions are only "original in emphasis, not in substance" (Rothstein, 1980, p. 426); Kernberg profusely cites others, including Kohut, and openly acknowledges his conceptual debt to his predecessors. Kohut began his theorizing within the confines of classical psychoanalysis and then went through a transitional phase where he began to question the traditional approach. In his final theorizing, Kohut disputed even such core psychoanalytic concepts as conflict, drives, the Oedipus complex, and interpretation and insight as the fundamental curative factors in psychoanalysis: Kernberg, in contrast, has progressively moved toward mainstream psychoanalytic theory while constructing conceptual bridges between contemporary ego psychology and British object relations theory. Kernberg's contributions are additive; Kohut's, potentially divisive.

Kohut and Kernberg clearly differ in their conceptualization of narcissistic personality disorder. Kohut eschews descriptive diagnosis and considers spontaneously unfolding transferences to be the only reliable tool in diagnosis: Kernberg provides detailed behavioral descriptions of such patients and regards descriptive diagnosis as complementary to the psychodynamic formulation. Kohut sees the etiology of the disorder in parental empathic failure, leading to a developmental arrest upon archaic forms of grandiosity and self esteem regulation. Kernberg regards such pathological grandiosity to have developed as a defense against paranoid anxieties consequent to splitting and projection of aggressive self- and object representations with secondary distortions of the Oedipus complex. Kohut emphasizes the reparative function of the analyst in the psychoanalytic treatment of narcissistic personality; Kernberg steadfastly underscores the interpretative function of the analyst. Kohut emphasizes empathy as a therapeutic tool; Kernberg regards it as a technical necessity for interpretation. Kohut makes reductionistic, linear reconstructions of childhood traumata from patient's conscious recall; Kernberg posits that narcissistic transferences at first activate past defenses against deeper relationships with parents and only then the real past relationships. Kohut appears to decode dreams from manifest content and does not provide adequate associative material to substantiate his conclusions; Kernberg proposes no deviation from traditional technique in the handling of dreams. When rage appears in treatment, Kohut views it as reactivate to empathic failures of the analyst that reactivate similarly traumatizing experiences from past; Kernberg views pregenital aggression as the basic, inciting agent against which the grandiose self is built as a defense. His suggested technique insists upon a thorough interpretation of negative transference developments in their defensive as well as recapituation aspects.

Though not addressed here, other differences exist between the views of Kohut and Kernberg. Most important among them is the implications of their theories for their respective views of fundamental human nature. For Kohut, man is born whole, full of potential, even happy and eager to joyfully actualize the blueprint of his destiny. If he is unhappy, it is because of environmental failure. All his conflicts are the end result of unfortunate, tragic disorganization caused by lack of parental empathy. For Kernberg, conflict is embedded in normal development. Lifelong struggle with intrapsychic and reality conflicts is unavoidable. There is no escape from aggression, both from within and from outside. Life, comprising the constant reactivations of the infantile conflicts as well as renewed challenges posed by reality, is, however, still interesting and possesses the potential for that greatest of human experiences, love. However, even love can never be totally free of early transferences. Need the reader be reminded that Kernberg's view of human nature is closer to what the founder of psychoanalysis envisioned?

REFERENCES

Akhtar, S. (1984), Self Psychology vs. mainstream psychoanalysis. *Contemp. Psychiat.*, 3:113–117.

—— (1988a), Hypomanic personality disorder. *Integr. Psychiat.*, 6:37–52.

—— (1988b), Some reflections on the theory of psychopathology, and personality development in Kohut's self psychology. In: *New Concepts in Psychoanalytic Psychotherapy*, ed. J.M. Ross & W. Myers. Washington, DC: American Psychiatric Press, pp. 226–252.

—— & Thomson, J.A. (1982), Overview: Narcissistic personality disorder. *Amer. J. Psychiat.*, 139:12–20.

Altshuler, K.Z. (1979), Panel report: The interrelationship between academic psychiatry and psychoanalysis. *J. Amer. Psychoanal. Assn.*, 27:157–168.

American Psychiatric Association (1980), *Diagnostic and statistical manual of mental disorders* (DSM-III). Washington, DC: American Psychiatric Press.

Atkin, S. (1975), Ego synthesis and cognition in a borderline case. *Psychoanal. Quart.*, 46:29–61.

Bacal, H.A. (1987), British object-relations theorists and self-psychology: Some critical reflections. *Internat. J. Psycho-Anal.*, 68:87–98.

Bach, S. (1977), On the narcissistic state of consciousness. *Internat. J. Psycho-Anal.*, 58:209–233.

—— (1985), *Narcissistic States and the Therapeutic Process.* New York: Aronson.

Baker, H.S. & Baker, M.N. (1987), Heinz Kohut's self psychology: An overview. *Amer. J. Psychiat.*, 144:1–9.

Balint, M. (1937), Early developmental stages of the ego: Primary object-love. In: *Primary Love and Psychoanalytic Technique.* London: Hogarth Press, 1952, pp. 90–108.

Bergman, P. & Escalona, S.K. (1949), Unusual sensitivities in very young children. *The Psychoanalytic Study of the Child,* 4:333–352. New York: International Universities Press.

Blashfield, R.K. & McElroy, R.A. (1987), The 1985 journal literature on personality disorders. *Comp. Psychiat.*, 28:536–546.

Brenner, C. (1976a), *Psychother. Soc. Sci. Rev.*, 10:13

_____ (1976b), *Psychoanalytic Technique and Psychic Conflict,* New York: International Universities Press.

_____ (1982), *The Mind in Conflict.* New York: International Universities Press.

Calef, V. & Weinshel, E. (1979), The new psychoanalysis and psychoanalytic revisionism. *Psychoanal. Quart.*, 48:470–491.

Cooper, A.M. (1983), The place of self psychology in the history of depth psychology. In: *The Future of Psychoanalysis,* ed. A. Goldberg. New York: International Universities Press, pp. 3–17.

_____ (1988), Review of *How Does Analysis Cure?* by H. Kohut. *J. Amer. Psychoanal. Assn.*, 36:175–179.

Deutsch, H. (1942), Some forms of emotional disturbances and their relationship to schizophrenia. *Psychoanal. Quart.*, 11:301–321.

Dorpat, T. (1976), Structural conflict and object relations conflict. *J. Amer. Psychoanal. Assn.*, 25:855–874.

Emde, R., Graensbauer, T. & Harmon, R. (1976), *Emotional Expression in Infancy.* New York: International Universities Press.

Fairbairn, W.R.D. (1944), Endopsychic structure considered in terms of object-relationships. In: *Psychoanalytic Studies of the Personality.* London: Routledge & Kegan Paul, 1952, pp. 82–137.

_____ (1952), *Psychoanalytic Studies of the Personality.* London: Routledge & Kegan Paul.

Freedman, A.M., Kaplan, H.I. & Sadock, B.J. (1975), *Comprehensive Textbook of Psychiatry/II.* Baltimore, MD: Williams & Wilkins.

Freud, A. (1965), Normality and pathology in childhood. In: *The Writings of Anna Freud,* Vol. 6. New York: International Universities Press.

_____ (1966), Some thoughts about the place of psychoanalytic theory in the training of psychiatrists. In: *The Writings of Anna Freud,* Vol. 7. New York: International Universities Press, 1971.

Freud, S. (1919), On the teaching of psychoanalysis in universities. *Standard Edition,* 17:169–173. London: Hogarth Press, 1955.

_____ (1923), The ego and the id. *Standard Edition,* 19:1–66. London: Hogarth Press, 1961.

_____ (1925), Some psychical consequences of the anatomical distinction between the sexes. *Standard Edition,* 19:241–258. London: Hogarth Press, 1961.

_____ (1940), An outline of psychoanalysis. *Standard Edition,* 23:139–207. London: Hogarth Press, 1961.

Gedo, J. & Goldberg, A. (1973), *Models of the Mind.* Chicago: University of Chicago Press.

Gitelson, M. (1962). The place of psychoanalysis in psychiatric training. *Bull. Menn. Clin.*, 26:57–72.

Greenberg, J.R. & Mitchell, S.A. (1983), *Object Relations in Psychoanalytic Theory.* Cambridge, MA: Harvard University Press.

Geenspan, S.I. (1977), The oedipal-preoedipal dilemma: A reformulation in the light of object relations theory. *Internat. Rev. Psycho-Anal.*, 4:381–391.

Grinspoon, L., ed. (1982), *American Psychiatric Associations 1982 Annual Review.* Washington, DC: American Psychiatric Press.

[GAP] Group for the Advancement of Psychiatry (1978), *Self Involvement in the Middle East Conflict,* GAP report 103. New York: GAP.

Grunberger, B. (1975), *Narcissism.* New York: International Universities Press.

Guntrip, H. (1969), *Schizoid Phenomena, Object Relations and The Self.* New York: International Universities Press.

Hartmann, H. (1939), *Ego Psychology and The Problem of Adaptation,* trans. D. Rapaport. New York: International Universities Press, 1958.

—— (1952), The mutual influences in the development of ego and id. *The Psychoanalytic Study of the Child,* 7:9–30. New York: International Universities Press.

Holzman, P. (1976), The future of psychoanalysis and its institutes. *Psychoanal. Quart.*, 45:250–273.

Jacobson, E. (1964), *The Self and the Object World.* New York: International Universities Press.

Jones, E. 91953), *The Life and Work of Sigmund Freud* Vol. I. New York: Basic Books.

Kernberg, O.F. (1967), Borderline personality organization. *J. Amer. Psychoanal. Assn.*, 15:641–685.

—— (1970), A psychoanalytic classification of character pathology. *J. Amer. Psychoanal. Assn.*, 18:800–822.

—— (1974), Further contributions to the treatment of the narcissistic personality. *Internat. J. Psycho-Anal.*, 55:215–240.

—— (1975a), *Borderline Conditions and Pathological Narcissism.* New York: Aronson.

—— (1975b), Melanie Klein. In: *Comprehensive Textbook of Psychiatry/II.* Vol. 1, ed. A. Freedman, H. I. Kaplan & B.J. Sadock Baltimore, MD: William & Wilkins. pp. 637–650.

—— (1976), *Object-Relations Theory and Clinical Psychoanalysis.* New York: Aronson.

—— (1977a), Normal psychology of the aging process revisited-II. *J. Ger. Psychiat.*, 10:27–45.

—— (1977b), Clinical observation regarding the diagnosis, prognosis and intensive treatment of chronic schizophrenics. In: *Traitements An Long Courses Des Etats Psychotiques,* ed. C. Chiland & P. Bequart. New York: Human Science Press, pp. 332–360.

_____ (1978a), Leadership and organizational functioning: Organizational regression. *Internat. J. Group Psychother.*, 28:3–25.

_____ (1978b), The diagnosis of borderline conditions in adolescence. *Adol. Psychiat.*, 16:298–319.

_____ (1979), The contributions of Edith Jacobson: An overview. *J. Amer. Psychoanal. Assn.*, 27:793–819.

_____ (1980), *Internal World and External Reality.* New York: Aronson.

_____ (1981), Structural interviewing. *Psychiatr. Clin. N. Amer.*, 4 (1):169–195.

_____ (1982), Supportive psychotherapy with borderline conditions. In: *Critical Problems in Psychiatry,* ed. J.O. Cavenar & H.K.H. Brodie. Philadelphia, PA: Lippincott, pp. 180–202.

_____ (1984), *Severe Personality Disorders.* New Haven, CT: Yale University Press.

_____ (1985), Hysterical and histrionic personality disorders. In: *Psychiatry,* Vol. 1, ed. J.O. Cavenar & R. Michels. Philadelphia, PA: Lippincott, pp. 1–11.

_____ (1988), Book review of *Borderline Psychopathology and Its Treatment* by G. Adler, *Amer. J. Psychiat.*, 145:264–265.

_____ Goldstein, E., Carr, A. Arthur, D., Hunt, H., Bauer, S. & Blumenthal, R. (1981), Diagnosing borderline personality organization. *J. Nerv. Ment. Dis.*, 169:225-231.

Klein, M. & Tribich, D. (1981), Kernberg's object-relations theory: A critical evaluation. *Internat. J. Psycho-Anal.*, 62:27–43.

Koenigsberg, H.W., Kernberg, O.F. & Schomer, J. (1983), Diagnosing borderline conditions in an outpatient setting. *Arch. Gen. Psychiat.*, 40:49–53.

Kohut, H. (1957), Observation on the psychological functions of music. *J. Amer. Psychoanal. Assn.*, 5:389–407.

_____ (1964), Some problems of a metapsychological formulation of fantasy. *Internat. J. Psycho-Anal.*, 45:199–202.

_____ (1971), *The Analysis of the Self.* New York: International Universities Press.

_____ (1972), Thoughts on narcissism and narcissistic rage. *The Psychoanalytic Study of the Child,* 27:360–400. New Haven, CT: Yale University Press.

_____ (1976), Creativeness, charisma, group psychology: Reflections on the self analysis of Freud. *Psychological Issues,* Monogr. 9. New York: International Universities Press.

_____ (1977), *The Restoration of the Self.* New York: International Universities Press.

_____ (1982), Introspection, empathy and the semi-circle of mental health. *Internat. J. Psycho-Anal.*, 63:395–407.

_____ (1984), *How Does Analysis Cure?,* ed. A. Goldberg & with P. E. Stepansky. Chicago: University of Chicago Press.

_____ & Levarie, S. (1950), On the enjoyment of listening to music. *Psychoanal. Quart.*, 19:64–87.

_____ & Wolf, E. (1978), The disorders of the self and their treatment: An outline. *Internat. J. Psycho-Anal.*, 59:413–425.

Kris, E. (1947), The nature of psychoanalytic propositions and their validation. In: *Selected Papers of Ernst Kris.* New Haven, CT: Yale University Press, 1975.

Lustman, S.L. (1956), Rudiments of the ego. *The Psychoanalytic Study of the Child,* 11:89–98. New York: International Universities Press.

Mahler, M.S. (1968), *On Human Symbiosis and the Vicissitudes of Individuation.* New York: International Universities Press.

_____ (1972), A study of the separation-individuation process and its possible application to borderline phenomena in the psychoanalytic situation. *The Psychoanalytic Study of the Child,* 26:403–424. New Haven, CT: International Universities Press.

_____ Pine. F. & Bergman, A. (1975), *The Psychological Birth of the Human Infant.* New York: Basic Books.

Meissner, W.W. (1976), The relationship of psychoanalysis to current changes in medical and psychiatric education—historical perspective. *J. Amer. Psychoanal. Assn.*, 24:329–346.

Nemiah, J.C. (1961), *Foundations of Psychopathology.* New York: Oxford University Press.

Pine, F. (1985), *Developmental Theory and Clinical Process.* New Haven, CT: Yale University Press.

Potter, H. & Klein, H. (1951), Toward unification of training in psychiatry and Psychoanalysis. *Amer. J. Psychiat.*, 108:193–197.

Reich, W. (1933), *Character Analysis,* trans. T. P. Wolfe. New York: Orgone Institute Press, 1945.

Robbins, M. (1980), Current controversy in object relations theory as outgrowth of a schism between Klein and Fairbairn. *Internat. J. Psycho-Anal,* 61:477–492.

Rothstein, A. (1979), Oedipal conflicts in narcissistic personality disorders. *Internat. J. Psycho-Anal.*, 60:189–199.

_____ (1980), Toward a critique of the paychology of the self. *Psychoanal. Quart.*, 49:423–455.

Segal, N.P. (1981), Book review of *Borderline Conditions and Pathological Narcissism* and *Object Relations Theory and Clinical Psychoanalysis, J. Amer. Psychoanal. Assn,* 29:221–236.

Selzer, M.A., Koenigsberg, H.W. & Kernberg, O.F., (1987), Initial contract in treatment of borderline patients. *Amer. J. Psychiat.*, 144:927–930.

Spitz, R.A. (1965), *The First Year of Life.* New York: International Universities Press.

Stein, M.R. (1979), Book review of *The Restoration of the Self. J. Amer. Psychoanal. Assn.*, 27:665–680.

Stern, D.N. (1976), A microanalysis of mother-infant interaction: Behavior regulating social contact between a mother and her 3 1/2 month old twins. In: *Infant Psychiatry,* ed. E. Rexford, L. Sanders & T. Shapiro. New Haven, CT: Yale University Press.

Stone, L. (1954), The widening scope of indications for psychoanalysis. *J. Amer. Psychoanal. Assn.,* 2:567–594.

Strassman, H., Mann, J., Madow, L. & Wood, E. (1976), The impact of psychiatric residency training on choice of analytic training. *J. Amer. Psychoanal. Assn.,* 24:347–356.

Strauss, G.D., Yager, J. & Strauss, G.E. (1984), The cutting edge in psychiatry. *Amer. J. Psychiat.,* 114:38–43.

Svrakic, D.M. (1985), Emotional features of narcissistic personality disorder. *Amer. J. Psychiat.,* 142:720–724.

Thomas, A., Chess, S. & Birch, H.G. (1968), *Temperament and Behavior Disorders in Children.* New York: International Universities Press.

_____ _____ & _____ et al. (1963), *Behavioral Individuality in Early Childhood.* New York: International Universities Press.

Tolpin, M. (1980), Discussion of "psychoanalytic developmental theories of the self: an integration" by M. Shane and E. Shane. In: *Advances in Self Psychology,* ed. A. Goldberg. New York: International Universities Press, pp. 47–68.

Volkan, V.D. (1980), Narcissistic personality organization and "reparative" leadership. *Internat. J. Group Psychother.,* 30:131–152.

_____ (1986), The narcissism of minor differences in the psychological gap between opposing nation. *Psychoanal. Inq.,* 6:175–191.

Waelder, R. (1930), The principle of multiple function: Observations on multiple determination. *Psychoanal Quart.,* 5:45–62.

Wallerstein, R.S. (1983), Self psychology and "classical" psychoanalytic psychology: the nature of their relationship. In: *The Future of Psychoanalysis,* ed. A. Goldberg. New York: International Universities Press, pp. 19–63.

_____ (1986), Book review of *Severe Personality Disorders: Psychotherapeutic Strategies. J. Amer. Psychoanal. Assn.,* 34:711–722.

Winnicott, D.W. (1953), Transitional objects and transitional phenomena. *Internat. J. Psycho-Anal.,* 34:89–97.

_____ (1960), Ego distortion in terms of true and false self. In: *The Maturational Process and the Facilitating Environment.* New York: International Universities Press, 1965, pp. 140–152.

_____ (1965), *The Maturational Process and the Facilitating Environment.* New York: International Universities Press.

_____ (1967), The mirror-role of the mother and family in child development. In: *Playing and Reality.* Middlesex, Eng.: Penguin Books, 1971, pp. 130–138.

Zonis, M. (1980), Some possible contributions of the psychology of the self to the study of Arab Middle East. In: *Advances in Self Psychology,* ed. A. Goldberg. New York: International Universities Press, pp. 349–446.

18

Lacan and Kohut
From Imaginary to Symbolic Identification in the Case of Mr. Z

JOHN P. MULLER

In comparing Kohut's work with the theory and practice of his contemporaries, one is eventually going to bump against the work of the French psychoanalyst Jacques Lacan. Not only do their lives overlap, both dying in the same year, but their work, too, shows remarkable correspondences, at least at first glance. Both were practicing analysts who drew upon their own experience to offer a reformist critique of mainstream psychoanalysis, especially of ego psychology. Both criticized making the ego the criterion for truth and reality, Kohut by focusing on a comprehensive notion of "self," and Lacan by elaborating a less accessible structure of "subject of the unconscious." Both men emphasized disintegration anxiety and put mirroring phenomena in the forefront of processes of identification that shape subjective experience. Both challenged the accepted notion of the patient's "resistance" and instead stressed the clinical importance of recognition. Both criticized the kind of training provided by psychoanalytic institutes and were equally critical of the "therapeutic maturity- or reality-morality" reinforced by such training (Kohut and Wolf, 1978, p. 423).[1] In their overall

[1]The reader is referred to the following texts to pursue similarities between Kohut and Lacan: in their criticism of ego psychology: Kohut (1984, p. 59, 65, 148); Lacan (1977, pp. 1–29, 128–129, 132, 306); in their critique of naive notions of "reality": Kohut (1984, p. 36, 173); Lacan (1977, p. 135, 230); on disintegration

characterization of contemporary existence, both Kohut and Lacan used the figure of "tragic man" (Kohut, 1984, pp. 45, 207–208; Lacan, 1953, p. 16; 1959–1960, p. 361). Finally, although both openly operated from a reformist position, each stressed his proper orthodoxy. While Kohut (1984) offers "a new definition of the essence of the self and a new conceptualization of its structural development" (p. 8), he maintains that his viewpoint "is placed squarely in the center of the analytic tradition, that it is in the mainstream of the development of psychoanalytic thought" (p. 95). Lacan (1977), critical of the neo-Freudians, reiterates that his effort consists of a "return to Freud" and to the foundations of psychoanalysis (p. 117). Lacan never abandoned this claim, even though he was considered a renegade by most analysts after he was excluded in 1953 from the International Psychoanalytic Association (Turkle, 1978).

The Freudian unconscious, according to Lacan (1977) is "structured in the most radical way like a language" (p. 234): the unconscious, as other to consciousness, as intruding on rational discourse, is an articulation governed not by biological instincts but by general linguistic patterns. Freud (1900a) described how the dream work follows the two governing principles of condensation and displacement; Lacan (1977, pp. 160, 258), applying the structural linguistics of Saussure (1916) and Jakobson (1956), reinterprets Freud's data in terms of metaphoric substitution and metonymic combination (see also Muller and Richardson, 1982). But the unconscious articulation, preserved in repression and insistently repeated in symptoms and parapraxes, is inscribed in a manner foreign to the conscious ego. The unconscious, therefore, is the "discourse of the Other" (Lacan, 1977, p. 172), and human desire is "the desire of the Other" (pp. 264, 312).

THE OTHER

The Other, with a capital O, is not any individual person (although the Other is often projected onto individuals), nor is it a kind of universal, like Mead's (1925) "The generalized other" (p. 193). For

---

anxiety: Kohut (1984, p. 16); Lacan (1977, p. 11, 137); on resistance: Kohut (1984, p. 144, 148); Lacan (1977, p. 78, 101, 143, 169, 235); on training and reform: Kohut (1984, p. 40, 164); Lacan (1977, p. 35–37, 76, 144); on "reality-morality": Kohut (1984, p. 208); Lacan (1959–60, p. 349; 1966, p. 677).

Lacan (1956), the Other is a field, "the very foundation of intersubjectivity" (p. 35), anchoring the place in which structure and meaning become possible. Lacan illustrates this with a joke of Freud's: " 'Why are you lying to me?' one character shouts breathlessly. 'Yes, why do you lie to me saying you're going to Cracow so I should believe you're going to Lemberg, when in reality you *are* going to Cracow?' " (p. 36; Freud, 1905, p. 115). To make sense of this joke, the listener must go beyond the words themselves, beyond their literal signification, and also beyond the speakers themselves into another dimension or position beyond words and speakers, into the field that structures words and speakers in meaningful ways. In understanding this joke, we affirm the status of the Other, not an other person in an I-Thou relation, but the Other as structural third, giving perspective on any I-Thou relation, the Other as a potential place to stand and judge the truth of any two-party contract. The very fact that it is possible to lie, Lacan reminds us, is an affirmation of this third position, for to tell a lie requires that the speaker take into account the perspective of truth, the perspective afforded by the Other. For this reason Lacan (1977) refers to the Other as "the guarantor of Good Faith" (p. 173) and "witness to the Truth" (p. 305).

This reference to "the Other" resonates with Freud's use of Fechner's phrase, *ein anderer Schauplatz,* (an other scene), in describing where dreams occur and as a general reference to the unconscious (Freud, 1900a p. 48; 1900b, pp. 50–51). As "the discourse of the Other," which transcends it, the unconscious articulates what is received from elsewhere and what is primarily received is "the desire of the Other." Desire, as we shall see, arises in an intersubjective context structured by the Other, by the field of language and the unconscious. Lacan (1977) writes that it is "as desire of the Other that man's desire finds form" (p. 311), that is, "it is *qua* Other that he desires" (p. 312). In the matrix of the mother-infant relation, one's desire finds its form, becomes unconsciously structured by, and as, the desire of another, and this identification of one's desire with that of another can never be completely dissolved, is the dynamism expressed in repetition, and persists as structured by signifiers.

Lacan illustrates the Freudian discovery by means of ex-centric circles, circles whose centers do not coincide and that cannot be subsumed and unified by a larger circle with a single center. He cautions that "if we ignore the self's radical ex-centricity to itself with which man is confronted, in other words, the truth discovered by

Freud, we shall falsify both the order and methods of psychoanalytic mediation" (p. 171). We cannot mediate this split as analysts by believing the patient can become a "whole person" or a "complete self." Lacan objects "to any reference to totality in the individual" (p. 80) because the in-dividuum is not conceivable given the split introduced by "the subject of the unconscious" (pp. 128, 299). Thus Lacan insists that the "radical heteronomy that Freud's discovery shows gaping within man can never again be covered over without whatever is used to hide it being profoundly dishonest" (p. 172).

FRAGMENTATION AND MIRRORING

How, then, does consciousness come to experience itself as a unity, as cohesive instead of as fragmented? Lacan (1977) claims the source for such experience of unity lies in the formation of the ego in what he calls the "mirror stage" of child development. Lacan's attention was drawn to mirroring phenomena by the French psychologist Henri Wallon (1934). Wallon's (1921, 1931; see also Voyat, 1984) early emphasis on the infant's visual precocity and sociality made it clear that there was no initial primary narcissism or autistic period of infancy (Lacan, 1938). The human infant is born into a linguistically structured social milieu in which its consciousness of "I" is shaped by what it takes itself to be as the object of the mother's desire. Beginning *in utero* as the object of the mother's fantasies (Ver Eecke, 1984, p. 76; see also Kohut and Wolf, 1978, p. 416), the visually precocious newborn moves toward psychological differentiation through the process of identification with the image of the whole human body as a Gestalt. Lacan (1953) claimed that between eight and eighteen months of age the infant becomes capable of recognizing its reflection in a mirror (for experimental data, see Muller, 1982) and that the decisive effect of such recognition and identification is the constellation of a formal structure that he calls the ego.

In the visual presentation of the human form (whether in an actual mirror or in the mirroring gaze of the mother),[2] the infant

[2]We can speculate about how the infant's own form is reflected in the pupils of the mother's eyes. Brown and Witkowski (1981) found that "slightly over one-third of the languages of the world equate pupil of the eye with a human or humanlike object" (p. 600), including "established figurative expressions translating literally as 'baby of eye,' 'girl of eye,' or 'doll of eye' " (p. 597).

catches sight of a coherence, unity, and mastery that is in contrast to its own motoric discoordination and helplessness occasioned by its necessarily premature birth.[3] The human form as a unified Gestalt captivates the infant's interest and becomes associated with what the infant perceives as pleasing to the mother. A social dialectic is inaugurated in which what is desirable becomes so precisely because it is desired by another and serves to reinforce one's status as desirable to another. In other words, processes of mirroring lead to the cementing of identifications, not just between the ego and its own image, but also between the ego and objects in the world. The ego takes onto itself from the mirror the attributes of coherence, substantiality and permanence and in turn projects these attributes of itself onto the objects of its world. The Lacanian ego is precisely what Freud (1923) describes it as being, namely, "first and foremost a bodily ego" and "the projection of a surface" (p. 26). That is, the ego arises with the image of the body to form a projected plane, the foundational grid of consciousness. This grid establishes consciousness of self as a staging arena in which an "I" coordinates the narrative sequence of experience, a stage on which this "I" creates representations that distort experience but enhance one's sense of mastery and effectiveness by exaggerating one's importance and, as repeatedly verified by the experimental work of social psychologists, by minimizing the positive contributions of others (see Muller, 1986).

Lacan (1961–1962) emphasizes certain consequences of this process of mirror identification. Since left and right are reversed, the reflection is distorted (p. 471). Since it takes place before the infant has an active role in making meaning through speech, the process is a compelling one: the infant is captured by its image, which lures its narcissistic investment. But because this image comes to it from another and is perceived as being "out there" as an other, some confusion persists about identities. Lacan (1977) writes that up to about two and a half years of age, children exhibit what he calls, following Charlotte Bühler and "the Chicago School," transitivistic behavior (1977, p. 17). In this confused period, the infant, identifying with the image of the body of another, will cry at the sight of another child falling or being struck as if he or she were suffering the injury.

[3]Gould (1976) argues that the human infant must be born about nine months prematurely so that the infant's cranium, only a quarter of its eventual size, can pass through the maternal pelvic cavity.

In this stage of ego development the child is learning to manage competitive aggression and to maintain self-esteem. The ego for Lacan plays a dynamic role in structuring a sense of imaginary identity with unity and coherence precisely because without its defensive armoring the child would experience bodily fragmentation, an experience of *corps morcelé,* the body in bits and pieces. To avoid this loss of coherence, the ego will strive to buttress its masterful position against threats from within as well as from others. In identifying with parental and other adult desires, the ego uses denial, repression, and projection to evade one's own desire. Contrary to Coen's (1981) claim (critical of Kohut) that maintaining cohesion "is not a predominant motivation for behavior" (p. 404), when experiencing an attack on its cohesion or preeminence, the ego mobilizes fantasies of the other's fragmented body in its counterattack. For Kohut (1984), aggression is "always motivated by an injury to the self" (p. 116). Likewise for Lacan (1938) aggression is "secondary to identification" (p. 39) and is a structural correlate of the ego; he (Lacan, 1977) defines it as "the correlative tendency of a mode of identification that we call narcissistic" (p. 16). The narcissistic investment in one's cohesive image, when threatened by the other, is turned into an effort to fragment the other. Aggressiveness, therefore, cannot be controlled by strengthening the ego, by reinforcing the ideal ego, but rather by shifting focus to "the pacifying function of the ego ideal" (p. 22), through "the oedipal identification," which is "that by which the subject transcends the aggressivity that is constitutive of the primary subjective individuation" (p. 23).

IDENTIFICATION AND THE EGO IDEAL

Before we go further with Lacan's thinking about "oedipal identification," we have to acknowledge that the notion of identification as such poses enormous difficulties. As Widlocher (1985) notes, "In psychoanalysis, the concept of identification is a blurred one, and will probably remain so for a long time to come" (p. 31). This confusion is especially prominent with regard to the concept of "primary identification," which "turns out to be anything but clear" (Etchegoyen, 1985, p. 5). In this instance, the psychoanalytic confusion appears to rest on the complexity of the history of the word itself. In the *Compact Edition of the Oxford English Dictionary* (1971) we read that identification is "the action of identifying or fact of being identified" (p. 1368). Two definitions follow: 1) the making, regarding, or treating of a thing as identical with . . . another, or of two or more things as identical with one another . . .; 2) the determination of identity; the action or process of determining what a thing is; the recognition of a thing as being what it is.

Identification thus means both being in a relation of identity with or *likeness* to another and being determined or recognized as being *separate,* as being what one is. The word "identity," which has as an obsolete form the word "idemptitie," derives from the late Latin word *identitas,* which is "peculiarly formed from ident(i)-, for [the Latin] *idem* 'same' + *-tas, -tatem.*" Its meaning is given as the "quality or condition of being the same . . . essential sameness; oneness . . . the condition or fact that a person or thing is itself and not something else." We are given an explanatory note regarding the origin of the word "identity" from the Latin *idem:* "Various suggestions have been offered as to the formation. Need was evidently felt of a noun of condition or quality from *idem* to express the notion of 'sameness,' side by side with those of 'likeness' and 'oneness' expressed by *similitas* and *unitas:* hence the form of the suffix." All of the psychological confusion of oneness, sameness, and likeness is packed into the history of the word itself, and Lacan therefore begins here in his attempt to make sense of the concept of identification.

He starts with the Latin root *idem* and then considers its Indo-European root *em,* found, for example, in the French word for "same," *même.* He then considers identification from the angle of recognizing someone, of determining that he is the "same," the very person one has taken him to be. He postulates that such "identity" of the subject rests on a signifier, a name, not on an appearance or on a consciousness of continuity. The "primary identification" is achieved through naming, through the use of a signifier. This form of identification is *symbolic* identification, it is the process whereby one is identified by a symbol and in fact is designated as "one" only through the use of a signifier (we shall take this up shortly). Such symbolic identification is also operative when one's identity is unconsciously constellated by other signifiers, bestowed by parents in specifically designated ways. We are all subjected to these words in childhood, and they structure a kind of unconscious symbolic map of desire that Lacan terms the ego ideal. It is the ego ideal that enables one to channel desire, and Lacan contrasts it to the ideal ego, which, in striving for competitive mastery, resists the assumption of one's desire. The ideal ego is the product of an *imaginary* identification, an identification *with* the image held by consciousness as a reflection of the mirror or the mirroring gaze of another.

In imaginary identification, a dual relation is established based on a likeness in which one or both poles are idealized, inflating the ego. Such imaginary identification cannot be primary since it occurs only with the onset of the mirror stage and ordinarily follows upon the decisive consequences of naming and kinship specification.

In Lacan's (1977) view, the oedipalization of the subject does not stimulate conflict but, rather, generates structure. If the mother's role in the genesis of the subject is to engage desire, then the father's role is to structure desire and symbolically individuate it through the action of what Lacan calls the "paternal metaphor" (p. 199). In metaphor, one signifier is substituted for another, which remains operative but in a repressed state. In the "paternal metaphor," the father's name is the signifier of the symbolic order, a consequence of which is the incest prohibition, the end of duality, and the introduction of a third. This structure of symbolization as such substitutes for a fusion of desires associated with what Lacan calls the "phallus." The phallus, the image of what is imagined to be lacking in the mother, is what the infant becomes for the mother in an imaginary identification. With the structure of the paternal metaphor, the infant "gives up" being the phallus, the latter then becoming repressed as a generalized signifier of the desire of the other. In repression it continues to function but now precisely as a signifier in unconscious associative networks of signifiers that follow the laws of displacement and condensation. As a consequence, the child becomes a subject, not simply of language, but of desire, and no longer just an object of the mother's or father's desire, as identified in an imaginary manner with their desire. The child can symbolize and experience the parent's absence now as a desiring subject. But the very possibility of imaginary identification, of experiencing oneself as complete and as the completing object of another's desire, rests on the more fundamental identification of oneself as *one*. To be identified with a name as *this one* is to be placed in a symbolic network that sets one apart precisely as not being someone else. Kinship relations, sex roles, social status, prescribed obligations and opportunities all rest on what Lacan (1954–1955), following Lévi-Strauss, calls "the symbolic order" (pp. 29, 326).

THE SYMBOLIC ORDER AND THE SIGNIFIER

The meaning of "the symbolic order" emerges most clearly when understood in relation to what Lacan offers (and many claim this is his chief theoretical contribution) as the three "registers," or dimensions, of experience: the imaginary, the real, and the symbolic. Up to this point, we have focused primarily on the imaginary register, or that aspect of experience structured by dual resemblance, point-to-point correspondences, mirroring reflections. The focus here is on the lure of likeness, on being liked or liking because of a likeness, on narcissistic preening, ostentatious display, competition and comparison. The imaginary register includes what is proper to the image, the sensuous play of light and sound that draws our interest and that constitutes much of what we call "reality," to be distinguished from what Lacan calls the "real."

The register of the real is what we from time to time encounter in horror as that which has no name. It appears in the breakdown of technology as the intrusion of loss of meaning, sudden catastrophe, death, such as in the moment when the space shuttle Challenger exploded before the gaze of millions or when hundreds of thousands were touched by the poison gas in Bhopal. The real is what remains when images and symbols carve out objects in experience, a margin of not just what is "undecidable" but what is impossible to symbolize or imagine. We are brought to this edge or margin in the work of the German painter Anselm Kiefer as he uses processes of negation to articulate the unspeakable horrors of Nazism. Ordinarily, the images and words provided by our culture shield us from contact with the real, but in psychotic states patients are often at the edge of the real; and the experience of being driven slightly crazy by psychotic patients is a response to their attempt to bring the treatment to that edge so that they can draw some kind of boundary there, to place some marker at that frontier (Muller, 1987).

The marker that sets off the real, that "introduces difference as such in the real" (Lacan, 1961–1962, p. 78) is the signifier, a semiotic term Lacan takes from Ferdinand de Saussure, the Swiss founder of modern structural linguistics. Saussure (1916) made a basic distinction between speech and language, insisting that speech is an individual psychomotor act whereas language is a system of signs that makes speech possible. The linguistic sign is composed of the junction of a signifier and a signified, a signifier being a phonetic sound-image, a concept being the signified. Saussure stressed that signifier and signified are related solely by convention, that is arbitrarily, without intrinsic connection. He also emphasized that each, in itself, is without positive substance but consists, rather, solely in its difference from the other units in the linguistic system:

> Everything that has been said up to this point boils down to this: in language there are only differences. Even more important: a difference generally implies positive terms between which the difference is set up; but in language there are only differences *without positive terms.* Whether we take the signified or the signifier, language has neither ideas nor sounds that existed before the linguistic system, but only conceptual and phonic differences that have issued from the system. The idea or phonic substance that a sign contains is of less importance than the other signs that surround it [p. 120].
>
> Putting it another way, *language is a form and not a substance*. . . . This truth could not be overstressed, for all the mistakes in our terminology, all our incorrect ways of naming things that pertain to language, stem from the involuntary supposition that the linguistic phenomenon must have substance [p. 122].

It is this "distinctive feature" of the signifier, the fact that it is established within the system not as an identity but as a difference, that distinguishes the symbolic register from the imaginary register, on one hand, dominated as it is by mirroring identities, and, on the other hand, from the register of the real, where there is no differentiation. This notion of the substanceless signifier as identity-in-difference finds its prime expression in music: a single note has no "meaning" in itself, it derives its value solely from its difference from the other notes in the scale system. I once heard a Japanese psychoanalyst describe this even more succinctly when he said that the music rests on the silence between the notes.

THE SUBJECT OF THE UNCONSCIOUS

Americans (and others) encounter great difficulty with this notion of pure difference used to define the subject. As we have seen, Lacan sharply distinguishes ego from subject and locates Freud's *Kern unseres wesens,* what Kohut (1984) likewise calls "the core of our being" (p. 140), not in consciousness but at the level of the subject. But this means that we are dealing not only with what Lacan (1954–1955) calls "a subject without a head" (p. 167; see also Richardson, 1983) but a subject without positive substance. The subject of the unconscious, the subject of psychoanalysis, is not constituted by positive attributes. Rather, it receives its identity through a process of symbolic identification whereby it is designated as one. Such symbolic identification is achieved through signifying differentiation, concretized in the conferral of a proper name. Lacan (1961–1962) states that "to name is first of all something that has to do with a reading of the mark *one* designating the absolute difference" (p. 148). Such identification, such "one-ing," is not founded on qualitative differences or representable content. Self and object representations (as used, for example, in object relations theory) are secondary to this more fundamental identification based on the signifying difference, "the inaugural identification of the subject with the radical [or root] signifier" (p. 38). What seems to be at stake here is the affirming of a structural basis for uniqueness, and Lacan finds it in the signifier: "It is as pure difference that the unit, in its signifying function, is structured, is constituted" (p. 58). This unit marks the subject as *one,* and this mark, given in one's name, is the least determined by any qualitative characteristic. Being so symbolically marked as "one" is the necessary condition of possibility for the subject to differentiate from others, and specifically from the field of the desire of the mother.

Lacan links his view of symbolic identification to Freud's (1921a) second type of identification. Freud writes that with this type "identification has appeared instead of object-choice, and that object-choice has regressed to identification" (p. 106–107). In other words, identification occurs in the place of the lost object, and such identification is "the earliest and original form of emotional tie" (p. 107). It can occur in relation to one who is loved or one who is not loved, but "in both cases the identification is a partial and extremely limited one and only borrows a single trait [*einen einzigen Zug*] from the person who is its object" (Freud, 1921a, p. 107; 1921b, p. 117). Lacan zeroes in on Freud's phrase *einen einzigen Zug* as suggestive of a single trace, *une trait unaire* in French, basically just a line or a mark. He searches for the origin of this mark, following the linguistic research of Leroi-Gourhan (1964, pp. 262–264), in the cuts or notches made on bones over 35,000 years ago perhaps to indicate *one* in a series of ones, keeping count, for example, of animal kills or astrological phenomena (see also Harris, 1986). The use of this trace or mark, Lacan speculates, gave rise to the experience of segmented temporality, narrative sequentiality, and firm object boundaries. This trace or mark is a signifier and as such has its status in the Other, "the locus of the signifier" (Lacan, 1977, p. 310), the semiotic field; and because this mark gives the first, radical structure to the subject, it is "the foundation, the kernel of the ego ideal" (Lacan, 1964, p. 256). By being designated one, one is affirmed as not being something or someone else. Psychotic structure appears to lack this mark, and therefore we find boundary blurring and fusion with a cosmic Other in psychosis. Ultimately the designation or mark of "one" rests on an act of writing, Lacan says, but that would take us too far from our task, although it is of great interest to see Lacan grappling with the relation between speech and writing as later would Derrida (1967).

THE ANALYTIC FIELD

The effect of this mark of "one" is not to unify but rather to make unique. Unification remains an illusion of the ego. Because he insists that the subject-ego split can never be healed, Lacan (1977) rejects a two-person model of analysis, "the field that our experience polarizes in a relation that is only apparently two-way, for any positing of its structure in merely dual terms is as inadequate to it in theory as it is ruinous for its technique" (p. 56). Lacan instead offers a four-cornered structure (pp. 139, 193), as follows: Position 1, the Subject corner, locates the patient as barred or divided ($) within himself or herself, that is, as irremediably split by repression and therefore incapable of full knowledge regarding who he or she is, what he or she is actually saying, why there is this symptom. Position 2, the Ego corner, is the place of the subject's ego as reflecting the so-called objective world but especially reflecting other egos. Position 3 marks the place of other egos, and specifically of the analyst's ego, which the patient's ego attempts to lure and maintain in a mirroring reflection with itself. In Position 4, Lacan locates what he calls the "Other" and from where "the discourse of the Other" can be articulated. Here the analyst as subject resonates with those sonorous and gestural, as well as thematic, aspects of the

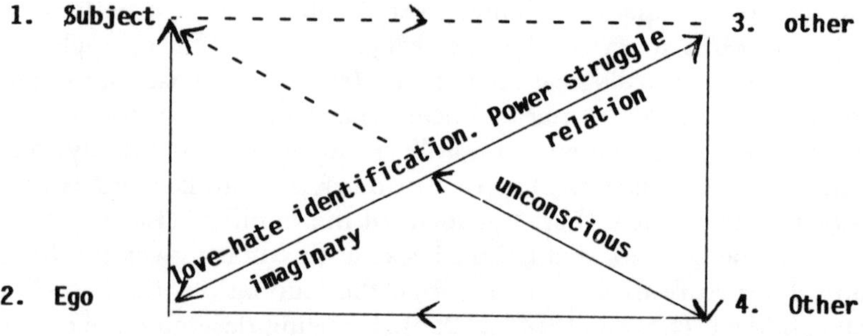

FIG. 1 Lacan's Schema L (modified)

patient's discourse that are not in awareness. The discourse of the Other is Lacan's way of calling attention to how language, as other than, wider than, not reducible to, the individual consciousness of any speaker, has already structured human experience and therefore has already channelled human desire. As we saw earlier, the discourse of the Other is that semiotic structuring of desire which Freud discovered in his analysis of dreams and symptoms as the unconscious. Lacan maintains that because the unconscious is structured like a language, the effects of the unconscious can be understood and interpreted. Position 4 therefore provides perspective on what is happening to the subject's desire in his or her symptoms as well as what is happening between the two individuals when they relate as egos, when the so-called real relationship between patient and analyst develops.

This "real relationship" Lacan calls an "imaginary relation," marked on both sides by narcissism and illusion, an effect of mirrors. On this axis linking the subject's ego and the analyst's ego we can observe all the emotional variations of what Lacan terms *haine-amouration,* an enamoration, that is, a love-hate relationship. Competition, coercion, power struggle, seduction, and imaginary identification are pursued on this axis of object relations. According to Lacan, the American emphasis on strengthening the ego, on encouraging the patient's ego to model itself on and identify with the analyst's ego, marks a fundamental betrayal of Freud and of the place of the Other, leading to loss of perspective regarding the subject of the unconscious, the subject as distinct from the ego. This American emphasis on getting the patient to identify with the analyst, with the analyst as a model for the patient, has a long tradition here and is still being maintained as a goal of treatment in mainstream American psychoanalytic writing (see Muller, 1985, for examples).

Kohut (1984) appears uneasy with the notion of identification, referring to "gross identification" when the issue is raised (pp. 101, 169; see also pp. 100, 160). It may be useful to introduce into Kohut's framework Lacan's distinction between symbolic identification *by* the Other and imaginary identification *with* an other with an imago of the Other or with an image held by the Other. Imaginary identification reinforces likeness and constrains the field of desire in a mirroring relation while symbolic identification structures difference and opens desire onto the field of substitution and displacement. The distinction is one that Kohut appears to make but only by separating "gross identification" from "transmuting internalization." Thus, for example, he describes a patient who "at the end of a long analysis during which there had been periods of gross identification with me, . . . said: 'Now I am similar to you only in one respect: I am an independent person just like you" (p. 169). The patient had gone from modeling himself as a reflection or image of the analyst in imaginary identification to assuming the status of one who is symbolically identified by the Other and so recognized by the analyst.

THE DESIRE OF THE OTHER

When recognition is effective it is because the other's desire has been recognized. The most dominant aspect of psychic structure is not the satisfaction or frustration of needs but the phenomenon of desire, and therefore desire is the dominant feature of transference-countertransference, as we shall see in Mr. Z's treatment.

How does desire arise? In distinguishing the three registers of real, imaginary, and symbolic, we can follow Lacan and argue for a parallel distinction among need, demand, and desire. Needs are physiological conditions, rooted in the organism's tissues and organs, and they are imperative: food, water, warmth, air, are essential for life, and there are no substitutes for them—we cannot live on their metaphors. These needs in infancy are met by a caretaking other (usually the mother), who nurtures in a cultural, familial, and intersubjective system of exchanges in which both the infant and mother learn to associate the infant's expressions of needs with organic and psychic states. Rhythm, touch, affect, and mutual responsivity quickly establish, in ways specific to the given culture, a semiotic framework of communication in which language is present from the beginning as structuring the mother's world. The child's cries soon become signifiers, with the result that the child's needs are channeled through "the defiles of the structure of the signifier" (Lacan, 1977, pp. 255, 309). One of Lacan's students expresses it this way:

> When the mother responds to the cries of the infant, she recognizes them in constituting them as a demand, but what is more momentous is that she interprets them on the level of desire: desire of the infant to have the mother next to her, desire that she bring her something, desire to aggress against her, or whatever. What is certain is that by its response the Other is going to give the dimension of desire to the cry of need

> and that this desire with which the infant is invested is always initially the result of a subjective interpretation, a function of just the mother's desire, of her own fantasm (Aulagnier, 1962, p. 401; my translation).

This development means it becomes impossible to directly express needs or directly respond to them. The state of need becomes partially articulated when addressed to an other and in this signifying form functions as a demand. The other can no longer respond only to the state as need but must respond to it as an articulated demand. In this responding, the other will of necessity indicate just how he or she is recognizing the one making the demand (as entitled, as appropriate, as delightful, as obnoxious). In turn, the child making the demand will obtain from the other's response proofs and disproofs of love and caring, evidence that the relationship affirms the child as desirable or undesirable.

With the constellation of the ego, as discussed earlier, the child seeks to maximize his or her position as the all-fulfilling object of the mother's desire. This will so intricate the child's desire with the mother's desire that we can then speak of an identification of the child's desire with the mother's desire. This identification necessarily takes place at the level of the unconscious, indeed as part of the process whereby the unconscious is structured: "It is through the bias of the unconscious of the Other that the subject makes its entrance into the world of desire, and he will have to initially constitute his own desire as a response, as an acceptance or refusal to take the place that the unconscious of the other designates for him" (Aulagnier, 1962, p. 401; my translation). Such a total identification may be supported by the mother's words and behavior and, if so, will absorb the child's desire, consciously and unconsciously, in the absence of any effective intervention by a third. This "third," for Lacan, is the presence in the mother's life of sociocultural frameworks that contextualize and delimit the role of the child in her life and is usually highlighted by the presence of the father, who ideally sets limits on the grandiose totalization of desire.

Specifically, it is the "symbolic father," or patrinomial function, that lays the foundation for differentiation by naming the child as occupying a particular place in a kinship system. As we have seen, such naming marks the child as other than all others, and in being so identified the child has the structural possibility of eventually assuming his or her own desire rather than being merged in the desire of the mother or of the father. This symbolic identification then enables the child to mobilize its ego ideal as a "signifying mapping" (Lacan, 1964, p. 272), which then takes over from the ideal ego the task of limiting and channeling one's desire according to the constraints of finite existence. This is how Lacan conceives of the oedipal resolution, whose outcome is "symbolic castration," structuring the subject as pluralistically related (no longer in a dual relation with the mother), as sexed (no longer being the phallus but rather having or not having a penis), and as capable of finding and combining substitute objects of desire (rather than claiming the wholeness of totalized desire and not desiring at all).

THE TWO ANALYSES OF MR. Z

In my reading of "The Two Analyses of Mr. Z" (Kohut, 1979; unless otherwise indicated, all subsequent quotations are from this text), a reading informed by my reading of Lacan, I find that desire occupied the central place both in Mr. Z's history and in the transference-countertransference relationship with Kohut. In so emphasizing the crucial importance of desire, I am drawing on Lacan's theory of desire in the spirit of Goldberg (1980) when he quotes Popper in affirming that "facts are interpreted in the light of theories; they are soaked in theory, as it were" (p. 91). In the first analysis of Mr. Z, despite his initial resistance, Kohut promotes an identification between himself and Mr. Z so that Mr. Z shifts his desire from his mother's desire to Kohut's desire. In so identifying with Kohut in the first analysis (henceforth designated as K1), Mr. Z reinforces Kohut's position as the one who is supposed to know, thus rendering him desirable, and, in turn, by identifying with his desire, Mr. Z also becomes more desirable in his eyes. This identification of desires constitutes an imaginary identification: it is based on Mr. Z's becoming like K1's model of him. Kohut acknowledges in the second analysis that Mr. Z's changed behavior is rightly called a "transference success" (p. 16). As he did when his desire was merged with his mother's desire, Mr. Z shows "an attitude of compliance and acceptance that he had now reinstated with regard to me and to the seemingly unshakable convictions that I held" (p. 16). Kohut writes:

> The improvement which resulted from the first analysis must therefore be considered in essence as a transference success. Within the analytic setting, the patient complied with my

> convictions by presenting me with oedipal issues. Outside the analytic setting, he acceded to my expectations by suppressing his symptoms (the masochistic fantasies) and by changing his behavior which now took on the appearance of normality as defined by the maturity morality to which I then subscribed (he moved from narcissism to object love, i.e. he began to date girls) [p. 16].

But in the second analysis, Kohut (K2) no longer promotes such compliance: he shifts from trying to be recognized to recognizing Mr. Z. After Mr. Z disengages his desire from K1 and from his mother, K2 promotes the process of symbolic identification in which Mr. Z's ego ideal can be affirmed and engaged to delimit his desire as his own.

Kohut emphasizes how he at first viewed the "analytic material entirely from the point of view of classical analysis" (p. 3), whereas the second analysis occurred after his shift to "a new viewpoint, which, to state it briefly, allowed me to perceive meanings, or the significance of meanings, I had formerly not consciously perceived" (p. 3). But what is at stake in this shift is not only a matter of perception, but more profoundly a shift in what Lacan (1959–1960, 1977, p. 252; see also Richardson, 1987) designates as the ethical fulcrum of psychoanalysis, namely a shift in Kohut's *desire*, a shift not so much in how he thinks as in where he desires, and this shift in desire has a profound impact on the patient.

Mr. Z's identification with his mother's desire is indicated by his fantasies of being a woman's slave with no will of his own, reinforced in childhood by his mother's reading aloud to him *Uncle Tom's Cabin,* which opens with the threatened separation of a slave-child from his mother. Indeed, Mr. Z's mother spent much time "reading to him, playing with him, talking with him, and spinning out fantasies with him about what his future would be like" and "in her imagery about him as a grown man, she had always taken totally for granted that, however great his successes in life, their relationship would never be altered, he would never leave her" (p. 14).

As the first analysis draws to a close, Mr. Z appears to be reluctantly complying with the desire of the analyst. The reluctance is signified in a dream that occurred about half a year before termination of the first analysis, a dream Kohut saw as the "most significant sign of his advance": ". . . he was in a house, at the inner side of a door which was a crack open. Outside was the father, loaded with giftwrapped packages, wanting to enter. The patient was intensely frightened and attempted to close the door in order to keep the father out" (p. 8).

The patient's associations pointed to the time when the absent father rejoined the family, and he also had "many associations referring to present experiences (including the transference) and to the past. Our conclusion was that it referred to his ambivalent attitude toward the father" (pp. 8–9) and therefore was taken as confirmation of the castration-anxiety theme proposed by K1. But what is the ambivalence about? I hear the "giftwrapped" in the dream as "gift-trapped": Mr. Z fears being bribed and trapped in the father/analyst's desire as he was in his mother's desire. It is not, as Ostow (1979) suggests, that "the patient sees the analyst (as well as the father) as an intruder into his attachment to the mother" (p. 532), but rather that he feels K1's desire is coercing him, as we can read for ourselves:

> And, in view of the overall image I had formed of the construction of his personality and of his psychopathology, I stressed in my interpretations and reconstructions especially his hostility towards the returning father, the castration fear, vis-a-vis the strong, adult man; and, in addition, I pointed out his tendency to retreat from competitiveness and male assertiveness either to the old pre-oedipal attachment to his mother or to a defensively taken submissive and passive homosexual attitude toward the father.
>
> The logical cohesiveness of these reconstructions seemed impeccable and . . . in line with . . . precepts that were then firmly established in me as almost unquestioned inner guidelines in conducting my therapeutic work . . . [Kohut, 1979, p. 9].

K1's desire here is to get Mr. Z to recognize him as the one who knows, who knows not only Mr. Z's character structure but also what constitutes reality and maturity, and Mr. Z eventually complies by acting in accordance with K1's desire.[4] Initially, Mr. Z

[4]In commenting on the case of Mr. Z, Gedo (1986) suggests that Kohut was handicapped by "an excess of certitude"; in his view, Kohut's self-criticism regarding the first analysis throws light "on the fact that attitudes of omniscience are out of place in psychoanalytic work" and, furthermore, that "Kohut was not alone in bringing these authoritarian attitudes to the analytic task—they are practically ubiquitous in a profession that draws upon the traditions of clinical medicine" (pp. 120–121). Gedo goes on to state that in the second analysis "the transference soon emerged in the form of fantasies of merger with the analyst, but

struggled to get the analyst to mirror *his* states, but in the end, as his desire becomes disengaged from his mother's, he identifies with K1's desire but risks feeling trapped again. Kohut senses something is "wrong" with the termination because it was "emotionally shallow and unexciting" (p. 9). But such a state would be congruent if, in fact, Mr. Z did not experience termination. That is to say, there was no cut between them since Mr. Z's desire remained identified now with K1's desire. As Lacan (1964) puts it, "such imaginary identification is merely a pause, a false termination of the analysis which is very frequently confused with its normal termination" (p. 145). This would also account for the lack of zest and "emotional depth," since Mr. Z did not experience the process as his own, as the realization of his own desire (Thompson, 1985). In short, Mr. Z as subject was not recognized in the dual, imaginary relation between positions 2 and 3 of Lacan's Schema L.

SECOND ANALYSIS

Four and a half years later, Mr. Z contacted Kohut to renew the analysis. At that time he continued to live alone in his own apartment, did not enjoy his work, and had a succession of affairs with women, but he felt his sexual relations with women were unsatisfying and shallow. We can see that he still had not claimed his desire as his own and was beginning to regress to an identification with his mother's desire: he felt increasingly isolated socially, just as his mother had become, one of the signs of her serious personality change, which included a set of circumscribed paranoid delusions. Kohut (1979) wondered whether Mr. Z "was being confronted with the loss of a still unrelinquished love object from childhood or with guilt feelings about having abandoned her" (p. 10), as if she were the object of his desire. In fact, as was determined later, Mr. Z felt relief in the face of his mother's growing disability, since it allowed him to disengage from her desire even more freely.

The material for the second analysis can be divided into two

---

a merger from which Mr. Z struggled to disentangle himself (p. 13)! It is in this context, replicating the patient's childhood enslavement by his mother, that anxiety about the possibility of disintegration was reexperienced" (p. 124). This formulation is consistent with the reading I am proposing, except for the issue of anxiety, which will be addressed shortly not as a repetitive moment but as a restructuring one.

phases, "the almost exclusive preoccupation with the mother" and "thoughts concerning his father" (p. 12; see also p. 20, 21: "Mr. Z's detaching himself from the mother and turning toward his father"). As we have seen, material about the mother was also plentiful in the first analysis; and in attempting to articulate what was different about its emergence in the second analysis, Kohut emphasizes "that between Mr. Z's first and second analysis my theoretical outlook had shifted" (p. 12). What was this shift about? "I had in the first analysis looked upon the patient in essence as a centre of independent initiative and had therefore expected that he would, with the aid of analytic insights that would enable him to see his path clearly, relinquish his narcissistic demands and grow up" (p. 12).

With this attitude, Kohut believes Mr. Z can choose to orient his desire; he sees "the patient's persistent attachment to the mother as a libidinal tie that he was unwilling to break" (p. 12). He assumes that Mr. Z's desire is his own, thereby presuming the very condition Mr. Z came into treatment to achieve. The shift, therefore, from K1 to K2 (which to me marks a decisive difference, contrary to Wallerstein's, 1981, efforts to harmonize the two phases) required two changes: first, in Kohut's own desire: "I was now able, more genuinely than before, to set aside any goal-directed therapeutic ambitions. Put differently, I relinquished the health- and maturity-morality that had formerly motivated me" (p. 12). The second change is in his view of the patient. He no longer sees the patient's self as "resisting change or as opposing maturation because it did not want to relinquish its childish gratifications, but, on the contrary, as desparately—and often hopelessly—struggling to disentangle itself from the noxious self-object, to delimit itself, to grow, to become independent" (p. 12). The shift in Kohut's own desire enables him to see the patient's desire differently: "Where we had formerly seen pleasure gain, the sequence of drive demand and drive gratification, we now recognized the depression of a self that, wanting to delimit and assert itself, found itself hopelessly caught within the psychic organization of the self-object" (p. 17)—caught, in other words, in the mother's desire.

The effort to give an account of this shift holds Kohut's attention as more childhood history is reported, having to do with the mother's intense scrutiny of Mr. Z's feces up to the age of six and then her searching his face for blackheads:

> We are again confronted by the puzzling question why this crucial material had not appeared during Mr. Z's first analysis.

> To be sure, it had indeed appeared, but—what is even more incomprehensible—it had failed to claim our attention. I believe that we come closest to the solution of this puzzle when we say that a crucial aspect of the transference had remained unrecognized in the first analysis [p. 15].

What was unrecognized in the first analysis? Kohut affirms that it was how his own convictions "had become for the patient a replica of the mother's hidden psychosis" (p. 16), with which the patient complied. But in a Lacanian framework the crucial transference issue that remained unrecognized was how Mr. Z's entanglement in K1's desire replicated his enmeshing with his mother's desire.

What does this perspective add to Kohut's formulation? It clarifies some of Mr. Z's symptoms. We have already seen how the "sexual masochism" is the enactment in fantasy of Mr. Z's position as object of mother's desire with no desire of his own. Kohut rightly notes that an object relations approach "fails to do justice" to this symptom as well as to the "chronic despair which could often be felt side by side with the arrogance of his demandingness" (p. 12). I suggest that Mr. Z's demandingness was his mother's demandingness with which he was identified (we are told that she "emotionally enslaved those around her and stifled their independent existence," p. 13), and his despair is precisely over this state of his desire. He cannot but act in accordance with the unconscious structure of his desire, formed by his mother's desire. Thus, when he reports with "the most intense shame" that as a young child "he had smelled and even tasted his feces" (p. 17), he is indicating just how his desire was identified with his mother's desire in taking such intense interest in his feces. When Kohut rationalizes that "he had come to understand for the first time in empathic consonance with another human being, that these childhood activities were neither wicked nor disgusting, but they had been feeble attempts to provide for himself a feeling of aliveness" (p. 17), he does not acknowledge (nor does Myerson, 1981) that Mr. Z's shame is over the fact that he was like her, that he desired what she desired.

While the structure of Mr. Z's desire is not explicitly posed, Kohut grasps its obvious import in relation to the mother: "His most significant psychological achievement in analysis was breaking the deep merger ties with his mother" (p. 25). And furthermore: "No independent self had gradually formed; what psychological existence he had managed to build was rooted in his attachment to the mother" (p. 23). His very status as a self—in Lacanian terms, as subject of desire—rested on the imaginary identification of desires. His mother's desire provided the psychic scaffolding on which he built an unhappy and fragile sense of himself. Because his experience of cohesion rested on this mirroring, reflective structure, he experienced "the deepest anxiety he had ever experienced" in a dream of "a starkly outlined image of the mother, standing with her back turned toward him" (p. 19). This occurred as Mr. Z was focusing explicitly in the analysis on his father. An immediate sense of the dream occurred to Mr. Z. that as he moved closer to his father, his mother turned her back on him, just as she used to treat him with "icy withdrawal" whenever "he attempted to step toward independent maleness" and her tactic, her "chilling look of disapproval" (p. 15) always brought him back emotionally.

But the "deeper meaning of the dream" concerned "the unseen, the unseeable frontal view of the mother" which, when the patient tried to imagine it, brought intense, nameless anxiety. When K2 (acting for the moment again like K1, perhaps, as we shall see, in response to the collapse of the structure of desire, which is what the dream shows) suggests "the horror of castration, of the sight of the missing external genital, of fantasies of blood and mutilation," in response "the patient brushed these suggestions aside"; while he agreed that "the imagery of mutilation, castration, and blood was related to the unnamed horror, he was sure that this was not the essential source of the fear" (p. 20). Another formulation was offered by K2: "When I suggested that the mother may not have lost her penis but her face, he did not object but responded with prolonged silence from which he emerged in a noticeably more relaxed mood" (p. 20).

I will attempt a Lacanian understanding of K2's approach: The images of mutilation relate to the experience of bodily fragmentation and ego disintegration and are, as the patient insists, secondary consequences of a more primary collapse. This primary fall is the loss of status as a desiring subject, being no longer embraced by the mother's gaze or addressed by her voice. The dream-trauma consists not in what was unseeable but in the fact that the mother was unseeing, no longer holding her son in her desiring gaze and no longer putting his face before her as her reflection—all of this implying, of course, that she never did see him as he was but only as her image. The very structure of Mr. Z's psychic consistency is here declared to be undone, and K2 points to this (by mentioning the loss of her face) and allows the prolonged silence to register the shift. While we doubt that "the unseen side of the mother in this dream stood for her distorted personality and her pathological outlook," since conscious acknowledgment rather than repression of her pathology had recently brought relief (p. 16), we can agree that the dream "expressed his anxiety at the realization that his conviction of the mother's strength and power [of her desire]—a conviction on which he had based a sector of his own personality [as subject] in intermeshment with her [desire]—was itself a delusion [as are all such imaginary identifications]" (p. 20). What *is* he, if he is no longer that something he was in his mother's desire?

The disengagement of Mr. Z's desire from his mother's desire now moves ahead differently than in the first analysis: K2 does not seduce compliance with his own desire but instead, by keeping his desire in the analytic place of the Other, he enables Mr. Z to engage in a process of retrieving the kernel of his ego ideal by focusing on his father. The issue of the father was posed at the beginning of the second analysis. The night before the beginning of the second analysis, Mr. Z had the following dream without action or words:

> It was the image of a dark-haired man in a rural landscape with hills, mountains, and lakes. Although the man was standing there in quiet relaxation, he seemed to be strong and confidence-inspiring. He was dressed in city clothes, in a complex but harmonious way—the patient saw that he was wearing a ring, that a handkerchief protruded from his breast pocket, and that he was holding something in each hand—perhaps an umbrella in one hand, and possibly a pair of gloves in the other. The figure of the man was visually very plastic and prominent—as in some photographs in which the object is sharply in focus while the background is blurred [p. 11].

Mr. Z's associations showed the figure to be a composite of a childhood friend, a camp counselor (based on landscape features relating to the summer camp), the father (his hair), and the analyst (umbrella, gloves, the handkerchief, the ring). Mr. Z also recalled the dream of his father "loaded with packages," and this "established a link with the terminal phase of the first analysis—announcing as it were that the second analysis was a continuation of the first one" and that "it took off from the very point where the first one had failed most significantly" (p. 11).

If the second analysis takes off from this point, then we must consider the dream as occurring just when the patient, feeling he is still the object of K1's desire, is once again going to confront the amorphousness of his own desire. If we can understand the first dream of the father "loaded with giftwrapped packages" in terms of Mr. Z's asking the question, "What does the other want from me?" then this dream presents the other as desiring nothing from the subject, as holding his gloves and umbrella, rather than gifts, in his hands. There may yet be a space for the subject's own desire to emerge.

IDEALIZATION AND THE EGO IDEAL

How does "the second phase of the second analysis" (p. 18) proceed? Having given up the ideal ego fashioned in mirroring response to and identification with his mother's desire, Mr. Z now attempts to recover and articulate the sources of his ego ideal, or, more specifically, what Lacan (1977) calls "the paternal identification of the ego-ideal" (p. 197). For a time Mr. Z's mood remains hopeless and despairing, specifically because "his father was weak, ... The mother dominated and subdued him" (Kohut, 1979, p. 18). He then focuses on his counselor friend briefly, and then begins "to express intense curiosity about me," about the analyst's past, his early life, his interests, his family, his relationship to his wife and children (p. 18). I hear this as Mr. Z's attempt to find out something about K2's desire, where it was, what sustained it, whether Mr. Z would again be seduced into compliance—all attempts to safely anchor his ego ideal. But K2 initially responded to this as K1 had earlier: "Whenever I treated his inquiries as a revival of infantile curiosity and pointed out the associative connections with the sex life of his parents, he became depressed and told me I misunderstood him" (p. 18). Gradually Kohut changed his view and "finally ventured the guess that it was his need for a strong father that lay behind his questions, that he wanted to know whether I, too, was weak, subdued in intercourse by my wife, unable to be the idealizable emotional support of a son" (p. 18). As I read it, Mr. Z's questions address Kohut about the following: 1) Am I still the object of your desire? 2) Are you a subject of desire, and do you have other objects of desire? 3) Do you have something I can pin my ego ideal on and mobilize my desire along signifying lines? In other words, Mr. Z wanted to make contact with the paternal function: did Kohut know how to use his penis, and was he able to set limits. Kohut set limits with "friendly firmness" in denying Mr. Z's requests for information. In response to Kohut's change in approach, Mr. Z dropped his demands and became dramatically less depressed and hopeless. He also "made do with certain bits of information which he had obtained either accidentally or via inference—my interest in art and literature, for example" (p. 18). "Art and literature" serves as the verbal bridge between his mother (p. 4), his counselor-friend (p. 7), and Kohut and, we can speculate, forms one kernel of his ego ideal.

At this point "the analysis took a new turn" and focused directly on Mr. Z's father, who until then had remained a shadowy figure. Mr. Z now began to talk about "positive features in his father's personality," and he did so "with a glow of happiness, of satisfaction" (p. 19). For Kohut, this was, "as can be judged in retrospect, the crucial moment in the treatment—the point at which he may be said to have taken the road toward emotional health" (p. 19). But on this road Mr. Z had "quasi-psychotic experiences in which he felt himself disintegrating and was beset by intense hypochondriacal concerns. At such times he dreamed of desolate landscapes, burned-out cities, and most deeply upsetting, of heaps of piled-up human bodies . . . he was not sure whether the bodies were those of dead people or of people still barely alive" (p. 19).

This description calls to mind Lacan's (1953) examples of bodily-fragmentation fantasies about which he writes:

> What struck me in the first place was the phase of the analysis in which these images came to light: they were always bound up with the elucidation of the earliest problems of the patient's ego. . . . Their appearance heralds a particular and very archaic phase of the transference, and the value we attributed to them in identifying this phase has always been confirmed by the accompanying marked decrease in the patient's deepest resistances [p. 13].

In Kohut's view, "Mr. Z was now relinquishing the archaic self (connected with the selfobject mother) that he had always considered his only one, in preparation for the reactivation of a hitherto unknown independent nuclear self (crystallised around an up-to-now unrecognized relationship to his selfobject father)" (p. 19). The moment has arrived for Mr. Z to let go of what has structured him as a desiring subject—his place in the eyes of his mother. At precisely this point Mr. Z's dream of his mother occurs in which she was "starkly outlined" like the dream of the standing man. In the aftermath of this third dream, which finally frees Mr. Z's desire from his mother's, and the ensuing relaxed mood, Mr. Z recalls positive memories of his father, "preceded and accompanied by his idealization" of K2, including a short-lived wish to become an analyst. This "idealization" is nothing like the grandiosity-building idealization of his mother (to which we shall return shortly) but is more properly a bringing into focus of the field of his ego ideal.

The main memory of his father to emerge at this point was of a trip to Colorado he had taken with his father at the age of 9. He spoke "with an increasing glow of joy" of his father's traits; as a "man of the world," he could amuse others with stories, was a good skier, showed "resoluteness, perceptiveness, and skill" in business dealings and, above all, Mr. Z recovered "the intensely experienced awareness that his father was an independent man who had a life independent from the life of the mother" (p. 21)—that is, that father had his own desire independent of his mother's. Then Mr. Z complained about how little he knew about his father and, after "a brief period of transference fantasies," he suddenly voiced the suspicion "that his father had a woman friend" who had been present during the trip to Colorado and that they met in a bar the night before leaving. Mr. Z never mentioned this episode to his mother when they returned. Although his father did not explicitly request this, "he felt that there was a silent understanding between them that he would be quiet about it" (p. 21). This experience suggests the presence of a number of key factors in the psychic structure of Mr. Z at that time: 1) he knew his father had a penis and knew how to use it, and therefore was a subject of desire, not just an object; 2) the sight of his father with this other woman demonstrated to Mr. Z his inferiority to his father, that his father possessed anterior sexual knowledge; 3) he could identify with a paternal prohibition by keeping the secret, but precisely because it was a secret it lent itself to repression; 4) in keeping the secret he won recognition from his father as being his ally. To be sure, this secret identification and identification through the secret must have rested on some earlier foundation of symbolic identification (such as sharing his name with his father), but we can agree that because of its secret status "this material represents, in terms of the structure of Mr. Z's personality, the deepest layer of the repressed" and that "no pathogenic oedipal conflicts still lay in hiding" (p. 22). The aforementioned ingredients of psychic structure suggest that the Colorado trip achieved symbolic castration for Mr. Z.

I question, therefore, Kohut's conceptualization of the outcome of this process as the result of an idealization. There is something amiss in the formulation of Mr. Z's "glow of joy and the invigorating sense of having finally found an image of masculine strength—to merge with temporarily as a means of firming the structure of his self, of becoming himself an independent centre of strength and initiative" (p. 22). The "glow of joy" indicates the mobilization of his own desire, not because of any additional merger (he has, with relief, just ended his merger of desires with his mother) but because he has constellated an ego ideal that delimits and anchors his desire and therefore facilitates his becoming a subject with "strength and initiative." That his recognition and affirmation of the paternal function were repressed and split-off seems likely, but this repression appears to be a product of his grandiose ego, fueled by the idealized mother with whom he was "enmeshed," "submitted to the role of being her phallus" (writes Kohut) and displaying "a grandiosity that was bestowed upon him by the mother so long as he did not separate himself from her" (p. 24). It would be inconsistent for his ideal ego to repress another idealization (since another idealization would only inflate his ego further) or that in the split-off sector he would have "preserved the idealizations that maintained a bond to his father" (p. 24).

Kohut understandably wants to go beyond an object relations formulation that rests on drive-cathexes of representable objects, but in its place he appears to make idealization serve the function of establishing ties, not between a drive and an object, but between a needy self and a self-object. It seems to me, however, that Mr. Z's recovery of the repressed is not the recovery of an idealization but of an identification. That identification is, furthermore, based not on "an image of masculine strength" for him to copy, but on some marking by symbols, including the penis as symbol of masculinity *versus* the phallus as symbol of the other's desire (see Julien, 1987; Lacan, 1938, p. 59). While I agree that the dream of attempting to slam the door on the gift-laden father "was not motivated by castration anxiety" (Kohut, 1984, p. 86), Mr. Z's reformulation of his dream (with which Ornstein, 1981, concurs), in which the danger in the father's return allegedly consisted in the traumatic state of being suddenly offered "all the psychological gifts, for which he had secretly yearned" (Kohut, 1979, p. 23), seems to be a lame argument. With the father back, there is no reason why "male psychological substance" could not have been gradually handled, provided the father could set limits. The *ad hoc* explanation of "too much, too fast" appears less compelling than one that emphasizes the structural effects of being identified with the desire of the mother, one effect being the kind of grandiose mutual idealization that would split off any delimiting third and that left the young Mr. Z without an operative ego ideal.

TERMINATION

The termination of the second analysis was different from that of the first one. The idealization of the analyst was short-lived and worked through with the analyst falling from being identified with the Other and the resulting gap providing a place for the subject's desire. There was no return of earlier symptoms (the underlying structure of desire supporting the sexual masochism fantasies had dissolved); there was no severe anxiety in the face of losing the analyst's presence. For several weeks the patient was sad about losing the analyst and regretted that, with his father dead, he would have no chance to develop a friendly relationship with him. Significantly, "for a few sessions he also expressed considerable anger towards me for having originally failed him, like his father in childhood" (p. 24)—a failure to disengage his desire from his mother's in the father's case, a failure by forcing compliance with his own desire in Kl's case. Months were spent reviewing the past and anticipating the future. During the last few weeks, Kohut "was very impressed by his expanded empathy with and tolerant attitude towards the shortcomings of his parents" (p. 24). Such contextualization in a symbolic matrix extended especially to his mother, with her pathology but also with her positive features, which he could see "without a trace of the idealizations with which he had begun his first analysis" (p. 25). The content of his ambitions and ideals, which

> had arisen in the matrix of the now abandoned merger relationship with the mother, persisted but the working through of his transference relationship to me [i.e., making the transition from K1 to K2] enabled him to reestablish a link with his father's maleness and independence, and thus the emotional core of his ambitions, ideals, and basic skills and talents was decisively altered, even though their content remained unchanged. But now he experienced these assets of his personality as his own [p. 25].

He had made his desire his own and could pursue its realization according to its own signifying pattern.

Returning to Lacan's Schema L, we can map onto it the

positions of K1 and K2 as we have come to understand them: In the first analysis, Kohut abandoned his analytic stance and coerced the patient's desire to identify with his own; in the second analysis, he successfully achieved symbolic recognition of Mr. Z as subject, not allowing himself to become lured by Mr. Z's grandiose ego into the imaginary collusion of "strengthening the ego." As a result, Mr. Z claimed his desire as his own in his efforts to realize his desire with others; this was made structurally possible by the constellation of an ego ideal that delimited his desire, giving it scope and direction. The ingredients of the ego ideal had their source in the symbolic matrix of the father/analyst—not that he can fill the place of the Other; on the contrary, his very limitations, as Kohut stresses, are the fulcrum for the shift brought about by "transmuting internalizations." In the end, the analyst becomes *an* other, one among many others whose significance to the patient, like that of his parents, is now contextualized in the symbolic order, no longer captivating him as isolated elements in the imaginary register. Here we see that the positive features of oedipalization and the goals of analysis overlap: to move from duality to plurality, from focus on the ideal ego to the ego ideal, from imaginary identification that represses desire in order to imagine oneself as like another to symbolic identification as being different in one's own desire.

Clearly, in many details Kohut and Lacan reveal a similarity of purpose, and in their assessment of psychoanalysis they say similar things, despite the obvious differences noted by Lacanians (see, for example, Laurent and Schneiderman, 1977; Harari, 1984; Cottet, 1985; Peraldi, 1987). Despite these differences, Kohut has provided us with invaluable documentation of what for Lacan is the

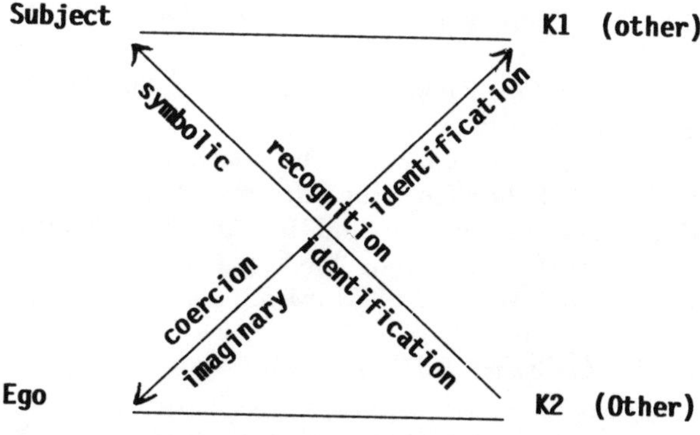

FIG. 2 Kohut and Schema L

essential analytic responsibility: to discern the effects of one's own desire. We are all pressed, at certain moments in every treatment, toward the K1 position: This is an effect of transference, an effect of the patient's desire that constellates the supposed knowing subject in us and engages our own narcissism in countertransference. Our only recourse (and the patient's as well) is to take note of just how we are (or were) being lured out of the K2 position. In such moments we learn most about our patients, about ourselves, and about the Freudian discovery.

REFERENCES

Aulagnier, P. (1962), Angoisse et identification. In: *Seminaire 1961–62. L'identification,* by J. Lacan. Unpublished manuscript. International Research Center. New York: International General, pp. 396–412.

Brown, C. & Witkowski, S. (1981), Figurative language in a universalist perspective. *Amer. Ethnol.,* 8:596–615.

Coen, S. (1981), Notes on the concepts of selfobject and preoedipal object. *J. Amer. Psychoanal. Assn.,* 29:395–411.

Compact Edition of the Oxford English Dictionary (1971). New York: Oxford University Press.

Cottet, S. (1985), Presentation: Le plus novateur des analystes américains. In: H. Kohut, *Les Deux Analyses de M. Z*,* trans. G. Laurent-Sivry & C. Leger-Paturneau. Paris: Navarin/Seuil.

Derrida, J. (1967), *Of Grammatology,* trans. G. Spivak. Baltimore, MD: Johns Hopkins University Press, 1976.

Etchegoyen, R. (1985), Identification and its vicissitudes. *Internat. J. Psycho-Anal.,* 66:3–18.

Freud, S. (1900a), The interpetation of dreams. *Standard Edition,* 4 & 5, London: Hogarth Press, 1953.

_____ (1900b), Die Traumdeutung. *Gesammelte Werke,* 2 & 3. London: Imago, 1942.

_____ (1905), Jokes and their relation to the unconscious. *Standard Edition,* 8. London: Hogarth Press, 1960.

_____ (1921a), Group psychology and the analysis of the ego. *Standard Edition,* 18:69–143. London: Hogarth Press, 1955.

_____ (1921b), Massenpsychologie und Ich-Analyse. *Gesammelte Werke,* 13:71–161. Frankfurt am Main: Fischer, 1940.

_____ (1923), The ego and the id. *Standard Edition,* 19:3–66. London: Hogarth Press.

Gedo, J. (1986), *Conceptual Issues in Psychoanalysis.* Hillsdale, NJ: The Analytic Press.

Goldberg, A. (1980), Letter to the Editor, *Internat. J. Psycho-Anal.,* 61:91–92.

Gould, S. (1976), Human babies as embryos. *Natural History,* 84:22-26.
Harari, R. (1985), *Discurrir el psicoanalisis.* Buenos Aires: Ediciones Nueva Vision.
Harris, R. (1986), *The Origin of Writing.* La Salle, IL: Open Court.
Jakobson, R. (1956), Two aspects of language and two types of aphasic disturbances. In: *Fundamentals of Language,* ed. R. Jakobson & M. Halle. The Hague: Mouton, pp. 53–87.
Julien, P. (1987), Entre l'homme et la femme il y a l' a-mur. *Littoral,* 23/24:25–34.
Kohut, H. (1979), The two analyses of Mr. Z. *Internat. J. Psycho-Anal.,* 60:3–27.
—— (1984), *How Does Analysis Cure?* ed. A. Goldberg & P. Stepansky. Chicago: University of Chicago Press.
—— & Wolf, E. (1978), The disorders of the self and their treatment: An outline. *Internat. J. Psycho-Anal.,* 59:413–425.
Lacan, J. (1938), *Les complexes familiaux dans la formation de l'individu.* Paris: Navarin/Seuil, 1984.
—— (1953), Some reflections on the ego. *Internat. J. Psycho-Anal.,* 34:11–17.
—— (1954–1955), *The Seminars of Jacques Lacan, Book II,* ed. J. A. Miller (trans. S. Tomaselli). New York: Norton.
—— (1956), Seminar on "The Purloined Letter," trans. J. Mehlman. In: *The Purloined Poe.* ed. J. Muller & W. Richardson. Baltimore, MD: Johns Hopkins University Press, 1987, pp. 28–54.
—— .(1959–1960), *Le séminaire: Livre VII. L'ethique de la psychanalyse,* ed. J. -A. Miller. Paris: Seuil, 1986.
—— (1961–1962), *Séminaire 1961–62. L'Identification.* Unpublished manuscript, International Research Center. New York: International General.
—— (1964), *The Four Fundamental Concepts of Psychoanalysis,* ed. J. -A. Miller (trans. A. Sheridan). New York: Norton, 1978.
—— (1966), *Ecrits.* Paris: Seuil.
—— (1977), *Ecrits, A Selection.* trans. A. Sheridan. New York: Norton.
Laurent, E. & Schneiderman, S. (1977), Parcours du self. *Ornicar?,* 11:95–101.
Leroi-Gourhan, A. (1964), *Le geste et la parole: Technique et langage.* Paris: Michel.
Mead, G. H. (1925), The genesis of the self and social control. In: *The Philosophy of the Present,* ed. A. Murphy. Chicago: University of Chicago Press, 1980, pp. 176–195.
Muller, J. (1982), Cognitive psychology and the ego: Lacanian theory and empirical research. *Psychoanal. Contemp. Thought,* 5:257–291.
—— (1985), Lacan's mirror stage. *Psychoanal. Inq.,* 5:233–252.
—— (1986), The psychoanalytic ego in Lacan: Its origins and self-serving functions. *Psychological Perspectives on the Self,* Vol. 3, ed. J. Suls & A. Greenwald. Hillsdale, NJ: Lawrence Erlbaum Associates, pp. 79–106.

_____ (1987), Language, psychosis, and spirit. In: *Attachment and the Therapeutic Process,* ed. J. Sacksteder, D. Schwartz & Y. Akabane. New York: International Universities Press, pp. 99–116.

_____ and Richardson, W. J. (1982), *Lacan and Language.* New York: International Universities Press.

Myerson, P. (1981), The nature of the transactions that occur in other than classical analysis. *Internat. Rev. Psycho-Anal.,* 8:173–189.

Ornstein, P. (1981), The bipolar self in the psychoanalytic treatment process: Clinical-theoretical considerations. *J. Amer. Psychoanal. Assn.,* 29:353–375.

Ostow, M. (1979), Letter to the editor. *Internat. J. Psycho-Anal.,* 60:531–532.

Peraldi, F. (1987), K.K.K. *Etudes freudiennes,* No. 30:181–212.

Richardson, W. (1983), Lacan and the subject of psychoanalysis. In: *Interpreting Lacan,* ed. J. Smith & W. Kerrigan. New Haven, CT: Yale University Press, pp. 51–74.

_____ (1987), Ethics and desire. *Amer. J. Psychoanal.,* 47:296–301.

Saussure, F. de (1916), *Course in General Linguistics,* ed. C. Bally & A. Sechehaye (trans. W. Baskin). New York: McGraw-Hill, 1966.

Thompson, M. (1985), *The Death of Desire.* New York: New York University Press.

Turkle, S. (1978), *Psychoanalytic Politics.* New York: Basic Books.

Ver Eecke, W. (1984), *Saying "No."* Pittsburgh, PA: Duquesne University Press.

Voyat, G., ed. (1984), *The World of Henri Wallon.* New York: Aronson.

Wallerstein, R. S. (1981), The bipolar self: Discussion of alternative perspectives. *J. Amer. Psychoanal. Assn.,* 29:377–394.

Wallon, H. (1921), La conscience et la conscience du moi. *J. de Psychologie,* 18:51–64.

_____ (1931), Comment se developpe, chez l'enfant, la notion du corps propre. *J. de Psychologie,* 28:705–748.

_____ (1934), *Les Origines du caractère chez l'enfant: Les préludes du sentiment de personnalité,* 2nd Ed. Paris: Presses Universitaires de France, 1949.

Widlocher, D. (1985), The wish for identification and structural effects in the work of Freud. *Internat. J. Psycho-Anal.,* 66:31–46.

19

Mahler, Kohut, and Infant Research
Some Comparisons

ESTELLE SHANE
MORTON SHANE

It is inevitable that psychoanalysts interested in developmental theory would seek correspondences between the work of Margaret Mahler (1979; Mahler and Furer, M., 1968; Mahler, Pine, & Bergman, A., 1975) and that of Heinz Kohut (1971, 1977, 1984), the two authors many recognize as having most significantly influenced American psychoanalysis in the current, postclassical era of object relations and self-development. Their methodologies, of course, were significantly different. Mahler based her theory on systematic observation and careful documentation of the psychologically relevant behavior of infants and toddlers in interaction with their parents, providing a view of the development of the "objective self," a concept we put forward in an effort at integrating Kohut and Mahler (Shane and Shane, 1980). The term objective self in our formulation was based on the vantage point from which these observations on the development of the self were made. Kohut, unlike Mahler, derived his theory exclusively from the psychoanalytic situation, creating a view of the development of the "reconstructed self," as we termed it in that same publication, based again on the vantage point from which his observations were made.

But despite this difference in their vantage points, because both Kohut and Mahler began their respective inquiries with the same general frame of reference, that is, psychoanalytic, and because both stress the significance of the infant-caretaker unit in the earliest period of life, congruencies between their investigative findings as well as their conceptual innovations were to be expected. And, in fact, it seems that both Mahler and Kohut had, at the beginning at least, that same expectation. Kohut (1980), in a discussion of our 1980 paper, described an interchange he had had with Mahler in the early 70's. Mahler had written Kohut a letter at that time asking him what he saw as the differences between her theory and his. Kohut answered Mahler's query in such a way that conceptual distinctions between them were played down, saying that he viewed himself and Mahler as "digging tunnels from different directions into the same area of the mountain" (1980). Thus, in the 1970s, he seemed to infer that the approaches of the observer of children and of the reconstructor of childhood might generate findings that could meet, or be integrated, the same position we had taken. The fact is, however, that Kohut, in discussing our 1980 paper, indicated that since the exchange of letters between himself and Mahler some years before, he had changed his mind about the possibility of integration between them, not because of the differences in his and Mahler's methods of data gathering, but because of differences that later evolved in their respective schools of thought.

In this chapter we will begin with a rather full review of the developmental sequence put forward by Mahler, using as much as possible her own language and theoretical underpinnings. Unless otherwise indicated the formulations are contained in Mahler, et al. (1975). We will then examine selected aspects of this developmental scheme from the viewpoint of Kohut's conceptualizations, noting where the views overlap and where they part company. At the same time we will assess Mahler's and Kohut's developmental postulates from the vantage point of current infant observation.

MAHLER'S DEVELOPMENTAL FORMULATIONS

Mahler's chief contribution to psychoanalytic developmental theory is her study of what she terms the separation-individuation phase, or process, which culminates in object and self-representations and stable identity formation. To this end, Mahler conceived a research design using analytically trained observers who applied classical, analytic, genetic-dynamic insights to infant-mother interactions. She discovered what she considered to be a normal, ubiquitous process occurring in children who successfully maneuver the first three years of life. As Harley and Weil (1979) stress, "Mahler's intent was not to add any new theory; to the contrary, her ultimate aim was to integrate into our existing body of developmental knowledge detailed and systematic findings on the beginning enfoldment of object relations" (pp. xiv–xv).

This separation-individuation phase, Mahler asserts, establishes a sense of separateness from and relation to reality, particularly in regard to the relationship between one's own body and the primary love object. This phase is never finished but occurs primarily from four months to 36 months of age. Separation, defined by Mahler as an intrapsychic achievement not to be confused with physical separation, refers to an emergence from symbiotic fusion with the caregiver; individuation refers to the child's assumption of his or her own individual characteristics. While these processes are intertwined, there may be either lag or precosity in one or the other. For example, a mother may interfere with separation strivings in her infant but may encourage progressive development of cognitive, perceptual, and affective function.

The Forerunners of the Separation-Individuation Process

Mahler identified two phases that precede separation-individuation, the normal autistic phase and the normal symbiotic phase, which phases were less systematically studied by Mahler through direct observation and therefore are less behaviorally detailed than the finely noted aspects of the subsequent developmental sequence, which is, after all, her main focus. The concepts of autism and symbiosis were derived for the most part through Freud's (1900, 1905, 1915, 1920, 1923, 1926) theories of early development and Mahler's own psychoanalytic reconstructions from the study of psychotic and borderline children and adults.

Mahler's normal autistic phase describes the initial state of the infant, who is viewed as existing in a monadic system (as contrasted to a dyadic system), self-sufficient in hallucinatory wish fulfillment. The principal task of this phase is the achievement of homeostatic equilibrium through somatapsychic mechanisms. Only gradually does the infant become aware of need satisfaction stemming from outside the self.

This dim awareness of the need-satisfying object marks the beginning of the normal symbiotic phase. Mahler is denoting a social symbiosis, a matrix of physiological and sociobiological dependency on the mother from which structural differentiation takes place, leading to a functional ego. The physiological need gradually becomes a psychological wish, and the affects become object bound. Concomitantly the body image is delineated. The infant's inner sensations from the core of the self remain the central crystalization point of the feeling of self around which the sense of identity will be established.

Normal autism and normal symbiosis are prerequisite to normal separation-individuation. The normal autistic phase promotes homeostasis; the normal symbiotic phase creates the ability of the human being to cathect the other within a vague, dual entity, creating the primal soil from which all human relationships form. The subsequent separation-individuation subphases are characterized by a steady increase in awareness of a self separate from others, which coincides with the origins of a sense of self and of true object relationships, as well as an awareness of a reality in the outside world.

Images of the love object, as well as images of a bodily, and later a psychic, self, emerge from the increasing memory traces of pleasurable and unpleasurable experience. But even the most primitive differentiation from the mother depends upon the matching of discharge patterns of mother and infant, and later interactional patterns discernable in mutual cueing. The mother's availability is thus essential to progression into the next phase.

The First Subphase: Differentiation and the Development of the Body Image (6-10 Months)

At the age of four to five months, the peak of symbiosis, differentiation is observed. By this time the achievement of the social smile indicates the establishment of a specific bond. A central core of dim body awareness is hypothesized, based on behaviors that demarcate self from other. For example, the infant is observed molding to his mother, distancing from her, feeling his own and his mother's bodies, and handling transitional objects.

Six to seven months is importantly marked by hatching, defined by Mahler as a gradual ontogenetic evolution of the sensorium, characterized by a new look of alertness, persistence, and goal directedness. The child is observed pulling at his mother's hair and ears, feeding her, straining back for a better look at her, all in contrast to the earlier molding into mother when held.

The child's creation at this time of transitional objects is a monument to his need for contact with the mother's body. In addition, the mother's preferred soothing or stimulating pattern is taken over, assimilated as a transitional pattern.

At seven to eight months, the infant develops a checking-back-to-mother pattern. Mahler calls this the most important normal pattern of cognitive and emotional development. The baby begins with comparative scanning, comparing mother with the other. He becomes more and more familiar with how she feels, tastes, smells, and looks.

Mahler writes that the well-documented stranger reaction and stranger anxiety developing at this period can also incorporate curiosity and eagerness to find out about the stranger, once the stranger has averted his or her gaze. When the infant is sufficiently individuated to recognize the mother's face and is quite familiar with her moods, he turns with more or less wonderment and apprehension to a prolonged visual and tactile exploration of the faces of others, always checking back to mother's face. With an optimal symbiotic phase and with optimal confident expectation, curiosity and wonderment predominate; in children whose basic trust is less than optimal, an abrupt change to the acute stranger anxiety made familiar by Spitz (1965) may occur, or, alternatively, prolonged mild stranger reactions, which interfere with inspective behavior, may take place. The infant's response to the stranger becomes evaluative both of his socialization process and his first steps toward emotional object constancy.

When symbiosis is delayed or premature, differentiation is similarly delayed or premature. Such disturbed symbiosis can be caused by the mother's indifference, ambivalence, intrusiveness, or unpredictability.

Mahler notes that as important as inborn potential is for eventual harmonious personality development, a favorable mother-child interaction also affects subphase adequacy. The mother, too, has to adapt, particularly at crucial periods.

Mahler and her colleagues (1975) conclude

> It is the specific unconscious need of the mother that activates out of the child's infinite potentialities those in particular that create for each mother "the child" who reflects her own *unique*

> and individual needs. This process takes place of course within the range of the child's innate endowment [p. 60].

The Second Subphase: Practicing (10-17 Months)

As the child enters the practicing subphase, he and his mother are less able to take undisturbed pleasure in their close physical contact with one another, but they can enjoy one another at a greater distance. A mother who has difficulty relating to her child tends to want him to grow up quickly as soon as he seeks to distance himself. Such children, in turn, find it difficult to give up a demanding closeness. On the other hand, children who have had the best relationships with their mothers can now venture the farthest from her; but when they become concerned about separation, they are able to turn to her once again. How the child perceives the widening world depends on mother, for while the thrust for individuation is an innate given, it can be experienced as painful if mother is not available to alleviate fears, falls, and hurts.

The central feature of the practicing subphase is the elated investment in the exercise of autonomous functions, especially motility, to a near exclusion of interest in the mother. Optimal distance allows for free exploration at the same time that it permits refueling, a "perking up" for further exploration. Mahler concludes that during this early practicing subphase, all children have some separation anxiety and require the use of the distance modalities of hearing and seeing mother in order to enable them to move physically from her.

The practicing subphase proper, from 10 or 12 to 16 or 18 months, is characterized by Greenacre's (1957) concept of a "love affair with the world" Children attain a new visual level in upright locomotion, which offers them continuously new and interesting sights. This period constitutes the height of narcissism, when the child invests his own functions and his own body, as well as objects and objectives of his expanding reality. Impervious to falls and other frustrations, he is more easily able to substitute other adults for his mother to get reassurance.

Mahler emphasizes the importance to emotional development of the capacity to walk, which allows the child to test reality and his own control and mastery of the world. Individuation and identity formation are augmented. The mother both renounces and continues to possess the child's body. Delay in the child's locomotion results in a concomitant delay in the experience of a love affair with the world. Walking thus has great symbolic meaning for both mother and child, indicating to the mother that the child will make it and adding to the child's developing self-esteem.

The child's mood can be described as low keyed in mother's absence. Gestures and performance are slowed down, interest in surroundings diminished, and the child appears preoccupied with inwardly concentrated attention, with "imaging." When a person other than the mother actively attempts to comfort the child, his emotional balance is lost, and tears result. The low-keyed state ends with mother's return. This state, and the inferred attempt to image the mother, is seen by Mahler as a miniature anaclitic depression and an attempt to hold on to the ideal state of the self.

A disturbed practicing subphase may include greater than average separation anxiety, more than average shadowing of the mother or impulsive darting away from her, and excessive sleep disturbance.

The Third Subphase: Rapprochement (17-24 months)

In the early rapprochement subphase, mother is no longer just home base, but also the person with whom the child wishes to share his discoveries, wanting her interest and participation. His elation with locomotion wanes, and he shifts to a wish for social interaction with his mother and with other children. For both boys and girls, the discovery of anatomical differences produces a sense of their own bodies. For girls, the penis symbolizes what other children have that they cannot get, and for both boys and girls a claim to gender identity ensues. The child shows a characteristic negativity toward mother, which results both from a sense of expanded autonomy and a more intense recognition of the father.

The child reacts more strongly to mother's absence, not with low-keyedness, but with increased activity and restlessness. Both responses indicate sadness, but the activity is seen as a defense instituted against that painful emotion. The child can now cope better and can relate to substitute adults and engage in symbolic play to master the separation experience. The period of early rapprochement ends at about 18 months and appears to be a temporary consolidation and acceptance of separation; however, harbingers exist of impending crisis, including almost ubiquitous temper tantrums, vulnerability, rage, helplessness, recurrence of stranger reactions, and beginning loyalty conflicts between mother and others.

As awareness of separateness grows, there is an increased need for the object's love. This constitutes the basis for rapprochement. During this period there is a strong need for optimal emotional availability of the mother. It is the mother's love of the toddler and her acceptance of his ambivalence that enables him to cathect his self-representation with neutralized energy. The father is of special importance also during this period.

Shadowing and darting away are two behaviors characteristic of this subphase and indicate the wish for reunion and the fear of reengulfment. Concomitant with the acquisition of skills and perceptual cognitive capacities, there has been an increasingly clear differentiation of the intrapsychic representations of object and self; thus, the toddler must cope with the world on his own, as a small, helpless, separate individual, unable to command relief merely by feeling the need for it.

The rapprochement crisis proper occurs from about 18 to 22 months and is characterized by conflicts deriving from the desire to be separate, grand, and omnipotent, and yet have the mother fulfill wishes without having to recognize that help comes from the outside. The child's mood changes to one characterized by dissatisfaction, insatiability, temper tantrums, and, especially, ambivalence. The mother is used as an extension of the self to deny separateness. The mother, too, shows anxiety about separation, and where mother is dissatisfied with her child, or anxious about him, or aloof from him, the normal rapprochement patterns become exaggerated.

During this period the child shows a realization of his own limitations and relative helplessness. A new capacity for empathy and higher level identifications develops. The child is especially aware of and sensitive to his mother's whereabouts. Piaget's (1952) object permanence is already achieved, so the child can conceive of mother being elsewhere and found again, which is often reassuring; but many demonstrate difficulty in leave taking from their mothers, with clinging behaviors and depression. Splitting as a defense is now possible. Other people become the bad mother; the good mother is longed for, but exists in fantasy only, and the real mother becomes a source of dissatisfaction on her return, leading the child either to ignore the returning mother or to avoid her.

As the rapprochement crisis is resolved, the child finds an optimal distance from mother, exercising autonomy and sociability and avoiding the ambivalence that proximity to mother might bring. By this age, children reveal less phase-specific behavior and more individual differences. Boys and girls seem very different for the first time, with boys being more disengaged from mother and girls being more engaged with her, demanding closeness in an ambivalent fashion and blaming her for the lack of a penis. Boys are less overtly concerned with sexual differences.

The developmental tasks for the child at the height of the separation-individuation struggle are enormous. Conflicts about oral, anal, and early genital drives all meet, and in addition there is a need to renounce symbiotic omnipotence. The belief in the mother's omnipotence, too, is shaken. Superego development begins with intensified vulnerability to the threat of losing the object's love. Where development has been less than optimal, the ambivalence conflict in relation to mother that became discernible during the rapprochement subphase is unresolved, as revealed in rapidly alternating clinging and negativistic behaviors. These reflect an ambitendency not yet internalized. Excessive splitting may be revealed as well.

The Fourth Subphase: Consolidation of Individuality and the Beginning of Emotional Object Constancy (24-26 Months and Beyond)

The tasks of this subphase are the achievement of definite, and in some ways lifelong, individuality, the attainment of a certain degree of object constancy, and structuralization of the ego and beginning development of the superego.

The establishment of object constancy depends on the gradual internalization of a constant, positively cathected inner image of the mother. It depends also on the cognitive attainment of object permanence, a stable sense of entity (self-boundaries), and a primitive consolidation of gender identity. Necessary attainments include as well unification of good and bad objects into whole object representations, fusion of aggressive and libidinal drives, tempering of hatred for the object when aggression is intense, and not rejecting the love object for another when the former is no longer satisfying.

Separations from the mother during the fourth, open-ended subphase are influenced by the degree of ambivalence in the relationship. When mother's leaving stirs up expressed or unexpressed anger and longing, the child cannot easily maintain her image in his mind. During this period, verbal communication develops rapidly, play becomes more purposeful and constructive, and fantasy play, role play, and make believe are initiated. A sense of time develops, along with a capacity to tolerate delay of gratification. The child is resistant to demands of adults and often reveals an unrealistic wish for autonomy. The recurrent mild or moderate negativism of this period is essential to the establishment of identity. Individuation proceeds.

During the earlier part of this subphase, the less predictably reliable or more intrusive the love object, the more does this object remain or become an unassimilated foreign body, a bad introject, and the child shows an increased tendency to identify and confuse the self-image with this bad introject. In such cases, during the rapprochement period, aggression sweeps away the good object and the good self-representation, as is indicated by an increase of temper tantrums and increase of coercion of mother to function as an external ego. Marked ambivalence may ensue, marring development toward object constancy and sound secondary narcissism.

The mother should be available to the child as a mental representation in the mother's absence, the first basis of this availability being the actual mother-child relationship. Threats to the establishment of object constancy and separate individual functioning stem from the pressure of drive maturation, confronting the child with new tasks (for example, toilet training) and new fears (for example, castration fears). Mahler demonstrates that these fears affect budding object constancy and self-development, particularly when there is developmental trauma. The achievement of both object constancy and individuality is easily challenged by struggles around toilet training and by awareness of anatomical differences, which awareness poses a threat to the girl's narcissism and the boy's body integrity.

KOHUT, MAHLER, AND INFANT RESEARCH

At this point we will discuss Mahler's formulations from the perspective of Kohut's developmental framework and at the same time from the perspective that current infant research provides not only for Mahler but for Kohut as well. We will take in turn each phase and subphase identified by Mahler.

Beginning with a comparison with Mahler's autistic phase, then, it must be said that Kohut never did posit a phase in which there is no psychological connection whatsoever to the outside world or to important others; rather, he (Kohut, 1971) postulated reconstructively, early in his articulation of self psychology, a primitive self-selfobject bond wherein the nuclear self experiences the other as part of its self in an egocentric fashion. This may be seen as a quasi-autistic phase in that, from the observer's objective point of view, there is a self and an other, but from the subjective view of the self, there is only an impersonal function in the surround that enhances the self.

By 1977, Kohut demurred entirely from such speculation on the self of the presymbolic infant, postulating only a "virtual self," that is, the self of the infant as envisioned in the mind of the parent. Other self psychologists have speculated more freely about the emergent self in the early months of life. They see, in contrast to Mahler, the infant as active, engaged, and intent upon communication (Basch, 1983), with a healthy cohesiveness (Tolpin, 1980), and immersed within a self-selfobject unit.

As to current infant research and Mahler's (1968) concept of autism, we need say no more than there has for decades been strong and increasing evidence that would sweep aside any notion of a normally endowed infant incapable of connection to the outside world. Numerous empirical studies demonstrate that the infant is an active, eager learner, prewired and well equipped for communications and interactions with the environment from the very beginning. Stern (1985), who has synthesized much current infant observation, puts forward an "observed infant" based on this synthesis. That this observed infant is consistent with "Kohut's baby" (Tolpin, 1971, 1980), much more so than with "Mahler's baby" is no accident. Self psychology has endeavored to remain *au courant* with infant research and to change its theories in accordance with it. Mahler and classical analysis attempt the same but carry complex theoretical baggage that makes this task more difficult. For example, Mahler incorporates Freud's (1900) postulate of the extremely young infant living initially in solipsistic isolation and employing hallucinatory wish fulfillment to satisfy need. To remain consistent with this Freudian idea, Mahler creates such concepts as delusions of fusion to defend against unbearable separateness. Further, she focuses on Freud's (1911) postulate of fantasy as primary and reality as secondary in the infant. All of this contrasts with infant research findings, which postulate the infant as not only, as previously stated, connected with others from birth on, but also as reality based from the very beginning. Current infant researchers hold that the infant's capacity for fantasy and defense formation, attributed by Mahler to the two-month-old, only originates at the age of 18 months, when the infant has achieved symbolic thought. Mahler's deep fealty to Freud seems to have locked her into a model inconsistent with current developmental observations; Kohut and self psychology, on the other hand, having less fealty, have been free to drop such outdated postulates.

It is in Mahler's concept of the symbiotic phase that she and Kohut, at least initially, appear to have been most closely linked theoretically. Kohut (1971) writes of the archaic self-selfobject merger in the mirror transference, which is conceptualized to resonate with a stage in normal development, dating back to the first years of life, characterized by a grandiose self in relation to a mirroring selfobject. While that formulation may have appeared consistent with the concept of symbiosis, the congruence in theory was weakened somewhat when Kohut (1977) demurred by postulating only the virtual self up to 18 months. Moreover, once self psychology's definition of the selfobject concept was reformulated so that archaic fusion was no longer viewed as an obligatory aspect of normal development, the two theories were more widely divergent.

Current infant research strongly supports the importance to normal development of the close connectedness between the child and the primary caregiver from birth on, consistent with the emotional significance of both Mahler's symbiosis and Kohut's selfobject merger; however, infant researchers, and Stern (1985) in particular, criticize the view of the infant as perceptually unable to distinguish self from other. Rather, Stern considers the human being to be equipped at birth with predesigned emergent structures that prepare him to develop very early totally separate cognitive schemas of self and other. Lichtenberg (1983) adds that the theory of symbiosis is contested by the active role of the infant as behavioral initiator of interaction.

All of this implies that a truly symbiotic phase in normal development *à la* Mahler is improbable and requires concomitant modification in important aspects of her separation-individuation process. That process postulates a need to separate out of *something,* to hatch out of *something,* and the something is conceived of by Mahler as a dual unity. The achievement of connectedness to the other is postulated as an epigenetic given in normal development. In contrast, infant research stipulates a self perceived as separate from the other almost from the start, with the achievement of autonomy being but one of the central tasks of the infant, on a par with, but *only* on a par with, the equally important task of achieving a capacity for interdependence. The state of interdependence, then, is not seen as happening automatically in the infant as a passive acquisition, but rather as a relationship the infant must actively endeavor to construct for himself or herself.

Again, self psychology, because of its comparative freedom to make theoretical change, has more or less adopted the view that infant observation brings to the field. It was for this reason, we believe, that the definition of the selfobject construct was rethought to eliminate the now discredited (at least by most developmentalists) notion of a normal developmental phase characterized by a perception of self merged with other. Self-selfobject relationships are still seen as imperative throughout the life cycle, but no normal self-other fusion or confusion is postulated as an inevitable phase of normal development.

We will now turn to the separation-individuation phase proper. Rather than contrast Kohut and Mahler specifically in terms of the subphases of separation-individuation as against the unfolding of the bipolar self, with its three sectors and concomitant selfobjects, we will instead focus more globally on a contrast of their respective views of development during that entire time period. We do so because Kohut did not, for the most part, so particularize and date events in the child's developmental course; he was not, after all, an observer of children, as was Mahler, but a reconstructor of the childhood of his patients. We assume a basic familiarity with the overall theoretical constructs of Kohut on the part of the reader, as we did not with Mahler.

To begin with, as we have seen, Mahler points to a gradually increasing independence from the primary caregiver as *the* important goal for the normally developing child. That is, Mahler identifies as the task of the first three years of life intrapsychic separation from the mother and the attainment of autonomy. Her formulations thus require, as indicated earlier, a separation out of a symbiotic unity. Kohut, on the other hand, conceptualizes the caregiver from the point of view of the self as supplying primitive selfobject functions, which, as maturation proceeds, are maintained increasingly by the self through the development of self-structure via transmuting internalization. In addition, there is a decreasing requirement for physical proximity to the primary selfobject caregiver as self-structure is consolidated, and selfobject need becomes less peremptory. But the main function of this structure building is to permit a developmental progression from primitive to more mature selfobject need and need fulfillment. The requirement for the selfobject function remains.

Thus, while there is an apparent similarity in view between Kohut's concept of improved and consolidated self-structure via transmuting internalization and Mahler's concept of increasing autonomy from caregivers via ego development, there is a difference between them; and it was this difference that was of vital importance to Kohut. Kohut viewed the goal of autonomy from supporting caregivers, so significant to Mahler and to mainstream analysis as well, as carrying with it a hidden moralistic stance, which self psychology, with its emphasis on the need for selfobject experiences throughout life, assiduously avoids. The issue of autonomy from supporting objects, recognized by mainstream analysis as a goal of normal development, versus Kohut's assertion of a normal lifelong dependence on selfobjects was for Kohut one indication of an overall difference in world view between his framework and that of classical analysis in general and Mahler in particular that made an integration between their developmental schemas impossible.

Infant research may help us resolve this difference between Mahler and Kohut. Kohut's position regarding the normality of lifelong selfobject needs seems to be confirmed by infant observation. Stern (1985) concludes, on the basis of his synthesis of this research, that from the very beginning, the individual's life is always social. In infancy, with development of the core self taking place from two to six months, most of what the infant does, feels, and perceives occurs in the subjectively perceived context of human relationships. And with the acquisition of cued memory at that time, henceforth, subjective experiences throughout life are largely social for all of us whether we are alone or not; the experience of self with a self-regulating other and a self-attuning other as a subjective reality is pervasive.

Stern's stance implies that the normal person, from birth to death, is never completely autonomous, always reliant for self-sustenance either on the internal, psychological presence of an other or on the external presence of an other. The other is not seen as fused with the self; rather, it is perceived as a separate entity that has an all-important role to play in self experience.

It is important to note here the basis for Stern's concluding from his reading of the newest infant observational research that the infant experiences the psychological presence of important others even when he or she is not in their company. Stern postulates that the infant has a capacity for an evocativelike memory, making it possible for interactions with significant others to be layed down in memory, to be retrieved spontaneously when only aspects, or cues, of the remembered experience are present.

For example, the mother and infant play together with a particular rattle, to the infant's delighted excitement. The interaction, occurring many times over, is generalized and layed down in the infant's memory. Subsequently, when the infant, now alone, plays with that same rattle, a presence of the mother, along with the excitement experienced with her, is evoked by the rattle, the infant subjectively experiencing the mother's active presence even in her absence. It is this capacity to evoke the mother's presence even in her absence that enables the child to progress without anxious disruption in the face of mother's not being there to soothe, comfort, stimulate, and amuse him at all times. Heretofore it was understood by cognitive psychologists (e.g. Piaget, 1952; Piaget and Inhilder, 1966) and accepted by mainstream analysts that such evocative memory was not possible until 18 months (the advent of object permanence). Positive affective attachment to the image of the mother as a reassurance in her absence, even in the face of subjective feelings of anger and hostility toward her, was not thought to be possible for the infant until 36 months, the advent of libidinal object constancy. Before that age, the infant is viewed by Mahler as unable to retain in his or her mind the picture of the ambivalently loved mother during her absence. And it is perhaps for this reason that the issue of the infant's separation from the mother has such high priority in Mahler's theory. Thus for Mahler, once the toddler has achieved object constancy, near the end of the separation-individuation sequence, the issue of separation has been for the most part resolved; with libidinal object constancy, the normally developing toddler can endure the mother's absence with relative comfort and without trauma. However, with the new discovery of early, evocativelike memory, the issue of separation ceases to be consigned to a particular time period and becomes, instead, an issue of potential importance throughout the life cycle. In self psychology terms, relatively nontraumatic versus traumatic experiences with separation from the other are mainly dependent on how successful or unsuccessful that other has been in supplying selfobject functions, and this is true from early infancy throughout adulthood. Autonomy, too, becomes a lifelong issue, not relegated to any phase or age; moreover, it no longer serves as a criterion for maturity.

Stern (1985) makes another point in the Mahler-Kohut disagreement concerning autonomy as a goal of development. He states that the normal infant, with its capacity for representation of experiences with important others always available to him in time of need, has an inborn ability to adjust to the requirement for either independence or interdependence, and that how much of each is required for adequate adaptation depends on the culture into which he is born. Thus, autonomy from and interdependence with others are best understood as relative issues. A moralistic stance is uncalled for, and it is just this avoidance of a moralistic position that will endure as Kohut's contribution to these issues.

We will now turn to specific concepts arising out of particular subphases in the separation-individuation process in order to contrast them first with Kohut's formulations and then with current data from infant observation. During the subphases of differentiation and practicing, Mahler focuses on the checking-back-to-mother pattern, calling it the most important normal pattern of cognitive and emotional development. Checking back is postulated to be a defense against separation anxiety. Kohut, obviously using Mahler's observations to support his own thinking, views checking back, instead, in support of his own concepts of the mirroring selfobject and the grandiose self, as the infant's way to achieve reassuring affirmation from the mother. The infant's developing capacity to become more and more physically distant from the caregiver is viewed by Kohut not as a diminution of anxiety because of increasing autonomy, as in Mahler's schema, but rather, as an indication of the progression from primitive to more mature selfobject ties. Hence, excessive stranger anxiety, seen by Mahler as a failure to acquire basic trust, becomes for Kohut (1984) an indication of self-fragility requiring a checking-back-to-mother for a mirroring reaffirmation of the selfobject bond. This is a subtle difference, with the emphasis in self psychology on the state of the self; whereas in separation-individuation theory, the emphasis is more on the trust in the new object relationship on the way to the achievement of object constancy and only secondarily on the integrity of the self. However, refueling and perking up—Mahler's phrases for the practicing subphase child's ability to use the mother as a means for reconstituting when the child feels threatened by new exploration—are similar to Kohut's concept of mirroring, which restores the self. Self-cohesiveness and self-constancy do seem to be closely related concepts, though based on different theoretical formulations (Shane and Shane, 1980).

Stern (1985), in his observation of children in this time period as they move away from mother and check back for refueling or mirroring, emphasizes that the child's need is not always for self-regulation in these instances, as is implied by Kohut, but is equally for intersubjective sharing and for verbal affirmation, more consistent with Mahler.

Mahler makes a valuable contribution, too, in terms of the rapprochement subphase, characterized by the child's ambivalent and uneasy return to mother after a period of confidence in turning toward the larger environment, as well as in her description of subphase resolution. Contained in this description are theoretical assumptions about an aggressive drive that create a nidus of divergence between her views and Kohut's theoretical frame of reference.

In writing about fusion of drive energies as prerequisite to resolution of the rapprochement crisis, Mahler seems faithful to the classical Freudian dual drive theory wherein an aggressive drive is postulated as co-equal with the libidinal drive, inborn, and not dependent on environmental frustration for activation. While Mahler herself did not emphasize this aspect of the aggressive drive, Kohut distinguished himself from Mahler in particular, and classical analysis in general, on this basis. Kohut pointed to the fact that the mainstream view of aggression as innately destructive does not fit with data he derived from the clinical situation. He asserted that there was no concurrence between his developmental views and those of Mahler, because, again, he distinguished himself from a world view that saw aggression as an inevitably destructive impulsion, committing himself instead to a view of aggression as reactive to frustration.

As a matter of fact, infant observation supports Kohut in this view. Parens (1979) conducted a developmental study on infants and children in interaction with their mothers that demonstrated the likelihood that destructive aggression is not inborn but instead is a reactive response deriving from unempathic interference with the child's assertiveness, which assertiveness *is* seen by Parens as inborn. What is interesting here is that Parens is a classical analyst whose research was organized by Mahlerian thinking. In turn, his work influenced Mahler and her co-workers, creating ultimately a closer fit between Kohut's views and those of Mahler in this regard (Shane and Shane, 1983).

As a final comment regarding these two theories of child development, it is important to note that Mahler conceptualizes the attainment of individuality, or self-constancy, as a lifelong task. This is not quite the same as Kohut's contention that the self requires selfobject functions throughout life, but perhaps their views are not that far apart after all. If self-constancy continues to require support from the environment, then autonomy, despite its importance to Mahler's developmental progression, is never fully attained. Mahler would postulate that dependency on the environment diminishes; Kohut would postulate that the dependency itself does not diminish, but rather that the quality of the required selfobject tie and selfobject sustenance achieves greater maturity.

We must conclude that the greatest difference between Kohut and Mahler, then, lies in their underlying theoretical frameworks, not in the particulars of their observations on the developing individual. We have followed closely the creative elaboration of these two psychoanalytic innovators; each has influenced as well as antagonized the other, and both have enriched the psychoanalytic world.

REFERENCES

Basch, M. (1983), Empathic understanding: A review of the concept and some theoretical considerations. *J. Amer. Psychoanal. Assn.,* 31: 101–126.

Freud, S. (1900) The interpretation of dreams. *Standard Edition,* 4 & 5. London: Hogarth Press, 1953.

——— (1905), three essays on the theory of sexuality. *Standard Edition,* 7:125–243. London: Hogarth Press, 1953.

——— (1911), Formulations on the two principles of mental functioning. *Standard Edition,* 12:215. London: Hogarth Press, 1958.

——— (1915), Observations on transference love. *Standard Edition,* 12: 157–171. London: Hogarth Press, 1958.

——— (1920), Beyond the pleasure principle. *Standard Edition,* 18:7–64. London: Hogarth Press, 1955.

——— (1923), the ego and the id. *Standard Edition,* 19:3–66. London: Hogarth Press, 1961.

——— (1926), Inhibitions, symptoms and anxiety. *Standard Edition,* 20: 77–175. London: Hogarth Press, 1959.

Greenacre, P. (1957). The childhood of the artist: Libidinal phase development and giftedness. *The Psychoanalytic Study of the Child,* 12:27–72. New York: International Universities Press.

Harley, M. & Weil, A. (1979), *The Selected Papers of Margaret S. Mahler,* Vol. 1. New York: Aronson.

Kohut, H. (1971), *The Analysis of the Self.* New York: International Universities Press.

_____ (1977), *The Restoration of the Self.* New York: International Universities Press.

_____ (1980), Reflection. In: *Advances in Self Psychology,* ed. A. Goldberg. New York: International Universities Press.

_____ (1984), *How Does Analysis Cure?* ed. A. Goldberg & P.E. Stepansky. Chicago: University of Chicago Press.

Lichtenberg, J. D. (1983), *Psychoanalysis and Infant Research.* Hillsdale, NJ: The Analytic Press.

Mahler, M. (1979), *Selected Papers of Margaret S. Mahler.* New York: Aronson.

_____ & Furer, M. (1968), *On Human Symbiosis and the Vicissitudes of Individuation.* New York: International Universities Press.

_____ Pine F. & Bergman, A. (1975), *The Psychological Birth of the Human Infant.* New York: Basic Books.

Parens, H. (1979), *Development of Aggression in Early Childhood.* New York & London: Jason Aronson.

Piaget, J. (1952), *The Origins of Intelligence in Children.* New York: International Universities Press.

_____ & Inhelder, B. (1966), *The Psychology of the Child.* New York: Basic Books, 1969.

Shane, M. & Shane, E. (1980), Psychoanalytic developmental theories of the self: An integration. In: *Advances in Self Psychology,* ed. A. Goldberg. New York: International Universities Press.

_____ & _____ (1983). The strands of aggression: A confluence of data. *Psychoanalytic Inquiry,* 4:263–281.

_____ & _____ (1985), Change and integration in psychoanalytic developmental theory. *New Ideas in Psychoanalysis,* ed. C.F. Settlage & R. Brockbank. Hillsdale, NJ: The Analytic Press, pp. 69–82.

_____ & _____ (1988), Pathways to integration: Adding to the self psychology model. *Learning from Kohut: Progress in Self Psychology, Vol. 4,* ed. A. Goldberg. Hillsdale, NJ: The Analytic Press, pp. 71–77.

Spitz, R. (1965), *The First Year of Life.* New York: International Universities Press.

Stern, D. (1985), *The Interpersonal World of the Infant.* New York: Basic Books.

Tolpin, M. (1971), On the beginnings of the cohesive self. *The Psychoanalytic Study of the Child,* 26:316–352. New York: Quadrangle.

_____ (1980), Discussion of psychoanalytic developmental theories of the self: An integration, by M. Shane and E. Shane. In: *Advances in Self Psychology,* ed. A. Goldberg. New York: International Universities Press.

Part V

Summarizing Reflections

20

Self Psychology
A Post-Kohutian View

JOHN E. GEDO

The task of evaluating Heinz Kohut's "self psychology" some five years after his death is particularly difficult for me, because I was Kohut's earliest adherent as well as the person he looked upon as the first apostate from his cause. Heinz never mastered his sense of betrayal as a result of my inability to become his disciple; this unspoken reproach was conveyed only in the tears of his widow when I belatedly offered her my condolences. Gallantly, she said that the outcome was not anyone's fault: "It could not be helped." And she asked me whether I had any idea of how much I had meant to her husband. Yes, I did.

De mortuis nil nisi bonum: I wish I could confine this essay to the testimony that in my view Kohut's personal contribution to psychoanalysis was so important that in the past two decades all pioneering work in the field deserves to be called "post-Kohutian." Of course, I already said as much at the celebration honoring Heinz on his 60th birthday (see Gedo, 1975a); for many years now, my own intellectual work has invariably focused on the specifics of the complex disagreements between us (see Gedo and Goldberg, 1973, chap. 5; Gedo, 1979, pp. 29–31, 165–67, 176–78, 181, 209–10, 220–21; 1980; 1981, chaps. 4–7; 1984, chap. 10; 1986, chaps. 7 and 8). The failure of contributions to the literature of self psychology ever to take note of this extended critique has not made it easier for me to remain dispassionate about these difficult matters.

Of course, I could place the emphasis on the other side of the coin: the invitation to contribute a chapter to this volume should constitute sufficient acknowledgment that I have given Kohut's contribution careful thought. Indeed, I have remained on excellent terms with some of the leading contributors to self psychology, so that I know that many of Kohut's present-day adherents in fact share some of my unfavorable opinions about various discrete aspects of Kohut's heterogeneous writings or the practices prevalent within the movement he founded. I can therefore empathize with the need of certain members of an embattled minority to ignore those who question the truth of its cause; whenever such a challenge comes from former supporters, it is particularly likely to be treated as anathema.

As a matter of fact, it was my initial articulation of disquiet about Kohut's treatment recommendations that led to the unpleasantness that compelled me to dissociate myself from Heinz's circle. To do him justice, Kohut himself never voiced any objection to my dissent; rather, he set about trying to rebut my point of view (see Kohut, 1977, chap. 1). In putting forth the claim that the appropriate end-point of the psychoanalytic treatment of disturbances involving the self—disorders that he was later to define so as to include all psychopathology!—is the erection of compensatory mental structures, Kohut abandoned the psychoanalytic consensus that the proximate aim of treatment is to *know,* in favor of the ambition to effect a cure. Kohut was admirably clear about his radical departure from Freudian premises and values; in the last decade of his life he consistently repeated that he wished to replace insight with *empathy* as the primary goal of his therapeutic enterprise.

Obviously, such differences of opinion are both legitimate and commonplace; similar disagreements about fundamental premises led to the ruptures between Freud and Adler (Stepansky, 1983) as well as between Freud and Jung (Gedo, 1983). In such circumstances, neither protagonist is right or wrong: both are involved in disparate enterprises. In the present instance, the unanswered question is whether Kohut's enterprise can still be regarded as part of psychoanalysis, in view of his rejection of some of Freud's basic goals and values.

I feel very uneasy about assuming the mantle of Grand Inquisitor—after all, some sectarians might very easily claim that my own work is too unorthodox for their taste!—and will therefore make no attempt to pronounce judgment on the psychoanalytic credentials of self psychology. Suffice it to say that there seems to be a degree of uncertainty on this very question, even among Kohut's heirs: on one hand, there are those who continue to see themselves as psychoanalysts and assert (as did Goldberg, 1978) that interpretation is the crucial curative factor in their work; on the other hand, there are many who feel no allegiance to psychoanalysis and openly declare their adherence to a new therapeutic discipline (see Baker and Baker, 1987).

If self psychology is a novel professional discipline offering a new brand of psychotherapy, I have nothing to say about it, just as I have nothing to say about its countless competitors in the clinical marketplace. Judiciously conducted (see Basch, 1980) or administered with sufficient charisma, it is a system that is doubtless just as effective as most others. It is quite a different matter to perform psychoanalysis in accordance with self-psychological assumptions, and that is the enterprise I propose to highlight in this essay. Unfortunately, in actual practice many clinicians obfuscate in this regard: for example, not long ago, as a guest instructor at a reputable psychoanalytic institute, I was presented a case report wherein the candidate-analyst (with the approval of his supervisor) decided, entirely on the basis of a brief history obtained in the initial consultation, on a therapeutic prescription of providing positively-toned "mirroring." I suspect that Kohut would have been horrified to learn of such misuse of his ideas to adulterate psychoanalysis with the dross of a manipulated "corrective emotional experience." At least, I hope so.

From my vantage point, one of the primary virtues of self psychology is its freedom from the legacy of the metapsychology that organized psychoanalytic thinking for some 75 years. This advantage was not easily gained: when he embarked on his pioneering work, Kohut was the heir apparent of Heinz Hartmann, and through 1972 his writings were carefully cast in the mold of Hartmann's psychoeconomic postulates. It was only after Hartmann's death and Anna Freud's rejection of his proposed clinical innovations that Kohut was willing to listen to those of his friends—Michael Basch, Arnold Goldberg, and I—who had for years been urging him to abandon these untenable hypotheses. Clearly, many theoreticians who do not accept Kohut's point of view about clinical issues concur with his rejection of Freud's metapsychology (see Gill and Holzman, 1976); in American psychoanalysis, priority in this regard belongs to the students of David Rapaport.

For a few years, Kohut pursued his clinical investigations—

which convinced him that drive theory was irrelevant to the issues he was attempting to conceptualize—without making a serious effort to think through the consequences of his findings for psychoanalytic theory as a whole. As a result of this choice of focus, he was content to use what he called two "complementary" theories (in analogy with the dual physical theories of light); this phase of his work was characterized by the distinction he made between "Tragic Man," unable to fulfill his own ambitions or to meet his ideals, and "Guilty Man," in conflict between his conscience and his appetites. In retrospect, this artificial dichotomy only divided the segment of the psychoanalytic field Kohut felt ready to view in terms of his own concepts from the residual issues he still saw as within the framework of traditional clinical theories.

In his posthumous book, Kohut (1984) reversed himself on this score: he abandoned the self-indulgence of using two uncoordinated theoretical schemata simultaneously in favor of a unified self-psychological conceptualization, based on the notion of self-selfobject relations. Before commenting on the adequacy of this proposal as a replacement for Freud's drive theories as a unifying framework for psychoanalysis, I should state that some of his students preceded Kohut in concluding that a psychology of the self must be able to account for all of the clinical phenomena encountered in the analytic situation. In particular, Terman (1976) showed that oedipal vicissitudes may be understood from the viewpoint of their impact on self-esteem and self-cohesion. My own earlier critiques of Kohut raised repeated objections to the artificiality of the Tragic Man versus Guilty Man distinction. I do not know, of course, whether Kohut bothered to read my publications after the estrangement between us, although I have very strong reasons to believe that my opinions continued to weigh heavily with him.

What did Kohut's ultimate psychological system, that of selfobject needs, selfobject functions, and self-selfobject relations, imply about human nature? Overall, this conception of mental life regards bonding with a need-satisfying object as the sole norm of human existence, the only source of significant motives, and the only potential cause of maladaptation. Even if Kohut had broader criteria for selfobject functions than in fact he did, this view of mental life seems exceedingly restrictive: as Stern (1985), among others, has concluded, much of human existence even during infancy presupposes solitude. But Kohut (1977, 1978) defined selfobject needs in an extraordinarily narrow manner, confining them to those issues implicated in the regulation of self-esteem, namely, the idealization and subject-centered grandiosity he encountered in the consulting room.

However ubiquitous these human propensities may be, they do not adequately encompass even those contingencies evoked in the dyadic context of the psychoanalytic situation. At the very end of his life, Kohut (1984) began to realize that his classification of selfobject functions was incomplete. As a first step to remedy this deficiency, he proposed elevating so-called twinship transferences to the same conceptual plane hitherto occupied by idealizing and mirror transferences alone. What he failed to acknowledge was the probability that the need for an alter ego is much broader and more fundamental than the "narcissistic transferences" he had previously described (Kohut, 1968, 1971)—that the search for "twinship" is a consequence of lacunae in the patient's psychological skills, whereas idealization of others and the wish for affirmation are merely secondary effects of developmental difficulties of that kind (see Gedo, 1988).

Kohut's ultimate legacy to his followers is therefore likely to be this warning from the grave not to congeal his writings into self-psychological dogma, for in the backlash of the condemnation of his work for reductionism, the attempted construction of a finished theoretical system threatens to obscure his valuable clinical discoveries. Arguments trying to prove that self psychology is less vulnerable on that score than are other reductionistic systems, such as Hartmann's ego psychology, are not likely to impress the coming generation of psychoanalysts, who will demand a clinical theory that accounts for the observations of every analytic faction.

From the clinical point of view, the greatest deficiency of Kohut's system is not its deemphasis of oedipal issues, as certain analytic traditionalists would have it. It is, in fact, perfectly feasible to deal with those conflicts through a self-psychological framework (see Terman, 1984–85). In my judgment, self psychology is weakest in its underemphasis on the effects of prior structuralization on the regulation of behavior. As a consequence, it promotes excessive optimism about the possibility of altering the personality by means of new (more empathic) experiences, without going to the trouble of painstakingly undoing existing pathogenic structures. Perhaps the most obvious example of this tendency is the neglect of patients' continuing hostile dispositions, or other current dynamics, in favor of stressing that these were brought about by various noxious experiences suffered in childhood. But this selective inattention is by no means unique; Kohut has, in general, taken insufficient note of the unfavorable consequences for later adaptation of early identifications. That is how he blundered into the untenable position about the Oedipus complex he adopted in his posthumous book (Kohut, 1984): he asserted that pathological outcomes of these developmental vicissitudes are invariably the results of the parents' unempathic responses to the child's *current* behavior. Life is more complicated than that—in many instances, even in early childhood, it is the shadow of the past that has fallen upon the present.

A second major problem left unresolved by self psychology is an internal contradiction concerning the young child's reactions to failures on the part of caretakers to provide optimal life experiences. Kohut (1978, p. 929; Kohut and Wolf, 1978, esp. p. 416) reached the conclusion that the resultant frustrations (and the psychopathological sequelae that follow) are bound to be felt as injuries inflicted by the unempathic and disappointing "selfobjects." Indeed, on occasion Kohut (1977, 1984) went further, actually endorsing the accuracy of such an infantile view of the world by asserting that caretakers can be expected to perform empathically enough to avoid the formation of psychopathology. At the same time, Kohut (1971) never repudiated his definition of selfobject as a term that denotes a caretaker experienced as part of the subject's volitional system. He often tried to illuminate this notion through the metaphor of a person's startled reaction to a paralyzed limb that no longer carries out his intentions. If this comparison of the reaction to a selfobject failure to a somatic catastrophe is apt, as I believe it is, it cannot at the same time be true that the victim of such a misfortune will attribute its causation to the caretaker/selfobject. He would, in fact, be more likely to experience it irrationally as a personal failure.

To be more precise: analysands may often try to blame their psychopathology on the failures of their caretakers, but just as frequently they may assign the blame to themselves, and in many cases they are well aware that the crystallization of the personality is too complex a matter to be understood in terms of causation by specific disappointments. In other words, patients' attitudes in adult life are not direct reflections of their initial childhood reactions to various crucial experiences, and those potentially pathogenic reactions cannot be eliminated from the mental life of analysands through empathy with childhood disappointments alone.

On paper, such exaggeration of the responsibility of caretakers for whatever goes wrong in early development may look like a relatively minor flaw in Kohut's system. I see it as a *major* problem because of its intimate connection with the role of empathy in Kohut's theory of treatment. Although he was at times explicit about the view that empathy is merely a method of cognition (see Kohut, 1971, p. 300), in the main Kohut (1978) avowed that the analyst should provide patients with "empathic acceptance" (p. 899). Goldberg (1978) defined analytic empathy as "the proper feeling for and fitting together of the patient's needs and the analyst's response" (p. 8). Consequently, self psychology seems to expect that infantile attitudes of entitlement have to be validated by the analyst, that the analysand's persisting rage should be understood as the only appropriate response to the frustration of "selfobject needs," and that all misfortunes in early life should have been mastered through empathic parenting.

I have little doubt that a substantial number of patients may accept such authoritative verdicts, experience some diminution of guilt and shame, and even become less rageful as a result of such reassurance. In other words, this approach is often therapeutic, but its beneficial results are obtained by means of a shared illusion, the echo of Rousseau's "noble savage" as the innocent babe. For even in those instances where childhood rage was provoked by parental failures (and, more emphatically, in all cases in which the childhood reaction was *not* caused by such errors), analysands can transcend these archaic transactions only if they grasp their inappropriateness in an adult context. And in the majority of cases children do not, in fact, end up disappointed with their caretakers; to the contrary, they tend to erect reaction formations against any disillusionment they may have suffered (see Gedo, 1975b).

En passant, it is worth mentioning that many self psychologists have espoused a view of therapeutic empathy that Kohut himself would certainly have rejected: in their minds, empathy requires the application of Kohut's interpretive schema (see Schwaber, 1987). To justify this ideological prejudice, they caricature alternative positions, usually by claiming that non-self-psychological theories are *ipso facto* experience-distant, incapable of articulating the analysand's subjectivity, and can only lead to an outrageously frustrating therapeutic ambience. To be sure, these self-promoting attitudes seldom find their way into print, but I have encountered them with some frequency in personal discussions, and I have even heard them expressed in public meetings.

Although Kohut himself never indulged in such ideological terrorism, he was guilty of accusing those who would not accept his dictum that reliance on selfobjects is expectable throughout the life span of being unable to see the truth because of personal psychopathology (Kohut, 1984). I wonder whether he would have admitted, in this ultimate period of his life and work, that his own viewpoint about the lifelong persistence of selfobject needs was a reflection of *his* personal preferences? Earlier in his career, when I was on the best of terms with him, Kohut was proud to acknowledge that his insights about what he then called the narcissistic disorders were gained through introspective, self-analytic work—in other words, that the selfobject needs he had first discerned were his own. It is scientifically risky to build a clinical theory on a putative understanding of one's own personality.

Kohut (1976) did not hesitate to point out that Freud's theory of neurosis had been shaped by the latter's inner life, but he seems never to have realized that his own psychological horizons were equally bound to be circumscribed, that his brilliant introspective insights should not be turned into universals. Kohut (1968, 1971) discovered that excessive ambitions develop in early childhood as a result of various vicissitudes unconnected with parricide or incest, that the failure to establish stable ideals is related to early disappointments with the caretakers, and that defects in self-esteem regulation are usually undergirded by tendencies to become disorganized or apathetic under stress. In my judgment, these were valid clinical observations that compelled Kohut's successors to reconsider the entire clinical theory of psychoanalysis. (For my version of such a reconsideration, see Gedo, 1979). Unfortunately, Kohut's own clinical theory focused too narrowly on issues previously understood under the rubric of "narcissism," presumably because these were the issues of paramount personal significance for him.

In conceiving of the psychological structure he called "the self" as bipolar, consisting of ambitions and ideals that must be fulfilled to achieve self-esteem, Kohut (1977) reduced human motivations to the single issue of seeking perfection and deliberately chose to ignore biological, preverbal (and *a fortiori* presymbolic) influences on structuring the personality. Kohut was slow to accept that his clinical findings demanded the postulation of a macrostructure formed before the secure differentiation of ego from id: as late as 1972, he still insisted that "self" refers only to a *content* of the mind (see Kohut, 1978). He acknowledged (Kohut, 1977) that he had left unanswered the question of how self-as-structure is formed. In the remaining years of his life, all he wrote on this score (Kohut, 1984, p. 70; Kohut and Wolf, 1978, p. 44) implied that it is the caretakers' empathic response to selfobject needs—that is, sufficient confirmation of the child's perfection and adequate maintenance of his view of their own—that determines self-formation.

Kohut's (1984) ultimate definition of selfobject was that of any entity that supports the cohesion, strength, and harmony of the self; in his view, the need for such supports is lifelong (Kohut, 1980a, p. 453; b, p. 473). What Kohut never tried to explain is *why* conditions wherein the caretakers can be idealized and the child is affirmed in his expansiveness or provided with a silent double enhance the self-organization in these ways, or how such experiences might lead to self-formation in terms of developing specific sets of ambitions and ideals. To put the matter somewhat differently, Kohut's hypotheses about self-organization are too adultomorphic: they apply clinical findings about adult patients with defects in self-esteem regulation to the mental life of preverbal children. The issues Kohut discerned, which were originally termed "narcissistic transferences," are properly referable to a phase of childhood wherein reflexive self-awareness already exists, a phase in which language is already available. In other words, ironically, self psychology fails to address the most fundamental issues of human existence, those matters that are built into the personality during infancy and form the core of "the self."

I can put this crucial point in still another way: Freudian psychoanalysis explored the intersystemic conflicts characteristic of the neuroses—the matters Kohut labeled the problems of Guilty Man. Kohut's clinical observations led him to realize that a whole range of narcissistic issues—those he called the problems of Tragic Man—antedated and underlay neurotic conflicts. Instead of trying to correlate his new findings with the accumulated data of psychoanalytic experience (but see Gedo and Goldberg, 1973, esp. c. 7), Kohut attempted to subsume all of mental life under the rubric of the vicissitudes of self-cohesion in various circumstances involving idealization/disillusionment and affirmation/lack of empathy. The inadequacy of this schema to explicate the totality of human mental life is most apparent from Kohut's failure to account for the structural defects that predispose people to the frequent episodes of faulty tension regulation he correctly observed: self psychology has had almost nothing to say about the disordered self!

To be sure, Kohut (1971) noted a wide variety of signs and symptoms of "fragmentation" or of emergency adaptive measures used to avert such disorganization, but he was not interested in the details of the regressive phenomenology or in their implications for the psychoanalytic theory of the mind. In parallel with this inattention to the antecedents of the cohesive self, in his statements about nosology, Kohut relegated conditions in which such self-cohesion has never been completely achieved to the category of psychoses—conditions about which he never wrote anything at all. It is true that Kohut (1984, p. 183) noted that so-called borderline patients are analyzable insofar as the analyst succeeds in organizing the bewildering phenomena presented by such analysands into some cognitive schema available to him, but Kohut never offered such a schema.

Kohut's pervasive tendency to ignore the work of most other contributors to psychoanalysis is nowhere more regrettable than in his failure to study the extensive literature on primitive personalities, where he could have learned about archaic mental states he did not seem to have encountered in his analytic practice. (I have in mind clinical contingencies in the so-called borderline spectrum as described, for example, by experienced therapists such as Searles, 1986.) Almost 20 years ago, Arnold Goldberg and I (1973) postulated that such syndromes do not constitute disease entities; rather, they are expectable modes of functioning, acquired in the course of early development, evoked throughout the life span by specific adaptive requirements. In other words, these archaic response patterns are potentially available to everyone; in every analysis that goes far enough or deep enough such contingencies can be expected to arise. The best therapeutic results are obtained in those analyses which evoke transferences from every developmental level, including those preceding consolidation of a cohesive self. This is why I do not trust Kohut's (1977) recommendation that the analyses of disturbances affecting the self may appropriately be terminated when compensatory adaptive devices have been acquired. A personality built on quicksand is not likely to stand.

Ultimately, the least satisfactory aspect of self psychology may prove to be the extraordinarily reified notion of self in Kohut's writings. Not only does he anthropomorphize this construct in describing "the self" as a sentient being, capable of enfeeblement or vigor; what is more grave, he conceives of the regressive loss of self-cohesion as a fragmentation, in a literal acceptance of certain patients' concretization of their subjective state during these crises. The self is thereby reduced to a china figurine, which when smashed into bits becomes a mass of dysfunctional shards. This notion is misleading, for neither analysands nor young children lose their functional capacities in a global way whenever they regress to a mode of organization that antedated self-cohesion.

Another way to state this objection to the reductionism of Kohut's view of human nature is to consider the inadequacy of his nosological system, particularly the one he promulgated after the creation of self psychology (see Kohut and Wolf, 1978). In this schema, the sole indicator of dysfunction is the patient's subjective state: is the self lacking in vigor, coherence or harmony? In other words, Kohut postulated that empathic parenting (in his terms, adequate provision for selfobject needs) would succeed in creating a cohesive self, albeit that maintenance of this state requires the continuing availability of selfobjects. If, as a result of selfobject failures, the infant does *not* develop a stable bipolar self, Kohut (1971) assumed that the resulting personality structure would be either psychotic or barely compensated by means of avoidant (schizoid) defenses designed to forestall injuries to self-esteem that would precipitate a psychotic decompensation.

In Kohut's (1971) schema, various forms of self disorder are accounted for by means of the concept of a "vertical split." As Basch (1967) was probably the first to point out, nonrepressive defenses such as disavowal are the mechanisms that maintain such mental conditions: splitting of the mind implies the simultaneous presence of mutually incompatible alternatives. In other words, Kohut was cognizant that a person's outward behavior may screen a broad spectrum of archaic mentation. On the other hand, he never acknowledged that in many instances we observe a primary failure to integrate the totality of personal aims into a cohesive self-organization, rather than the consequences of the defensively motivated splitting of a unitary hierarchy of aims (see Gedo and Goldberg, 1973, p. 99).

As I have tried to show in some detail elsewhere (Gedo, 1988), archaic pathology generally persists precisely because of a failure of integration of the relevant functions into the cohesive self, the aspect of mind that continues to mature with experience. In other words, the occurrence of islands of malfunctioning such as psychosomatic conditions, actual neuroses, or tics (to mention only a few of the more obvious types of archaic symptomatology in the presence of generally age-appropriate mental organization in adults) is best understood in terms of the frequent coexistence of separate subsets of "self nuclei" (Gedo and Goldberg, 1973), one of which may undergo regression without involving the other in the process. These are the mental dispositions that permit the persistence of a "psychotic core" within an otherwise nonpsychotic personality, as Winnicott (1952) long ago noted. Complexities of this kind are left out of account in Kohut's work.

To recapitulate: Heinz Kohut deserves great credit for a

decisive breakout from the restrictive paradigm of the transference neuroses. His work through 1972 lent clinical substance to the gathering movement to revise psychoanalytic theory (for example, Klein, 1976; Schafer, 1976; Gill and Holzman, 1976; Rosenblatt and Thickstun, 1977; Gedo, 1979), not only in the direction of abandoning the metapsychology based on Freud's physicalistic postulates but also by taking into account data from cases beyond the boundaries of the neuroses (see Gedo and Goldberg, 1973). Kohut's (1971, 1977; Goldberg, 1978) clinical material dealt with issues more archaic than the infantile neuroses familiar to psychoanalysts. He convincingly demonstrated that some of these problems could be dealt with in psychoanalytic treatment conducted in the traditional manner if the transferences he defined as narcissistic were given due weight. Because these archaic mental dispositions are focused on the stability of the sense of self as well as on issues of self-esteem, Kohut began to call his work "the analysis of the self."

This choice of psychoanalytic emphasis became transformed into the dissident school now named self psychology when analytic conservatives failed to accept Kohut's viewpoint. Probably in reaction to this polarization within the analytic community, Kohut attempted to formulate a clinical theory of universal applicability on the basis of his new findings. This effort eventuated in a premature closure—a reductionistic theory, which, like its traditional predecessor, fails to take into account the legacy of all developmental phases, concentrating instead on derivatives of the specific nodal point in development that give rise to the adaptive difficulties found in the particular cases whose study led to the formulation of the theory.

As I have tried to point out for many years (see Panel, 1971), psychoanalytic clinical theory must integrate the data of our observations with children and adults of every type of personality organization. Derivatives of different developmental phases need to be integrated in a hierarchical manner. The findings and concepts of Heinz Kohut should find their proper place within such a hierarchic view of self-organization. Alas, there are more things in heaven and on earth than are dealt with by self psychology.

REFERENCES

Baker, M. & Baker, H. (1987), Heinz Kohut's self psychology, *Amer. J. Psychiatry,* 144:1–9.

Basch, M. (1967), On disavowal. Presented at the Chicago Institute for

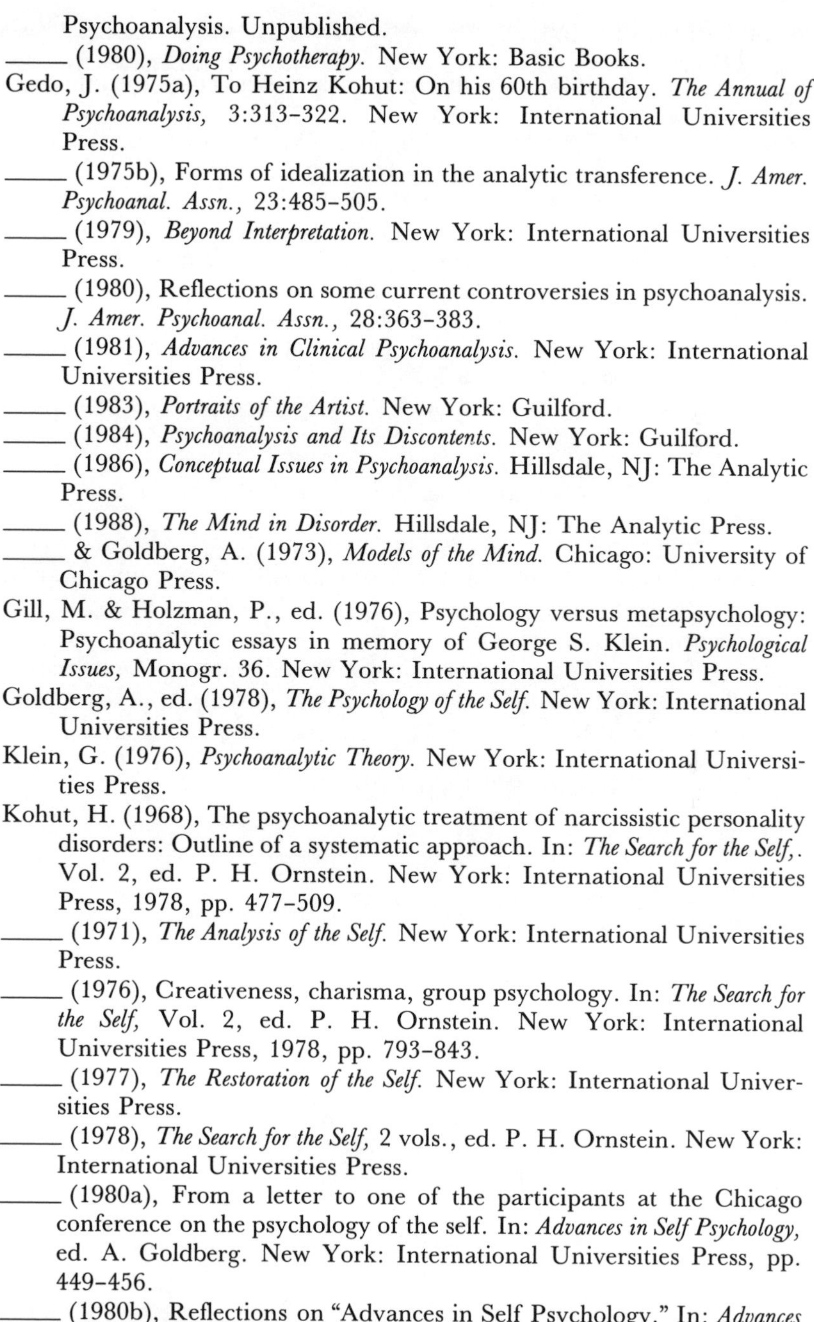

Psychoanalysis. Unpublished.

_____ (1980), *Doing Psychotherapy.* New York: Basic Books.

Gedo, J. (1975a), To Heinz Kohut: On his 60th birthday. *The Annual of Psychoanalysis,* 3:313–322. New York: International Universities Press.

_____ (1975b), Forms of idealization in the analytic transference. *J. Amer. Psychoanal. Assn.,* 23:485–505.

_____ (1979), *Beyond Interpretation.* New York: International Universities Press.

_____ (1980), Reflections on some current controversies in psychoanalysis. *J. Amer. Psychoanal. Assn.,* 28:363–383.

_____ (1981), *Advances in Clinical Psychoanalysis.* New York: International Universities Press.

_____ (1983), *Portraits of the Artist.* New York: Guilford.

_____ (1984), *Psychoanalysis and Its Discontents.* New York: Guilford.

_____ (1986), *Conceptual Issues in Psychoanalysis.* Hillsdale, NJ: The Analytic Press.

_____ (1988), *The Mind in Disorder.* Hillsdale, NJ: The Analytic Press.

_____ & Goldberg, A. (1973), *Models of the Mind.* Chicago: University of Chicago Press.

Gill, M. & Holzman, P., ed. (1976), Psychology versus metapsychology: Psychoanalytic essays in memory of George S. Klein. *Psychological Issues,* Monogr. 36. New York: International Universities Press.

Goldberg, A., ed. (1978), *The Psychology of the Self.* New York: International Universities Press.

Klein, G. (1976), *Psychoanalytic Theory.* New York: International Universities Press.

Kohut, H. (1968), The psychoanalytic treatment of narcissistic personality disorders: Outline of a systematic approach. In: *The Search for the Self,*. Vol. 2, ed. P. H. Ornstein. New York: International Universities Press, 1978, pp. 477–509.

_____ (1971), *The Analysis of the Self.* New York: International Universities Press.

_____ (1976), Creativeness, charisma, group psychology. In: *The Search for the Self,* Vol. 2, ed. P. H. Ornstein. New York: International Universities Press, 1978, pp. 793–843.

_____ (1977), *The Restoration of the Self.* New York: International Universities Press.

_____ (1978), *The Search for the Self,* 2 vols., ed. P. H. Ornstein. New York: International Universities Press.

_____ (1980a), From a letter to one of the participants at the Chicago conference on the psychology of the self. In: *Advances in Self Psychology,* ed. A. Goldberg. New York: International Universities Press, pp. 449–456.

_____ (1980b), Reflections on "Advances in Self Psychology." In: *Advances in Self Psychology,* ed. A. Goldberg. New York: International Universities Press, pp. 473–554.

_____ (1984), *How Does Analysis Cure?* Chicago: University of Chicago Press.

_____ & Wolf, E. (1978), The disorders of the self and their treatment: An outline. *Internat. J. Psycho-Anal.*, 59:413–426.

Panel (1971), Models of the psychic apparatus. S. Abrams, reporter. *J. Amer. Psychoanal. Assn.*, 19:131–142.

Rosenblatt, A. & Thickstun, J. (1977), Modern psychoanalytic concepts in a general psychology. *Psychological Issues* Monogr. 42/43.

Schafer, R. (1976), *A New Language for Psychoanalysis.* New Haven, CT: Yale University Press.

Schwaber, E. (1987), Review of "Kohut's Legacy: Contributions to Self Psychology," edited by Paul E. Stepansky and Arnold Goldberg. *J. Amer. Psychoanal. Assn.*, 35:743–750.

Searles, H. (1986), *My Work with Borderline Patients.* Northvale, NJ: Aronson.

Stepansky, P. (1983), *In Freud's Shadow.* Hillsdale, NJ: The Analytic Press.

Stern, D. (1985), *The Interpersonal World of the Infant.* New York: Basic Books.

Terman, D. (1976), Distortions of the Oedipus complex in severe pathology: Some vicissitudes of self development and their relationship to the Oedipus complex. Presented to the American Psychoanalytic Association (December).

_____ (1984–85), The self and the Oedipus complex. *The Annual of Psychoanalysis,* 12/13:87–104. New York: International Universities Press.

Winnicott, D. (1952), Psychoses and child care. In: *Collected Papers.* London: Tavistock, 1958, pp. 219–228.

21

Self Psychology, Psychoanalysis, and the Analytic Enterprise

Douglas W. Detrick

Arnold Goldberg, in his foreword to this volume, has said, "Heinz Kohut has made us take notice." Indeed, as a survey of the contributions to this volume bears out, Kohut's ideas not only have engaged proponents of the many viewpoints that shape contemporary psychoanalysis, but also both the major ideas and contemporary philosophy, on one hand, and all of the seminal, historically important psychoanalytic figures on the other.

Taken together, these contributions provide a remarkable background of intellectual and scholarly discourse against which to approach a variety of issues regarding self psychology and its place in the psychoanalytic enterprise.

THE ESSENCE OF SELF PSYCHOLOGY

The elements of Kohut's self psychology can briefly be set forth as follows:

1. The centrality of the empathic vantage point in the psychoanalytic process (Kohut, 1959).[1]

[1]A case can be made that this should not be included among the points unique to self psychology (Meissner, 1985; Goldberg, 1988; Kohut, 1984). I have included it

2. The discovery of the selfobject transferences (Kohut, 1968, 1971, 1977), which provide new, in-depth understanding of a variety of classes of psychological disturbance (Kohut, 1977).
3. Three new developmental lines (mirroring, alter ego, idealizing) generalized from the study of the selfobject transferences (Kohut, 1971, 1977, 1984).
4. Certain attributes of the mature personality (creativity, humor, mature empathy, wisdom) that are the end result of specific selfobject developmental lines (Kohut, 1966, 1971).
5. The motivational-experiential core of the personality as a bipolar structure; the bipolar nuclear self (Kohut, 1977, 1984). The ambitions form one pole, the ideals the other.

Another way of describing Kohut's achievement is to say that it has brought together and given unity to the three main streams of modern psychological thought: the existential-humanistic perspective, systems-communication theory, and clinical psychoanalysis. His discovery of the structure and dynamic essence of the nuclear self provides the theoretical context to understand the centrality of the human need to actualize one's personal destiny. Kohut's discovery of the self-selfobject unit and that the self in both health and disturbance must be understood in the context of the surrounding selfobject environment brings systems-communication theory in direct connection with the existential-humanistic tradition. In other words, human destiny and authenticity are not antagonistic to, but rather *require,* one's embeddedness in the human culture or "system."

Finally, the third strand, clinical psychoanalysis, is woven with the other two by virtue of Kohut's discovery of the selfobject transferences. Flaws in the organization and dynamic essence of the nuclear self are healed by the psychoanalytic process. Our understanding of the essence of this process is based in systems theory (Basch, 1988; Goldberg, 1988). Also, the development of the self both in health and disturbance was first discovered in the psychoanalytic situation.

---

for two reasons. First, ego psychology/object relations theory characteristically takes the vantage point of an external observer and the associated "objective" viewpoint (Schwaber, 1983). Second, the role of the empathic vantage point has become strategically central in the analysis of self-disturbances in a way that is not in the analysis of the structural neuroses (cf. Basch, 1988, ch. 9, 10.)

THE HUMAN MIND: AN EVOLUTIONARY PERSPECTIVE

Before we can proceed further in defining the scope of psychoanalysis and placing self psychology within its context, a view of the evolution of the human mind must be presented.

To focus on the evolution of the human mind requires that two separate but related aspects be considered. The first is the development (evolution) of modern consciousness. This has admirably been done by Jaynes (1976), who describes how modern consciousness (that is, being aware of being aware) emerged out of what he calls the bicameral organization of the brain.

The second aspect in the evolution of the modern mind is the evolution of the bipolar nuclear self. I believe that the modern nuclear self, the motivational core of the personality consisting of a bipolar structure embedded in a selfobject matrix, is the result of a relatively recent shift in the organization of the personality. There has been a gradual change from the original archetypal organization of the personality to its present modern form.[2]

Eliade (1954) has described the archetypal organization of the self out of which the modern form slowly emerged. He points out that the significance of all of the actions of "archaic humanity" derived from their being put into an archetypal framework. For example, the birth of a child is significant not because of the personal impact on the lives of the parents, but rather because it often parallels the birth of the world at the beginning of time or the birth (rebirth) of the world each year in the spring. With respect particularly to the concepts of sacredness and profanity, Eliade discusses the relationship of mundane, everyday activities with the archetypal background of human experience:

> You might say that the archaic world knows nothing of 'profane activities': every act which has a definite meaning—hunting, fishing, agricultural; games, conflicts, sexuality—in some way participates in the sacred. . . . Take the dance, for example. All dances were originally sacred; in other words, they had an extra human model. The model may in some cases have been a totemic or emblematic animal, whose motions were repro-

---

[2]In this regard I should like to note that according to Weintraub (1978), the first autobiography to reflect fully a modern individuality was written in the 18th century by Goethe.

> duced to conjure up its concrete presence through magic, to increase its numbers, to obtain incorporation into the animal on the part of Man. In other cases, the model may have been revealed by a divinity or by a hero [pp. 27–28].

In other words, all human activity originally obtained its *meaning* by being imbricated with the archetypal domain.

I believe that until the modern era, the archetypal collective unconscious organization was more or less adequate for humans both in the cultural and personal domain. However, this organization was slowly undermined over the last two millennia by the expansion of the personal unconscious. The personal unconscious pushed back the role of the archetypal collective unconscious in human affairs. This broadening of the personal unconscious was the direct result of the expansion of the affective interplay between parent and child. The personal unconscious in human mental organization is a direct result of the enlarged selfobject matrix.[3]

Although the self, the archetypal center of the personality (Jung, 1946), has existed for millennia, only recently has both its intrinsic bipolar structure and its central organizing function entered the *personal* unconscious.

The idealizing aspects of the nuclear self as realized in its relation to the archetypal center were consolidated long before the ambitions pole. As the self emerged as the center of the personality in the expanding selfobject (affective) matrix, the role of individual human destiny became increasingly central in human experience. Or it would have, had not a turn away from the ambitions pole taken place, allowing the essence of human destiny to be anchored in the human community rather than disrupted. It was the body self and its search for sexual satisfaction that was the most dramatic form of the individual's search for grandiose exhibitionistic need gratification two to three millennia ago. The rejection by the great religions of the body (sexuality!) came at a time when the human community would have been irreparably disrupted by this form of individual quest for destiny, because the self was still not sufficiently anchored in the selfobject universe. Once the selfobject environment that human beings now need for their very sustenance

[3]Freud's (1905) observation that the "ancients laid the stress upon the instinct itself, whereas we emphasize its object" (p. 149*n*) can be understood in the larger context of the shifting organization of the human personality and its deepening embeddedness in the selfobject milieu.

and existence expanded (the two poles of the bipolar self are essentially linked to the human community by way of the selfobject unit), then the quest for human individual destiny could emerge. The modern thinker whose work provides an understanding of the transition from the archetypal organization to the modern organization of the bipolar self is Carl Jung (1946). Jung's work is transitional because one aspect of it is anchored in the earlier organization of the collective unconscious and archetypes, and the other aspect is anchored in the thoroughly modern concept of the centrality of destiny in human existence. He discusses the latter issue as "individuation."

MODERN CULTURE: THE EXISTENTIAL-HUMANISTIC MEDIUM

Over the last few millennia, the slow expansion of the personal unconscious has been at the expense of the collective unconscious (archetypal organization).[4] This major shift in the human mental organization is primarily the result of the strengthened affective bond between the child and caretaker. The selfobject transferences and their correlated selfobject developmental lines are a manifestation of the emergence of this type of human personality organization.

Freud (1911-1915) discovered the tools for exploring the personal unconscious. Why his theories focused the drives (especally sexuality) will be discussed in the next section. Let it be said that Freud's (1923) basic personality theory (id-ego-superego) is at odds with the central issues of 20th-century thinking, that is, the idea of individual destiny, or individuation.

It was Carl Jung and the existential-humanistic philosophers who were first in touch with modern humankind's despair and experience of meaninglessness. Jung's theories harkened back to an earlier organization, in which human meaning was derived from the individual's life being embedded in the archetypal matrix. The existential-humanistic thinkers took a very different tack. Kierkegaard is arguably the first existential philosopher (Rubin, this volume). His focus on religion in general and Christianity in particular denotes his preoccupation with the archetypal domain of

[4]In this context note Kohut's comment, "We misunderstand the essentials of the ancient Greeks. . . . we have missed something that's completely out of our understanding" (Strozier, 1985, p. 266).

experience. His concept of "leveling," the malaise of the modern generation, needs to be understood as the result of the loss of the archetypal embeddedness of the relationships among family members and among humans in a larger cultural context. There is also little doubt that his focus on the varieties of meaningful lives or commitments (spheres of existence) is directly related to the individual's destiny and authenticity.

Subsequent to Kierkegaard, there are two major overlapping areas within existential-humanistic philosophy. One is characterized by a concern with the core of human experience, especially insofar as it is authentic and fulfills one's individual, unique destiny. The existential philosophers Heidigger and Sartre emphasize this dimension of human experience. The other focus of interest of the existential philosophers has to do with the human being as an observer (data gatherer) of other human beings. Husserl and Merleau-Ponty emphasize this side of existential-humanistic thought. This area of philosophic inquiry is often referred to as phenomenology and is seen in the context of a reaction against the idea that human beings can be observed and understood within a "natural science" framework (McCall, 1983).

Kierkegaard's work preceded the more recent flowering of existential thought and its bifurcation into two domains of interest. His work is focused not on the issue of phenomenology, but rather on the instability of the core of the personality of modern man. Heidigger (1927) and Sartre (1943) both discuss threats to the organization of the core self in a philosophic rather than psychological context. On one hand, they see these threats as resulting from the impact of nonhuman modes of psychological organization. On the other hand, they see the threat as coming from human sources in which the authenticity of the individual is given over to the demands to adapt to another's needs.

Rogers's (1980) work can be characterized as attempting to bring existential phenomenology and "humanistic" (self-actualizing) issues into the centrality of the psychotherapeutic situation. Like Jung, he emphasizes the importance of the patient's experience as the primary observational data. And also, like Jung, he emphasizes the self-actualizing (in Jung's theory, individuation) need at the core of humanness. However, unlike Jung, he does not utilize the theories or concepts of the collective unconscious and archetypes. In this regard, Rogers focuses on the modern psychological organization in the context of psychotherapy. As pointed out by Kahn (this volume), there are two major differences between Kohut and

Rogers. One is Rogers' belief that all that is necessary for cure is acceptance and empathy; interpretation is not necessary. The second difference is that Rogers rejects the concept of the transference as useful in understanding the therapeutic process that leads to cure. In this regard, Rogers differs not just with Kohut but with mainstream clinical psychoanalysis. The centrality of interpretation and the analysis of the transference in the cure of psychological disturbance goes back to Freud, and it is to him I now turn.

FREUD, FREUDIANISM, AND THE "HISTORICAL DISSIDENTS"

Freud, the originator and primary developer of psychoanalysis, far outstripped in importance any of the talented workers that became attracted to psychoanalysis in its first few decades. Freud's contribution not only was immense in the domain of clinical theory, but ranged from the very methodology of this new science to the larger and much more difficult to see *Weltanschauung* (world-view).

Basch (this volume) begins with an overview of the various categories of Freud's contribution in the origination and development of psychoanalysis. Basch rhetorically asks, which Freud are we to compare Kohut with? Is it the Freud who emphasizes the centrality of the method of psychoanalysis, based on the analysis of the transference utilizing the data-gathering tool of free association? Or is it Freud the biologist, who saw the essence of human experience as a battle with the instincts of sex and aggression? In addition, there is Freud the theoretician of a general psychology, who put forward ideas regarding the normal cognitive and emotional development of human beings.

Basch underscores Freud's two central findings that must be retained as the defining characteristics of the clinical science of psychoanalysis: the dynamic unconscious, and the analysis of the transference. From this point of view, there is no doubt that, as Basch concludes, self psychology is "very much an extension of and a corrector for traditional psychoanalytic practice." Kohut's understanding of the resistances to mobilizing the childhood experiences in the transference, his specifying the types of transferences that are mobilized in the analysis of the self-disorders, and his emphasis on the working through of these new transferences are all consistent with the idea of what constitutes a clinical psychoanalysis.

Basch has made the fascinating discovery that Freud's general psychological theory in its essential form predated his turning to the treatment of the neuroses by psychological methods. Freud's theory was derived from his understanding of the disturbances in the cerebral cortex leading to the aphasias. Also, Basch suggests, it was Freud's need to anchor his new psychoanalysis solidly in the "natural sciences" that led him to emphasize the instincts (especially sexuality) as the central guiding force in human motivation. Basch notes that the

> self-appointed guardians of Freud's legacy were quite right to object to Kohut's empathy and introspection paper. Resting as the instinct theory does on simplistic and long-since falsified biological speculation, and on an epistemological fallacy, it was (and to some extent still is) supported only by the belief grounded in the convention—any threat to that belief could bring the whole house of cards tumbling down.

Basch has taken the position that the rigid adherence to instinct theory and the correlated rejection of self psychology by the psychoanalytic establishment is the result of the isolation of psychoanalysis from the mainstream of modern-day science. In numerous publications (Basch, 1975, 1976a, b, 1977, 1978, 1981, 1985, 1986, 1988), he has cogently criticized the instinct theory and offered an alternative theoretical foundation derived from affect theory and our understanding of modern neuropsychology. In particular, he has underscored the view that the brain's normal function is to process information on nonsymbolic and symbolic levels and that the notion that an instinct (id) is required to explain human motivation is now outdated.

My own belief is that the Freudian adherence to the instinct theory is only one aspect, though the central one, of a cultlike group dynamic existing within the body of scientific psychoanalysis. I call this mental health cult "Freudianism." Like all cults, Freudianism can be comprehended by the explication of three elements: the apotheosis of a leader, a ritual, and an ideology. Sullaway (1979) has discussed, in the context of "the myth of the hero," how Freud and his achievements have taken on "heroic" import within the Freudian community.[5] The ritual of Freudianism is, of course, the lying on "the couch." Adherents to Freudianism feel this is the sine qua non of clinical psychoanalysis. They have apparently forgotten

[5]See Kohut (1984) for a discussion of the role of the training analysis in this process.

that Freud introduced the couch because he could not tolerate being looked at all day (Jones, 1955). Freudian dogma is contained within a general attitudinal context geared toward the analysand that is an important element in all "brainwashing" techniques (Lifton, 1963). I have jokingly referred to this attitude as, "The customer is always wrong." No matter what analysands say about themselves, their world, and their feelings, the purveyor of Freudianism negates it. This negation is rationalized theoretically by way of the concept of the unconscious.

The second characteristic of the general viewpoint of Freudianism is that all ideas and behaviors are defensive. In other words, the justification for the rejection of the analysand's experience and opinions is that everything is "defense." Whatever the analysand reports, it is a defense against some other, deeper material. Early in the development of psychoanalysis, this argument took the form that all behaviors and fantasies are defenses against unconscious sexual and aggressive wishes. A latter-day variant of this point of view is that many behaviors are a defense against "helplessness" secondary to "separation." Of course, if all human behavior is the result of defenses against unconscious fears, then control over oneself rests with somebody else; that is, one is always fooling oneself and must always rely on some authority.

The specific ideology of Freudianism is, of course, the instinct theory. And it is here, as Basch (this volume) notes, the reactionary members of the Freudian establishment take greatest offense at self psychology. Whereas Basch sees this reaction as the result of modern science's ignorance about brain function and human development, I find a more specific factor. I believe that the instinct theory is necessary for Freudianism because it is intrinsically linked to a group dynamic characterized by guilt and confession. Freudianism, with its searching out of unconscious sexual and aggressive wishes assumed to be at the center of the human personality, and with its exposure in a guilt-inducing context, brings about a type of group cohesiveness whose strength should not be underestimated.[6]

I have sketched out the elements in the cult of Freudianism as they exist within the body of contemporary psychoanalysis, for two reasons. The first is that by demonstration of this reactionary impediment to scientific psychoanalysis, the purpose of freeing

---

[6]Beyond the scope of the present work is a discussion of two other elements in Freudianism: one, the negative view of women (see Hillman, 1972), and, two, the view that adult patients are reporting *fantasies,* not real events of child abuse (see Miller, 1984).

psychoanalysis will be served. The second reason is that I believe that the instinct/guilt/confession/intensified group cohesiveness dynamic played a crucial role in the evolvement of the modern mental (self) organization.

Strangely lacking in Freud's work is a recognition and appreciation of the centrality of the individual's destiny in human experience. Freud's biologically based speculations gave no role to the concept of self-actualization as we now understand it. His comment, "Anatomy is destiny" was primarily a deprecation of what we now have come to see as the human being's never-ending search for meaning and the realization of personal destiny.

In the phylogeny of the human self, the transition from the archetypal organization to the bipolar nuclear self (characterized by each person's actualizing his nuclear program) put in jeopardy and hence threatened the existence of the human community because of the originally asocial nature of the strivings for individual achievement. One indication of this threat is that pride is the most serious of the sins among the Mycenean-Greek civilization. There are similar inhibitions and prohibitions against taking pride in oneself throughout the world at that level of cultural development.

The great religions, whose cultural institutions derived from the emergence of the self archetype's increasing importance in human mind, turned against the body in the preoccupation with the sin of sex, thus suppressing the archaic grandiose self's (the body self) seeking out its own destiny, that is, sexual pleasure. It took more than a thousand years in the West, the so-called "Dark Ages," before the selfobject matrix had evolved to a point where the individual's destiny was not antagonistic to the cohesion of the group. Rather, it became dependent upon it. In other words, the sex/guilt/confession dynamic in the evolution of the human community provided a necessary impediment to the individual's searching out his own needs, until the maintenance of the selfobject environment became essential for the individual's very psychological survival. One can see the almost uncanny contention and conflict between the instinct/guilt dynamic of Freudianism and the centrality of the need to actualize one's nuclear program (personal destiny) of the self psychologies as enacting in microcosm the great tensions in human culture over the last several millennia.

In one way or another, each of the historical psychoanalytic "dissidents" has put forward a contribution in reaction to elements of psychoanalysis that we can now characterize as Freudianism. Although I evaluate the contribution of Jung differently from the contribution of other dissidents (because of his emphasis on the archetypal foundation of human experience), a number of his ideas can also be seen as a reaction to Freudianism, such as his accepting the reality of the analysand's accounts as valid, rather than attempting to see it as *necessarily* distorted and wrong. His emphasis on individuation is in direct contradiction to Freudianism's negation of the centrality of the need to actualize personal destiny.

The great gap between Jung and Kohut resides in Kohut's total emphasis on the personal unconscious.[7] There is no doubt that much of human experience—motivation—is archetypal in its origin. However, I believe that the archetypal domain has been more or less replaced by the personal unconscious characterized by the self-selfobject matrix. In the domain of psychotherapy, the Jungian notion that the important work is done on the level of the archetypes (Edinger, 1973, 1985) is no longer valid for most patients. Psychological disturbance must now be traced back to events in the person's development and correlated flaws in the organization and development of the personal unconscious.

I found it both a humbling and an awe-inspiring experience to read the chapters in this volume on the historical dissidents to see how brilliant the contributions were and how, in many instances, their authors had accurately seen flaws in Freud's opus. All the contributors saw the invalidity of the centrality of the instinct theory and the correlated Oedipus complex. They all reevaluated the role of childhood sexuality in a way much more consistent with modern findings. All of them also saw, in one way or another, that the response to childhood trauma was to attempt to protect the integrity of the core of the personality.

Rank's work, as described by Menaker, is a far-reaching one. He emphasizes the role of creativity in human experience. "It is Rank's special contribution to a philosophy of therapy that he emphasizes the uniqueness of the individual and sees as a major function of psychological treatment the fostering of the growth of the self and its free expression in the creative wheel." However, several vestiges of Freudianism remain in Rank's work. One is that creativity is a "defense." Menaker states that, for Rank, creativity "is the human creature's response to the fear of separation, especially the fear of the final separation, namely death." Self psychology's view of creativity and the search for meaning, consistent with

[7]Jung also has no concept comparable to the self-selfobject unit.

modern existential-humanistic thought, is that these are an essential attribute of human experience.[8]

The second vestige of Freudianism in Rank's work is his notion that guilt is necessarly evoked by creative activity. Although in many cases, one can find this link, it is not an invariable one. Most disturbances in creative productivity are not the result of creativity's being guilt-inducing but rather are the result of either the overstimulating nature of creativity (see Elson, 1987) or of the feared withdrawal of the selfobject's responsiveness. Guilt in many instances can be seen as being in the service of restoring a lost or threatened selfobject tie (see Goldberg, 1988).

Rachman (this volume) points out a number of similarities between Ferenczi's thinking and self psychology. Two of the most important similarities are the emphasis on empathy in analysis, and the belief that in certain instances, the "Freudian analytic situation re-created the original trauma for the analysand who had suffered childhood abuse." The deliberately "restrained coolness, professional hypocrisy, the focus on the patient's criticisms of the analyst as resistance, the clinical facade behind which the analyst hides from a genuine interpersonal encounter, all contribute to producing a nongenuine and therapeutically limited experience." It is in this context that Ferenczi discusses the role of empathy, what he calls "tact." It is unfortunate that the word "tact" has a meaning very different from that of "empathy." Tact requires empathizing with the other person and should always be a consideration in giving interpretations. Empathy in self psychology, however, has become a much more strategic concept owing to the nature of the self-disturbances that are being presented for analysis.

Kohut (1984) had remarkably little to say about actual child abuse. His comments regarding the return to the seduction theory, and that patients in fact—not merely in fantasy—had been damaged by their parents, were meant to be understood in the terms of failures in empathy and selfobject responsiveness. Ferenczi's (1933) pioneering work in the damage and continuing effects of childhood sexual abuse is beyond anything else found to this date in the self psychological literature. The theoretical work on the impact of childhood sexual and physical abuse (leading to the defense of dissociation) on the organization of the nuclear and more peripheral

[8]One might say that viewing the creative endeavor and the search for meaning as defensive is analogous to saying that a fish's swimming in the sea is a defense against flopping around out of the water on the beach.

sectors of the self remains to be done. We do not yet have a theoretical comprehension of the interrelationship between the dissociative defenses resulting from child abuse and the better known defensive and compensatory structures resulting from flaws in parental selfobjects.

Karen Horney's work is discussed in the section on "Historical Dissidents," although she actually seems to lie closer to the English object relations school. She never had the close relationship with Freud that Jung, Adler, Rank, and Ferenczi did. Her ideas were not merely a reaction against Freudianism, but also were weighted in the direction of the cultural (object relations?) schools. Had she emigrated to England instead of the United States, there is little doubt that she would be seen as a leading figure in the English Object Relations school. Also she would have also been spared the ostracism of the American Psychoanalytic Association. Perhaps if she had resided in England her ideas, especially those recasting the psychoanalytic development of women, would have been palatable to more analysts in the United States. As described in this volume by Paul, Horney's work is also a "self psychology." In addition to rejecting the centrality of Freudian instinct theory, she eventually came to the concept of the "real self," which needs to "realize its potential." Paul states, "Thus the real self is a process of movement or directed growth orientation which in the final analysis is not truly analyzable."

All of the "historical" dissidents made important observations and advanced fundamentally correct theories, which now, in retrospect, we can see with clarity. Why did none of the dissidents have more influence than they did? First, none of them advanced the truly cohesive theory that Kohut's self psychology represents. Without the clinical concept of the self-selfobject matrix, and especially selfobject transferences, many of the observations and insights of these thinkers could not be maintained within a psychoanalytic context.

It was with Kohut's work that the *specific* developmental lines leading to the organization of the self and the correlated transferences indicating developmental disturbance were sufficiently detailed for clinicians to utilize them. (The importance of supporting details in the acceptance of scientific theory should not be overlooked. For example, the theory of evolution had been around since the time of the Greeks, but it was only with Darwin's gathering of an enormous amount of data that it became a scientifically acceptable theory.)

Also, the distinction between real childhood trauma and self-pathology based on faulty affective attunement (Basch, 1988) required the theoretical distinction between the defense of dissociation and the defense of repression and disavowal. Many instances of actual childhood physical and sexual trauma bring about the defense of dissociation in which hypnosis is necessary to gain access (Bliss, 1986). In many cases of actual childhood abuse, free association is inadequate ever to mobilize the traumatic material. Also, Ferenczi's insistence on the importance of *real* childhood trauma was overshadowed by his "active" attempts at therapeutic reparenting.

Perhaps even more important is the role of historical factors in the rejection or acceptance of ideas. After all, Ferenczi's plea to accept the reality of widespread child abuse fell on deaf ears. Perhaps it takes the passage of many decades before a new generation, a generation symbolized by the little boy in the story "The Emperor's New Clothes," can emerge and push forward.

THE ENGLISH OBJECT RELATIONS THEORISTS

Brandchaft (this volume) notes that the term object relations theory first arose in an attempt to set apart the work of such authors as Baliant, Fairbairn, and Winnicott, from that of Melanie Klein and her followers. He writes that although Klein's theories are very much in the tradition of Freudian drive theory, "She established that the archaic tie was foundational when she concluded from her psychoanalytic investigation and treatment of small children that the basic structures of normal and pathological development were laid down in earliest infancy. She thereby signalled her departure from Freud and the theory of the centrality for development of the oedipal conflict in the fourth and fifth year." The work of Balint, Fairbairn, and Winnicott can all be seen as reactions to the influence of Melanie Klein's work and as attempts to move away from an instinct-based to a relationship-based model of human development and functioning (see also Greenberg and Mitchell, 1983).

Of all the historically important figures discussed in this book, perhaps none was as close to being a self psychologist as was Donald Winnicott. As Bacal (this volume) states:

> There is in fact compelling evidence that Winnicott understood the idea of early selfobject functioning in much the same sense that Kohut did, but did not, so to say, organize the ideas so precisely. Winnicott's well-known comment that there is no such thing as an infant, but only the infant mother unit, is very much in line with self psychology's concept of the self-selfobject unit. . . . Although Winnicott did not conceptualize the subjective object of the experience as being provided the essential functions that affect the sense of self, he gave extensive indirect expression to this in his understanding of the self-sustaining and growth-enhancing functions of the early maternal environment in his ideas of the ordinary devoted mother, the good enough mother, the holding environment, and the mirroring function of the mother's face.

Another area of apparent similarity between self psychology and Winnicott's work is in the notion of Winnicott's true and false self. Winnicott's concept of the true self, however, is directly related to drive theory, and his understanding of the relationship between the true self and the false self is at a considerable distance from self psychology's understanding of the need of all selves, whether nuclear or not, to be embedded in the self-selfobject matrix. Winnicott [1960] states, "In particular, I link what I divide into a True and a False Self with Freud's division of the self into a part that is central and powered by the instincts [or by what Freud calls sexuality, pregenital and genital], and a part that is turned outwards and is related to the world" (p. 140). The Kohutian (1971, 1977) false self is referred to in self psychology as the vertical split. Bacal does not seem to consider Kohut's "vertical split" as a false self organization.

However, in both of those areas, Kohut adds elements that are crucial to both theoretical advance and technical refinement. Kohut's ideas regarding the varieties of selfobject developmental lines and the correlated disturbances in empathy or selfobject responsiveness give conceptual tools to the working therapist that Winnicott's ideas do not. Knowledge of the *specific* transferences that can be potentially mobilized is of central importance to the therapist. In this regard, Kohut's theories add a specificity to an understanding of the organization of the vertical split (false self) and, in addition, an understanding of the transferences mobilized, once the nuclear self is accessed (i.e., true self).

That Kohut's conception of the self *requires* a selfobject matrix and that the self's internal organization is bipolar, with a correlated set of skills and talents (Kohut, 1977), are theoretical advances not found in Winnicott's work. Winnicott's best-known concept is that of the "transitional object." Although seemingly conceptually close to Kohut's concept of the selfobject, it is essentially linked to a misguided dichotomizing of human experience into internal psychic reality and external reality. Winnicott saw the transitional object as an early stage in the development of what he called "illusion." As Bacal (this volume) notes, Winnicott considered this capacity for illusion "as of the greatest importance for healthy development." Winnicott (1951) states that the transitional object and transitional phenomena are characterized by "an intermediate area of experiencing to which inner reality and external life both contribute. It is an area . . . that shall exist as a resting place for the individual engaged in the perpetual human task of keeping inner and outer reality separate yet interrelated" (p. 230).

Winnicott has confused the dimension of perception, that is, external reality versus internal fantasy, and the dimension of "meaning," that is, the affective recruitment of situations. The world of meaning, of symbolization, is not primarily defined by the dimension of internality versus externality. My belief is that the transitional object symbolizes the most archaic form of feeling about material possessions. We all have special feelings of "me-not me" about our personal possessions. Sometimes they take on a selfobject quality. However, Kohut's concept of the selfobject and its role in the maintenance of the cohesion and the vitality of the self is on a more fundamental level of personality organization. In other words, although sometimes material possessions can act as selfobjects, many, if not most, selfobject experiences are unrelated to material possessions.

All the English objects relations theorists have attempted to replace Freudian instinct theory with a theory based on the interaction of the child or the adult with other people. Although in a general sense, self psychology is an object relations theory, in the specific sense it is not. Self psychology emphasizes the individual in the particular domain where others are experienced as a part of oneself. These other people are included by virtue of providing functions to the self. The English object relations theorists never make this distinction. They also never advance a detailed clinical theory that includes the nature and types of transferences mobilized in the analysis of the self disturbances. (See also Brandchaft, 1986.) Moreover, the English object relations school does not address, in the major way self psychology does, the individual's need to actualize one's nuclear program, one's destiny.

CONTEMPORARY CONTRIBUTIONS

Bromberg's essay brings the modern version of the school of thought begun by Harry Stack Sullivan to bear on self-psychology. Bromberg describes a number of points of similarity between interpersonal psychoanalysis and self psychology. Perhaps the most important area of correspondence is that both theoretical contributions are in essence field theories. In other words, it is the human being embedded in the matrix of human culture or the human system that is the central aspect of all human experience. Another point of convergence is that both approaches emphasize that "the analyst's participation is seen as an ongoing element in the field of observation and inseparable from it. What the analyst must be trying to listen to in his basic stance includes the immediate and residual effects of his own participation."

Bromberg, however, goes on to discuss how the mode of analytic listening is essentially atheoretical. He quotes an anecdote from Bonaparte regarding Freud to the effect that "the appropriate stance for the analyst 'taking in the scenery,' " as when that "consists simply in not directing one's notice to anything in particular and maintaining the same 'evenly suspended attention' . . . in the face of all that one hears." Whether or not empathic listening is theory based is a major topic, both with critics of self psychology and with its supporters (see Goldberg, 1988).

Kohut's (1984) ideas in this area are significant because he divides the therapeutic enterprise of psychoanalysis into two related components. The first is the understanding phase of pure data gathering, characterized by "empathy." In this phase, the analysand must feel that the analyst understands and affirms the reality of the analysand's primary experience. (See also Schwaber, 1983.) The second phase he terms the explanation. The explanatory phase is also known as the interpretive phase. Although it is now recognized that one can not perceive without some preconception (such as a theory) of what one will see (or hear), I believe that the first, "understanding" phase is much less anchored to an explicit theoretical formula than is the second "explanatory" phase.

In my own teaching, I characterize the first phase as the "what" phase, and second phase as the "why" phase. Thus, in the first phase, the analyst must be experienced by patients as understanding what they are saying about themselves and their experience. As Bromberg notes, insofar as the analyst is accurate in this first phase, new and significant material will emerge. The second phase, the explanation or interpretive phase, can be understood as always directly answering the question "why" with "because." Generally speaking, there are three domains of interpretation in this second, "explaining" phase. The first involves the patient's day-to-day interactions away from the therapy. The second domain of interpretation involves the interactions between the analysand and the analyst, the so-called transference. The third domain is the material from the patient's early life, the so-called genetic point of view.

The two phases can be brought together. For example: you felt happy and relieved when I told you I would be taking a vacation next month [the understanding phase], *because* you experience me as someone who is trying to undermine your self-esteem by not giving you enough support in your life [the explaining phase].

Kohut's emphasis on empathy and the empathic vantage point was specifically aimed at a group of patients who had suffered a lack of affective attunement during some point of their early development (Basch, 1988). Such a lack of affective attunement is not significant in those patients suffering from the structural neuroses. Yet, knowing that these patients suffer from a disturbance of affective attunement would be insufficient to analyze successfully most of the self-disturbances. It is here that the second phase, the explanatory phase, utilizing the concept of the selfobject developmental lines and the selfobject transferences, becomes crucial. In the strictly psychoanalytic sense, self psychology is not an "interpersonal" theory. Feelings about, and interactions with, other people are viewed as contributing an essential aspect to the patient's own self-organization (Goldberg, 1988). Self-selfobject relationships are different from self-other relationships. Interpersonal theories bear only on the latter. Kohut always felt that self-other (object) relationships were very important in human experience. One type of pathology involving self-other interactions is the structural neuroses. I must confess disappointment in learning that the interpersonal school of psychoanalysis has not made further headway in understanding the developmental lines, characteristic transferences, and psychopathology of such "self-other" relationships as those involving care, friendship, and love.

Gediman's chapter focuses on one aspect of clinical theory, the role of conflict versus deficit pathology and how they can be intertwined in any specific patient's disturbance. She believes Kohut's approach, which she characterizes by quoting his ideas on Tragic Man versus Guilty Man, is too simple. She notes that Kohut's conclusion was that, for the most part, patients presented either with symptomatic disturbance or character pathology related to either conflict or deficit organization. There is no doubt that, although one can find many instances of references to "deficit and conflict," the central aspect of Kohut's clinical contribution in this area is the differentiation of object libidinal relationships and their correlated psychopathology versus the self-selfobject relationships and their correlated psychopathology. My own belief is that in discussions on such a high level of sophistication as Gediman's, one must give up the manifestly metaphorical terms conflict and deficit and rely on those specific types of transferences mobilized in the analytic situation. In other words, rather than looking at conflict versus deficit pathology in the analytic situation, one should organize the data along the lines of object versus selfobject transferences mobilized.

Gediman goes on to use the concept of "annihilation anxiety" (in Kohut's terminology, disintegration anxiety) as a way of discussing the issues of conflict and deficit pathology. In this context, she urges us to attempt to integrate conflict and deficit models by not forgetting "Freud's view that the experience of the anticipation of traumatic intensity of excessive stimulation and the corresponding feeling of psychic helplessness as a narcissistic catastrophe underlies all the dangerous situations." She states that

> narcissistic catastrophe . . . refers to the vulnerability of the psychic structure of the person in the face of undischarged accumulated need tensions and situations of psychic helplessness. The unconscious or the manifest experiential content known as annihilation anxiety refers to powerful affects, that is, the quantitative intensification of anxiety, associated with representations of all four of the traditional danger situations.

Gediman continues,

> My reconciliatory position contains two basic assumptions. One, both narcissistic and neurotic manifestations of anxiety, in the broader sense, are implicated in conflict and compromise formation, although manifestations may differ with respect to the relative preponderance of pre-oedipal or oedipal conflicts.

> Two, both narcissistic and neurotic annihilation anxiety reflect a certain degree of traumatic excitability deriving even from traumatic failures of empathy or any other trauma, or from other factors such as rigid defenses. . . .

In summary, Gediman is attempting to integrate conflict and deficit pathology by suggesting that disintegration and conflict-based anxieties are found throughout the various types of psychological disturbance. In particular, relying on Freud's (1926) first psychoeconomic theory of anxiety, she suggests that disintegration anxiety is to be equated with helplessness and is therefore part and parcel of all psychological disturbances. Although this is certainly a justifiable position, I believe that the crucial issue is whether the anxiety is derived from conflict with a separate person and the dangers implied in that, or from the loss of another person who is being experienced as a part of oneself in the self-selfobject system.

Another perspective can be gained on the understanding of the distinction between conflict and deficit pathology, on one hand, and disintegration anxiety versus other forms of anxiety, on the other, by turning to the domain of metapsychological formulation. Metapsychology consists of those theories not derived from protracted empathic immersion with another, that is, not derived from a psychoanalytic situation (see Basch, 1988). For example, Piaget's theories of cognitive development, neuropsychology, systems theory, and affect theory all are systems of thought relevant to explicating psychoanalytic clinical findings and clinical theory, although they are not derived directly from protracted empathic immersion (see Basch, 1977, 1981). Tomkins's (1981) theories regarding the nature of affect, combined with cybernetic models of brain functioning, lend an excellent metapsychological pespective on self psychology's clinical findings. Figure 1 shows Tomkin's theory of affect. The various qualitative differences among the affects are initially quantitative differences resulting from the density of neural firing as a function of time in the context of information being perceived and integrated by the brain.

Figure 2 shows the same information as Figure 1, except that the brain's optimal range of processing information has been superimposed. This optimal range of processing is the result of both biological factors and learning. As Kohut (1977) has described, the total personality consists of innumerable selves, sectors, and segments. He has termed the nuclear self as that self which resides at the very core of the personality and is, in a sense, responsible for the

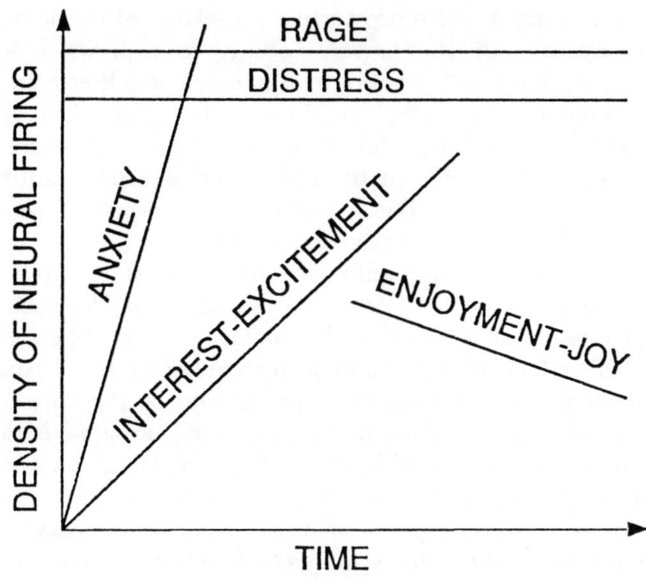

FIG. 1 (from Tomkins, 1981)

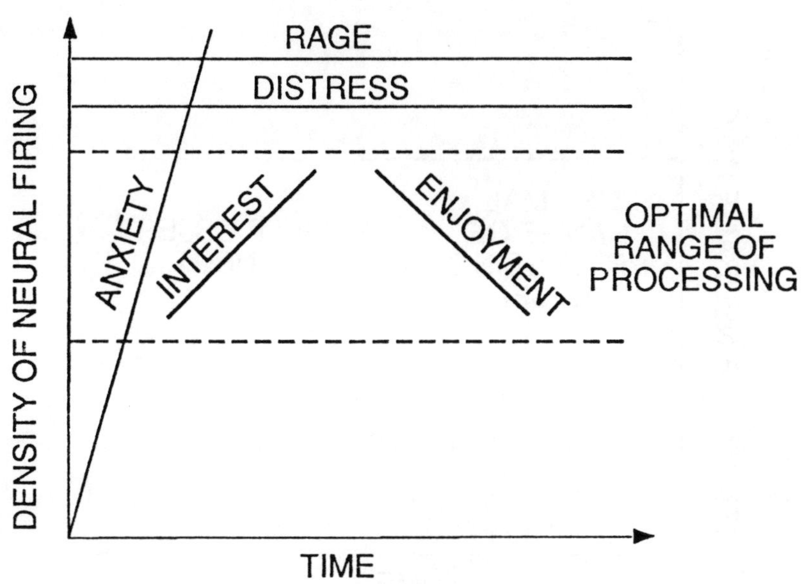

FIG. 2

smooth functioning of the more peripheral selves. Also, the nuclear self is responsible for the person's ability to experience life as meaningful, as lived with a more or less resilient self-esteem. The "optimal range of processing" might also be referred to as the "optimal range of selfing," for it is the process of organizing experience optimally that can be understood as "maintaining the cohesion of the self." As Basch (1976a) has discussed, self is a reevocation of "selfing." (See also Basch, 1978).

Figure 3 includes the selfobject function as a part of the cybernetic feedback system necessary to maintain "cohesion" or optimal processing at the level of the nuclear self. A "cohesive" and vital nuclear self is metapsychologically explained as the maintenance within the optimal range of processing of the core of the personality. This "selfing," or maintenance of cohesion, is dependent on the input of a specific kind of information into the self system (located in any particular individual's brain). This information, described from the point of view of clinical theory, is the selfobject function. When the selfobject's function does not provide the necessary information to the information-processing brain, "fragmentation" occurs.

The personality is made up of a complex hierarchy of peripheral and superficial selves or sectors of processing organized around

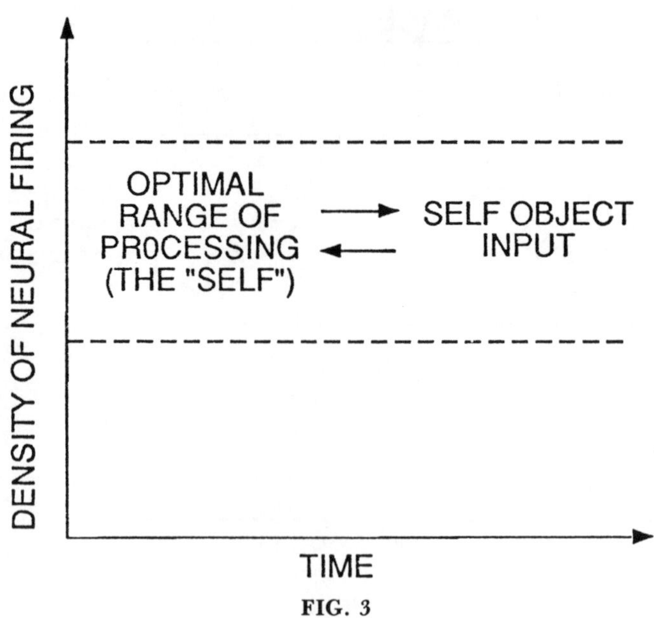

FIG. 3

the core central "nuclear selfing." Disintegration, or annihilation anxiety, is the result of a disruption in the nuclear self-selfobject feedback cycle. Conflict or neurotic anxiety can result from the inability to organize experience in superficial layers of the personality. Neurotic anxiety is helplessness that does not affect the very core of the personality.

In the last section of her paper, when discussing the issues of psychoanalytic technique, Gediman states, "When the dissolution of the self metaphor is contained in interpretations that the analyst offers to narcissistic patients, patients often tend to respond narcissistically, with any one of a number of 'entitlement' fantasies." She goes on to state, "If the analyst were to neglect latent content and the role of conflict in the kind of incomplete, one-sided interpretations aimed only at addressing developmental arrests, he or she could produce an "iatrogenic effect" in helping along the patient's expectation of being treated either as defective or as an 'exception.' " Most self psychologists, I believe, would see Gediman's caveat as an impediment to maintaining the empathic stance and would view "the patient's expectation of being treated either as defective or as an exception" as the welcome emergence of disavowed aspects of the self that might be indications of the mobilization of any one of the varieties of the nuclear selfobject transferences (see Schwaber, 1983).

Muller's comparison of the work of Kohut and Lacan, using the vehicle of a reinterpretation of Kohut's (1979) "The Two Analyses of Mr. Z," involves the reader directly in the obscure complexity of Lacan's ideas. It seems to me that Lacan's notions regarding the "imaginary, the symbolic, and the real" are meant as metapsychological concepts (see Basch, 1973), whose truth can be validated only outside the the psychoanalytic situation. In other words, these three terms and their interrelation need to be compared and contrasted with the work of, for example, Piaget (Piaget and Inhelder, 1969), Tomkins (1981), and Vygotsky (1934).

Lacan's theory of motivation employs the concepts of "need" and "desire." The former is a biological concept, whereas the latter is the psychological result of the biological impulsion. These motivational concepts are also part of a metapsychological system that is not derived directly from psychoanalytic observation. An alternative, one that seems more consistent with the findings of clinical psychoanalysts, is to anchor the concepts of motivation in both instinct and affect (Basch, 1976b, 1978, 1983a, 1988; Tomkins, 1981).

To focus on another point, so far as I can judge there is little correspondence between Lacan's mirror stage and Kohut's concept of the selfobject's mirroring developmental life. Whereas Lacan describes the young child's interaction with its own image in the mirror, Kohut's concept of mirroring stresses the child's relationship with another vital, enthusiastic human being who is experienced as providing a function that the child does not have within itself.

Muller (this volume) questions Kohut's explanation of the source of the anxiety in the dream of the returning father with gifts being held out of the room by the boy's pressure against the door. Muller overlooks the inchoate self's vulnerabilities in which overstimulation and "flooding." are a threat equal to that of loss. Figure 2 shows that the self-organization (or "selfing") is maintained only within an "optimal range of processing." The overstimulation caused by "too much, too soon" can potentially destroy the organization of the self. (See also Elson, 1987.)

Although all the theoreticians discussed in the Contemporary Contributors section have engaged in an ongoing dialogue with self psychology and Kohut, perhaps no dialogue has gained more attention than the "Kernberg-Kohut debate." Fitting the importance of this debate, Akhtar's essay is of exceptionally wide range. He discusses not only the different conceptions of such clinical issues as the development and structure of the character pathology known as narcissistic personality disturbance, but also their relative emphasis in citing early contributors and involvement with general psychiatry.

The relationship of psychoanalysis to general psychiatry is an old issue starting with Freud himself. Also an old issue, although still the subject of some controversy, is that of medical analysis versus lay analysis. The intensity of this latter debate has shifted over the last several decades, the attempt to keep psychotherapy a medical subspecialty now being of historical interest. The interrelation among psychotherapy, psychoanalysis, and psychiatry is a complex one. There is no doubt that Kohut (1977) was a purist in insisting that psychoanalysis is not only a therapy but also preeminently a scientific endeavor. (See also Eissler, 1965.)

Related to the relationship of psychoanalysis to general psychiatry is the relationship of psychoanalysis to general psychotherapy. In the past decade not only has the understanding of the role of psychopharmacology in a variety of psychological disturbances increased significantly, but also awareness of childhood trauma and the associated defense of dissociation has grown. The traumas resulting from childhood physical and sexual abuse are often defended against by encapsulating dissociative defenses incapable of remobilization and integration in the transference through the techniques of empathy and free association. Hypnosis is often necessary for access to the childhood traumas. And it often is a crucial intervention either prior to or during analytic work. In my view, all therapists should be trained in hypnotic techniques and become sophisticated in their application. Certain cases of child abuse lay deeply hidden, and the working psychoanalyst may not be able to gain access to them without utilizing hypnosis (Bliss, 1986).

Kohut (1977) was not only aware of other contributors to the psychology of the self, but initially attempted to incorporate them.

> At first I tried to orient myself in the area of my interest with the aid of the existing psychoanalytic literature. But, finding myself floundering in a morass of conflicting, poorly based, and often vague theoretical speculation, I decided there was only one way that would lead to progress: the way back to the direct observation of clinical phenomenon and the construction of new formulations that would accommodate my observations (p.xx-xxi).

The substance of Akhtar's chapter pertains to clinically relevant issues. In regard to the role of conflict, Akhtar suggests that Kohut plays down the role of conflict. Akhtar states, "Kohut proposes that, given optimal parental responsiveness, the growing child is internally conflict free." Kohut's views are actually the opposite of this. Kohut felt (1984) that conflict was omnipresent in human experience but in many situations would lead to maturity and growth. What Kohut did say is that with proper selfobject responsiveness, these inevitable, ubiquitous conflicts would not lead to characterological or symptomatic psychopathology. Kohut would agree wholeheartedly with the viewpoint that Akhtar ascribes to Kernberg: "Kernberg regards intrapsychic conflicts to be a necessary and inevitable aspect of mental life, and not merely an enforced byproduct of faulty parental responsiveness to the growing child."

In regard to the role of the oedipal complex in development and psychopathology, there is a substantial difference in the views of Kernberg and Kohut. Kohut views the pathogenic oedipal complex not as an inevitable part of human development. Akhtar is quite right when he states, "Little mention is found in his writings of penis, vagina, urinary stream pleasure, infantile theories of childbirth, penis envy, primal scene, castration fears, and the like." According to Kohut (1977), these issues play a central role in the analysis of the structural neuroses, but a peripheral to nonexistent role in the analyses of the narcissistic disturbances.

The differing views of Kernberg and Kohut regarding the role of the oedipal complex in normal and pathological developments is part of a much wider difference. Kernberg adheres to the Freudian drive theory as his central motivational construct in his clinical theory, whereas Kohut has determined that in a certain widely found type of psychopathology, the self-disturbances, infantile sexual development is not the major domain of fixation and regression.

As an aside, Akhtar quotes Greenberg and Mitchell to support the common misunderstanding that Kohut sees instinctual wish as the result of pathology. Kohut very much supported the idea that the wish for and seeking out of sexual gratification should be seen as a healthy human wish, the self seeking a particular pleasure. Kohut (1977), however, emphasized in his writings—writings that focused on clinical psychoanalysis and the cure of a certain type of character pathology—that *drives in isolation* (pp. 122, 171–173) reflect underlying pathology. That is, drives that emerge directly from a rupture in the self-selfobject bond are part and parcel of a defensive move on the part of the narcissistically wounded patient to restore self-cohesion.

In his final section, Akhtar discusses the treatment technique differences between Kernberg and Kohut. Whereas Kernberg emphasizes the need to confront the patient with distortions in reality, Kohut (1984) emphasized the need for the analyst to accept and enter into the patient's world. Reality "distortion" must always enter into the analyst's consideration of the material that the patient presents. Except when the patient's or someone else's life is threatened, however, this viewpoint is rarely a *directly* relevant one. Perhaps distortion is an issue of lack of "age-appropriate responsiveness," rather than reality "distortion." As the analyst accepts and moves into the patient's experience and tries to see the world as the patient does, defenses recede and feelings are mobilized in a way not allowed for by an "objective," reality-based approach (see Schwaber, 1983).

Akhtar concludes that Kohut feels that interpretation is no longer a relevant aspect of psychoanalytic technique. Kohut does refer to certain analyses when interpretations seem to play a minimal role. However, his contribution to technique, the "basic therapeutic unit" (Kohut, 1984) gives equal weight to the role of interpretation and the role of the empathic bond.

Akhtar closes his essay by asking, "Need the reader be reminded that this latter (Kernberg) view of basic human nature is closer to what the founder of psychoanalysis had envisioned?" Unquestionably, Kernberg's ideas on such issues as the oedipal complex, the instinctual drives, and the very essence of humankind lie closer to Freud's than Kohut's do. Whether or not this means that Kohut's work in self psychology should not be considered psychoanalysis and is less in tune with the essence of modern human experience and its disturbances is a question each of us must decide (see Basch, 1986).The ideas of Kohut and Kernberg have been a major force in modern psychoanalysis. Most of the contributions that these two men have made have flowed from the psychoanalytic situation. This is natural, of course, inasmuch as both men have been committed to the tenet that clinical psychoanalysis is in a fundamental way a legitimate *scientific* enterprise.

Because clinical psychoanalysis utilizes the transference in both an observational and a conceptual fashion, it is only natural that its findings will sooner or later need to be compared and contrasted with observations of children (see Kohut and Wolf, 1978). The work of Margaret Mahler has dominated the psychoanalytic developmental literature for the past several decades. Many clinical psychoanalytic theoreticians have relied heavily on her work (Kernberg, 1980; Masterson, 1981). The Shanes' chapter compares the work of Kohut and Mahler. As the Shanes note, as Kohut's work became increasingly embedded in the empathic point of view—what the patient is experiencing to the exclusion of extrospective viewpoints—Kohut (1980) felt that his work could not be reconciled with Mahler's. To make just one point among many that could be made in regard to this comparison: Would the concept and domain of the self-selfobject experiences ever have been discovered using the methodology that Mahler adopted? No. Furthermore, the concept of the selfobject matrix, which is essential to understanding the self's developments or disturbance, gives a vastly enriched understanding of the so-called issues of separation and individuation.

I am reminded of the difference between the unconscious before and after Freud's own conceptions of the dynamic unconscious. There is no doubt that many thinkers had talked about mentation and experience proceeding outside of awareness (Whyte, 1960). However, it took Freud's *theory* of the *dynamic* unconscious, plus the innumerable observations of people both in analysis and outside to give the proper depth and relevancy to the concept of the unconscious. This is also true of Kohut's conception of the central role of self-selfobject experiences in human developmental life. This theory of Kohut's focuses on the same terrain as Mahler's ideas of separation and individuation. But, Kohut's theory has allowed us a deeper understanding of these dimensions of human experience that, like Freud's concept of the dynamic unconscious, both enhances our appreciation of its role in everyday human experience and gives us a tool for understanding certain processes in a clinical psychoanalysis.

Felicitously, the Shanes did not stop at comparing the theories of Mahler and Kohut. They also included a comparison of how both Kohut's and Mahler's ideas measure up to those of modern developmental researchers, especially Stern (1985). As the Shanes demonstrate, the work of sophisticated infant and child developmental researchers has a vast and central relevance for psychoanalytic clinical theory. This work provides yet another perspective on developmental and psychopathological theories developed within the psychoanalytic context (reconstructions based on material mobilized in a clinical analysis). Infant researchers should not, of course, be viewed as judges of the observations and theories derived from clinical analysis. Although in a certain sense the observations of the analytic researcher are more limited than those of the developmental researcher, they may also be much richer. To state the obvious, infant and childhood researchers do not observe the large sectors of human experience that emerge in adolescence and adulthood. Necessary is an ongoing dialogue in which the clinical and academic researchers can mutually enhance and correct the contributions of the other.

Klein's chapter on the work of Masterson clearly shows the importance of the work of Mahler to Masterson's clinical theories. It may not be an exaggeration to suggest that the validity of Masterson's clinical theories stands or falls on the validity of Mahler's developmental theories. Recently, perhaps under the influence of Kohut's work, Masterson (1985) has focused on the concept of the "real self." Descriptively, Masterson's "real self" and Kohut's "nuclear self" are almost indistinguishable. Both concepts have to do with core vitality, cohesiveness, and the need for self-actualization. The major difference is that Kohut's nuclear self is essentially embedded in a selfobject supportive-responsive matrix, whereas Masterson's "real self" is independent and autonomous. In addition, Kohut's theory of the nuclear self includes its differentiated structure (bipolarity) and the correlated defensive and compensatory structures. Masterson's concept of the real self relies more on the constructs of self and object representations. In fact, he (Masterson, 1985) states, "The real self is defined as the sum of the self and object representations, intrapsychically, and their related affective states" (p.171). The nuclear self is only one among many different self-configurations within the personality, although it resides at the very core of the personality (Kohut, 1977).

Klein also describes what he believes is a difference in the concept of cure between Masterson and Kohut. He suggests that Kohut focuses on the "missing structure" in the self-disturbances. "In contrast, the essence of the work and treatment of the personality disorders is the working-through of the abandonment depression, the fundamental roadblock on the developmental pathway that underlies all the disorders of the self." Kohut (1984) spoke about a variety of archaic configurations that are engaged and worked through in the analysis of the self-disturbances. Perhaps his most comprehensive statement is the following: "I want to emphasize the essential importance of . . . working through the lethargies, depressions, and rages of early life via the reactivation and analysis of their archaic traumatic self-selfobject relationships in the transference" (p. 5).

It also seems as if Masterson's approach with borderlines contains significantly more "confrontation" than self psychology. Rather than using confrontation with the severely disturbed, self psychology employs empathic responsiveness. Kohut (1984) emphasizes that often with the severely disturbed, long phases of "just understanding" are necessary before the nuclear transferences become mobilized. (See also Brandchaft and Stolorow, 1984.)

In his chapter, Gedo takes issue with a variety of points of view identified with self psychology. His perhaps most important point is carried in his final sentence: "Last, there are more things in heaven and on earth than are dealt with by self psychology." Gedo feels that Kohut's clinical experience was quite limited and ignored the contributions of others. Kohut may have been unaware of widespread childhood physical and sexual abuse. For example, Kohut's discussions of the conversion hysterias are consistent with Freud's and ignored the childhood sexual abuse that often provides the bedrock for these disorders. (However, see Freud, 1896). Gedo is also on the mark in noting that many members of the "self psychology school" bend to see Kohut's ideas as the alpha and omega of both clinical theory and therapeutic technique.

It is difficult to evaluate the basis for Gedo's contention that self psychology relies too much (exclusively?) on empathy (affective attunement). There are various opinions on this matter. However, Kohut himself, by introducing the concept of the basic therapeutic unit (understanding and explaining), certainly implies that although it is essential for the patient to feel the analyst has grasped his experience, the analyst is under no obligation to agree with it or affirm its essential logic.

I believe that Gedo is correct in noting that Kohut's discussions of psychosis are inadequate. For example, Kohut often talks about the borderline as having a "psychotic core." Kohut does not distinguish impaired reality testing from thought disorder or nonspecific states of chaos characterized by rage and disintegration anxiety.

Perhaps the most important lack in Gedo's own models, at least from the point of view of the self psychologist, is his restricting the self-selfobject unit to circumscribed archaic areas of pathological functioning. There are several points at which I believe Gedo misunderstands self psychology. First, Gedo states, "In this (nosological) schema, the sole indicator of dysfunction is the patient's subjective state: is the self lacking in vigor, coherence, or harmony?" The categorization of the patient's self-state can be, and often is, made by observation, without its being correlated with the subjective experience of the patient.

Second, Gedo also states, "In Kohut's scheme, various forms of self-disorder are accounted for by means of the concept of a vertical split." While this is true, Kohut (1977) also felt that self-disorder could manifest itself by virtue of "defensive structures" and certain pathological interactions with others (Kohut and Wolf, 1978).

Gedo's own contributions to clinical psychoanalysis (Gedo, 1979, 1981; Gedo and Goldberg, 1973) employ a hierarchical schema of interrelated developmental levels, defensive organization, psychological needs, and a variety of other variables. Self psychologists could learn from this approach and attempt more sophisticated conceptual understandings of the development of human psychological functioning using a hierarchical model.

SUMMARY AND CONCLUSION

In this chapter, I set myself two major tasks. The first was to discuss each of the foregoing chapters with an eye to verifying self psychology's relationship to the specific theorist being discussed. In a sense, this task can be seen as a "critique of the critiques." The second major task was to place self psychology and the modern developments in psychoanalysis in the larger context of the phylogeny of the personal unconscious, on the one hand, and the bipolar nuclear self, on the other. I discussed how the shift from the archetypal organization of the personality to the modern organization included both an expansion of the personal unconscious at the expense of the collective unconscious and a shift from a unitary, archetypal self to the bipolar nuclear self. On the metapsychological level (Basch, 1988), both of these shifts can be explained by the expansion of the role of the affective (self-object) tie in human development over the last three or four millenia.

In his final paper (Kohut, 1984), Kohut illuminated his shift away from the Freudian psychoanalytic theory of the drives by contrasting the Sophoclean Oedipus with the Odysseus of Homer. His central point was that the great tragedy of King Oedipus began early in his life when, seen as a threat to his father, he was sent out into the woods to be killed. The tragic events of his final demise formed an unbroken continuum with the early rejection of his infantile healthy self. The destructiveness of the Oedipus complex results from the rejection of the child's healthy strivings. In contrast, Kohut underscored the healthy parents' response to the child by citing Odysseus' avoiding killing his infant son by the plow after Palamedes had placed him in the furrow to test Odysseus' sanity. It was the very act of avoiding injury to his son that signaled to the Mycenean warriors that Odysseus was indeed feigning insanity (Kohut, 1983).

Perhaps, for the modern reader, the saga of *E.T.: The Extraterrestrial* is a more appropriate referent. This extraordinarily popular movie portrays ". . . a ten-year-old child, Eliot, growing up in a family characterized by a harried, overworked mother and the recent departure of his father. E.T., the extraterrestrial, then arrives, surely symbolizing the regressively transformed inner experience of the boy. Rather than experiencing himself as a joyful, growing child, Eliot feels like a charming yet ugly being left by cruel fate on a distant planet far from his own kind" (Detrick, 1985, p. 240). The regressive pull of the addictions is portrayed in the scene with E.T. binge-eating and becoming drunk. Eliot's pseudomaturity in both love and work is symbolized by his activities at his school. Throughout the movie, the helping adults are portrayed as faceless, whether the schoolteacher or the NASA scientists. It is only at the end, when one of the scientists takes off his helmet (the act of empathic bond represented by the human face), that the tide is turned. Eliot is allowed to see E.T. E.T.'s vitality is restored.

Within the larger human context, empathic bonds both sustain the individual's essential humanness and catalyze the individual's innate initiative and creativity (Kohut, 1973). Within the confines of the psychoanalytic situation, that restricted and special process which was the focus of Heinz Kohut's lifelong commitment, he always emphasized "scientific" empathy. He asserted:

> But scientific empathy, the broadening and strengthening of this bridge toward the other human being, will be the highest ideal. If the analyst will lead the sciences of tomorrow into this direction, he will most significantly have entered the decisive battle of the future: the struggle between the human world, a world in which the varieties of psychological experience are cherished, and a non-human world. . . . whose regimentations and regularities resemble the inexorable laws that established the organization of inorganic matter. We cannot predict how this battle will end, or where the victory will ultimately lie. But we do know on which side the psychoanalyst must fight, upon which side psychoanalysis, this new son among the sciences of man, will shed its understanding warmth and its explaining light [p. 684].

REFERENCES

Basch, M. F. (1973), Psychoanalysis and Theory formation. *The Annual of Psychoanalysis,* 1:39–52. New York: Quadrangle/New York Times Books.

_____ (1976a), Psychoanalysis and communication science. *The Annual of Psychoanalysis,* 4:385–421. New York: International Universities Press.

_____ (1976b), The concept of affect: A re-examination. *J. Amer. Psychoanal. Assn.,* 24:759–77.

_____ (1977), Developmental psychology and explanatory theory in psychoanalysis. *The Annual of Psychoanalysis,* 5:229–63. New York: International Universities Press.

_____ (1978), Psychic determinism and freedom of will. *Internat. Rev. Psychoanal.,* 5:257–64.

_____ (1981), Psychoanalytic interpretation and cognitive transformation. *Internat. J. Psycho-Anal.,* 62:151–75.

_____ (1983a), Empathic understanding: A review of the concept and some theoretical considerations. *J. Amer. Psychoanal. Assn.,* 31:101–26.

_____ (1983b), The perception of reality and the disavowal of meaning. *The Annual of Psychoanalysis,* 11:125–54. New York: International Universities Press.

_____ (1985), New directions in psychoanalysis. *Psychoanal. Psychol.,* 2:1–13.

_____ (1986), Can this be psychoanalysis? *Progress in Self Psychology,* Vol. 2. New York: Guilford Press, pp. 18–30.

_____ (1988), *Understanding Psychotherapy.* New York: Basic Books.

Bliss, E. (1986), *Multiple Personality, Allied Disorders, and Hypnosis.* New York: Oxford University Press.

Brandchaft, B. (1986), British object relations theory and self psychology. *Progress in Self Psychology,* Vol. 2. New York: Guilford Press, pp. 245–272.

_____ Stolorow, R. (1984), The borderline concept: Pathological character or iatrogenic myth? In: *Empathy II,* ed. J. Lichtenberg, M. Bornstein & D. Silver. Hillsdale, NJ: The Analytic Press, pp. 333–357.

Detrick, D.W. (1985), Alterego phenomena and the alterego transferences. In: *Progress In Self Psychology,* Vol. I, ed. Arnold Goldberg. New York: Guilford Press, pp. 240–256.

Edinger, E. (1973), *Ego and Archetype.* New York: Penguin.

_____ (1985), *Anatomy of the Psyche.* LaSalle, IL: Open Court.

Eissler, K. (1965), *Medical Orthodoxy and the Future of Psychoanalysis.* New York: International Universities Press.

Eliade, M. (1954), *The Myth of the Eternal Return.* Princeton, NJ: Princeton University Press.

Elson, M. (1987), *The Kohut Seminars.* New York: Norton.

Ferenczi, S. (1933), The confusion of tongues between adults and children. In: *Final Contributions to the Problems and Methods of Psychoanalysis,* Vol. 3, ed. M. Balint. New York: Basic Books, pp. 156–167, 1955.

Freud, S. (1896), The aetiology of hysteria. *Standard Edition,* 3:191–221. London: Hogarth Press, 1959.

_____ (1905), Three essays on the theory of sexuality. *Standard Edition,* 7:130–243. London: Hogarth Press, 1959.

_____ (1911–1915), Papers on technique. *Standard Edition,* 12:89–171. London: Hogarth Press, 1958.

_____ (1923) The ego and the id. *Standard Edition,* 19:12–59. London: Hogarth Press, 1961.

_____ (1926), Inhibitions, symptoms and anxiety. *Standard Edition,* 20:77–178. London: Hogarth Press, 1959.

Gedo, J. (1979), *Beyond Interpretation.* New York: International Universities Press.

_____ (1981), *Advances in Clinical Psychoanalysis.* New York: International Universities Press.

_____ & Goldberg, A. (1973), *Models of the Mind.* Chicago: University of Chicago Press.

Goldberg, A. (1988), *A Fresh Look at Psychoanalysis.* Hillsdale, NJ: The Analytic Press.

Greenberg, J. & Mitchell, S. (1983), *Object Relations in Psychoanalytic Theory.* Cambridge, MA: Harvard University Press.

Heidegger, M. (1927). *Being and Time.* New York: Harper and Row, 1962.

Hillman, J. (1972), *The Myth of Analysis.* Evanston, IL: Northwestern University Press.

Jaynes, J. (1976), *The Origin of Consciousness in the Breakdown of the Bicameral Mind.* Boston: Houghton Mifflin.

Jones, E. (1955), *The Life and Work of Sigmund Freud,* Vol. 2. New York: Basic Books.

Jung, C. (1946), The psychology of the transference. *Collected Works* Vol. 16. Princeton, NJ: Princeton University Press.

Kernberg, O. (1980), *Internal World and External Reality.* New York: Aronson.

Kohut, H. (1959), Introspection, empathy and psychoanalysis. In: *The Search for the Self,* Vol. 1, ed. P. Ornstein. New York: International Universities Press. pp. 205–232.

_____ (1966), Forms and transformations of narcissism. In: *The Search for the Self,* Vol. 1, ed. P. Ornstein. New York: International Universities Press, pp. 427–460., 1978.

_____ (1968), The psychoanalytic treatment of narcissistic personality disorders: Outline of a systematic approach. *The Psychoanalytic Study of the Child,* 23:86–113. New York: International Universities Press.

_____ (1971), *The Analysis of the Self.* New York: International Universities Press.

_____ (1973), The future of psychoanalysis. In: *The Search for the Self,* Vol. 2, ed, P. Ornstein. New York: International Universities Press, pp. 663–684.

_____ (1977), *The Restoration of the Self.* New York: International Universities Press.

_____ (1979). The Two Analyses of Mr. Z. *International Journal of Psychoanalysis,* 60:3–18.

_____ (1984), *How Does Analysis Cure,* ed. A. Goldberg & P. Stepansky. Chicago: University of Chicago Press.

_____ & Wolf, E. (1978), The disorders of the self and their treatment: An outline. *Internat. J. Psycho-Anal.,* 59:413–425.

Lifton, R. J. (1963), *Thought Reform and the Psychology of Totalism.* New York: Norton.

Masterson, J. (1981), *Narcissistic and Borderline Disorders.* New York: Brunner/Mazel.

_____ (1985), *The Real Self.* New York: Brunner/Mazel.

McCall, R. (1983), *Phenomenological Psychology.* Madison; WI: University of Wisconsin Press.

Meissner, W. (1985), Psychoanalysis: The dilemma of science and humanism. *Psychoanal. Inq.,* 5:471–498.

Miller, A. (1984), *Thou Shalt Not Be Aware.* New York: NAL, Penguin.

Piaget, J. & Inhelder, B. (1969), *The Psychology of the Child.* New York: Basic Books.

Rogers, C. (1980), *A Way of Being.* Boston: Houghton Mifflin.

Sartre, J.P. (1943), *Being and Nothingness.* New York: Washington Square Press, 1966.

Schwaber, E. (1983), Psychoanalytic listening and psychic reality. *Internat. Rev. Psychoanal.,* 10:379–392.

Stern, D. (1985), *The Interpersonal World of the Infant.* New York: Basic Books.

Strozier, C. (1985), *Self Psychology and the Humanities.* New York: Norton.

Sulloway, F. (1979), *Freud: Biologist of the Mind.* New York: Basic Books.

Tomkins, S. (1981), The quest for primary motives: Biography and autobiography of an idea. *J. Personal. Soc. Psychol.,* 41:306–324.

Vygotsky, L. (1934). *Thought and Language.* Boston: MIT Press, paperback edition, 1962.

Weintraub, K. (1978), *The Value of the Individual.* Chicago, IL: University of Chicago Press.

Whyte, W. (1960), *The Unconscious Before Freud.* New York: Basic Books.

Winnicott, D. (1951), Transitional objects and transitional phenomena. *Collected Papers: Through Paediatrics to Psychoanalysis.* New York: Basic Books, pp. 229–242, 1958.

——— (1960). Ego distortion in terms of true and false self. In: *The Maturational Processes and the Facilitating Environment.* New York: International Universities Press, pp. 140–152, 1965.

Author Index

A

Abraham, K., 233, 243, *256*
Adler, A., 50, 51–54, *72*
Akhtar, S., 331, 333, 335, 344, 353, *357*
Alexander, F., 101, *106*
Altshuler, K. Z., 334, *357*
Andersson, O., 6, *20*
Angel, E., 210, *211*
Ansbacher, H., 113–14, *126*
Ansbacher, R., 113–14, *126*
Anzieu, D., 96, *106*
Arthur, D., 332, *360*
Atkin, S., 338, *357*
Atwood, G. E., *158,* 176, *190,* 194*n,* 196, 197*n,* 208, *211,* 234, 238, 239, *256*
Aulagnier, P., 377, *392*

B

Bacal, H. A., 218, 219, *226,* 249, *256,* 259–69, *270,* 335–38, 341*n,* *357*
Bach, S., 301, *308,* 341*n,* 348, *357*
Baker, H. S., 333, *357,* 417, *426*
Baker, M. N., 333, *357,* 417, *426*
Balint, M., 90, 94, 102, *106,* 242–49, 250, *256, 257,* 262*n,* 337, 339, *357*
Barande, I., 90, *106*
Barrett-Lennard, G. T., 283, *290*
Barton, A., *190*
Basch, M. F., 4, 6, 7, 10, 11, 14–19, *20, 21,* 89, *106,* 224, *226,* 405, *412,* 417, 425, *426, 427,* 430, 435–36, 442–43, 446, 448, 450, 451, 455, 459, *460, 461*
Bauer, S., 332, *360*
Bergman, A., 312, 313, *327,* 336, *361,* 395, 396, 399, *413*
Bergman, M. S., 90, *106*
Binswanger, L., 178, *190,* 210, *211*
Bion, W., 236, 256, *257*
Birch, H. G., *362*
Birnbaum, J. H., 98, *107*
Blashfield, R. K., 333, *358*
Bliss, E., 442, 453, *461*
Blumenthal, R., 332, *360*
Bollas, C., 89, *106*
Boss, M., 178, *190,* 210, *211*
Brandchaft, B., *158,* 194*n, 211,* 232, 234, 238, 239, *257,* 442, 444, 457, *461*

Brenner, C., 305, *308,* 338, 342, *358, 359*
Breuer, J., 6, *21*
Bromberg, P. M., 277, 282*n,* 285, 289, *290, 291*
Brown, C., 366*n, 392*
Burgess, A. W., 98, *106*

C

Calef, V., 330, 338, 341, *358*
Carr, A., 332, *360*
Chess, S., *362*
Chessick, R. D., 89, *106*
Chomsky, N., 41*n, 45*
Coen, S., 368, *392*
Cohler, B. J., 89, *106*
Cooper, A. M., 330, *358*
Corbett, L., 24, *45*
Cottet, S., 391, *392*

D

Davis, M., 262, 266, 269, *270*
Demos, E. V., 84, *87*
Derrida, J., 373, *392*
Detrick, D. W., 15, *21,* 166-67, 170, *172,* 459, *461*
Deutsch, H., 338, *358*
Dilthey, W., 68-70, *72*
Dorpat, T., 344, *358*
Dreyfus, H. L., 141, *149*
Duhem, P., 66, *73*
Dupont, J., 96, 98, *106*

E

Edinger, E., 439, *461*
Einstein, A., 157, *172*
Eissler, K., 452, *461*
Eliade, M., 431, *461*
Ellenberger, H., 210, *211*
Elson, M., 14*n, 21,* 137*n, 149,* 440, 452, *461*
Emde, R., *358*
Epstein, L., 279, *291*
Erikson, E., 113, *126*
Escalona, S. K., *357*
Etchegoyen, R., 368, *392*

F

Fairbairn, W. R. D., 113, *126,* 249-55, *257,* 311-12, 313, *327,* 336-37, 338*n,* 339*n, 358*
Federn, E., 53*n,* 63, *74*
Feiner, A. H., 279, *291*
Ferenczi, S., 89-106, *107,* 440, *461*
Fordham, M., 29, *45*
Freedman, A. M., 332, *358*
French, T. M., 101, *106*
Freud, A., 112, *126,* 219, 297, 300, *308,* 334, 344, *358*
Freud, S., 5-10, 12, *21, 22,* 34, 37, *45,* 53*n,* 59, 60, 63, *73,* 78*n, 87,* 91-92, 95, 185, 188, *191,* 233, 242, *257,* 278-79, *291,* 293, 297-300, 302, 307, *308,* 333-34, 336, 347, *358,* 364, 365, 367, 373, *392,* 397, 405, *412,* 432*n,* 433, 435-36, 448, 457, *461*
Friedman, L., 287, *291*
Furer, M., 344, 395, *413*

G

Gediman, H. K., 294, 297, 303, 304, *308,* 447-48, 451
Gedo, J. E., 93, 96, 105, *107,* 151, *172,* 344, *358,* 380*n, 392,* 415, 416, 419, 421-26, *427,* 458,M *461*
Ghent, E., 277, *291*
Gill, M. M., 219, *227,* 277*n, 291,* 294, *308,* 417, 426, *427*
Giorgi, A., 184, *191*
Gitelson, M., 334, *358*
Goldberg, A., 14*n, 22,* 277, *291,* 344, *358,* 378, *392,* 415, 417, 421, 423-26, *427,* 429*n,* 430, 440, 445, 446, 458, *461, 462*
Goleman, D., 278, *291*
Gordon, R., 29, 34, *45*
Gould, S., 367*n, 393*
Graensbauer, T., *358*
Gray, S. H., 280-81, *291*
Greenacre, P., 400, *412*
Greenberg, J. R., 351, *359,* 442, *462*
Greenspan, S. I., 344, *359*
Grinspoon, L., 332, *359*

Grossman, W. I., 303, *308*
Groth, N. A., 98, *106, 107*
Grunberger, B., 348, *359*
Guntrip, H., 112, *126,* 223, *227,* 249, *257,* 264, *270,* 337, *359*

H

Hanley, C., 23, *45*
Hanly, C., 210, *211*
Harari, R., 391, *393*
Harley, M., 397, *412*
Harmon, R., *358*
Harris, R., 373, *393*
Hartman, F. R., 90, *106*
Hartmann, H., 64-65, 70*n, 73,* 112, *126,* 336, *359*
Heidegger, M., 178, 180, *191,* 193, 195-203, *211,* 434, *462*
Heimann, P., 232, 234, 235, 240, 243, 250, *257*
Held-Weiss, R., 283, *291*
Hesnard, A., 175, 189, *191*
Hillman, J., 437*n, 462*
Hodges, H., 68-70, *72, 73*
Holborn, H., 69, *73*
Holmstrom, L. L., 98, *106*
Holzman, P., 338, 341, *359,* 417, 426, *427*
Horney, K., 111, 114-26, *127*
Hunt, H., 332, *360*
Husserl, E., 152-54, 156-62, 165, 168-69, 171, *172, 173,* 180-82, 186, *191,* 197*n,* 198, *211*

I

Inhelder, B., 7, 18, *22,* 41*n, 47,* 409, *413,* 451, *463*
Isaacs, S., 232, 234, 235, 243, 250, *257*

J

Jacobson, E., 338-39, *359*
Jacoby, M., 24, *45*
Jakobson, R., 364, *393*
James, B., 98, *107*
Jaynes, J., 431, *462*
Jones, E., 4, *22,* 92, 96, *107,* 249, *257,* 300, *308,* 333, *359,* 437, *462*
Joseph, B., 243, *257*
Julien, P., 389, *393*
Jung, C. G., 23, 24-45, *46,* 76, *87,* 432, 433, *462*

K

Kächele, H., 67, 68, *74*
Kahn, E., 89, *107,* 213, *227*
Kalshed, E. D., 34, *46*
Kant, I., 171, *173*
Kaplan, H. I., 332, *358*
Kaye, C., 113, *127*
Keller, E. F., 160*n, 173*
Kernberg, O. F., 113, *127,* 312, 313, *327,* 330-33, 338-41, 345, 347, 349-50, 352, 254-55, *359, 360, 361,* 455, *462*
Khan, M., 242, 245, 249, *257, 258*
Kierkegaard, S., 131-*49*
Kirschenbaum, H., 215, *227*
Klein, G., 194*n, 211,* 426, *427*
Klein, H., 334, *361*
Klein, M., 112-13, 232-42, 243, 250, *257,* 259*n,* 260, 265, *270,* 300, *309,* 311, 312, 314, 320, *327,* 338, 341*n, 360*
Klein, R., *328*
Kluback, W., 69, *73*
Koenigsberg, H. W., 332, 333, *360, 361*
Kohut, H., 3-4, 13, 14*n,* 15, 17-20, *22,* 24-33, 35, 37, 38-39, 41-42, 44, 45, *46,* 54-57, 61-69, 70*n,* 71, 72, *73,* 80, 84, 86-87, 93, 95, 99-105, *108,* 113, 114, 125-26, *127,* 132, 133, 136, 137, 142, 143, 147, 148, *150,* 151-53, 156, 160, 162, 164, 165*n,* 166, 168, 169-70, 172, *173,* 176-77, 179, 183-85, 187, 188, 190, *191,* 194*n, 211,* 216-18, 220-22, 224-26, *227,* 240-46, 248-49, 253-56, *257,* 260-63, 268, 269, *270, 271,* 276-77, 283, 284, *291,* 294-97, 298, 299, 302-5, 307, *309,* 314, 318, 319, 322, 324, 325, *327,* 330-32, 336-40, 343, 344,

346–53, *360,* 363, 364, 368, 372, 375–76, 378–83, 386–91, *393,* 395, 396, 405, 406, 410, *413,* 416, 418–26, *427, 428,* 429, 430, 436*n,* 440, 443–45, 448, 451–55, 457–60, *462*
Kris, E., 342, *361*
Krull, M., 96, *108,*
Kugler, P. N., 24, 30, *45, 47*
Kuhn, T., 58, *73,* 142, *150,* 177, *191*

L

Lacan, J., 363–80, 381, 386, 387, 389, *393*
Lachmann, F., 38*n, 47,* 94, *109,* 298, *309*
Lakatos, I., 58, *73*
Langer, S., 7, *22,* 77, 81, *87*
Laudan, L., 58, 63, *74*
Laurent, E., 391, *393*
Leowald, H. W., 162, *173*
Leroi-Gourhan, A., 373, *393*
Levarie, S., 339, *360*
Levenson, E., 281, 289, *291*
Levine, F. T., 303–4, *309*
Levy, S. T., 92, *108*
Lichtenberg, J. D., 406, *413*
Lifton, R. J., 437, *462*
Lustman, S. L., *361*

M

McCall, R., 434, *462*
McElroy, R. A., 333, *358*
McGuire, W., 60, *74*
Maddi, S. R., 226, *227*
Madow, L., 334, *362*
Mahler, M. S., 312–17, *327,* 336, 344, *361,* 395, 396–412, *413*
Mann, J., 334, *362*
Masek, R. J., 176, 177, 179, 184, *191*
Masson, J. M., 23, *45,* 95–97, *108*
Masterson, J. F., 46, 311–15, 317–26, *327, 328,* 455, 457, *462*
May, R., 178, 181, *191,* 210, *211*
Mead, G. H., 364, *393*
Meissner, W. W., 111, *127* 334, *361,* 429*n, 462*
Menaker, E., 79, 81, 82, 86, *87*
Menaker, W., 82, *87*
Merleau-Ponty, M., 175–90, *191*
Miller, A., 437*n, 463*
Miller, J. P., 218, 222, 225, *227*
Mitchell, S. A., 351, *359,* 4442, *462*
Modell, A., 259*n,* 260, *270,* 286, *291*
Muller, J., 364, 366, 371, 375, *393, 394,* 452
Myerson, P., 383, *394*

N

Nasjleti, M., 98, *107*
Nemiah, J. C., 348, *361*
Newman, K. M., 260, 262*n,* 268*n, 270*
Nissim-Sabat, M., 151, 165, *173*
Nunberg, H., 53*n,* 63, *74*

O

Ornstein, A., 286, 287, *291*
Ornstein, P. H., 94, 95, 102, 104–5, *106, 108,* 137*n, 150,* 224, *227,* 286, 287, *291,* 389, *394*
Ostow, M., 380, *394*

P

Papousek, H., 14, *22*
Parens, H., 411, *413*
Paul, H., 115, 123, 125, *127*
Peraldi, F., 391, *394*
Piaget, J., 7, 18, *22,* 41*n, 47,* 402, 409, *413,* 451, *463*
Pine, F., 312, 313, *327,* 336, 341*n, 361,* 395, 396, 399, *413*
Plaut, A., 42, *47*
Polanyi, M., 49–50, 65, 72, *74*
Portnoy, I., 116, 122, *127*
Potter, H., 334, *361*

R

Rachman, A. W., 89, 91, 92, 96, 98, *108, 109,* 440
Rae, A. I. M., 159, *173*
Rangell, L., 294, *309*

Rank, O., 76-*87*
Redfearn, J. W. T., 26, *47*
Reed, G. S., 303, *309*
Reich, W., 348, *361*
Rendon, M., 115, *127*
Richards, A., 293, *309*
Richardson, W. J., 364, 372, 379, *394*
Ricoeur, P., 167-68, 169, *173,* 285, *291*
Riviere, J., 232, 234, 235, 243, 250, *257*
Roazen, P., *47*
Robbins, M., 336, *361*
Rogers, C. R., 213-21, 223, 224, 226, *227,* 434-35, *463*
Rosenblatt, A., 426, *428*
Rosenblatt, B., 162, *173*
Rosenfeld, H., 243, *257*
Rothstein, A., 335, 351, 352*n,* 355, *361*
Rubin, J., 133, 134, 138-41, 142*n,* 144*n, 149, 150,* 433-34
Rubins, J., 119, 120, 12, *127*
Rush, F., *19,* 98

S

Sabourin, P., 90, 96, *109*
Sadock, B. J., 332, *358*
Samuels, A., 23, 29, *47*
Sander, L., 238, 244, *257*
Sandler, A.-M., 296, 306, *309*
Sandler, J., 162, *173,* 296, 306, *309*
Sartre, J.-P., 193, 195, 197*n,* 203-10, *211,* 434, *463*
Saussure, F. de, 317-72, *394*
Schafer, R., 194*n, 211,* 288, *291,* 426, *428*
Schneiderman, S., 391, *393*
Schomer, J., 332, *360*
Schur, M., 96, *109*
Schwaber, E., *158,* 176, *191,* 237, 239, 276, *291,* 421, *428,* 430*n,* 445, 451, 454, *463*
Schwartz-Salant, N., 24, *47*
Searles, H., *428*
Segal, H., *158,* 232, 234
Segal, N. P., 338, 341, *361*
Selzer, M.A., 332, 333, *361*
Sgyoi, S. S., 98, *106*
Shane, E., 395, 410, 411, *413*
Shane, M., 395, 410, 411, *413*
Shlien, J. M., 219, *227*
Simitis-Grubrich, I., 90, *109*
Slap, J. W., 303-4, *309*
Spiegel, L., 113, *127*
Spitz, R. A., *361,* 399, *413*
Steele, R. S., 36, *47*
Stein, M. R., 335, *361*
Stepansky, P., 52*n,* 53*n,* 59, *74,* 416, *428*
Stern, D. N., 46, 114, *127,* 261*n, 270,* 316, 317, *328, 361,* 405, 406, 408-9, 411, *413,* 418, *428, 463*
Stewart, W. A., 303, *308*
Stolorow, R. D., 38*n, 47,* 89, 94, *109, 158,* 176, *190,* 194*n,* 196, 197*n, 211,* 213, 220, *227,* 234, 238, 239, *256, 257,* 298, *309,* 457, *461*
Stone, L., 329-30, 355, *362*
Strassman, H., 334, *362*
Strauss, G. D., 331, *362*
Strauss, G. E., 331, *362*
Strozier, C. B., 14*n, 22,* 433*n, 463*
Sullivan, H. S., 279, 284-85, *291*
Sulloway, F., 96, *109,* 436, *463*
Svrakic, D. M., 348, *362*
Sylwan, B., 96, *109*
Symonds, A., 114, 116, 119, *127*
Symonds, M., 114, 119, *127*

T

Terman, D. M., 218, *227,* 269*n, 270,* 418, 419, *428*
Thickstun, J., 426, *428*
Thomä, H., 67, 68, *74*
Thomas, A., *362*
Thompson, C., 91, 96, *109*
Thompson, M., 381, *394*
Thomson, J. A., 331, *357*
Tolpin, M., 343*n, 362,* 405, *413*
Tomkins, S., 448, 449, 451, *463*
Toulmin, S., 155, 158-59, 163, 169-72, *174*
Tribich, D., 338, 341*n, 360*
Turkle, S., 364, *394*
Turvey, M., 30, *47*
Tuttman, S., 113, *127*

V

van den Berg, J. H., 180, *192*
Ver Eecke, W., 366, *394*
Volkan, V. D., 330, *362*
Voyat, G., 366, *394*
Vygotsky, L., 451, *463*

W

Waelder, R., 298, *309,* 344–45, 354, *362*
Wallbridge, W., 262, 266, 269, *270*
Wallerstein, R. S., 304, *309,* 341*n,* 342, 344, 345, 351*n,* 353, *362,* 382, *394*
Wallon, H., 366, *394*
Wayne, M., 92, 98, *109*
Weber, M., 71, *74*
Weil, A., 397, *412*
Weinshel, E., 330, 338, 341, *358*
Weintraub, K., 431*n, 463*
Wertz, F. J., 190, *192*
Whitmont, E., 114, *127*
Whyte, W., 455, *463*
Widlocher, D., 368, *394*
Winnicott, D. W., 113, *127,* 238, 249, 250, *258,* 259–69, *270,* 300, *309,* 312–13, 318, *328,* 337, *362,* 425, *428,* 443, 444, *463*
Witenberg, E. G., 290, *291*
Witkowski, S., 366*n, 392*
Wolf, E. S., 14*n, 22,* 99, *108,* 188, *191,* 220, *228,* 331, 343, 349, *360,* 363, *393,* 420, 422, 425, *428,* 455, 458, *462*
Wolf, F. A., 160, *184*
Wood, E., 334, *362*

Y

Yager, J., 331, *362*
Yates, F. E., 29, *47*

Z

Zimmerman, 113, *127*
Zonis, M., 330, *362*

Subject Index

A

Abandonment depression, 313–14, 326, 457
Abuse, child. *See* Child abuse
Academic psychiatry
  Kohut vs. Kernberg's affiliation with, 332
  relationship between psychoanalysis and, 333–34
Actualizing tendency, 214, 215–16
Aesthetic sphere, 139–40
Affect, Tomkins's theory of, 448, 449
Affective attunement, disturbance of, 446
Afterimage (*Nachbild*), 69
Aggression
  Adler on, 51–52
  elemental, 241
  Kernberg on, 341*n,* 352
  Kohut on, 241, 411
  Lacan on, 368
  as "narcissistic rage", 55–56
  nondestructive, 241
"Aggressive Drive in Life and Neurosis, The" (Adler), 51
Aggressive drives, 8
Aggressive persecutory ego, 251
Alchemy, Jung on, 28
Alienation
  neurotic development and, 118–19
  from self, 118–19, 122–24
Alter-ego personalities, 349
  Kohut and Husserl on, 166–69
Alter ego transference, 15
Ambivalence conflict, 345
  in relation to mother, 402, 403
American Institute for Psychoanalysis, 114
American Journal of Psychiatry, 332
American Psychiatric Association's 1982 Annual Review (Grinspoon), 332
American Psychoanalytic Association, 339, 441
Analysand, Fairbairn on, 251–52
Analysis
  Horney vs. Kohut on, 126
  Kohut on, 61–62, 84
  need gratification in, 224–25
  neutrality of therapist in, 224–26
  personal questions of patient in, 223
  role playing in, 224
Analysis of the Self, The (Kohut), 13, 55, 70, 176

Analyst
attitudes of omniscience in, 380*n*
Balint on role of, 244–45
client-centered therapy and, 214–15
as corrective selfobject, 94
Freud on appropriate stance of, 278–79
impact of psychiatric involvement on analytic work ego of, 334–35
interpersonal listening stance of, 277–82, 285
Jung on function of, 44
Kohut on role of, 239–40
patient's subjective experience of, 254–55
restoration of self by, 143
self-disclosure, 98
Analytic field, Lacan on, 374–76
Analytic neutrality, 224–26
Analytic situation, 85
Ferenczi's view of, 98–99, 103–4
Anguish, Sartre's concept of freedom and, 205
Annihilation anxiety, 297–304, 447, 448, 451
Antilibidinal ego, 251, 254
Anxiety
annihilation, 297–304, 447, 448, 451
disintegration, 297, 298, 305, 447, 448, 451
existential, 297
extinction, 300
Freud's first and second theories of, 299, 302
Heidegger on, 200–201
Horney's theory of, 116–17, 121, 122
instinctual, 300
Kierkegaard vs. Kohut on, 147
neurotic, 451
psychotic, 300
Rank's search for paradigm for, 77–78
separation, 400
stranger, 399, 410
Aphanisis, 300
Archaic grandiosity, 263, 264
Archaic humanity, 431–32
Archaic mental states, 424
Archaic pathology, 425
Archaic selfobject functioning, 262
Archaic self-selfobject relationship, Winnicott's subjective object compared to, 261–62
Archaic tie, 232–33
Archetypal collective unconscious, 432
Archetypal transference, 37–41, 42
Archetypes, 25, 30
"numinous" property of, 39
Archives of General Psychiatry, 332
Art and Artist (Rank), 77
"Artist, The" (*Der Künstler*) (Rank), 76–77
Association for the Advancement of Psychoanalysis, 114, 119
Associative process, 104
Attachment, obstinate, 254
Attitude, natural, 181
Attitudes of omniscience in analyst, 380*n*
Authentic self, 199, 200–201
Autistic phase, 397, 398, 404–6
current infant research and concept of, 405–6
Kohut's perspective on, 404–5
Autonomy
current infant research on, 408–10
Mahler vs. Kohut on, 408–10
Awareness of self, introspection and evolution of, 82–84

B

Bad faith, Sartre's concept of freedom and, 205
"Basic fault", area of, 245, 246, 248
Behavior disorders, 12
Being, nature of, Heidegger on, 196–203
Being and Nothingness (Sartre), 195, 203–10
Being and Time (Heidegger), 178, 195, 196, 202, 203
Being-for-itself, 204, 206, 207
threat of reduction to, 207–8
Being-for-others, 207
loss of freedom and imprisonment of subjectivity in, 208
Being-in-itself, 204, 205, 206

Being-in-the-world, 198
Being-with-Others, 199
Bipolar nuclear self, 438
evolution of, 431–33
Birth experience, Rank on, 77–78
Body image, development of, 398–400
Bonaparte, Princess Marie, 278
Borderline personality disorders, 313
dimensions of difference between narcissistic and, 322–26
distinctions between narcissistic and, 320–22
Borderline triad, defined, 313
Breuer, Josef, 6
British Psycho-Analytical Society, 260

C

Call of conscience, 202
Care, attitude of (*Sorge*), 198
Caretakers
alterego self-selfobject relation and, 166, 169
communication between infant and, 18
exaggeration of responsibility of, 420–21
See also Mother-child relationship
"Case of the Slovenly Soldier, The" (Thompson), 91
Castration, symbolic, 378
Central ego, 251
Centrality of perception, 179–80
Character types of Horney's theory, 123
Charcot, Jean Martin, 4–5
Checking-back-to-mother pattern, 399, 410, 411
Child abuse, 440–42, 453, 457
Ferenczi's empathic plea for reality of, 95, 96–98
"China" as a Symbol of Vagina (Gray), 280–81
Christian insights, secularized version of, 133
Classical psychoanalysis
Horney's shift away from, 117–18
Kohut's involvement with, 339–40
Client-centered therapy, 213, 214–16
Coherent framework of theory, 233, 240, 241
Cohesion, fragmentation vs., 134, 136
Cohesive self, 32, 94, 296, 423, 425, 450
Collective unconscious, archetypal, 432
Commitment
essential contingency and, 145
Kierkegaard on, 131–32, 135, 141–44
world-defining, 135, 136–37
Communication between infants and caretakers, 18. *See also* Empathy
Complex
Jung's notion of, 31
unintegrated, 32
See also Oedipus complex
Comprehensive Textbook of Psychiatry II (Freedman, Kaplan, and Sadock), 332
Conceptual levels, mixing of, 303
Concern, stage of, 265
Concretization, 238
Conditions of worth, 215
Conflict
of ambivalence, 345
in relation to mother, 402, 403
intrapsychic, 342–46
intrasystemic, 344
Kohut on, 453
Kernberg vs., 342–46
object-relations, 344
Conflict and deficit models of psychopathology, 293–309, 344–45, 447–48
annihilation anxiety, problem of, 297–304, 447, 448, 451
therapeutic technique and, 304–7
Congruence, Rogers on, 215
Conscience, call of, 202
Consciousness
development of modern, 431–33
phenomenological concept of, 158, 161–62
primacy of perceptual, 181
radical freedom of, 205, 206–7
Sartre on, 203–10
Consensual validation, 284–85
Consolidation of individuality, 403–4
Contact-shunning personalities, 343, 349
Contingency, essential, 145

Contributions of predecessors and contemporaries, Kohut's vs. Kernberg's regard for, 335–39, 424
"Contribution to the Theory Resistance" (Adler), 54
Corrective emotional experience, 101–2
Countertransference
in interpersonal psychoanalysis, 279–80
Kohut and Jung on, 42–43
Countertransference analysis, 98, 102–3
Creativity
guilt and, 86, 440
Kohut on, 86–87
Rank on, 77, 85–86, 439–40
transference of, 86–87
Cultural school of psychoanalysis, Horney and, 115–17
Cultural sciences, Dilthey on, 68–70
Culture
modern, 433–35
reciprocal relationship between individual and, 82–84
"Cutting Edge in Psychiatry, The", 331

D

Danger situations of childhood, 298
Dasein (being-there), 196–203
Defense mechanisms, 9
Balint on, 243
Freudianism and view of, 437
Klein on, 233–34, 235
Deficit and conflict models of psychopathology, 293–309, 344–45, 447–48
annihilation anxiety, problem of, 297–304, 447, 448, 451
therapeutic technique and, 304–7
Deintegration, Fordham's theory of, 29
Dependence, developmental shift from absolute to relative, 269
Depression, abandonment, 313–14, 326, 457
Depressive patients, constriction in temporal horizons of lives of, 180
Depressive position, 235–37, 265
Depth psychology, 61
Desire of the other, 376–78
Despised image, 123
Destructiveness
developmental significance to infant of, 265–66
infantile, 241
See also Aggression
Development
ego, 51, 336
Fairbairn on, 253–54
Klein on, 232–42
Kohut on, 13–17, 319
Mahler's formulation of, 312, 396–404
consolidation of individuality and beginning of emotional object constancy, 403–4
differentiation and development of body image, 398–400
forerunners of separation-individuation process, 397–98
from perspective of Kohut's developmental framework, 404–12
practicing, 400–401
rapprochement, 401–3
needs from early, 14–17
as profoundly intersubjective in nature, 239
psychoanalytic view of, 11–12
Winnicott on, 260–69
Developmental arrest phase in borderline and narcissistic disorders, 322–24
Developmental object relations theory, 311, 315, 317, 320–21
Differentiation, 398, 399
Kohut vs. Mahler on, 410–11
leveling vs., 134–36
Difficult patients, Ferenczi on empathy in treatment of, 91
Disintegration anxiety, 297, 298, 305, 447, 448, 451. *See also* Annihilation anxiety

Dissidents, historical. *See* Historical "dissidents"
Divine child, mythic image of, 41
Dreams
  interpersonal interpretation of, 289-90
  self-state, 336
  state-of-affairs, 336-37
Drive psychology phase of evolution of psychoanalysis, 111-12
Drives
  Adler on, 52, 53-54, 57
  Freud on, 8
  Kohut on, 54-57
DSM-III, 333
Dual instinct theory, 233-34
Dynamic perspective, 187

E

E.T.: The Extraterrestrial (film), 459-60
Eclecticism, 185
Ego, 9
  Adler on, 51, 52
  aggressive persecutory, 251
  antilibidinal, 251, 254
  central, 251
  Fairbairn on, 251
  ideal, 369-70
  Jung on, 25, 33
  Lacan on, 366-68
  libidinal, 251
  as translation of *Ich,* 113
Ego and the Id, The (Freud), 279
Ego development, 51, 336
Ego ideal in "The Two Analysis of Mr. Z", 386-90
Ego-object-relations movement, 113
Ego psychology, 65, 112-13, 176
Ego-relatedness, 262, 264
Ego-self axis, 25
Ego-self merger, 41
Emotional object constancy, beginning of, 403-4
Emotional void, 132
Empathic data-gathering, 67-68
Empathic failure as trauma, 98-103
Empathic immersion
  Kohut's method of, 44-45
  protracted, 35
Empathy, 151-72
  alterego phenomenon and, 166-60
  capacity for, 166
  cyclical stages of, 283-85
  as defining psychoanalytic field, 163-64
  Dilthey's definition of cultural sciences from standpoint of, 68-70
  ethics and, 169-72
  Ferenczi on role of, 90-93
  Goldberg's definition of analytic, 421
  grounding the scientific status of, 152
  Husserl on, 152-53, 165
  interpersonal nature of, 282-85
  interpretation as supplement to genuine, 222
  Jung on, 37
  Kohut on, 35, 37, 61-62, 66, 93, 153-54, 164-65, 166, 420-21, 445, 446
  maternal, 262, 351
  precondition for ability to empathize, 266
  problems with overemphasis on, 353-54
  Rogers on, 214
  science and, 154-59, 164
  scientific, 460
Empiricism
  positivist, 156-57
  radical, 156-58
English object relations theorists, 231-71, 441, 442-45
  Balint, 242-49
  Fairbairn, 249-55
  Klein, 232-42
  Kohut's disregard of, 336-38
  Winnicott, 259-69
Entitlement
  fantasies, 306, 451
  feelings of, 122
Environment-mother, 265
Envy
  Klein on, 236-37
  penis, 303
Essential contingency, 145
Ethical sphere, 140

Ethics, empathy and, 169–72
Evocative memory, 409
Evolution of human mind, 431–33
Evolution of psychoanalysis, 111–14
  drive psychology phase, 111–12
  ego psychology phase, 112–13
  self psychology phase, 113–14
Existence, spheres of, 138–44, 145, 146, 148–49
Existential analysis, 210
Existential anxiety, 297
Existential-humanistic thinkers, 129–228
  Heidegger, 193, 195, 196–203
  Husserl, 152–54, 156–72
  Kierkegaard, 131–32, 134–49
  Merleau-Ponty, 175–90
  Rogers, 213–26
  Sartre, 103, 195, 203–10
Existential-humanistic tradition, 430, 433–35
Existentialia, 197–98
Existential-phenomenological systems, 193, 194–95
  in Heidegger, 195, 196–203
  in Sartre, 195, 203–10
Existential self, 138–44
Expansive character solution, 123
Experience of life histories, Kierkegaard vs. Kohut on, 137–38
Explanatory phase, 187, 188, 445, 446
Exploration in interpersonal psychoanalysis, 285–90
Extinction anxieties, 300
Extrospective reality, 156, 160

F

Fallacy of parallel importations, 303
Falling (*Verfallen*), 199–200
False self, 263, 264, 268, 337, 443
Fantasies
  entitlement, 306, 451
  fragmentation, 387
Fantasy selfobject experience, 267
Fragmentation, 423, 424
  cohesion vs., 134, 136
  fantasies, 387
  Lacan on, 366
Free association, Kohut on, 62
Freedom, Sartrean doctrine of man's, 204–6, 207, 209
Freudianism, 436–38
  historical "dissidents" in reaction to, 438–42
Functioning intentionality, 182

G

Gender identity, 401
Genetic perspective, 188
Global theories, 58
Goal of analysis or therapy
  for Fairbairn, 254–55
  for Horney, 121
  for Kierkegaard, 135–36
  for Kohut, 136, 138
Goal of self psychology, Kohut's view of, 143
Good-enough mother, 264, 265
Grandiose self, Kernberg on, 352
Grandiosity
  archaic, 263, 264
  healthy, 263
Gratification, need, 224–25
Gross identification, 375–76
Growth orientation of Horney, 114–15, 125
Guilt, creativity and, 86, 440
Guilty Man, 295, 344–45, 418, 423

H

Hatching, 398–99
Hermeneutics, 158
Hierarchically ordered two-reality view, 237–38
Historical "dissidents", 3–127, 438–42
  adler, 49–74
  Ferenczi, 89–109
  Horney, 111–27
  Jung, 23–47
  Kohut and Freud compared, 3–22
  Rank, 75–87
Holding environment, 262
Holistic-dynamic orientation of Horney, 115
How Does Analysis Cure? (Kohut), 176
Humanistic disciplines, scientific status of, 160–61

Humanistic psychoanalysis, 95. *See also* Existential-humanistic thinkers
Humanness, sense of, 166

I

Id, 9
Ideal ego, 369–70
Ideal-hungry personalities, 349
Idealization in "The Two Analysis of Mr. Z", 386–90
Idealized image formation, 120, 121–23
Idealizing parent imago, 41, 100
Idealizing transference, 15, 216–17
Ideas Concerning a Descriptive and Analytic Psychology (Dilthey), 69
Identification
  Freud's second type of, 373
  gross, 375–76
  imaginary, 369–70, 375, 378
  Kohut on, 375–76
  Lacan on, 368–70
  mirror, 366–68
  primary, 368, 369
  projective, 236–36
  symbolic, 372–74, 375, 377–78, 379
Identity
  gender, 401
  Kohut vs. Kierkegaard on, 136–37
Id-satisfaction, 368
Illusion
  capacity for, 444
  Winnicott on nature and function of, 266–68
Imaginary identification, 369–70, 375, 378
Impingement, reactions to, 262
Inborn selfobject needs, 217, 218
Incongruence, Rogers on, 215–16
Individuality, consolidation of, 403–4
Individuation
  Jung's concept of, 24, 25, 34
  Langer on process of, 81
  Mahler's definition of, 397
  See also Separation-individuation
Infant
  communication between caretaker and, 18
  meeting omnipotence of, 264
  self of, Winnicott on, 263–66
Infantile destructiveness, 241
Infantile object ties, 233–335
Infant research, 395–413, 456
  confirmation of self as primary in, 84–85
  Mahler's developmental formulations, 396–404
    consolidation of individuality and beginning of emotional object constancy, 403–4
    differentiation and development of body image, 398–400
    forerunners of separation-individuation process, 397–98
    from perspective of Kohut's developmental framework, 404–12
    practicing, 400–401
    rapprochement, 401–3
Instinct theory, 8, 9
  Basch's criticism of, 436
  dual, 233–34
  Freudianism and, 436–37
  Horney's deemphasis of, 115
  Kohut's challenge of, 3–4
Instinctual anxiety, 300
Institute for Psychoanalysis, 119
Intentionality, functioning, 182
Intergenerational modification of self psychology, 65
Internalization, transmuting, 318, 350, 407, 408
International Psychoanalytic Association, 59
Interpersonal life, Sartre's image of, 207–9
Interpersonal psychoanalysis, 275–91, 445
  countertransference in, 279–80
  empathic communication and, 282–85
  exploration and interpretation in, 285–90
  interpersonal listening stance, 277–82, 285
  transference in, 279–80
Interpretation, 454–55
  domains of, 446

Interpretation (*continued*)
in interpersonal psychoanalysis, 285-90
medical model and, 221-23
Intrapsychic conflict, 342-46
Intrapsychic experience of self, 27-28
Intrapsychic separation, 407
Intrapsychic splitting, 30-33
Intrasystemic conflict, 344
Introjection, processes of, 235
Introspection
evolution of awareness of self and, 82-84
Kohut on, 61, 62
vicarious, 153, 164, 165
"Introspection, Empathy, and Psychoanalysis" (Kohut), 3, 62
Introspective reality, 156, 160

J

Jesus as paradigm, 142*n*
Journal of American Psychoanalytic Association, 341
Journal of Nervous and Mental Disease, 332

K

Kiefer, Anselm, 371
"Kinship libido", 28

L

Lebenswelt (life world), 154, 156, 157-58, 162-64, 165*n,* 169, 171, 179, 180
Leveling, 132, 141, 434
differentiation vs., 134-36
Kierkegaard's definition of, 134-36
See also Nihilism
Libidinal ego, 251
Libido
Freud-Jung disagreement over, 34-35
"kinship", 28
narcissistic, 34
Listening stance, interpersonal, 277-82, 285
Locus of the signifier, 373
Love, primary, 246-47, 338
moving to mature, interdependent love from, 247

M

Mach, 157
Manic patients, expansion in lived space afforded to, 180
Materialist schools of psychological thought, 194
Maturational process, Winnicott's use of term, 265
Maturation of self, 222-23
Medical model, interpretations and, 221-23
Memory, evocative, 409
Mental health, Horney vs. Kohut on, 126
Merger-hungry personalities, 349
Metaphor, personal, 370
Metapsychology, 11, 448
Kohut and, 17-19, 351, 417
reification of, 303-4
Mind, evolution of human, 431-33
Mirror-hungry personalities, 349
Mirroring, Lacan on, 366-68
Mirror transference, 14-17, 41-42, 216-17
Modern condition, diagnoses of, 131-32
Mother
ambivalence conflict in relation to, 402, 403
maternal empathy, 262, 351
pathogenic personality disorder in, 351
Mother-child relationship
empathic failure in, 98
Kohut-Freud similarities on, 336
Mahler's developmental formulations and, 396-404
Winnicott on, 260-66, 268-69
similarities with Kohut, 337
Motivation
Husserl's concept of, 165-66
Kohut on, 80
Lacan's theory of, 451

origin of psychoanlytic theory of, 7–10
Rank on, 80
tension-reduction theory of, 8–9
Mutual analysis, 98
Mythic image of divine child, 41
"Mythology" of psychoanalysis, 9. *See also* Instinct theory

N

Nachbild (afterimage), 69
Nacherziehung, 12, 17
Narcissism, 132, 133–38
Balint on primary, 242–43
Kohut on, 276
during practicing subphase, 400
transformations of, 34–35
Narcissistic catastrophe, 298–99
Narcissistic libido, 34
Narcissistic personality disorder, 12, 80, 283
clinical features, 348
closet, 321–22
diagnostic criterion of, 331
distinctions between borderline and, 320–22
dimensions of difference, 322–26
Kohut on
goal in treatment, 136
Kernberg vs., 348–55, 356
pathogenesis and metapsychology, 350–52
phenomenology, 348–50
terminology in describing, 331–32
treatment technique, 352–55
temporality of, 138
Narcissistic rage, 55–56, 348–49
Narcissistic transference, 43, 352–55
Natural attitude, 181
Natural science, 156, 159–61
Nature, uniformity of, 156
Needs
from early development, 14–17
gratification, therapeutic value of, 224–25
Lacan on, 376–77
selfobject, 217, 418–19, 422
inborn, 217, 218
Negative transference, 217–18
Nervous Character, The (Adler), 52*n*
Neurosis and Human Growth (Horney), 120–21
Neurosis(es)
alienation and development of, 118–19
Charcot on, 4–5
Horney on, 116, 119, 120, 121–22
Kohut in contrast to, 125
Jung on, 30, 31–32
Rank on, 78
structural, 446
Neurosogenesis, Adler's development perspective on, 53
Neurotic anxiety, 451
Neurotic "claims", 122
Neurotic Personality of Our Time, The (Horney), 116–17, 118
Neurotic trends, 120
Neutrality, analytic, 224–26
"New beginning, the", 245, 248
New Ways in Psychoanalysis (Horney), 117, 118
New York Psychoanalytic Society, 119
Nihilism, 132, 133–38
Noetic-noematic relation, 161–62, 163
No Exit (Sartre), 208
Nondestructive aggression, 241
Nosological system of Kohut, inadequacy of, 424–25
Nosologic terminology
of Kernberg, 333
of Kohut, 331–32
Nuclear self, 138–44, 318, 337, 448–50, 456–57
bipolar, 431–33, 438
Nuclear selfing, 451
Nuremberg Congress, 59, 60

O

Object constancy, beginning of emotional, 403–4
Objective reality, 234, 238
Objective self, 395
Object-mother, 265
Object-relations conflict, 344

Object relations theory, 112–13, 231, 232
developmental, 311, 315, 317, 320–21
See also English object relations theorists
Object Relations Theory of the Personality, An (Fairbairn), 249
Object representations, 323
Observation
Kohut's characterization of, 184–85
participant, 288–89
Obstinate attachments, 254
Odysseus myth, 347, 459
Oedipal resolution, Lacan's concept of, 378
Oedipus complex, 96, 459
Adler on, 53–54
healthy oedipal stage vs. pathological, 57
Horney vs. Kohut, on, 126
Kohut vs. Kernberg on, 346–48, 453–54
self-psychological approach to, 56–57
Omniscience, analyst's attitudes of, 380*n*
On Aphasia (Freud), 6, 7
"On Narcissism" (Freud), 34
"On Neurotic Disposition: A Contribution both to the Etiology of Neurosis and the Question of the Choice of Neurosis" (Adler), 52
Operational analysis, 168
Ordinary devoted mother, 264
Organismic experience, 215
Other, the
desire of, 376–78
Lacan on, 364–66, 373–75
Our Inner Conflicts (Horney), 120
"Oversensitive" organs, 52
Overstimulation, 452

P

Paradigms, Kierkegaard's discussion of role of, 142–43
Parallel importations, fallacy of, 303
Paranoid-schizoid position, 235, 236
Parent imago, idealizing, 41, 100
Parents, trauma of interpersonal relations with, 99–100. *See also* Mother-child relationship
Participant observation, 288–89
Pathogenic personality disorder in mothers, 351
Paul, conversion on way to Damascus, 83
Penis envy, 303
Perception, centrality of, 179–80
Perceptual consciousness, primacy of, 181
Persecution, feelings of, 235
Persona, 32
Personal aspects of transference, 37–38
Personality
change in, 83–84
contact-shunning, 343, 349
creative, Rank on, 85–86
as dynamic sculpture, 25–26
narcissistic, types of, 349
Personality adjustment, Rogers theory of, 215
Personality disorders, 311
Kohut on, 319
Masterson on, 314, 320–22
pathogenic, in mother, 351
See also Borderline personality disorders; Narcissistic personality disorder
Personal metaphor, 370
Personal questions of patient, 223
Personal unconscious, 432, 439
Person-centered approach, 215
Persönlichkeitgefühl (self-feeling), 52–53
Phallus, Lacan on, 370
Phenomenal field, 182
Phenomenological psychology, Heidegger and, 178
Phenomenological reduction, 157, 181–83, 186
Phenomenology, 434
alterego-self relation explained in, 168–69
concept of consciousness in, 158, 161–62
Husserl's view of, 152–53

of Merleau-Ponty, 177, 178–80
as radical empiricism, 156, 157
science and, 159–61, 169–72
self psychology and, 155–56, 161–64
homology between, 152–53
Phenomenology, philosophical, 195, 210–11
Phenomenology, psychoanalytic, 193–211
existential-phenomenological thought and, 193, 194–95
Heidegger and, 193, 195, 196–203
Sartre and, 193, 195, 203–10
situating Merleau-Ponty within, 180–83
Picket fence model, 6
Pleasure-unpleasure principle, 8–9
Polarization of people
annihilation anxiety as test case to document, 297–304
tendency to, 295–96
Positive transferences, 218
Positivism, 157, 163, 186
Positivist empiricism, 156–57
Post-Kohutian view of self psychology, 415–28
Practicing subphase, 400–401
Kohut vs. Mahler on, 410–11
Predecessors, Kohut's vs. Kernberg's regard for contributions of, 335–39, 424
Preruth, stage of, 265
Presence-to-hand (*Vorhandenheit*), 198–99
Pride, neurotic, 122–23
Pride system, 123
Primacy of perceptual consciousness, 181
Primacy of self development, 80
Primary identification, 368, 369
Primary love, Kohut vs. Balint on, 338
Primary maternal preoccupation, 262
Primary object love, 246–47
"Primary" process, 11
Progress and Its Problems (Laudan), 58
"Project for a Scientific Psychology" (Freud), 6, 7
Projective identification, 235–36
"Protracted empathic immersion", 35
Psychiatry
Kohut vs. Kernberg in relationship to general, 331–35
psychoanalysis and, 333–34, 452–53
Psychoanalysis
defining characteristics of clinical science of, 435
general psychotherapy and, 452–53
historical background of, 4–6
Kohut and
insistence on scientific status, 156, 159
Kernberg vs., in relation to mainstream, 339–48
operational perspective, 66, 68
traditional vs. Kohutian technique, 352–55
motivation, origin of theory of, 7–10
psychiatry and, 452–53
academic, 334–34
as science of introspective reality, 156
self psychology as extension of and corrective for traditional, 20
thought formation, origin of theory of, 6–7
widening scope of, 329–30, 355
Psychoanalytic method
origin of, 10–12
widening application of, 12–17
Psychoanalytic phenomenology. *See* Phenomenology, psychoanalytic
Psychoanalytic situation. *See* Analytic situation
Psychotherapy, relationship between psychoanalysis and general, 452–53
Psychotic anxieties, 300

Q

Quantum physics, 153–54, 159–60

R

Radical empiricism, 156–58
Radical freedom of consciousness, 205, 206–7
Rage, narcissistic, 55–56, 348–49

Rapprochement subphase, 401–3
Kohut vs. Mahler on, 411
Reactions to impingement, 262
Readiness-to-hand (*Zuhandenheit*), 198–99
Reality
introspective and extrospective, 156, 160
Kohut vs. Jung on, 36–37
objective, 234, 238
subjective, 238
Real relationship, 219–21
Real self, 315, 456–57
Reduction, phenomenological, 157
Merleau-Ponty on, 181–83, 186
Reductionism of Kohut's view of human nature, objection to, 424–25
Reductive analysis, 36
Reflective aesthetic, 139–40
Regression to expose area of "basic fault", 245
Reification of metapsychology, 303–4
Relationships
Kierkegaard on, 131–32
Kohut on, 132
transference, 219–21
See also Mother-child relationship
Relativism, Fairbairn's focus on, 250–51
Relaxation therapy, 101, 104
Religiousness A, 140–41
Religiousness B, 141–44, 145
Repression, 9
Research tradition
analysis as, 61–63
changing core of, 63
defining, 66–67
Kohut's perspective on psychoanalysis as, 66–68
Research tradition, psychoanalytic, 71–72
Research traditions, distinction between theories and, 58–59
Resignation, 123
Resistance
Fairbairn on, 254
Ferenczi on, 90–91, 103–6
Kohut on, 62k 104–6
shame, 306
Responsibility for becoming fully functioning self, 146–47
Restoratin of self, 143
Restoration of the Self, The (Kohut), 55, 56, 70*n*
Role playing, 224

S

Schema L, Kohut and, 391
Schizoid condition, Fairbairn on, 250
Science
empathy and, 154–59, 164
natural, 156, 159–61
phenomenology and, 159–61, 169–72
postmodern, 159–61
Scientific empathy, 460
Seduction hypothesis, 95, 96–98, 440
"Selected Problems of Self Psychological Theory" (Kohut), 57
Self
alienation from, 118–19, 122–24
cohesive, 32, 94, 296, 423, 425, 450
Dilthey on, 69
evolution of awareness of, introspection and, 82–84
existential, 138–44
false, 263, 264, 268, 337, 443
fully functioning, 146–47
functional definitions of, 113
grandiose, Kernberg on, 352
Horney on, 114–26
importance of valuing the, 213–26
inattention to antecedents of cohesive, 423
of infant, Winnicott on, 263–66
intrapsychic experience of, 27–28
Jung on, 24–29
Kierkegaard's views of, 138–49
Kohut vs., 144–49
Kohut on, 24–29, 144–49, 296, 319–22, 422, 424
Masterson on, 315, 319–22
maturation of, 222–23
Merleau-Ponty and, 175–90
nuclear, 138–44, 318, 337, 448–50, 456–57
bipolar, 431–33, 438

objective, 395
origin and development of, 29–30
paradigms and creation of, 142–43
as primary, confirmation in infant research of, 84–85
real, 315, 456–57
restoration of, 143
spontaneous individual, 119, 120
"they-self" vs. authentic, 199, 200–201
true, 263, 264, 318, 337, 443
use of term, 81–82
virtual, 405

Self Analysis (Horney), 119
Self development, primacy of, 80
Self-disclosure, therapist, 98
Self disorders, 243
Self-effacing character solutions, 123
Self-experience, 215
Self-feeling, 52–53
Self-idealization, 122
"Selfing", 450, 452
nuclear, 451

Self nuclei, coexistence of separate subsets of, 425
Selfobject
Kierkegaardian paradigm vs. Kohutian, 142–43
Kohut's conception of, 27, 28, 423
objection to continuation and prolongation of notion of, 317
Winnicott's understanding of transitional objects and, 267–68

Selfobject functions, 262, 418
Selfobject needs, 217, 418–19, 422
Selfobject relationship, 262
Selfobject theory, 260*n*
Selfobject transferences, 93–95, 145, 188, 218–19, 430
Self psychology, 14
Adlerian critique, key elements of, 55–57, 61
controversy between proponents and opponents of, 49–50
ego psychology and, 176
essence of, 429–30
as extension of and corrective for traditional psychoanalytic practice, 20
Ferenczi's contributions to evolution of, 89–106, 440
of Horney, 121–26
humanistic disciplines and, 152
intergenerational modification of, 65
interpersonal psychoanalysis and, 275–91, 445
empathic communication and, 282–85
exploration and interpretation in, 285–90
interpersonal listening stance, 277–82, 285
phenomenology and, 155–56, 161–64
homology between, 152–53
post-Kohutian view of, 415–28
problems left unresolved by, 419–26
quantum physics and, 153–54, 159–60
Rank and, 76–87
Winnicott and, 259–69

Self psychology phase of evolution of psychoanalysis, 113–14
Self representations, 323
Self-selfobject relations, 418
caretaker's comportment and formation of, 166, 169
phenomenological explanation of, 162–63

Self-selfobject transferences, 188
Self-state dreams, 336
Separation
intrapsychic, 407
Mahler's definition of, 397
during rapprochement subphase, 401–3

Separation anxiety, 400
Separation-individuation, 312
borderline triad and, 313
of borderline vs. narcissistic patients, 323–24
current infant research concerning, 408–12
forerunners of, 397–98
incorporation of psychology of self in, 315
Kohut's lack of acknowledgment of, 336

Separation-individuation (*continued*)
  Mahler on, 396, 397–404
    consolidation of individuality and beginning of emotional object constancy, 403–4
    differentiation and development of body image, 398–400
    from perspective of Kohut's developmental framework, 404–12
    practicing, 400–401
    rapprochement, 401–3
  theory, 315–18
Sequential analysis, 306–7
Sex-role stereotypes, analytic neutrality stemming from, 225–26
Sexual abuse of children, 95, 96–98, 440–42, 453, 457
Sexual drive, 8
Sexuality
  Adler on, 52–53
  as basis for all motivation, 8, 9
  in Freud's time, 75
Shame resistances, 306
Signifier, 371–72
  locus of, 373
Social smile, 398
Socratic position, 133
Spheres of existence, 138–44, 145, 146, 148–49
Splitting
  intrapsychic, 30–33
  selfobject transference and, 94
  subject-object split, 161
  vertical split, 31, 32, 425, 443
Spontaneous individual self, 119, 120
State-of-affairs dreams, 336–37
Stereotypes, sex-role, analytic neutrality stemming from, 225–26
Stranger anxiety, 399, 410
Streamlining, 123
Structural model of psychopathology, 293–94, 297
Structural neuroses, 446
  Kohut's distinction between narcissistic disorders and, 351
Subjective object, mother experienced by infant as, 260–62
Subjective reality, 238
Subjectivity of patient, Kohut and Jung on importance of, 35–37
Subject-object split, 161
Subject of the unconscious, 372–74
Sublimation, 9
Superego development, 403
Susceptibility to trauma, 100
Symbiosis, Mahler's use of term, 316
Symbiotic phase, 397–98, 406–7
Symbol, Jung's conception of, 27–28
Symbolic castration, 378
Symbolic identification, 372–74, 375, 377–78, 379
Symbolic order, Lacan on, 370–72
"Symbols of Transformation" (Jung), 34
"Synthetic" approach, 36

T

Tact, 440
Talion law, 235
Tension-reduction theory of motivation, 8–9
Termination of second analysis of Mr. Z, 390–92
Theories
  distinction between research tradition and, 58–59
  global, 58
Therapeutic alliance with borderline vs. narcissistic patient, 325
Therapist. *See* Analyst
Therapy. *See* Analysis
"They-self", 199, 200–201
Thought formation, origins of psychoanalytic theory of, 6–7
"Thoughts on Narcissism and Narcissistic Rage" (Kohut), 55
Thrownness (*Geworfenheit*), 198
Topographic model, 6, 296
Towards independence stage, 269
Tragic hero, Kierkegaard vs. Kohut on, 147–48
Tragic Man, 295, 344–45, 418, 423
Transcendental field, 182
Transference, 10, 216–19
  alter ego, 15
  archetypal, 37–41, 42

of borderline vs. narcissistic patients, 324
of creativity, 86–87
defining, 219
idealizing, 15, 216–17
in interpersonal psychoanalysis, 279–80
kinship libido and, 28
Kohut and Jung on, 37–43
mirror, 14–17, 41–42, 216–17
narcissistic, 43, 352–55
negative, 217–18
personal aspects of, 37–38
positive, 218
relationship, 219–21
self-object, 93–95, 145, 188, 218–19,430
self-selfobject, 188
Stolorow and Lachmann's definition of, 38*n*
therapeutic interaction and, 37–43
twinship, 419
Transformations of narcissism, 34–35
Transitional object, 266–68, 399, 444
Transitivistic behavior, 367
Transmuting internalization, 318, 350, 407, 408
Trauma, susceptibility to, 100
Trauma of Birth (Rank), 77
Trauma theory, 95–103
empathic failure as trauma, 98–103
Kohut on, 99–101
True self, 263, 264, 318, 337, 443
12th International Psychoanalytic Congress, 95
Twinship transferences, 419
"Two Analysis of Mr. Z, The" (Kohut), 378–92, 451
idealization and ego ideal in, 386–90
second analysis, 381–86
termination in, 390–92

U

Unconditional positive regard, 214, 215
Unconscious
archetypal collective, 432
Jung and Kohut on, 26*n*
Lacan on Freudian, 364, 365
personal, 432, 439
subject of the, 372–74
Understanding phase, 185, 445–46. *See also* Empathy
Uniformity of nature, principle of, 156
Unintegrated complex, 32

V

Validation, consensual, 284–85
Vertical split, 31, 32, 425, 443
Vicarious introspection, 153, 164, 165
Vienna Psychoanalytic Society, 51
Freud's commentary on Adler's summary lectures before, 59-60, 63-64
Virtual self, 405
Vulnerability, Kierkegaard vs. Kohut on, 147

W

Walk, capacity to, emotional development and, 400-401
Wholeness, idea of, in Jung and Kohut, 33-35
Will
earliest expression of, 79
inhibition of, 84
Rank on, 78–79
Words, The (Sartre), 208
Working through, with borderline vs. narcissistic patients, 325–26
World-defining commitments, 135, 136–37